"God is rich in mercy; because of His great love for us, He brought us to life with Christ when we were dead in sin. Both with and in Christ Jesus He raised us up and gave us a place in the heavens, that in the ages to come He might display the great wealth of His favor, manifested by His kindness to us in Christ Jesus." (Ephesians 2:4-7)

Untold Mercy
The Diary of
Father Leonard Gadfly

By
Father Leonard Gadfly

Based Upon A True Diary

"Because God and my father confessor have commanded me to write the pitiable account of my life, it will be well enough to say, and thereby include everything, that since I have been a great sinner and received a sea of graces from His Divine Majesty, everyone will clearly see the grandeur of His unlimited mercy." St. Charles of Sezze

Maria Regina Pacis Publications

Untold Mercy
The Diary of
Father Leonard Gadfly

Quotations from the *Diary of Saint Maria Faustina Kowalska, Divine Mercy in My Soul* used with permission of the Marian Fathers of the Immaculate Conception of the Blessed Virgin Mary. Stockbridge, MA USA.

Vilnius Divine Mercy Image, used with permission of the Marian Fathers of the Immaculate Conception of the Blessed Virgin Mary. Stockbridge, MA USA.

Cover Image the Child Jesus: The artist of the cover image is unknown. All attempts have been made by Maria Regina Pacis Publications to locate and give credit to the artist. In the event that the identity of the artist becomes known, all due recognition will be given in future editions.

Act of Consecration to St. Joseph by Fr. Donald Galloway, in his book, *Consecration to St. Joseph,* used with permission of the Marian Fathers of the Immaculate Conception of the Blessed Virgin Mary. Stockbridge, MA USA.

Quotations from *The Autobiography of St. Charles Sezze,* translated by Fr. Leonard Perotti, OFM, used with permission of Mediatrix Press.

Cover photo of *St. James Church, Medjugorje* used with permission of Medjugorje Orbis 3 Hotel, Medjugorje

Cover photo of *Handwriting in a Notebook;* back cover photo of *Apparition Hill, Medjugorje;* back cover of *Monstrance During a Holy Hour at St. James, Medjugorje,* by an anonymous helper.

© 2023 Maria Regina Pacis Publications

All rights reserved. No part of this book may be reproduced or transmitted in any form by any means, electronic, mechanical, photocopying, recording or otherwise, without written permission of the author.

ISBN: 9798865365068
First Edition
Second Printing
Printed in the USA

MARIA REGINA PACIS PUBLICATIONS
FatherGadfly@gmail.com

Tua, Domine, propitiatione et beate Mariae semper Virginis intecessione, ad perpetuam atque praesentem haec oblatio nobis proficiat prosperitatem et pacem. Amen.

By thy gracious Mercy, O Lord, and the intercession of blessed Mary ever Virgin, may this offering be of avail to us for welfare and peace now and for evermore. Amen.

DEDICATION

To the Blessed Virgin Mary, Our Lady Queen of Peace and Mother of Mercy, this diary is affectionately dedicated, and consecrated, in the hope that through Her Immaculate Heart and the Sacred Heart of Jesus, it may conduce to the growth of sanctity in numerous souls, help them trust in God's infinite mercy, and God's mercy will be extolled throughout the world.

THE TRIUMPH OF MERCY

"I know very well what I am of myself, because for this purpose Jesus has opened the eyes of my soul; I am an abyss of misery, and hence I understand that whatever good there is in my soul consists solely of His holy grace. The knowledge of my own misery allows me, at the same time, to know the immensity of Your mercy. In my own interior life, I am looking with one eye at the abyss of my misery and baseness, and with the other, at the abyss of Your mercy, O God." *The Diary of St. Maria Faustina Kowalska*, (#56)

MER-CY

There is a song called, *I Can Only Imagine*, by the Christian group, MercyMe. The main singer states the group received the name MercyMe, because it was a phrase his grandmother used to say. When something shocking would occur, my mother, Carmen, at times, would say "Mercy" pronounced "Mer—cy". I often told friends, when I was born, my mother must have cried out "Mercy" and many other times in my life as well, which caused her heartache. My only desire in making this collection of stories in my diary public, is to extol, glorify, and give praise to God's unfathomable mercy. The diary is not about me, it's about God's mercy. I claim only my misery and my sins, all else is God's grace and mercy. Father Leonard Gadfly

TRUE STORIES FROM A REAL DIARY

Ladies and gentlemen: the stories you are about to hear are true. Only the names, places, and organizations were changed, including the name of the author.

TABLE OF CONTENTS

PREFACE

Before reading the diary, it is helpful to understand the meaning of mercy. The Latin "misericordia" means "mercy". "Miseri" means "misery" and "cordia" means "heart". To be merciful means to open one's heart to the misery of others and to relieve that misery by acts of kindness. Whenever someone performs a deed of mercy, the giver of mercy, is moved with compassion to relieve the misery of others.

God creating the universe and creating man are acts of mercy. After the fall of Adam and Eve, God opened His heart to relieve the misery of souls in different ways. Through salvation history (the flood washing away evil; freedom from slavery by crossing the Red Sea; God providing manna and quail in the desert; God giving judges, kings, and prophets for His people; their entering the Promised Land, etc...), are all events of God's mercy for His people when they were in misery. "With mighty hand and outstretched arm, for his mercy endures forever; Who split in two the Red Sea, for his mercy endures forever; And led Israel through its midst, for his mercy endures forever; But swept Pharaoh and his army into the Red Sea, for his mercy endures forever; Who led the people through the desert, for his mercy endures forever;, etc..." (Psalm 136 12:16)

God the Father, sending the Redeemer into the world was an act of mercy. God became man, so He could unite Himself to us through His creation, forgive our sins, restore our friendship and union with God, and we can become a member of God's family. "For in goodness you created man and, when he was justly condemned, in mercy you redeemed him, through Christ the Lord." (Common Preface II)

Foreseeing Our Lord's redemptive act on the Cross, God applied the merits of redemption in advance to the Virgin Mary, who was conceived without original sin and never sinned in Her life. This action of God preventing Our Lady from any sin is a marvelous act of mercy.

Our Lord's crucifixion on Mount Calvary was the greatest act of God's mercy because it conquered sin, death, and the devil to allow mankind to be relieved of these miseries.

The Church was born through the wound in the side and Heart of Christ, and so gave us the seven sacraments. Jesus opened His Heart on the Cross to relieve our misery, to be with us, and give us graces in every generation through the sacraments.

For sinners, God sees the misery of every soul in need of forgiveness. The sacraments, especially Baptism, the Eucharist, and Confession are the primary fonts of mercy.

Anointing of the Sick likewise forgives sins and through the Apostolic Pardon all punishment of sin is washed away.

Only God can wash away original sin and personal sin through Baptism. St. Caesarius of Arles said, "At our first birth, we were vessels of God's wrath; reborn we became vessels of His mercy. As I said earlier, before Christ redeemed us, we were the house of the devil, but afterward, we merited being the house of God. God Himself in His loving mercy saw fit to make of us His own home."

Only He can forgive personal sin through Confession, and, only God can forgive the sins of an unconscious person dying through Anointing of the Sick.

The Holy Mass is a tremendous source of mercy, because the re-presentation of Calvary becomes present on the altar, and in Holy Communion, we are united with Jesus in the most profound way possible on earth. The Eucharist is Jesus, Himself. During union with Jesus in Holy Communion, our venial sins are forgiven, and we receive untold graces.

The greater the sinner, the greater God's mercy. The greater the offense, the greater the mercy we can give or receive. St. Mary Magdalene was a prostitute and possessed by seven demons, but Jesus delivered her, forgave her, and even appeared to her before appearing to the apostles. Forgiving Mary Magdalene was an act of mercy because her sins were numerous and grievous. Another act of mercy is that she beheld the risen Lord. In her misery, she longed to see Him again.

The feast of Divine Mercy, the Sunday after Easter, given to us through St. Faustina, is an incredible once a year, event of mercy. On that day, when one goes to Confession, during Lent, and up to and including Divine Mercy Sunday, and then receives Holy Communion, in the state of grace, our soul becomes like it was at Baptism. It will be completely free from sin and all the punishment due to sin. All is washed away in the ocean of God's unfathomable mercy.

Apparitions, visions from God, mystical experiences are fascinating, and are small acts of mercy, as they give consolation to the soul and can be beneficial for the Church. But they are nothing compared to God's mercy through the sacraments and through sufferings accepted with love.

Pain and sufferings are really gems of mercy given to us by God, and are much more precious and valuable than visions, etc…, when embraced. When pain and sufferings are united to the sufferings of Jesus on the Cross, they are redemptive for our miserable soul and souls of others.

A car accident, that caused a person to change one's life; a physical healing; an answered prayer; casting aside judgmental or negative thoughts; deliverance from an evil spirit; overlooking faults of others; and all non-sacramental moments of grace, are really acts of mercy. Through actions of love, misery is relieved.

St. Faustina said we are to prepare for the Second Coming by doing deeds of mercy. St. Augustine also explains that we are to prepare for our judgment and the Second Coming, by doing deeds of mercy. (See Appendix A)

The Church gives us seven corporal and spiritual works (deeds) of mercy to help us to relieve misery in others, to prepare us for our judgment and the Second Coming.

We are to feed the hungry; give drink to the thirsty; clothe the naked; shelter the homeless; visit the sick; bury the dead; visit prisoners; counsel the doubtful; forgive injuries; pray for the living and the dead; admonish sinners; bear wrongs patiently; instruct the ignorant; comfort the sorrowful.

In the diary of Fr. Gadfly, by God's providence, and grace, invalid sacraments (the Holy Sacrifice of the Mass, Confession, Baptism, Marriage, Anointing of the Sick) are uncovered and restored to validity. Through a mere simple lowly insignificant miserable sacramental priest, God's people can now receive His infinite and unfathomable mercy.

The proclamation of the truth by way of homilies, books, talks, and other means inspire virtue, admonish sinners, instruct the uneducated, comfort the sorrowful, inspire faith and move hearts to practice deeds of mercy.

As you read the diary, think of ways you had not previously known how God has been merciful to you and open the eyes of your heart to recognize ways you can be merciful to others.

INTRODUCTION

In 1991, a young man not educated in the Catholic faith, nor did he practice it, received a call from God to become a priest at Medjugorje.

As a child, a confession experience by his pastor caused Leonard to not go to Confession for 20 years. Due to an alcoholic father and an abusive neighbor, his early life is marred by emotional wounds and a poor self-image. Working on the family pig farm and a local chicken hatchery, he eventually attended college, but dropped out. He scheduled an abortion and then due to drunkenness wrecked his car that nearly killed three people. His life was spared, when he was about to end it. Being present at the death of his grandmother led him to learn how to pray the Rosary.

Through the alleged messages of Our Lady Queen of Peace, he returned to Confession and followed a call to become a Franciscan brother. But after making perpetual vows, he left the order. He wrote about his interesting experiences, during seminary, as a Franciscan, and as a seminarian for the Diocese of Rolling Hills.

Once ordained a priest, due to preaching the truth, his homilies were controversial. As pastor, he dealt with problems in his parishes standing up for what was true, right, and just, for the salvation of the souls of his flock, but wasn't supported. He began four Eucharistic Adoration Chapels, helped close two abortion clinics, and by his pastoral leadership brought about the conversion of many in a parish. Fired twice as a Catholic hospital chaplain, he explains what happened at the hospital during the COVID-19 pandemic. When patients were treated unethically, he attempted to address hospice heartaches with the hospice, hospital, and his bishop. However, due to his imprudence, he was demoted as a "sacramental priest". Through the intercession of St. Anthony, the bodies of two dead were found. Appearances of the Divine Child Jesus, demonic attacks, souls wanting Masses, and saints interceding are just a few of the many fascinating stories in the entries of his diary.

The Diary of St. Maria Faustina Kowalska and *Autobiography of St. Charles of Sezze* helped him to more fully understand God's mercy and were an inspiration to him. He found emotional healing and deliverance by the "prayer of feeling", an adaption of St. Ignatius discernment of spirits method.

While writing his autobiography, Jesus told him, "I desire you to extol my mercy." By the entries of his life stories, his diary reveals God's Untold Mercy and how God used a weak and miserable man to "extol" it.

Within *Untold Mercy, The Diary of Father Leonard Gadfly–* are a collection of true stories written as entries, that he originally kept to himself and his spiritual director, but now revealed. No doubt the Virgin Mary helped him accomplish this task, as he mentions in his diary.

The manner in which the diary began, was that he originally wrote interesting stories about his life, he had hoped to pass on to his family. But after his spiritual director read them, he suggested to Father Gadfly, to write his autobiography. And after it was completed, Father Gadfly continued to write, in what he called his diary. Because it's a diary, there are no chapters, but rather entries. Some entries have subheadings because at times, he wrote about multiple topics in one entry. Entries were numbered in the order written. As with any diary, he wrote about his thoughts and events of the day.

Some stories may seem insignificant to some, but to others, they will be very meaningful. Because half of his life was without God, he wrote much about his life before his conversion. The editor chose to leave these stories in the diary, to allow the reader to have a glimpse into the depths of his miserable life and sins, so at to come to understand God's infinite mercy in relieving them. The editor also kept as faithful as possible original wording and therefore much of the diary wasn't edited, so the reader could experience his personal authentic style of writing.

He especially mentions his sins, how he offended the Lord, and hurt others, but he also shows how God's mercy triumphs over them. "We triumph over all these things through Him who loved us" (Romans 8:37)

Despite living a miserable life without God, God called him to become a priest, as an instrument of His mercy, and be an example of one who gives glory, honor, and praise to His infinite mercy. Through many difficulties in his ministry, and ethical dilemmas, he learned to love and sacrifice himself for the sheep entrusted to his care to help them obtain salvation.

It is abundantly clear the Virgin Mary and Jesus in the Most Blessed Sacrament are the foundations of the priest's life and ministry. This diary will be helpful to religious, seminarians, priests and lay people to grow in their love of God and better understand His infinite and unfathomable mercy.

Editor's Note

As you begin to read the Diary, it is good to recall the reason the editor chose to not remove many of the original stories prior to the conversion of Fr. Leonard Gadfly, is to show the reader that almost half of his miserable life was without God. Therefore, God's mercy is made known in greater light when one comes to understand the misery of a person's life prior to having a relationship Jesus. And how God, out of His love for each person, reached down to relieve Leonard's misery and did great things for him and through him for others. God's mercy meets misery and relieves it. This is the actual diary.

Special Note

Items numbered are not chapters, but rather entries from a real diary. Some entries were not numbered because more than one topic was written during specific entries. Sentences could have been constructed better by the author. At times, words are missing from sentences, and commas may be out of place, but these were not edited to respect the exact wording from the diary.

#1 BIRTH AND BAPTISM

"Before I formed you in the womb, I knew you; Before you were born, I sanctified you; I ordained you a prophet to the nations." (Jeremiah 1:5)

In the *Diary of St. Faustina*, #85, Jesus said, "Write down at once what you hear: I am the Lord in My essence, and immune to orders or needs. If I call creatures into being—that is the abyss of My mercy."

I, Father Leonard Joseph Anthony Gadfly, was born Feb. 30th, 1963 to Joseph Anthony Gadfly and Carmen Anne Tosmercka at Hasten County Memorial Hospital, in Crossroads City, Ohio. I was named after my grandfather Leonard Gadfly. My middle name is my father's first name, Joseph Anthony Gadfly. At the time I was born, we were living on a farm near Loretta, Ohio, that had a small Catholic church called Our Lady Help of Christians. I was given the gift of baptism by my parents on March 3rd, 1963, (Feast of St. Katherine Drexel) just a few weeks after I was born. I was baptized by an Irish-born priest, Fr. Michael O' Murphy. My godparents were Belinda Dott and Bert Smickel.

#2 SIBLINGS (BROTHER AND SISTERS)

My siblings are Anne, Marie, Margaret, Sue, Louis, Gail, and Jean. I am the fourth child and oldest boy, who came into the world after Margaret, and before Sue.

#3 MY PARENT'S FAMILIES

My Parents' Families
"Now will I praise those godly men, our ancestors, each in his own time: These were godly men whose virtues have not been forgotten; Their wealth remains in their families, their heritage with their descendants; Through God's covenant with them their family endures, their posterity, for their sake. And for all time their progeny will endure, their glory will never be blotted out; Their bodies are peacefully laid away, but their name lives on and on. At gatherings their wisdom is retold, and the assembly proclaims their praise." (Ecclesiastes 44:1, 10-15)

My mother, Carmen Anne Tosmercka, was the daughter of John and Sarah (Vatal) Tosmercka. She had 8 siblings. Mom's mother, my grandma Sarah, died in April 1964. Since I was one year old, I don't remember my grandmother. She died of an apparent heart-attack. Her husband, John (Pappy) died of a heart attack in October 1980. As a child about the age of 3, I remember seeing Mom's brother, Larry, in a casket. He drowned at the age of 18. I recall seeing his face discolored and purple.

My dad, Joseph Anthony Gadfly, was the son of my grandfather, Leonard Gadfly and Scholastica (Schwinderspoon). He had four siblings. Leonard died in April 1955, the year my father was to graduate from high school. But due to the funeral, my father was unable to complete his classes and never graduated. The school lacked mercy toward young Joseph, despite the death of his father. The sudden death of Leonard due to a bleeding ulcer would cause a deep emotional wound in my father. Ever since that happened, he didn't want anything to do with doctors or hospitals, and rarely went for a doctor's visit.

Dad never said anything negative about his father, except for the time he and his brother James got into a fist fight at their home. Their father, Leonard, would have none of it. He threw both of his sons against the wall so hard it put a whole in it. Grandma Scholastica let her husband, have it with some German words used only when she was upset.

At times Dad told us, "I love you." He said, "I want to tell you I love you because my father never said that to me, though I knew he loved me."

Grandpa Leonard ran a "beer joint" (bar) and a radiator and tire shop. It seems he suffered from ulcers, which my father would inherit, but would later be cured of due to an antibiotic. Uncle James would suffer from stomach problems as well.

Leonard Gadfly married Scholastica Schwinderspoon. Scholastica was the daughter of Paul and Petrina (Steakclub) Schwinderspoon. My grandmother, Scholastica, died January 1990. Paul's mother and father were John Schwinderspoon and Mary Blender.

Dad used to tell the story of how John Schwinderspoon and Mary Blender, the parents of Paul, met on a boat headed from Russia to the United States. They were German Russians, who settled near the Volga River. Neither knew each other and decided to come to the US on a boat. Traveling alone on the boat by herself, Mary worried about coming to the US alone. She asked the Virgin Mary for help, and while on the boat, she had a vision of the Virgin Mary, who said, "Do not be afraid. You will meet a man by the name of John on this boat. You will marry him, and he will take care of you." By God's providence, they met on the boat and settled in Hasten County, Ohio.

Grandpa Leonard's grandmother, Archangelina Hisman married Linus Gadflie. She gave birth to three children. When she was pregnant with her fourth child, Archangelina and her unborn baby died. There are two stories that explained how Archangelina and her unborn baby died. One story indicated great-grandfather Linus beat her and punched her in the stomach, resulting in both the death of her and their unborn baby. The other story indicated that she fell off a step stool and landed on her stomach causing an internal hemorrhage and the death of the baby.

After his wife and child died, Linus abandoned his children to relatives and moved away because he wanted to marry a "mail-order bride". Grandpa Leonard was so angry with his father, Linus, for giving up he and his siblings, and especially because they treated him as a hired hand, rather than as a son, he changed his last name from Gadflie to Gadfly.

Both Parents Lose a Parent at a Young Age

My father, Joseph, lost his dad, Leonard, when Dad was 18. My mother lost her mother, Sarah, when Mom was only 21. My father didn't have his father and my mother didn't have her mother to help them during their young adulthood, and therefore, it must have been difficult to raise their young family. But my parents did a fantastic job as parents not having one of their parents to turn to.

#4 PARENTS ARE MARRIED

My Parents Are Married and Their Early Marriage

My father, at the age of 20, and my mother, at the age of 16, conceived my eldest sister, Anne. Due to the pregnancy, Pappy (Grandpa Jack Tosmercka) told my father he was required to marry his daughter. My parents were married Jan. 6th, 1957 by Fr. Ferdinand Tosmercka, Mom's brother at Holy Moses Catholic Church in Tucom, Ohio.

My mother mentioned that grandpa Tosmercka never spoke to his grandchildren born of Mom and Dad, but spoke to his other grandchildren. This was due to my parent's premarital pregnancy and the embarrassment and shame caused to the family. I remember him seldom speaking. I recall the smell of tobacco from his pipe, and remember listening to his grandfather clock, *tick-tock, tick-tock,* due to a lack of conversation.

Due to the circumstances of Mom and Dad's marriage, there was more than one reason why their marriage was most likely invalid from the beginning and why an annulment was granted. Most likely, premarital pregnancy pushed my parents into getting married. My mother's father, grandpa Pappy, tried to force them to get married. Perhaps their immaturity at the time of marriage would have been a serious reason. And my father's alcoholism at the time of the marriage could have been a cause for my parents to not give oneself totally to the other during their vow exchange.

#5 MY MOTHER

Carmen Anne (Mom)
"As one whom his mother comforts, so I will comfort you." (Isiah 66:13)

As a child, my mother suffered grievously from her brothers who taunted her and from her sister who ignored her and treated her badly. Over the years she mentioned some things they did to her, and it seemed she had difficulty forgiving her siblings.

My mother was very loving and compassionate, and at times, wet her fingers with saliva to knock down my rooster (hair sticking up), just before we entered the church for Sunday Mass. She was just like a mamma cat who licked her kittens.

As a child, I remember many hugs and kisses. My mother was a religious person. She loved religious art, and had a large, beautiful picture of Jesus' Agony in the Garden, she hung on the wall in the living room. She surrounded the picture of Jesus with each of our school photographs. She had a set of pictures of the Sacred Heart of Jesus and the Immaculate Heart of Mary, that were incredibly beautiful. At times, she lit a candle in her room.

Every year after the Christmas Midnight Mass, Mom took my siblings and I up to the manger, and she would just gaze upon the scene and wanted us to do the same in silence. It was so moving to me. She would not say a word, and wanted us to look carefully at the Child Jesus, Mary, and Joseph, and the animals in the stable.

She made sure we attended Mass every Sunday, that is-- until serious problems began to occur between her and Dad.

When we became older and moved out of the house, Mom wanted to always have Easter every year at her home, and after I became a priest, I was rarely able to attend. I asked her why she wanted the family to gather every year on Easter at her home. I thought she would say something about how meaningful it was for the family to gather. But she said, "Because He is risen! He's alive." It made me realize how she took her faith seriously and wanted us to take it seriously as well.

A few years after I was ordained a priest, I encouraged Mom to go to Confession at her parish, and so I said, "Mom, have you thought about going to Confession before Christmas?" And she said, "Na Yah!!! I did that already. We were supposed to confess our sins before celebrating Christ's birth." I didn't know she went to Confession, as she never talked about it. But I learned, that she did, in fact, go to Confession. I realized I had been judging her and felt bad about it.

When Dad was working, my mother would gather us to kneel before a statue of Mary on what was called the buffet. She taught us the Rosary, and I very much enjoyed praying it.

During a very difficult time in her life, when Mom suffered terribly from my father's alcoholism, she told me one night she was awakened and saw the face of Jesus in her bedroom. She cried because she thought it meant she was going to die soon. This happened a few years after I graduated from high school and not too much from the time her and Dad divorced. I told her I thought it meant Jesus was with her in her great time of distress.

A few years before that occurred, while I was still at home, one night, Mom was crying and Dad was saying, "Don't do it. Don't take those pills." Mom had a bottle of pills and was threatening to kill herself. Dad's relentless drinking and the abuse she suffered pushed her over the edge. At times, she would stay in bed until noon, mostly due to depression. Consequently, she failed to keep the house clean. She became so distraught by the mental anguish she suffered, she was near a nervous breakdown.

One evening, when I was in high school, as we were all sitting around the table eating dinner, Dad criticized each of us, one by one, as we sat around the table. I had enough of it, and exclaimed, "Stop criticizing us! We are sick and tired of you putting us down." I couldn't believe what came out of my mouth. It was the first time I finally stood up for Mom, my siblings, and me. Mom's reaction was stunning. She took her plate filled with food and threw it at him across the table. The plate crashed against the wall near his head. When I left the table, my sister Sue came with me. We got in the car, and drove around town talking about what had happened. After an hour, I dropped off my sister, purchased beer, as I was 18, the legal age at the time, and became drunk. When I returned home after midnight, Dad was waiting for me. I looked at him, and stupidly said, "See how drunk I am. Now you know what we have to put up with!" He never said a word, and I went to bed.

One Christmas, my father purchased a mink coat for my mother. After opening the gift, she said, "I would rather you stop drinking, then have this mink coat." That Christmas, Dad passed out in the bathtub and when he got dressed, Mom pushed him outside on the concrete porch. He slipped on ice, fell, and hit his head, which began to bleed.

Many nights, we heard Mom and Dad arguing, and Mom crying. I should have helped her but didn't. I was too fearful of my father, and not strong enough to come to my mother's aid. For years, I regretted not helping her. I used to want to treat her like a queen. When I was in college, we went to the cinema to watch a movie together, and I took her out to eat.

When in high school, I helped Mom at the pig farm, and often rode with her to various places to deliver baby chicks from the hatchery where she worked. These times together helped create a mother and son bond.

Due to Dad putting Mom down frequently when he was drinking, and because she never graduated from high school due to her per-marital pregnancy and abrupt marriage, she had a negative opinion of herself and thought she was stupid.

Once, Mom and Dad came to Fort Hickok, picked me up, and we drove around the city in the family station wagon. As Dad was driving, they asked if I thought they should get a divorce. I didn't know what to say. I didn't want them to get a divorce, yet they fought terribly. Months previously, there was a Rosary I found on the ground and gave to Mom. She wrapped it around the rearview mirror, and as I was sitting in the back seat, the Rosary kept reflecting the sun, and shining on my face. Finally, I said, "Consider all the fighting you do. I think you would have more peace if you didn't live together." I couldn't believe I said that. I wish I had told them to pray the Rosary together, but I didn't think of it at the time. I came to realize after the divorce, it was the right thing for them to do. I later came to believe the divorce was a blessing because both were happier after it. Eventually, Dad became sober for many years, and found God. Mom found another man she loved and was finally able to live in peace.

"Can a woman forget her nursing child. And not have compassion for the son of her womb? Even should she forget, Yet I will not forget you." (Isaiah 49:15)

As Mom was going through her depression and nervous breakdown, at times, when she became angry, she would beat my sister Marie, and brother Louis with a belt. I often wondered if she was taking out her anger and frustration on them. During this time, she seemed confused, and especially after the divorce, she wasn't thinking clearly, and failed to provide adequate food for Louis, Gail, and Jean, who lived with her. At times, my brother obtained food from Dad. He eventually moved in with him. My eldest sister, Anne, made up a story saying someone reported Mom to SRS (Social Rehabilitative Services) and that SRS was threatening to take Gail and Jean away from her. Mom believed Anne, who then allowed her to take Gail and Jean into her home, to feed and care for them.

Over time, it seemed all three healed from the heartache of being taken away from Mom. I think they came to understand Mom was grievously hurt emotionally from the abuse of Dad. She was a wreck and could not help what she was doing. It would have been best, to have her admitted to a hospital for a nervous breakdown. But, back then, nobody understood it.

Due to the divorce and their inability to pay monthly house payments, my parents lost their home and had to transfer ownership of it to the bank. During this time, I failed to help Mom emotionally and financially, when she really needed it. She became a single mother on food stamps. Only when the severity of it all was brought to light, did I begin to help Anne financially care for my two sisters.

Eventually, Donald Huntsman moved in with Mom, was taking care of her financially, and helping her emotionally to recover from a very difficult time in her life. Yet, to live together before marriage was immoral.

Mom and Dad eventually received an annulment and consequently, Mom and Donald Huntsman were married on July 4th, 1992, at St. Francis Church in Budapest,

Ohio. On the day of the wedding, he was baptized, made his First Communion, was Confirmed, and married my mother.

Despite her failings, I love my mother. She was the best mother I could ever have. The perfect mother for my family. And by far, the best cook ever.

#6 MY FATHER

Joseph Anthony Gadfly (Dad)

"As a father has compassion on his children, so the Lord has compassion on those who fear him." (Psalm 103:13)

My father was baptized Joseph Anthony Gadfly. He used to tell us, that he never crawled as a baby, but rather, just stood up and began to walk. As a toddler, one day his parents couldn't find him and looked everywhere. They finally found him asleep in the church. He began to sleepwalk at a young age.

My father was a wonderful man who loved his family. But there was a dark side to him that even he did not understand. He worked hard to provide for our needs and was paid little by his greedy boss. His father, Leonard, ran a radiator, tire repair shop and beer joint. As a boy, Dad worked at the shop repairing bicycles and tires.

While in high school, Dad began to work for Clement Schneider at Schneider's Hatchery and Feed Supply. Dad was very popular and well known for his willingness to do anything for anyone.

When I was young, I recall my father repairing our bicycles and putting on new tires for them. While barefoot, he used to want us to race him down the street.

He often said he was proud of me and loved me. He said, "My father never showed affection, and, well, I want to show affection to my children."

He, likewise had a keen ability to just know things, others couldn't perceive, and pick up on things, others didn't. He could almost always guess the gift I purchased for his birthday, Father's Day, or Christmas. Furthermore, he could tell if a pregnant woman was going to have a boy or a girl, and was right, over 90% of the time. He would say, "If her eyes are watery, it will be a boy. If her eyes are dry, it will be a girl. If she is "hanging low", it's a girl. And, if high, it's a boy." After eight children of his own, he must have somehow figured that out.

When my mother was pregnant with my youngest sister, Jean, Mom's water broke (amniotic sac ruptured), and we had just installed our first telephone at our home. Mom asked my oldest sister, Anne, to call my father, and tell him to come home right away because her "water broke". My sister called Dad, and said, "Mom wants you to come home right now. Her water broke." Dad responded, "Tell Mom to shut off the water, and I will get there, when I get off work."

All the local farmers knew my dad and loved him. He would deliver their feed any day of the week, and no matter how late. While working at the feed mill, he inhaled a tremendous amount of grain dust, and often, coughed up large hunks of brown phlegm.

Later, when he was working for Co-op, he inhaled pesticides and herbicides. He smoked cigarettes as well, and over time, developed lung and brain cancer. Who knows what caused the cancer, most likely a combination of cigarette smoke, grain dust, and chemicals he inhaled.

When my father was not drinking, he was very kind, funny, witty, and wise in practical things of life. He enjoyed hunting, fishing, and camping. He wanted his children to have fun together and took us on vacations to Six Flags Over Texas, Worlds of Fun, Mount Rushmore, Nebraska, Colorado's Royal Gorge, and Missouri's Caves.

The time I spent with my father working at the hatchery, feed mill, and hog lot, was a wonderful time of learning and joy. He taught me how to work hard, and to be honest and loving toward others.

As I was about to be on my own, he wanted me to take over the family pig operation. But, I didn't want to. For profits, Clement Schneider, his boss, abused his kindness and hard work, over many years. He treated us and my father like slaves. He never paid us for all the hard work we did at the hog lot. When Dad realized what was happening, on occasion slaughtered a pig and put in our freezer to help feed our poor family.

When my father would drink, he was a different person. It was almost like a demon would take control of him to persecute the family, whom Dad loved.

Over time, he began to drink more and more, and soon, it became apparent he had a drinking problem. He drank mostly beer, but at times hard liquor. Despite his excessive drinking, he was always faithful to his job and never missed work. Most nights of the week, after late hours at work, he stopped by the "beer joint" and stayed there until midnight when the bar closed. When he came home drunk, he expected Mom to get out of bed, and fry him a T-bone steak, fried potatoes, and cottage cheese.

I used to look for, and find his whiskey bottles that he hid. At first, I dumped them down the drain. When Mom found out, she scolded me. She said he would only waste money buying more. Nevertheless, I kept dumping half of the bottle out, but refilling it with water, so he wouldn't get drunk as easily.

Before long, most every night our home became a nightmare. My parents would yell at each other. We listened for Dad's truck, and when we heard it coming, (due to a damaged muffler), we quickly turned off lights and acted like we were sleeping. Poor Mom had to endure his hateful words, and condescending remarks. At times, he came to my room, and I acted like I was sleeping.

He worked very hard, but his addiction to alcohol got the best of him. It was not only a cross for him. It was a cross for Mom and the family. Night after night, there was screaming and hollering. I couldn't wait to move out of the house, and felt I often betrayed my mother for not standing up for her, like I should have.

Dad couldn't help it, but would occasionally sleepwalk. At times, he walked out of the bedroom, only in his underwear, or even nude, and then would urinate outside, or in different locations in the house. At times, he would even go outside in freezing weather and sit in the car. The poor man would come back in the house very embarrassed and act as though nothing had happened. He said, "It sure is cold outside." We could tell when he was sleepwalking when he had a strange blank look on his face, as though he was not there. Mom said we should never wake him while he was sleep-walking, as she understood that it was dangerous for sleepwalkers to be suddenly awakened. This was truly a cross for him and us, because we worried he may start the car and drive off, but he never did.

We had horses at the farm and Dad had the habit of driving down into the ditch with the car or pickup to park near the fence, to feed the horses. One winter day, we had heavy snow, and Dad had too much beer. I was driving the family Pontiac station wagon, with him sitting in the passenger seat. The ditch was nearly full of snow, but Dad told me to veer the car into the ditch to feed the horses. I warned him, saying, "Dad, the ditch is almost full of snow. We should just park on the side of the road. We will get stuck." And he said, "No, this car is heavy. We won't get stuck." For fear of his drunken rage, I did as he asked. The car nosedived into the ditch, and snow flew everywhere. We tried opening the doors, but couldn't, due to the snow level above the doors. I used the automatic button to roll down the back window and crawled over the seats. I then took a feed scoop and did my best to remove the snow by the doors, so Dad could get out. Then I attempted to remove the snow behind the wheels of the car. Dad attempted to back the car out of the ditch, but to no avail. He then crawled over the back seat and out the back door. He got a tractor from the farm and tied a chain from the tractor to the car. I sat behind the wheel of the car, and accelerated the motor, causing the wheels to spin, and he, at the same time, tried pulling the car out with the tractor, but the station wagon wouldn't budge. A farmer happened to drive by with his tractor and hooked his tractor to Dad's tractor. I got behind the wheel of the car and hit the accelerator. Finally, the family station wagon came out of the snow, but it took two tractors. A truly hilarious scene.

Once Dad was very drunk and as we were returning from the farm and heading into town, he passed out while driving his pickup. I was sitting in the passenger seat and immediately tried to wake him up, but to no avail. The pickup began swerving while speeding about forty-five miles per hour. It gradually slowed down, but not enough. I couldn't reach the brakes, and we came closer and closer to the main intersection of the two highways. The pickup slowed down to about twenty-five miles per hour, and I kept shaking Dad. I just knew we were going to drive right through a stop sign and crash into another car. A few blocks before the intersection, I quickly turned the pickup down a side road and when I did-- the pickup swerved so badly, firewood on the back of the truck flew off landing on the highway. We nearly missed mailboxes that lined the street. Another stop sign was ahead, and I finally shouted with all my might, and Dad woke up. He slammed on the brakes just as we entered the intersection. The pickup spun on the sand, and we ended up spinning and stopping in the same direction it was originally heading. Dad remarked, "I just wanted to see if you were paying attention." I thought, "Yeah, right. You were out cold." Although it was frightening, later I thought about what had happened, and saw it as a hilarious event. Even today when I just think about it, I have a good laugh.

My sister, Anne, told me she called the police on Dad. He came over to Mom's house and was choking her. Due to this, I became very angry at my father. A few weeks after the incident, I went to his house and told him, "If you ever choke Mom like that again, I will never speak to you, as long as I live." He was furious with me and denied having choked her. He said I had no right to talk to him like that. I didn't care and walked away as he was yelling.

Later I wrote him a letter. In the letter, I told him I was proud of all the hard work he did for the family. But, said that he seldom came home to be with his wife and children. We just wanted him to be a father to us. What I meant was that he was not at home, due to staying out drinking after work and that he would come home drunk. I told him he was not a good father because of his drinking and that he needed to get help to stop.

Nearly thirty years later, a week after his death, my sisters discovered that letter in his wallet. Over the years he changed his life and became the best father he could be. He was a good father. For years, he no longer drank any alcohol and helped many through Alcoholic Anonymous (AA). Towards the last five years of his life he had occasional drinking spells. He manfully carried his cross to the best of his ability. He turned to God, his higher power, and God helped him. I burned the letter on the porch of the rectory and felt as though that little letter helped change his life. However, he mistakenly thought I meant that he had not been a good father his whole life, but that wasn't true. Although, he often said he was proud of me, I never told him I was proud of him and wished I had.

I later learned he had alcoholic blackouts. Consequently, when he was drunk, he couldn't remember his behavior. At first, this was hard for me to believe, but then later, I came to discover it was true. If he could have remembered his actions, he most likely would not have been able to live with himself, for all the harm he did to himself, to us, especially my mother and one of my sisters.

The more difficult to love someone, the greater the love. I grew in love for my father, to forgive, and to pray for him. I pray every day, since now that he has died, that, God in His mercy, will give him the gift of eternal life.

When I discovered my call to the priesthood, I decided to break the news to my father, and made sure he was sober when I told him. Unfortunately, he was furious and told me I had to pass on the Gadfly name, and didn't want me to be a priest. My mother was supportive, telling me that she was happy with whatever I wanted to do. Eventually, after my brother and his wife conceived and had a boy, I had Dad's support. To show his support, he even drove all the way to Louisiana twice, for my religious professions. I was very proud of him.

Once when I was in seminary, I was thinking about Dad and having angry thoughts. I began to pray for him and asked Jesus to help me to forgive. At that moment I had a spiritual experience. I suddenly saw Jesus, hanging from the Cross in my room and saw myself and my father standing beneath the cross. I prayed, "Jesus, help me to forgive. I am sorry, for not forgiving my Dad." Jesus said, "Forgive him, for he knew not what he did." Dad looked up at Jesus and said, "Lord, I'm sorry." Dad then looked at me, and said, "Please forgive me." I looked at my father, and said, "Dad. I forgive you." We then hugged each other and the cross vanished. At that moment, I felt like I finally forgave him.

Later, at times, I still had angry thoughts and wondered if I really forgave him, but realized I did and those were just feelings. I chose to forgive, and eventually over time, the angry feelings slowly went away. The hurtful feelings were the result of being wounded. It took time for the emotional wounds to heal.

As the years went on, after Dad stopped drinking, at times he would fall by getting drunk. A few years before he died, I noticed at times, he repeated himself and said incoherent things. I suspected he was getting dementia, but I was wrong. It was something else.

#7 PAGE TORN OUT AND MISSING

#8 THE TOWN OF CROSSROADS

The town of Crossroads received its name by French immigrants due to roads that crossed at the edge of the city. When I was growing up, it had a population of nearly 1,800 people. In the late 1960s and early 1970s, there were many businesses: two grocery stores, a movie theater, a drive-in movie business, two lumberyards, three gas stations, three "beer joints", two liquor stores, various shops, and businesses, including multiple clothing stores, a "Dime Store", two ice-cream stores (Tasty Freeze and Dairy King). The city had two motels and a hotel. The hotel was owned by a Catholic family with 12 children and each child had their individual room. It was located next to the railroad tracks. The train came through our farming town to haul railroad cars full of grain, especially wheat, the primary grain grown in the area. There were two competing grain companies (Co-op and Schneider's Grain) in town. By looking at their sign placed in their window, the owner of Schneider's would undercut the Co-op by 5 cents a bushel.

The town had a Sale Barn, where farmers brought their cattle, pigs, and sheep, to be sold on Fridays. There was a bakery that sold bread, donuts, and cakes.

When a high school sports team went to the state championship, all businesses closed except gas stations. On Sundays, only gas stations were open. High school youth would drive their cars up and down Main Street called "dragging Main", especially during summer.

The fairgrounds, and softball fields were popular during the summer, as adult teams played one another for fun, and families came to the annual fair for rides, and enjoy livestock shows farmers used to compete for ribbon prizes.

There was a Catholic, Methodist, Presbyterian, and Christian church in town. During Christmastime, the city put up large metallic Christmas trees with glass bulbs on all light poles on Main street. The city had a large nativity scene placed on public property. When a fuss was made, about it being on public property, a local businessman purchased the ground to keep the nativity scene up every year.

The town had a hospital with a doctor, who did surgeries and delivered babies. Dr. Baker performed the required physicals, so the youth could go out for sports. My first physical in 7th grade was the bare minimum. I sat in the waiting room, until it was my turn. The doctor opened the door and pointed to the scale. He took my weight, and then listened to my heart with his stethoscope. He said, "How do you feel?" I replied, "Fine." He held out his hand, and said, "Five dollars." I gave him a $5 bill, and he gave me a paper with his signature, stating I was fit to play sports.

Immorality was rampant in the town. In the 70s, there were numerous high school students who smoked marijuana, and even smoked it in the restrooms at school. In my class of 34 students, there were only two who did the drug. When I was a freshmen in high school, the senior class, was very promiscuous. Half of all the girls in that class became pregnant before graduating from high school. In my class, one girl became pregnant before graduating. When a younger sister of mine, became a senior, she became pregnant. Her boyfriend proposed on her graduation day. Beer was available easily for those over 18. The town was plagued with many who went to bars and came home intoxicated.

There was a paved black-top runway at the airport a mile out of town. It was believed the sheriff and police permitted drugs to be flown in, and then dispersed the drugs in the region. A local car dealer not only dealt in cars, but also drugs. Finally, the FBI caught several police officers, who were arrested, as well as the auto dealer. The sheriff somehow escaped from being charged, though everyone knew he was guilty.

Crossroads had its own power plant, that would, at times, stop working, and the electricity would go out unexpectedly. People would chuckle, saying, "The squirrels didn't get fed again. They stopped running in the squirrel cage." They joked as though squirrels were making the power plant operate. The city had town sirens to warn of tornadoes and were used to call volunteer firemen to fight fires. The sirens blared every day, but Sunday, to remind citizens, it was time for lunch at noon.

When the locals heard a siren of an ambulance or firetruck, they would get in their cars, and follow the ambulance or fire truck to see what was going on. Numerous vehicles would drive by to see whatever was happening. My mother called it, "Gawking."

Most shopped locally, until a dirt road connecting to the next northern county was paved, which resulted in vehicles traveling twenty-four miles to Fort Hickok to purchase merchandise and food. There they found malls, and large grocery stores with lower prices, that smaller stores could not compete. Residents from Crossroads, traveling to the larger city with cheap gas, caused an economic disaster for the town. Over the years, the once bustling city became like a ghost town, as more and more shops and businesses closed. By the 1990s, the population decreased by 600 residents to 1,200.

#9 EARLY MEMORIES

Earliest Memories

One of my earliest memories as a child, was when we lived on the north side of town in an old white house. These memories were from the age of 3 or less.

I recall a wonderful neighbor, Smitty Sherman, and his wife, who gave my siblings and I, a little red wagon with fruit and candy in it for Christmas. We loved that wagon and played with it regularly. We had a next-door neighbor, Maurice, who owned the house we lived in. He was very kind, and at times, invited us into his home. I can remember the smell of his house, and the fascinating things he had on his desk, such as a glass giraffe, canceled checks and pens.

Oh! Rats!

The first house we lived in at Crossroads City unfortunately had rats. Not mice, rats. There were even holes in the walls where they would come in and out, especially at night. Sort of like Tom and Jerry rat-holes. At times, we could hear them gnawing on wood.

On my 2nd or 3rd birthday, Mom made a birthday cake for me. She stored the cake in the oven while it was turned off to prevent insects and the rats from getting to it. Unfortunately, the oven had a hole in it where the electric oven light socket used to be. Sometime during the day, a rat came through the opening of the hole in the oven and ate some of my birthday cake. When Dad came home, I remember Mom telling Dad, "That's it, we are moving! We are not going to live in this house anymore."

Hanging by the Ears

My father would take me to grandpa's tavern and put a dime in a peanut machine, causing peanuts to spill out onto his hands. To show off, Dad told the men at the bar I was a tough kid and wouldn't cry easy. He picked me up off the ground by both ears, and oh, it was painful. I didn't cry. I wanted Dad to be proud of me. I recall one man saying to my father, "You should not do that to your son!" The Tavern was fun to be in, as I would watch adults play pool, and a table game, called shuffleboard. The smell of beer and cigarettes was part of the atmosphere.

New House

My parents found a house for us, and we moved. It was located at 514 E. 6th, and it was either new or almost new when we moved in. We moved to the new house when I was either 2 or 3 years old. One of my first memories at the house involved me getting upset about the food I was supposed to eat and throwing it on the floor.

Dog Food and Dog Poop

I was sitting in a highchair at supper time and threw my bologna sandwich on the floor, saying, "I'm sick of eating bologna all the time." Dad would have none of it, and not knowing the sandwich landed on dog poop, picked it up, and shoved the poop and sandwich in my mouth. I began to cry, trying to tell him there was poop in the sandwich, but he didn't hear me. He said, "You're not going to waste food in this house. Now stop your crying and eat it!" You have no idea how gross it was for me to swallow that sandwich with poop on it. But I did, and learned never to complain again about the food we were given. That episode made me realize our family really could not afford other kinds of food.

I recall my mother buying cereal and making oatmeal often. We seldom had fried eggs or bacon. We thought that kind of food was only for rich people. Mom rarely made pancakes. She made homemade syrup out of sugar too. She melted the sugar in a saucepan, and it was fantastic!

Evening meals were warm meals. Lunch was either leftover food from the day before, or most often sandwiches. On Sunday evenings we had a big dinner, such as roast cooked in a crock pot or fried chicken with mashed potatoes and gravy. We had three meals, breakfast, dinner, and supper. The word "lunch" was not in our vocabulary, and I later learned the new word, when I went to school and had lunch at school.

When we ate together as a family, we didn't have napkins, but rather, had "the community rag". We passed the rag around the table whenever anyone wanted to wipe their mouth. It sounds gross, but at the time, seemed normal for a German and Bohemian family.

Because our family was poor, there were a few times we had no food to eat. Consequently, Dad would go fishing and bring home some fish. At times, he shot wild rabbits and pheasants to eat. I loved that food, it was great!

One time my mother went hunting with us, and she shot a rabbit, but when we picked up the dead rabbit, a bullet hole could not be found. Finally, Dad chuckled and pointed to the anus of the rabbit, and it was where Mom shot the rabbit. Oh, how funny, but true!

Our weekly dessert was usually fruit: apples, oranges, and bananas. Very rarely did we have cake, cookies, or ice cream. Cake and ice cream are for birthday celebrations or Christmas and Easter.

When I was about the age of 5 to 7, I discovered dog food tasted pretty good. The dog food, in twenty-five-pound bags, had a sweet taste to it. Perhaps, it had molasses mixed with the hard nuggets. Dog food made by *Super Sweet* was the best. I used to enjoy eating it numerous times. I tried *Purina* dried cat food a few times but didn't really care much for it.

One day, while eating dog food, I noticed hair in the dog food, and was told it was animal hair from pigs or cattle, the dog food was made from, which caused me to discontinue eating it.

Later, as I became older, from 5 to 18 years of age, I became very aware of my parents' financial situation, and purposely ate less food, so that my siblings would have enough to eat.

I chose to be the last one to put food on my plate to make sure others had enough. I kept this to myself and let no one know I did it. Often I went to bed hungry but kept it to myself. Later, after I had a job, I used my own money to purchase food and hid it in my bedroom dresser, so that I would let my siblings eat as much food they wanted from Mom's cooking.

#10 CHILDHOOD THROUGH HIGH SCHOOL

Baths and Not Showers

To save money, our family had a community bath. Each person would take their turn using the same water for their individual bath. We did this to save money on water. My siblings and I fought, as to who went first, and who was last. No one wanted to be last. The water would be dark and dirty. Years later, Dad would install a shower, but it didn't work well due to inadequate water pressure.

Temper Tantrums

When I was just a toddler, I threw temper tantrums a few times. Once I pretended I was going to hang myself with the curtain rope, but my parents and sisters just laughed at me. That didn't work. At other times I banged my head against the wall over and over to get my way. That didn't work, and it really hurt my head. My mother would scream, "Stop that!"

Touched by Grace

When I was about 3 or 4 years old, I had a favorite little toy I played with outside on the grass but lost it. I looked over and over in the grass but could not find it. Just when I was about to give up, something told me to look down, and there it was, right in front of me. I intuitively felt and believed this as a spiritual experience. I knew someone, or something, put it right there. Was it Jesus? Was it my guardian angel, or St. Anthony? At that age, I had not heard of St. Anthony, and did not know I had a guardian angel. I just knew it was a spiritual event and I sensed it. Later in life, I came to give St. Anthony credit for it, as he often helped me find things, even when I did not ask him. When I understood who St. Anthony was, once I found an item, I knew it was St. Anthony who helped me.

When I was about 5, I went *Trick or Treating* on Halloween, and stopped by the convent of the Dominican sisters located next to the church. They used to teach at the Catholic school at St. Gabriel's in Crossroads City. It closed the year before I was to attend Catholic school. My older sisters attended the school, and used to wear the little white veils (mantillas) to Mass.

I knocked on the door of the convent, hoping to receive candy from a religious sister wearing a white habit and a black veil. She went to get candy in another room, and at that moment, I experienced God's presence. I knew beyond a doubt God was in that house. Did I sense Jesus in the Tabernacle, from within their Chapel? At that age, I didn't know anything about the presence of Jesus in the Eucharist, but later in my life I came to believe that back then I sensed His presence in the Eucharist.

I was dumbfounded and didn't know what to say to the sister when she returned with the candy. Due to the spiritual experience, I left with no concern for the candy. But rather, I was delighted to have had the received a spiritual treat.

I had so many wonderful memories as a child. When I was less than 5yrs old, I was fascinated with the statues and the Stations of the Cross in the church. I didn't pay attention to the homily or what happened at Mass. But, enjoyed just gazing upon the statues and the Stations. For some reason, they touched my little heart, in ways I did not understand, at the time.

At the age of 7, I began to take Confraternity of Christian Doctrine (CCD) classes. During the religious education classes, I enjoyed reading and learning about spiritual and holy things. At times, the priest came to visit each class, and when he asked a question, I prided myself on knowing the answer to them. Though I didn't think about becoming a priest as a child, I was certainly interested in spiritual things.

Roaches and Mice

The newer house we had moved into slowly became run down. We started to have roaches and mice. And, I mean, many roaches and mice. Mom thought the mice came home with Dad in his clothes from working at the feed mill. Once I set a mousetrap, and within about ten steps as I walked away, I heard it snap. When I came back to see what had happened, there were five mice caught in that little trap. Hard to believe, but true. Finally, Dad told Mom, we are getting a mouser (cat). When we got the cat, we didn't feed it for a week, which caused the cat to instinctively begin to catch the mice and eat them. The cat got rid of all the mice, but the roaches remained.

Deliriously Sick, Sick on My Birthdays and Pretending to be Sick

When I was attending kindergarten, I became very sick with a bad fever. The teacher took me to the office, and checked my temperature, which was 104 degrees. Mom came to the school to pick me up and took me home. We never had a phone at the time, so I suspect the school called a neighbor and asked the neighbor to notify my mother.

While at home, I became delirious. I saw faces and people laughing in the closet and began to cry. Mom came to my room and held me, trying to convince me there were no ghosts or people in the closet. A few days later the fever finally broke, and I was fine.

I loved my kindergarten teacher, Mrs. Closter. She constantly had to put up with children who wet their pants. She taught me to tie my shoes and learn the alphabet. I don't recall wetting my pants at school.

When I was young, I was often sick on my birthday. One year, I had the flu. The next year I had an upset stomach. Another year, I had chickenpox, and the next year, I had chicken pox again. One year, I had the mumps (only on one side of my face) and the next year, I had the mumps again (on the other side of my face). All these illnesses were on my birthday. I thought you were supposed to only have chicken pox or mumps, once in a lifetime, but not me. I was often sick on my birthday. What's up with that?

There were also times I didn't want to go to school in grade school and high school, and therefore pretended to be sick. I would mess up my hair, and keep rubbing my eyes until they were red, and then when Mom would take my temperature, I rubbed the thermometer, so it would go above 98.6. While at home, I laid on the floor in the living room, watched movies all day, and slept a lot, wrapped in a blanket. Mom made *Campbell's* chicken noodle soup for me.

Feeling the Baby Move Within My Mother

"As soon as the sound of your greeting reached my ears, the baby in my womb leaped for joy." (Luke 1:44)

I had six sisters, three older and three younger and one brother. After Mom had four girls, I very much wanted to have a brother. When my mother became pregnant, I was so excited about the possibility of having a brother. She used to let me feel the baby move around in her tummy. I was fascinated by it all and wondered how the baby got inside of her. Naturally, I was told a stork put the baby there, but didn't believe it. When my brother was born, I dreamed of playing sports with him.

Play House with My Sisters – Or Else!

My sisters wanted me to play house with them, or should I say they forced me to play house with them. They made me play with their dolls, and then later, I began to play with the dolls by myself, and then realized how stupid it was. My second-oldest sister, Marie, made fun of me for playing with the dolls, so, I grabbed her favorite doll, and with a pair of scissors, cut off its hair. Oh man, was she upset.

For years, even when I was in my 30s, she reminded me I ruined her *Skipper* doll. I apologized numerous times, but she mentioned it regularly. Finally, I realized I had not made restitution for the harm I caused and decided to purchase a new *Skipper* doll to give to her on Christmas. I wrapped it up, and when she opened it on Christmas, she cried, and cried. She was very appreciative of receiving the doll. After she received her *Skipper* doll, she never mentioned it again. It was a lesson for me on the importance of restitution.

There is No Santa Claus and No Easter Bunny—My First Concussion

When I was about 5 years old, I climbed on top of the kitchen counter to see what was in the cabinets. When I opened the cabinet door, I discovered Easter candy. At that moment, I came to know there was no Easter Bunny and no Santa Claus. It was so shocking to me, I fell off the counter top backwards, and hit my head on the floor. Due to the discovery, I became upset because I wondered, "If Mom and Dad lied about the Easter Bunny and Santa Claus, what else did they lie to me about?" After that event, I began to wonder whenever my parents told me something, if it was true or not. The funny things children think of.

As a family, we enjoyed playing games together, such as cards (Blitz and Pitch), but also Checkers, Chess, Operation, Sorry, UNO, and Battleship. But there was one board game, I wish my parents would have never brought home, the Ouija board.

Butchering Chickens and Rabbits
(Running Around Like a Chicken with Its Head Chopped Off)

When in high school, we used to butcher chickens by the hundreds in our backyard. What a mess! To kill the chickens, we took a pole of a rake, and put the neck of the chicken under the pole, and then pulled the chicken by its legs, causing its head to remain under the pole on the ground. The body of the chicken, without its head, jumped around our backyard with blood squirting from the neck. After being pulled off, the chicken's head would lay on the ground and blink its eyes staring at us for a minute or two until it stopped. Dad purchased a homemade "chicken plucker", which had rubber fingers that spun in a circle powered by an electric motor. After the chickens died, and before plucking their feathers, we soaked them in hot water, making it easy to pull the feathers out.

Rabbits were also butchered at home. Dad knocked them out, hitting their head with a hammer, and then nailed their legs to a tree. In a matter of minutes, he then cut open their belly, cleaned out their insides, and then skinned their furs. He butchered them in the front yard on the tree, near the street. I wondered if people who passed by were horrified at the "crucified" rabbit on the tree. The rabbits were not pets.

Toe Nail Falls Off – A Bloody Mess

When in 2nd grade, I accidentally dropped a can of vegetables on my big toe. It slowly turned more and more black and blue. I never told anyone, and the toenail slowly started coming off and bled. My second-grade teacher was shocked to see a pool of blood under my chair. She hollered, "Oh my, what happened to you? Did you get hurt?" I said, "No, why?" She noticed blood on the floor, took off my shoe, saw how my toe was bleeding, and then put a Band-Aid on it. She asked if I had told my mother about it, and I replied that I didn't.

The Purpose of The Cry Room at Church Is to Make Children Cry
When They Misbehave

When I was about 2, I used to crawl under the pews at church, and Dad would reach over and twist my ear, to make me straighten up. I can remember going to the cry room once, and Mom giving me a whoop on the butt, that made me cry, hence I thought "cry room" is a place to make children cry.

Problems Reading, Writing & Arithmetic – Summer Classes

When I was in third grade, several events caused great pain in my life. One event was that I could not understand multiplication and division, and had a difficult time reading. I felt everyone was smarter than I. Summer reading classes were a burden for me but were needed to catch up with the other children. I was so nervous, I felt like I was going to wet my pants. Other children knew how to solve the problems, and could read much better than I. Consequently, I developed the idea, I was stupid.

Junkyard (Trash Dump)

When I was between the age of 7 and 13, at times our family went to the local junkyard. The junkyard always smelled of burnt ashes, as often those tending the junkyard were burning trash. In the American way of living, our family was somewhat poor. Mom, Dad, my siblings, and I went through the garbage dump looking for old toys, furniture, lamps and all sorts of things. We wondered how those rich people could throw away items still usable. People threw things away just because they didn't want them anymore, and to us, that was a shock. Back then, there was no such thing as *Good Will* stores or thrift stores. Once I found an old hard rubber car, and it still had all its wheels. Mom found lamps and even a chair for the living room. Dad found an old fan to use in the house. The cord of the fan was shredded, but Dad repaired it, and we used the fan. Occasionally, I accidentally stepped on something that would cause a small cut in my foot, but it never became infected.

#11 ABUSED

"It would be better for him if a millstone were hung around his neck and he were thrown into the sea than for him to cause one of these little ones to sin." (Luke 17:2) "What you do to the least of my brothers, you do to me." (Matthew 25:40)

I was abused by two people when I was a child. The first abuse occurred when I was between the ages of 5-7. My father was the first to abuse me. I felt like I was trapped and was extremely repulsed by the situation. No matter how hard I tried to get away, he would not let me go. Only after he fell asleep, could I finally get away. This occurred multiple times.

Even up to the point of Dad's death, I was repulsed when he laid his hand on me, even though it was an innocent pat on the back. As an adult, whenever there was any situation where it seemed like there was no way out, I overreacted, as to sort of "break free" of the situation. I felt like superman in a phone booth, and if I was locked in the booth, I would destroy the booth to get out.

Later, after being healed of this behavior I realized even if there seemed to be no way out of a situation, I could wait on the Lord to solve the problem, rather than to try to break free at all cost. It was a psychological problem I endured until the Lord healed me of this fear, thanks to the St. Ignatius Discernment of Spirits method.

I was also abused by an older boy who invited me over to his house to play. We used to play catch with a softball and shoot baskets. We went to the creek and caught tadpoles and turtles with our bare hands and caught fish with nets. I greatly enjoyed doing these boy activities.

However, abuse events occurred from 7 to 10 years of age. He was much larger and stronger than I. In fact, when he was in 7th grade, and I was in 5th grade, he could pick up objects weighing up to 150 pounds and toss them over his head. He had me hang onto one of his biceps and he would pick me off the ground. At that time, I weighed about 80 pounds, and he weighed about 150. When spending the night at his house, he began to molest me.

These two events caused a thorn in my side for many years. By the grace of God, when I was 55 and did the "Discernment of Spirits Retreat", I was delivered from this demon which caused so much grief for most of my life. Because these childhood wounds were healed, the demons were no longer able to affect my mind as before. I no longer wanted to look like other men. I was finally content, with the way God made me. When I was in a situation where I felt trapped, I could now wait for the Lord to act and not force my way out of it. This healing occurred because I consecrated the source of these wounds to the Immaculate Heart of Mary and the Sacred Heart of Jesus. Within a few weeks after that, I did the Discernment of Spirits Retreat which helped me to gain freedom. Thank you, Jesus and Mary!

I forgave Dad and the neighbor boy who hurt me. They were seduced by an evil spirit. These events allowed me to develop an empathy towards abuse victims, and I could understand how an innocent person could feel guilty (false guilt) and unclean when they hadn't done anything wrong. I could also give advice to victims of abuse who were deeply hurt and help victims to forgive the perpetrator. I am now able to help victims obtain emotional and spiritual healing. God permitted these things to happen to me, so in the future, I could help others. Thank you, Jesus! This was a beautiful example of the Triumph of God's Mercy over evil.

#12 BOYHOOD ACTIVITIES AND FRIENDS

First Girlfriend from 4th Grade to 8th Grade

A pretty girl with long dark brown hair and dark brown eyes, by the name of Bonnie Bean, and her family, moved to town just a block from my home. I became friends with her. She became my first girlfriend. I bought her a ring that came from a toy machine operated by placing a quarter in a slot and by turning the handle causing the toy to drop out. It was like a gum ball machine, but for toys. I purchased a necklace for her at the Dime Store. We used to hang out at her house and talk about all sorts of things.

She later became interested in a new kid in our class, William Bronson. He became the only blonde boy in our class and owned a motorcycle, which made him popular among girls. I became angry at him for stealing my girlfriend and treated him badly. I instigated a fight with him off school property, so the school couldn't do anything about it. Neither of us were hurt by the fighting because a teacher broke us up.

Oh, God, forgive me, and please bless him for treating me with forgiveness and mercy. Bonnie later became known for dating boys in high school and having relations with them. I was glad we broke up. Back then, we called girls like her "sluts". How bad for her and us who gave her such a title. During that time of my life, I never prayed for her or for other youth that I hurt by my bad behavior.

Boy Activities and Friends

In grade school and high school, I enjoyed riding my bicycle, and at times did long-distance running on my own. In high school and into my early 20s, I ran 10K (6.2 miles), two to three times a week. I enjoyed running down the country roads near my hometown as I listened to and watched wild animals. The fresh air was such a blessing. I took a camera with me, and many times took photos of sunsets and wildlife that were spectacular gifts from God.

As did other boys, I drove my first car, a 1964 Ford Galaxy 500, down Main Street, in what we called "dragging" Main. During high school years, most boys had mag wheels and 8 track tape players in their cars. In order to purchase the car, I took out a loan from the local bank and eventually paid off the loan through my high school job.

God only knows how often I wanted to do other things with other youth my age, but was unable, either due to work, or having few friends. Due to work, I was unable to go to school activities. The Lord gave me a friend in grade school (not the boy who abused me) and a different friend in high school. He also gave me a friend in college. God always provided a friend during my life. I was never really alone, but wished I had more friends, and did more things with other youth my age. God used this isolation to prepare me to live alone as a diocesan priest. As a priest, though at times lonely, I have always been content knowing I have as my best friend, Jesus, and because of Him, I'm never alone.

I Sent a Kid to the Hospital & Sports

I was unable to play sports with my father. He often worked late, and after work, he didn't come home right away, as he spent the rest of the evening at a bar. Certainly, he would have liked to have spent time with me, but it was necessary for him to work late and provide for our family. I wanted to go out for basketball and football and was permitted in 7th grade to go out for both of these sports activities. I didn't play much and really didn't understand the games like other boys.

At one of the football practices, the coach told me to hit the other guy as hard as I could, and I did. The poor kid doubled over and couldn't get up. His mother happened to be at the practice watching. She took her son to the hospital, and he had to have an emergency appendectomy. Since then, I no longer desired to play football and didn't want to cause someone to nearly die.

My father didn't want me to play sports because he said I needed to work to financially help the family by taking care of my own financial needs. Because of work, I couldn't attend homecoming games. Once my father and I had a big argument about it, and then I finally realized nothing could be done, so why mention it again. I should have been more willing to sacrifice myself for my family. Now I greatly value the work ethic instilled within me at a young age.

"Seven Seas" The Dreadful Play
"I Don't Want Her, You Can Have Her, She's Too Fat for Me"

In 3rd grade, our public grade school had a play called the Seven Seas. It was about a man who became stranded on an island. I had a very minor non-vocal part. The teacher chose me, the skinniest boy, to dance with the fattest girl. She was supposed to sit on my knee, and I barely supported her during the play. Obviously, the teacher did it to get a laugh out of the people, but it embarrassed me. The day before the play one of the main characters became ill, and as a result, the music teacher asked me to play his role. I told her I couldn't memorize all the lines before the next day. She said, "Don't worry, the other main character will whisper the lines to you during the play, and you just say them out loud." I was relieved. However, once the play began, the other main character said the words loud enough for the audience to hear, and then I repeated what he said. Every time I spoke, the people laughed. The crowd thought it was funny, but I didn't. I was embarrassed. The longer the play, the more people laughed at me, and the more embarrassed I became. Then, when the fat girl sat on my knee, I couldn't take it anymore. I kept doing my part, but inside I was crying. When the play finished, I went behind the curtains, and balled my head off. The teacher asked why I was crying. I told her I ruined the play and made everyone laugh. For many years up until I was 55 years old, I had great difficulty standing before a crowd of people, especially when I was to say anything. However, thanks be to God! The emotional wounds of this event were healed during the Discernment of Spirits Retreat, many years later after I was ordained a priest.

Music Festival Disaster

When I was in 5th grade, the same music teacher who asked me to be a main character in the 3rd grade play, insisted I sing for the music festival. I told her I couldn't sing. She, another pianist, and I practiced over a period of weeks. I couldn't memorize the song, and I couldn't sing. The day came for the music festival, and as I sang, I watched the judges shake their heads. When it was over, my score was 4 minus. The lowest grade a person could receive was 4. I was once again humiliated. I felt worthless and believed I had no gifts.

Swimming Pool- "Your Skinny"

I went swimming at the local city pool when I was in 3rd grade. A girl my age noticed my skinny body and yelled at others, pointing at me, she said, "Oh, look at his ribs, his bones are sticking out. See how skinny he is." The other children looked at me and laughed. Since then, when I went swimming, I was never shirtless. But rather, I always wore a shirt when swimming. I had the fear that other children would make fun of my skinny body. I also was never shirtless at home or on vacation, as I was embarrassed due to my skinny appearance. This event, combined with the envy of the physical appearance of the neighbor boy, caused years of inner turmoil.

Later in life, even when I was at a normal weight for my age, I viewed myself as being skinny, though I wasn't. I developed sort of the opposite view of Anorexia, where girls view themselves as fat, though they weren't. I viewed myself as skinny, though I wasn't.

After, ordained a priest, I was healed of this problem, using the Discernment of Spirits meditations. Enduring this difficulty helped me to have empathy towards others with body image difficulties. As a result, I could give them spiritual advice. With His mercy, God reached out to heal my misery, so He could use me, to help Him heal the misery of others.

Wrestling, Undefeated, Sort Of

My brother was six years younger than I. Because of the age difference, we never played sports or boys games together. When he was about 5, and I was about 11, we wrestled. And of course, I would always win. I learned how to wrestle from the neighbor boy across the street.

When I was in grade school, during physical education classes, we learned to wrestle "school" style, which was much different from the professional wrestling style we watched on TV. Wrestling had not yet become a sport in many smaller public schools at that time. Even though I was small and skinny, no one was able to defeat me. Due to my finesse, I was fast, and called "fast Lennie". I could get out of holds and pin my opponents. In fact, I never lost a match in grade school, except one.

The coach was very proud of me. However, he began to bet money on my wrestling matches. When I found out, I felt like he was using me, like a dog at a racetrack. He decided to have me wrestle against the largest kid in my class, and was sure I would beat the boy. He bet money on me. I didn't want anything to do with it. The kid's name was Carl Touser. He was a kind and gentle soul. He outweighed me by at least 50 pounds. As we began to wrestle, I decided to throw the match. At first, I attempted to pin him, but soon I realized he wasn't going anywhere. Consequently, I just laid down and let Carl pin me. I often wondered later, had I given my all, maybe I could have defeated him, or perhaps he would have been the victor. I doubt I could have won, but only God knows. Coach Sebastian was furious with me, as he figured out I threw the match.

Wrestle with Neighbor

When I was in the 5th grade, the neighbor boy who was in 7th grade would wrestle with me, and he could easily pin me. He gave me what was called, in pro-wrestling, the bear hug, by picking me off the ground and squeezed me against his chest and belly, for what seemed like 15 minutes. He was about two feet taller than I and outweighed me by at least 70 pounds. There was no way I could get out of his hold. It didn't cause any pain, but I became frustrated I couldn't get out of the hold, or, do it to him. I wanted to overpower him but couldn't. When he finally let me down, I decided to punch him, as hard as I could in the stomach. Other times, he would tighten his stomach muscles, and wanted me to punch him in the gut, as hard as I was able, to show me how strong he was. With stomach muscles tightened, he could take a good punch with no reaction. This time, I wanted to see how strong he really was without tightening his stomach muscles for a hit. I backed up and, with all my might, sunk a fist as hard as I possibly could into his very soft belly. To my astonishment, he didn't flinch. But he must have felt pain, as he immediately sunk a fist into my skinny belly. I doubled over and lost my breath. He immediately felt bad and apologized. He could have hit me much harder but didn't. I deserved the punch from him. I went home crying, and he kept apologizing as I went.

Sadly, the result of this incident damaged our friendship. I became envious of his strength and wanted to change my appearance to look stronger. I purchased a flexible stretching device through the mail, that was supposed to help build pecs and other muscles, rather than purchasing metal weights. Back then, many 5th grade boys purchased their own weightlifting set (which I could not afford) or they used the public high school weights.

Rock Fight – Knock Out

Due to each of us hitting one another, I didn't want to play with him anymore, and he became angry because I wouldn't. So, he started throwing rocks at my mother's garden ruining her flowers and in turn, I became angry. I began to throw rocks at him and his cousin, who happened to be visiting, and he too joined in. The two began to throw rocks at me and mom's garden and I threw rocks at them. I was outnumbered. Then, out of desperation, I picked up a brick and hurled across the street. I could not believe it, but I actually hit his cousin on the head and the brick knocked him unconscious. I thought I killed him and ran to hide in the creek. Just like Adam and Eve who went to hide after they had done something terribly wrong, I ran and hid in the bushes. I heard screaming from his mother, and then I heard my mother come out, and they talked to each her. They carried the boy in the house and my mother came looking for me. She hollered, "Where are you? Come here! Don't worry, I won't spank you!" Trusting her words, I came out of from the creek. But she must have immediately changed her mind or just lost it, and spanked me like I was never spanked before. I deserved it. Later, as an adult I often wondered what happened to that kid. Did he suffer brain damage? Was he okay? Did he have seizures from his concussion? What a terrible thing I did out of desperation! At that time, I didn't know Jesus and never prayed for the boy.

Girly Magazines

In 7th grade, the neighbor friend, who abused me, introduced me to girly magazines. He gave me his *Hustler* and *Playboy* magazines, and I secretly kept them under the mattress of my bed. I eventually started to purchase them myself and was surprised they sold them to young boys at the grocery store. Back then there was no internet, nor websites to view porn. Sadly, the virtue of purity was never on my mind during that time. However, after about a year, I threw them in the trash because I felt guilty. Each person should be respected and not looked upon as an object of pleasure. Rather, we should see God in all persons, who are created in His image and likeness. I can honestly say, by the grace of God, I never looked up porn as a seminarian or a priest. "Blessed are the pure of heart, for they shall see God." (Matthew 5:8). If we look at others with a pure heart, we will see God within them.

Sadly, after we were adults, one of my sisters told others that I had magazines with male pornography when I was a child, but this is totally false. Never in my life did I ever have nor look at male pornography. How gross!! This is absolutely abhorrent to me. She also told others I was gay. She never started saying such things until after I became a priest. I think the reason she began saying such nonsense was because the priest in her parish abused boys. Due to the scandal of her parish, she left the Catholic Church and joined the Methodist church. I found all of this very hurtful.

Due to the Church sex abuse crisis, what happened at her parish, and due to her wild imagination, she came up with these stupid ideas. I forgave her and I love her, despite the harm she did to my reputation.

My Own Bedroom "The Living Room"
After the rat ordeal at the old house on 12th street, located one block from Main Street, we moved to a newer "pink" 3-bedroom house, on 6th street. Pink was my grandmother's favorite color, so I suspect the color influenced my father and mother to purchase it. I didn't like the color of the house.

As the years went on, my brother and I slept in bunk beds, and with Mom's motherly touch, she added a light switch cover that had a plastic owl whose eyes glowed in the dark, and put up boy curtains with a cowboy theme.

Later, after I graduated from 8th grade, I asked my parents if I could sleep in the living room. I wanted my own bedroom (the living room). Every night for four years, I slept on the couch in the living room. My dresser was in my previous bedroom. At first, I enjoyed my own space, but due to the television, I was always last to fall asleep, as I needed to wait until the last person went to bed. Because of my "bedroom" location, I was privy to the many arguments and fights of my parents. At times, I wanted to go to sleep early, but never had that opportunity. It was nice, I could stay up watching TV, and had the whole room to myself, but lost sleep because of it. During those years, I only prayed for one intention and didn't have a relationship with Jesus. Before falling asleep, I prayed one Our Father, Hail Mary and Glory be, so my father would stop drinking.

#13 PETS AND FARM

S and G Hog Company – Here! Piggy! Piggy!

My father entered into an agreement with his boss Clement Schneider, and they began a hog lot (pig farm). We raised pigs from birth to feeders to be sold at the weekly Sale Barn. Much of the work was daily feeding and watering hogs, moving them from pen to pen, cleaning pig pens by throwing the manure on the back of a pickup truck, and then dumping the manure on a field. I became known as the "shit slinger" due to the fact, I had to sling the manure from the pen onto the back of the truck and could do so more rapidly than others.

Due to the barn remodeling, a large pit under the barn captured manure with urine and water. The thick watery sewage in the pit at times filled up and needed to be pumped out by a "honey wagon" (manure spreader) connected to a tractor. One Christmas Eve, the manure pit filled up and was overflowing. I found myself pumping out the manure into the honey wagon and spreading it on the field until dark. At least the pigs had a Merry Christmas. I did too, as I felt I helped them in their time of need. Mom, some siblings, and I, did hog chores at the pig farm regularly. We fed the pigs by operating augers or carrying bags of grain to the pig feeders. We emptied the bags of pellet food for the sows and boars. And, likewise, carried many buckets of grain daily to various pig pen locations. All we had to do was yell, "Here, piggy, piggy, piggy!" And, they came running for their food.

Dad taught me to castrate young pigs. This prevented young gilts from getting pregnant before being sold at the Friday Sale Barn Auction in Crossroads City.

When I was about 7 or 8 years old, we had a pet pig called Frank, short for frankfurter (pork used for hot dogs). It was a farm pet, and so, we never brought it to our home in town. Pigs are smart and like dogs can answer to names. When we hollered for Frank, he ran up to the gate of the pig pen. The pig farm was S & G Hog Company (Schneider and Gadfly) because it was operated by my father and his boss. We had Frank trained to come next to the gate, and stand there, until we climbed on top of his back. We then grabbed his ears to keep from falling. He ran around the pig pen with one of us on his back. At the end of each sibling's turn, he dropped each of us off at the gate for the next sibling to ride him. He loved it, and so did we. When it was very hot outside, we weren't thinking about how the heat could affect Frank, but kept riding him over and over despite the hot temperature. The pig liked it, but it was obvious he was exhausted. The next day we called for Frank, but he didn't come. We found him dead. Dad suspected he died from a heat stroke from all the running around the day before. We were crushed.

Because I had only one pair of shoes in high school, I also used them at the farm. Often times, my shoes had a pig manure on them. After returning home from the farm, I cleaned them to the best of my ability, but they still smelled like pig manure. Because of the odor from my shoes, other youth my age avoided sitting next to me in class. I even went to the extent of spraying Mom's hair spray on my shoes to cover up the smell, but that really didn't work. It made my shoes smell like hog manure and hair spray.

#14 FIRST CONFESSION & HOLY COMMUNION

First Confession and First Communion

"On that day you will realize that I am in my Father, and you are in me, and I am in you." (John 14:20)

Before my First Communion, I made my first Confession. When I made my first Confession, I don't recall the sins I confessed. A few months after my first Confession, I made my first Holy Communion. With all the other children in our second-grade class, kneeling next to each other at the altar rail, I received Jesus on the tongue, which was customary at that time. Back then, no one received Communion on the hand.

The outside light above the door indicated if someone was in the confessional. When I entered the confessional for the first time, I was surprised it was completely dark inside. There was no light within the room, which was just large enough to kneel. I had to kneel before closing the door to see where I was to confess my sins to the priest. Then after confession, I had to feel around to find the door knob to open the door and exit the little room.

I don't recall having a spiritual experience or even praying after receiving Jesus in Holy Communion. I don't believe I understood what I was doing, nor can I recall anything special about receiving the Eucharist at that time. Unfortunately, my greatest impression when I received my First Communion was the cute little girl kneeling next to me. Later, after we graduated from high school, we went swimming together in a locked city pool.

However, soon after my First Communion-- I became interested in spiritual things. I used to enjoy looking at the statues, the large Crucifix and the Stations of the Cross in the church. I found them more interesting, than the priest's homily.

I remember what I confessed when I did my second Confession. I stole a walnut at the local grocery store and wanted to confess that I stole it. Not much after that confession, we had a new priest come to the parish, who severely damaged my view of Confession.

Confession Changed – No Confession for 20 years

The new priest who came to St. Gabriel's parish constructed what was called the "Reconciliation Room". The room had chairs placed in a circle. The priest gathered my classmates for Confession and said to the child on the end, "You go first. Tell everyone your sins." Then after the first child confessed publicly, he pointed to the next child, and said, "Confess your sins." Each child my age confessed as they went. When it came my turn, I froze, and didn't know what to say, so I made up sins I really didn't commit. When all finished confessing out loud to each other, the priest said, "Your penance is one Hail Mary." He then gave all of us collectively absolution, with the sign of the Cross, and said, "Okay, you can all go now and play." I was shocked by all this, and thought confession changed. From that time on, I never saw anyone stand in line for confession. My parents never went to confession, that I know of-- nor did they encourage my siblings, or I, to go.

8th Grade and the Sacrament of Confirmation (He lost his head!)

My 8th grade graduation and Confirmation occurred the same year. My parents wanted me to take Saint Denis for my Confirmation name, due to Denis being the name of my Confirmation sponsor. For many years, I didn't know who St. Denis was. I later found out, he was a bishop from France, martyred by having his head cut off. The holy bishop picked up his head and began to carry it for miles.

When I was in 8th grade, there was a young man, about the age of 18 decapitated from a car accident. Despite our age difference, we were about the same size. After his death, his mother needed money and had a garage sale. My mother purchased his used light green dress suit for my 8th grade Graduation and Confirmation. It fit perfectly. How fitting to wear the suit to my Confirmation, since my confirmation saint was decapitated, and since the previous owner of the suit was decapitated in a car accident. God's providence! I didn't realize this was the case until years later. How strange! It felt strange, to wear the suit of a dead man, but how fitting for the occasion, since both he and my confirmation saint lost their heads.

During the Confirmation Mass, I had an interesting experience. When the bishop laid hands on my head, I felt heat come down on my head, and had an indescribable joy. I thought everyone else had the same experience, but later discovered they didn't.

After my Confirmation, my parents mistakenly told me, "Now that you are an adult, you can decide for yourself if you want to keep going to CCD classes." Naturally, as a young kid, I decided not to attend anymore, which was a big mistake on my part. I certainly wasn't an adult, and shouldn't have had the ability to choose for myself, if I would attend religious classes or not. This false understanding was promoted in CCD books, and from priests at the time. It spread throughout the Church and the false idea would linger for decades.

The Sacrament of Confirmation is an out pouring of the Holy Spirit to strengthen and make firm baptismal graces, so we may become a witness for Christ. It is one of the three sacraments needed to complete initiation into the Church, but, it does not mean one becomes a mature adult when confirmed.

#15 TABERNACLE AND CRUCIFIX MOVED

Moving the Tabernacle and Crucifix at St. Gabriel's Church

Priests came and went at my hometown parish of St. Gabriel's church. A beautiful Crucifix hung above the altar. The Tabernacle was directly behind the Altar in the center. When a new priest came, he moved the Tabernacle to the side where the statue of Mary was located, and placed the Crucifix against the wall where the Tabernacle was previously. However, when the next priest came, he moved the Tabernacle back in the center and placed the crucifix directly above the altar. The third priest came, and again the Tabernacle was moved to the side, the Crucifix went against the wall, and the priest's chair was moved to the center, where the tabernacle had been.

In the late 1960s and early 70s the pastor began to offer Mass in Latin and English, and we could follow along in the missalette with both languages. Then a few years later, the Mass was offered only in English, and no Latin.

Just a few years ago, in the 2020s, they moved the Crucifix at St. Gabriel's parish and the Tabernacle again. However, this time both are now on the wall. The crucifix is in the center and the Tabernacle is now about four feet to the left of the crucifix. Poor Jesus in the Eucharist is moved around like He's an object of decoration, rather than a person. Since it's His house, He should be in the center!

#16 FAMILY FAITH

Family Faith

For the first 14 years of my life, my family attended Mass every Sunday at 10am in Crossroads City at St. Gabriel's Church. We always prayed before meals and sometimes Dad added, "Good food. Good meat. Good God. Let's eat". My siblings and I attended CCD classes, but unfortunately, I didn't learn much. At times, someone came to my class to play the guitar, or we had singalongs played on a record player.

One of my favorite songs was *Whatsoever You Do, to the Least of My Brothers, That You Do Unto Me.* By the time I finished CCD classes, I didn't know the 10 Commandments, the Seven Sacraments, the mysteries of the Holy Rosary, the Holy Days of Obligation, the difference between a mortal sin or venial sin, or if you missed Mass on Sunday, it was a mortal sin. I remember being taught that Jesus loves me.

When I was a youth, I enjoyed spiritual things, and when the priest came to our classroom, I was always one of the first to answer the priest's question. I didn't realize it at the time, but the content of what we learned was very watered down. As I grew up, I never heard of Eucharistic Adoration or a Holy Hour. I didn't have an understanding of Jesus' true presence in the Tabernacle. My family wasn't involved in parish activities, and so, I never knew what parish life was like outside of Mass. I didn't know why we genuflect when we entered and left the church.

A Father's Spiritual Advice

When I was working as a manager at the hospital in Hickok, an employee under my supervision was causing problems in the sterilizing department. When asking my father for advice on how to deal with the person, I said to him, "I can't stand working with her. I'm going to find a different job." But, Dad said, "Pray for her". I said, "I can't stand her. I will not pray for her." And Dad repeated, "Pray for her." I reluctantly told him I would pray for her every day. About a month later, I could not believe what happened. She and I sat down and we talked. We shared our feelings and concerns with each other about work. From that moment on we became friends. Prayer changed her heart and mine. It was a good lesson I learned from my father.

Hearts of Jesus and Mary

Mom was given large pictures of the Hearts of Jesus and Mary from her brother, Father Ferdinand, a priest. I loved images very much. Years later, after Mom and Dad lost the house due to a foreclosure, my eldest sister, Anne, was given the pictures. I was secretly jealous Mom gave them to her. When I went to college, I stopped at a garage sale, and noticed a set of those exact pictures, and purchased them for next to nothing. I hung them on my wall in the living room of my rented house, and enjoyed looking at them. But over a period of time, and because I wasn't practicing my faith, I felt like they were too religious to be seen by friends who came to my home. I didn't need all that religious stuff anymore. How sad! I removed them from the wall and placed them beside the outside garbage can. I can't believe I did this.

As soon as I returned inside the house, I saw a woman stop and get out of her car. She was obviously shocked to see the beautiful pictures by the garbage can. Thanks be to God, she took both with her, and I was glad they didn't go to the dump.

Years later, not much after my conversion and became a practicing Catholic, while in Medjugorje, I saw the two Hearts of Jesus and Mary in the sun. I will speak about this event later. I felt terrible about setting them with the garbage, and later, after I became a priest, I noticed a set for sale on the internet. I purchased and framed them.

Now, I have I devotion to the Hearts of Jesus and Mary, and have had many prayers answered by consecrating situations to the Hearts of Jesus and Mary. One example of my prayer answered was that after my concussion, while I was pastor of St. Veronica Giuliani Catholic Church in Brushwood City and St. Anthony in Jericho City, I had serious problems with my emotions. Due to the head injury, I would laugh inappropriately, lose my temper, or cry easily, etc.... The doctor prescribed at least six different medicines over several years, but none did any good.

I decided to consecrate my head injury to the Immaculate Heart of Mary and the Sacred Heart of Jesus, and within a month, on May 13th, 2013, the doctor prescribed a new medicine, Gabapentin. It worked. I am now back to my normal self. May 13th is the anniversary of Our Lady of Fatima, who promoted devotion to Her Immaculate Heart and the Heart of Jesus. This is just one of many prayers answered by consecration to the Hearts of Jesus and Mary. (See Appendix B – Consecration Prayers)

#17 JOBS

Work, Work, Work

"Whatever you do, work at it with your whole being. Do it for the Lord rather than for men, since you know full well that you will receive an inheritance from Him as your reward. Be slaves of Christ the Lord." (Colossians 3:23-24)

My first job at home was to dump the trash every week, and didn't do it as often as needed. About the age of 7, my second job was to help Mrs. Charmen with her yard. I was paid $5 to mow the yard and pull weeds, and was given a peanut butter and jelly sandwich with toasted bread.

Schneider's Hatchery, Feed Mill and Grain Co.

When I was about 10yrs old, in 1975, I began to work with my father at Schneider's Feed Mill and was paid by Clement Schneider $20 a week for 54 hours. I dumped sacks of grain in the mixer, loaded customer sacks of grain mixed by my father, cleaned the feed mill, and accompanied my father delivering truckloads of grain to feed bins used to feed cattle and pigs at farmsteads.

When I was in high school, my salary increased to $2.00 an hour (minimum wage) working 54 hours a week, with no overtime pay. I also worked for the chicken hatchery and grain elevator. I did daily chores of feeding chickens, shoveling manure out of chicken houses, carried off dead hens, daily gathered eggs in baskets, washed eggs at the hatchery, fed baby chicks in brooders, changed their poop trays, carried bags of feed to farmer's vehicles, unloaded semis of bagged grain, loaded grain cars and dumped grain trucks at the grain elevator. During this time, I enjoyed getting to know many farmers. By the end of 6 years working for Mr. Schneider, I was making $4 an hour, while my father, who had been working there for over 30 years, getting only $6 an hour. I decided to work at the local grocery store at the end of my junior year and therefore chose to quit. On my last day at Schneider's, I decided to ask Clement to give my father a pay raise. My father had no idea I would do that. The last 30 minutes before the store closed for the day, I said to Clement, "Will you give my father a raise? He is only making $2.00 an hour more than myself, and has 8 children to feed. He has no idea I'm asking this." Clement's response was anger, yelling and colorful language that caused me to blush. Later, when Dad found out, he said, he was proud of me. My father actually received a good pay raise.

To Kill a "Mocking" (Myna) Bird (Mr. McGregor)

The feed store and hatchery was the home of a myna bird, Mr. McGregor. The bird would mimic all sorts of sounds including the soda pop machine, and make a wolf call whistle, some, but not all, thought humorous.

One day, a woman came in the store, heard the bird whistle, and thought Clement did it. In response, she slapped him in the face.

Patrons could feed the bird popcorn or a few grapes. As the bird began to age, it was no longer able to sit on the bars in the cage. I decided to feed it to see how much it would eat. It ate all the popcorn and most of the grapes contained in the bowl. The bird finally stopped eating. The next day, the bird was found dead at the bottom of the cage. I suspect he ate too much, and his little body couldn't take all the food it had eaten. I thought the bird would have been smart enough to know when to stop eating. I felt terrible, despite unintentionally killing the bird.

Killing of the Innocents (Baby Boy Chicks) -- Pharaoh for a Day

"Throw the males in the water!" "Then Pharaoh gave this order to all his people: "Every Hebrew boy that is born, you must throw into the Nile, but let every girl live." (Exodus 1:22)

While in High School and working for Schneider's Hatchery and Feed Store in Crossroads City, I was asked to do something I did not want to do. Have you ever wondered what happens to all those baby roosters, due to every farmer receiving one rooster per ten hens? Everyone wants hens to lay eggs, and only a few roosters. Hatchery workers counted the number of tips on the chick's wings to determine if they were male or female. About half of all chicks hatched were male, and the other half female. Because no one wanted to purchase male baby chicks (roosters) and mostly wanted egg layers (hens), the owner of the hatchery would kill the male baby chicks by the hundreds.

One day, I was asked to kill the male baby chicks. A large metal trash can was half filled with water. Then, all male baby chicks that could not be sold were dumped into the can, and the worker took a broom, and continually swished the water around, until all baby boy chicks drowned. As I did this, I was horrified. I kept swishing the water around until, I thought they were all dead. However, when all were no longer moving, water was drained, and deep in the middle of the trash can, I heard one baby chick cheeping. It greatly bothered me. I searched the can filled with hundreds of dead chicks, but could not find the one chick still alive. After I did this dirty job, I went to Clement and told him I could never do it again. I told him he could fire me if he wanted, but I refuse to kill chicks again. He didn't fire me.

Later, as I reflected on this, I felt like the one cheeping chick was Moses, who survived from getting drowned in the water. What sorrow this caused my heart to know I did such a terrible thing. Man has dominion over creatures, but should they all die like that if no one wants them? Perhaps today they are raised and given to chicken companies to make breaded chicken patties. Back then, baby male chicks couldn't be raised. The meat of a rooster is very tough to eat, no one would want it, and it would be a substantial expense for the business.

A co-worker and I were collecting eggs from the nests of a hen house and as we normally placed them in wire baskets, he threw an egg and hit me in the head. I threw an egg at him, and he threw another egg at me. Before we knew it, we had thrown multiple baskets of eggs at each others, splattering them all over the inside walls of the chicken house. Since it was their future chicks, the hens were beside themselves in cackling. Due to frigid weather with ice on the road, we made up a story that the company station wagon filled with baskets of eggs, slid on ice and crashed against the curb, breaking eggs in the wagon. Clement believed us. Vandalism of the eggs and lying. Forgive us! O Lord.

Dickey's IGA Grocery Store

My first day on the job, I was asked to stack wooden crates of glass pop bottles. At that time, they were worth 10 cents a bottle when returned after use, and sent back to the manufacture and refilled. I placed the last of seven crates on top of each other, causing the stack to slowly sway until the entire stack came crashing to the ground, ruining many glass bottles and making a mess. The owner came to see what happened, smiled, and said, "Don't worry, those things happen." I was relieved.

He was a wonderful boss and due to my hard work, I was quickly promoted from bagger, to stocker, to checker, and then eventually became the assistant manager. I became friends with the other workers, which opened up a new world of friendships that I didn't have attending school. I had dreams of becoming a grocery store chain owner, and wanted to give away food to the poor at each of the store locations.

A friend and I, while working at the store, regularly stole packages of *Little Suzie Brownies* and ate them. The owner realized we were doing it and questioned us, but we denied it. O God, forgive us. I eventually made restitution by mailing cash anonymously to the owner.

Due to my positive experience at the store, I decided to go to college at Fort Hickok. I wanted to be a wealthy grocery store owner.

"Lord Jesus Christ, you brought the repentant thief from the suffering of the Cross to the joy of your kingdom, Lord, when we die, may we who confess our sins be brought to you through the gates of heaven, that we may have eternal joy in that kingdom where you live and reign forever and ever." Friday, Week 1, Midafternoon Prayer of the *Liturgy of Hours*.

EZ Mart

"Lord, remember me when thou comest into thy kingdom." (Luke 23:42) "Amen I say to thee, this day thou shalt be with me in paradise." (Luke 23:43)

While working at the grocery store, I decided to work at a convenience store to save extra money for college. My boss was fabulous. I enjoyed getting to know many people of the local area.

I came to know specific purchasing habits and likes of customers. One customer was known for his Winston cigarettes. Another guy had the habit of regularly purchasing chewing tobacco. I discovered most people always drank the same beer or pop, and purchased the same things when they came to the store. Creatures of habit, we are.

A friend and I stole rolls of quarters out of the register to play the video game, *Pac-Man*. We thought the owner didn't lose any money, since we just gave it back to him in the machines, but later discovered he received only a portion of the money from the machines. I made restitution by anonymously sending money in the mail to the owner. Later, I was greatly troubled when another employee, a cousin, was blamed for stealing the quarters and was fired. I should have confessed to spare her grief, but didn't. O Lord, forgive us, for we were ignorant in our youth.

Bob Gart's Grocery Store

Before going to college, I quickly found a job as a bagger and stocker at a grocery store in Fort Hickok. I moved up in ranks and became the Dairy Department manager, and then later, was promoted to Produce manager. However, one summer I went custom cutting wheat, but returned to work at the grocery store.

Stupidly, with the permission of the store manager, when I was produce manager, I decided to advertise a ladies bathing suit contest at the store. One woman came wearing a swimsuit, and she won the contest. That was not a very pious thing to do, which I regret. The manager, who was married, and I, hoped many more young girls in their bathing suits would come for us to admire. O God, forgive us for promoting and encouraging immodesty.

Nedley Regional Medical Center

While in college, I quit at Bob Gart's Grocery and began to work at Nedley Regional Medical Center, one of the two hospitals in Fort Hickok. While working in the purchasing department, I stocked carts with medical supplies, delivered supplies to nursing units, unloaded boxes, and re-stocked shelves in the purchasing department. I eventually was asked to work in the Central Supply Department and after a few years, became manager. The Central Supply department sterilized surgical instruments and kept track of important supplies for the operating room. This Methodist hospital was run mostly by Catholics, who worked there. I had a terrific Catholic boss. The hospital was known for its high-quality medical care and friendly atmosphere.

However, the destruction of the Catholic and Methodist identities at both hospitals occurred when the two merged. It was a disaster for both hospitals. 90% of the employees at Nedley Regional Medical Center discontinued working there. The Catholic hospital lost its identity. Its Tabernacle, statues and Crucifixes were removed. Immoral surgeries began to be performed at both facilities, such as tubal ligations and vasectomies. Planned Parenthood asked the Nedley hospital campus to sterilize surgical instruments. I told my Catholic boss, if what we were doing for Planned Parenthood was publicized, it would be a public relations disaster. He agreed, and we no longer sterilized the instruments. I was employed at Nedley when I received my call to the priesthood.

A funny event happened at the hospital. I received an urgent call from a ward secretary who said a patient card machine was stuck and smoking. I asked her to call maintenance. She said she did, but nobody came, and urgently needed someone to shut off the machine before it would cause a fire. When I arrived at the nursing unit, the machine was smoking. There was no on/off button on the device. It was plugged in beneath the counter top. I pulled out the drawer, crept inside the hole from the drawer, and was able to unplug the machine. Unfortunately, however, I was unable to back out of the cabinet hole. I was stuck. No matter how I tried, I could not get back out. I began to panic and told the secretary to call maintenance. Instead, she placed one of her feet on the top of the ledge and suddenly grabbed my two legs and raised them in the air and tried to pull me out. Ouch! It didn't work. My ribs got bruised. Finally, after about 15 minutes, I slowly turned my hips until I was able to back out, but not without a few bruises and scrapes. When I stood up, I thanked the secretary, and said, "You ought to be glad I never farted when you pulled on me like that!" Years later when I happened to see her, she reminded me what happened and what I said. Our words are remembered by individuals, but also recorded in the Book of Life and opened at our judgment.

#18 HIGH SCHOOL YEARS

Have You Ever Thought About Becoming a Priest?
When I was in high school, my uncle, Fr. Ferdinand Tosmercka, my mother's brother, asked me, "Have you ever thought about becoming a priest?" I looked at him straight in the eye, and said, "Father, that's the last thing I would ever want to do." While I was young, I was drawn to spiritual things, but not in high school. Later, after I discovered I had a call to the priesthood, Fr. Ferdinand was very supportive and prayed much for me. He never lived to see my ordination, and died shortly after his 50th priesthood anniversary. While he was known for his orthodoxy, some photos after his death with another priest shockingly scandalized the family. The photos caused us to believe he

was gay and had a gay priest friend. I inherited his chalice. My grandmother's wedding ring was soldered on the base of the chalice after his mother, my grandmother, Sarah (Vatal) Tosmercka, passed into eternal life, a year after I was born.

Broken Picture

Due to poor self-image when I was in high school, I threw a dart at my class picture on the wall. It broke the picture glass creating a hole in the photo on my face. Later, when my mother saw what I did, she cried, and asked why I did it. I said, "I'm ugly, and I'm stupid." She cried all the more, and hugged me, trying to convince me, I was not that way. I believe I felt that way due to being rejected by classmates, being called skinny, my inability to have a girlfriend, being made fun of by other boys, my father calling me "dumber than a box of rocks", etc. Looking back, I realize I didn't share any of my difficulties with either parent or any friend, and think things could have been different had I confided in someone. In my opinion, children should be encouraged to share their difficulties with others, especially parents. Back then, I didn't believe my parents ever wanted to listen to me. I may have been very wrong.

Poor Self-image

"Does the clay say to the potter, 'What are you making?' Does your work say, 'The potter has no hands'?" (Isiah 45:9)

By the time I was in high school, I developed a strong negative image of myself. It can be summed as "Unloved, Sad, Self-Hatred, Angry, and Stupid". I felt unlovable because girls did not express an interest in me, which I presumed had to do with my skinny appearance, and my perception of my not so handsome face. I wanted to be strong like other boys, which I believed attracted girls to them. Besides their appearance, I believed it was also their personality and ability to communicate effectively. This caused girls to be interested in them. I felt sad due to not having many friends, and was unable to participate in youth activities my age due to work. I also felt sad as a result of my parents having problems with their marriage, and also, I didn't get along with my siblings. My siblings and I fought a lot, and I received blame for things I didn't do. I felt all alone. I felt stupid because my grades were poor, but the primary reasons were I seldom studied and didn't like to read. When my father was drunk, he said I was "dumber than a box of rocks". When in seminary, I learned St. Thomas Aquinas was called, a "Dumb Ox", which gave me consolation. I had self-hate as well. I didn't like my appearance, and thought I was ugly. Not only that, I hated my appearance and was angry. I thought my parents never listened to me, and felt I had no one to talk to. My mother had to deal with Dad's torments, and I didn't dare say anything to him while he was drunk.

I later discovered other high school youth also had problems in their families, and at times, they too felt alone and unloved. The unloved, the sadness, self-hatred, anger and feeling stupid haunted me for years.

This baggage was brought out in the open, when I was a Franciscan of Perpetual Victim Martyrs. Some brothers, a few extern sisters (non-cloistered), and I were giving talks at a high school. I lost my temper at a high school age boy, who was picking on a girl, and realized I had anger issues due to the times I never defended my mother from my father's mistreatment toward her.

Over the years, I made progress with some of these negative ideas about myself. For example, I learned why I felt like I was stupid. It was due to the times I was told I wouldn't amount to much, and I was "dumber than a box of rocks" and therefore, began to believe these things. I eventually learned to counter these negative thoughts with true thoughts.

I kept playing the same negative thoughts over in my mind like a record on an invisible record player. But realized it could be corrected, with practice. To change the record, whenever I called myself stupid, I corrected myself, saying in my mind, "I'm not stupid, I just made a mistake, or I wasn't thinking." Or, if I felt unloved, I reminded myself my parents loved me and God loves me. I learned to change my way of thinking, due to a story I read in *Reader's Digest*, that explained how we can change our negative way of thinking about ourself.

The Discernment of Spirits Retreat helped to get to the bottom of many of these negative and erroneous views, and I found permanent healing from Jesus through the meditations. And many times, healing occurred at the time of the meditation.

High School Happenings and Shenanigans
"Do not remember the sins of my youth and my rebellious ways; according to your love remember me, for you, LORD, are good." (Psalm 25:7)

For the most part-- my first two years in High School were uneventful. I had a crush on a girl and invited her to come with me to "Snow Ball", a winter dance. She said she would think about it, and let me know later. When the day came for her to give the answer, I told her I didn't want to know what she decided. I felt unworthy of taking such a nice girl to the dance and asked her to forgive me for asking in the first place. Afraid she would say no, I didn't want to be crushed by rejection. I always wondered what her answer would have been. I had very low self-esteem at the time, which hindered relationships.

School Studies & The Third Book

The first two years of high school, I didn't get in trouble and just minded my own business. I rarely did any homework unless it was absolutely necessary. The entire time in high school I only read two books, *The Grapes of Wrath* and *Little Women,* which were both required. I didn't like to read and never read the assignments. I tried to recall the information spoken at class for the tests, and did papers by skimming through books, and then writing about what I skimmed. My grades in high school were average, and really should have been much higher had I read the assignments and studied for tests. My parents were unconcerned about my grades and were not involved in my studies. The third complete book I read was the *Holy Bible* given to me by my eldest sister Anne. Sadly, after I read it from front to back, I didn't pick it up again for 9 years.

School Organization

I was a member of FFA (Future Farmers of America), but was not involved in any other school organizations or functions. While in high school, I had to work both at the pig farm (hog lot) and my grocery store job. I had little time to do much of anything else.

Karate Kid

During one semester, one day a week, I took Kickboxing (Karate Boxing) classes at night. During class, I was undefeated. Although I was small and thin, the other boys were afraid of me as I hit as hard as I could. I was tenacious. Each player who landed a punch or a kick would obtain points depending upon where and how (with a punch or a kick) the person was hit in the stomach, on the head, leg, etc.

During class, I punched an opponent, bigger and more muscular than I, so hard he fell down. I don't recall if it was a blow to the head or stomach, but the coach yelled, "You're not supposed to hit the other man as hard as you can! You're only supposed to make contact with your opponent, to receive points." I thought we were supposed to hit our opponent as hard as we were able.

From that moment on, I was afraid I may hurt my opponents and began to lose all matches even though I wanted to win. One fella took advantage of my weakness, noticing I was afraid of hurting others, and gave me some good hard punches during a match. But it didn't bother me. Up to that point, I was vicious and unconcerned about hurting others, and didn't care about the feelings of my opponents. I somehow wanted to beat my opponent and win by conquering at all cost, and nothing would stop me. It was as though every punch I landed was directed toward the one who abused and overpowered me when I was younger. The coach's correction was a reality check, and opened my eyes to see how I can hurt others due to my desire to get even and conquer the one who had hurt me years before. I began to see others in the light of viewing them as persons with feelings, who suffered pain. I could now see they can be hurt by a ruthless boxer, someone who wanted to get even with his neighbor, and who always won whatever game we played.

Purchased My Own Clothes and Shoe Size Too Small
I purchased my clothing from the time I was a freshman through high school. I wore size 6 ½ shoes because that's the size my parents purchased for me in 8th grade and didn't realize until I went to college and was measured at a clothing store that my actual shoe size was 8. For all those years, I wore shoes that crimped my toes. I had no idea shoes were worn in any other way. When I put on size 8 for the first time, it felt like I had too much room in my shoe, but later, they felt more comfortable than the 6 ½'s.

Animal House
During my junior year, I watched a movie called *Animal House,* which lead to behavior change. The movie motivated me to want to have fun, or so I thought. By the time I was a senior, I began to do crazy things. I knew first-hand how television can affect personal behavior.

Car on the Sidewalk
After watching the television program *Duke's of Hazard,* I decided to have fun with my car. I came up with a stupid idea of driving down the sidewalk to scare people, and I actually did just that. I drove on the sidewalk in front of the grocery store. Thanks be to God, no one came out of the store. Otherwise, I may have killed them. What an inconsiderate and uncaring thing to do.

Chickens
When I was a senior, I came up with the idea of taking a few chickens from the hatchery and letting them lose in the high school at night. A friend and I took a chicken coup and captured some chickens at a chicken house. Earlier in the day, I unlocked a window in the restroom of the school, so I could crawl through it at night. It appeared to be locked, but wasn't. The poor janitor had a mess to clean up the next day. I didn't care if I made his life and job miserable. I just wanted to have fun at the expense of others.

Dead Calves
The night before graduation, I again unlocked a window and found a couple of dead calves in the alley behind the veterinary clinic. After entering the school, I placed a calf on a toilet in the girl's restroom and the other in the middle of the gym floor where graduation was to be held the next day.
Weeks later, someone later broke into the school and set off fire extinguishers. I was later accused of it, but had nothing to do with it. I have no idea who did it. I personally consider it vandalism, because it caused damaged to property, which I didn't do.

Prom Night

After Prom was over, my cousins and some friends went to eat at a restaurant at Fort Hickok, and since we were 18, we all had too much beer. Coming back from Fort Hickok, I decided to show off and drive my car faster than the 20 MPH city speed limit, and sped over 70. The railroad track is elevated on Main Street and when we hit the tracks, the car became airborne. I couldn't believe it. The car landed on the back end of the vehicle, hitting the gas tank and rear wheels first, and then it jumped up and down on the highway until all four wheels were on the road. All of us hit our heads on the roof of the car, while beer flew all over inside. The engine died, but to my surprise it started once we slowed down. How stupid of me. I could have killed everyone in the car. O Lord, thank you, for in your mercy, you spared us!

After the flying car incident, we entered inside the school through an open window and took the handcrafted staircase made from wood and cardboard used as a prop, and also took a large blue cloth that said, "Stairway to Heaven", our prom theme. We placed the stairway on top of the car, and drove down Main Street. Although it was about 3am, it just so happened my father had stopped at an intersection and watched as I drove my car with the staircase on top of it. He later never said anything about it. I think he was curious as to why I wasn't home at that time, and knew I was up to no good. We dumped the staircase outside of town in a ditch, and then placed the blue cloth around the life-size Statue of Liberty in the city park of Crossroads. Our crazy antics did not at all, help us climb the stairway to heaven. St. Rose of Lima said, "the Cross is the only stairway to heaven".

Dated A Girl From My Senior Class

Betty Brunella, who I knelt next to when I made my First Holy Communion, was someone I later enjoyed doing fun things together in high school. Once, we asked the high school secretary to retrieve something from inside the walk-in safe and to look up something for us in a file. While she was inside the safe, we slowly closed the door on her, flipped on the intercom switch, and in unison, said really loud, "It don't matter!" The principal had warned students to avoid apathy. The truth is, no one really had it, we just acted like it. So, when we said, "It don't matter", it was a purposeful jab at the principal. She and I ran out of the office to quickly hide in the science lab. We acted as if we were performing lab tests. But the principal figured out we did it, and told us we were not going to walk across the stage to get our diploma on graduation day and said it would be mailed to us. Both of us went to graduation anyway, hoping he wouldn't follow through with his threat. To our surprise, our names were called. We called his bluff. Neither one of us told our parents what happened.

About a month later, I decided to take her out on a date. She made it known we were to only be friends, and do nothing more than what friends would do. I took her to the local city swimming pool at night, and after removing most of our clothing, we sneaked in under the fence and went swimming, when suddenly a spotlight shone upon us while in the pool. It was Brady, the town police officer. We fled the pool, entered my car, and drove several blocks. But soon, red lights were flashing, and so I pulled the car over and parked next to the curb. He warned us, we could be arrested for trespassing, but when he saw we were in our skivvies, he chuckled and let us go.

Betty had large, pretty blue eyes, and I told her she had Betty Davis eyes. But she seemed unimpressed. I asked a friend, older than 21, to purchase champagne for me. I bought plastic martini glasses, which I placed in the car before picking up my date. As we dragged Main Street, we sipped the champagne. (It's against the law to drive with an open container and against the law to drink the percentage of alcohol in the champagne.) We both looked at each other and said, "I don't like champagne, do you?" Both of us said, "No". Therefore, we decided to open the car door, and pour it down the center of Main Street as though we were christening the street with our last hurrah before we were to go our separate ways.

I had always wanted to take a girl to "Lover's Lane", a dead-end dirt road about three miles out of town. Couples would park in that romantic spot at night and gaze upon the moon and stars together, and maybe do a few more things boys and girls like to do together. Yet, I knew that wouldn't happen with Betty Brunella. I pray, if I had taken a girl there, we would have just admired God's creation, especially the moon and stars together in love.

A Hole in One, The First Time I Golfed by Myself
(No Footprints in the Sand) – Not a Poem

While working at the local grocery store, I met a fella two years younger than I, who became my best friend. We did everything together. Unfortunately, when I turned 18, I introduced him to alcohol. But, I never purchased any for him. We enjoyed working together, going to concerts and skiing together in Colorado. He introduced me to golfing and taught me how to golf. I never golfed on my own. However, he convinced me to go by myself. Because he bought new clubs, he gave me his old set. As I started the game on my own, on the first hole, I swung and the ball went flying. Surprisingly, it went in the direction of the hole, but I thought I over shot it. When I was looking for the ball, I happen to see an old man near the first hole, so I said to him, "Have you seen my ball?" He said, "Yes, it's in the hole. I saw the whole thing." I laughed and said, "Okay sir, really, have you seen my ball?" He said, "Yes, it's in the hole. You got a hole in one." I said, "No way, this is the first time I came out by myself. That can't be." He said, "Look, I will show you." He showed me where the ball landed on the sand green and pointed how it left jump marks in the sand and went in the hole. There were no footprints in the sand. We both had a good laugh.

Graduated 1981 from Crossroads High

Our class theme was chosen by popular students. Although I had nothing to do with naming of the theme at that time, I agreed with it. The theme was "Sexy girls, booze and fun, we're the class of 81". In March of that year, President Reagan was shot and then about a week before graduation, Pope John Paul II was shot. At the time of these events, our history teacher allowed our class to watch live television through local programming from nearby larger cities. These events seemed to somehow cause more instability in the lives of people my age.

Adult Store

When a group of friends went to snow ski in the mountains, sadly, the leader of our group from Crossroads took us to a very awful place called *"Bare and Boogie."* While inside the place, if you gave the attendant money, you could look at an unclothed girl behind an adult glass play pen. She was obviously drunk or high. When we all returned to the bus, no one said a word. All of us felt terrible. We felt bad for her, the life she was living, and how we contributed to it. We also felt bad because we used our money to pay for something so sinful. O Lord, forgive us, for we know not what we do!

Guilt by Association

After I graduated from High School, one summer night, I parked my car on the side of Main Street and was enjoying watching other high school youth drag Main, when a man, Boris Smithson, who was two years older than I, and a group of his friends, came up to a friend and I, and encouraged us to walk through town with them. After walking with them for only a block, I realized something wasn't right. At first, I didn't realize it, but later came to understand this fella was drunk, and I felt uncomfortable tagging along with him and his friends. I never hung out with him or his friends before. As we walked down an alley behind Main Street, he suddenly rammed his shoulder against the back door of Dickey's IGA Grocery Store, where I had previously worked. The door immediately broke and popped opened. I was shocked and wanted to leave. He and some of his friends went inside the store and came out with pop and snacks. Not able to find my best friend, I assumed he was inside and went in the store looking for him, so we could take off and leave the group. He wasn't inside. When I came out of the store, I found him and said, "Let's get out of here! This is not right." Boris went on to do more damage throughout the town, including damaging train track signals and knocking over a phone booth. After the grocery store was broken into, we departed from them.

The next day, a policeman approached me and said I was to come with him to the police station. When I arrived, he read my rights, but I went ahead and explained all that had happened, and how I did not want to have any part in it.

A court date was set, and all who were at the grocery store that night had our individual court hearing. Explaining to the judge that I didn't want to be there and had

55

nothing to do with the door being broken, I said the reason I went inside the store was to find my friend, so we could leave. Although, I told him I didn't steal anything, he ordered me to pay restitution for the damaged door, and charged me with stealing a can of pop, even though I didn't steal any or take any from anyone. He said I should have fled and called the police when it happened, and was guilty by association.

I was angry, because I felt I hadn't done anything wrong, and I just happened to be in the wrong place at the wrong time. We should have never joined the group of guys who I had never been with before.

I eventually paid to have my record expunged, and then later when I was in seminary, I told my formation advisor about it the incident. He said it was not a problem, and when a record is expunged, the law considers it as though it never happened. To me, the expungement is like a Plenary Indulgence, a way of bestowing mercy. With a Plenary Indulgence, God forgives and forgets the sinful act and the punishment due to it-- and by His grace-- is erased forever.

Even though I had paid for the expungement, I later found out it remained on my record. An elderly friend from a town called Apache, Iowa called his lawyer friend, and as a favor, the lawyer removed it from the official courthouse file. Thank you, Jesus, for bailing me out!

#19 MOVED OUT OF THE HOUSE

Moved out of the House

When I was 17 my father told me, "When you turn 18 you have to move out of the house. We have other mouths to feed, and you can provide for yourself." After my 18th birthday in Feb. of 1981, my father reminded me he wanted me to move out of the house and do it before graduation. Perhaps it was due to me telling him to stop criticizing us at the dinner that Mom threw her plate at him. Or maybe, it was financially necessary due to our large family.

Once graduated, I began to search for a place to stay. I rented a small single bedroom house 3 blocks away and paid the deposit for electricity and gas. I didn't own much, so I just brought with me the few clothes I owned and a few other things and moved out. It all fit in just a few boxes. I was upset my parents didn't seem to want me, so when I moved out, I didn't tell them when I was moving. I moved out and didn't come back home for a month. When I came home, I asked Mom if she missed me. She said, "What do you mean?" I said, "I moved out a month ago in a house 3 blocks away." She said, "You did! I didn't even know you moved out." This situation reminded me of the television programs called *Ma and Pa Kettle*. The Kettles had so many children, they forgot their names and couldn't keep track of them. Dad had a habit of calling me by my brother's name, Louis and calling Louis, by my name. Louis and I used to joke about it saying, "It's not like there's a bunch of boys, there's only two of us."

Car Accident - Saved by Angels

"For he will command his angels concerning you to guard you in all your ways."
(Psalm 91:1)

When I was 18, in the fall of that year, I was invited to an underage alcohol party in Center City. When I arrived, I was given hard liquor I hadn't consumed before. I drank Schnapps, Whiskey with coke and Ever Clear with orange juice followed by a few cans of beer at that party. I decided I shouldn't be drinking hard liquor, but it was too late. I soon felt loopy. Because I realized I was getting drunk, I wanted to return to Crossroads City. Another fella younger than myself wanted to come with me. We never hung around together before that night. He was a decent young man, so I gladly took him with me to Crossroads City. Unfortunately, I was someone he probably should not have trusted. The more we drove, the more intoxicated I became. I chose to take dirt roads back to prevent an accident. We crossed the main highway without slowing down or stopping at the stop sign, and suddenly another vehicle zoomed passed in front of our vehicle, missing us by inches. Their truck swerved and went into the ditch, but we kept going. I was afraid they were coming to chase us down, so I turned off the lights as we drove down the dirt road. The moonlight made it possible to see the edges of the road. Suddenly, I saw a car with no lights parked on the road and I slammed on the brakes, but it was too late. We rear ended their vehicle and my passenger and I hit our heads on the windshield. I also hit my chest against the steering wheel. A bone was broken in my sternum, but I never told anyone. Years later, it would pop out of place randomly. My passenger's head cracked the windshield, and it broke his eyeglasses. He and I received a concussion and were temporarily confused. I couldn't remember why we were on the road and what we were doing there. I opened the door and discovered I slammed into the back of a car of a classmate. They had their lights off before the collision. What do you think they were doing at night in the middle of the road without lights? Parking! They were making out! I opened the door, but due to my concussion, I wasn't thinking about what they were doing or why I was there, and said to the female passenger in the other car, "What are we doing here?" The young girl slapped me in the face, and said, "You idiot, you ran in the back of our car." They were a little bruised as well as my passenger, but everyone was okay. My passenger acquired a black and blue eye and a bruise with a large bump on his head. A few years later, the couple married. When the police arrived on the scene, the policeman asked me, "How many drinks did you have?" I held up three fingers, and said, "two". The police officer took us to the police department. We weren't arrested and neither the other driver nor I received a ticket. The officer said we were both at fault. I guess he was unable to tell I was intoxicated.

The policeman suggested I call someone, and so I called my mother and said, "Mom. You need to sit down. Something bad happened". She said, "I'm not going to sit down. What did you do? Did you get a girl pregnant?" I said, "No, I had a car accident, and it's totaled (ruined and unable to be repaired)." She said, "Oh, no, not the Plymouth Duster. I really liked that car." My mother had helped me pick it out several years before at a car dealer. She never asked how I was doing or if I was injured, but kept saying, "Oh, that car. I can't believe you wrecked it." I guess she figured I was fine, since she heard my voice on the phone. There is no doubt angels were working overtime to protect all of us that dreadful night. How many other youths died in car accidents throughout the country due to alcohol? And yet, we were protected. Lord, why did you preserve me? Your infinite mercy, helps me to see how miserable I am.

The accident was a wake-up call. The adjuster said if I had been traveling a few miles faster, the other car's gas tank would have exploded, and we would have burned to death. I felt horrible. I ruined both cars, hurt three people and me. Had the gas tank exploded, we would have burned alive and most likely three of us (the couple acting in impurity and I) would have been burning in hell forever.

Due to the accident, I stopped drinking alcohol, even though I rarely drank before the accident happened. In the early 1980s, the legal age to drink alcohol in Ohio was 18. Consequently, whenever I went to a party or bar, I drank soda, at least for a while. After I joined a college fraternity, I wouldn't drink alcohol, except occasionally. On those occasions, in order to "fit in", I acted drunk at frat parties. Rarely, I became intoxicated again after the car accident.

After my car accident, I asked to move back home to save money to buy a car, but when I did, I was told I had to pay rent. Every month for a year, that I lived with my parents, until I went to college, I paid $135 rent. From the time I was a freshman in High School until I moved out for good, I paid for my clothing, car, school tuition and books, car insurance, snacks and some of my food. It was a good lesson and helped me to be responsible for myself and at the same time helped the family.

During this time in my life, I never asked the Lord for forgiveness, I never prayed for those I hurt, and in fact, didn't pray at all.

Thank you, Lord, for protecting all of us. Oh, the infinite mercy of God! You, dear Lord, allowed the accident to prevent me and others from death and the fires of hell. And You protected me from a life of drunkenness.

The Easter Vigil I Never Knew – A Girl's House on a Double Date
"Put to death whatever in your nature is rooted in earth: fornication, uncleanness, passion, evil desires, and that lust which is idolatry. These are the sins which provoke God's wrath. Your own conduct was once of this sort, when these sins were your very life." "What you have done is put aside the old self with its past deeds and put on a new man, one who grows in knowledge as he is formed anew in the image of the Creator." (St Paul's Letter to the Colossians, 3:5, 10)

Over the years, I had dating relationships with girls. Often times they were short relationships and sadly inappropriate. When I was 18, my best friend suggested I take a 16-year-old on a date with him and his girlfriend. Because I was 18, I was able to purchase *Malt Duck* beer. I drank a little too much, but wasn't drunk. However, my date became drunk. Oh, my. She invited the four of us to her home since her parents were away for the weekend. She and I went to her bedroom and began to make out, but by the grace of God, we didn't have relations. My best friend and his girlfriend made out in the other bedroom too.

The next day, Easter Sunday, I called her and told her I was sorry. She didn't say anything. What I attempted to do on the most sacred of nights, the Easter Vigil, was terrible and sad. I wonder if it wasn't the power of the Resurrection that prevented us from making a colossal mistake. I hurt my Lord on this most holy of nights, and He rescued me and her from the power of darkness. At that time, I had no understanding of an Easter Vigil. For an 18-year-old to attempt to have relations with a 16-year-old is surely despicable and against the law, though at the time, it never crossed my mind. I pray for her and hope she found a man who respected her in a way I didn't. I nearly did the same as my father. When my dad was 20 and my mother was 16, Mom became pregnant with my older sister, and my parents were forced into marriage, as that is what was expected when a teenage girl became pregnant. The father of the child was to take on the responsibility of raising the child and providing for the girl. God in His mercy preserved my date and I from such a life changing and heartbreaking experience. God's mercy prevented a life of misery.

Grandma's Gas

My grandmother, Scholastica Gadfly, never drove a car, but walked everywhere, which was good for her health, except in the winter and during the summer heat, and I worried about her. She lived frugally because her income was very low. She had a leaky kitchen faucet and collected drops of water into a large sauce pan, and then used the pan filled with water to boil eggs. Furthermore, she had a five-room house. During the winter, she closed off the living room and her bedroom to heat three rooms: the dining room, with a gas furnace, and a bathroom and kitchen. She slept on a cot in the dining room next to the table because her bedroom was closed off. At times, water pipes froze, which resulted in no running water. When I found all this out, I became upset with her children (my aunts and uncles) for not taking care of her needs.

Consequently, I decided to take matters into my hands and called the gas company. I put her gas bill under my name, and told the gas company to mail me the bills. I sent her an anonymous note telling her, she won the prize of free gas for the rest of her life. But it didn't last long. She had to move to Apache, so that one of her daughters could help her, as she was going blind due to untreated cataracts. She moved to a low-income housing unit. Every year at Christmas, grandma sent every grandchild a dollar in a

Christmas card. It's all she could afford, and even today, it brings tears to my eyes because she was so thoughtful despite her poverty.

Cigarettes, Chewing Tobacco, Marijuana, and Drugs

Second-hand smoke from my parents caused me to hate cigarettes. I very much disliked when my parents smoked in the house and in the car causing my sisters, brother, and I to gag and cough.

A neighbor handed me something, he said was candy. He said it had a minty taste to it. The container said, *Skoal*. I had never heard of that kind of candy. Knowing it would make me sick, he told me to eat and swallow it, and I did. I suddenly became sick to my stomach so bad I couldn't go to the game. I felt like vomiting, but didn't. This prevented me from ever using chewing tobacco.

While working at the chicken hatchery, a high school co-worker smoked cigarettes, and asked if I wanted to try one. I lit one, smoked it, and immediately became ill. I was glad I became sick, as it made me never want to smoke. God's mercy in disguise!

When in high school, while attending a band concert at Fort Hickok, I happened to sit between a man and woman smoking marijuana. They kept passing the lit weed in front of me. I was shocked they did it in front of their little boy, who was about 2 years old.

Years later, while in college, a fraternity friend came to my house and brought with him some whiskey and without my knowledge marijuana. He suddenly pulled out the marijuana and lit two of them. He asked me try one, I hesitatingly took it and began inhaling. I recognized the same odor from the concert. Suddenly, I began to laugh and laugh and laugh—for no apparent reason. Then I had the munchies and wanted to eat dry cereal and any food that was around. I then desired whiskey with it, and he told me no. He said you can't mix the two. After this event, I felt bad and never smoked marijuana again, and in fact, no longer befriended him. I felt like it ruined our friendship, because I didn't want a friend who would encourage illegal behavior and was unconcerned for my well-being.

While in college, my high school best friend from Crossroads called and said he wanted me to meet him at a motel in Fort Hickok. I was curious as to why he was staying in a motel, since he just lived twenty-four miles away. When I arrived at the motel, I realized he wasn't staying there, but rather his friend used the room as a place to do drugs. He held out his hand, with what appeared to be candy, that had the form of white crosses. I said, "What is that?" He said, "It's a drug called White Cross". "Take it, you can have it for free. It will make you have fun experiences." I looked at him with sadness and said, "I will not take it. And after today, if I find out you continue to take drugs, you will no longer be my friend. I don't want a friend who's a druggie." I walked away and felt deep sadness. A few weeks later when I saw him, I asked whether he continued to take drugs, and he said, "No. I will never do that again." Praise God!

Even though at that time I was not going to church, I believe I received a grace from God to save our friendship and help him turn away from something that could have ruined our lives. At that time, I wasn't praying and never said a prayer for him. God in His mercy prevented both of us from grave danger.

Human Respect-Terrible Choice-Death of a Baby

One of my friends was popular among girls and nearly always had a girlfriend. He and one of his girlfriends had relations, and she became pregnant. What a disaster! They didn't know what to do. They were 16 years old. The girl was Catholic and didn't want to tell her parents. She said, her father would be very angry, she would not be able to attend college, and was torn, not knowing what to do. They thought about obtaining an abortion and wept over the circumstance. Privately, he cried when he was with me, and said, "I don't want to kill my baby son or baby daughter. But what can I do?" He was silent for about 5 minutes and then asked me to help them to get an abortion in Rolling Hills.

I was young, stupid, and valued friendship more than God, and had little concern for the baby or the spiritual welfare of my friends, so I said, "I don't agree with abortion, but since you are my friend, I will help you." I couldn't believe what came out of my mouth. It was human respect at its worst!

A few days later, I called the abortion clinic from a pay phone and scheduled the abortion. I told the lady on the phone the girl was only 16. She said, "Don't worry, we won't ask her age and she can just tell us she's 18, and will do it for her. We take credit cards or cash. It costs $300.00" After saying this, the woman without any other concern, hung up the phone. I gave my friend the information for the day and time of the appointment for the abortion.

As time went by, I never heard anything and wondered if they had the abortion. I hoped it wouldn't happen. Finally, I mustered up the courage and asked him, "Did she get the abortion?" He said, "No, we didn't need to. She had a miscarriage." I was relieved, but only partially. I felt horrible I attempted to help kill their baby and felt bad the baby died. Not much later, the two broke up.

I later came to understand despite her taking the pill, she became pregnant and most likely the miscarriage happened due to the chemical from the pill. The pill, the IUD, the patch, and birth control injections are used to prevent pregnancy, and also irritate the lining of the mother's womb. Despite the chemicals from the birth control, a woman at times is still able to conceive a child. It normally takes 5 days for a newly created child to pass through the Fallopian tube to reach the lining of the womb. But due to the irritation of the womb, the child is unable to attach, dies and is expelled, and the mother never knew she was pregnant. And yet, there are times when a woman uses contraception, conceives, and becomes aware she is pregnant due to her not having her normal cycle.

At times, she can conceive, and the child attaches to the womb, but may end up dying later because the chemical causes the womb to not give nutrients to the child as needed, and therefore, the child dies resulting in a miscarriage. This is what may have happened to his girlfriend's child.

Years later, after my conversion, when I went to seminary, I told the rector about what happened because I became aware canon law had a rule preventing a man from becoming a priest if he helped procure an abortion. The rector said since the abortion never happened, the incident was not an obstacle. But this event caused a deep wound in my soul and with God's mercy, it was used to propel me to do as much possible to save the lives of unborn children in the future. During the time of the pregnancy crisis, I never prayed for my friend, his girlfriend, or the baby. I should have been a true friend and tried to obtain the help they needed and should have tried to protect the baby from the danger the child was in. I had not heard of crisis pregnancy centers at the time, but if I asked for help from a priest, perhaps I could have pointed them in that direction. Today, when a child is adopted the birthing mother bares no costs for the labor and delivery, because the health insurance of the adoptive parents cover medical costs.

#20 FAMILY ACTIVITIES GOOD AND BAD

Family Activities Doings

My family was poor compared to most families in my hometown of Crossroads, but not as poor as many others in the world. We had Christmas stockings with candy filled by Santa Claus on Christmas and Easter baskets with homemade colored eggs and all sorts of candy the Easter bunny would leave. Mom decorated the large front room window for Easter, Christmas, Thanksgiving, and Halloween. She used to make homemade reindeer using wishbones from turkeys. She made holidays special for my sisters, brother and I. One Easter, Dad left a trail of rabbit poop (little balls of poop) on the front porch and sidewalk, so we would think the Easter Bunny had come. He obtained the rabbit poop from the rabbit hutch we had in the backyard.

Ouija Board

"There shall not be found among you anyone who makes his son or his daughter pass through the fire, one who uses divination, one who practices witchcraft, or one who interprets omens, or a sorcerer, or one who casts a spell, or a medium, or a spiritist, or one who calls up the dead. For whoever does these things is detestable to the LORD." (Deuteronomy 18:10-11)

My parents had no idea how bad it was, nor the problems it could cause, when they purchased the Ouija board. My siblings and I played the game a few times. I believe we unknowingly unleashed demons to enter our home to attack our family. Exorcists have warned the Ouija board is a doorway and channel for demons. One exorcist said it can even cause possession if played often.

One night when our parents were away, we were playing it and the plastic device began to move on its own. A lamp near the location where we were playing the game, began to flicker on and off which gave us the heebie-jeebies. To play such a game is a sin against the loving providence of God. The person who plays the game does not place their trust in God, but rather an inanimate object. Lord, thank you for your mercy in forgiving us for this sin against your First Commandment, please protect other families and children from such "games" and may we always trust in your Divine Providence.

Other Games

Our family had a volleyball net, ping pong net, and other fun games. We had bicycles, basketballs, bats, and balls. We played softball together at times. Mom and Dad on separate occasions would join us in shooting baskets. We also played card games such as "blitz" or "pitch". Playing games brought us closer together as a family. Working together at the hog farm also built-up love and sacrifice in the family.

Family Reunions

The Schwinderspoon Family Reunion was always held on Thanksgiving Day. While the adults played cards and drank beer in the basement of the church, younger children and cousins played games in the old church converted into a gym years ago. The Schwinderspoon Reunions were fun and the food from the many families were delicious. I enjoyed getting to know my cousins, aunts, uncles, grandmother, and great-grandfather.

We began Gadfly reunions and went camping at a lake spending time with aunts, an uncle, their families, my cousins, and my own immediate family. It was very enjoyable, except for the times, my father would get drunk and embarrass us.

We are Family—Mama, Papa, Sisters, Brother and Me!

Peter began to say to Him, "Look, we have left everything and followed You." "Truly I tell you," said Jesus, "no one who has left home or brothers or sisters or mother or father or children or fields for My sake and for the gospel will fail to receive a hundredfold in the present age—houses and brothers and sisters and mothers and children and fields, along with persecutions—and in the age to come, eternal life...." (Matthew 10:29-30)

I was the oldest boy and fourth child. My three older sisters are Anne, Marie, and Margaret. My younger siblings are Sue, Louis, Gail, and Jean. Like other youth our age, we fought like most brothers and sisters, especially in our teenage years. After high school, we all became good friends, but that would soon change as each sibling began to have their family and the seed of dysfunction began to sprout into a wild bush with all sorts of thorns.

Working together on the farm, playing board games and persevering through family hardship and Dad's drinking kept us close when we were young. Our parent's divorce, Dad's drinking, and each sibling having their own family, began to pull us apart. None of us were faithful in attending Mass or going to confession during that time in our lives. The family was rocked by turmoil, and we didn't turn to God, when we needed Him the most. The lack of forgiveness, thievery, jealousy, lying, hurtful comments due to raw emotions took a toll on everyone.

In my opinion, God can only do so much with us. He can't make us forgive. He can't make us renew relationships, especially with those who fail to practice their Catholic faith.

I pray someday, we may be healed of this dysfunction, and have ordinary relationships with each other. But I also realize, it will probably only be in heaven, where we will all be part of God's family, in perfect union, and love each other the way God intends.

My family really does not know me at all. They have no idea what my priestly life has been like. I am actually closer to people from past parishes, and they know me better than my family. As a "spiritual father" of many whom I serve, at times, I am more at home with them than my natural family.

I pray God's mercy will pierce the hearts of my family members and move my heart to love ever more. As far as my priestly vocation, for a time, I wanted to be close to family and to be a priest in the Lakota City diocese. However, over time I realized God spared me from much family turmoil and purposely kept me away from them to better serve the people of God, for peace in my family and peace in own mind.

#21 PAGE TORN OUT AND MISSING

#22 JOIN THE ARMY

You're in the Army Now – Not So Fast! Our Lady of Fatima
My Mother Wears Combat Boots

In 1983, while working at Bob Gart's Grocery, in Fort Hickok, I wanted to join the US Army. I knew the government would pay for my college education and I also wanted to serve my country, which I am very proud of. Many times, when I hear the national anthem, for some reason tears well up in my eyes. This happens especially when I think about all who laid down their life for our good ole USA. Even today, I am moved when I see an American flag.

I went to the recruiting station in Fort Hickok and signed up to serve in the Army for two years. The Army paid for my flight from Fort Hickok to Ohio City to get a physical. When I arrived in Ohio City, I was excited about a new venture with the prospect of defending my country.

At that time, due to the AIDS scare, some thought that the purpose of the military health tests was to discover the potential soldier had AIDS or not. But this wasn't why blood and urine were tested. The military personnel drew blood and recruits had to urinate in a plastic container, and then wait for the results. The time for mine seemed longer than the others, and my number was 13. Finally, a soldier called my number, and said in front of everyone, "Sorry, but you are DQ'd (disqualified)".

Everyone looked at me as though I had AIDS, and some even moved away from where I was seated. The soldier escorted me to a doctor, who said my urine test showed that I had too much sugar in it. He said I was probably diabetic. He said, "See your personal physician, and if he writes a letter to us saying you don't have diabetes, you can join the army."

Back then, I had no insurance, so when I returned to Fort Hickok, I paid for my doctor's visit and lab tests to determine if I was diabetic. My doctor said I did not have diabetes, but most likely I may become diabetic in the future, but probably not for many years. The US Army paid for my flight back to the Ohio City medical recruiting station, so I would be approved by the Army doctor. Nevertheless, I was required to take another physical. The urine test came back, and I was told again that I had too much sugar in my urine.

Even though my personal doctor stated in his letter I didn't have diabetes, the Army doctor said, "Unless you pass the urine test here, you cannot join." The disregarded the letter from my doctor, and I was disqualified. I was disappointed and angry.

When I returned to Fort Hickok, I stopped by the recruiting center and gave the poor soldier a piece of my mind, telling him how stupid it was the Army paid for my second flight, even though, I gave them a letter saying I wasn't diabetic, only to be told I'm "DQ'd" because I didn't pass the urine test a second time.

Later, I saw the hand of God in me not becoming a solder at that time. The number 13, was not seen any longer as bad luck, but as a sign from Our Lady of Fatima, who appeared on the 13th of every month to three children. She was guiding me toward a path to the priesthood, but I didn't understand it at the time.

If I had joined the Army, I believe my life's direction would have gone differently. However, because I went to college, I ended up with thousands of dollars in debt due to loans. Providentially, when I felt the call to become a priest, I believe it was Our Lady who took care of the debt. She didn't want me to join the US military, but rather wanted me in Her spiritual army. She is our Mother in combat boots, guiding her little army to help Her crush the head of Satan. I would not carry a gun, but a Rosary. I would not follow, the commands of an officer, but rather, follow the Commander in Chief of the Spiritual Army, Jesus Christ Our Lord.

#23 COLLEGE YEARS

Fort Hickok University and Sigh Fi Gamma Fraternity

While working at Bob Gart's Grocery store, in Fort Hickok, a co-worker friend invited me to join the Sigh Fi Gamma Fraternity. They broke my dorm contract, so I could live in the fraternity. At the fraternity, I quickly made good friends and enjoyed my time there for the most part. The beer parties and dances were fun, at least I thought they were at the time. I didn't drink alcohol for a year due to my car accident, as I was determined to now allow alcohol to ruin my life. However, I eventually started drinking some and became drunk a few times.

Fort Hickok was known for several large bars and due to the drinking age of 18, there were many college students who were often out partying, rather than studying. Being a German community, Fort Hickok was nationally known, for its high consumption of alcohol. The city held the record for many years for the most alcohol consumption, per population in the US.

Occasionally, I pretended I was drunk in order to fit in. At one party, someone brought a "beer bong". It had a hose attached to a funnel. A can of beer or two would be poured into a funnel, and the hose was placed in the drinker's mouth. The beer was released and immediately swallowed in a matter of seconds. After a few times, I quickly became drunk. Despite this behavior, many who lived in the fraternity were fine young men, but there were a few who were a pain in the neck.

Most young men came from rural farming areas and were not contaminated by drugs, alcohol, or immoral activity. Many of them graduated with high honors and acquired future careers in the world. They would marry wonderful women, most of whom they met at college sororities. The fraternity was a place of getting to know other young men my age, studying together, and helping each other with life's difficulties. Every year we had a canned food drive for Thanksgiving that helped hundreds of poor people in the community. The fraternity did not haze like the other fraternities. In fact, some of the secret things we did for initiation (I- Week)-- were spiritually inspiring.

While in the fraternity, there came a time when I didn't have any money because of the monthly fraternity bill, auto repairs, car payments and insurance, etc. and I had only $20 to my name for a whole month. With the twenty bucks, I purchased a hundred-pound bag of potatoes and stored it in my frat room. Every day for a month, I ate potatoes. Little did I know, in a small way, I imitated St. John Marie Vianney, who ate only potatoes for years. At that time in my life, I had never heard of St. John Marie Vianney.

Every year, the fraternity had Derby Days, which involved playing games on campus. During the "Derby Chase" a girl from a sorority came running after me to remove the derby from my head. She succeeded by tackling me, but my elbow accidentally landed on her nose and broke it. I felt horrible, I broke a girl's nose. I purchased some flowers for her, and one of her sorority sisters responded, saying, "First you break her nose, and now you give her flowers!" The young lady forgave me. She was an American with German ancestry, like myself. The incident caused me to meet another girl I would date and had high hopes to marry.

At Fort Hickok University, my grade point average was 2.3 (not so good) as I worked full-time and attended college full time at the grocery store and also part-time at the college work study program as a janitor cleaning teacher offices. I rarely studied, went to parties often, and my grades showed it. On one occasion, I asked a fraternity friend for help in creating a paper for an English Composition class. He ended up writing the entire paper for me. I handed it in as though I did it. I cheated. The graded paper was returned, as an F with a note, to see the teacher after class. I thought, "He was a good writer, how could he have received an F on my paper?" The teacher said, "I know you didn't do this paper. This is not your work." She said, "You have a choice. You can either re-do it or take the F. If you don't re-do it, I will notify administration, and you will be kicked out for cheating, and then no other college will accept you. Or you can re-write it and the highest grade I will give you will be a B, that is, if you do well on it." I said, "But, I'm stupid. I don't know how to write a good paper." She said, "You're not stupid. Just remember, your paper needs to have a beginning, a middle, and an end. You can do it. I believe in you."

I spent hours typing the paper and handed it in. I was shocked to receive a B with the note on the paper, "Original idea. Paper was well-thought-out!" That teacher not only made me realize it was wrong to cheat and the consequences to it, but she gave me confidence in myself. She believed in me. God's mercy through that woman was so abundant.

The fraternity had a wonderful German cook. Her food was delicious! We affectionately called her, Mommie Aggie, but her real name was Velma Augustus. She was not just a cook, but also a "housemother" and took her role as mother seriously. Whenever she heard one of the frat brothers do something out of line, she would let him know his behavior was inappropriate. We loved her as a mother. Her favorite ingredient in her soups was pepper, and her second favorite ingredient was pepper. Lots of pepper.

Living in the fraternity gave me many opportunities to get to know girls, and I had a girlfriend who I met due to the broken nose incident. I thought I would someday marry her. We never did anything immoral together. She didn't talk much. I dreamed of being with her for the rest of my life and having eight children together. She was a Catholic girl.

However, one day I went to one of the local bars, DJ's, and saw her with her old boyfriend. It crushed me. He was tall and strong and much better looking than I. So that they would know I saw them together, I went up to them, just stood there and looked at them for about 5 seconds and then walked away. She hung her head and I knew it was over. There was no way I could fight him because he probably outweighed me by at least 100 lbs and mostly muscle. Fighting is not the way to win a girl. I learned to fight wasn't the way to solve any problem. She wanted to be with him and not me. That night as I left the bar, I knelt under a tree in a nearby darkened yard and cried. I decided to go to a nearby church (St. Joseph's) to talk to God about it. But the church was locked, and this caused me to become angry. I thought, why lock the church to keep people from praying? I just wanted to be with God because I knew He would understand how I felt. At that time in my life, I had no understanding of the Lord's true presence in the Tabernacle, and yet somehow was drawn to Him and didn't even realize it. This sorrowful event caused depression that made me feel unlovable, and I began to believe I would never get married.

At the beginning of a college semester, Kenneth, a fraternity friend (who later came out of the closet as gay-- to my shock) and I decided to find a bank to open a checking account and deposit our college loan and grant checks. We drove down a city street of Fort Hickok and haphazardly picked out a bank. As we exited our vehicle, we noticed an armor truck unloading money on a cart. I happened to reach under my shirt and rubbed my stomach saying, "I'm hungry. When we are finished, let's get something to eat." Suddenly, we heard the security guard yell, "Freeze!" We turned and looked at him, and he was pointing a gun at us. He was nervously shaking the gun like Barney Fife on the *Andy Griffith Show*. I thought he was pointing at someone behind us. I looked behind and no one was there. And my friend said, "He's pointing at you, why did you rub your stomach like that? He thinks you have a gun." We slowly walked to the front of the bank and when we entered the lobby the security guard was pointing at us. We cautiously walked to the nearest teller, who was shaking out of fear. I looked at her, and said, "We would like to open up a checking account." She breathed a big sigh of relief, and said, "Sure". The security guard walked away as though relieved. Ironically, my friend later became the president of a bank.

After my second year in the fraternity, I wanted out. I roomed with a man who had a different girl in his bed almost every night. Ugh! Not only that, I couldn't stand the noise (the banging of the springs going up and down) and the immorality of it all. Oh, how gross!

One evening an alumnus, known as a homosexual, suddenly sat beside me on the porch, and put his arm around me. I bolted away from him and ran in the house. He complained to one of the leaders of the fraternity, who said I had no right to treat an alumnus like that. And I responded saying, "He had no right to treat me like that! I'm straight!!!" That was the last straw, and so I moved out as quickly as possible, as I wanted nothing to do with the fraternity anymore.

Kenneth, the fraternity friend who went with me to the bank, eventually married and had several children. I was in his wedding. It was truly a blessed time. He wasn't Catholic at the time and eventually became Catholic years later. We were friends for many years, and I used to visit his family and the family would come to visit me. They came to my ordination, but afterwards we lost touch.

During college, I changed my major three times. My first major was biology because I wanted to be a biology teacher, just like my high school biology teacher, Mr. Frankston. Then I changed my major to Computer Science, and finally changed it to Business Management. I dropped out of school after 5 years when I was offered a job as the Central Supply Manager at Nedley Regional Medical Center. I had two semesters left and would have graduated. I thought, "Why keep going to school, when I have a good paying job".

During the last year of classes, my grades improved because I purchased a VHS tape from an infomercial called *If There's A Will There's an A*. I then applied the principles from the tape to my studies, and my grades increased higher than anticipated. I learned how to obtain good grades, without reading much. These methods would become very helpful when I later entered seminary.

I made several long-lasting friends from the fraternity. But later, as a seminarian, I totally renounced my Sigh Fi Gamma membership, because I no longer wanted to be connected to the immoral activity that occurred in it. The fraternity certainly had many positive sides to it, but there was also the dark side and I didn't want to be associated with it.

Youthful Future Hopes and Dreams

After reflecting upon what I believed I wanted to do in the future, I recalled enjoying my work at Dickey's IGA Grocery Store and also at Bob Gart's Grocery Store. I dreamed of owning a grocery store chain. And, if I that would happen, I wanted every store, I hoped to own, to give free food to the poor, who would come when they needed it. This is one of the reasons why I changed majors in college.

Fight Over a Girl in College

My second fight occurred was when I was in college. At night, I went to a local bar called DJ's, which was a disco place. Unfortunately, I went there to look for a girl to date. After having a few beers, I kept walking around the inside of the bar looking for pretty girls. There was one red head I was attracted. When her boyfriend noticed, he came up to me and said, "You're looking at my girlfriend. She's mine!" I said, "Well, she's pretty." He said, "Stop looking at her." He said, "You're gay!" To call me gay are fighting words. I wondered, "Why are you calling me gay, when I find your girl attractive". It was one thing I couldn't stand if someone calls me gay, and besides, I'm obviously not since I was looking for girls and was attracted to that red head. I said, "Do you want to fight about it?" He said, yes. We went outside and began to fight. He landed several punches on my mouth. He was quick and obviously did street fighting before. I moved into my wrestling mode and grabbed him, and we fell to the ground. I was not yet able to land a punch, when the police came. He ran off. The officer saw my bloody mouth, and said, "What is his name?" I knew his name, but said, "I don't know". He said, "Do you want to press charges?" I said, "No."

Fort Hickok - Living on My Own

I moved to the basement of the Terry Legee family house on Winston Street. A wonderful couple with a young boy lived upstairs. But the boy was learning to play drums, and the noise kept me awake at night.

To help them realize it was annoying, I decided to record the drumming noise through air conditioner vents. Then later, after all went to bed, I re-played the beating of drums from the tape recorder through the vents. When I started playing the recording, I heard the father scream, "Stop playing your drums, I told you to go to bed". The boy yelled, "But I'm not". I turned off the recording as soon as the yelling started. However, I started it back up again when it was quiet. The poor boy got blamed for playing the drums, even though he wasn't playing them at all.

Also, at this house a real freaky thing happened. One night, my wall phone (cell phones were not yet invented), rang and when I answered it, no one was there. It kept repeatedly ringing within minutes of the other rings. I thought someone was just playing with me. But then I unplugged the phone, and as I held the disconnected cord in my hand, the phone rang, which was impossible, I thought. I cried out, "Ah!" and dropped the receiver. How could a phone ring without being plugged in the wall? After a few minutes, I mustered the courage and plugged it back in, and called a friend to tell him what happened. I thought it might be a ghost. But, he responded, "It was probably a plane with radar flying over. Some planes cause phones to ring like that." That relieved me.

Guardian Angel Saved My Life on My Birthday

"For it is you who light my lamp; the Lord my God lightens my darkness." (Psalm 18:28) "...through the tender mercy of our God, when the day shall dawn upon us from on high to give light to those who sit in darkness and in the shadow of death to guide our feet into the way of peace." (Luke 1:79)

After I discontinued college and was living in Fort Hickok, in the basement of the Terry Legge family home, on Winston Street, one night I lit a small votive candle and placed it on a wall mount. The next day was my birthday, and I was having back pain.

Consequently, I decided to sleep on the floor in the same room the candle was lit. Early in the morning of Feb. 30th, I was awakened, and gazed up at the candle. As I was looking at it, the candle fell on the ground. Since it happened so quickly after I had awakened, I was still very groggy and thought I was dreaming. I decided to get up to see if I really saw the lit candle fall to the ground, and there on the ground was broken glass and the carpet was starting to burn from the candle still lit. I immediately threw water on it dousing it. Had I just gone back to sleep or had I not been awakened just before it fell, everyone in the house could have died. Thank you guardian angel.

Haunted House

I found a cheaper place to live, and thought it would be quieter, since an older lady lived alone upstairs, while I rented her basement. It was located on 27th street in Fort Hickok. The lady was really nice, but I noticed when I was away and came back, some things were moved in the apartment. Apparently, she watched for me to leave and then entered the basement and looked around. This greatly annoyed me. I used clear tape and placed small pieces of it on the edge of the doors leading to her side. This way, I could find out for sure if it was happening, and it was, as the sealed tapes were broken open when I returned. I decided to give her something to look at. Consequently, I took twine string and hung it across the living room. Then I used clothes pins to hang my clean underwear on the string. After she saw this, when I was away from the apartment, she made a comment to someone who told me she didn't like my underwear hanging in the house.

A friend, his wife, and infant baby, came to visit while I was renting the basement of this same house. Rather, then spending the night in a motel, I told them they could sleep on the bed with their baby, and I would sleep on the floor in a sleeping bag. After I turned off the lights, I saw a black figure move across the basement window, blocking out the streetlight, and said, "What are you doing getting up?" He said, "I'm not up, you're up." I said, "No, I'm down here." Both of us realized, he was in the bed, and I was on the floor, and simultaneously all three of us screamed. I quickly turned on the light, and no one was there. There were other times, I saw a black figure, but this incident took the cake. All three of us had seen it. I was convinced I needed to move. We surmised it was her deceased husband, who didn't want me renting the basement.

At College, Time with A Girl – Saved by Grace, Giant Hickey

When I was in college, I went on a date with a girl, Cammara. We went to a fraternity function and then to someone's home with other college students to sit in their whirlpool. She invited me over to her house, and we went outside to lay on a blanket in her backyard to look up at the stars. The next thing I knew, we were making out. She asked if I ever had a hickey and I said no. She said, "Let me give you one." We started to do inappropriate things. Suddenly, I realized I was sinning and stopped. It was like a freight train experience. I just froze and recognized something bad was about to happen. She said, "Is it me?" I said, "No, it's me. I can't do this." Praise God, we never had relations. We were prevented by God's grace from doing something terribly wrong. "Lord, thank you for preserving both of us, and please forgive us for getting carried away." She gave me such a large hickey that I was able to make up the story I got hit in the neck by a baseball. All believed the lie.

About 10 years after I was ordained a priest, a priest friend from another diocese said a girl I dated in college became a religious sister. I suspect it was this girl. He wouldn't tell me her secular name, so I never found out who she was. I think both of us received a special grace that night when we were looking up at the stars. I never had relations with a girl in my life, though twice I came very close, but by the grace of God was prevented.

Rubber Band and "Peanuts" Stopped Cussing Like a Sailor
"But now ye also put off all these; anger, wrath, malice, blasphemy, filthy communication out of your mouth" (Colossians 3:8).

While in college, I developed a very foul language and often times used the "F" word. One evening, I went to visit a friend, his wife, and two little girls at their apartment. As we were talking, out of my mouth, I said the F word. His wife pointed to the door, and said, "Out you go! You will not cuss like that in front of my children!" I said, "I'm sorry, I won't do it again." She said, "Out now!" Feeling ashamed, I left the apartment. That was the first time, I realized how cussing hurts others and gives bad example. After a few weeks, I was allowed back into their apartment, and kept my dirty words to myself.

But I still had a problem with cussing, but not in front of them. At that time, I wasn't going to confession, and so did not receive sacramental grace to stop the bad habit. One day, I happened to have a rubber band on my wrist, and when I cussed, I snapped it. I decided to snap it every time I cussed. The first several weeks were brutal, and my wrist was aching. But, by the end of the month, for the most part, I stopped cussing. Then, every once in a while, out of my mouth, when I least expected, came a foul word. Praise God! Today, I never use foul words.

There was an old man, Jake Smoldergrass, who used to play Bingo at the Crossroads Veteran's Club. I played Bingo with my grandmother there, and whenever someone else would Bingo, out of Jack's mouth came, "Peanuts!" At the time, others and I, thought he was crazy. But, later in my life, I realized he was smart. At least he never cussed when he was angry. Eventually, I learned to do something similar. I learned to replace a cuss word with a neutral word that didn't hurt God or anyone else. For example, when I was upset, I would say, "Jumping Jelly Beans" or "Scott Malloy" (a fictitious person) or "Glipin Globbin" (a made-up word). The silly words reduce stress, calm the anger, and don't hurt anyone.

Later as a priest, I began to tell people who confessed cussing, to replace foul words with other harmless words. After I reflected upon snapping the rubber band on my wrist, once I began to practice my Catholic faith, I realized every time we sin, it's like causing pain in the wrist of Jesus. And if we commit a big sin, it's like nailing His wrists to the Cross.

#24 IMPURITY TO PURITY

Impurity to Purity (Confession and the Virgin Most Pure)
The Power of the Sacrament of Confession

"You heard it was said, 'Do not commit adultery,' but I say to you that everyone who looks at a woman in order to covet her has already committed adultery with her in his heart." (Matthew 5:27-28)

As a boy, I looked at girlie magazines, but did not have the habit of impure actions. Later, after I dropped out of college, I began to watch certain weekly television programs that caused me to do impure actions. It became a dreadful habit and before long I was doing it two or three times a night. I fell into this bad habit for about six months. It disgusted me. I tried to stop and would quit for a week or so, and then do it again. At that time, I was not going to confession, and relied on myself to stop. I wasn't praying, but I knew it was wrong.

One night I watched a sports event on television, and one of the players became injured, and was bleeding from his side. It reminded me of the wound in the side of Jesus (it made me feel guilty for offending God by my sins) and I made my best effort to stop. I began to think how my impure actions were hurting Jesus. I did not think of going to confession. I was too far away from God, and still believed we had to confess in a group, as it was when the new priest came to my hometown parish. Still, the habit would not go away. Only after confessing, on Jan. 1ˢᵗ of 1991, when my conversion began, I finally stopped impure actions. The grace of confession resulted in a complete break from purposeful impure actions. I struggled with lustful thoughts and wet dreams through seminary, but never did impure actions. As a priest, I never purposely viewed pornography, but struggled with impure and lustful thoughts. There were times, I accidentally saw pornographic images. From 1991 to 1993, I confessed monthly, and when I became a religious brother, I began to confess weekly and continued weekly through my entire priesthood.

As a priest there were times I struggled greatly to remain pure. The television and computer are occasions of sin and the devil uses them to entice us to desire a false pleasure. I use an image blocker on my computer that prevents inappropriate images and avoids temptation. I thank Our Blessed Mother, who greatly helped to become more and more pure. St. Alphonsus Ligouri said those who I pray three Hail Marys every day in honor of Her purity and for the gift of purity will always receive the gift of purity. By these daily 3 Hail Marys, Mary helped me to become more and more pure. I continue to pray these prayers every day. "Live in accord with the spirit, and you will not yield to the cravings of the flesh. The flesh lusts against the spirit and the spirit against the flesh; the two are directly opposed." (Galatians 5:16-17)

#25 DEPRESSION

The Man in the Glass (I Saw the Face of Death)
"In the day of my distress, I will call, and surely You will answer me." (Psalm 86:7) "For Your love to me has been great; You saved me from the depths of the grave." (Psalm 86:13) "Eternal God, in whom mercy is endless and the treasury of compassion inexhaustible, look kindly upon us and increase Your mercy in us, that in difficult moments we might not despair nor become despondent, but with great confidence submit ourselves to Your holy will, which is love and Mercy itself." (St. Faustina, #950)

After I discontinued attending college, I became more and more depressed, as I couldn't seem to find a girlfriend. I badly wanted to love a girl and a girl to love me. But the harder I tried, the more it seemed I was unlovable. I began to think I was ugly and unlovable, and therefore, would never get married. I wanted a wife and many children. Every night, at about 2am, I heard the train whistle as it traveled through Fort Hickok. I hated myself because I thought no girl could ever love me, and started to think of ending my life. I didn't have any concern, nor did I think about how it would affect my family. My parents were having problems and divorced, and I felt like they were unconcerned about me (though, that really wasn't true). I no longer had friends, as they moved away, and believed I was all alone in the world.

With the intention of ending my life, I put on a black coat, black pants and a black stocking cap and decided to walk to the train tracks and lay on them. The black clothing would not allow the locomotive engineer to see me laying down on the tracks. I put everything on and, about 1:30am, started to walk out of the house to be there for the 2am train. Suddenly, I stopped, and decided to look at myself in the mirror to see if I was serious in going to do it. When I looked at myself in the mirror, I was horrified because at that moment, I saw the face of death. I knew I was going to do it. I turned to walk out of the house, when suddenly (by the grace of God) I turned around, went back to my bedroom, fell on the bed and began to cry. I prayed, which I rarely did at the time, and said a simple prayer, "Jesus, help me. I don't want to die." I cried myself to sleep, and when I woke the next day, I was still depressed, but thought, "Well, I'm alive today. I'll just live today." From that day on, I still didn't have hope for the future, but decided to live day by day. That is, until, I went to confession a few years later, on Jan. 1st, 1991. The moment I went to confession, the depression immediately disappeared, and I was never depressed like that again. When I received absolution from the Franciscan priest, I had joy in my heart, that I didn't have since I was a child.

Before my confession, black was a symbol of death and after my confession black remains a symbol of death, but a different kind of death. Rather than a hopeless death, now it's a death of dying to myself and my desires. Now it's a death to the world, death to the devil and hope for heaven. Ironically, I was dressed in black and wanted to commit suicide. And now today, as a priest, I wear black pants, black shirt, black socks and black shoes all the time, as a reminder, I am to die to myself for love of God and the salvation of souls. From a sign of despair, came a sign of hope. After my confession, I was no longer a slave of sin, but, became a slave of Christ, which is why priests wear collars, as slaves wore many years ago.

St. Francis of Assisi said, "...where there is doubt, faith; where there is despair, hope; where there is darkness, light; where there is sadness, joy; O Divine Master, grant that I may not so much seek to be consoled as to console; to be understood as to understand; to be loved as to love. For it is in giving that we receive; it is in pardoning that we are pardoned; and, it is in dying that we are born to eternal life." His words are about self-gift, rather than self concern. Later, I read the poem, "The Man in the Glass" which reminded me of how the Lord saved my life. O Lord, in your infinite mercy you saved not only my life, but especially my soul from eternal fire. Thank you, O God of mercy!

When you get what you want in your struggle for self
and the world makes you king for a day
Just go to the mirror and look at yourself
and see what that man has to say
For it isn't your father or mother or wife
who judgment upon you must pass
The fellow whose verdict counts the most in your life
is the one staring back from the glass
Some people may think you are a straight-shooting chum
and call you a wonderful guy
But the guy in the glass says you're only a bum
if you can't look him straight in the eye
He's the fellow to please, never mind all the rest
for he's with you clear up to the end
And you've passed your most dangerous, difficult test
if the man in the glass is your friend
You may fool the whole world down the pathway
of life and get pats on the back as pass
But your final reward will be heartaches and
tears if you've cheated the man in the glass.
by Peter Dale Wimbrow, Sr.

#26 GRANDMOTHER'S DEATH – BEGINNING OF CONVERSION

Grandma's Death Caused Me to Think About Heaven

My grandmother, Scholastica Gadfly, died Jan. 30th of 1990. On that day, I went to visit her in the hospital after she received a pacemaker. My father, aunts, uncles, and cousins were there. When visiting with her after surgery, I promised to pray the Rosary for her. However, I forgot how to pray it. I went back to the waiting room, and suddenly an old religious Dominican Sister came in the room and said to all present, "She's passing. If anyone wants to be with her when she dies. Come now." Everyone went but me. I was determined to not watch my grandmother die. She and I were close. She regularly wore a fake pearl necklace that I gave her and rubbed it so often the paint on it started to chip off. Everyone came to her room, but me. I finally relented, and as I entered her room, the old religious sister began to pray, saying, "Go to Jesus. Go to the light. Jesus is waiting for you." In just a few minutes, grandma slowly stopped breathing and died. I watched as the monitor showed her breathing had stopped, but her heart kept beating, so we thought. But it was the pacemaker causing the monitor to appear as though her heart was beating.

After she died, I thought, "This is grandma's body, but this not my grandma. Where did she go?" Later that year, I wanted to pray a Rosary for her, but didn't know how to pray it. I went to a Catholic church in Hickok and asked the priest how to pray the Rosary. I was surprised when the priest insisted on knowing why I wanted to learn how to pray the Rosary and finally told him I wanted to pray for the soul of my grandmother. He acted as though he thought, "Why do you want to pray that thing!" He handed me an instruction sheet, but I couldn't figure out how to use it. Although I was 26 years old, when looking at the pamphlet explaining the Rosary, I had no idea the meaning of the Assumption of Mary or the Ascension of Jesus. A few months later, I happened to turn on the television and watched a program of nuns praying the Rosary on EWTN, and this is how I learned how to pray it.

I started praying the Rosary more often and whenever I prayed the Sorrowful mysteries, I felt bad for my sins. I had the desire to confess, but would not do it, because it was 20 years since my confession. I still believed we had to confess as a group. This was because the priest in my home parish changed how children went to confession from an individual to a group.

I heard Pope John Paul II was coming to San Antonio, Texas and went to the papal Mass. His homily was about Confession. He said we should confess monthly, and he talked about the beauty of God's mercy. But I still would not go to confession. That is, until the day I saw a woman go to confession in a confessional, and thought they changed confession back from group confession to individual confessions.

Is Missing Mass a Mortal Sin?

"Tell the Israelite's, 'Surely you must observe My Sabbaths, for this will be a sign between Me and you for the generations to come, so that you may know that I am the LORD who sanctifies you." (Exodus 31:13)

Until I was 27, I did not know if you missed Mass on Sunday, it was a mortal sin. I do not recall learning it was mortally sinful to miss Mass on Sunday when taking my religion classes as a child, nor did I hear it said at Mass. That being said, I always enjoyed attending Mass on Sunday, but in college, I avoided attending Mass by myself. I didn't want others to see I was alone.

The Virgin Mary Intercedes to Bring About My Spiritual Awakening (Conversion)

"Do whatever He tells you!" (John 2:5)

Occasionally, a college fraternity friend, a good Catholic, invited me to attend Sunday Mass with him. I always went when he asked, but only when he asked. One Easter, we watched a movie about Fatima on regular TV. The movie was hosted by Vincent Price. I thought, how amazing it would be if Mary appeared today like she did to the children of Fatima. Later, I found a newspaper with an article by Wayne Weible called "Miracle at Medjugorje" about Mary's alleged apparitions in Medjugorje. I wanted to try to live Mary's messages, as indicated in the newspaper. At the end of the year, I decided to make some New Year Resolutions, and wrote them down. First, I planned to start dating again, and believed I could find a girl at a local bar. (Not the best way to meet girls). Second, to return to Confession and then confess every month as Mary asked. Third, start attending Mass every Sunday. Fourth, pray the Rosary daily. Fifth, fast on bread and water on Wednesday and Friday. Sixth, read the bible daily. Seventh, pray with the heart. Due to learning how to pray the Rosary, Mary interceded to bring me to Her Son in Confession and then to receive Jesus in Holy Communion. When I prayed the Rosary, especially the Sorrowful mysteries, it caused me to be sorry for my sins, and it placed a desire in my heart to confess them. The messages from Our Lady Queen of Peace in Medjugorje, coupled with the death of my grandmother, would be the cause of my conversion.

Return to Confession & Mass on Jan. 1st Mother of God

"I will praise you, Lord, because you rescued me." (Psalm 30:1) "Let the weak, sinful soul have no fear to approach Me, for even if it had more sins than there are grains of sand in the world, all would be drowned in the unmeasurable depths of My mercy." (Diary of St. Faustina, #1059)

I happened (providentially) to go to St. Joseph church in Fort Hickok to pray. I don't understand why I went inside the church, but I did. As I knelt looking at the beauty of the church, a woman came in the back of the church, genuflected and then knelt down in a pew to pray. After a few minutes, she went inside the wooden box confessional located on the side of the church and a red light came on. Then as she departed, the red light went off, and a green light came on. She knelt down in the pew, prayed, and then left. I was stunned. I thought, they changed confession back to being private again. For all those years, since the priest in my parish made us children do a group confession, I thought that was how it was done. And now, I believed they changed it back. This shows the great harm a priest can do by departing from the normal and traditional way to perform the sacraments. How dangerous for a priest to do his way of doing things. Although I could now confess privately, as when I made my first Confession, I still did not return to the sacrament.

A few years later, on Jan. 1st, (Solemnity of Mary, Mother of God), a Holy Day of Obligation, almost a year after my grandmother died, I went to confession. I had no idea how to go, nor did I know Jan. 1st was a Holy Day. The Franciscan priest, Fr. Fidelis, at St. Joseph church helped me to confess my sins. For my penance, I was to look at the large crucifix in the Church for 15 minutes. As he said the words of absolution, I felt something spiritual happen inside. I suddenly felt as though all burdens were lifted, and became instantaneously joyful. I felt a spiritual action within me, and the feeling of it caused me to want to come back to church. Looking at the Crucifix was a penance I will never forget. Gazing upon the sufferings of Jesus helped me to realize how my sins hurt Jesus, but also, I understood His immense love for me. Since then, every time I received Holy Communion, I felt l spiritually charged. I began to attend daily Mass and enjoyed hearing homilies. I felt like a new person. Once I confessed my sins, I never had the thought of killing myself ever again. I felt like a new man, had hope for the future and discovered I had a friend, Jesus.

These spiritual experiences and how they affected my life gave me the inspiration to travel to Medjugorje, where the Virgin Mary was allegedly appearing. Her messages changed my life and amazingly for the better. I stopped going to bars to look for a girl to marry. But rather, started attending church functions such as chili suppers, etc. in hopes of meeting a girl there. I began to feel the need to help others and volunteered to mow the cemetery near the little town of Anthony, Ohio without payment. But, the priest insisted I be paid. I volunteered to "Senior Sit" during Advent, so the wife of the handicapped man, could go shopping or enjoy time with her friends. I enjoyed helping others and felt good about myself for doing something for them. Helping others in need, became a powerful means to overcome depression, and gave me self-worth.

Because my life changed so drastically, and I was filled with joy, I wanted others to have that same joy. I ordered over 1000 newspapers with the "Medjugorje Miracle" article by Wayne Weible and distributed them throughout Fort Hickok by tossing them in driveways throughout the city. The story about Mary's apparitions and Her messages played an important role in bringing about my conversion. Later, when I went on pilgrimage to Medjugorje for the first time, it is there I discovered my call to the priesthood.

Since my conversion occurred on the Solemnity of Mary, the Mother of God, it was clearly wrought, through the intercession of the Virgin Mary, who saw the misery of my soul and obtained for me the grace to be reconciled with Her Son, the King of Mercy.

Jesus Calls at Night, But I Do Not Understand His Call at the Time

When Samuel went to sleep in his place, the LORD came and stood there, calling out as before: Samuel, Samuel! Samuel answered, "Speak, for your servant is listening." (1 Samuel 3:9-10)

One night, while sleeping, I suddenly awoke to a man's voice saying my name, "Leonard". I thought it must have been a dream. A few seconds later, I heard the voice again say, "Leonard". This time, I knew I was fully awake. The hearing of my name spooked me, and I wondered if someone was in my room. But, who could it be, no one ever called me Leonard. Strangely, no one ever called me Leonard, though it was my legal name. As a child, I was called, "Lennie" and then later in High School and College, I went by "Len", but never "Leonard". My parents never called me "Leonard". Later, after reflecting upon this event, I believe it was God calling me, by name, to follow Him by becoming a priest.

Strange Occurrences After Conversion

Some months after I started practicing my Catholic faith, unusual occurrences began. One night, I had a dream or something like a dream, as it seemed I was awake, when it happened. I felt as though my body lifted off the bed and I became, as though in a bubble, and could move around in every direction within it. I didn't see the bubble, but felt like I was in something safe, something that surrounded me with love. It was like being underwater, where you can move in every different direction. Then suddenly I was fully wake lying in my bed and felt joy. Later, after reflecting upon this, I believe the experience is what an unborn baby would feel in his mother's womb, to move about in any direction without any kind of hindrance.

On another occasion, due to back problems, I decided to sleep on the floor. Just as I turned off the lights in the bedroom, I felt a warm sensation go over my body, and as it did, the covers of my blanket moved, as though a gust of warm wind was blowing. Though it was dark in the room, I looked up at the light fixture on the ceiling in the middle of the room, and in it, I saw something like sparks of lightening coming from it. At first, it frightened me because I didn't know what it was. But, the warmth of the wind blowing (no windows open) and the blanket moving on me, gave me comfort and

I quickly fell asleep. Later, after reflecting upon this, I thought perhaps it was the Holy Spirit moving over me.

On still another occasion, one night I woke to what felt like an evil presence in my bedroom and there was a stench that came with it. The odor was like rotten eggs, or a rotten smell that comes from women's perms. The evil presence would not allow me to speak. No matter how hard I tried to say the name of Jesus, I could not. I felt pressure on my chest. A brown scapular was located on the nightstand and immediately put it on. And once I did, I was able to cry out to Jesus for help. Then the evil presence immediately departed.

When my conversion occurred, I was living on 20th street, a block from Branch St. The house was really nice. It had one-bedroom and somewhat new. It was here I was saved from suicide, but also the remarkable floating event occurred in it. It was in this house I came to accept Jesus into my life.

I moved again, this time to an upstairs apartment on 8th street in Fort Hickok close to Taco House restaurant near campus. It was a small one-bedroom apartment. I met a young man about my age by the name of Samuel. He told me he was Catholic and was involved in the occult, but wanted to stop. He said whenever he entered a Catholic church, he started to sweat and felt nervous. I convinced him to go to Confession, and we made an appointment with a Franciscan priest at St. Joseph parish. I accompanied him to the church office, but the priest was late. He finally came, but said he couldn't hear his confession, as he was too busy. Both of us were hurt and upset. A short time later, I moved to Louisiana, and never knew if Samuel ever made his confession. I resolved, that if I would become a priest, I would never do what that priest did to him. Here was a man who desperately wanted to be reconciled with God, to turn away from evil, and was ready to confess his sins, but was turned away. How sad!

#27 DAD STOPS DRINKING

I Prayed for Dad's Sobriety, One Our Father, Hail Mary and Glory Be, Every Day
For many years through high school and beyond, I prayed every day one Our Father, Hail Mary and Glory be, asking the Lord to help my father stop drinking. The day finally came when he checked himself in at an alcohol sobriety unit at St. Joseph's Hospital in Helena, Ohio. During family week, Marie, Sue, Gail, Louis, Jean, and I came to visit. We were told alcoholism is inherited (a disease). We learned to separate the disease from the person and were taught to treat an alcoholic as one suffering from an illness. Furthermore, we were told to hate the disease, but love the person. During a meeting at the unit, my siblings and I, were required to tell Dad how he hurt us. After we shared our feelings, we wept many tears. It was healthy for us and for Dad. When he was dismissed from the hospital, he was a different man who wanted to be involved

in the lives of his children. But, his children were not ready for it. For the next five years, he was sober and made attempts to be part of our lives, but most rejected him.

My father and I were reconciled, and we finally began to talk to each other more than ever. I had my father in my life. Most of my siblings kept him at bay and did not know how to treat him. They were afraid they would get hurt. I was astonished at how few gave him the time of day. One Thanksgiving Day, he had nowhere to go. No one invited him to their house. So, I invited him. I purchased some Turkey drumsticks from a meat department at the local grocery store and I attempted to bake them. We had mashed potatoes and gravy and I boiled some canned corn. But Dad was depressed. He wanted badly to be part of the family. To him, he was rejected, and he could not understand why, after all, he was no longer drinking. A few years later, he began to drink occasionally. For the most part, much of the time, he was sober, but at times, wasn't. He joined several AA groups and became well known throughout the state for helping many alcoholics to regain sobriety. Most of my siblings could not understand alcoholism was his cross, and it was permanent. He did his best to carry it. He knew when he fell carrying it, he had to ask God the Father, who he called "the Old Man Upstairs", to help him to continue to carry his cross.

#28 MEDJUGORJE FIRST TRIP

Trip to Medjugorje

I sold some furniture, a camcorder, and worked two additional jobs to save money to go to Medjugorje. In addition to working at the hospital, as a Central Supply Manager, I worked at Domino's Pizza as a delivery boy in the evening and got up early in the morning before Mass to throw newspapers for *The Hometown Times.* My pilgrimage to Medjugorje was from Sept. 10th through Sept. 19th, 1991. Before I departed, I had heard about supposed solar phenomena, and rosaries turning to gold. However, I decided I wasn't going there for that. But rather, wanted to enjoy myself and attend some apparitions, if possible.

Confession in Medjugorje –Sept. 13th

One of the first things I did, when I arrived in Medjugorje was go to Confession to a Franciscan priest, Fr. Svet. In Confession, Fr. Svet said, "What are you doing with your life?" I said, "I'm a hospital worker." He said, "No, no, are you married or single?" I said, "I'm single." He said, "While you are here, pray, and ask God if He wants you to be a priest." I was shocked by what he said, because I never thought about becoming a priest. I was reluctant to do as he asked, especially because I wanted to get married and have children. Not having a girlfriend is what caused me to want to commit suicide. Now I had a renewed hope of getting married, and this priest is asking me to give up a wife and children! I was not excited at all. But I began to pray about the possibility of becoming a priest.

In Medjugorje – Feast of the Triumph of the Cross

"When Jesus saw His Mother and the disciple whom he loved standing nearby, He said to His Mother, "Woman Behold Your Son", "Behold Your Mother" (John 19:26-27)

On the Feast of the Triumph of the Cross, Sept. 14th, a village Mass was held at the top of Mt. Krizevac "Crucifix". As I journeyed up the rugged rocky path toward the top, I helped an elderly woman, a member of our group, to make it to the top of the steep mountain. We came to the large concrete Cross where Mass was going to be held.

Later, as I reflected upon helping the elderly woman to the top of the mountain with a cross, it was as though I helped the Virgin Mary walk up the hill of Calvary to stand with Her at the foot of the Cross of Her Son. And since Mass was offered at the base of the Cross, I felt Mary's presence at Mass, which is the re-presentation of Calvary. There I was with Mary, at Mass, at the foot of the Cross, just like St. John stood with Her at Calvary.

In Medjugorje Sept. 15th Our Lady of Sorrows - Miracle of the Sun (Beating Hearts)

"It was then, when the LORD delivered up the Amorites to the Israelites, that Joshua prayed to the LORD, and said in the presence of Israel: Sun, stand still at Gibeon, Moon, in the valley of Aijalon! The sun stood still, the moon stayed, while the nation took vengeance on its foes. This is recorded in the Book of Jashar. The sun halted halfway across the heavens; not for an entire day did it press on." (Joshua 10:12-13)

On the following day, Sept. 15th, we went to Siroki Brieg, the church of the Assumption located at a friary, where Franciscans were martyred during World War II by communists. In the sanctuary, I heard Fr. Jozo, a Franciscan priest, give a talk. Seeing his love for Mary, the Eucharist, and the Cross, and being moved by his penitential habit, I wanted to be like him.

After his talk, I needed to use the restroom, and while waiting in the monastery, I saw an old statue of St. Francis of Assisi. I don't know why, but I was impelled to say this prayer in front of the statue, "O St. Francis, please help me. If God is calling me to be a priest, please give me a sign from God, so I know what He wants me to do." After we left the church, we were taken to the site where many Franciscans were martyred and burned to death. When I went down into the cave where they were martyred, I was moved by the giving up of their life for Jesus. I thought, what a blessing to die for Jesus as a martyr.

Probably due to fasting on bread, water, and a little fruit, I developed a tremendous headache. When we boarded the bus to return to Medjugorje, I thought much about Fr. Jozo's talk, and the martyred Franciscans.

We arrived back in Medjugorje and disembarked off the bus. Everyone went their own way, except for two young women and I. One was single and the other married. I was walking with them, when suddenly the married lady said, "Look at the sun, it's spinning." I said to myself, "I am not going to look at the sun, and ruin my eyes."

Then the other young lady said, "Wow, it's spinning." Still, I was reluctant to look, but with a hand over my eyes, I looked and was astonished to see the sun spinning without harming my eyes. First there was a darker spot in the center of the sun that appeared to be spinning, but then, the sun became brilliant white, and for some reason, one of the ladies said, "It's the Eucharist". It was a beautiful white. Then as we watched, the sun became red and there appeared what looked like a crown of thorns around the sun. The sun took the shape of a human heart and to my astonishment, it began to beat and throb. I later came to believe it was the Sacred Heart of Jesus. I didn't know what to say. Then, the sun split in two, yet stayed connected, such that there were two pieces of the sun, that formed two hearts. One heart had a crown of thorns, the other did not. They both began to pulsate and beat, yet were attached to each other, similar to Valentine hearts. Then the sun returned to its normal appearance. Yet, there were sparkle colors within it. I said to the ladies, "We should kneel, we are seeing a miracle." All three of us knelt. The sun returned, as it was when we first saw it, with a dark disc in the center that began to spin, and finally, the sun returned to its original brightness, and we could no longer look at it. I don't know how long this lasted, perhaps five to ten minutes. We were so dumbfounded by what we saw, we agreed to not tell others.

Later, women, as they are, talked about it and some questioned me wondering if I saw what they reported. My reply, at the time, was, "I don't want to talk about it."

That night, I decided to walk back to the place we were staying and wanted to pray about what we saw. I wondered, "Was this the sign, God was giving me, to be a priest?" Yet, I was overwhelmed by my past sins, and thought, there is no way God would call someone like me to become a priest. On the path at night, barely lit by a flashlight, I happen meet by God's providence, a Franciscan priest. I thought there was no way he would talk to me, after all, he probably didn't speak English. However, he was an American, who became a Franciscan and was living with the friars in Medjugorje. He said, "Let's go up to Apparition Hill and talk". When we arrived at the top of the hill, I told him what happened, and he told me his story, how he was very wealthy and gave up everything to become a Franciscan. As we looked at the lights of the little village from the top of the hill, where Mary first appeared, I told him what I had seen with the two ladies. I said I felt unworthy to be a priest. He explained to be a priest is a calling, and if we respond with an open heart, we will know deep inside if that is what God wants or not. I began to cry, and told him, "I am unworthy to be a priest". I had lived a terribly sinful life. He said, "All of us are unworthy." God was revealing His mercy to me, and I hard a difficult time understanding God could be so merciful.

By the time we left Medjugorje, I believed God was calling me to be a priest. But not so much because of what we saw in the sky. But, rather, what I believed God was saying inside my heart. God's mercy touched my heart, and He used it to call me to the priesthood. It was through the intercession of the Blessed Virgin Mary, I came back to the Church, and it was through Mary's intercession at Medjugorje, I discovered my call to the priesthood. Oh, I cannot ever thank you enough for loving me, so much that you would help me, O Mary.

In Medjugorje - Perpetual Adoration Chapel
God Touches My Heart, I'm Loved by God
"Then you will look and be radiant, your heart will throb and swell with joy; the wealth on the seas will be brought to you, to you the riches of the nations will come." (Isaiah 60:5)

Considering all that had happened, another experience helped me to understand that Jesus is truly present in the Eucharist, and He loves me. I don't recall what day, but someone from our group encouraged me to go to the Adoration Chapel. I had no idea what an Adoration Chapel was. One of the ladies, not married, and who also witnessed the sun event, showed me the Adoration Chapel. We both went inside. She went to pray in a different pew. I knelt down and looked at the Host, which was in a small metal box (Tabernacle). The door of the Tabernacle contained an opening, so the Host could be placed in a small door, allowing the Host to be visible. I said a few prayers, closed my eyes and started to pray the Rosary. As I began to pray the Rosary, it seemed as though someone was shining a flashlight on my closed eyes lids. I kept my eyes closed, and kept praying the Rosary. It was not a flashlight. The light raced across my eyelids, and as I meditated on the mysteries of the Rosary, the mysteries became as though alive in my mind. I could see Jesus come out of the tomb, His ascension into heaven, etc... as though watching a movie in my head. When I finished the Rosary, as I kept my eyes closed, I began to feel-- warmth coming from the light and that warmth went to my heart. I began to feel love. I do not know how to express this, except I felt love. My heart started to beat faster, as though I was in love. As the love increased, my heart started to beat faster, and faster and faster. I did not know what was happening to me. I felt like my heart was going to explode. The love was intense. I thought I was going to die. If love had increased anymore, I would have died of love. Slowly the love diminished, and my heart began to slowdown. I was overwhelmed with emotion and had to leave the Chapel. I knew if I would stay, people would see me crying and so, I quickly went outside and sat on a bench and cried and cried and cried. I cried, because I never felt love like that before, and felt like a tiny ant in the middle of an ant pile. Out of love, God reached down, picked me up from among all the ants, and held me in His hand giving me His full attention.

My reaction, after I stopped crying was rather odd. I began to think, "Who do those people think they are? They should warn us that when you go in there, this happens." I became angry, as I thought people need to be aware before they enter the chapel what will happen to them and not be shocked by it.

The next time I saw the leader of our group, I said to her. "Why didn't you tell us, what happens before we go into that Chapel?" She said, "What things?" I said, "You know, when we feel love and then the heart beats fast like that!" She looked at me, and said, "What are you talking about?" I tried to explain to her what happened and quickly realized, it didn't happen to everyone who went to the Chapel.

Return to the USA After Medjugorje Trip and Return Trips to Medjugorje

When I returned to the USA, I tried to process all that happened and didn't know what to do. I spoke with several priests who encouraged me to not share these experiences with just anyone, but only with a spiritual director. I decided I wanted to be a priest, and believed Our Lady helped me in Medjugorje to come to know I had a vocation to the priesthood.

Invited to attend a vocation gathering with priests and the bishop of the Helena Diocese, I was excited. However, my experience at the event was terrible. The priests were drinking hard liquor and many became intoxicated. Some were making negative comments about their bishop, within a few feet of his presence. This greatly turned me off. I started to think maybe God wanted me to be a religious priest like Fr. Jozo. I looked at the newspaper, *Our Sunday Guest,* and it had an article about new religious orders. One order was a group of Franciscans, who had a devotion to Mary and the Eucharist. I decided to visit the community. It was called the Franciscans of the Perpetual Victim Martyrs.

I eventually returned to Medjugorje 7 times. One time I was asked to give a written testimony about my conversion and call, since it occurred in Medjugorje. On one trip, the St. James church pastor told me, I was the 81st priestly vocation from the USA.

When I returned to Medjugorje after I was a priest, it was moving to be able to offer Mass at St. James Church and give the homily. I offered a Mass of Thanksgiving to thank Our Lady for my vocation.

#29 SPIRITUAL HAPPENINGS AND EVENTS AFTER TRIP TO MEDJUGORJE

Heart Palpitations

Occasionally, while in Catholic churches, while praying before Jesus in the Tabernacle, or during Eucharistic Adoration, my heart would begin to suddenly beat rapidly out of love for Jesus truly present in the Eucharist. On several occasions, my heart started to beat rapidly when I read Luke 10:1-12. This particular Gospel was read at a Mass during my first trip to Medjugorje, and when it was read at other times, it reminded me, God wanted me to be a priest. On a few occasions, the beating of my heart before Jesus in the Tabernacle, was so intense, and I felt God's love in such a way, it caused me to blush due to the feeling associated with it.

St. Francis of Assisi

When I returned from Medjugorje after my first pilgrimage, I found a book, *The Little Flowers of St. Francis,* in the back of the church of St. Joseph in Fort Hickok.

Due to my experiences in Medjugorje with the Franciscan priests, going to confession to a Franciscan priest at St. Joseph church, and due to *The Little Flowers of St. Francis,* I was intrigued and wanted to be a follower of St. Francis. I was drawn to his life of poverty, humility, and penance. I came to understand, I needed to do much penance because of the many sins from my youth, and thought that if I become a Franciscan, I could make reparation for them and be like Fr. Jozo, to speak about Mary and the Eucharist. I wanted to die a Franciscan martyr, like the Franciscans martyred at the Siroki Briege monastery in Bosnia-Herzegovina.

Red and White Rays Emanate From the Eucharist - Who is St. Faustina?

The following event happened after my trip to Medjugorje. When praying during a Eucharistic Holy Hour at St. Joseph's Church, I saw two rays of light come out of the Host. One ray was red and the other white. I had no idea what it meant. When I visited with my spiritual director, Fr. Mark Sercowski, he asked if I heard of Sister Faustina. I told him, that I had never heard of her. Years later, I discovered who she was, and was astonished to hear she had the experience of seeing white and red rays coming from the chest of Jesus, but I saw emanating from a Host during Eucharistic Adoration. I later discovered the Eucharist is a font of mercy and personally saw how Jesus pours out His mercy through the Sacred Host during Eucharistic Adoration.

Holy Hours

"As the deer longs for streams of water, so my soul longs for you, O God. My soul thirsts for God, the living God. When can I enter and see the face of God? My tears have been my bread day and night as they ask me every day, "Where is your God?" (Psalm 42:2-4)

While in Medjugorje on my first pilgrimage, I recognized a woman, Anna Mae, from Rolling Hills, who introduced me to her friend, Juliana. I told the two about my experiences in Medjugorje, and they introduced me to praying an hour before Jesus in the Blessed Sacrament, they called a "Holy Hour."

While living in Fort Hickok and Milo City, I felt drawn to be with Jesus in the Sacred Hosts in the Tabernacle, and at first, began to make a weekly Holy Hour before Jesus in the tabernacle, and then would do more Holy Hours until I was praying a Holy Hour daily.

While living at Milo, Ohio, in a house near St. Mary's church. Monsignor Vincent La Pew, the pastor of the parish, became my spiritual director, and taught me much about the Blessed Virgin Mary. It was at this church, I entrusted my bills to Our Lady, and She paid them off. I asked Monsignor if we could have continuous Eucharistic Adoration in church. After promoting it, we ended up having 12 continuous hours of Adoration every week. He was hesitant at first, but decided to give it a try. It was a huge success. I prayed many would sign up for Adoration. My prayers were answered.

When I entered the Franciscans of the Perpetual Victim Martyrs, it was customary for the postulants and novices to pray two Holy Hours a day. From then on, 1993, until today, I have faithfully prayed two Holy Hours every day. Over the years, a few times I prayed only one Holy Hour due to illness or a busy schedule, almost every day I continue to pray two Holy Hours consecutively. When I pray for two hours I pray the *Liturgy of the Hours*, the Rosary (usually the 7 Sorrows), the Stations of the Cross, a meditation on Sacred Scripture and just sit, adore and listen to Jesus. As a Franciscan of the Perpetual Victim Martyrs, I was introduced to making short visits to Jesus in the Tabernacle. St. Maximilian Kolbe made 10 visits a day. As a brother, visiting Jesus in the Blessed Sacrament often was a joy, and I received many inspirations from doing so.

Consecration to Mary – If I Pray to Mary, Will I Ignore Jesus?
"My soul magnifies the Lord and my spirit rejoices in God my Savior." (Luke 1:46)

Anna Mae and Juliana from Rolling Hills encouraged me to consecrate myself to Jesus through Mary. It was also recommended by Fr. Luke Zambeze while in Medjugorje. Fr. Zambeze said something to me in Medjugorje I will never forget. While going to confession to him, he said, "You have a devotion to Mary, just like Pope John Paul II." At that time, I had no idea what kind of devotion Pope John Paul II had of Mary. Fr. Zambeze allegedly was able to read souls.

Before doing the consecration, I read *True Devotion to Mary* by St. Louis de Montfort. However, about halfway through the book and halfway through the consecration, I had a dilemma. I suddenly decided it was wrong to pray to Mary. If I did, I was ignoring Jesus. Out of desperation, I pleaded with Jesus, and said, "Lord, if you want me to pray to your Mother, show me!" I opened up my bible and my finger landed on this: "My soul magnifies the Lord, my spirit rejoices in God my Savior." This scripture helped me to see Mary is like a magnifying glass. All our prayers go through Her, and She magnifies Jesus and makes Him easier to see and understand. She also magnifies our prayers and makes them more pleasing to God. From that moment on, the doubt vanished, and I had no problem in praying to Mary. The day came for the consecration. After going to Confession and receiving Jesus in Holy Communion, I consecrated myself to Jesus through Mary on Dec. 8th, 1992. All of my good actions, merits, virtues, life, soul, were all entrusted to Her to do with as She pleases.

Franciscans of the Perpetual Victim Martyrs Pilgrimage

Anna Mae and Juliana went with me to Canterbury, Louisiana to visit the men's religious order. When I arrived, I went into the Adoration Chapel. I was astonished when I looked up at the Monstrance. I said to my friends, "Déjà vu." This is so weird. I feel like I've been here before or seen this place before." My friends chuckled, and said, "Len, this is Mother Annunciata's Monastery." I felt stupid, as I had no idea the men's religious order was at the same place. We had a good laugh at my ignorance.

Before leaving, I met with Fr. Patrick Maccaroni, who prayed over me. While praying aloud, as though speaking on behalf of the Virgin Mary, with what was thought to be a locution, he said, "My child, I am calling you to this community. Do not be afraid. I am your mother. I am calling you to follow my Son." After visiting the brother's religious community, and staying in their monastery with Fr. Patrick, I believed God wanted me to become a member, but not due to Fr. Patrick's prayer.

The Virgin Mary Paid for My College Education, I Had Hoped the Government Would Pay by Joining the Army

As the days went on after my consecration, I felt more and more like I had a call to religious life, especially to the Perpetual Victim Martyrs. However, I had $6,900 worth of college loans and knew it would take years to pay them off.

I read about St. Maximilian Kolbe and how he needed a certain amount of money to start his printing press. He knelt before a statue of the Immaculate Virgin Mary, asking Her for the money for his press. And then, when he stood up to leave, he noticed, an envelope lying on the altar next to the statue of Mary. It contained the exact amount of money needed to purchase the printer.

While living in Milo, Ohio, one night out of desperation, I entered St. Mary's church. The Virgin Mary's statue on the side altar was barely aglow due to candles beneath the statue in the darkened church. I knelt in front of the statue and out of desperation prayed, "O Mary, I consecrated myself to you. When I made the consecration, I gave you everything. I gave you my body, my soul, my possessions and all that I am. But there is one thing I did not give you….my bills." I put my hand on my hip, and said, "I give you my bills. If God wants me to be a Franciscan priest, you take care of them! As of today, they are no longer my bills, but your bills. You now owe $6,900."

I stood up, I looked with trust and hope on the altar near the statue, expecting to find an envelope with $6,900 dollars needed to pay off my school loans, so I could go to seminary, but it wasn't there. I rudely walked out of the church and could not believe I treated Mary in such a manner.

Amazingly, within two weeks after I prayed this prayer, the two hospitals in Fort Hickok merged and became one. Due to the excess number of employees, administration encouraged employees to quit, so they wouldn't need to lay off anyone. They decided if an employee would quit, the person would immediately receive their pension. I was employed for only 6 years, so I didn't believe I had a pension. But when I went to the Human Resources Department, I discovered I had a $10,000 pension. I said to the HR department lady, "So, do you mean if I quit, I will receive $10,000?" She said, "Yes". I said, "How long before I receive the money?" She said, "The day you quit." I thanked her and went directly to my boss, and asked to meet with him. I said, "I quit. You have a two-week notice, or longer if you like." He was shocked, and said, "Why do you want to quit?" I said, "I want to be a priest." His mouth dropped open, and stuttered saying, "Really!" In my mind, I knew it was a woman who paid off my bills to become a priest—The Virgin Mary, the greatest and most loving of all women.

St. Mary's Church – I'm Loved and I Give My Love
Perpetual Adoration Chapel in Fort Hickok

Before my conversion, one of my greatest heartaches was the desire to love someone and to be loved, and not having that desire fulfilled. I wanted a wife to love, who would love me back. After my conversion and after my pilgrimage to Medjugorje, one night while praying in the church of St. Mary's in Milo, I was pondering the desire to be loved and to love. I was feeling down, since I didn't feel loved and greatly wanted to love someone. In the silence of the darkened church, I sensed Jesus was lonely and wanted to be loved.

I recalled my experience in the Adoration Chapel in Medjugorje and how I felt loved. Now, I felt God wanted to be loved here in the church, and I too will be loved. God loves me and I love Him. I wept as I thought, finally I have someone I can give my love and someone who loves me.

Since that experience in the Adoration Chapel in Medjugorje I began to make a daily Holy Hour. Every day I came to receive love and to give love. When before Jesus in the Tabernacle, two lonely hearts were together in love. I wanted others to experience His love and began to pray Fort Hickok would someday have an Adoration Chapel.

Every day, I prayed intensely for Perpetual Adoration, so many could experience the love of Jesus in the Eucharist. I spoke about Perpetual Adoration to the Queen of Peace Prayer Group, of which I was a member in Fort Hickok.

The group decided we would try to start an Adoration Chapel and together every week, we made a Holy Hour before Jesus in the tabernacle, praying the Holy Rosary and Chaplet of Divine Mercy for the intention of starting Perpetual Adoration at our parish of St. Mary's.

After a year went by, Lilly Gillgall, the prayer group leader, asked the pastor if the parish could have Perpetual Adoration, but he refused. Since he declined, we decided to fast on bread and water on Wednesday and Friday of every week for the priest. The following year, we asked the pastor again, and this time he said yes.

We invited Alicia Schlooper and Silli Quinn to come and speak at the Masses. While giving their talks at Holy Mass, some of us prayed the Rosary for them as they spoke. After the overwhelming number who signed up on Feb. 28th of 1993, the Adoration Chapel began in a closet near the back door of the Convent of the Sisters of St. Agatha. The room was so small only two people could pray in it. Eventually, when the Sisters of St. Agatha abandoned their convent, Perpetual Adoration was moved to their Convent Chapel. Some thought Jesus kicked out the liberal sisters who had no devotion to Jesus in the Eucharist, so the people could pray comfortably adoring Him in a larger Chapel. Later, when St. Mary's built their new church, they created a new and beautiful Chapel.

Before my conversion, after breaking up with a girl whom I thought I would marry someday, out of desperation I went to the church to pray at night, but it was locked. I was angry because I couldn't enter and be with God when I needed Him the most. Now, years later an Adoration Chapel is available to welcome anyone distressed, so they can be with Jesus, 24 hours a day, 7 days a week—even in the wee hours of night. The Lord was now able to receive visitors to give His love, and visitors could now be with Him to receive His tender love.

#30 ST. MARY'S PARISH IN FORT HICKOK

Unconsecrated Hosts Placed with Consecrated Hosts in the Tabernacle

After returning from my first pilgrimage to Medjugorje, not much after my conversion in 1992, I had the wonderful habit of attending daily Mass. One Sunday after Mass, I stayed in the church to pray, and I noticed the sacristan take the remaining unconsecrated hosts from the entrance of the church that were not brought up during the offertory. She opened the Tabernacle and placed them in the Ciboria with consecrated Hosts. I was shocked she didn't know the difference. I immediately went to the priest and told him what I witnessed. He quickly dropped what he was doing and visited with the sacristan. He was horrified it happened. This would be the beginning of my defense of Jesus in the Eucharist and in defense of His Precious Blood. It also made me aware of problems that can happen with lay people having access to Jesus in the Tabernacle.

#31 PERPETUAL ADORATION "MIRACLES"

"Miracles" Due to Adoration at Fort Hickok

About a year after adoration started, a man went to the Adoration Chapel in Fort Hickok to pray for his protestant friend who needed a heart transplant. During his Holy Hour in the Adoration Chapel when he was praying to Jesus in the Sacred Host, asking Our Lord to grant his friend a new heart, the Chapel phone rang. His friend called and asked him to drive him to Helena, Ohio, where he was to receive a new heart.

The grandmother of a young boy, about the age of ten, went to the Adoration Chapel at Fort Hickok to pray. During her Holy Hour, she prayed for the safety of her grandson who was helping with the wheat harvest. Little did she know, during her Holy Hour, a wheat truck ran over her grandson. When the family heard the news, they rushed to the hospital, expecting the worst.

After all x-rays and CT scans were complete, the doctor came to speak to his tearful parents and said, "The boy's torso was run over by the back wheels of a grain truck, but there is nothing wrong with him, except a few scrapes. And I can't explain how he is not injured."

None of these so-called miracles were ever investigated, but many believe they were true miracles.

#32 BECOMING PRO-LIFE

Pro-Life

"For thou didst form my inward parts, thou didst knit me together in my mother's womb. . . .My frame was not hidden from thee, when I was being made in secret, intricately wrought in the depths of the earth." (Psalm 139:13,15)

When I was working at Nedley Regional Hospital in Fort Hickok, Ohio, after I had discontinued attending Fort Hickok State, my job was to clean surgical instruments. One day, the surgical nurse brought back instruments and a large suction canister filled with blood. Normally, I dumped the blood from the canister down the hopper in the sewer, and did so as usual. However, when I dumped the canister, I noticed large chunks falling into the hopper, but presumed they were blood clots. When the nurse returned, she said, "What did you do with the contents of that canister!" I said, "I dumped it down the drain." The nurse immediately began to cry. And said, "Oh, no! There were parts of a baby in the canister. The mother had a miscarriage, and we needed to have surgery to remove the baby." I was horrified and apologized profusely. She said not to worry since I didn't know. Then, when I was cleaning the surgical instruments from that surgery, there on a curette, I noticed at tiny hand or foot attached to it. I was shocked and I too began to cry.

#33 ENTERING RELIGIOUS LIFE AND DEPARTING FROM IT

Entered the Religious Order of the Franciscans of the Perpetual Victim Martyrs
After the Virgin Mary paid off my college loans, I called Fr. Patrick Maccaroni, the superior of the religious community, the Perpetual Victim Martyrs, founded by Mother Annuciata. Her religious community of St. Clare Nuns have as their apostolate to Adore the Holy Eucharistic Face of Jesus. The sisters and the brothers religious communities share the same grounds and were located in Canterbury, Louisiana.

Fr. Patrick had told me to come when I am able. I arrived May 25th, 1993 (the birthday of St. Padre Pio). I was an observant of the community until July 16th, the feast of Our Lady of Mount Carmel, when I became a postulant.

Postulants wear a white shirt, tie and black pants. Around our neck we wore a silver crucifix with Mary standing at the foot of the cross. In less than a year, on March 25th, the Solemnity of the Annunciation, I became a novice and was clothed with the habit of St. Francis. I received the name Br. Antonio Maria Padua of the Sweet Heart of Mary.

During my postulancy, the community voted to add Franciscan to its name. The community became known as the Franciscans of the Perpetual Victim Martyrs. Before their name change, novices and professed wore a black cassock with an emblem. Sadly, Fr. Maccaroni was abruptly transferred to Rome by his religious superior, which was devastating to the little religious community, to Mother Annunciata, and her sisters. It was the only time I ever saw Mother Annunciata cry. Fr. Giuseppe Mary Barker, just ordained a priest a few months before Fr. Patrick's transfer, was made superior of the community.

One day, when I was a postulant, I had a severe headache and asked Fr. Patrick for permission to take Tylenol. He said, "Let's see if the Lord wants to take it away first." He laid his hands on my head and prayed over me. I felt heat come upon my head, and within a minute, the headache that had been excruciating, almost completely disappeared. Apparently, he had the gift of healing and I experienced it firsthand. His homilies were inspirational. And he had the knack of defusing conflicts with his sense of humor.

Many years later, it came to light why Fr. Maccaroni was transferred. Decades before becoming the superior, of the Franciscan Perpetual Victim Martyrs, while he belonged to another religious community, it is believed he sexually abused a child. This came to light after his death. It was truly a shock to me and many people. I never would have suspected he had done such a thing.

Fr. Paschal Buchanan was a priest who gave retreats for pilgrims. He belonged to a different religious community, the Order of Our Lady of the Snow. He knew the entire Bible by heart and not only gave talks for retreatants, but regularly gave a Bible study to the brothers as well. Fr. Paschal was well-loved by everyone. At times, he would get caught up in his homily at Mass and would begin weeping, especially when speaking about the Passion of Jesus.

After Fr. Paschal died it was also revealed he too was accused of sexually abusing a child. This came to light about ten years after I was ordained a priest for the Diocese of Rolling Hills. I witnessed the deep devotion of these two priests toward the Eucharist, and the Blessed Virgin Mary, as well as their dedication as a religious. If it was true of their sexual deviancy years previously, both seemed to have changed their lives. Still, I became angry they did such terrible things to innocent children. When I found out about these scandals, I was totally dumbfounded and felt deeply sad, I felt sorry for the allegedly abused.

During the time I was a member of the religious community, and also while in seminary, I was naïve and unaware of how homosexual priests and religious caused so much damage to Holy Mother Church, and the lives of innocent people and their families.

March 25th, 1995 was my first profession, vowing poverty, chastity, and obedience. I was excited my mother and step-father came, as well as my father and his friend. Being clothed in the habit, I felt protected by Our Lady from many temptations.

I greatly enjoyed religious life, especially the challenge of living out the vows in a community of men. How difficult it is to live with other men with personalities much different from mine and who had very odd ways of doing things. At times, I wanted to scream due to their foibles. I am sure I also drove some of them nuts. However, I received many consolations, especially when I had persevered through some trial, which usually involved obedience. I had great zeal to be holy, motivated by Mother Annunciata's example and words. She told us we should all strive to be saints.

Once, when I was a postulant, Fr. Giuseppe asked me to be the cook. However, I hardly ever cooked for myself before entering religious life, and had no idea how to cook for fourteen men. I said, "Father, I hardly ever cooked before. I can't do it." He said, "I have confidence in you." I then said, "Did you pray about this?" He looked at me, and said, "You will be the cook." And I said, "Father, I think the devil put you up to this." I think he was shocked at what I said, and then looked at me, saying, "You're starting tomorrow." As I lived religious life, I became more tactful in dealing with things.

A previous brother who was the cook decided to bake a turkey. He took a frozen turkey out of the freezer and put it directly in the oven. He failed to thaw it out. Four hours later, when it was time to eat, he removed the turkey from the oven. He tried to cut up the turkey, but it was still frozen in the middle. We ended up using an electric knife to cut it up into small pieces and then broiled it. Nobody became sick.

After I took my first vows, I attended St. Robert Bellarmine Seminary in Pittsburgh, Massachusetts for two years. The brothers then started their House of Studies and then later we began to attend Mary's Meadow Seminary, in Quakers, Virginia.

One of my greatest difficulties in religious life was feeling the need to be liked. Nothing was more difficult when I felt a superior ignored me, or even at times put me down due to, what I believed was jealousy. I kept the pain of it all in my heart and in the ears of my confessor. Due to disagreeing with the superior at times, interiorly, I became angry and had thoughts of not obeying, but outwardly always did what was asked. Exteriorly, I was a model of obedience, but interiorly, there was a raging storm. In this way, and many other ways, religious are to die to themselves and be crucified with Christ, so that Christ may live within us.

There was a time I lost my temper with a brother, and he never forgot it. Most of us learned to forgive each other, and to love each other as brothers in Christ. Often times, I was inspired by the virtue of the brothers, and at the same time I felt that I gave bad example often, which may not have been the case. I enjoyed striving to grow in holiness and virtue and living out my vows of poverty, chastity, and obedience. Up to that point, there was no other time I believed I grew in purity so quick as when I was a brother. I felt spiritually protected.

During this time the Lord gave me some spiritual gifts which are difficult to explain. At times, the Lord would tell me things in advance. For example, He would let me know this brother or that brother will be leaving the community soon, and just as the Lord revealed, it would happen within a few days. It seemed the Lord wanted me to know about some of these events in advance, so I would not be as shocked by these situations.

When I was praying for Fr. Jarod Shortnecker, I suddenly saw (in my mind) maggots coming out of his mouth. I was horrified by this image and could not understand what it meant. Within a week he left the brothers and the priesthood, and moved in with a woman, and then they later married. This was the first great scandal I ever dealt with. Fr. Jarod was popular and known for his gift of healing. His homilies were spiritual and practical. However, in the monastery, I noticed he hadn't been praying the *Liturgy of the Hours* with the brothers, and I hardly ever saw him make his Holy Hour or spend any time in the chapel. He stopped praying and became excessively preoccupied with helping pilgrims who came to the monastery.

At the friary, the brothers fasted on Wednesday and Friday, with Friday being more strict. As a postulant, I really wanted to prove my love for Jesus by fasting more than what was asked. Consequently, on Wednesday and Friday, I fasted strictly on bread and water, while the other brothers had soup and a light meal.

However, I began to be tempted by the evil one, to think I was better than they, after all, I could fast better. After reading books about the lives of saints and a few books on religious life, I realized it was a temptation to do more than what was expected of the brothers, and in that, was the fault. It is important for religious to not do less or more than others. Otherwise, pride can creep in. I quickly realized I needed to do the same as the others and to be faithful to the rule and its practice to the best of my ability, not doing anything more or less.

I was always punctual to meals, prayer, and work. When it was time to go to prayer or to finish work, when I heard the bell signaling to stop or start an activity, I dropped what I was doing out of obedience. Obeying the superior, the bell, and being prompt for everything is how one accomplishes God's will. I was told the devil can imitate humility, but never obedience. I was always in the Chapel when it was required and never late. Unfortunately, the superiors often didn't show up until after prayer had begun, or not at all. It was as though they were so busy and had much more important things to do. Later I realized it was a fault on their part and was not a good example for the brothers.

As a religious, I learned the power and beauty of obedience. While taking Spanish classes out of obedience at a local college, I wondered where the nearest Tabernacle is located, so I could turn my mind to the physical presence of Jesus while taking class. I said a simple prayer, "Jesus, where are you located?" Not much after pondering where the physical presence of Jesus might be, the superior asked me to drop off food and clothing at a place ran by the Sweet Consolation Sisters, who would then distribute them to the poor. The place I delivered the items was just a few blocks from the college where I was taking classes. And this is how I discovered a Tabernacle was located very close to the college. I saw how the Lord used obedience to answer my prayer to help me know where the nearest Tabernacle was located.

The brothers sent their seminarians to St. Robert Bellarmine Seminary and then later switched to Mary's Meadow Seminary and still later started their House of Studies. The leaders of the community, as well as I, perceived God was calling me to be a priest.

At St. Robert Bellarmine Seminary, I went through some turmoil because I was accused of throwing holy water on a priest and because of it, wasn't allowed to renew my vows. I was told I was going to be pulled from seminary, and I may not go on to the priesthood. Yet, once they heard the truth of the matter, that no one was present in the room when I sprinkled Holy Water, they said I could make my perpetual vows.

As I look back at the time just before I made my perpetual vows, I believe I was bound and determined to make my Perpetual Profession (as they say, hell or high water) and therefore was not so attuned with what God may have been saying to me at the time. My father and his friend came to my Perpetual Profession on Aug. 14th, 1998 (the feast of St. Maximilian Kolbe). I had often wondered why the profession wasn't scheduled on the Solemnity of the Assumption, and thought perhaps it was due to the professions of the St. Clare Nuns of Adoration of the Eucharistic Face of Jesus, and to have both on the same day would be overwhelming for both communities.

In the period of time just after my Perpetual Profession, a great storm in the community occurred. Mother Annunciata asked the brothers to establish a friary at their new monastery near Smithville, about an hour drive away. The Franciscan

Perpetual Victim Martyrs council took a vote and told her no. If you know anything about Mother Annunciata, especially since she was the founder of the men's religious order, you don't tell your founder no. Mother was furious, and so were many of the brothers.

To convince the brothers to locate a new friary at her new monastery, she came to the friary for dinner with the brothers and asked us to please come and serve the sisters. She wanted the priests to offer Mass for the sisters, and she wanted the brothers to take care of the grounds and to serve guests who would come. But, again, they told her no. The superiors of the order told us, "We are maturing as a community and now make our own decisions." Soon, brothers began to leave. At that time, we had twenty-four brothers and within six months half of them left.

In response to their no, Mother decided to start another religious community of brothers and called them Guardians of the Holy Grail, who would serve the sisters at their new monastery. Mother decided to ask the religious community from Kentucky, the Fathers of Love, to offer Mass for the sisters.

I decided I too had to leave. A community unfaithful to their founder was not for me. I felt if we lose the reason we are founded, we inevitably cannot grow in the holiness God destined for us, and in fact, could go to hell. Because I had just made my Perpetual Profession five months previously, and because I was thinking of leaving the brothers, I decided to visit with Mother one on one, and told her of my decision to leave. She said I should not leave, but I chose to leave anyway.

In addition to this turmoil in the community since Fr. Giuseppe became superior, he drastically changed the community schedule. When I first entered the community, the brothers were making two Holy Hours of Eucharistic Adoration a day. Together we prayed the Chaplet of Divine Mercy, Morning Prayer, the Office of Readings, Daytime Prayer, Evening Prayer with the Rosary and Night Prayer. However, just before leaving the community, only Morning Prayer, the Office of Readings, Evening Prayer, and the Rosary were held in common. We no longer even had a community Holy Hour. Each brother was supposed to pray it on our own. I felt like the community I joined was not the same, and were no longer obedient to our founder. I became confused and didn't know what to do. I missed singing the Salve Regina at the end of Night Prayer. It always filled my heart with joy to sing to Our Lady as a community of brothers.

The morning I was to leave the brothers, while shaving off my beard, it was announced they would now start a friary at Mother's new monastery. Since I already made my decision, I left that day. This decision would haunt me for many years, especially since I had made my Perpetual Profession and promised God to stay there for the rest of my life. I later thought myself as disobedient and lacking in humility when I left. I received permission to leave from my spiritual director, from the religious community, and also from the bishop. But, I felt like I failed the Lord and turned my back on the vocation He called me to, especially since I had made my Perpetual

Profession nine months previously. The moment I left, my soul entered into a deep darkness, and believed God abandoned me.

God's Ocean of Mercy

"Oh, give thanks to the LORD, for He is good! For His mercy endures forever. Oh, give thanks to the God of gods! For His mercy endures forever. Oh, give thanks to the Lord of lords! For His mercy endures forever: To Him who alone does great wonders, For His mercy endures forever; To Him who by wisdom made the heavens, For His mercy endures forever;" (Psalm 136)

After I became a Franciscan of Perpetual Victim Martyrs, I came to enjoy and appreciate the Divine Mercy devotion so much that I asked a Divine Mercy picture be placed in the friars' Chapel and the superior placed in it there. It was a picture I brought with me when I entered the order.

An Abortionist and God's Mercy

"See that you do not despise one of these little ones. For I tell you that in heaven their angels always see the face of my Father who is in heaven." (Matthew 18:10)

While at Mary's Meadow Seminary, Bernard Nathanson, a former Jewish abortionist who became Catholic, came to the seminary and spoke to all seminarians about his conversion to the Catholic faith. The cold manner he spoke about abortion gave me chills. As a former abortionist, he admitted to killing over 70,000 babies. And yet, when he was baptized at St. Patrick's Cathedral in New York, by Cardinal O' Conner, all of his sins and the punishment due to his sins were forgiven and washed away in the ocean of God's mercy. On Divine Mercy Sunday, if any Catholic goes to confession during Lent, and especially the very day of Divine Mercy Sunday (the Sunday after Easter), and receive Holy Communion on that day, while in the state of grace, all their sins and the punishment due to their sins are forgiven. People have done the most horrible things to themselves and others. Yet, God's mercy endures forever and is infinite. If God can forgive a man who killed 70,000 innocent children, He will forgive anyone. Jesus told St. Faustina, "The greater the sinner, the greater his right to God's mercy." (#423) I rejoice in the fact, Jesus forgave me all my sins and the punishment due to them, and I can never appreciate enough His untold mercy. Every day, I try to pray the Chaplet of Divine Mercy during the 3pm Hour, not only for myself, but for the sick and dying and the whole world. Thank you, Jesus, for Your infinite mercy! As you are merciful to me, should I not be merciful to others?

#34 MOTHER ANNUNCIATA AND I

Life with Mother Annunciata

"I am espoused to him whom the angels serve." (Morning Prayer antiphon feast of St. Agnes)

I could write several books on my six years of getting to know Mother Annunciata when I was a brother. She was a deeply spiritual woman with great faith, great trust, and unimaginable courage. Mother Annunciata encouraged Catholics to stand up against liberals, who she said were damaging the Church. She taught the brothers and sisters the importance of defending the Church and our faith. The witness and zeal she demonstrated at speaking events, and in person, made us proud to be Catholic.

Her deep love of Jesus in the Blessed Sacrament, love of the Church, practical wisdom and way of making the scriptures come alive had a tremendous impact on how I came to view the Church and live out my life as a Christian, religious brother, and future priest.

Almost every week, on Wednesday, the brothers enjoyed their "Wednesday Audience" with Mother. On Wednesdays, the brothers went to a cloistered room used for guests, and Mother Annunciata gave us a talk. These talks and her holy example, as a religious, were profoundly spiritual, played an important role in preparing me for the priesthood, molding my spirituality, and helped to develop a spiritual life.

There are so many stories I could share about Mother. Here are a few of them. A pickup truck carrying a marble corpus of Jesus Crucified from a church in Chicago that rejected it arrived at the monastery. When it arrived, Mother came out of the cloister, and kissed it. It was moving to see her reaction to the Crucifix. She said the Lord spoke to her saying, "At last I have a home." It's my understanding the pastor of the church was going to throw the Crucifix away, so a layman rescued it and delivered it to Mother. Later, she built the Holy Cross Shrine, whereby the Crucifix was attached to a wall with black background. The shrine had stained-glass windows, and an altar used for outdoor Masses for Corpus Christi Sunday benediction. At times, some employees and I stood before the large corpus and prayed the Chaplet Divine Mercy at 3pm.

One day, Fannie Suzuki and I came to pray the Chaplet at 3pm. As we prayed the chaplet, and as we were gazing upon the face of Jesus, suddenly the upper portion of the torso of the corpus appeared to expand, and return as if it took a breath, and exhaled. The chest of Jesus rose and fell. I could not believe my eyes. Fannie said, "Did you see that?" I said, "Ah, yeah, I did." She said, "Did you see Jesus take a deep breath?" I said, "Yes!"

The local home school families gathered regularly for a potluck meal, pray the Rosary, and then one of the brothers would give a talk. I gave a talk for multiple Catholic families at one of their homes. After the talk and meal, I returned to the friary

Chapel, to pray night prayers before retiring, but no one was in the Chapel. Usually, at that time, brothers were saying their prayers, but no one was around. As I left the Chapel, I ran into a brother in the hallway, and said, "Where is everybody?" He said, "Don't you know what happened at the pilgrim center where Mother gives her talks?" I said, "What are they doing there?" He said, "Mother Annunciata was healed, and can walk without her crutches." I said, "Yeah. Right." I didn't believe what he said, and went to my cell, thinking he made up the story.

The next day, after Morning Prayer (Lauds), when I came down to the Chapel for Holy Mass, it was filled and overflowing and many were talking about the healing. During Mass, all wanted to see Mother walk without the crutches to receive Holy Communion. When it was time for her to come forward to receive Her Spouse in the Eucharist, she stood up and walked unaided without any difficulty. There was a collective gasp by the crowd. The crutches were lying on the steps in front of the Tabernacle on the cloistered side. Interestingly, it took a year for me to believe it was a real miracle. During that year I had many doubts and tried to rationalize she never really needed the crutches, and now wanted attention. It was a sad way of thinking due to doubts.

However, I met a young girl who came out of the Chapel with her mother. Her name was Dani Beardson. A year previously I met her for the first time. The young girl was from Canterbury, Louisiana. Fr. Giuseppe Barker and I paid a visit to her at the hospital after she had an esophageal surgery because she was born without an esophagus. During the hospital visit, Fr. Giuseppe held out a Franciscan Crucifix for her to look at. In the location where the blood came from the side of Jesus on the San Damiano Crucifix, she kissed it, saying, "I want to make Jesus feel better." Now, a year later, when I came upon her and her mother exiting the chapel, she looked fine. Her mother said, "Dani, tell Br. Antonio what happened." With eyes downcast, she didn't say anything. Her mother asked her again, and finally, she said, "Jesus healed me." Her mother explained the day after Mother Annunciata was healed, Dani received a healing when a visionary prayed over her, and Dani was completely fine. The visionary who prayed with Mother Annunciata also prayed with Dani, and both were healed.

From that moment, I began to wonder if Mother really did receive healing. The little girl's miracle increased my faith to begin to believe maybe it was true, Mother really was healed. Soon after seeing Dani healed, I was walking down the corridor of the House of Studies where the brothers took seminary classes, when I saw the backside of a sister who was somewhat heavy and briskly walking. Since she was walking fast as though youthful, I presumed she was a young sister. As I was walking behind the sister, I was unable to see her face and wondered who she was. I quickly caught up, tapped her on the shoulder, and said, "Hey sister, who are you?" The sister turned around and looked at me. I was shocked to discover it was Mother Annunciata. It was at that moment the doubting Thomas within was healed, and I finally believed the miracle. This event caused me to ponder how, during the time of Jesus, what it was like, for some to see people they knew healed by Jesus. Maybe I experienced some of the doubts they had, until finally the day came, when all believed wholeheartedly.

When I was a postulant, on the feast of St. Clare, August 4th, while attending Mass, suddenly there was a great thunderstorm, flashes of lightening and loud thunder. There was a great crash, the lights went out, and the Chapel became dark due to the dark clouds obscuring the morning sun. The priest had just finished the homily and intercessions and was now standing at the Altar. The candles on the altar barely provided enough light for him to continue to offer the Mass. However, during the Holy, Holy, Holy (Sanctus), one light in the Chapel came on and was directed toward the Altar, making it easier for the priest to see the words from the Roman Missal. The light shinned on the Altar during the Eucharistic Prayer. We were amazed, but not as amazed as later when we discovered lightening hit the building and caused serious damage to the wires on top of it. The electrician told Mother there is no way the little light bulb could have worked during Mass. The wire to it was completely severed by the strike. But it worked, and we were all witnesses to it. The little light lit up the Altar on the feast of St. Clare, whose name means "light".

Without her knowing about it, Br. Pedro Mary of the Lamb of God, decided to purchase a lamb for Mother Annunciata. Br. Pedro heard Mother mentioned to the sisters that the original group of nuns who came to found the monastery used to have lambs, and now Mother and the sisters missed having them.

As Mother Annunciata gave her "Wednesday Audience" to the brothers, Br. Pedro was absent, and no one knew why he wasn't there. About halfway through the talk, there was a knock at the door, and when it was opened, Br. Pedro was holding a little lamb. He said, "Mother, this little lamb is a gift to you." She didn't know what to say, but accepted it. When he put the lamb on the floor, it walked directly to Mother and bowed down to her, bending its two front legs. All of us were astonished and Mother blushed. Some thought the lamb mistook Mother Annunciata for its mother, and wanted to be nursed. Others wondered if God directed the lamb to show reverence to Mother, just as the mule bowed before the Eucharistic presence of Jesus, as St. Anthony of Padua held the Sacred Host.

Once, as I was taking flowers from the sister's Chapel to the brother's friary, I happen to meet Mother on the pavement in front the monastery outside the cloister, which was very rare. The brothers received week old flowers that came from the sister's monastery. We used them for the Altar of our Chapel. I quickly walked up to her, and said, "Mother, I would like to give you a flower. Please take one." Without any hesitation, she grabbed the most wilted flower and sniffed it, and then walked away without saying anything. I was miffed, and didn't know what to think. But later, I came to believe she wanted to teach me to not desire worldly things.

When I made my Perpetual Profession, Mother came out of the cloister to meet our families and congratulate us. She walked up behind me, and I suddenly felt her hand go through my hair as she messed it up. At that time, I allowed one side of my head of hair to grow longer, than the other, to cover the bald spot on my head. She chuckled as she walked away. Unfortunately, I became a little angry, but quickly realized she was teasing me, rather than trying to embarrass me. It was a cute and playful moment I had not experienced from her. About a year later, she spoke at an event about the vanity of men and how they try to cover their bald spots. It was then I finally figured out she was giving me a lesson on vanity. From then on, I cut my hair short without having excess to cover the bald spot.

#35 UNUSUAL EVENTS IN RELIGIOUS LIFE GOOD & BAD

The Special Christmas with the Franciscans of the Perpetual Victim Martyrs (1997)
One Christmas Eve, I was assigned to take care of Br. Martin, a brother who had cancer making it impossible for him to walk. While using his electric wheelchair, he always carried with him a urinal, as he never knew when he would suddenly need it. At times, he would pull out the urinal, cover it with his habit, and use it in the oddest places. During Mass, he stayed in the sacristy located near the front of the chapel, which gave him a good view of the altar and priest. An assigned brother stayed in the Chapel near the sacristy, so if in a moment's notice he was needed, he would get up during Mass to help him.

The Christmas Midnight Mass was beautiful with Mother Annunciata singing her Christ Child solo and the sisters voices sounded like angels. Sr. Isabel played the violin, as Sister Gabriel hit the highest notes. I was moved to tears hearing the Latin hymns, the sisters singing, the incense, and the reverence. Just as I was deeply entering into the mystery of the Mass, suddenly came the bellowing no brother wanted to hear during Mass, "Brother! Brother!" Br. Martin was calling for the brother who was assigned to care for his needs. It was me. I quickly came to see what he wanted. He had dropped his urinal on the floor, and urine was everywhere. I was dismayed, but as I cleaned up the mess, I heard everyone singing the Pater Noster (Our Father) in Latin, and I joined in on bended knees, cleaning up the urine singing, "Pater Noster, qui es in Caelis". The sad event took on a spiritual meaning which filled me with joy. It was as though I was cleaning up the wet pants of baby Jesus on Christmas, the day of His birth. My heart was filled with joy. My Holy Communion was special, since the Lord humbled me before I received Him. It reminded me of another Christmas many years ago, where I had to pump pig manure with a honey wagon (manure spreader) from the underground pit below the barn, so the pigs too could have a good Christmas.

I can't count the number of times I received consolation from the beautiful Masses, serving Holy Hours at Our Lady of Seraphim Monastery and listening to the sister's voices at Mass. To hear Sister Gabriel sing, and Sister Isabel play the violin, many times moved me to tears. My time in Louisiana, with the brothers and sisters, made me feel like I was in heaven. I tremendously grew in my faith because of Mother, the sisters, brothers, and the faithful who came on pilgrimage.

Blow Up at High School

Before I entered seminary, while I was still a brother, I was invited to give a talk with Sr. Mary Clarity, Sr. Mary Purity, and Br. Lionel Mary at a high school in New Orleans. I gave my talk, which I thought went well, and then Sr. Mary Clarity began to talk to the youth gathered in the gym, about the love of God. As she was giving her inspirational talk, I saw a teenage boy picking on a girl, and his annoyances caused her to become greatly upset. Suddenly, and catching even myself off guard, I yelled, "Stop picking on her! If you don't stop what you are doing, the next thing you know, you will end up doing worse things that offend God, and if you're not careful, you can end up in hell!" I shocked the entire group of about a hundred children, teachers, and the principal. Sr. Mary Clarity completely got thrown off her topic. I couldn't believe what came out of my mouth, and there was a sudden eerie silence. The boy was terrified, but the girl was relieved. Yet, she too was shocked at my words. I immediately apologized to everyone. I didn't understand why I did it. Why did I overreact so terribly, I wondered?

After Sr. Mary Clarity finished her talk, I told the principal how I was deeply sorry and asked if I could personally apologize to the boy. He took me to the boy's classroom, and I apologized. The poor kid cowered when I walked up to him. I felt so bad. The principal was very kind, and said, "Those things happen. Don't worry about it." When I returned to the monastery, the superiors had already heard about it. Within a few days, they held a council to discuss the incident, and decided I needed to see a psychologist. They knew a psychologist in Pittsburgh, Massachusetts, I could see when I begin to attend seminary. Consequently, when I entered seminary for the first time, at St. Robert Bellarmine Seminary, I had regular meetings with the psychologist. He helped me to understand the reason for my outburst, had to do with not dealing with emotions, caused by my father's alcoholism. The counseling resulted in me attending Al-anon meetings while at seminary.

#36 ATTENDING TO ST. ROBERT BELLARMINE SEMINARY

St. Robert Bellarmine Seminary

"Exiit Qui seminat (the sower went forth to sow) is indicative of the young priest who leaves the seminary for his missionary labor."

The Franciscans of Perpetual Victim Martyrs sent their brothers to St. Robert Seminary in Pittsburgh, Massachusetts, because it's orthodox (faithful to the Catholic Church) while many other seminaries across the country at that time were not.

At the seminary, the philosophy and Latin professors were terrific, but some Scripture professors were not. I needed to re-take English classes that I had at Fort Hickok, including a writing class. Fr. Winston Pastrami was the English teacher for the seminary. His teachings during class and his homilies were without spirituality, and his personality was odd. By taking his English classes, I learned how to prepare papers, but I didn't like him as a teacher. There was something strange about him. A few years later, after I was no longer attending St. Robert, it became known he left the priesthood. And about ten years later, I discovered he sexually abused young boys, and he was doing it at the same time I was in seminary! I knew he was strange, but never would have thought he was doing such a horrid thing. Oh, how upset I was when I learned this. I was outraged that a priest I actually had contact with could do such things to children.

In addition to this, two other St. Robert Seminary priests left the priesthood. Fr. Henry Crackle, my Formation Advisor and Fr. Ted Bourgeois, the Spiritual Director of the seminary, both, later left the priesthood. Both married women with whom they had a relationship, that we later discovered was occurring while ministering at the seminary. While these were scandals, their scandal was nothing in comparison to Fr. Pastrami's.

Not knowing what these men were doing, while I was in seminary at St. Robert, I felt an evil presence in that seminary. The rector, Msgr. Paul Maroony, gave the most bizarre homily. The homily not given at the time of Halloween was creepy. In it, he spoke about a child committing suicide, hanging from a rope and never once mentioned anything about Jesus or anything that had to do with God.

Some of our formation advisors were truly nuts. Fr. Zed Mariachi used to climb a tree to spy on seminarians. During Formation Class, we usually sat in chairs in a circle, Fr. Mariachi had us pass around a stuffed rabbit. He handed it to the seminarian on the end, and told him to pass it to the next seminarian, until it went around to each man. As each seminarian received it, Fr. Zed wrote down in his notebook how each seminarian handled the rabbit. I quickly passed it to the next seminarian. One seminarian decided to push the priest's "buttons" and acted like he was choking the rabbit, causing him to feverishly write in his notebook. The Formation Room was half filled with sand, in sort of, a large sandbox. We were told the sand helped us relax. How bizarre!

A seminarian from Alamo, Texas was kneeling on a prie-dieu before the Tabernacle, when Fr. Mariachi came up to him, and said, "What are you doing?" The seminarian said, "I'm praying to Jesus making a Holy Hour." The priest said, "You don't need to pray before THAT, you can pray in your room or anywhere. Don't you know God is everywhere?"

My Introduction to Sacred Scripture class was taught by a priest, Fr. Thomas Scriptura, who used to say odd things about scripture, and even heretical things. The class was supposed to read Raymond Brown's *101 Questions About Jesus.* In the book, he said something like, "If the body of Jesus were found today, would we still believe in the Resurrection?" And the author's response was, "It would make no difference if the body of Jesus was found today, since the Resurrection was a spiritual event."

To protect the class from demons, as a consequence of bad theology being taught in the room, I decided to go to the classroom early to sprinkle Holy Water in Fr. Scriptura's classroom, without anyone knowing about it. I later confided to one of the brothers, what I did. But he couldn't keep a secret and mentioned it to our religious community superiors. Except, he told them I sprinkled the teacher with Holy Water, which wasn't true. The room was empty, when I sprinkled Holy Water. When it came time to renew my vows on March 25th, a year after I originally made my First Vows, they had no plans for me to renew them.

However, due to their false understanding of what happened and despite the fact, I didn't renew my vows, they decided I would make my Perpetual Profession on Aug. 14th, the feast of St. Maximilian Kolbe, but I would not be returning to seminary, after completing the second semester of that year.

While in seminary at St. Robert, I never noticed any man suspected of being gay, nor did I see any inappropriate relationships. At the time, I had no idea what was going on in the Church. However, I had heard the seminary in Bartlesville, New Jersey was called the "Pink Palace", due to the many homosexuals who attended it, and they literally painted many of the buildings pink.

At St. Robert, we were forbidden to genuflect on both knees during Eucharistic Adoration. Otherwise, it was a formation issue. It was also a formation issue to pray the Rosary silently during Adoration, which motivated some seminarians to secretly pray it, as they held the beads in their pocket. The real formation issues, were the nutty formation advisors.

While attending St. Robert Bellarmine Seminary, my apostolate was to minister in a nursing home. The experience was wonderful and blessed. The seminarian, who went with me, on the apostolate, was kind, compassionate, and orthodox. However, after he was ordained, within just a few years, he left the priesthood. I never understood why. I thought perhaps he couldn't deal with all the liberal antics of his bishop, and other liberal priests in his diocese.

St. Robert Spiritual Directors

I had two spiritual directors in two years at St. Robert Bellarmine Seminary. My first spiritual director was Fr. Thaddeus Magoo, a Marian and Thomas Aquinas theologian, who was a friend of Mother Annunciata, and encourager of seminarians. He was very helpful to me and many seminarians. He never minced words. If he was unhappy with the seminary, or a seminary teacher, or anyone who he felt did someone wrong, he plainly said so. As a religious brother, we never had a spiritual director before entering seminary, consequently, Fr. Magoo was my first spiritual director after I entered religious life. There were a few times, he became visibly angry with formation advisors at St. Robert's, and also at one of my superiors. His Mr. Magoo rounded thick glasses, his spunk, and passion to help seminarians, made him admired, and it encouraged us to see a priest with a personality. He deeply loved the Blessed Virgin Mary. On one occasion I told him, when I pray, in my mind couldn't see the face of Jesus. He began to think I had psychological problems. Since he was seeing other brothers, I wondered if one of them, told him I sprinkled Holy Water on a priest. And he believed him, rather than I. I began to feel uncomfortable in sharing personal things about my spiritual life, and that motivated me to find a different spiritual director. I think Jesus was hiding His face, to help me search for His face, ever more.

Fr. Gaspard Romero became my next spiritual director. He was a deeply spiritual man, who had a tremendous love of Our Lady and Our Lord in the Blessed Sacrament. He was a genuinely happy priest and terrific mentor. His example as a religious, gave me inspiration to imitate his vows of poverty, chastity, and obedience. He was a tenderhearted orthodox priest, who enjoyed being religious.

During my time with Fr. Magoo and Fr. Romero, I took Al-anon classes. I was asked by my superior to remove my habit and wear secular clothes before attending the meetings, to not be an embarrassment to the community. The meetings allowed me to work though some difficulties I had with my father's alcoholism. Due to my father's alcoholism, he picked on my mother. When I witnessed the boy pick on the girl at the school, it was as though I needed to stand up, and correct the injustice, that I failed to correct with my parents. However, I over-reacted by yelling at the boy, rather than reasonably discussing with him, the error of his ways. I thank God, I was awarded the opportunity to work through this difficulty and became stronger by overcoming it. Truly an untold mercy!

St. Robert Seminary Appeal

At St. Robert Seminary, every year all seminarians gave a seminary Appeal Talk in assigned parishes on a particular weekend. We were to give a talk at the end of every Mass throughout the archdiocese of Pittsburgh. I was assigned to speak in the parish of St. Stanislaus. Since I was a religious, I was an anomaly to the diocesan priest pastors. Some of the information we were to say was scripted by the seminary, but we could add our thoughts. Before the Masses that weekend, and due to my quiet nature, I overheard the pastor say to his associate priest, speaking of me, said, "I think he's retarded." I guess he expected me to be more outgoing like himself. At the end of the weekend, I was shocked to discover the pastor put the entire money collected by the appeal in a bath tub. He said, "Well, I suspect we won't get much. Each parish has to give all that is collected. I disagree with that, I think the parish should keep some of it." He was so overly focused on money, every time I saw him, he mentioned something about it. However, something happened to change his mind. When the weekend was over, he was thrilled, and kept saying, "We never got so much money for the Appeal before. You did an outstanding job!" I wrote him a thank-you letter for allowing me to speak at his Masses and said I learned money isn't everything.

St. Robert Bellarmine Seminary, Great Trials at Seminary
The Origin of Lactose Intolerance & Parents Almost Died

In 1994, I saw a doctor because I had great difficulty urinating. The doctor suspected I had a severe prostate infection, and therefore, he prescribed a new strong antibiotic to take every day for a month. Within a few days of taking the medicine, I began to have diarrhea, terrible abdominal pain, and much gas. I started to have blood in my stool, and days later, also came flesh in my stool with blood. The doctor asked me to take all sorts of medicines, including ox bile pills, to stop the diarrhea. The loose stool became so bad, within an hour of eating food, —it ended up in the toilet. It was painful from the time I ate until I passed it. I went from 160 to 130 pounds, losing 30 in a month. Several doctors couldn't figure out what was wrong. Over a period of time, I became lactose intolerant, and also couldn't eat spicy or acidic foods without severe pain.

Also, during this time, I received a call from my sister, who said my mother had a heart attack and consequently, I asked my superior Fr. Barker permission to return home to be with her, but I couldn't. A week later, I received another phone call saying my father was in the hospital, and almost died from a bleeding ulcer. I asked my superior again if I could go home, but was denied as well. I became angry, felt helpless and went to the Chapel at St. Robert at night, and praying aloud told the Lord how I felt, and begged Him to help my parents. Praying aloud gave me peace, and I later discovered both parents pulled through their dilemma.

All of this took place at the same time of my newly developed bowel problems and the urination problem. The urination issue cleared up in a month, but the lactose intolerance and diarrhea worsened. For many years, I had diarrhea and rushed bowel movements, even including up to 2019 just before I received a physical healing of my colon from Jesus.

In 1998, when I met a Nurse Practitioner, volunteering at the Sisters of Good Deeds home for AIDS, where my apostolate was located while attending Mary's Meadow Seminary. She told me she had taken the same medicine for an infection which ruined her colon. She said she also had blood and flesh in her stool, and lactose intolerance developed. Finally, after seeing multiple doctors, none of whom helped, I discovered it was caused by the antibiotic used for infection of the prostate. The medicine was originally approved by the FDA, and then later removed from the market. I also discovered I never had an infection back in 1994, but rather, my prostate became swollen due to *Benadryl*, that I was taking for allergy medicine. This was discovered when I took *Benadryl* for allergies years later.

If this was not enough, in 1994, the trials increased when I was told I couldn't renew my religious vows, because I was accused of throwing Holy Water on a teacher, which I didn't do. Looking back, I could see all these events of my parent's medical issues, of not being able to be with them, my health problems, and the false accusation, as a means to draw me closer to the Lord. And they even gave me the grace to desire ever more fervently the gift of ordination to the priesthood that God was offering to me. It was truly by God's grace, I persevered. I can now look back on these trials with thanksgiving to the Lord for using them to draw me closer to Him, to learn to persevere through suffering, and to trust Him who loves me.

#37 ATTENDING MARY'S MEADOW SEMINARY

Mary's Meadow Seminary in Quakers, Virginia

Although there was the bump in the road with the brothers, I was able to continue seminary by attending Mary's Meadow Seminary in Quakers, Virginia, which was a fantastic seminary. The brothers switched to the Meadow since some teachers at St. Robert Seminary were openly anti-Mother Annunciata, and even made it known to other seminarians in class. Next to the seminary was the college called Mary's Meadow College and University. Between the seminary and the college is a soccer field used by young lady college students to sun bathe in their swimming suits when the weather is favorable. This activity was often a topic of discussion among the seminarians. Some secretly enjoyed seeing the young ladies, while most seminarians saw it as a temptation. The rector wouldn't dare bring it up to the college administration, nor would any priest say a word about the problem, except in jest. Their failure to address the issue of immodesty was a silent lesson for seminarians on what to do as priests. Ignore it.

Formation was very different at Mary's Meadow compared to St. Robert Bellarmine! There were no goofy scripture teachers, no screwball advisors, and no sand boxes in the formation room! Rather, we had a daily Holy Hour and Rosary. Both of which were optional, but almost all seminarians attended. I spiritually flourished.

Everyone who attends "The Meadow" learned the "Meadow Hospitality". All seminarians and teachers greeted the new men with joyful enthusiasm and were extremely helpful to them. However, college classes were not as good, as I had a teacher who was a former priest. He taught philosophy. Some college teachers taught ideologies contrary to the faith. The Grotto behind the Meadow was one of my favorite get-a-way places. I went to the Grotto almost every day to pray before the statue of Our Lady of Lourdes. Over the many years since the seminary began, miracles are reported from the water at the Grotto, including the healing of a boy with AIDS, while I was at "The Meadow".

The Meadow formed young men to be manly, and many of the seminary teachers and priests truly cared about forming good priests. All of us knew the Meadow was protected, because it was Mary's Meadow, and She watched over her priest sons to be.

At this seminary, there were several men I thought were gay but neither went on to be a priest. The seminary caught a seminarian viewing child pornography and was immediately dismissed. Considering what was occurring in other seminaries at the time, though most of us had no idea, this seminary was a blessing. I learned much about my faith at the holy seminary.

Every year, on the Solemnity of St. Joseph, the seminarians and staff went to the Sisters of Love Convent, that was located at the Shrine of St. Philomena, for dinner and talent show. During the talent show, I decided to borrow a guitar from another seminarian for a spiritual meditation. Rather than using strings, I used the back wooden part of the guitar to make the sound of a heartbeat. I asked the crowd to close their eyes, and I slowly repeated the Seven Last Words of Jesus on the Cross. Gradually I made the heart beat sound beat slower, until the last words of Jesus spoken, "Father, into your hands, I commend my spirit." When the heart beat stopped, I walked away. Many had tears in their eyes and I believed it was a good meditation, especially since it came from the heart. One of the teachers, a religious sister, Sister Marie Grumpy, said she was moved by it and enjoyed it. However, about a week later after visiting with other faculty, she changed her mind and told me it was a formation issue since it was supposed to be a talent show with funny skits. A spiritual meditation at an event meant to be funny was an issue. The rector said it was a "morbid" skit.

The Meadow is a seminary named after the Virgin Mary, and yet there wasn't a crowning of the Virgin Mary in May. I took it upon myself to ask the Dean of Students, Fr. Robert Grandiose permission to organize the coronation of the Virgin Mary during the first week of May. I asked one of the secretaries at the Meadow to create a crown made of flowers. She made copies of prayers and hymns for the event. Since I was not yet a deacon, I asked a deacon to perform the ceremony. We advertised it on bulletin boards at the seminary, and to my surprise, many seminarians came for the crowning of Mary. The deacon performed the rite from the *Order of Crowning an Image of the Blessed Virgin Mary,* and we all sang several hymns and prayed the Litany of Loreto. The following year, after I was ordained a deacon, I had the privilege of performing the ceremony myself. The seminarian organization, the Legion of Mary, asked if their organization could organize the ceremony every year. Since then, the Meadow has had a crowning of the Virgin Mary. I thank the Lord, He used me to begin the yearly activity honoring His Holy Mother.

At the Meadow, there was a plaque dedicated to Fr. Stanley Rother. While at seminary, I never came to know anything about him. Years later, while serving in the Diocese of Tantrum, Idaho, he was beatified in 2017. I was privileged to travel and attend the beatification Mass in Oklahoma City. When I heard about his story, I regretted in failing to learn about a fellow Meadow priest, who became a martyr and I secretly wished I too could be martyred like him someday.

Brother John Mary of the Holy Archangel Chokes

As a Franciscan of the Perpetual Victim Martyr, the brothers and I who were attending Mary's Meadow Seminary, decided to eat out on a Sunday at Meadow Gate Family Restaurant in Thermos, Virginia, not far south of Quakers. We decided to eat breakfast at the restaurant. Sitting across the table from me, was Br. John Mary of the Holy Archangel. He was a large and tall man, probably weighing close to four-hundred pounds. During the meal, I noticed he stopped talking and was quiet, and I looked at him. His face was red, and he even began to turn a purple green color. He was motioning to me. I said, "Are you choking?" He nodded. I said, "Do you want me to give you the Heimlich maneuver?" He nodded again. I walked around the table and stood behind him and realized he was about to pass out. He was unable to say a single word. He stood up, and I reached around his large stomach.

I was barely able to grasp both of my hands around his stomach, and then I gave a quick one time thrust to his stomach, and suddenly from his mouth, popped out, a full-size sausage link landing directly in his plate. He sat down and resumed eating as though nothing happened. I think he was very embarrassed by it all. Later, I reflected upon what had happened and realized I most likely, by God's grace and providence, saved his life. God in His mercy, used me to save a life.

Rolling Hills Massacre – A New Friend Murdered

Every year, the seminary had a big celebration in honor of Mary's Immaculate Conception, usually on Dec. 8th or the night before. The Chapel on campus named Immaculate Conception is incredibly beautiful. I was so happy and blessed to be ordained a deacon by Bishop Basil Braveheart in this blessed Chapel, Nov. 6th, 2003.

In the year 2000, the vocation director for the Diocese of Rolling Hills brought some men, who were potential seminarians for a "look and see" to discern, if they had a vocation to the priesthood. One man from Rolling Hills, who felt a call to the priesthood, was Baron Von Flanders. The evening of the celebration, I happened to sit across from Baron at the formal dinner. We had a wonderful visit. It was quite the strange event for me. As we talked, it seemed as though we had known each other for years. Perhaps it was due to his charisma or personality, but we became new friends. I never made a friend before in such a short time. He was determined to come to the Meadow in January with the beginning of the new semester. I was anticipating, with hope, to his coming to seminary, getting to know him better and to share spiritual things with each other.

But, a week later, on Dec. 15th, the city of Rolling Hills, and especially the Catholic world, was horrified to hear of the murder of Baron and three others. It was on national news and called the "Rolling Hills Massacre". I had also met Millie Nordstram, the secretary of the college Campus Center, who was killed with him. They died a horrific death by the Jalopy brothers, who stole their money, and forced them to use an ATM to withdraw funds. The four, college age young people, were shot, and ran over by the Jalopy brothers' vehicle in a soccer field.

I had terrible feelings of anger and revenge in my heart. The devil tempted me to become racist, to view all blacks as bad. No matter how hard I tried, I could not forgive. I wept bitterly because I could not forgive. I felt helpless and did not know what to do. How could I forgive these men who killed four innocent people for drug money? It took a month before I was able to forgive.

I begged the Lord for help and finally realized, I couldn't forgive on my own, I needed to ask Jesus for the grace to forgive, and at the very moment I prayed that prayer, I saw in my mind an image of Jesus hanging from the Cross, and heard in my heart His words, "Forgive them, for they know not what they do." It was then I realized, the killers were high on drugs and drunk. They had been abused by their parents. What they did was monstrous, but I forgave them because if they had known these wonderful people, they murdered, and, if they were in their right mind, they never would have killed them. My heart was open to see not only the misery of those who died, but the misery of the killers. My wounded heart became a fountain of mercy, which flowed from the wounded Heart of Jesus on the Cross.

Jesus in the Tabernacle (Holy Hour) at Mary's Meadow Seminary
I received a letter from Sally Manning in Mitchell, a small town south of Rolling Hills, Ohio. When I first joined the diocese of Rolling Hills, as a seminarian, I was assigned to St. Michael's parish in Mitchell for two summers. While at seminary, a letter arrived from Sally, who asked me to pray for her, so she would have a quick and pain-free delivery for her fourth child. She was due in a few weeks.

Consequently, I made a Holy Hour before Jesus in the Tabernacle, and offered the graces of the Holy Hour for her and the baby, so she would have a quick delivery with little pain. I sent a letter to Sally indicating the exact day and hour I made the Holy Hour for her and the baby. A few weeks later, she wrote a letter back, and said, "I cannot believe it. I gave birth to my son, Peter, during the exact time you prayed the Holy Hour. The delivery went so quick, we barely made it to the hospital, and I had hardly any pain with it either. In less than an hour, from the time labor began, Peter was born."

Heart Attack? Healed by Anointing of the Sick?
One Our Father, Hail Mary and Glory Be for the Grace of a Happy Death
At seminary, while doing exercises, I suffered a possible heart attack. My skin became cold and clammy, and pain shot down from my chest to my back and forearm. I

collapsed on the floor and could not regain my strength for about 5 minutes. When I regained strength, I went to the Student Health Center on campus, and an appointment was made to see a doctor.

Every time I exercised, I had the same symptoms: clammy skin, sweating, weakness, and sometimes pain in my chest. I discontinued exercises for fear the symptoms would return.

At that time, I had very inexpensive health insurance, that would cover only $1000 in medical bills. The doctor preformed an echocardiogram and said there was a shadow over the bottom portion of my heart, where a heart attack occurred, and part of the heart died. The doctor wanted to do a heart-catheter surgery, but I didn't have the money for it. It cost $10,000. My vocation director suggested I obtain a second opinion.

My spiritual director gave me anointing of the sick. I made an appointment with a different doctor, who performed another echocardiogram. He said there was no shadow on my heart. Since the shadow was no longer there, he surmised my rib caused the shadow on my heart from the previous echocardiogram. But once I received the Anointing of the Sick, I never again had the same symptoms. Did Jesus heal me through the Sacrament of the Sick? I think so, but only God knows.

From that day on, even until today, I pray one Our Father, Hail Mary and Glory be, for the grace of a happy death. Back then, I had heard about the practice and decided to do it daily. After all, there is nothing more important than having a good Judgment, and receiving the grace of a happy death.

#38 LIED TO THE BISHOP

The Only Time I Ever Lied to A Bishop
"You shall not bear false witness against your neighbor" (Exodus 20:16)

Bishop Basil Braveheart made yearly trips to the seminary and met with each seminarian privately, especially on his way to the Bishop's Conference in Bartlesville, New Jersey. About a year after studying for the Diocese of Rolling Hills, Ohio, he came to visit seminarians from our diocese.

During my meeting with him, he asked, "Do you still think about being a religious?" I wasn't ready for his question and I still had longings for religious life, but said, "No." and immediately realized I lied to the bishop and felt horrible. I believed it was very wrong to lie to the bishop.

After I left the meeting, I immediately went to the Chapel to pray, and felt I needed to tell him I lied. When I returned to the room where he was meeting seminarians, he was gone. I decided I had to tell him I lied. It was the right thing to do. I was able to obtain his cell number, and called him while he was driving. He admonished me and reminded me, saying he is the spiritual father of all his seminarians and priests. Saying, I should not be afraid to tell the truth, but to trust him.

#39 SPIRITUAL PRACTICES DEVELOPED AT MARY'S MEADOW SEMINARY

Stations of the Cross

While at Mary's Meadow Seminary, I read an article stating Fr. Emil Kapaun, a military chaplain during the Korean War, may become a Saint someday. It stated he prayed the Stations of the Cross every day. From that time on, I try to pray a short version of the Stations of the Cross every day. I pray just one Hail Mary at each station and pray, "We adore thee O Christ, and we bless thee, for by thy Holy Cross, thou hast redeemed the world." And then after the Hail Mary, I pray, "Lord Jesus Crucified, have mercy on us!"

A Desire to be a Martyr, Began to Pray One Our Father, Hail Mary and Glory be

"Precious in the Eyes of the Lord is the death of his faithful." (Psalm 116)

After my heart incident, I developed the desire to be martyred, and for many years after that, I began to pray one Our Father, Hail Mary, and Glory be, to be martyred. I realize it's a total gift from God and unmerited. But I want to die for Jesus, who died for love of me and to save my miserable soul by His mercy. After I was ordained a priest, I confided to a priest friend that I pray prayers to be a martyr every day, and he told me I was prideful for doing so. Because of his comment, I changed my prayer that when I die I would go straight to heaven. I secretly hope to be martyred, but I trust in God's mercy He can and will, if He so desires it, to take me straight to heaven, even if I'm not martyred. Later, my spiritual director said he didn't believe it was prideful to pray to be martyred.

In Honor of 28,430 drops of Blood Shed by Our Lord for Grace
To Go Straight to Heaven

Jesus said to St. Gertrude, "I will concede to all those faithful, who shall recite for three years, each day two Paters (Our fathers), Glorias (Glory Bes) and Aves (Hail Marys), in honor of the drops of blood I lost, I will concede the following 5 graces: 1. The plenary indulgence and remittance of your sins. 2. You will be free from the pains of Purgatory. 3. If you should die before completing the said three years, for you, it will be the same as if you had completed them. 4. It will be upon your death, the same as if you had shed all your blood for the Holy Faith. 5. I will descend from Heaven to take your soul and that of your relatives, until the fourth generation." I began to daily this prayer in Nov. of 2016.

Mary's Purity and for the Gift of Purity -3 Hail Marys Everyday

In a book written by St. Alphonsus, *The Glories of Mary*, I read, that if a person prays three Hail Marys every day, in honor of Mary's purity and for the gift of purity, one will always receive that gift. I have prayed these prayers ever since seminary at Mary's Meadow. Later, after I was ordained a priest, I often suggested to penitents who struggle with purity to take up the practice. The Virgin Most Pure will intercede for those who desire to be pure. Oh, how pure a priest should be when he offers the Holy Sacrifice of the Mass! I can joyfully say, I have grown more and more pure over the years and rarely have lustful thoughts. Thank you! Blessed Lady!

Pray One Our Father, Hail Mary and Glory Be & Father Kapaun (to not commit a mortal sin)

I read that Fr. Kapaun daily prayed one Our Father, Hail Mary, and Glory be, everyday asking God to help him, so he would never commit a mortal sin. When I heard how he prayed these prayers, I took up that practice, and pray it every night before going to bed, while kneeling before an image of the Blessed Virgin Mary.

#40 GOD'S PROVIDENCE WHILE ATTENDING SEMINARY

My Car During Seminary & God's Providence

I owned an old 1987 Buick while in seminary. It was purchased for $500, but ran well. With nearly 200,000 miles on the car, I drove it back and forth from Quakers, Virginia to Rolling Hills, Ohio because I could not afford airplane tickets like the other seminarians.

One day, the starter of the car went out and I took it to the local auto repair shop. I had only $30. The mechanic said it would cost $50, including labor, but he decided not to charge for the labor, and installed a used starter. When I left the shop, I had no money at all. However, when I returned to the seminary from the auto repair shop, I checked my mail, found a check for $30 from the Knights of Cortez, who faithfully sent $30 every month while I was in seminary.

When returning from seminary, after 16 continuous hours of driving, as I was parking at St. Tarcisius parish, in Rolling Hills, the entire head liner inside the car fell down. Had I been driving on the highway, it could have been disastrous. But, thanks to the Lord's protection, I had just stopped and turned off the car when it fell down.

Eventually, the air conditioner went out in the car, making a very miserable 16-hour drive from Quakers to Rolling Hills.

Another providential event happened after I finished my last seminary year, and had just arrived at Happy Soul Retreat House, after driving sixteen hours, the engine quit working. I didn't realize it, but the engine was blown, and it just so happened, by God's providence, the engine died just as I pulled into the parking lot. The car was eventually towed to the salvage yard, and I was paid $100 for it. After driving all those miles for four years and since I paid only $500, I was happy it lasted that long. I used to say, "I drive cars until they quit". I thank the Lord for His divine providence in preventing the car from breaking down in a location far from the seminary or the diocese.

My Trench Coat Got Run Over by an Airplane

My step-father, Donald Hunstman, gave me a brand-new trench coat. I really liked it. When I arrived at Quaker airport in Virginia to fly back to Ohio for Christmas break, the ticket agent said I couldn't bring the trench coat on board the plane. This was due to having another carry on (a small Duffel bag). Consequently, she gave me a cardboard box to place the coat, to be placed with the baggage under the plane.

As I sat in the terminal watching planes come and go and baggage vehicles driving to and from planes, I noticed a box fall from a baggage vehicle and a few minutes later a plane unknowingly ran over the box. I felt bad for the person who owned the box and was certain the item in the box would be crushed beyond recognition.

When the plane landed in Rolling Hills, I went to retrieve my baggage and the box with the trench coat at the baggage claim carousel. I was shocked to discover the box containing the coat was totally flat and had tread marks on it. To my surprise, the box I saw fall from the baggage truck and ran over by the plane was mine! I was sure it was ruined, but when I opened the box, there was nothing wrong with it.

A few months later, after returning to seminary, while wearing the trench coat, a seminarian saw it and said he wanted to buy it. Since I had almost no money, I sold it to him for $100. I didn't have the heart to tell him it was run over by an airplane.

#41 SPIRITUAL DIRECTORS AT MARY'S MEADOW SEMINARY

Spiritual Directors at Mary's Meadow Seminary

At Mary's Meadow Seminary I had two spiritual directors. Fr. Andrew Goodsheperd was my first spiritual director. He greatly helped confirm my vocation to the priesthood. He was a very wise priest, who helped me to discern leaving the Franciscans. I told him, "You are wise beyond your years!" He had a little smile on his face when I said that. Later, he became the bishop of the Diocese of Helena, Ohio and was later promoted to the Archdiocese of Millsburger, Idaho. I received the grace to completely open up to him, with regard to everything going on in my soul, which gave me tremendous peace. On one occasion, I mentioned something to him in confession. But outside of confession, he accidentally mentioned what I told him in confession. The contents didn't have anything to do with sin. But it caused a great disturbance in my soul. I felt the need to obtain a different spiritual director and decided to ask Fr. Matthew Mann.

Fr. Mann was very encouraging and had a constant joy about him, that always raised my spirits. He too was very wise. It was through his help I began to notice small ways the Lord was working in my life. When I mentioned some words about my soul or experience, he would suddenly stop me and say, "There you go again! You said the Lord did this or the Lord did that." I had a hard time understanding what he meant, until I realized later not everyone experienced their life with Jesus as I did.

Despite these experiences, while in seminary there was a deep darkness I never shared with my spiritual directors. I felt God abandoned me when I left the Franciscans of Perpetual Victim Martyrs. It sounds contradictory, to recognize Jesus in daily experiences. But to feel His presence and to try to understand if you are doing His will is another, which I greatly lacked. Both spiritual directors played important roles in helping me to become a priest.

#42 APOSTOLATES AT MARY'S MEADOW SEMINARY AND STEWARDSHIP

Apostolates at Mary's Meadow Seminary

One of my apostolates at Mary's Meadow was "Gift of Joy", a home for AIDS patients ran by the Sisters of Good Deeds. I ministered to AIDS patients and enjoyed being around the sisters. It was very inspiring to see how they live out their vocation of poverty, chastity, and obedience. They took a fourth vow to take care of the poor.

While at Mary's Meadow, I taught 8th grade CCD at St. John's in Eastwindsor, Virginia. A parent of one of the students complained, as a result of me telling the children they should not play the Ouija board. Thanks be to God, the seminary formation priest backed me up and helped her to understand the dangers of the game.

One Wednesday, when we arrived to teach, the CCD Director told all CCD teachers and children to come to an assembly in the gym. The request was very unusual, and we had no idea what was going on. Police officers gave the assembled group a talk. The officers said five teens from their parish died from an overdose of heroin, several other teens were in ICU on life support, and one teen shot and killed his mother to obtain money from her to purchase heroin. He said that when the batch of heroin was made, it was excessively potent and warned the youth to throw away any heroin they might have, as it was deadly. They also reminded students it was against the law. The policeman told us heroin destroyed the lives of many.

While teaching at St. John's, there was 8th grade boy in my class who had ADD (Attention Deficit Disorder). He had such a severe case of it, he was removed from regular school, but continued to come to CCD. The kid was the nicest boy, but constantly caused disruption in class. I happen to run across a CD on ADD and learned that ADD children needed extra things to do in class, and at the same time, the teacher was to ask the child to pay attention to what is being said, since they could do both. The boy was an artist. I asked him to paint images during every class and also pay attention to the lesson of the day. He did outstandingly well, with both listening to the lesson and painting. However, he eventually figured out why I wanted him to do both, was to keep his attention and from disrupting the class.

Another apostolate while at the Meadow was at St. Teresa's parish in Jewellsburg, Virginia. Two seminarians and I were assigned to St. Teresa's and were to "shadow" the pastor. He was an outstanding Monsignor, and the best pastor I ever met. He allowed us to sit in on his marriage prep classes and other meetings he had with parents. We also went with him to anoint and visit the sick. The three of us learned much from him. He was truly a stalwart priest whom Jesus helped to become holy over the years. He was joyful, kind, compassionate, which helped me to be a good teacher and pastor.

I had another apostolate, a soup kitchen, while at the Meadow, which was also in the city Jewellsburg. I very much enjoyed working with the poor. There was another seminarian, a brother from my order, Br. Tarcisius Mary who came with me. The director was a black, no-nonsense lady, whom the homeless and poor deeply respected. They called her the Mother Teresa of Jewellsburg. She knew how to keep order at the soup kitchen and would not take any guff from patrons.

I asked her a simple question, and she took it wrong. Unbeknownst to me, she confused Br. Tarcisius and I. She thought he asked the question. She ended up making it a "formation issue" and Br. Tarcisius had no idea what she was talking about. Unfortunately, she was diagnosed with cancer and was dealing with the stress of it, and therefore, I believe she wasn't thinking clearly when this happened.

When Br. Tarcisius told me that she said things about him that weren't true, I finally realized I was to blame, but decided to keep my mouth shut, and didn't tell anyone. I should have spoken up in his defense and also clarified my question. I can't remember what I asked, but whatever it was --she misunderstood it, most likely due to her emotional state and concern for her health.

My last apostolate while at Mary's Meadow Seminary, was at St. Nathaniel's parish with Fr. Matthew Beetle. While assigned at his parish, I was ordained a deacon at the Meadow, and his parish would be the first parish I assisted as a deacon. I absolutely loved it. Fr. Beetle was the best priest faculty at the Meadow, and all the seminarians loved him. He was most helpful in cutting through the mustard of what the seminary wanted us to do, and making practical applications. Three unfortunate incidents happened while at his parish.

I decided to prepare a homily on Natural Family Planning verses Contraception. Just as Mass began, as we were processing down the aisle, he asked what I was going to preach about, and I whispered to him what I was going to say.

As we are walking down the center of the aisle to the altar, he berated me with soft words, saying, "What are you thinking, these are old people at this Mass, they don't need to hear what you have to say." The closer we came to the altar, the louder he berated me. I didn't know what to do, since it was all typed out. Consequently, I decided to make up a homily. When I gave the sermon, it was terrible. As we were processing out, he berated me again saying, "You should have given your prepared homily. You were an embarrassment to me. They knew you just made it up, as you went." I learned my lesson of knowing my audience and the pastor, also to not make up a homily at the last minute.

Also, at St. Nathaniel parish, in a homily during Lent, I unintentionally made a statement that offended Fr. Beetle, though I had no idea it offended him at first. I pointed out the sin of gluttony with other sins to try to help parishioners overcome them during Lent. But, since he was overweight, he took it personally, and it hurt his feelings.

After distributing Holy Communion at St. Nathaniel's, I missed a step in the sanctuary, fell face down on the ground, and landed on my stomach. When I hit the floor, I heard a collected gasp by the people, saying "Oh!", as I went down. Thanks be to God, I never dropped a Host nor did my fingers (which touched the Sacred Host) touch anything. I smiled as I picked myself up, and they chuckled.

Fr. Mann, my spiritual director, told me that Fr. Beetle saved my vocation. Some faculty members didn't want me to continue on to the priesthood, due to what some referred to as "pre-Vatican II homilies", but Fr. Mann explained that Fr. Beetle went "to bat" for me and changed their minds. Fr. Beetle never said a word about it. When I thanked Fr. Beetle, he told me Fr. Mann should never have said anything.

Seminary Stewardship

While in seminary, many seminarians volunteered performing stewardship functions for other seminarians. All seminarians were encouraged to give the traditional Meadow welcome to guests, priests of the seminary, new seminarians, bishops, and college students. It was called "Meadow Hospitality". We willingly enjoyed helping anyone who came to the Meadow, to unload and load up items of other seminarians, or give tours to college students or visitors, etc...

For stewardship, I was a newspaper carrier. I delivered the *Quakers Post* going door to door for seminarians and priests at the seminary. I also was responsible for food donations to the local food pantry in Quakers. Seminarians would donate canned food, cereal, and other food items etc.... and then I delivered them to the St. Vincent de Paul pantry at St. William's Church a few miles from the seminary. I was inspired to collect food for the poor due to working with Mother Maryanne's sisters in India and also at the Gift of Joy house in Quakers, Virginia as one of my apostolates. A deacon seminarian, who graduated, asked if I would take on the task, which I greatly enjoyed.

#43 PILGRIMAGES WHILE IN SEMINARY

Fatima – Relic of Jacinta and Francisco

While at Mary's Meadow Seminary, I noticed a flier hanging on the bulletin board, that said, "Free Trip to Fatima". I could not believe it, but it was true. Benedictine abbot, Fr. Edmund Munjor and some of his friends were inviting any seminarian to go to Fatima for free. I called the number and received permission from my vocation director, and was able to make the pilgrimage.

While in Fatima, I prayed to Our Lady, and asked Her for a relic of Francisco and Jacinta. I said, "If I get a relic, then I know for sure I am called to the priesthood." I asked some local people how to obtain a relic, but they said it's only for priests and churches. Finally, a local person directed me to the house of an old priest. He was the Monsignor in charge of the beatification process. Mustering up the courage, I knocked on his door. He opened the door, invited me in, and said, "What can I do for you?" I said, "I am a seminarian, and I would like a first-class relic of Francisco and Jacinta." He sternly said with an accent, "No, No, No!" This is only for parishes and religious houses. You can't have one." I sheepishly, said, "Oh, okay." And then, he suddenly changed his mind, and said, "Okay, you can have one. But they are not for personal use. You have to promise that others will venerate the relic. When we were children, I was a friend of Francisco. He gave me a branch from the holm oak tree, Our Lady stood on, and, it is now used for relics. The wood you see in the relic with the names Francisco and Jacinta came from their caskets." I was elated and deeply grateful.

I participated in the Corpus Christi Procession, the Candlelight Procession and did penance walking on my knees. I didn't realize it, but my knees became so scraped and torn, blood was visibly coming from the knees of my pants. It was embarrassing.

Many times, I was blessed to help carry the statue of Our Lady of Fatima with three other men during the nightly processions. Once, while helping to carry the statue, I was very rude to a lady by pushing her out of the way as she kept trying to touch the statue. I felt ashamed for my behavior in a holy place while carrying the statue of Our Lady.

Years later, when I returned to Fatima after I was ordained a priest, I was able to offer Mass at the Capellina (the chapel originally built at the request of Our Lady and location where Mary appeared on the holm oak tree).

Jubilee Year 2000 & Trip to Rome

"You will declare this fiftieth year sacred and proclaim the liberation of all the inhabitants of the land. This is to be a jubilee for you" (Leviticus 25:9-11).

Many seminarians were traveling to Rome during the Jubilee year, but I couldn't afford it. I very much wanted to go. Therefore, I prayed to Our Lady and asked Her to somehow make it happen. I had $500 to my name, and it cost nearly $2000 to go with a

Catholic travel agency. A seminarian suggested I check airfares because airlines were giving big discounts due to the Jubilee year. The airlines, with the Italian government, wanted to help as many tourists to come to Rome to spend money in their country. I couldn't believe it, but I found a ticket for $450 round trip from Washington, DC to Rome. Without thinking about hotel or food expenses, I purchased the ticket to go to Rome over spring break. After paying the airfare, I had only $50 left. A seminarian from the Meadow, who knew seminarians studying in Rome, made the suggestion that I contact seminaries there, but all were full. I emailed, Rodrick, a seminarian in Rome, who was a former brother of the Franciscans of Perpetual Victims Martyrs.

On my behalf, Rodrick asked a wealthy friend if she would pay for my hotel expenses. She not only paid for my hotel room, but also paid for a train ticket to Assisi and paid for an overnight stay with the Bridgetine Sisters.

I loved Assisi and felt a special peace there. The church of San Damiano, the Basilica of Our Lady of Angels and the Basilica of St. Francis caused within me a longing to be a Franciscan again.

Because I didn't have much money, I brought canned goods and a can opener in my carry-on my bag. I directly ate out of the can without warming up the food. The food in Assisi was included in the trip, but not in Rome. While in Rome, I ate a small cheese-less pizza (rosa pizza). It cost just a few dollars.

I feared taking taxis and couldn't afford one, so I walked to the many holy sites, especially St. Peter's Basilica, where I attended the beatification of a martyr, Pedro Calungsod, and came close to Pope John Paul II as he was driving by in his pope-mobile. A funny thing happened, as Pope John Paul II was driving by and waving to the crowd, a group of religious sisters from Poland and I, stood on chairs to see the pope. As we waved at the pope, he looked directly at me, as if he was thinking, "What are you doing standing on that chair!" His facial expression said it all. After his glance, I felt like crawling under the chair.

I walked all over Rome, looking at churches and attending Mass and Eucharistic Adoration. I happened to enter a church containing the incorrupt body of Blessed Maria Taigi.

Thank you, Mary, for a wonderful trip to Rome. Not only did you provide a place to stay, but provided someone to pick me up at the airport, and take me to Assisi.

Calcutta & Saint Mother Teresa

"When I was hungry, you gave me food, when thirsty, you gave me drink." (Matthew 25:31) Jesus said to St. Faustina: "... I demand from you deeds of mercy, which are to arise out of love for Me. You are to show mercy to your neighbors always and everywhere. You must not shrink from this or try to excuse or absolve yourself from it." (Diary of St. Faustina, #742)

Someone attached a note to the seminary bulletin board asking seminarians if they would be interested in working with Mother Teresa's sisters in Calcutta during the Jubilee year, for a month during summer. I was excited about the possibility of doing missionary work, and it was free! I asked Our Lady to obtain the gift of serving the poor in India. I received permission from our diocesan vocation director, to go, but I would lose out on a month's income serving in a parish during the summer. However, I trusted and went. The experience was life changing. Many stories could be told about my experiences with the poor. A priest and two other seminarians and I went for the missionary trip.

To see abandoned children in a large building filled with beds was heart-wrenching for me. Many children were crying for attention and wanted to be loved. Handicapped adults were placed in a shelter run by the sisters. Otherwise, they would die in the streets because no person or organization would care for them. Every day, I helped care for patients at the home of the dying. The heat, lack of food, mosquitoes and bad water caused many to die. The sisters took the dying off the street, so they could die with dignity. I saw a man with a hole on his forehead and maggots were in the hole. A sister used tweezers to remove them.

A severely malnourished baby, about 6 months old, was left alone on the sidewalk and appeared to be dying. I attempted to get the attention of passersby by, so someone would help the baby. The next thing I knew, a large crowd was standing around the baby and I. The people seemed angry and no one seemed to understand what I was trying to say. Finally, an English-speaking Hindi man interpreted my concerns to the people. He said the people were under the impression I wanted to steal the baby and were threatening to kill me. With the interpreters help, I tried to convince them to take the baby to the Mother House of Mother Teresa to give the child medical care. Thanks to his intervention, I was spared from the mob. After most had left, the mother of the child came back. She had been pumping water about a half a block away. Looking back, I wish I would have picked up the baby and held the child in my arms, but if I would have, I may have been beaten.

I prayed every day at the tomb of Mother Teresa, located at the Mother House in the chapel of the sisters. The sisters prayed two Holy Hours a day, and we prayed with them. They had no hot water, air conditioning or fans while the temperature was over 100 degrees almost every day with dense smog and humidity at nearly 100%. The conditions were truly miserable. The sisters slept in beds raised above the floor to prevent rodents from bothering them. Nets covered their beds to prevent rats and mosquitoes from injuring them.

It was there, I met Sister Mary Patristic, MC, whom Sister Marshmella introduced to me. The superior of the community assigned her to offer all her prayers and sacrifices throughout here entire religious life for my priesthood and ministry. How humbling! We received the permission to write each other several times a year at Christmas and

Easter. I had her name engraved by the chalice company, on the bottom of my new chalice, so I would remember her at every Holy Mass offered. I offer two Masses for her every year on Sept. 5th (Anniversary of Mother Teresa's death) and Oct. 7th (anniversary of the founding of their religious community).

In Calcutta, I saw the corporal works of mercy in action, and learned to love the poor and see Jesus in their disguise. And, by their daily Holy Hours, I saw spiritual works of mercy, which motivated me to be faithful to my Holy Hours. Again, the Virgin Mary interceded for another trip, which gave me the experience of corporal works of mercy with holy sisters. Sister Marshmella also gave me two relics of the Mother Teresa. One relic was a piece of her hair, and the other blood from her vomit when she was dying.

#44 GRADUATE DEGREE FROM MARY'S MEADOW SEMINARY

Bachelor's Degree in Philosophy 233 Credits!

For various reasons, including low grades, only one year of college classes transferred from Fort Hickok University to St. Robert Bellarmine Seminary. I had to re-take three years of classes. After attending St. Robert for two years, I needed another year of school to graduate with a degree in Philosophy. When the Franciscans of Perpetual Victim Martyrs started their St. Joseph Seminary, I took a year of classes there, and believed I would graduate from their seminary. However, the community later realized classes taken at their seminary were not accredited. Therefore, a degree could not be given from the seminary, nor could credits from classes taken be transferred to another seminary. Oh! My! The following year, when I began to attended Mary's Meadow Seminary, I needed to retake those classes as well.

Consequently, by the time I received my Bachelor's Degree in Philosophy at the Meadow, I had accumulated 233 credits. You would be surprised at how different the same class can be taught. As one who doesn't like to read nor write, if I could receive a grade for perseverance and patience, I hope I would have obtained an A+ because I never complained. By the grace of God, I did what I was told for His glory and honor. I used to tell seminarians, if someday I become a priest, and if I become a saint, I could easily be a patron saint for seminarians to help them with their studies.

#45 PASTORAL YEAR – YEAR OF DISCERNMENT

Ordination of Diaconate Delayed
"For His sake, I have forfeited everything." (Philippians 3:8)

After I had left the brothers, joined the Diocese of Rolling Hills and completed three years of theology at the Meadow, I was about to be ordained a deacon. A month before my diaconate ordination, I read an article that caused me to feel unworthy to become a priest. I copied the article, and sent it to Bishop Basil Braveheart. We later had a profitable conversation about it. In the back of my mind, I was also wondering if maybe someday I might get married. Our diocesan vocation director was furious, and recommended to the bishop that I should never be ordained in the future.

However, the wise bishop requested I make a Pastoral Year, teach at a local Catholic high school, reside at the Church of the Ascension and help out at the parish in Rolling Hills for a year. The plan for me was to discern if I had a call to the priesthood.

During that year, I contemplated whether I had a vocation to marriage. I had always wanted to get married and have a large family (eight children, just like my parents). At one point during the year, I decided to discontinue on the road to the priesthood, with the hope I would find a wife. But, the longer I thought about not continuing on to the priesthood, the less peace I had. When I finally decided to make the sacrifice of not getting married, nor having children, I had peace. And, this how I finally realized and accepted God's call to the priesthood. I also came to understand God calls sinners to be His disciples. None of us are perfect, but we do our best as one of His followers. My experience at the Catholic high school helped me to understand how to teach, and also how to discipline children, so that teaching would be profitable for students. But, I also learned to trust in God's infinite mercy. Jesus wanted me to put behind the sins of the past and have confidence in His unfathomable mercy.

Lessons Teaching High School

During my Pastoral Year, I was assigned to teach at the east side Catholic school, and was not permitted to wear clerics. The children treated me as they would any teacher. Every teacher prepares a lesson for the day, but at times, the youth give lessons of a different kind to the teacher. I taught two classes, with freshmen and sophomore students intermingled in each. One semester, I taught the New Testament and the following semester, I taught Liturgy and the Sacraments.

Before the year started, a very experienced teacher, told me give out demerits generously. I decided to take her advice for one class, but the other class I thought I would just be very kind to the students, and hoping they would listen to me, if I politely asked them to behave.

The class that I gave demerits generously, I was able to maintain control and teach the students much. However, the other class I didn't give demerits, I lost control by the end of the semester. I was wrong in thinking if I practiced kindness, they would listen and obey.

While praying in an Adoration Chapel, I asked the Lord for help in control the behavior of the students. In the chapel, I happened to find a Catholic magazine that explained the philosophy of St. John Bosco, on the behavior and teaching of children. In the article, it said the teacher should take away privileges and never raise one's voice. It also said it was important to lay out rules of the class, and to follow through with consequences for misbehavior. It said, failing to do so, the youth would not respect the teacher. I quickly applied these rules, and had good success in the class that I took away privileges and generously gave out demerits.

The school had a mixture of poor black youth and rich white youth, both on the east side of the city. The Catholic school, on the west side, had all white students with average income households. In the school I taught, some rich youth at sporting events would pull out their credit cards, chanting, "We have credit cards, and you have trailer houses. We will beat you, because we have success!" Most of the time at sporting events, the east side Catholic school with the rich youth and very poor youth, lost to the west side Catholic school. The principle at the east side school would later correct the youth for their misbehavior during games.

One day, a rich girl kept talking in class, and I repeatedly reminded her to discontinue, or she would receive a demerit. I gave her one demerit, and then, she talked again, so I gave her another demerit. Then she argued with me about the demerits, and I requested that she go to the office. In response, she pulled out her cell phone, and started dialing it, saying, "I'm calling my mother to tell her how you are treating me." I said, "Not here in class. If you want to call your mother, go to the office." She stomped out of the classroom dialing her phone, as she left, saying, "My mother will be unhappy with you." About 15 min. later, she returned and sat in her chair without saying a word. Her mother apparently supported me, and told her to return to class and be quiet.

A sixteen-year-old-girl came to class as it was about to begin, and said, "Today is my birthday!" I said, "Happy birthday!" She said, "I got a new Porsche with a sunroof, and my boyfriend and I went for a ride in it." I said, "You received a new car for your birthday? You have a boyfriend?" She said, "Yes, he's in college." I said, "Do your parents know, that your boyfriend is in college and that he went for a ride in your Porsche?" She said, "Yes, my parents let me do whatever I want."

I repeatedly asked a girl to stop talking in class. While I was teaching, occasionally she would stand up and visit with other youth around her. This was in the class I didn't give demerits, but had hoped the youth would listen if I politely asked them to behave. Out of anguish and desperation, I could not believe what came out of my mouth. I said, "Would you sit down and shut up!" The whole class stared intently at her, and me, and for the remaining time of the class, all behaved well. After class, I apologized to her, but told her to be quiet from now on during class.

In the other class, I used the demerit system and took away privileges. It allowed me to teach the class without interruption, and the young people learned much. The class with demerits given and privileges taken away, respected me, while the other class that I failed to give out demerits, didn't respect me. The lesson I learned is that youth yearn for boundaries, and once they have them in class, they feel safe and are less apt to act out. To be merciful sometimes means to discipline out of love.

Mouse in the House

"Of the creatures that swarm on the ground, the following are unclean for you: the rat, the mouse, the various kinds of lizards." (Leviticus 11:29)

During my Pastoral Year, while residing at the rectory of Church of the Ascension in Rolling Hills, when Fr. Walter German, the pastor, was out of town, I was watching the news at 10pm and eating *Triscuit* wheat thins, sitting on the couch. Knowing I was the only one in the rectory, I suddenly felt a tapping on my right shoulder. I slowly turned my head, to see who was behind me, and no one was there. It was creepy. I kept watching the news, when again I felt tapping on my right shoulder. I slowly turned my head and saw a mouse sitting on my shoulder, reaching for a "wheat thin", I was holding in my hand. I stood up, and yelled, "Ah!" The sudden movement from quickly standing up, caused the mouse to fall to the floor, and I immediately gave it a hard stomp with my foot and killed it. Thank God, I was wearing my shoes. I picked up the deceased mouse, threw it in the trash, and cleaned up the bloody mess on the floor and my shoe. I felt bad for killing the poor thing.

Battle with Spiders

"His confidence is but a gossamer thread, his trust is a spider's house." (Job 8:14)

One morning, when I was awakened by the alarm, I noticed tiny baby spiders all over the bed and on me. I received 34 spider bites while sleeping. I surmised a spider laid eggs in the bed skirting and the baby spiders hatched at night. The recluse spider bites caused scabs to appear and wounds that kept getting larger over time. A doctor prescribed an oral and topical antibiotic for the wounds. After three months, they finally disappeared.

A few months after the spider biting event, I noticed during the night what appeared to be large dead spiders in various places on the floor, but discovered recluse spiders play dead when lights are turned on. To exterminate them, I sprayed the entire house with bug spray, but they returned night after night. I ended up using a strong spray with a terrible odor. The odor was so intense, one night I became nauseated and slept in a room at the church. Because Fr. German was away for a week, he wasn't around during the battle with the spiders. I decided not to tell him what happened, since I didn't think he would understand why I slept in a room at the church.

During his time away, visiting priests came to offer daily Mass. But the spiders continued to appear despite spraying the house multiple times. None of the insecticides were successful. I mentioned the spider problem to an elderly lady of the parish, who recommended I sprinkle *Seven Dust* insect powder (normally used for vegetable gardens) around the entire floor base. It worked! Oh, the wisdom of the elderly! Dozens of dead spiders were everywhere. They walked through the dust and returned to their hidden places, killing themselves and other spiders with them. Praise the Lord!

Visiting Priest & Peeing for All To Hear

"There is nothing concealed that will not be revealed, nor secret that will not be known. Therefore, whatever you have said in the darkness will be heard in the light, and what you have whispered behind closed doors will be proclaimed on the housetops." (Luke 12:2-3)

Because Fr. Walter German was away, several visiting priests came to offer daily Mass at the Church of the Ascension. As a seminarian, I helped the visiting priest before Mass. One morning, an elderly priest was preparing for Mass. After he was vested with Alb, vestment, and microphone, he needed to use the restroom, but he didn't remove his microphone or priestly attire. Unknowingly, the microphone was on, and everyone in the church could hear what he was doing. They heard the door of the restroom close, and then they heard him urinating in the toilet. I yelled through the door, "Father, your microphone is on!" And the people heard that too. Because he was hard of hearing, he didn't hear what I said. Hearing everything, the people in the church chuckled. To the relief of everyone, they heard water running with the washing of his hands, the using of the towel dispenser, the toilet flushed, and the restroom door open and close.

#46 THE DARK NIGHT FOR 5 YEARS

Darkness in My Soul – I Felt the Lord Abandoned Me for 5 Years

"If I say, "Surely the darkness shall cover me, and the light about me be night," even the darkness is not dark to you; the night is bright as the day, for darkness is as light with you." (Psalm 139:11-12)

I left the Franciscan brothers after only ten months of taking Perpetual Profession due to severe turmoil in the religious community, not caused by myself, nor was I involved with it. The moment I left the brothers, a darkness came over my soul that I have never been able to fully describe. I felt abandoned by God, although it was I who abandoned my vows and the community. There were no spiritual consolations and no signal graces to guide or help me to know whether I made the right decision to leave. Even though I received permission from my spiritual director, the bishop of the diocese of Bakersville, Louisiana, and from the community, this decision would cause great anguish in my heart for many years. Even though I had no inspirations that felt like they were of God, I continued to believe God was calling me to the priesthood. It also made me stronger inside because of it.

Only when I was ordained a deacon did the darkness disappear. Later, as I reflected on those five years, I believe they were five years of purification. During that time, I was unknowingly drawn ever closer to Jesus, my faith increased, and by God's grace conquered some sins I didn't believe were possible. Due to the darkness in my soul, I sought Jesus ever more and attempted all the harder to turn away from sin, and desired to please Him as much as I could. When I left the brothers, I prayed, and asked the Lord to help me to know which Diocese He wanted me to serve as a priest. I could have returned to my hometown diocese of Lakota, Ohio, but didn't want to be under a liberal bishop, nor go to a liberal seminary where they sent their men. I wanted to return to Mary's Meadow Seminary, where I knew I would have excellent formation and education to be a good priest. A deterrent to the Dioceses of Lakota and Helena is the requirement for seminarians to pay their own way through seminary. But once ordained, the diocese would reimburse the priest. I certainly didn't have the money to pay my tuition, and had no idea, if and how, I could take out a loan. The Diocese of Rolling Hills paid for the seminarians to attend seminary, and this was also a major reason why I believed the Lord wanted me in this diocese and an added benefit was their bishop wasn't liberal. While in seminary, I became friends with seminarians from Rolling Hills. They were fine young men, who, I believed, would accept me in their diocese.

#47 ORDAINED A DEACON AT MARY'S MEADOW SEMINARY

Ordained to the Diaconate

"In the tender compassion of our God, the dawn from on high shall break upon us..." (Luke 1:78)

Due to teaching for a year at a Catholic high school, when I returned to seminary, there was a discussion between my bishop and the seminary, about when and where I was to be ordained a deacon. Bishop Basil Braveheart decided I would be ordained Nov. 6th, 2003 at the Meadow, in the Chapel of the Immaculate Conception with several other men, who also had delayed ordinations.

On the day of the ordination, I had no idea how to vest in an Alb or a cincture. My spiritual director happened to be there and showed me what to do.

During Mass, as I lay prostrate on the floor, I was overwhelmed with doubts, and the darkness that I felt for five years, seemed to fall on me all at once, and I thought, "Lord, do you really want me to be a priest? You should not do this! Lord, is this truly Your will for me? Help me Jesus!" As I was laying on the floor, now and then, I looked at the other men prostrate next to me, to see if they had stood up.

When all stood up together (I felt like I came out of a tomb) the darkness in my soul vanished, and I immediately experienced a consolation with the understanding, it truly was God's will. It was as though a light suddenly broke through clouds and a rainbow appeared.

I felt humbled, the Lord chose me. I immediately felt confidence. As of this writing, nineteen years later, I have never once doubted my call to the priesthood.

Sadly, Bishop Basil Braveheart was transferred to the diocese of Rapid Water, Michigan just two weeks after my ordination as a deacon. Because I knew that my parents, nor any family could attend, I didn't notify them, when I was to be ordained a deacon, and only told them afterwards.

After the ordination Mass, I served tables, in the fashion of being a deacon, for my six guests who came. Two elderly fellas, Lonnie and Lance, from Ohio took an Amtrak train to travel to the event in Virginia. Fr. Walter German from Rolling Hills and his parents came, as well as a woman from his parish. The bishop enjoyed the dinner held in a classroom. There was no other room at the seminary to use at the time. I gave money to a seminarian to purchase Kentucky Fried Chicken with the fixins for those who came from Ohio and served them.

#48 A FEW WORDS TO JESUS WITH BIG CONSEQUENCES

About a year before I was ordained a deacon, I told Jesus how I felt, but it was just a side comment to Him that I really didn't think much of. When gazing upon the beauty of the Immaculate Conception Chapel at Mary's Meadow Seminary, in Quakers, Virginia. I said, "O Jesus, this church is so beautiful, I wish I could be ordained a deacon here." I didn't say it with any sort of insistence, but only, as a side comment. But then later, I backed out of my deacon ordination. And then, when I came back to seminary, Bishop Basil Braveheart decided to ordain me, and two other men in the beautiful Chapel at the Meadow. The prayer was answered in an unexpected way.

Another prayer I prayed to Jesus early on, when I joined the diocese of Rolling Hills, and then later found out Bishop John Fidelity had retired. I said, this little prayer. "O Jesus. I was hoping that Bishop Fidelity would be ordaining me, and now, that he is retired, that can't happen." Bishop Braveheart was transferred to Rapid Water, Michigan, shortly after my deacon ordination at the Meadow. Consequently, we were without a bishop. It was then they decided, Bishop Fidelity, although retired, would ordain us four men from the Diocese of Rolling Hills. Jesus answered both of these prayers in a way I never could have imagined. Thank you, Jesus, for listening even to the smallest sighs of the heart, and answering them with your love.

#49 ORDINATION TO THE PRIESTHOOD

Letter to Pope John Paul II Asking for His Blessing and Relic Received
"Peter, you are rock and on this rock, I will build my Church." (Matthew 16:18)

Before I was ordained to the priesthood, a seminarian told me that if a deacon sent an invitation to his ordination to Pope John Paul II, he would give his Apostolic Blessing. About two months before the ordination, I sent the pope an invitation with the hope, the blessing would arrive before the ordination or even on the day of the ordination, but it didn't. Every day I kept looking in the mailbox for the letter.

One night, I dreamt I walked up to Pope John Paul II, knelt before him, and he made the sign of the cross over me giving me his blessing. I was so refreshed when I had awakened, and thought at least I had the consolation of receiving his blessing in a dream. But then, that same day, after I had the dream, when I went to the mailbox in the afternoon, the Apostolic Blessing of the Pope was in the mail.

About a year after I was ordained, in 2005, Pope John Paul II died. We all felt as though we lost our father. Several years later, when I was assigned to St. Charles of Sezze Parish, I decided to request a relic of Pope John Paul II, and I sent a donation to the postulator of his cause. I was very much hoping to obtain a relic. Then on May 29th, 2007, the third anniversary of my ordination to the priesthood, I received a relic of Pope St. John Paul II in the mail the same day. I told parishioners, when he was alive, he didn't quite get the day right. His blessing was a few weeks late, but now, since he went to the Father's House, he hits it perfectly on the anniversary of my ordination by giving me a relic of him.

The people of the Church of the Ascension paid for a new chalice to be made for me. I was humbled by the unexpected gift. When the chalice was to be made, four handmade medallions were placed on the base of the chalice purchased by the people of the Church of Ascension. On their own, they took up a separate collection to purchase a new chalice for my ordination. I was humbled by their generosity and had engraved "Church of the Ascension" on the bottom of the chalice. One medallion is that of Pope Saint John Paul II, as I believed he would someday become a saint. The other medallions are the Heart of Jesus, Heart of Mary and an image of Our Lady of Grace.

Ordination to the Priesthood
"The LORD has sworn and will not change his mind: "You are a priest forever, in the order of Melchizedek." (Psalm 110:4)

There are four dioceses in Ohio. The Diocese of Rolling Hills, the Diocese of Lakota City, (my original home diocese), the Diocese of Helena, and the Archdiocese of Ohio

City, Ohio. I was ordained May 29th, 2004 at the Cathedral of the Immaculate Conception in Rolling Hills, Ohio for the Diocese of Rolling Hills.

I was excited to be ordained in 2004, because Pope John Paul II declared the Year of the Eucharist from the summer of 2004 to the summer of 2005. I was very much looking forward to preaching about the Eucharist to try to draw as many as possible to Jesus in the Most Blessed Sacrament.

Preparations for my ordination included a deaconate retreat, a general confession, making my own invitations, preparing for my First Masses, and preparing a dinner, although I had no idea how to pay for it. By God's providence, everything fell into place. Monsignor McGillacutty told me to ask the Men's Club at St. Tarcisius parish to pay for the dinner, and they did. I later attempted to reimburse the club with a monetary donation, but they refused it.

I decided to offer three First Masses. St. Tarscisus parish would be the first of the three on the same day as the ordination. Church of the Ascension, would be the next day, and a week later, at St. Michael's parish in Mitchell City.

The First Mass of Thanksgiving was at St. Tarcisius parish in the evening I was ordained. The Congregation of the Sisters of Virtue were to sing in choir. Unlike other sisters in our diocese, they wore their habit, veil, and Rosary. The Mass booklets were printed at a business owned by a parishioner from St. Tarcisius parish. He owned the company, and gave a large discount.

I created holy cards at the library of the seminary using their printer. On the front was an image of a priest's ordination from the book, *The Imitation of Christ*. On the back was the date of the ordination and the prayer of St. Francis of Assisi, "Let everyone be struck with fear, let the whole world tremble, and let the heavens exult when Christ, the Son of the living God, is present on the altar in the hands of a priest! O wonderful loftiness and stupendous dignity! O sublime humility! O humble sublimity! The Lord of the universe, God, and the Son of God, so humbles Himself that for our salvation He hides Himself under an ordinary piece of bread! Brothers, look at the humility of God, and pour out your hearts before Him! Humble yourselves that you may be exalted by Him! Hold back nothing of yourselves for yourselves, that He Who gives Himself totally to you may receive you totally!"

St. Francis felt unworthy to be a priest, but was ordained a deacon. I had hoped to have at least a portion of his love for Jesus in the Eucharist and be willing to accept suffering as he.

The cost of refurbishing the Chalice, inherited from my uncle, Father Ferdinand Tomerscka, was provided by my mother and step-father. Since my mother played a role in obtaining the chalice, after my uncle's death, I told her it was her chalice, and I would borrow it for my priesthood.

The night before the ordination, a seminarian classmate, good friend, and current brother of the Franciscans of Perpetual Victim martyrs, helped me practice offering Mass. We stayed up late practicing and I began to feel sick that night.

The next day, of the Ordination Mass, I had a terrible sinus infection and a horrible headache. Since I was the oldest seminarian, I was first to be ordained by the bishop. The ceremony went well. We prostrated on the floor and everyone recited the Litany of the Saints.

The bishop then laid his hands on our heads and placed chrism oil on our hands. We wiped the chrism on a cloth to be given to our mothers during our First Mass. We made the promise of obedience, and the bishop completed the ritual as prescribed.

My spiritual director, Fr. Matthew Mann, clothed me in the priestly vestment. How incredible to stand next to the bishop and concelebrate reciting the words of consecration. That was my real first Mass I offered, and my family had front-row seats.

I was ordained with three other men. One went to seminary with me at the Meadow, while the other two went to a different pontifical seminary. It was all so surreal. I felt much joy in my heart, loved by God and chosen by Him, to be a sacramental disciple. Why did Jesus choose me, with a terrible past, to become a priest? God's Mercy alone can explain how He would do such a thing. It was my moment of Mt. Tabor, forgetting the cross, victimhood of the priesthood and basking in the joy and glory of it all.

During much of my adult life, my siblings and I rarely spoke to each other. Usually, I visited with each sibling maybe once a year and for less than fifteen minutes on the phone, as they apparently didn't seem interested in talking to me. I surmised they didn't want much to do with me, especially since I tried all sorts of ways to get them to practice their faith when I was a brother and seminarian.

Therefore, when my family came forward to receive Holy Communion at the ordination Mass, I was stunned because a brother-in-law who I knew wasn't Catholic, came forward. I wondered if he became Catholic, and I didn't know about it. One of my sisters, not married in the Church, and her son, who I didn't believe was baptized, both came up for Communion. Caught off guard, and not knowing what to do, I gave all who came forward Holy Communion, only to discover later the brother-in-law had not become Catholic, my sister was still living with a man outside of marriage. Her son wasn't baptized. I felt I betrayed Jesus in the Blessed Sacrament. It was a sad moment that marred the wonder of the day. I didn't know how to deal with it when it happened, but ever since, I never gave Communion to a non-Catholic again. After that day, if I discovered a non-Catholic came forward for Holy Communion, I would whisper to them that I would give them a blessing and explain after Mass why they could not receive. And to Catholics, who I perceived were non-practicing, I still gave them Communion, because I had no way of knowing if they had just gone to confession or not. I can't judge their soul, for only God could do that. After the ordination Mass, the other priests took pictures with the bishop, but my family wasn't interested in taking photos. Consequently, I went to the Cathedral hall to give First Blessings. What a joy to see so many families and friends come to the ordination. My sister who lived in Texas made the day extra special because she hadn't been home for many years and all were delighted to see her and her son.

My brother and his wife weren't married in the Catholic Church. A few years before my ordination, they invited me to attend their backyard wedding. But, since it was an invalid wedding, I refused. Consequently, my brother nor the woman he married invalidly came to the ordination.

I explained to them why I could not attend their wedding. My brother was fine with it, but his "so called" wife was angry and became especially infuriated when after the ceremony, I addressed postal letters to them as Louis Gadfly and Lydia, rather, than Mr. and Mrs. Louis Gadfly. I was saddened they didn't come, but trusted God would do something in the future, and later He did, in a way I never anticipated.

#50 FIRST CONFESSIONS AND FIRST MASSES

First Confessions

"Peace be with you. As the Father has sent me, so I send you." And when he had said this, he breathed on them and said to them "Receive the Holy Spirit. Whose sins you forgive are forgiven them, and whose sins you retain are retained." (John 20:21-23)

Thirty minutes before my First Mass of Thanksgiving at St. Tarcisius parish, I heard Confessions for the first time. The Confessional was built in such a way, only behind the screen Confessions were possible, which I greatly enjoyed. As a child, I abhorred being required to go face to face and publicly confess my sins in a group. What a supernatural joy to be an instrument of mercy! After all the sins of my life, Jesus was using me to forgive the sins of others, and reconcile them back to God. Incredible! Oh, the infinite and glorious mercy of God. In the confessional, I had my little paper with me, to be sure I would say the absolution words properly. I never would have thought, after not going to Confession for twenty years, I would someday be a priest in the confessional.

First Holy Mass

"For I received from the Lord what I also handed on to you, that the Lord Jesus, on the night he was handed over, took bread, and, after he had given thanks, broke it and said, "This is my body that is for you. Do this in remembrance of me." In the same way also the cup, after supper, saying, "This cup is the new covenant in my blood. Do this, as often as you drink it, in remembrance of me." For as often as you eat this bread and drink the cup, you proclaim the death of the Lord until he comes." (I Corinthians 11:23-26)

I decided to have my First Mass of thanksgiving at St. Tarcisius parish, where I resided as a seminarian when home from seminary.

I chose to have the First Mass of thanksgiving the same day of the ordination, the Vigil of Pentecost, the Saturday evening of my ordination, as I didn't believe my family would stay for my First Mass, which was evident the following day.

Only my mother and my step-father came the next day, to my second Mass at Church of the Ascension. My family had a long trip back to western Ohio, and so I didn't blame them for wanting to leave early Sunday morning to return home.

I asked a seminarian friend to greet my family before Mass, and explain to them, what my parents were to do during Mass. During the procession of the gifts, my father was to carry an altar cross and my mother and step-father would carry up the chalice they paid to be refurbished.

I hate to make an excuse, but due to the long day, the headache, the sinus infection, and the little sleep at night, just before Mass, out of anger I snapped at the seminarian for not telling my parents what to do. But, I realized he had no idea who my parents were since I failed to introduce him to them. I sang the Mass, partially in Latin and in English, and the Sisters of Virtue led the people in singing some Mass parts in Latin and hymns in English and offered the *Jubilate Deo Mass* of Pope Paul VI.

During the consecration, as I held the Host in my hands for the first time, and said the sacred words of Jesus, "This is My Body", I was overwhelmed with emotion and nearly began to cry, but held back tears.

Wow! God used me to make His sacrifice present on the altar, to change bread and wine into His body and blood, and as Fr. Kapuan said, "Not even the Immaculate Virgin Mary did that, nor any of the angels in heaven, and yet, He chose me! Who am I?"

During the Mass after Holy Communion, I set flowers before a statue of the Blessed Virgin Mary and gave my mother flowers, naturally causing her to cry. I knelt before the statue of Our Lady of Grace and consecrated my priesthood to Her, and thanked Her for helping me to the Altar.

Some parish ladies helped frame images of the Sacred Heart of Jesus and the Immaculate Heart of Mary, that I gave to those who helped serve Mass. To promote Jesus in the Eucharist, I gave to all who attended the Mass, the book, *Jesus Our Eucharistic Love.*

During Mass, I gave my father the confessional stole used for my first Confessions, and my mother the linen (manutergium) used to dry my hands from the Chrism at the ordination. The tradition of giving these items to parents is that when each parent goes to their judgment, they will present them to the Lord. His father holding his stole and his mother holding the manutergium in their hands, will remind Jesus they gave their son to the Church for the Sacred Priesthood for the service of the Church.

Years later, when my father passed from this life and was in the coffin, the stole and his Rosary were placed in his hands. My mother is currently still living.

After Mass, during the ordination dinner in the basement of the church, I introduced my family and gave first blessings for those who didn't receive them at the Cathedral earlier in the day. It was an indescribable a joy to celebrate, what the Lord did for the Church and for me, ordaining a new priest!

During dinner, suddenly tornado sirens blared, as a tornado was reported southeast of Rolling Hills near the city of Mitchell. I announced to those present, that they were safe to stay, since we were in the basement of the church, but if they wanted to leave it was understandable. Fr. Matthew Mann, my spiritual director from Mary's Meadow Seminary, attended the ordination, First Mass and dinner. He was such a help in my journey to the priesthood. May God reward him for all the young men, he helped become holy priests over the years that he taught theology at the Meadow. Since he taught theology, he used to call himself, "God Man."

Shadow Over My First Mass

Monsignor McGuillicutty, pastor of St. Tarcisius parish, was diabetic and consequently, decided to add water to the wine, so the accidents of the wine wouldn't affect his blood sugar. I regularly witnessed him mixing water with the wine. It appeared, large quantities of water were added to the wine, and began to wonder if it caused invalid Masses. I had planned to use wine directly from a new bottle before Mass started, but due to the first Confessions and excitement, and not feeling well, I forgot to be sure that only pure wine would be used. How sad to think my First Mass may have been invalid. Only Jesus knows the sadness caused in my heart for many years. I had wished I would have spoken to him about his mixing of water and wine, when I first noticed he was doing it. Back then, I was afraid it could cause a stumbling block to the priesthood. I also should have been concerned about other Masses that were offered when using the mixed water and wine. At times, seminarians were told to stay "under the radar" before ordination. However, I needed to learn to speak up, especially when it involved serious problems with the sacraments. It was just as much my fault, as his, for not saying anything. This event would impel me in the future to speak out about invalid Masses due to wine not made from grapes. I would later be confronted with invalidity problems in a monastery and at a parish and also need to deal with other invalid sacraments like baptism, marriages, and anointing of the sick not properly performed.

Second Mass of Thanksgiving – Church of the Ascension on May 30th 2004

The day of my ordination and First Mass of Thanksgiving was overwhelming and the following day when the other three priests had their First Mass, I had my second Mass. I wanted to give thanks to the people of the Church of the Ascension, who helped in the discernment of my call to the priesthood. The wonderful people pulled together to purchase a new chalice for me, and so I had engraved "Church of the Ascension" on the bottom of the chalice. The chalice would not arrive until about six months after I was ordained. Fr. Walter German, pastor of Church of the Ascension, was very gracious and made the second Mass special. For a second day in a row, I caused my mother to cry, when she received flowers again, after I had also placed flowers before an image of the Virgin Mary in the Church of the Ascension.

First Homily as a Priest May 31st 2004

He (Jesus) stood up to read and was handed a scroll of the prophet Isaiah. He unrolled the scroll and found the passage where it was written: "The Spirit of the Lord is upon me, because he has anointed me to bring glad tidings to the poor, He has sent me to proclaim liberty to captives and recovery of sight to the blind, to let the oppressed go free..." (Luke 4:17-18)

My first homily as a priest was May 31st, the Visitation of Mary. Due to a sinus infection, sore throat and talking to so many people, my voice could barely be heard, as I offered the Mass without a concelebrating priest. Due to laryngitis from talking and sinus infection, almost nobody heard the homily.

Third Mass of Thanksgiving – St. Michael's in Mitchell City, Corpus Christi Sunday

Due to spending two summers at St. Michael's in Mitchell, when I joined the diocese as a seminarian, I wanted to show my appreciation for those who helped me feel at home in the Diocese of Rolling Hills. Consequently, the following Sunday, Corpus Christi Sunday, I offered my third Mass of thanksgiving followed by a Eucharistic Procession.

When I blessed the people with the Monstrance, I almost passed out. I later discovered it was due to a pinched blood vessel in my spinal cord. As I blessed the people, blood supply to my brain was cut off, nearly causing me to collapse. After the procession, we had a nice meal and celebrated together God's mercy in ordaining me a priest.

#51 YEAR OF THE EUCHARIST AND FIRST PRIEST ASSIGNMENT

June 10th, 2004 Pope John Paul II Proclaims Year of the Eucharist

How wonderful, Pope John Paul II declared "The Year of the Eucharist" just 12 days after I was ordained.

It gave me the opportunity to preach often on the Eucharist, help the pastor of my first assignment with Forty Hours Devotion, do a Nine-day Novena of Holy Hours for a new Supreme Court Justice, and help stop the Eucharistic Sacrileges occurring at St. Gertrude Parish in Rolling Hills.

First Assignment as a Priest & Scandal followed by Scandal
The Intertwining of Priest Assignments

When I was a deacon at Mary's Meadow Seminary, I went on pilgrimage to the Shrine of St. Gertrude and prayed before the altar, where her relics are located.

Because I had a devotion to the saint, I traveled to the shrine a few times and would go to the gift shop, make a donation, and obtain a relic of the saint. I gave the relics away as gifts. When it came time to get one, for myself, the sisters said they had no more relics. I was so disappointed. Here I was promoting devotion to her and ended up without a relic for myself.

Fast-forward about seven years after I was ordained, when I was the chaplain for the Holy Nuns of St. Therese, I was thrilled when the Solemnity of All Saints, the sisters gave me relics of St. Gertrude, St. Francis of Assisi, St. Therese, St. Maria Goretti and St. John Neumann.

When I was a deacon, and went to pray before the relics of Gertrude located in an altar of the shrine. I prayed, "O Saint Gertrude, please grant that my first assignment as a priest be a good one." After I was ordained, my first assignment was at St. Gertrude parish in Rolling Hills. St. Gertrude answered my prayer. Little did I know, the meaning of "good one" was different from what I anticipated.

I was excited to meet my pastor. Everyone I had visited with said, "Oh, you will love Fr. Bill Cody. He's a great priest." About a week before my assignment, I decided to go to St. Gertrude parish and meet the pastor. Upon entering the office, I met the lovely secretary, and said to her, "I'm your new associate priest. I would like to meet the pastor." She said, "We are so happy to have you! Have a seat. He's busy." After a few minutes, she looked at me with a whimsical smile, and said, "He's always busy. He may not have time for you. I will let him know you're here." After a few minutes, he came out of his office. I stood up reached over the front desk to shake his hand, and said, "I'm Fr. Leonard Gadfly. I'm your new associate. It's a pleasure to meet you." He looked at me with a blank look on his face, reached out his hand to shake mine, and then just before our hands connected, he suddenly pulled his hand back, turned around and walked away. I was quite miffed by it all, and didn't know what to do. He never said a word. He never smiled and never shook my hand. I thought, "What the heck was that all about!" The secretary looked at me as though embarrassed, and didn't say a word. I didn't know what to do, so I just walked out of the office and left. I thought, "Boy, is this going be fun." This was my first prophetic thought as a priest. I had no idea what recently happened in the parish before my arrival, that may explain why the pastor acted so strange.

After I moved into the rectory, occasionally, I was awakened about 1am with a knock on my bedroom door. When I went to open the door, no one was there. Finally, one night I happened to be awake when I heard the knock, and quickly opened the door to Fr. Bill Cody standing there. I asked him what he wanted. He said, "I was just checking to see if you were in your room." Since then, I made sure my door was locked, because I thought his actions were very strange. The other associate pastor eventually explained why he was checking on me. It was due to the previous associate who would stay out until 3 or 4 am many nights. I suspect he wanted to know if I was doing the same.

Despite this, I later discovered the pastor's deep dedication and self-sacrifice for his people. He rarely laughed or smiled, but over a period of time, I was able to get him to laugh due to some of my stupid jokes. He gave good homilies, was a good micromanager and was gifted in being able to accomplish many things, despite the various parishioner personalities.

He gave me assignments in the parish, and would always say, "I will back you in your decisions." But after twelve times of not backing any of my decisions, I stopped counting. I was angered and felt it wasn't virtuous on my part, to count the number of times he failed to support me, even though every time he said he would.

One example of him not supporting one of my decisions, had to do with the CYO (Catholic Youth Organization). Some very talented young men were in a band that played Christian pop music at the monthly CYO Mass for teens. To make the Mass more reverent, I suggested they play ordinary Catholic hymns at Mass, and I asked the CYO youth to lead the singing. Then, after Mass, the youth could have a concert in the parish hall where they could play their Christian pop music and invite youth from other parishes to attend. The youth were excited about it, but not the CYO leader. She came to my office crying, saying I wrecked their Mass. The pastor sided with the CYO leader.

A year later, I discovered Fr. Jonathon Vanderbilt, who I replaced at St. Gertrude due to his transfer to another parish, had an affair with a married woman at St. Gertrude before my arrival. The woman and her family were traumatized due to the priest's "improper relationship" with her. The priest who he replaced at St. Gertrude was Fr. Albert Brandmueller was also accused of improper relationships with women, but at different parishes. Both priests would eventually be assigned as pastor to St. Veronica parish in Brushwood and St. Anthony in Jericho City, and both priests would also leave their "damage" there.

You will never guess where my first assignment as pastor would be? St. Veronica in Brushwood City and St. Anthony in Jericho City. Once again, I followed both priests, who had caused scandal and both ended up becoming the pastor of St. Veronica and St. Anthony as well. Fr. Brandmueller left the priesthood while he was pastor of St. Veronica and St. Anthony. He abruptly left the week before First Holy Communion at St. Veronica due to an improper relationship with a woman in a different parish where he had been an associate. His time at St. Veronica was also a time of scandal at that parish. The cleaning lady at St. Veronica, told me he came to see her teenage daughter after midnight when everyone was in bed. She thought it was strange he came to their house so late at night. He eventually returned to the priesthood and became a strong witness in preaching the truth of the Gospel. However, Bishop Athanasius Courageous made him a "Canceled Priest" due to parishioners complaining about his homilies. He had quoted saints, who said few people go to heaven, as the road to heaven is narrow, and the road to hell is wide. During Mass, he allegedly threatened to sue parishioners for making up lies about him and telling them to the bishop. There may have been other things I was unaware of that would cause the bishop to want to remove him as pastor.

When I later concluded my time as pastor of Immaculate Heart of Mary parish in Wheatland and was transferred to St. John of God Hospital in Tantrum, Idaho, Fr. Brandmueller followed me as pastor of Immaculate Heart of Mary. Interestingly, Fr. Jonathan Vanderbilt followed Fr. Brandmueller when he was transferred to a different parish. God's irony of ironies. How two priests and I continued to be intertwined in parish assignments was weird.

Fr. Jonathon's time as pastor of St. Veronica was also a time of upheaval at the parish. People who knew about his improper relationship at St. Gertrude came to St. Veronica and held signs of protest saying he raped a parishioner from St. Gertrude, which a police investigation concluded had no credence. He also made bad choices at the parish. His interactions with youth, caused more anguish in the lives of the people of that parish. For example, he had a sleep-over for high school youth at the parish hall and church basement, and it was reported he stayed up with them all night. I followed both of these men at St. Gertrude and also St. Veronica in Brushwood City, and they followed me at Immaculate Heart of Mary in Wheatland City.

First Day at St. Gertrude

As a newly ordained priest, I chose to wear a cassock regularly and when I arrived the first day at the parish, Fr. Bill Cody was more welcoming and took me to the rectory (priest's house). He gave a tour of the parish and school. He said I was expected to eat dinner with him, and the other priest, Fr. Anthony Birkenstock several days a week. The parish had a maid, who cooked, did laundry and cleaned the house. It was strange to have a woman in the house. I felt like a plantation owner who was served by servants, and wondered how poor parishioners viewed such extravagance. The average person in the pew didn't have hired workers to take care of their house.

He looked at my cassock and said, "I wouldn't wear that if I were you. It's a lightning rod for all sorts of things." I had no idea what he meant. I said, "Are you telling me to not wear it?" He said, "No. I'm just saying I wouldn't wear it, if I were you." Fr. Cody concelebrated my first daily Mass at the parish, and he seemed pleased with the manner I offered the Holy Sacrifice. During Mass, he was helpful and made me feel at ease.

#52 THANKSGIVING TO OUR LADY FOR PRIESTHOOD

Mass of Thanksgiving to Our Lady of Guadalupe

A few months after I was ordained, I learned about newly ordained priests going to Rome, but I couldn't afford it. I wanted to thank Our Lady in some way for my vocation. Consequently, I found a pilgrimage headed by Fr. Peter Arapaho, CFR, (Franciscan of the Renewal) who was leading a group to Mexico to the Shrine of Our Lady of Guadeloupe. The cost of the trip was only $450 for everything including the plane ticket, food, lodging. It was a great deal.

While on the pilgrimage in Mexico I beheld the beautiful image of Our Lady of Guadalupe and offered Holy Mass at the shrine. When he came to the shrine years before, I purchased a digital life-size replica of the image previously blessed by Pope St. John Paul II. Upon my return to Rolling Hills, a shop created a traditional looking frame for it. I eventually gave the framed image to the Diocese of Rolling Hills Respect Life Office, and at times they took it to the abortion clinic.

At the shrine it was incredible to see Aztec pyramids where thousands of men, women, and children were sacrificed to false gods. In the 1500s, due to her apparitions, Our Lady stopped the abomination. The sacrifice of innocent people was replaced the sacrifice of Jesus on the altar. Over ten million Indians became Catholic through the apparition of Our Lady of Guadalupe, and I was able to gaze upon the actual image in person that caused many conversions. I hoped and prayed through Mary's intercession She would end the slaughter of innocent unborn children in the USA, in our state, and, around the world, who were being sacrificed for convenience. She is the patroness of the Americas.

#53 SACRAMENTAL RECORDS
LEARNING TO GIVE HOMILIES & CONFESSIONS

Keeping Sacrament Records

"It is no longer I who live, but Christ lives in me." (Galatians 2:20)

When I became aware St. Maximilian Mary Kolbe kept track of every Mass he offered, all his baptisms, and weddings, etc., I decided to keep my sacramental records as well. Sacramental records are kept in every parish, but I wanted to keep my own in imitation of St. Maximilian. At St. Gertrude from June 2004 until October 2005, I had 43 baptisms. At St. Charles of Sezze parish from Oct. of 2005 to June 2007, I had 83 baptisms. I had 12 weddings at St. Gertrude and 16 weddings at St. Charles. By the time I was ordained 19 years, I offered 9,627 Masses, did 400 baptisms and 70 weddings. Praise God! In the first three years I was a priest I heard over 5000 confessions. Jesus did these sacraments through me and how humbling it was, to be an instrument of the Lord. Oh, the untold mercy and grace poured out through a priest, who lived a terribly sinful life before my conversion. By God's redemption of my soul's misery by way of His mercy and through my ordination, He used me, a sinner, to redeem the misery of countless souls.

Homilies at St. Gertrude

"Preaching, therefore, is a duty that is apostolic, angelic, Christian, divine. The word of God is replete with manifold blessings, since it is, so to speak, a treasure of all goods. It is the source of faith, hope, charity, all virtues, all the gifts of the Holy Spirit, all the beatitudes of the Gospel, all good works, all the rewards of life, all the glory of paradise: Welcome the word that has taken root in you, with its power to save you. For the word of God is a light to the mind and a fire to the will. It enables man to know God and to love him. And for the interior man who lives by the Spirit of God, through grace, it is bread and water, but a bread sweeter than honey and the honeycomb, a water better than wine and milk. For the soul it is a spiritual treasure of merits, yielding an abundance of gold and precious stones. Against the hardness of a heart that persists in wrongdoing, it acts as a hammer. Against the world, the flesh, and the devil, it serves as a sword that destroys all sin." St. Lawrence of Brindisi

As I was learning how to prepare homilies, I quickly discovered people of the parish take to heart what I say. It really surprised me. However, at first, I naively thought they will do what I tell them because I'm preaching as Jesus would preach to them. Most really listened to what I said. It humbled me to think people listen to someone they don't know from a hill of beans. I learned quickly not all agreed with what I had to say, but most actually listened.

My first Sunday homily at St. Gertrude was on the 4th of July (Independence Day). I never stood before so many people in a congregation who all looked at me. I was absolutely terrified. My hands and legs were shaking when I gave the homily. I think there were more people at that one Sunday Mass than the entire population of my hometown of Crossroads City. In my mind, I pictured the people throwing tomatoes and booing at me while I gave the homily. All were looking at me like deer staring into headlights. They came to see the new baby priest give a homily. Despite being nervous, the homily actually went over well, since I had not yet given a homily with sparks and fireworks.

I always typed out my homilies in advance and read them, since I am unable to preach effectively without reading word for word from a printed homily. I attempted many times over the years to preach spontaneously, and am unable to do so, with rare exceptions. Each priest has their gifts and each priest has his deficiencies.

After Masses, people came up to me to tell me how they enjoyed my homilies, but soon it started to get to my head. I thought, I'm good at doing this. That is, until I preached my first homily on contraception and the fireworks began. In that Sunday homily, I said those who use contraception are dancing with the devil. And when the dance is over, the devil will swoop you off your feet, and then let you drop into the fires of hell. I quoted from the *Catechism of the Catholic Church* about the evils of contraception, and spoke about how Natural Family Planning can strengthen marriages. After Mass, I believed it was well received, as I only received compliments.

But, little did I know, those who didn't like it, wrote letters and left nasty phone messages on my phone extension. One man wrote a letter saying, "Thanks to your homily, I decided to leave the Catholic Church. It was a wake-up call, since I do not believe a lot of what Catholics believe. I converted to Catholicism because my wife made me convert. And from now on, I'm going to follow what I have believed all along. I just want to thank you for helping me to see, I don't belong in the Catholic Church." I was devastated and thought, I'm just a new priest learning how to give homilies. Surely, he would understand, I could have said things better. His wife later came up to me in tears, and I told her what he said. She said, "Don't worry, father. Your homily was spot on. He just can't accept what the Church teaches." I prayed hard for him, his wife, and their family, as well as others who were more critical, and some who were out right mean in sharing what they thought. I prayed ever harder, God would help me to give better homilies, and the hearts of the people would be open to the truth. (See Appendix C – First Homily Given as a Priest on Contraception, August 1st 2004)

As the presidential election was coming up, I decided to give a homily on the importance of voting and explained the most important issue in the election was the issue of life. As I gave the homily, I somehow could read the people, and realized they were all paying close attention to my every word. I quoted Archbishop Capitulate of the Archdiocese of Wilmont, Colorado, but didn't mention that it came from him. I said, "It's a sin requiring confession before receiving Holy Communion, if one votes for a pro-abortion candidate while the other candidate is pro-life." When I finished the homily, and just as I sat down, suddenly people began to stand up and clap. Then more and more people stood up and clapped. To be honest, I was embarrassed and dumbfounded. I could not believe it. I received a standing ovation for a homily. When they finished clapping, I lead the congregation professing our faith praying the Creed. After Mass when greeting people, I quickly found out not all agreed with those who clapped. A man came up and said, "You crossed the line. You got into politics." He said, "You said, we can't vote for democrats." My homilies were always written out, and I read them word for word, so I knew I didn't say what he said. This was my first experience of learning that what priests say at Mass and what people hear-- can be two totally different things. I responded to his comment, saying, "Sir. I didn't mention Democrats, nor Republicans. I just said we need to vote for life and life is more important than the economy and even more important than feeding the poor." I proceeded to say, "Without life, one cannot eat, nor enjoy the things of life." The man's face indicated he was furious, and I thought for a moment, he was going to hit me.

Then, a little old lady who was listening to the conversation said to the man, "You ought to be ashamed of yourself for talking to a priest like that. What father said in the homily was right." She then took her fingers and forcibly banged them into his chest. The humiliated man walked away, as a dog cowers with his tail between his legs. The old woman had gumption. I suspected she was Italian.

A few days later I received letters in the mail, and they were not good. One man said, "I'll bet you were just gloating over your stupid homily. I am sure you just loved the applause. Well, I wasn't applauding. Your homily was terrible." In response, I wrote a letter to him, saying, "You're right, the homily was not very good. I could have certainly done better. Please forgive me, as I am just learning how to give homilies. I really was very embarrassed when people clapped and could not understand why they did. I will try to do better." I later heard after the man received my letter, he was surprised I thought I didn't do well, and was embarrassed.

Then Fr. Bill Cody, the pastor, made an appointment with me. During the meeting, he said, "I have gotten all sorts of letters, phone calls and emails about your homily. None of them were positive. I just thought I would let you know, so you learn something from this homily." I wondered, "What about all those people who stood up and clapped. Didn't they write anything positive? I guess Fr. Cody never knew almost everyone stood up and clapped, and I wasn't about to tell him otherwise."

Learning to Hear Confessions

As a young priest, when I began to hear confessions, I was in awe. I preferred to not hear confessions face to face, and therefore, fastened a sign in the confessional telling people I wanted to hear confessions only behind the screen. I wanted penitents to have the awareness, Jesus is behind the other side of their screen, and it was Jesus, who absolved their sins, and it was Jesus, who gave them counsel in the sacrament.

Several things surprised me about hearing confessions. First, I was humbled by the openness and trust people have in telling their sins. It was, and continues to be, truly inspiring. I am often times moved by their honesty and good self-knowledge. Something else that surprised me, is that, at times, I became aware Jesus speaks through me while giving advice. There were times, I said things I never thought of, and was surprised at how tender and loving I spoke, while at the same time wisdom came out of my mouth I didn't expect. Truly, it was not me, but the Lord. God used me, a miserable instrument, to bestow His infinite and incomprehensible mercy on souls, who, in their sinfulness, trusted in His mercy. At times, people would tell me, after they went to confession, how the Lord spoke to them, through me, but at those times, I was unaware of it.

Amazingly, if I happen to know the penitent, I rarely remembered their sins. Some priests call it "holy amnesia". I truly would not remember, nor did I want to remember, and was happy I didn't. By hearing confessions, it has helped me to confess my sins better.

At times, people who have been away from confession for a long period of time, might say something like, "I'm a good person. I keep all the commandments. The only sin I can remember is I lied once." For the first ten years as a priest, my response to something like that, was usually, "I encourage you to make an examination of conscience at the end of every day, and ask God for forgiveness. When you begin to go to confession monthly, you will have a list of sins to tell the priest."

While this wasn't bad advice, I could have given better advice, helping the penitent examine their conscience while in confession. For example, I could have gone through the Ten Commandments and asked questions. When I began hospital ministry, I learned how successful this method can be in helping people make a good confession. I wish I would have used this method as a young priest.

Occasionally, I heard something that caused deep grief and pain as I felt so bad for the person confessing, it caused me to later weep about it. When these things happened, I prayed much for the person, and sometimes even offered a Mass for a special intention, which was for the person whom I heard their confession. God knows the crosses placed on the shoulders of priests in confession, but He gives us the grace to carry them, and turn to Him, trusting in His love and mercy.

Something people don't think about, is that we priests who hear confessions go to confession to other priests. Ever since I was a religious brother, which began in 1993, I confess weekly, and after I became a priest, I continued this practice. Some priests would not give me any advice in confession, as they believe they shouldn't give advice to another priest, because they felt each priest should already know about how to overcome certain sins, but I never liked that. I believe the Lord uses priests to speak to the penitents, including other priests.

Sadly, some priests do not use the proper absolution, and rush through the sacrament. It is very common for some priests to say a formula like this, "I absolve you of your sins, Father, Son, Holy Spirit." But this is not the proper formula. The proper formula is, "I absolve you from your sins, in the name of the Father and of the Son and of the Holy Spirit." When I mentioned to priests, their erroneous words of absolution, a few scolded me for suggesting such a thing. At times, I would re-confess my sins to another priest for fear the absolution may not have been valid. I learned to confess to younger priests, who were more apt to say the words properly. But if they didn't, I would feel more at ease in reminding them to use the proper formula, if they failed to say it as required by the Church.

#54 EUCHARISTIC SACRILEGES AT ST. GERTRUDE

Eucharistic Horror at St. Gertrude During the Year of the Eucharist

Over a period of three months, after Mass, parishioners kept finding Hosts in hymnals. Twenty-two Hosts were found in hymnals, and an additional Host was found under a pew in the back of the Church. Then on Christmas Day, a Host was found in the parking lot. The three priests of the parish were very upset by all this, and it caused tension between us. At the Pastoral Council meeting, I suggested we purchase security cameras to see who was doing it. But, a council member said, "That's a waste of money for such a purpose" and the pastor sided with her.

We started to preach about how seriously sinful it is to remove a Host out of one's mouth, and place it in a hymnal. All three priests preached on the subject, but it continued.

Finally, the pastor spoke to the Administrator of the Diocese, since we were without a bishop, and asked how we should respond. It was agreed at all Masses we would tell the people, whoever is doing this is automatically excommunicated. The two associates, Fr. Anthony Birkenstock and I, hoped the diocese would temporarily not permit Communion in the hand, but that would never happen. We were to read a prepared statement from the Diocesan Administrator.

When I read the statement from the pulpit that was prepared by the Administrator, without thinking, I extemporaneously said, "If this does not stop, it's possible Holy Communion in the hand could be temporarily discontinued." The administrator's sister who attended the Mass thought I said, "Communion in the hand will be discontinued." which I didn't say. I really didn't think about it, before I said it. I should have only read the statement without a comment on my part. I received a letter of reprimand from the Diocesan Administrator indicating what I said, was not what he said. And I had no right to change what was said. That was my first experience of how people in the chancery treated priests. He never called me to ask about what happened or asked what I said. I could not defend myself. I felt thrown under the bus. And this throwing under the bus would become a habitual thing that would happen through my entire priesthood. Yes, I made a mistake, but how nice it would have been, if we could have just talked about it, and if I was allowed to explain what happened, and even apologize for it. But, it was good for my proud soul to be reproved.

Fr. Bill Cody told me to burn the dried-up Hosts removed from the hymnal and then bury them. The Hosts were attached to pages from the hymnal, because they were first placed in someone's mouth, then removed from their mouth, and placed in a hymnal. I carefully removed the Host, as well as I could, and then consumed it.

Since I was only ordained a few months, not thinking things out, and doing what my pastor suggested, I took a match and started to burn the paper attached to the Host, and then immediately realized this was not right, and stopped. I don't believe any Host was actually burned. From then on, I removed the Host to the best of my ability, consumed it, then soaked the paper in a bucket of water, and then buried the paper. The incident of burning the paper caused grief in my heart for many years. I wondered if particles of the Host were burned. Poor Jesus, being treated so cruelly by a parishioner, and also a priest! First, He is taken out of the Communicant's mouth, and then stuffed in a hymnal to be found by an unsuspecting parishioner, who would be shocked by it all. Then a stupid priest, who did what he was told, without thinking, treated the Lord so terribly.

Did I burn my Lord? Was I excommunicated? Oh, the interior anguish, for years I suffered from this. After mauling over this many times, I believe what actually happened, was no Host, nor any particle were actually burned. The pastor meant well, but it was certainly wrong advice.

We can burn religious objects, and bury them, but never the Sacred Host because the Host is a living person, Jesus Christ, the Son of God. After confessing this to a canon lawyer, I finally had peace, knowing I was not excommunicated, since my intention wasn't to purposely harm the Sacred Host and didn't know if any particle was actually burned.

In the end, we thought, perhaps the person who was treating the Hosts sacrilegiously was either mentally ill, or, some young person, who did not understand what they were doing. To our relief, it finally stopped. I offered Masses of reparation, and asked parishioners to come to the Adoration Chapel and make reparation for these sacrilegious occurrences. Surely, the devil was behind this terrible sacrilege.

#55 PARISH HEARTACHES AND GRACES AT ST. GERTRUDE

Harry Potter Books and the Diocesan Superintendent of Catholic Schools
A parishioner told me the school library at St. Gertrude had the collection of *Harry Potter Books* and wanted to know if I could do something about it. I had previously read how Cardinal Ratzinger, the head of the Congregation of the Faith, and also Fr. Gabriel Amorth, the chief exorcist in Rome, warned parents that children should not read these books. Therefore, I naively decided to send a letter to Mr. Verbose, the Superintendent of Catholics Schools for the Diocese, asking him to tell pastors of parishes to remove these books from the school libraries. He responded with a sharp letter, saying there was no problem with the books and I had overstepped by authority by making the suggestion.

Eventually, his vice superintendent resigned, and was replaced by a liberal democrat from Wheatland, who was favorable toward abortion. The vice superintendent was a parishioner of Immaculate Heart of Mary when I was pastor there.

Fire Alarms and Donuts Don't Mix

At St. Gertrude, fire alarms went off often in the middle of the night several times a month (24 times a year) and firemen with their trucks arrived to investigate. An emergency response phone worker from the fire and security system called the rectory to warn us of a possible fire. But there was never a fire. The alarm would go off by mice running through a room or balloons flying around due to the motion detector after weddings. I repeatedly asked church personnel for the fire alarm code, so I could shut off the alarm before the fire trucks arrived, but they would never give it to me.

We had our Pastoral Council meeting and during the meeting, we had donuts, which I heartily ate. It was a big mistake to eat the heavy sugar-coated donuts since I was a borderline diabetic. When it came to the discussion about the fire alarms, as the sugar increased, so did my temper. Finally, out of my mouth came, "I have repeatedly asked for the code to the fire alarm and no one ever gives it to me. Will you give me that damn code!" All were shocked, including Fr. Anthony Birkenstock and I. We later chuckled, as we surmised it was the result of the donuts. Church workers never gave me the code and when I was transferred to the next parish, at my farewell reception, I received an old fire alarm emergency handle as a gift.

St. Gertrude Sacristans

In the sacristy, I decided to discontinue using book matches to light candles and began to use stick matches, which were easier for the altar servers to light. When using the book matches, since they had little experience lighting them, some servers accidentally burned their fingers or dropped a lit match on the floor. The sacristan came in the sacristy and noticed the wooden strike matches and said, "Who got these?" I said, "I did. The altar servers burn their fingers and drop lit book matches on the floor since they don't know how to use them." She grabbed the wooden box of stick matches, threw it in the trash, saying, "We are not going to use those because we have always used book matches."

On another occasion, the sacristan noticed my new vestments made by nuns in Mexico. They were high quality, but inexpensive. However, she was unaware how much they cost. After noticing the new vestments, she pointed to my chalice, and said, "My, my, what an expensive chalice." I looked at her and said, "The Lord deserves the best. These vestments were made by nuns in Mexico for less than half of what they cost in the US." Then I said, "How much did you pay for your car?" She said, "I'm not telling." I said, "Well, this chalice cost $6,900 and was a gift from the people of the Church of the Ascension. I didn't ask them to buy the chalice. They did it on their own because they wanted me to have a new one. I would rather spend $6,900 for a chalice for the Blood of Jesus to rest, rather than $20,000 you spent on your car, to sit on your butt." My humility seemed non-existent, but I felt I defended the Lord. St. John Vianney would purchase expensive statues and vestments, while he went with little food and shabby clothes, since he also believed the Lord deserved the best. But, I doubt he would have responded as I.

5000 Plus Confessions St. Gertrude and St. Charles of Sezze Parish

The first three years of my young priesthood, I heard many confessions. I was assigned to the two largest parishes in the diocese, and on average, I heard ten confessions a day, except for my weekly day away from the parish. Priests were required by Bishop John Fidelity to take one day off a week from ministry to rest. And so, within three years, I heard well over 5,000 confessions. The longest I heard confessions in those three years were four continuous hours, and when the four hours were complete, I wasn't tired at all. Amazingly, God preserved my stamina. To me, hearing confessions is unlike performing other sacraments. For example, to offer two or three Masses in one day is very physically exhausting for me. I never tire of hearing confessions and believe it is a gift!

Strange Behavior of St. Gertrude Pastor at the Death of 16-year-old Boy

Just before I was transferred from St. Gertrude to St. Charles of Sezze parish, a couple from St. Gertrude invited me to their home for dinner. They had three boys. One died unexpectedly earlier in the year, before I was assigned to the parish. They told me their son died suddenly in his bedroom from a genetic abnormality. Furthermore, they called Fr. Bill Cody to come to their home when it happened. They said Fr. Cody asked them if he could wash the body of the 16 yr. old boy who had just died. The parents were shocked and traumatized by his death, and now their pastor wanted to remove his clothes and wash his body! They had no idea why in the world he wanted to do such a thing. There was no mention of fecal matter, that can at times, evacuate after death. There was also no mention of vomit associated with the incident. The parents didn't know why Fr. Cody wanted to wash the boy's body.

Due to their distress, they allowed him to do it, but later regretted it. I was so taken aback by what they said, I didn't know what to do, or what to say.

Finally, I said I thought it was very strange behavior and I had no idea why he would want to do such a thing. I didn't tell them, but I thought, maybe there was some morbid pedophile motivation by Fr. Cody.

#56 TRANSFERRED TO ST. CHARLES OF SEZZE PARISH

Transfer to St. Charles of Sezze Parish

At the end of every year, priests are asked to fill out a form from the bishop, and rate their satisfaction in their assignment, or if they want to move to another assignment, or express what sort of ministry he may be interested. When I filled out the form, I asked for a transfer. With the bizarre things the pastor was doing, and his failure to support me, as a young priest, I wanted a better experience, and to learn from a good and holy pastor, rather, then be shocked by his strange behaviors and be angered when thrown under the bus. Little did I know, the times I was thrown under the bus, God was preparing me to deal with the future or more of the same. Because I asked for a transfer, I felt I failed. After the bishop read my form, he indicated he wanted me to stay.

However, a scandal occurred at St. Charles of Sezze parish. It just so happened, by divine God's providence, a new priest was ordained in October. Consequently, on November 21st, (the Presentation of Mary), I was transferred to St. Charles of Sezze parish, and the new priest replaced me at St. Gertrude. When I was transferred to St. Charles in November 2006, the new pastor requested I lead and teach RCIA. It was an absolutely wonderful experience.

I was transferred because a priest associate at St. Charles of Sezze parish, who was teaching RCIA, had an affair with a married Catholic woman from the parish, causing her to obtain a divorce. He then left the priesthood and also the Catholic Church. He became an Orthodox priest and married her. This event caused great harm to the people of St. Charles, and especially the RCIA group he was teaching, along with the RCIA leaders. The people were confused, not only because he abandoned them, but also scandalously abandoned the Church. I felt totally inept, and didn't know how to deal with the scandal of a priest.

Before and even after I was transferred, the bishop, nor the pastor said anything about what had just happened in the parish. I ended up hearing about it from the leaders of RCIA and parishioners.

The Holy Name of Mary

"The angel Gabriel was sent from God to a town of Galilee called Nazareth, to a virgin betrothed to a man named Joseph, of the house of David, and the virgin's name was Mary." (Luke 1:26)

After I had left the Franciscans and was ordained a diocesan priest for the Diocese of Rolling Hills and due to the example of St. Louis Marie de Montfort, I added "Mary" to my middle name. Now my name became Fr. Leonard Joseph Anthony Denis Mary Gadfly. I wanted to make Her name part of mine in honor of, and in love of, Our Blessed Lady, who first loved me. Religious take on a new name to signify their devotion to a particular saint, and I thought there is no better saint than Mary to assist me with my priesthood and help me obtain heaven.

Invalid Marriages

"Any man, who divorces his wife, and marries another woman, commits adultery; and the man who marries a divorced woman, commits adultery." (Luke 16:18)

I started to look through the sacramental records of Catholics from the parish, because some parishioners and their non-Catholic spouses needed to obtain annulments of their marriages. It was then, I noticed a couple from the previous year, who became Catholic, but had not obtained an annulment. However, their marriage was recorded at St. Charles of Sezze without having obtained an annulment.

I met with the couple to find out what happened. The couple said the priest, who left the priesthood and the Church, witnessed their marriage in his office, without witnesses, and he had not applied for an annulment for them. Then, I found another couple who had a similar circumstance. But, they applied for their annulment, but it was refused by the tribunal office. The couple, whose annulment was refused, also had their marriage witnessed in the priest's office without any witnesses.

I found three invalid marriages recorded as sacramental marriages, and spoke with the pastor, who recommended I explain to the couples their marriages were invalid, they need to abstain from relations until their marriages could be witnessed properly in the Church, and to inform the bishop of the situation. Consequently, I sent the letter to Bishop Augustine Traditiones explaining what happened, but did not tell him the pastor asked me to tell the couples their marriages were invalid. The bishop phoned me and was furious. He said I never should have told the couples their marriages were invalid, and I should have left them in ignorance. I thought of telling the bishop the pastor asked me to do it. But to avoid getting him into trouble, I never said a word. My first year at St. Charles of Sezze parish, I felt like I was picking up pieces of glass, and would occasionally get cut by it. However, the Holy Spirit was working because all seemed to turn out well by the end of the year.

My second year at St. Charles was tremendously blessed. Over fifty men, women, and children were taking RCIA classes and wanted to become Catholic. At the beginning of the year, the team, and I consecrated RCIA to the Immaculate Heart of Mary and the Sacred Heart of Jesus, and the fruits were incredible!

Tragedies

I dealt with several tragedies at St. Charles of Sezze parish. The first tragedy occurred when I received an emergency call to come as soon as possible to anoint a man who was shot. The person who called said it just happened ten minutes before calling. It took about ten minutes to arrive, and therefore twenty minutes after it happened, I was on the scene.

A police officer said a man shot himself in the head in front of an eight-year-old girl, and his wife wanted a priest to anoint him. I went to the backyard, and he was lying on the ground with portion of his skull missing. He was dead. I spotted the fleshy chunk from his head lying against a nearby tree. The scene was strange, because there was no blood on the missing part of his head, nor on the portion blown off. Although shocked and horrified and since it is unknown how long the soul remains in the body, I anointed him, as I was told a priest can anoint a person up to thirty minutes after an apparent death. However, it was pretty obvious he was dead. I felt it was useless to anoint him, but because of the shock of it all, I did it anyway.

Knowing he killed himself in front of an innocent little girl, I became furious he would harm a child in such a manner. The uncanny thought occurred to kick his dead body because of what he did to the child. Of course, I didn't do such a thing. I then felt bad for having such a thought, and reminded myself only a mentally ill person could do something so horrible to a little girl, and his culpability is lessened because of his mental state.

The officer tried to make things better for the young girl, telling her he was shooting at a bird and accidentally shot himself. The wife didn't want to visit with me, so I departed the scene. The horror of it was seared into my mind, and the image was constantly before me at every waking moment for about a month. I prayed for his wife, the little girl, and for his soul. This event made me realize, how police, and EMTs have to witness these kinds of tragedies regularly, and must get traumatized by it. I know how it affected me. Finally, after about a month, and with prayer, the terrifying image in my mind slowly went away.

The second tragedy involved a plane accident that occurred when some youth and an adult parent were flying to a concert in another state. A sixteen-year-old boy had a pilot's license, and was flying the plane when the accident happened. Apparently, due to fog, the plane hit tops of trees and crashed. The adult father of the boy who was flying the plane died instantly. The boy piloting the plane was seriously injured. Several of his friends suffered broken bones, but were okay. Since it was night and foggy, searchers were unable to find the crash site until the sun rose in the morning. Because it was freezing weather, the boy who flew the plane, decided to lay on top of another boy to keep him warm. He died helping his friend to survive.

I was at the home of the wife and mother, when police came to tell her the news her husband and son died. It was devastating to her and her friends.

A few days later, when the bodies of her husband and son arrived at a Rolling Hills funeral home, the pastor suggested I go to the funeral home to be with the woman who wanted to see the bodies of her husband and son. When she opened the door of the room, she saw two opened caskets, looked at me, and said, "Which do I go to first?" Not knowing what to say, I said, "It doesn't matter. Perhaps go to your husband first." The poor lady sobbed and wailed at the site of her loved ones. It was a horrible sight to see. Amazingly, the event motivated her to grow in her faith, and she began to attend daily Mass. I admired her strong faith and witnessed how parishioners rallied around her. It was the first double funeral I concelebrated, but not the last.

Associate Priest Stealing Money

After a Sunday Mass, I went to the church office, and when I opened the door, I noticed an associate priest counting money. I thought it was odd. He quickly put the money in his pocket and left. A few weeks later, I again happened to come to the church office on a Sunday, and when I opened the door, he was again pocketing cash. He stared and gave me a stern look, but neither of us said anything.

I informed the pastor and mentioned, that I caught the other priest twice over the past several weeks, stealing money, but the pastor responded saying, "He's Mexican. He's probably getting extra cash to send home to his family. Let him have it." I was shocked by his response. Years later, the priest was caught stealing money in two different parishes where he had become pastor. The last time he was caught, he had to go to court. It became a scandal in the news. I wondered if the pastor from St. Charles had addressed the problem years ago, when I first told him about it, maybe the priest could have received help to deal with his stealing addiction.

Dream of "Ecce Homo"

Jesus therefore came forth, wearing the crown of thorns and the purple cloak. And he (Pilate), said to them, "Behold the Man!" (John 19:5)

As an associate at St. Charles of Sezze parish, one night, I had a dream. I saw Jesus as *Ecce Homo* (Behold the Man). His hands were bound with a rope. He had a crown of thorns on His head, and blood was flowing from His head, down to His face. He wore a red cloak, and His body was lacerated. I will never forget His sorrowful eyes. When I awoke, I wondered if I had offended the Lord so grievously and why I had such a dream. During this time, I was overeating much, and exercising to become more muscular, and suffered terribly from vanity.

Trip to the Holy Land

While at St. Charles of Sezze parish, I longed to go on pilgrimage to the Holy Land, but couldn't afford it. I recalled the many times Our Lady brought me to other places on the other side of the world, so I began to ask Her for help to go to the Holy Land. I then happen to run across a website asking for a priest to lead a pilgrimage to the Holy Land. They said it would be free, for the first priest who signed up, to be their chaplain for the trip. I called, signed up, and acquired a free trip to the Holy Land.

The trip was unbelievable. In the Holy Land, I literally walked in the footsteps of Jesus. I offered Mass in the Church of the Annunciation, and preached part of St. Bernard's sermon on the annunciation during the homily. I offered Mass at the Church of the Nativity at the side Chapel where St. Jerome translated the bible. It is also the place where the Holy Innocents were buried. There I offered Mass to close the abortion facility in Rolling Hills. The night before, I offered the Mass, I dreamt the abortionist at Rolling Hills repented. Before the dream, I didn't know the following day, we were to go to the Church of the Nativity.

A few days later, I offered Mass in the side Chapel at Calvary in the Church of the Holy Sepulcher and placed my hand in the hole, believed to be where the Cross of Jesus was planted on Calvary. I was moved to tears, when I touched that spot directly underneath the altar. The many sins of my past flooded my mind, and saw how I crucified the Lord, because of them.

When I offered Mass at the side altar on Calvary, during the homily, I preached on the Seven Last Words of Jesus. As I was preaching, it suddenly dawned on me, here, by God's power given to every priest, Calvary will become present on the altar, and at the same time, I was physically present at Calvary. How many would like to be in this holy location, but could never afford to travel here? Yet, at every Mass, all of us are truly there. Mass is the re-presentation (not representation) of Calvary.

During the pilgrimage, we rushed from place to place, and because of it, I felt like I didn't have the opportunity to meditate and ponder the events that occurred at the places we visited. But nevertheless, the Lord gave special graces.

We boarded a replica of a fishing boat from the time of Jesus on the Sea of Galilee. As we were boarding, suddenly a large dark shadow under the water near the boat came near us, and we became frightened. The guide told us it was a large school of fish. It reminded me of the event the apostles caught the miraculous fish that nearly broke the net. The trip was life changing. Everything came alive to be in the same places Jesus walked and lived. Thank you, Mary, for bringing me to the land of Jesus, your Son!

Down in Adoration Falling

I presided during a Holy Hour and had two 7th grade altar boys serving it. As we were kneeling at the beginning of Eucharistic Adoration, the boy to my right, suddenly fainted. He wasn't injured when he fell, but was a bit shook up. I whispered to him, to go to the server room, remove his alb, drink some water, and sit in a chair. After the Holy Hour was finished, I returned to the sacristy, and he was sitting in a chair. I said, "Are you okay? How are you feeling?" He said, "I'm doing fine now." He said, "I just did what we were supposed to do. When I fainted, I was "Down in Adoration falling." I thought his remarks were funny and witty. *Down in Adoration Falling* is the name of the ending hymn sung during Holy Hours.

#57 ANTI-ABORTION ACTIVITY

Novenas to Close Abortion Clinics & Our Lady of Guadalupe Prevents Clinic From Opening, Supreme Court Justice Novena

While at St. Gertrude, I decided to do a Novena of Holy Hours and Rosary with the people of the parish so that the president would choose a new Supreme Court justice who would be pro-life. On the last day of the Novena, Justice John Roberts was nominated by the president. It was announced by news outlets during the last Holy Hour that we, as a parish, prayed. For years, he seemed to support pro-life issues, but, later, his position apparently changed to pro-abortion.

Closing of the Broadway Street Abortion Clinic

In May 2005, I decided to ask parish secretaries throughout the diocese to include in their bulletins a nine-day novena-- praying the Rosary of Our Lady of Sorrows to close the abortion clinic on Broadway in Rolling Hills. The night before, I intended to notify *The Catholic Eagle* (our diocesan newspaper) about the novena, I had a terrible demonic experience. Thoughts kept coming into my mind all night, suggesting not to do the novena. Some thoughts made me think the bishop would be angry, the novena would be a waste of time, and pro-aborts would harm me, etc. Upon awakening the next morning, I was nearly convinced to not do it. But after praying, I decided to do it anyway. The novena was from May 17th to May 24th and was advertised in *The Catholic Eagle*. On the last day of the novena, May 24th, (former feast of Our Lady Help of Christians) the clinic closed for good. Thank you, Jesus, for answering our prayers, through the tears of Your Most Holy Mother.

The Closing of Schindler's Abortion Clinic

I began diocesan-wide novenas, with approval of the bishop, to close Schindler's Abortion Clinic. Parishes were asked to offer a Mass during the novena, such that, each day of the novena, at least one Mass would be offered. The response was greater than anticipated.

In parish bulletins, it asked lay people to pray a Rosary during the novena, go to confession, pray the Chaplet of Divine Mercy, attend daily Mass, to fast on Wednesdays and Fridays of the novena, and make a weekly Eucharistic Holy Hour. The last novena started on May 13th (feast of Our Lady of Fatima) 2009, and ended on Ascension Thursday (for the universal Church) of that year. During that novena, 33 Masses were offered by parishes throughout the diocese. But one parish, who wanted to participate in the novena, could not schedule a Mass during the nine days. They scheduled their Mass to close the clinic on May 31st. After the thirty-fourth Mass was offered, on May 31st, Pentecost Sunday that year, and also the Feast of Visitation of the Virgin Mary, Dr. Greg Schindler unexpectedly died.

Since the clinic was closed, due to his death, it did not allow pro-lifers to celebrate. The closing of the clinic on the day two unborn children are celebrated in the Church (Jesus, less than five days after conception, and John six months after conception) was certainly mysterious. The clinic remained closed for almost four years, but re-opened in April 2013.

Novena to Keep Abortion Clinic Closed and Statewide Novenas

There were rumors a local doctor wanted to re-open Schindler's Abortion Clinic. Consequently, I made sure several nine-day novenas of Masses occurred throughout the diocese. I sent out an email and letter to every parish in the state, asking all parishes to do a statewide novena to close all abortion clinics in Ohio. During that novena, over ninety Masses were offered throughout the state.

Our Lady of Guadalupe Prevents Dr. Morbid Fresien From Performing Abortions in Rolling Hills

Dr. Morbid Fresien, a local doctor, decided to perform abortions, and people began to pray outside her office building. Turning to Our Lady for help, I went into the Cathedral, knelt down and prayed before the image of Our Lady of Guadalupe. I recalled watching the video, *The Living Bread*. It's about the fruits of Perpetual Adoration in San Antonio, TX.

In the video, it explained how a teenage girl intended to have an abortion, but her friend went to their Adoration Chapel during the time of her appointment, and prayed that her pregnant friend would change her mind. While adoring Jesus in the Eucharist, she asked Jesus to scare her out of it, if He had to. During the Holy Hour, the girl who was to have the abortion, became frightened when she saw the long needle, changed her mind, and immediately left the clinic. She later gave birth to a healthy little boy. Remembering this story, as I knelt before the image of Our Lady of Guadalupe, I asked Mary to not let Dr. Morbid Frisien perform abortions, and if needed to scare her out of it, if She had to.

In December, I attended a pro-life prayer vigil in front of Dr. Frisien's office building. We prayed the Rosary and sang hymns. When it was finished, I went to a Catholic religious store and purchased a few Christmas presents for my family. I noticed a statue of pregnant Virgin Mary sitting on a donkey and St. Joseph holding the leash. The image is called La Posada, which is a Mexican custom by which a couple represents Mary, who is pregnant with Child, and Joseph knocking on the door of the church on Christmas Eve in imitation of the Holy Family trying to find room in an inn. The statue was created to represent this event. When I saw the statue, it occurred to me, I could purchase it, wrap it as a Christmas present, to send to Dr. Morbid Frisien requesting that she not perform abortions. I mailed the package with the statue to her office, and wrote a friendly note wishing her Merry Christmas, asking her to not perform abortions. I wrote my name on the box with the return address of the Cathedral, where I was assigned as an associate.

A week later, I presided at a funeral located at St. Veronica in Brushwood. As the funeral was ending, and as I was walking to my car to drive to the cemetery, a policeman in an undercover vehicle came up to me, and said I needed to call a police officer in Rolling Hills. I had no idea why, and worried something may have happened to a family member. When I called the officer, he asked if I sent a package to Dr. Morbid Frisien, and, I said, "Yes". He said, "You need to come and open it now." I said, "I can't, I'm in Brushwood about to perform a burial at the cemetery." He said, "You don't understand, this is official police business, and besides that, the entire block is cordoned off. The SWAT team is here!" He said, "What's in the package?" I said, "A statue of Jesus, Mary, and Joseph with a note wishing the doctor Merry Christmas, and asking her to not perform abortions." I was horrified they thought the package had a bomb in it, and perceived it as a bomb threat. He said, "Don't worry about it, when you get back to Rolling Hills, we will have police officers come visit you." I said, "Please tell everyone, I am sorry. I had no idea this would happen." In my mind I pictured local news stations showing the doctor's office cordoned off, and my picture and name blasted on the bottom of TV. I decided to immediately drive back to Rolling Hills after the burial, and go to the chancery and explain to the bishop what happened.

On my way back, as I was praying the Rosary, my cell phone rang, and it was Bishop Augustine Traditiones. Raising his voice, he said, "Fr. Gadfly! What is going on!" I played stupid, a really dumb thing to do, and said, "I'm at St. Veronica in Brushwood, and I just finished a funeral." He said, "You know what I am talking about!" I said, "Yes, bishop, I do. I was on my way to come to the chancery, and immediately tell you what happened." After I explained everything, there was silence on the phone, and I thought we lost our cell connection. I kept saying, "Bishop, are you there? Bishop, are you there?" Finally, he said, "Yes, I'm here. I don't think you did anything wrong." I let go, a sigh of relief, and he said, "When you hear from the police, call me, and let me know what they say." I said, "Okay." He then said, "When you get back to the Cathedral, you need to talk to the staff because they are upset. There were multiple police officers looking for you, and they didn't say why they were searching for you." When I returned to the Cathedral, I found out the secretary, cook, and a priest associate was questioned by police. I explained to them what happened. The police asked the employees at the Cathedral, if I was acting strange lately. All said, "No". However, Fr. Brendan O' Malley told the police, "Not any stranger than usual." I thought what he said was humorous.

A few weeks after the police event, at Midnight Mass, I planned on concelebrating the Holy Sacrifice of the Mass with the bishop at the Cathedral. Just before Mass, when the Bishop walked up to me, I said to him, "Bishop, the police are here. They want to take me away." With a shocked look on his face, he said, "Really?" I said, "No, I'm just kidding!" He responded in a way I didn't anticipate. With a furious look on his face he screamed, "Oh!"

During the homily of that midnight Mass, he accidentally referred to Jesus as a human person, which is not theologically true. Jesus is a divine person, with both a human and divine nature. I decided it would be best to not correct him after Mass. The baby Jesus gave me a Christmas gift that year. He taught me prudence, and Dr. Morbid Frisien changed her mind and decided to not perform abortions. In my opinion, Our Lady of Guadalupe scared her out of it.

Novena to Close Abortion Clinic
Aug. 14th (St. Maximilian Kolbe) to Aug. 22nd (Queenship of Mary) 2019

During abortion novenas, there were always four things that happened. 1. There is a demonic attack. 2. Something bad would happen to someone in the family. 3. I developed a potential personal health crisis. 4. I have some sort of problem with the bishop. This novena was no different.

As the Novena progressed, I felt anxious while praying my personal daily Holy Hours before Jesus in the Blessed Sacrament. Every day, the anxiety seemed to worsen.

However, when sitting in a chair, I decided to pray a prayer from the book, *Prayers Against the Powers of Darkness.* I prayed, "…I pray, I may not be shrouded in the darkness of demons, but always seen to stand in the bright light of the freedom that I received from you. Through Christ, Our Lord." As I prayed this prayer, my body began to convulse; my arms and legs became stiffer than a board, and my limbs turned in-- towards each of them. Then a demon screamed. I grabbed a Holy Water bottle, and before I sprinkled it, a demon screamed, "No! No!" When I poured the holy water on my head, the demon screamed ever more violently. It immediately departed. My body returned to normal. To say the least, I was terrified.

During that week, a close relative attempted suicide. Then later, I found out another close relative attempted suicide. A priest, who was pastor of Immaculate Heart of Mary called me. He said when he met with the bishop about problems with his current assignment, the bishop made a negative comment about me, saying, "The people are afraid that I might close the parish, especially because of all that happened when Fr. Gadfly was pastor." I had a health scare caused by fainting spells, when I moved my head, looking up. I was referred by my doctor to a cardiologist, and after tests, the cardiologist said the heart monitor I had worn for several weeks indicated I needed a pacemaker due to bradycardia (too slow of a heart beat). But this information was not correct. In fact, I did not need a pacemaker. The doctor is known for putting pacemakers in patients who don't need them. A different cardiologist believed I had a blood vessel blockage in my brain, but that was not the cause either. A neurosurgeon believed I had "Bow Hunters Syndrome", where a blood vessel in the neck gets kinked, and can cause a person to faint when the head and or neck move in the wrong way. Only God knew what was causing it. A few months later, the problem went away after I used the Discernment of Spirits prayer method.

#58 WEDDINGS

The Joy of Weddings
"Husbands, love your wives, as Christ loved the church and gave himself up for her..." (Ephesians 5:25)

Every wedding is memorable in its own way. Here are a few examples I will use to highlight how some weddings are more memorable than others.

The first wedding I witnessed was at St. Gertrude. Something happened at the wedding I later used an example during marriage preparation classes of what not to do during the ceremony. At the wedding, Lachelle and Armond exchanged vows and entered into Holy Matrimony.

During their marriage preparation, I warned the couple to not allow the best man to hold the wedding rings before they were needed at the ceremony, especially if he might do a shenanigan with them. I suggested the rings be placed on top of the altar before Mass. But they said they trusted the best man.

During the ceremony, when it came time to bless the rings, I asked the best man to hold them out for me to bless them. But, he said, "Oh no. I can't find them". He pretended to rustle through his pockets, searching for the rings. The groom knew he had them, and angrily shouted before the whole congregation, "Will you give me the damn rings!" Some in the assembly chuckled, but others were unhappy with the groom's anger, and the best man's behavior.

Another wedding I witnessed at St. Gertrude was between two lawyers. During their marriage prep, I warned them to not kiss lustfully after they exchanged their vows, since some don't like it. I said, "Just give each other a nice peck." But they didn't. In fact, it was quite embarrassing the way they kissed each other in church, causing some people in attendance to whistle. Others didn't like the whistling and expected kissing to be reverent while in church. When the wedding concluded and the couple were greeting people in the gathering space, a little old lady (probably Italian) came up to the groom, and forcefully slapped him in the face. She said, "You should know better than doing that, in church!" Since then, I always tell couples, during marriage preparation, the story of the little old lady.

The wedding of Kateri and Todd Rodriguez at Immaculate Heart of Mary in Wheatland went well during Mass, except during the homily. As I was preaching, I noticed some people were looking at me, and laughing, and then more and more began to laugh. I couldn't figure out what was going on. I hadn't said anything different, then at any other wedding. Realizing their laughing had something to do with what was behind me, I turned around, and noticed a bird flew in the church, and landed on a light chandelier directly behind where I was preaching at the ambo. I went to the sacristy located near the sanctuary, opened the door, and the bird immediately flew out. I looked at the people, and said, "A bird came to witness the love-birds." After the Mass, everyone kept saying it was a sign for the couple. One non-Catholic couple and their children who attended the wedding, were so moved by the experience, they decided to leave the Methodist Church and become Catholic. The following year, the whole family entered the church. God works in mysterious ways, even through a bird at a wedding.

Many priests refer to Bridezilla, the bride who forcefully dominates every detail of the wedding. I only had one Bridezilla, and she was at St. Veronica in Brushwood. At the wedding rehearsal, I started to explain to the wedding party what we were going to do during the wedding, where they would sit, and when and how they were to come forward, etc. But no, Bridezilla took over. She told me when and where I was to stand, and had every detail of the wedding completely planned out. I looked at her poor future husband, and thought, "Man, that fella does not have a chance. He's more of a man than me to marry her."

After the last marriage prep class with the couple, I always took the couple out for dinner at a restaurant, as a celebration for finishing their classes, and then would find out where they were planning to go for their honeymoon.

One newlywed couple was poor. He had just signed up as a soldier in the US Army, and she had a low paying job. Other than having a wedding dance, or wedding reception, they had a cookout at her parents' house. The young man was shy, and the young girl was not. When they took the Marriage Preparation Test, they only missed one question, so I presumed they cheated. Never had any couple ever missed just one question, and in fact, most missed about ten questions. So, I asked, "How is it, you only missed one question on the test?" Normally, he never spoke, and always let her talk, but this time he spoke up, and said, "Father, we never talked about the test at all. We have a good relationship. She asks me questions, and I give her the answers. And in this way, we get to know each other well."

Once, when I was preparing a couple for marriage, the future groom said, "Father, I read the vows and there is something missing." I said, "What's missing?" He said, "It doesn't say obey. She is supposed to obey me." I said, "Both of you, are to obey each other." He said, "No, she is the woman, and she is supposed to obey me, the man." I tried to explain, but to no avail, that in marriage each is supposed to sacrifice their will for the other. But his mind could not be changed, at least before marriage.

Before I was a priest, I went to Medjugorje for a second time, and was present at a wedding of one of the visionaries. During the wedding, as they exchanged their vows, they held a crucifix between their hands, a Croatian custom. Doing so, is a reminder of

157

the love Jesus has for them, that He should be at the center of their marriage, and that love is sacrificial.

Every couple I witnessed their marriage, I always asked if they would like to hold a crucifix when they exchanged their vows, and suggested they place it on the wall next to their wedding picture, as a reminder of the need to forgive each other, and love each other sacrificially, as Jesus laid down His life for His bride, the Church. Most couples, even non-Catholics, wanted to exchange their vows holding a crucifix that I gave them as a gift and I made a suggestion to the couples to honor the Virgin Mary with some flowers. At times, I provided a Consecration prayer to consecrate their marriage to the Virgin Mary. When they were to pray before the statue of Mary, I made the suggestion that the cantor sing the Ave Maria.

Many priests mourned the fact, either the bride, groom, or someone in the wedding party would faint during the ceremony. This has never happened for any wedding I witnessed, and that's because the Lord gave me the "secret" to prevent it. The secret is food. I told every couple, if they don't want anyone fainting during the wedding, they need to be sure everyone eats something two hours before the wedding. I strongly requested the bridal party get together a few hours before the wedding, and eat pizza, sandwiches, or hamburgers, but never pasta. Pasta can cause blood sugar fluctuations, which can cause some to faint.

#59 SACRAMENT OF THE SICK

The Sacrament of the Sick – Sad Lesson and Amazing Healings
"Are there sick people among you? Let them send for the priests of the Church, and let the priests pray over them anointing them with oil in the name of the Lord. The prayer of faith will save the sick persons. If they have committed any sins, their sins will be forgiven them." (James 5:14-15)

Ordained only a few months, I was asked by the pastor of St. Gertrude to visit a woman at her home who had terminal cancer, anoint her, and give her Holy Communion. When I arrived, the woman appeared healthy, and we had a nice talk. She didn't even look sick. I anointed her, and gave her Holy Communion. The following day, she died. I was shocked by her sudden death, and realized I didn't administer Viaticum with the Apostolic Pardon. I erroneously believed the Apostolic Pardon should not be given unless the sick person was immediately dying. I prayed much for her soul. Ever since that happened, anytime it became known to me that if someone was terminal, or whose life was seriously threatened, I gave the Apostolic Pardon with Holy Communion, as Viaticum.

At seminary, we were taught the Sacrament of the Sick can do three things: give the person grace to endure their sufferings; forgive sins if they are unconscious or conscious but unable to confess; and if it would be for the good of their soul, Jesus may physically heal the person.

During the first nineteen years of my priesthood, nine people had immediate healing from receiving the Sacrament of Anointing of the Sick. A high school girl kept passing out during physical activity such as sports. The doctor in Brushwood discovered she had a problem with her heart. On their way to Charity Children's Hospital, in Ohio City, Ohio, her parents and their daughter stopped by the church and I anointed her. When the tests were completed in Ohio City, the doctors said, the girl had nothing wrong with her heart. The doctor in Ohio City accused the doctor in Brushwood of sending the wrong test results, since he said the girl's heart was totally fine. After that, the girl never had heart problems, nor with fainting again while doing sports activities.

A man developed a severe infection in his body and blood. I believe it was called septic. The doctor told the family, he had only a 30% chance to live. I anointed him and gave him the Apostolic Pardon. Knowing him, I noticed when I visited him in the ICU, he didn't look himself. His body was swelled, and his face had a bluish green color. I prayed with the family and departed, but decided to return the next day because I thought he may die soon, and believed the family would need consolation. But, when I arrived at the hospital, and came to his room, he was awake and talking. At first, I thought I had the wrong room. He looked like a different person because all the swelling was gone, and his face looked normal, as though not even sick. When I arrived, he said, "Hi, father! How are you?" Dumbfounded, I didn't know what to say. Without telling him he looked like he was dying yesterday, and now today he looked fine, I quipped, "I'm great, and you look good today." When I visited with his daughter, I asked if the doctor gave him a different antibiotic, and she said, "No, all the infection went away on its own. His white count is normal. The doctor said he has never seen anyone improve so rapidly, and the only explanation is that a miracle occurred." I said to the daughter, "Yes, Jesus healed your dad through the Sacrament of the Sick."

A woman with alcohol poisoning passed out, while outside, during 100-degree temperatures, and was unconscious. She had severe sunburn, but that was not the worst of her problems. The doctor informed her boyfriend she was brain-dead and suggested he allow the nurse to disconnect the ventilator, to allow her to die. I anointed her and gave her the Apostolic Pardon. The man decided to wait a few days, and thanks be to God, he did. The day after I anointed her, she woke up, and I heard her confession. Within three days, her only medical issue, when dismissed, was sunburn. This is one reason, why I have difficulty with doctors declaring a patient brain-dead, and encouraging the patient's family to remove medical care.

#60 FUNERALS

The Misery of Funerals

"The Lord is my shepherd, I shall not want; he makes me lie down in green pastures. He leads me beside still waters; He restores my soul. He leads me in paths of righteousness for his name's sake. Even though I walk through the valley of the shadow of death, I fear no evil; for thou art with me; thy rod and thy staff, they comfort me." (Psalm 23:1-4)

While ministering to families of deceased loved ones, I felt like a true shepherd helping poor suffering sheep, mourning the loss of a loved one. However, funerals often times caused me misery and anxiety. People want to do the oddest things during funerals to try to grasp onto something from the deceased whom they deeply cared for, and they struggle to let go. Ordained just months prior at one of my first funerals, just before the funeral was to begin, a family member walked up to me with a giant metal sign, that said, *Dave's Washing Machine Service*. The sign was about four feet by six feet. They wanted the sign and the deceased man's fishing equipment brought up in a procession during the offertory.

Since the funeral was just about to begin, and as a new priest, I was flabbergasted and thought, "I know, I will tell the pastor, and he will bail me out by telling the family it can't be carried up during Mass".

I quickly went to the office of the pastor, and explained what they were asking, and, he said, "Oh, father, as a new priest, you must learn that you have to always give the family what they want at a funeral; otherwise, they will remember the bad priest, who caused them to leave the Church." From the time the funeral Mass began, until the offertory, I kept wondering what I was going to do with the sign as they carried it up. If I set against the altar, that would be disrespectful to the Eucharist, and would prevent people from seeing the top of the Altar. If I put it behind the Altar against the wall near the Tabernacle, that too would be disrespectful, and people would look at it, rather than looking at the Holy Sacrifice on the Altar. I prayed intensely, begging the Lord to help me to know what to do. Then, just as it was handed to me, I realized I could just lay it on the floor under the Altar, and so I did.

At a Rosary Vigil, for a different funeral, the family wanted to play a song on a CD player. Of course, the pastor said they can play what they want. Assuming it was going to be a Christian song, without finding out the name of it, before playing it, I told the family they could play the CD, and it would be mic'd, so it could be heard over loudspeakers. After the Rosary, they turned on the CD player and, suddenly, I heard, "We don't need no education. We don't need no thought control." It was Pink Floyd's "Another Brick in the Wall". I felt sad I allowed such a song to be played in the house of God.

On another occasion, a woman died, and the family was poor. Only the son and a few relatives came to the Rosary Vigil, with the embalmed body of his mother to view. That night, the mortuary cremated the body. The next day, the son was to bring the urn to the church for the funeral, but he was late. I wondered what had happened. Finally, he arrived, looking pale, and he said, "Father, I am sick to my stomach. This morning, when I went to pick up the urn, it was still hot from the remains. I felt like I burned my mother's body, and I just kept vomiting because of it." The poor young man was beside himself.

The day after the funeral, he called, and said, "They won't let me on the airplane with the urn. They want me to open it up, and look inside. I started crying, telling them it was mother's ashes. Finally, they let me on the plane without opening it. Now I am in Phoenix, and we want to bury Mom tomorrow, but they want hundreds of dollars, and I can't afford the cemetery plot. What do I do?" Not knowing what to say, I immediately said a prayer to Jesus. Then I said, "I am so sorry, you are going through all this. Do you have enough money to purchase a small shovel?" He said, "Yes." I said, "Well, when you are sure no one is looking, dig a hole about three feet deep above your father's casket, and then bury the urn in the hole." I said, "And if you get caught, please let me know." The young man called me back a day later, and said, he buried his mother without any problems.

When I was an associate at St. Charles of Sezze parish, I had the funeral of an elderly woman, who was a devout Catholic. At the end of the funeral, a daughter wanted to speak, and I presumed it would be another eulogy, which are not to be given at funerals; and so, I tried to discourage her from doing so. But, she said, (as many others have said), "The pastor from my parish lets us do it." Since there was no diocesan rule, and since they certainly wouldn't support an associate priest refusing them to give a eulogy, I went ahead and let her speak. She began making subtle negative comments about her siblings, and when she finished, she invited everyone to accept Jesus Christ as their personal Lord and Savior. She closed her little talk by telling everyone the location of her non-Catholic church, and invited all to join it. Furthermore, she was a fallen away Catholic, who "discovered Christ" in a non-Catholic church.

All eyes were on me, as to what I was going to say or do, and I stood up, and said, "Let us pray". Then I gave the final commendation, as though I never heard what she said.

After the funeral Mass, Catholics said they thought I handled it well. I thought it would be better to not bring any more attention to it, which later seemed prudent.

When I was assigned as pastor of St. Veronica in Brushwood City and St. Anthony in Jericho City, within a year, I had twelve funerals, four times the number as usual at that parish within a year. Due to the many deaths, a home-bound lady, whom I brought Holy Communion weekly, said to me, "Father, we want you to leave our parish. We believe you are bad luck, since so many people have died from our church." The funny thing was she wasn't kidding. And so, I said to her, "I am sorry, so many have died, but I haven't killed anyone. It makes me wonder who will be next. How's your health?" She did not know what to say, and was thinking, I may have cursed her or something, but then she said, "Oh, you're kidding, right?" I said, "Sweetheart, only God knows why He called so many home from St. Veronica. Perhaps, He wanted them all in heaven to enjoy each other's company."

I received a phone call about a woman from the parish of St. Veronica who died. The family said they wanted to delay the funeral until the July 4th weekend, so the entire family could come together to enjoy their time, out at the lake. When the weekend arrived, the family brought the urn to the church, and placed it near the Altar for the funeral. They said they wanted to scatter the ashes, but I told them it was forbidden by the Church; otherwise, we could not have a funeral Mass.

After the funeral, the family wanted a private burial, which they wanted two hours after the funeral. When I arrived at the cemetery, a hole had been dug. I then waited for someone to bring the urn.

Finally, the deceased's son came up to me, handed me a small pill box, and said, "Here's Mom". I said, "Where's the urn?" He said, "We decided we wanted to keep the urn, and so we put all the ashes in here." I thought to myself, "There is no way, all the ashes would fit in that small box." I shook my head in disbelief, and let them know, not by words, but by my motions, I didn't believe them. I was tempted to open the pill box, and give a good blow to an empty box. I went ahead and did the burial of the pill box and surmised they were probably going to scatter the ashes.

Another funeral at St. Veronica in Brushwood was a disaster. The family had a priest friend from another diocese who wanted to be the main celebrant of the funeral. Being a young pastor, I chose to allow him to be the main celebrant, while I concelebrated. During the consecration, the priest held the host in his hands, and moving his hands in a semicircle (not proper according to the rubrics), he said, "Take this all of you and eat of it, for this is OUR body, which will be given up for you." He altered the proper words of consecration which should have been, "This is my body, which will be given up for you." I was shocked and didn't know what to do during Mass. Should I stop the Mass and tell him to re-say the proper words. I kept silent and later notified his bishop. Was it valid? I was later told if a concelebrant says the proper words, when the celebrant fails to say them correctly, it's valid. Only proper Church authority can determine if that would be the case. As soon, as I was able, I re-offered the Mass privately for the soul of the person who died. I was told by a priest friend, the pastor should not allow a priest, who he doesn't know, to be the main celebrant of his own parish. I can see why. I prayed much for the priest and hoped and prayed it was a valid Mass.

There was a woman I gave weekly Communion at her home. Because she was home-bound, she asked me if it was okay if she could be cremated, as she couldn't afford a regular funeral. I told her it was okay, as long as she believed in the resurrection of the body, and the ashes would not be scattered. She agreed. After I was transferred to another parish, I later learned of her passing, and no one contacted me about her death, until about two years later. The family called, and said, "We don't know what to do. We can't find Mom's ashes." Finally, after conducting a diligent search, they found the urn. It was on the fireplace mantle, but they thought it was just a regular jug. We had the funeral and burial, and she was finally laid to rest. Thanks be to God, not long ago, the Vatican came out with new guidelines requesting the funeral and burial, be conducted in a timely manner after death.

#61 TRIED TO GET MY BROTHER A NEW JOB BY WRESTLING

Wrestle My Brother For A New Job
"Someone wrestled with him until the break of dawn." (Exodus 32:25)

When my brother, Louis, and I were young (roughly he was 6, and I was 12) occasionally, we wrestled on a mattress. Since I was six years older than him, and unbeatable in PE (physical education) at wrestling while in grade school, I could always easily beat Louis. He had in mind, that someday when we were older, he would be strong enough to pin me down.

After I was ordained for about four years, when I was assigned to St. Charles of Sezze parish in Rolling Hills, I was greatly tempted to vanity and worldly appearance. I gained weight due to a lack of exercise, and I purposely over-ate, since I believed I was skinny, and didn't want to look that way. I believe this was due to the girl, who made fun of me in 3rd grade. Over the years, even though I wasn't skinny, I perceived I was, and fell into the temptation of being jealous of the appearance of other men. I decided to exercise by doing push-ups, and other types of exercises. I kept gaining weight with fat and muscle. After about a year, I went from 165 pounds to 185 pounds. During this time, my brother was working as a security guard at the Ohio State Mental Hospital for the criminally insane. A small man, he weighed 125 lbs.

When I prayed for him, I kept thinking someday, he's going to get attacked, and could get killed at his job, he's too small to be doing that kind of work, and so, occasionally, I reminded him to look for a different job. He agreed, but, he said, "I'm trained in self-defense. I can handle myself, and them too." I said, "These men are criminally and mentally insane, and any man over 200 lbs. can easily hurt you. Because of their mind, they can be unusually strong and fearless." But he disagreed, saying he was trained, and the security guards would help each other, if attacked.

I went to visit Louis at his home and brought up the subject to try to convince him to get a different job. He showed me some of his moves to defend himself. He said, "I'll show you. I can put you in moves you can't get out of." He said, "I want to wrestle. I can beat you!" I didn't think it was a good idea and thought a priest shouldn't be wrestling; it's not dignified. But then, I thought of Jacob in the Old Testament, and since he's my brother, I didn't believe it was morally wrong, and perhaps could use it to convince him to get a different job. I removed my clerical shirt and collar. Wearing my white t-shirt and black pants, we wrestled. I was surprised at my strength, and his too. He put me in one of his new holds, and I was unable to move much at all. But I just kept flexing my arms and chest, and with all my strength, tried to get out of the hold, until finally, it happened. I overpowered him by sheer strength, and freed myself from the hold, which caused him to lose confidence. I don't know how much I could bench press at the time, but most likely I could bench my weight of 185 pounds. I found myself picking the little man of 125 pounds over my head and realized at that moment I could accidentally hurt him, and then slowly put him down, and forced him to the ground. His arms were pinned, he couldn't move, and I said, "You have to quit your job." "If I, who am a priest, and who am gentle, could easily pin you down, and could have thrown you across the room, how much more could that happen to you, at your work?" He agreed, and said he was going to get a different job.

Sadly, he didn't do it in time. Six months later, on Ash Wednesday, he was attacked by a two-hundred pound criminally insane prisoner, and received a traumatic brain injury and a broken shoulder. When the prisoner attacked Louis, another security guard came to help him, but my brother was knocked to the ground, and both fell on my brother's head. Almost four-hundred pounds came crashing on his head. When he and I wrestled, I truly believed the Lord was trying to warn him, and did not want that to happen. Due to his injuries, Louis was no longer able to work, and was permanently disabled.

#62 FRANCISCANS OF THE MOST PURE HEART OF MARY

A Call to Join the Franciscans of the Most Pure Heart of Mary?

During my time at St. Charles of Sezze Parish, I absolutely enjoyed serving as an associate pastor there. The office staff were very helpful and welcoming. The pastor was helpful and gave good example. The other associate and I got along well. The school was large, and filled with children who enjoyed growing in their faith. But deep down, I felt a call to religious life, one that never seemed to go away. After speaking about it with my spiritual director, he suggested I mention the desire to become a religious to Bishop Augustine Traditiones, and my spiritual director encouraged me to follow through with the desire. I received permission from the bishop to join the Franciscans of the Most Pure Heart of Mary. They were much more austere than the Franciscans of Perpetual Victim Martyrs, and more contemplative. They were orthodox "truly Catholic" and faithful to the Church in their teachings, a rarity among religious orders.

As a postulant, I learned the importance of doing penance in the life of a priest, and also developed a greater devotion to the Blessed Virgin Mary. A few of their priests unknowingly developed the Jesuit way of preaching theology. But, rather than doing it in a liberal way, they promoted what I called "high theology", which the average Catholic would not understand, and in my opinion, caused more confusion among the faithful. That kind of theology was not for me, and although I realized not all were like that, it caused me to be uncomfortable with the religious order, and I felt I had to leave.

During the 6 months I was at the religious order, I was able to offer Masses for my personal intentions. When I left the order, I had offered exactly 100 Masses to close the abortion clinic in Rolling Hills. And later, saw how the Lord used my interest in religious life to offer Masses to help save babies.

The Franciscans of Most Pure Heart of Mary (FMPHM), as a penance, scourged themselves on Fridays. I was not permitted to do it because I was a postulant. After leaving the Friars, with the permission of my spiritual director, I now scourge my back with a cord during the length of seven Hail Marys. I do it as a penance for my sins. It never draws blood, and just smarts a bit. I do it on Wednesdays and Fridays as well as abstain from meat on those days, and sometimes also fast on Wednesday and Friday. The Friars taught me the need for corporal penance for the sake of loving and appreciating the pain Jesus endured for love of me, and to make reparation for my own sins, and the sins of others. As I scourge, I either look at a Crucifix or the Ecce Homo "Behold the Man" picture in my rectory bedroom. I believe I am detached from it. If my spiritual director would tell me to stop scourging, I wouldn't have a problem discontinuing, and, at times, forget to do it.

With regard to doing penance for our sins, St. Jerome said, "Do not despair of his mercy, no matter how great your sins, for great mercy will take away great sins [cf Luke 7:41-47]. For the Lord is *gracious and merciful* [Joel 2:13] and prefers the conversion of a sinner rather than his death. Patient and generous in his mercy, he does not give in to human impatience but is willing to wait a long time for our repentance. So extraordinary is the Lord's mercy in the face of evil, that if we do penance for our sins, he regrets his own threat and does not carry out against us the sanctions he had threatened." (See Appendix D)

To be willing to accept suffering, as it comes throughout the day is important. It helps to accept times when suffering is forced on us, and certainly struggle to accept all kinds of suffering.

The Angel of Fatima told the children to pray, "Oh Jesus, for love of you, I accept this suffering, in reparation for sins committed against the Immaculate Heart of Mary and the Sacred Heart of Jesus, and for the conversion of sinners." I pray this prayer often.

After I left the Franciscans to return to the Diocese of Rolling Hills, I was assigned to St. Tarcisius Parish in Rolling Hills.

#63 ST. TARCISIUS PARISH

Associate Priest at St. Tarcisius Parish

When I arrived at St. Tarcisius parish, I met Monsignor Adolph Newman. He had worked in an office in Rome and used to appoint US bishops. He was holy, spiritual, communicated well with people and was a fantastic pastor to serve under.

After a few short months at the parish, I noticed he received a call on his cell phone. He quickly went to his office, then darted out of it, and went to the Adoration Chapel. I happen to go to the Chapel a few minutes later to pray. While in the Chapel, he was noticeably praying intensely about something. And Jesus told me, "He received the call to be a bishop." These were not audible words; but Our Lord spoke in the silence of my heart, and I firmly believed it.

That night, when Monsignor Adolph and I were watching Ohio State and Ohio University play basketball, I decided to try to get it out of him (that he had received a call to become bishop). I said, "So, what happens when a priest gets a phone call to become a bishop? How does that work?" He acted like I just asked a dumb question, and replied, "Well, there is a process they go through, and usually three priests are selected. Their names are given to the pope, and then the pope selects one. Then the apostolic nuncio calls the priest, and asks him to be a bishop." He had no idea that I knew he received the call, and he presumed, I was asking, because he thought I wanted to be a bishop. I found that hilarious, as I never wanted to be a bishop. And furthermore, I don't believe I have such gifts to be a bishop.

A few weeks later, he made the announcement to the parish, that he received the call to be auxiliary bishop of the Archdiocese of Wilmont, Colorado. When he left for his new assignment, I became the administrator of St. Tarcisius parish, and during that time, discovered many parishioners don't listen to the priest, but do their own thing. It was a subtle preparation to become a pastor for the first time a few months later.

A memorable homily I gave in Lent, while Monsignor was still pastor, I preached about contraception and the mercy of God. I said, if one had used contraception, and if it was never confessed, it should be confessed, since God desires that we give Him that sin, so we can have peace. After that Mass, we heard confessions, as was customary during Lent, and the lines were much longer than usual. Later, Msgr. Newman said, "What did you tell the people?" He could not believe, so many came to confession due to the homily. My time as administrator was short at St. Tarcisius Parish, but I quickly made friends with many parishioners, and renewed my friendship with those I had known when I was a seminarian at St. Tarcisius. Bishop Newman would become an outstanding good bishop in the US. As bishop, he promoted "ad orientem" Masses (priest faces toward the east—away from the people, and toward God), the extraordinary form of the Mass, and encouraged his pastors to start Perpetual Adoration in every parish in his diocese.

#64 PASTOR OF TWO PARISHES

Pastor of St. Veronica Brushwood City and St. Anthony in Jericho City
"I am the good shepherd. A good shepherd lays down his life for the sheep. A hired man, who is not a shepherd and whose sheep are not his own, sees a wolf coming and leaves the sheep and runs away, and the wolf catches and scatters them." (John 10:11-12)

After being ordained four years, I was assigned by Bishop Augustine Traditiones to become pastor of two parishes, St. Veronica in Brushwood City and St. Anthony in Jericho City. Within months after I arrived, I discovered how difficult it was to be a pastor.

On the first weekend, at the end of all the Masses, I stood in the gathering space at St. Veronica to greet the people and was shocked only one person walked up to me to introduce himself. Everyone else dodged by, and left without saying anything to their new pastor. I was befuddled by it, but later discovered they treated me like this since the people had many terrible experiences with priests at their parish. I had a long way to go to build trust.

Within a year, I had to fire the secretary for telling lies about me, and for refusing to do simple things when asked. I had to remove the paid parish cleaning lady due to theft. I tried to restore confidence in their pastor after the parish had multiple pastors known for scandal.

The people did not trust me, since when they saw a priest, they immediately surmised he was like their previous pastors. The families of their ancestors who founded the parish tried to run the parish and didn't want any changes. They pushed aside everything the pastor wanted to do, and they caused all sorts of problems. Because their great-grandparents founded the church, they felt entitled to run the parish and didn't want to take any advice from the pastor. The chancery agreed to their way of doing things, to the detriment of parishioners and the pastor.

Because the parish was without a pastor for a year, due to a priest, Fr. Brandmuller, leaving the priesthood, several families took over the running of the parish, and did not want to relinquish their "power".

Also, at St. Veronica, multiple families claimed their houses are haunted by a little girl. I also inherited the mystery of trying to figure out what to do with two haunted rectories, and I needed to complete the new rectory, which Fr. Vanderbilt had begun.

To help bring about the conversion of the people, we started an Adoration Chapel in the parish, and began the stewardship way of life. I thought the best way for them to be drawn closer to Christ, was to literally bring them to Christ in the Eucharist. In the midst of preparing to start Perpetual Adoration, I had a serious concussion, which caused even more problems.

The Altar Society at St. Veronica was a nightmare. They were dysfunctional and did almost nothing for the Altar. I asked the Altar Society to water flowers and plants that parishioners donated for the Altar, and asked them to remove dead flowers and plants, but they refused. I asked them to purchase wine, hosts and candles, but they refused. I asked them to purchase a new altar cloth because the parish had only one, and they refused. Yet, they took in thousands of dollars from their dinner events.

I was invited to attend one of the Altar Society meetings, and surprisingly, they asked if I could help them improve their organization. I told them, "Ladies, you do a fabulous job with your dinners, and they are very popular and delicious. Your baked goods sale is always well done, and the people love the food. But, I think you should change your name? Instead of calling your organization the Altar Society, I think you should call your organization the Dinner Society." They said, "Why do you say that, father?" I said, "Because you don't do anything for the altar."

About a month later, they decided to pay for hosts, wine, and candles, but they still refused to do anything with the flowers, and refused to purchase a new altar cloth. Later that winter, a Hispanic family decided, on their own, to purchase an altar cloth that would be used on feast days on behalf of their mother's birthday, but the Altar Society was furious.

I specially trained boy altar servers, and we started a group called the Knights of the Holy Altar. Several fathers helped the boys build a platform to process a statue of Our Lady of Fatima, which they carried at times in honor of the Virgin Mary. They also carried the Corpus Christi canopy when we processed the Eucharistic Jesus on Corpus Christi Sunday.

Parishioners of St. Anthony in Jericho reacted to their new pastor very different from the parishioners of St. Veronica in Brushwood. They were very welcoming and thrilled when I began to stay in their rectory. Bishop Traditiones said, I should not reside at the new rectory at St. Veronica until it was completed. I was to stay at the rectory at St. Anthony. The bishop also told me to not stay in the old rectory at St. Veronica. But I soon discovered the two old rectories are haunted, and the bishop apparently knew about it, but didn't say anything to me.

We started Family Theater night hosted by the Knights of the Holy Altar and began a new organization for girls called the Little Flowers of the Holy Altar. The girls made a Corpus Christi Canopy used for both parishes. The Altar Society of St. Veronica was jealous of the girls at St. Anthony, but decided to make a donation to them. The girls also made new laced altar cloths, chalice veils, and burses for the Mass.

St. Anthony's church was recently renovated before my arrival. We started an Adoration Chapel, the stewardship process, created a grotto to Our Lady of Lourdes, and built a garage.

One evening, I drove up to St. Anthony church after traveling from Brushwood to Jericho City, and noticed a large amount of dirt and a hole near the old rectory. Some men with shovels and other tools were standing next to the hole, beside the old rectory, across the street from St. Anthony. I asked the men, "What are you doing?" They said, "We're going to build you a new garage." I said, "You should have talked to me, your pastor, before spending the church's money without my knowledge. Something like this needs to be discussed by the Pastoral Council before it begins." They said, "We talked it out, and the church has the money, so we are building you a nice garage you can park your car." Believing it was a bygone conclusion, I never said another word.

Six months after they completed the garage, I again came from my journey from Brushwood to Jericho City and noticed the garage was painted pink. I said to myself, "What the heck!" When I found out who painted it, I said to him, "Why did you paint the garage pink?" He said, "It's not pink, it just looks pink. They didn't quite get the color I wanted at the local hardware store. They didn't mix the colors well." I said, "Whose idea was this, and who was all involved in making this decision?" He said, "No one, father, just me." Again, I thought this was another bygone conclusion, and I couldn't do anything about it. He gave his time and talent painting the garage, and I wasn't going to ask him to paint it again with a different, more manly color. Nor should I ask another parishioner to do it either.

I went to the hardware store and asked the manager, "Why did you mix the colors to make it pink? I ask that you please don't permit parishioners to charge anything to the church, unless I am first contacted". The hardware store manager said, "It's not pink, it just looks pink. And the people of your church are your problem. I ain't telling them to not charge anything to the church. These are good people, and you're going to create a mess, if you treat them like that. Now hold your horses, pastor. You need to re-think what you are doing. You need to let them know your thoughts and work with them." I realized the man was right, and put a note in the bulletin saying no one was to charge anything to the church without first gaining my approval, unless it was something inexpensive, such as Kleenex, toilet paper, soap, etc.

I asked permission from Bishop Traditiones to offer daily Mass in both parishes. I offered a 6:30am Mass at St. Anthony and a 5:00pm at St. Veronica, with confessions 30 min. before each Mass. The bishop said permission isn't needed, as long as there was a pastoral reason to daily offer two Masses. He was pleased with my efforts to help both parishes grow closer to Jesus in the sacraments of Confession and the Holy Eucharist. But it was a daily twenty-mile drive in one direction and therefore a forty-mile daily round trip. I could pray two Rosaries in the car driving from one parish to another, and also enjoyed the view.

Once, as I was traveling from Brushwood to Jericho City, there was a group of wild turkeys in the middle of the road, and needed to stop abruptly. They wouldn't get off the road even when I honked the horn. In fact, they thought the automobile as an enemy, and attempted to attack the car. I slowly drove the car, pushing them out of the way, to not injure them. It was quite a funny scene for sure.

The land between the two cities had hills and prairie grass, making it a beautiful, scenic trip. On the hills were cattle ranches, and at times, when traveling between the two cities, ranchers would move cattle across the road. The ranchers would place feed on the back of one of their trucks, and honk the horn, causing the cattle to follow the truck from one pasture to another, to a better area to graze. The cattle learned, that when the truck honked, they were going to be fed, and to follow the truck to get their food. It was an easy and swift way to move a large herd. Vehicles traveling on the road needed to wait until all the cattle crossed before continuing to their destination. Ranchers became images of the Good Shepherd, leading their sheep (cattle) to verdant pastures.

The non-Catholic communities of Jericho City and Locust Falls (a small city just a few miles away) saw St. Anthony as the church community to turn to for all their needs. Multiple Catholic families helped the parish be a strong witness in the non-Catholic community. They began a citywide Thanksgiving Day dinner at the Parish Hall, that gave the poor and isolated members of the community the opportunity to enjoy a delicious dinner and companionship.

#65 PARISH EVENTS AT ST. VERONICA & ST. ANTHONY, THE GOOD & BAD

Suspicious Death

The Altar Society president at St. Veronica acted very strange at the death of her husband. I was called to their home where her husband had just died. He was lying dead on the floor, had wounds on his hands, and there was blood on the floor in the kitchen. His wife was sitting on the couch in the living room, and when I sat beside her, she said, without a tear, "Isn't this something." The whole time I was at their home, she never shed a tear. Weeks before he died, she told me she wished she had never married him. Because his body was found without anyone being present, normally an autopsy would be required, but his wife strongly requested they do not do it. The sheriff and EMT (Emergency Medical Technicians) were all Freemasons, as well as her husband. She suggested he may have forgotten to take his heart medicine. The medicine bottle was opened on the table, as if someone had opened it, and conveniently either placed it there, or he had opened it, just before his death. It all seemed rather fishy. Oddly, after I was transferred to a new assignment, this woman would become the parish secretary. I later discovered her previous husband also died under strange circumstances, and due to his death, she inherited a large sum of money from his Life Insurance policy.

St. Veronica and the Battle for Modesty

"Charm is deceptive, and beauty is fleeting; but a woman who fears the Lord is to be praised." (Proverbs 31:30)

When I arrived at St. Veronica, I was introduced to some CCD teachers. A woman in her forties, taught high school CCD. The woman was frankly not attractive at all, but wore immodest clothing often (tight and low-cut). As the new pastor of souls, I decided I needed to address the problem of her immodesty. I spoke to her on the phone, and the conversation went like this: I said, "I called to thank you for giving your time and talent to teach high school youth, and also wanted to ask for a favor." She said, "Sure father, what is it?" I said, "Since you teach high school, I would like to remind you to wear modest clothing." The phone became silent, and I said, "Are you there?" Finally, she said, "Yes." I said, "Did you hear what I said?" She said, "Yes. Okay, father. Thank you." I thanked her and the conversation ended. I was astonished and thrilled it went so well, and was fretting she might be offended or argue against it, but she didn't.

However, a few weeks later, she called, and said, "I thought about what you said on the phone, and I disagree with you. I want to come and talk to you in your office". I said, "Okay." A few days later, she came for an appointment. She asked her Catholic friend, who was the church janitor at the time, to be with her. I would later catch her friend, the church janitor, stealing. She sat down, and said, "I disagree with you for wanting me to wear modest clothing. Are you telling me, my clothing is immodest?" Dumbfounded, I didn't know what to say, and said, "Well, you teach high school boys, and teachers should not wear immodest clothing revealing cleavage." She said, "There is nothing wrong with my clothing. Look at my daughter. Do you think she is wearing immodest clothing?" Her daughter, who was about eight years old, was playing outside the office. I said, "She is just a child. Nobody would think bad thoughts about the clothing she is wearing. But, if she were to wear clothing like that, when she is in high school, it would be inappropriate." I said, "If high school boys see women who are dressed immodestly, they can later have lustful thoughts, and then act out on them." She said, "I am not going to teach! I'm not going to wear different clothes. I teach sex education to boys in high school, and I know how they think." I said, "You are welcome to teach if you wear modest clothing." Her friend piped in on the conversation, and said, "I agree with father. You do at times wear clothing that is not very appropriate." Her comment made the woman furious, so she got up and left.

She later called the bishop's office, and left an obscene message on his secretary's answering machine. Bishop Traditiones called, indicating he wanted to come to the parish and visit with me, but didn't say why he wanted to meet with me, but that it was a surprise visit. When he arrived, I stupidly sat in the pastor's chair, while he sat in the chair in front of my desk, not an act of humility, for sure. I should have invited him to sit in the pastor's chair, and didn't even think about it, until after he left. He handed the typed-out message, that she left on the answering machine, and I read it.

At first, it was accurate; then suddenly I read the horrible, disgusting and obscene comments, she claimed I said to her. I said, "Bishop, the first part of this is true, but all this other disgusting stuff is not. I do not talk like that, and I never said those things." Bishop said, "She says this, and you say that, I think the truth is somewhere in between." It reminded me of Pilate, who said, "What is truth?"

I was deeply hurt the bishop didn't believe me, and told him there was a witness to the conversation, and we could ask her to come to the office to speak with him, or I could ask her to call or write a letter to him. He said not to bother her with it. He said, "I was never a pastor. Therefore, I don't know how to deal with a situation like you had. But in the future, when you have a situation like this, call an experienced pastor, and ask him what to do."

Green Light Special

"As the Father has sent me, even so I send you.' And when he had said this, he breathed on them, and said to them, "Receive the Holy Spirit. If you forgive the sins of any, they are forgiven; if you retain the sins of any, they are retained." (John 20:21–23).

Years ago, in my teenage years, *K-Mart* used to have "Blue Light Specials". A blue light would flash and people would come to see items on sale for a short period of time. I read that when St. John Vianney was a young pastor, at first, he used to give big penances, and then later much smaller ones. He had certain periods of time, when he announced he would give light penances in Confession to get people to come. He secretly did the penance for the penitents, rather than asking them to do it.

Knowing this, on several occasions, in the bulletin, and at Mass, I announced on a particular weekend, I would hear confessions before, and after Masses, and it didn't matter what was said in Confession, they could obtain a "Green Light Special", which meant it didn't matter what they said, their penance would be only one Hail Mary. I was shocked at how many people came to Confession. I kept track of prayers that I normally gave for a penance, and then prayed the prayers on behalf of the penitents. Soon parishioners would say, they felt they needed to do more penance, and when they discovered I was doing the penance for them, they felt guilty. However, the "Green Light Special" was a big success.

The Heart of the Infant Jesus Beats in My Hands at Midnight Mass

"And we all, who with unveiled faces contemplate the Lord's glory, are being transformed into his image with ever-increasing glory, which comes from the Lord, who is the Spirit." (1 Corinthians 3:18)

As pastor of St. Anthony in Jericho City, a statue of the Divine Child was given to me as a gift from a lady in the parish. When we started our Adoration Chapel, I decided to name the Chapel, Chapel of the Divine Infant. After all, the Divine Child appeared to St. Anthony of Padua. We started adoration in January of that year, then later the same year, at the Christmas Midnight Mass, Dec. 25th 2009 at St. Anthony's parish, during the consecration, right after I said the words, "This is my body..." I immediately felt the Host beating in my hands. As I elevated the Host above the altar, I was astonished at the feeling of the Host beating in my fingers. During Mass, I kept thinking, "Oh, I am pressing the Host too hard in my fingers. I must be hurting Jesus." But then I thought, "Wait a minute. I'm not supposed to feel Jesus in my hands."

After Mass, the event was bothering me so much, I decided to take a non-consecrated Host and press it between my fingers to try to feel that throbbing again. But, no matter how hard I attempted to create the feeling of beating on my fingers, or how hard I pressed the non-consecrated host with my fingers, I couldn't re-enact the throbbing sensation. I later came to believe I felt the Infant Heart of Jesus beating in my hands.

#66 EMILIA GORETTI, HEROIC VIRTUE? FUTURE SAINT?

Emilia Goretti – Future Canonized Saint?

At St. Veronica in Brushwood City, when I first arrived to the parish, I was asked to give Holy Communion to a teenage girl, who stayed in the cry room during Mass, and wore a stocking cap.

She had cancer and wore the hat due to hair loss. Over a period of months, I came to know her and her family. Her parents were devout and the family prayed the Rosary together every day. Her brothers and one of her sisters were altar servers. Her father was very involved in the parish, and taught CCD (Confraternity of Christian Doctrine), also known as Catechism Classes.

When she was at a children's hospital, I drove to Ohio City to visit Emilia. At the hospital, the doctor told her the cancer was terminal. As soon as he departed, she immediately took all the money from her purse, gave it to her father, and said, "Dad, you can have this. I don't need it anymore." Despite the fact she had just heard she was going to die, she never cried. Detached from material things, and due to the family's low income, she wanted to help the family.

The previous year, she won the "Children's Make A Wish Contest" and had the choice of going on a vacation with the family or receiving a free motor home. She chose the motor home because she wanted the family to enjoy it after her death.

I went to the local hospital in Brushwood to give her Holy Communion, and in the sacristy, there were two pyxes. In one pyx, I just placed a Host from the Tabernacle, to deliver it to her, at the hospital. The other pyx was empty. When I arrived at the hospital, I noticed Emilia was in terrible pain and said, "Are you sure you can take Communion today?" She said, "Yes, I want to receive Jesus." After I said prayers from the *Pastoral Care Book* to be read before giving the Eucharist in a hospital, I opened the pyx, and the Host was not in it. I did not understand what happened, and then realized I accidentally took the empty pyx, left the pyx with the Host on the sacristy counter, and told Emilia I would be back in fifteen minutes with Jesus. When I returned, she was no longer in pain, and I said, "Did the nurse give you medicine for your pain?" She said, "No. I am no longer in pain. I was suffering because you left Jesus at the parish, and now that you are back with Him, the suffering is gone."

It was later brought to light when parishioners were discussing their experience at the Goretti home, and sharing their experiences, they realized Emilia always wanted whoever came for a visit to pray the Rosary with her. The parishioners later figured out Emilia most likely prayed up to seven rosaries a day with visitors, but not letting on, she asked others to pray it with her.

Once, I asked Emilia, "What causes you the most pain?" She immediately responded without any hesitation, saying, "When my uncle takes God's Name in vain."

On a hospital room wall, Emilia had a calendar she circled May 20th. As the month of May progressed, each day she crossed the current day out, leading up to May 20th. It seemed God revealed to her the day of her death because that would be the day she died.

A few weeks before her death, when she was in the hospital, she overheard her mother saying she did not think she could bear staying at her side when she dies. Consequently, the day Emilia died, she told her mother to go home. But her mother said, "No, I am staying here until your father arrives." Emilia insisted her mother leave, until her mother finally relented, saying, "Well, your Dad is on the way, and he will be here in a few minutes." However, by the time her mother left the hospital, and before her father arrived, Emilia died. It was as though, she knew it was her time, and didn't want her mother to see her go.

After her death, I called the bishop and told him about the many mysterious events surrounding her life, and spoke graciously about her virtue. I asked the bishop if he could preside at the funeral whenever that would be, and he agreed. But the day the family chose for the funeral, was the same day as the priestly ordinations in Rolling Hills, and so, the bishop could not come for the funeral. Suspecting Emilia may become a saint one day, we recorded her funeral Mass.

Within a few weeks before she died, a cousin came to visit her. He said to her, "When you get to heaven, please ask Jesus to help us find the killer of Geraldine Pollen." She was a relative of the family murdered a few years prior. With the passing of years, Geraldine's death became a cold case. Emilia agreed, when she enters heaven, she will ask Jesus to help them find the killer of Geraldine. Within an hour after Emilia's death, the killer randomly confessed he killed Geraldine Pollen to an ambulance crew taking the man to a hospital due to some serious illness. The bishop later gave permission to ask her intercession to obtain favors.

#67 CHRISTMAS BLIZZARD

Christmas Blizzard

In 2008, when I was pastor of St. Veronica in Brushwood City and St. Anthony in Jericho City, Christmas Midnight Mass was at 8 pm at St. Anthony in Jericho City and Midnight Mass at 12am at St. Veronica in Brushwood City. But the weather prediction was dire due to an expected large snow storm. To be sure I could make it to Jericho City, I asked a parishioner from Jericho City to pick me up at Brushwood with his four-wheel drive, and then drive me back to Brushwood after the Mass. He was more than willing, since he wanted Mass at St. Anthony on Christmas Eve night. We had at least two feet of snow in the midst of a blowing wind. After offering Mass at St. Anthony, when I arrived at St. Veronica, I heard Confessions as previously scheduled before the Midnight Mass. As I sat in the confessional, I didn't expect very many to come, and was pleased I heard several confessions. After confessions, to my astonishment, there were only three parishioners who came to Mass. A car, from one of three parishioners who were there, became stuck in the snow a block from the church and had to walk. Who could blame anyone for not coming? It was a very unusual and special Christmas Midnight Mass, with just four of us present. It moved me to tears, they wanted to come to the Midnight Mass to celebrate the Birth of Jesus, despite the weather.

#68 CONCUSSION

One, Two, Three, You're Out! Concussion, Concussion, Concussion

In January 2009, perhaps on the feast of the conversion of St. Paul, on the 25th, I suffered three concussions in one day. They happened just before we started the Adoration Chapels at St. Anthony in Jericho City and St. Veronica Giuliani in Brushwood.

One night, I decided to sleep on the floor to relieve terrible pain in my neck and back. I placed a pillow under my head, and covered myself with a blanket. During the night, I stood up to make my way to the restroom, and was disoriented due to sleeping on the floor. Somehow, I stumbled, perhaps over the blanket, and fell headlong into the corner of the dresser, and knocked myself out. I fell to the ground, rolled under the bed, and was unconscious for hours.

As I was awakened by the morning alarm, I hit my head on the bottom of the bed (2nd concussion). I didn't recall the first concussion, and didn't think I hit my head very hard on the bottom of the bed, but I was confused and nauseated. I had the 6:30am Mass at St. Anthony to offer and needed I drive the twenty-mile trip. As I was driving to St. Anthony, due to dizziness and being sleepy from the concussion, I nearly drove off the road multiple times.

During Mass, I was confused, but able to offer the Holy Sacrifice. Just before the Consecration of the Sacred Host, I needed to sneeze, but did not dare let it go on the Sacred Species on the Altar, out of respect to Jesus in the Eucharist. However, after the Consecration of the Host, when I genuflected, I sneezed, causing my head to quickly thrust forward. There was the sound of a crack, as my head hit the corner of the Altar (third concussion) really hard. The result of the unusual scene provoked a few people to snicker. I also heard gasps the moment my head hit the altar. A parishioner later informed me, that as I said prayers from the *Roman Missal,* immediately after the hit, the words became garbled; but I was unaware my speech changed. I don't recall much after the concussion at the Altar.

A year later, a parishioner present at the Mass of the concussion, said she noticed before Mass, there was a large bump on my forehead the size of an egg, and that when I hit my head on the altar, I hit it on the exact location of the bump. I was unaware I had a bump on my head, and later came to the conclusion, it was caused by the first concussion on the dresser.

For months, after the concussions, I had difficulty with short-term memory, was confused, and extremely forgetful, and for a short time developed paranoia. Since I didn't recall items in various locations, I thought someone entered the priest's residence while I was away. Some items appeared to be missing from where I had left them. Other items seemed to be placed in locations, I didn't believe I put them. I discovered a burner on the stove left on, about an hour after I stopped using it. Cabinet doors and car doors were left open.

I became paranoid, thinking someone wanted to harm me, and that they moved things around and opened doors.

Because I couldn't remember the concussions, I wondered if someone had hit me in the head with a baseball bat at night, while I was sleeping, after all, some parishioners had keys to the rectory and were upset with me. I was confused, could not think clearly, and did not know what had happened to me.

During a weekday Mass, as I was giving the homily, in my mind I imagined the congregation yelling at me. None of them did such a thing, but my mind perceived something much different. Sadly, I yelled at the congregation, saying, "You people should have more respect for priests and not yell at us during Mass!" I remember seeing the look of shock on their faces, and when I sat down in the presider's chair, it was at that moment, I knew something was seriously wrong.

I didn't remember any of the three concussions, but knew something was wrong with my mind, and I had no idea what. Out of desperation, I called my doctor and visited with him on the phone. Not recalling my concussion, I told him about my forgetfulness, how I yelled at the congregation, and was often confused and paranoid. He bluntly said I may have a brain tumor and wanted me to come to Rolling Hills the next day for a CT scan. The following day I drove to Rolling Hills, but while there, I forgot why I came to the city.

I knew where I was, but didn't know why I came to the city. I became frightened, but remembered I had an appointment for the CT scan, and arrived at the appointed time.

About a year later, I slowly started to recall more about my first concussion. I remembered hitting my head on something wooden, but did not know what it was. Over time, the forgetfulness became less, my memory began to improve, and the paranoia disappeared, but I felt I could not effectively be a good pastor. Because I didn't feel like I was able to be a pastor, I sent a letter to Bishop Traditiones explaining that I had a concussion, and wanted to meet with him. He took me out to lunch, and as we met, I explained what I knew about the concussion and the forgetfulness. To my surprise, he said, "You are making this up. You just want to get transferred. How is it, if this happened a year ago, and you are now just telling me about it? You did fine this past year and never said anything, and now you're telling me you're not."

Due to his reaction of disbelief, I asked the new secretary to write a letter to the bishop and explain what she knew about my condition. I told her she had an obligation to tell the truth, as she saw it, and not sugar coat anything. She wrote the letter, which I never read.

Due to the concussion, I was unable to control my emotions. At times, I unexpectedly cried, laughed inappropriately, or lost my temper.

I repeatedly asked the organists to play a Communion hymn dedicated to Our Lady. They said they would, but never played any hymn to Our Lady. After the fourth time of reminding them, and after, I had just asked an organist hours before Mass, to play the hymn; and then when she didn't play it, it seemed as though they were purposely not playing them. As soon as Mass was complete, I went to the choir loft and yelled, "What the hell are you doing? Why don't you listen to me? I asked you four damn times to play a hymn to Our Lady during Communion, and you won't do it. Please explain, why you will not do it?" The organist and choir members were shocked, and so was I. I immediately apologized, and said, "I'm sorry. I don't know what's wrong with me. That was very inappropriate. Please forgive me." Due to the bishop receiving letters of complaint, and due to the secretary's letter, the bishop was finally convinced that it was time for me to leave the parish.

One weekend, in the bulletin, I explained to the people of the parish about my concussion and apologized to anyone I may have hurt. The people were very understanding and forgiving. The CYO group gave me a going away present on my last weekend at the parish. Inside the box was a high school football helmet with the inscription, "Father Crash". It was a cute idea only young people would have thought to do, and it helped me realize some were understanding and empathetic. I was proud of the youth.

Finally, three years after the concussions, I recalled hitting my head on the dresser the night I slept on the floor. But I continued to have difficulty recalling events from the past and had terrible anxiety. Because of these symptoms, I was referred to a neuropsychologist, to take three hours of tests that involved puzzles, fill-in-the-blank questions, and memory tests. When the testing was complete, the doctor pointed to my forehead, and said, "You had a concussion right here." I said, "How did you know the exact location?" She said, "Based upon the testing, you damaged part of your brain in this location." She said, "Before your concussion, you had higher than average intelligence, and after the concussion, you now have average intelligence." I thought, but did not say, "If the average person thinks like this, no wonder the world is in terrible shape."

I was assigned to Mother of Misery Healthcare for a few months and then later resided at the Cathedral and helped offer Masses and heard Confessions. I was then assigned to be the chaplain of the Sisters of St. Therese and help a pastor who had three rural parishes.

Three years after the concussion, due to the sudden death of the pastor of Immaculate Heart of Mary parish, and because the bishop had confidence in me, I was assigned as pastor of the parish. But I continued to have great anxiety and difficulty controlling emotions, though the emotions had improved. A year after I became pastor, I finally received a prescription, that I called, the "miracle pill", Gabapentin. Within a month of starting the medicine, I was back to my normal self before the concussion. For 3 years, my doctor prescribed at least 5 different anxiety/emotion medicines, but none of them worked, until I started taking Gabapentin.

The best way to describe the anxiety, is to use the analogy of a swimmer, in a pool of water six inches deeper than the height of the person, and for the swimmer to breathe, he would need to continuously go underwater, and push himself from the bottom of the pool to get air above the water. The anxiety made me feel like a swimmer in the slow process of drowning.

I received an inspiration from God, to consecrate the head injury to the Immaculate Heart of Mary. A few weeks later, I was prescribed, the new medicine, Gabapentin, May 13th, the feast of Our Lady of Fatima. Except for some minor forgetfulness, I am back to normal. O blessed Lady, thank you for your intercession! Years later, when I discontinued the medicine for a brief time, I discovered my forgetfulness was caused by a side effect of the medicine, and no longer the head injury.

#69 PILGRIMAGE TO LOURDES

Lourdes

Elisha sent him (Naaman) the message: "Go and wash seven times in the Jordan, and your flesh will heal, and you will be clean." (2 Kings 5:10)

Before receiving any medicine and due to concussion symptoms, I prayed Our Lady would obtain for me the grace to travel to Lourdes, France, where the Virgin Mary appeared to St. Bernadette. At Lourdes are bath houses with miraculous waters. Our Lady obtained for me the grace to go to the Shrine of Our Lady of Lourdes. While at Lourdes, just before Mass, the priest in charge of the outdoor shrine, asked if I wanted to be the main celebrant, and to give the homily. I was terrified, since I always wrote out my homilies and read them at Mass. And now, I had just a few minutes to read the Gospel before the Sunday Mass began, and then come up with an extemporaneous homily. I secretly and fervently, turned to Our Lady, and said, "O Mary, help me!" I couldn't pass up a once-in-a lifetime opportunity, so I quickly read the Gospel, and Mass started. As the reader was proclaiming the first reading, I begged Our Lady to help me give a good homily for the people. Suddenly, peace came over me, and thoughts came, as to what to say. After I read the Gospel, I couldn't believe what came out of my mouth. It actually made sense, was well organized and inspirational. When Mass was over, several pilgrims asked for a copy of it. But there was no copy to give, since nothing was written in advance. For me, it was truly a miracle.

The Virgin Mary told St. Bernadette, "Go and drink at the spring and wash yourself there!" At the bath houses, men and women were separated, and each group went to their own changing room. I was dunked by immersion three times by the shrine volunteers. It was as if they were waiting to see an immediate miracle. Although I bathed in the miraculous waters, I didn't receive a physical healing for my concussion. There was no immediate change in my health. However, I received the grace to accept the suffering and embrace it.

I met a group from the US, who had a woman from their group that was healed of her hip condition. She was scheduled to have surgery, but after she came out of the water, she had no pain, and it immediately disappeared.

I enjoyed the candlelight processions, a Eucharistic Procession, and Healing Service within a Holy Hour. I heard confessions at the shrine.

At Lourdes, I decided to drink lots of tea because I enjoyed the taste of it. It was a European thing to do, and I wanted to do as they did. However, on the way back to the US, while on the plane to return home, I started to feel uncomfortable, but couldn't explain why. When I landed in Rolling Hills at 2am, I decided to sleep overnight at the old rectory at St. Charles of Sezze Parish. I wasn't going to wake up the pastor and I knew he would allow me to stay there, since there was no one staying there at the time. I was too tired to drive back to Brushwood City, an hour and a half drive. I knew where the keys are located and so entered the Adoration Chapel, prayed, and was able to enter the church. I found the key to the rectory in the normal location.

Just as I laid down in bed, suddenly, I had to run to the restroom. First, a sudden bowel movement; then, I had terrible back pain. The pain increased, and I felt like vomiting. I never had such terrible pain in my life. On a scale of 1 to 10, it was a 10. I thought I was dying. I quickly grabbed my things and drove to Mother of Misery Healthcare System, St. Camillus de Lellis Hospital.

Barely able to walk to the *Emergency Room (ER)*, when I saw the ER nurse, she took one look at me, and said, "I know what's wrong with you!" I said, "How can you know, I haven't told you my symptoms." She said, "You have a kidney stone. I should know, I just had one. They're worse than having a baby." After lab tests and a CT scan, she was right. I had a kidney stone. It took several weeks to pass the stone. Then, periodically, I had more stones, but not as painful. I discovered the kidney stones were caused by tea. No more tea. No more stones.

What a grace, I made it back on soil from my flight to Lourdes just before the terrible pain occurred. I can't imagine going through that pain on a plane. Our Lady took care of me, and I was able to offer up my suffering! And my, was it a colossal suffering to offer up. I came to understand Lourdes wasn't only a place to be healed of physical ailments, but also spiritual ailments, by accepting the sufferings of this life, and be willing to offer them for others. It's a true healing when we can accept our crosses of life, rather than reject them.

#70 DAD'S DEATH AND FUNERAL

Dad's Death
"When they pray this Chaplet in the presence of the dying, I will stand between My Father and the dying person, not as the just judge but as a Merciful Savior." (The Diary of Saint Faustina, #1541)

While kneeling before a statue of the Blessed Virgin Mary and gazing at Her Immaculate Heart at St. Veronica Giuliani Catholic Church in Brushwood City, my cell phone rang. As I knelt before the statue, my sister, Marie, called. She said Dad had been suffering from carbon monoxide poisoning from the heater in his home (which is why he was often confused) and she said, the doctor also found cancer.

When I went to see Dad at the hospital, it was then, the doctor told him, he had just a few months to live. He told my sister that he just knew I wanted him to get chemo and fight the cancer. I surprised him, by telling him, "Dad, it's your life. I'm not going to tell you what to do." At times, he would bring up the letter, which I wrote to him, many years ago. He would say, "You always wanted me home, but I couldn't be there. I had to work to feed the family." However, that isn't what I meant, by the letter. In the past, whenever we talked, he always wanted to argue, but, as he was dying, I didn't want that to happen, so I rarely talked when I came to visit him. I wanted very much to tell him it was not because of his work, but because of his staying out at bars after work, which prevented him from being with us at home. I decided to let him find out when he went to his judgment what I really meant. I didn't want to cause him to get upset when he was dying. Maybe it would have given him peace. Or it would have brought him to repentance. Or it would have caused him to be even more upset. I feared the latter.

While he was in the hospital, my sisters moved some of his things to a nursing home in Crossroads City. He was transported to the nursing home by way of an ambulance, because he could no longer walk. At the hospital, he said, "If you put me in a nursing home, I will call my friends. And my friends will get me out of there, and you won't know where I am." When we arrived at the nursing home, he kept repeating, "I don't want to be here. Get me out of here!" A nurse came to his room, and asked if he wanted coffee, and he said he did. When she returned, he took a sip, and looked around at us, and said, "This coffee is good. I guess I will stay."

After two months had passed, he told me, "I'm going to call that doctor and have a word with him. The doctor said I had two months to live. Well, two months have passed, and I'm still alive!" During those last months of his life, I drove home often to see him, and at times, spent the night in the hospital before driving back the next day to Brushwood City.

While at the parish, at times I would get a call saying, "He's dying. Come right away." I would come, and by the time I arrived, he had a sudden rebound. This was truly agonizing to go through.

On another occasion, when I went home, he kept repeating over and over, "God, help me." My sister, Marie, who was also there, told him, "God is helping you."

When I came to see him, often times I anointed him and gave him the Apostolic Pardon. And he would say, "You just anointed me a few weeks ago, you're going to anoint me to death!"

The last dreaded call came, and when I arrived, on the evening of Sept. 16th, he was slowly going.

He was no longer conscious. I anointed him and gave him the Apostolic Pardon. I prayed the Rosary silently, and also the Chaplet of Divine Mercy. His skin color became blotchy and his breathing irregular. My sisters and I prayed the Lord's Prayer and three Hail Mary's, and just as we finished the last Hail Mary, suddenly, at 7:27am, Sept. 17th, 2009, he opened his eyes, and looked at my sister Sue, and closed his eyes and died. I felt as though, I saw Jesus die on the Cross. We all wept.

Born Sept. 7th, 1937, he died Sept. 17th, 7:27am, at the age of 72. Notice, the similarity of the numbers!

After he died, I frantically prayed rosaries for him, offered Masses for his soul, and yet, I did not have peace. Until one night, I dreamt, I saw Dad. He hugged me in the dream, and when I woke, I felt at peace.

Dad's Funeral

When the funeral was scheduled, I asked the pastor if I could be the priest celebrant and also give the homily, which he permitted. I led the Rosary Vigil the night before during the Funeral. In the casket, they placed in his hands, the confessional stole, I had given to Dad at my first Mass. It was used for my first confessions, before my First Mass. It was a reminder, when he died, he would go to his judgment, and show Jesus my stole, and say to the Lord, "I gave you my son, to be a priest."

The homily I gave at Dad's funeral was excessively long. It was the worst homily I ever gave. Although I wrote it out beforehand, I spoke little about Jesus, and rattled on about Dad. If I had to do it over again, I would have given a much different homily.

Years later, my heart broke, knowing the Mass I offered for his funeral was invalid, due to the wine made of strawberries and cherries, the pastor used at that parish. The knowledge of that made me physically ill and angry.

I presided over his burial at the cemetery, and it was there I cried after it was all over. Strangely, in ten years, the ground above where he was buried never grew any weeds or grass. For all those years, the ground looked as though he was just been buried.

His tombstone has an image of him fishing, and if that were possible, in heaven, he would certainly be doing it there. There were three hundred people who came to his funeral. Due to the Altar Society of St. Gabriel's parish desiring to make extra money from funerals, for his funeral dinner, we received a bill for $1500 at $5 a plate. It's understandable, out of charity, we should help pay for the dinner. But since many brought covered dishes, the dinner cost to the Altar Society, would have been no more than $300, at the most. So glad we could support the Altar Society due to my father's death!

Over the years, I offered many Masses for his soul and during the month of Sept. in 2019, I offered 30 Masses (Gregorian Masses) in a row for his soul. There is a promise, that if 30 Masses are offered in a row, for a specific deceased soul, the soul will obtain heaven once the last Mass is offered. While we don't know for certain if this is true, it is certainly a consoling devotion. I deeply loved my father. I would not have wanted a different one. Despite all the terrible events at home, he was what was best for me and my family. All the good and bad experiences helped me to be a better man, and to learn perseverance and unconditional love. These experiences helped me to endure the sufferings of bishops, who are spiritual fathers. My father helped me to understand mercy.

In addition to the Gregorian Masses I offered, the people of the two parishes were very generous and kind during my time of sorrow. They contributed over 80 Mass intentions for my father's soul. Praise the Lord!

#71 ASSIGNED TO "CATHOLIC" HOSPITALS

Mother of Misery Healthcare System, St. Henry Campus, Saint Mother Cope Campus, Crucifixes, Invalid Baptisms, Euthanasia

I was transferred from St. Veronica and St. Anthony parishes in June 2010 to become a chaplain at Mother of Misery Healthcare System, St. Henry campus, Saint Mother Cope campus, and helped out at the Saint Camillus de Lellis campus.

When I arrived at the hospitals, I had no idea there was controversy at the health system. The hospital was in the process of removing the names of saints from the hospital buildings and removing a large Cross at the top of St. Henry's hospital. The Cross was a local landmark. In addition to this, one of the Sisters of Misery said administration was going to remove all crucifixes and replace them with the resurrected Jesus image attached to a cross. The new Maryanne Cope Campus was not to have any crucifixes with a crucified Jesus. But, rather, a resurrected Jesus affixed to a cross.

Patients and staff confided in me, about the disintegration of Catholic identity. Staff said if they accidentally answered the phone, saying, "St. Henry's Hospital", they were reprimanded. The hospital was no longer to be called St. Henry's. But, rather, the Mother of Misery hospital on Hamilton street.

Everyone was upset, except for most Sisters of Misery, and the administrators of the hospital, who were behind the scenes eliminating Catholic identity to make the hospitals more "acceptable" for non-Catholics, at the cost of causing Catholics to be offended.

One patient said, "Father, why are you taking down the Cross and removing the saint's name from the hospital?" I said, "It's not me. I don't like it either." She said, "Why don't we start a petition, and ask administration to keep the names?" I said, "That's a great idea." Consequently, I started a petition to keep the names of the hospitals and keep crucifixes throughout the hospital and patient rooms, and asked local Catholic book stores to make the petition available for people to sign. And soon people began to sign it.

After the petition began, I thought it would be best to speak directly with the CEO of St. Mother Cope hospital, and ask him to not put up the new the resurrected crosses, but rather crucifixes. I made an appointment with him, and at the meeting explained what I was doing. To my surprise, he started crying. I didn't know what to say. He said, "You need to speak with Sister Susan, of the Sisters of the Weeping Madonna, and tell her what you are doing." I said, "Okay."

I made an appointment with her. When the meeting began, I didn't have a chance to say a word. Sister Susan berated me for 45 minutes. She wouldn't allow me to say a word, except, "Yes, sister. Okay, sister." She said, "Do you realize we can fire you for insubordination! You should have come to us first. This decision is not mine to make-- it comes from the sisters at headquarters." A week later, I received a phone call from the bishop's secretary stating that Bishop Traditiones wanted to meet with me. At the meeting, he said, "Father Gadfly, the health system wants to fire you over the crucifixes. Is it true you developed a petition for people to sign to keep the crucifixes?" I said, "Yes, bishop." He said, "You have three choices. One: You can let them fire you, and I will reassign you. Two: You can humbly apologize, and maybe they might just keep you. Three: I can reassign you. What do you want to do?" I said, "I would like to pray about it."

About a week later, after I prayed about it, and spoke to my spiritual director, I called the bishop and said, "Bishop, I'm not sorry, for what I did. I probably should have spoken to them first. But, I'm not sorry, for trying to keep the crucifixes. You can just reassign me."

Before the crucifix mess occurred, I discovered some baptism certificates that read, "Baptized in the name of the creator, redeemer, and sanctifier". Others said, "Baptized in the name of Jesus." And still others said, "Baptized in the name of the Father, and of the Son, and of the Holy Spirit." I spoke about this problem to a Catholic lay "chaplain", who told me she baptizes in all three ways, dependent upon the religion of the patient. I told her, "But two of these methods are invalid; you can't do that." She said, "I will do it the way I want. We have always done it that way." I then spoke to Sister Valerie.

Sister said, "Well, father, we have done this for years. We aren't going to change." In response, I called the Director of Worship for the Diocese, and asked him to give a talk to the lay chaplains on how to validly baptize, and he was willing to do it. Instead, he mentioned the invalid baptism situation to Bishop Traditiones. The bishop called, and said, "Father Gadfly! Why didn't you call me about this! This is a serious problem! I am the bishop of this diocese, and I'm responsible for the sacraments to make sure they are offered validly!" He said, "I will take care of this!" A few weeks after the crucifix fiasco, I was transferred, and I never heard if, or what, he did about it.

For a valid baptism, water must be poured three times over the person's head saying, "first and middle name, I baptize you, in the name of the Father (pour water on the head), and of the Son, (pour water) and of the Holy Spirit (pour water). Amen." Under extreme circumstances, when it's not possible to pour on a person's head due to an emergency such as "Code Blue", any part of the body may be baptized.

Before the transfer happened, I noticed a subtle form of euthanasia at Woebegone Hospice on the 8th floor of St. Camillus de Lellis hospital. I substituted several days every week when the other priest chaplain was away and quickly realized something was rotten in the state of Denmark.

At Woebegone Hospice, I anointed and gave Communion to patients who were not receiving nutrition or hydration, when they could benefit from them, even though they were living up to 2 weeks before death, which is contrary to Church documents. Only if a patient is imminently dying (within 3 days), and only if they will not benefit from nutrition and hydration, should they be removed. A lack of nutrition and hydration should not be the cause of death, but rather, the disease or illness. In many cases at Woebegone Hospice, a good number of people died because of a lack of food and/or water that would have helped them to endure their last days with dignity and comfort. Receiving food and water artificially gives true comfort care. Whereas, not giving a patient food and water, when they can benefit from them, will cause great discomfort and agony. And their response was to give so much medication, to keep them unconscious for up to two weeks.

A problem at St. Henry Hospital involved the purification of linen. Purificators, corporals, and altar cloths used during the Holy Sacrifice of Mass are to be purified by soaking overnight, before washing, so that the particles of the Sacred Host and drops of the Precious Blood of Jesus that may be on them, are dissolved, as required by the Church. Sister Millie, of the Most Stubborn Heart washed and ironed the linen. I asked her how they were purified, and she responded, saying she places them directly in the washing machine without any soaking or purification. I explained to her the linens used at Mass need to be first purified by soaking. She refused to do it any other way. She said she cleaned the linen the same way for decades. Knowing how she sacrilegiously washed used linens from the Holy Mass, I kept used purificators and corporals in a different hidden location; soaked them, and then washed and ironed them at the priest's house, and then replenished the linen. So she wouldn't know the difference, I replaced dirty linen with clean crumpled up linen in the container she used to wash linen, and therefore she washed only clean linen. All for the love of Jesus in the Holy Eucharist, who is in each Sacred Particle, no matter how small.

#72 CHILD JESUS APPEARED TO ME

The Child Jesus
"Amen, I say to you, unless you turn and become like children you will not enter the kingdom of heaven." (Matthew 18:3)

When I was a Franciscan of Perpetual Victim Martyrs, I prayed in Our Lady of the Seraphim Monastery in Canterbury, Louisiana, and looking up at the Sacred Host, praying, "Jesus, do You want me to have a devotion to You as a child?" Within five minutes of the prayer, a brother came to me while I was in the Chapel and said that all brothers were summoned to the Friary. When I arrived, an employee from the shrine, who had recently returned from Rome, had a relic for each brother. He handed me a relic from a piece of wood from the manger in Bethlehem. I saw this as a sign, the Lord wanted me to have a devotion to Him as a Child. Despite this event, I never really prayed to Him as a child until years later, except, of course, during the Christmas season.

After I left the brothers, and was a seminarian for the Diocese of Rolling Hills, my uncle, Fr. Ferdinand Tosmercka died. I was given his chalice and his statue of the Infant of Prague. The statue was large and in good condition. At the time, I knew almost nothing about the statue, and was even turned off by it, since I thought the statue appeared to be wearing a dress, and thought the boy-child should not be wearing a dress. I kept the statue of the Infant of Prague in a box for years, and then later, after I became a priest, I gave the statue away.

A few years after I gave the statue away, my father died. After his death, my sisters divided among themselves Dad's things. I was given the Infant of Prague, as a memento from my family. I liked this statue because it didn't have a "dress". However, one of the fingers was broken. Years later, I eventually read an article about the statue, and where the Infant of Prague originated. But I still did not have a devotion to the Divine Child or to the Infant of Prague. However, He seemed to have a devotion to me, and kept showing up, when I least expected.

About the time we were to start Perpetual Adoration at St. Anthony, a woman made a pilgrimage to the shrine of the Infant of Prague in Oklahoma and purchased for me another Infant of Prague. I decided to name the adoration chapel, "Divine Infant Chapel" and gave the statue to the parish to put in the adoration chapel. Then that Christmas Midnight Mass, I felt the Heart of Jesus beating between my fingers. The Heart of an Infant on Christmas.

Several years after my concussion, when I was assigned to the Cathedral of the Immaculate Conception, I became depressed. Not at all suicidal, but depressed.

I think some of it was caused by the concussion, but also, I felt sad, since I didn't think I would ever be a pastor again, and also believed the bishop wanted me to retire due to my head injury. I didn't know where I would go or what I would be doing and was heartbroken. Not only that, I had visited religious communities, thinking maybe God was using the concussion to help me realize I had a vocation to religious life, and I thought I could do well in a religious order despite my concussion. But I was depressed.

On January 1st, 2011, the Solemnity of Mary, the Mother of God, I went to the Cathedral. I had a vision of the Child Jesus, His Holy Mother, and the Blessed Trinity in heaven. As I knelt before the Tabernacle to pray, a great calm came over my soul, and everything except the Tabernacle disappeared before me. Because I was having problems with my memory, I later decided to record what I experienced for fear, I would forget what happened. And this is what I recorded:

"There was a mistake in the bulletin, which made it appear we had Mass at 10 am at the Cathedral. Just before 10 am, I decided to go to the cathedral to see if anyone was there, and to maybe hear confessions, if anyone wanted. No one was in the church, so I decided to go before the Tabernacle and pray. Just as I knelt, I had something like an intellectual vision, as it was not outwardly seen by myself, but, rather interior. I was dry in prayer for many months and I never seemed to get much of anything in prayer at all. This was especially difficult because I had been trying to discern over the past three months if I had a vocation to religious life, and if so, where. I also felt God had abandoned me, and was unconcerned about me—though I knew this was not true. But, today was different.

When I knelt by the communion rail, I saw the Divine Child Jesus standing directly in front of the Tabernacle on the marble ledge. He had the most beautiful blue eyes, with curly blondish brown hair. He had a wonderful smile, and both hands were extended out. It was just as though He was really there. He was wearing a long pink garment, and was moving about. He pointed His hands up, as in prayer, and laid His head upon His hands, as though He wanted to tell me something about sleeping. Furthermore, He kept pointing to me, and at the same time folding His hands in prayer, while He gently laid His head on His hands. Curious as to what He meant, I thought, "What do you mean, Jesus?" He then pointed to me, and began the same motions with His hands. It was then I realized, He was telling me I need to get more sleep.

Once I understood His message, He began to sort of jump, like a little Child. To my surprise, He jumped off the marble top, and directly landed in my arms, and began to cuddle in my arms, and he smiled at me, and laid His head against my chest. His face was radiant. His eyes so blue, and His hair was soft. He then jumped out of my arms into the air, and landed in the arms of the Blessed Virgin Mary, who had suddenly stood next to the Tabernacle. Mary held the little boy Jesus in Her arms. They smiled at each other, and Mary began to touch the nose of Jesus with Her finger, and Jesus playfully kept trying to grab Mary's finger. But, She moved it such that He couldn't grab it. He then jumped out of Mary's arms, and took me by the hand.

I walked with Him, and He led me, until we came to some clouds, which opened as we walked through. The clouds were not only on the ground, but also on both sides of me, such that I couldn't see everything in heaven. We walked to the center, where there were three thrones. On the left throne, God the Father was seated. The throne in the center was empty, since it was for Jesus, who was standing a little in front of me, and next to me, as we held hands walking. The throne, on the right of Jesus, was for Mary. She was seated, on a large throne. These chair-like thrones were enormous. When Jesus let loose of my hand, He jumped into His large throne, His feet were dangling from the chair, and He continued to smile at me. It was so cute, as to what happened next. God the Father took the hand of Jesus and Mary took the other hand of Jesus. They were sort of gently swinging His hands. I then thought, Jesus is the Son of the Father and the Son of Mary. The Holy Spirit was slowly flying above as a dove, around the thrones. I saw in heaven, so many people and angels everywhere; yet I was not permitted to see everything in heaven. I thought I saw my father there, but when I saw him, it happened so fast, I was not certain it was him. The Divine Child came down from the throne, and we walked out of heaven.

He then showed me some things that made me sad. He showed me people killing each other over food. People starving to death. People dying by disease. He showed me so many Christians that were beginning to be killed, and many churches which were bombed. He then showed me two nuclear clouds, indicating a nuclear war. I then saw Pope Benedict, whom some men came to take. He went with them; but, Jesus, although a little Child, was angry at the men.

When we were finished seeing these things, I found myself with the Divine Child Jesus in front of the Tabernacle. He jumped on the marble ledge in front of the altar, and began to motion to me, as though He wanted me to get more sleep.

He then showed me and image of myself wearing a brown habit, but that I was lying in a coffin and being carried out of a large church, and it was placed into a walled sarcophagus. I asked him how I died, and though I am uncertain if what I saw caused my death, I saw a man with a gun.

I then once again saw the Child Jesus hopping around in front of the Tabernacle. He did something I didn't understand. With one of His hands, He kept picking up one of His feet and showed me His big toe and the toenail was gold. Furthermore, He kept smiling and moving about, as though He was one or two years old. He then opened up the Tabernacle door, went inside, and closed the door. He took the lid off the ciboria and then went inside in the form of Hosts. From inside, He reached out, and grabbed the lid of the ciboria and put it on, so I could no longer see the Hosts. Then the door to the Tabernacle closed, and I was suddenly back to my surroundings at the Cathedral.

Considering the gold toenail, I wondered if it had anything to do with the toenail that fell off when I was a child. As a little boy, I dropped a can of beans on my toe, and it turned black and blue. It eventually fell off, and would bleed at the most inappropriate times. When at school, in second grade, it bled so much, it came through my shoe and blood seeped all over the floor, though I didn't realize it, until the teacher was shocked to see it. She took off my shoe, and wrapped my toe with a Band-Aid. I wondered if it was because I kept my pain and suffering to myself as a child, maybe I should be more attentive to doing so as an adult. I wondered if Jesus showed me His toe to remind me that it was pleasing to Him for me to suffer as a child, without telling others about it. And that He felt the pain and suffering I went through as a child.

This vision caused me to be greatly humbled, and I began to thank the Lord for being so good to me. After praying and thanking, I got up, knelt down, and kissed the floor and left the Cathedral. Fr. Leonard Joseph Anthony M. Gadfly."

As a result of the vision, the depression immediately vanished when it was over, and I never had depression like that again. The dryness in prayer also immediately left. My interpretation of this vision is that some things are symbolic, while others are not. I believe, that the part indicating I died wearing a brown habit may mean one of two things. Perhaps, the Lord wanted me to die to my personal desire of returning as a Franciscan of Perpetual Victim Martyrs. And, although I may never actually wear a habit again, I will die as a member of the Franciscans of Perpetual Victim Martyrs. The Lord perhaps accepted my desire, and validated it, though it may never be in this life.

In Feb. of 2013, Pope Benedict resigned, and many believed he was pressed into resigning by evil clerics in the Vatican. Only God knows what really happened.

About a year after the vision, when assigned to the Doorway to Heaven Nursing Center, I became chaplain of the Holy Nuns of St. Therese, and also drove every weekend to St. Peter in Lionel City, St. Timothy in Browbeat City, and St. Titus in Mustard City, to help the pastor of those parishes with Masses and Confessions.

During that time, I went to Confession to Fr. John Blacksmith. It was an ordinary confession; and for my penance, he suggested I invite Jesus wherever I go. And so, I did, but then I began to have more experiences with the Divine Child. These experiences caused me to have a conversion in my priesthood, where I was able to see Jesus (not always as an image of a child, but became aware of Him, who was present everywhere I went). I talked to the Lord almost continuously wherever I went. The Divine Child began to appear in His pink gown at various times in the most unexpected circumstances.

For example, I went to visit a new resident of the nursing home to anoint her, and on my way to visit her, as I walked through the corridor, the Divine Child Jesus was suddenly in my arms, and His face was all black and blue. I said, "This can't be you, Jesus." I said, "If you are of God, stay. If you are not of God, leave!" The Child Jesus smiled at me, but didn't say anything. He stayed. As I entered the elderly lady's room, the Child left, and I was shocked to see the woman with the same bruises, and black and blue marks, the Child Jesus had on His face. I immediately realized Jesus wanted me to know, He was suffering in the woman, who had fallen on her face.

The Divine Child appeared to me many other times. Sometimes in the car, other times, as I was walking. One day, I was upset with the Lord about something, and when the Divine Child Jesus appeared to me, I said, "Go away! I'm angry at you." Jesus immediately left. I felt so bad I treated Him like that. Eventually, the visions discontinued, and I missed them. I realized, often times in the past, He would appear to me when I was going through some distress. For years, He did not appear to me again.

However, one day, when I was making a Discernment of Spirits Retreat in Nebraska, I asked Jesus why I acted so childish when my prayers weren't answered. I did a novena to the Divine Child, and my prayer was not answered; therefore, I became upset and placed my statue of the Divine Child (purchased at the monastery of Mother

Annunciata) in the closet, as well as a picture of Mother Annunciata, who had passed, and who I had asked her intercession. I put both in the closet, since I was upset they didn't answer my prayer. When I was doing the Discernment Retreat, the retreat master told me to ask Jesus why I treated Him like that.

That is when He appeared to me again. He showed me two times in my life when I threw temper-tantrums as a child. He showed me how I would bang my head against the wall when I didn't get my way. But, when I did the meditation as prescribed for the day of the retreat, He appeared as a Child, and placed His hand between my head and the wall. It caused me to apologize for my sin as a child. Then in my meditation, the Divine Child (wearing His pink gown), and I, began to play football together. In this vision, we threw the football back and forth to each other. It gave great joy to my heart since as a child, I had always wanted a friend to play sports.

As I write this, I am secretly hoping He appears to me again, and I pray I never treat Him so badly like that again. I always have such joy in my heart when He appears, and He always makes me feel good when He comes.

Once, I made a pilgrimage to the Shrine of the Infant of Prague, in Prague, Oklahoma. Due to my petitions I left at the shrine on several occasions, my prayers were answered.

I use the relic of the manger, given to me when I was a religious brother, every year for Christmas, and set it near my personal nativity set at the rectory. I can't help but think about my mother's silence before the parish Nativity scene after Midnight Masses when we attended St. Gabriel's Church in Crossroads City when I was a child in my hometown parish. Her witness to the Divine Infant laid the grounds for me to eventually have a devotion to the Child Jesus. The little Boy, God, sought me out, though I didn't seek Him out. That is, until after I came to know He wanted to be part of my life, as a little Child. As a priest, I have preached homilies about the Divine Child, the unborn Jesus, and how we should pray to the unborn Jesus for an end to abortion.

Interestingly, about 10 years after I had the vision of Jesus at the Cathedral, my right big toenail became yellow and fell off. Most likely, it was caused by fungus. It grew back over time. When I saw Jesus with the yellow (golden) toenail, did He later want me to know that would happen to my toe?

#73 NURSING HOME, THREE PARISHES AND CHAPLAIN FOR NUNS

Doorway to Heaven Nursing Center
Three Parishes & Chaplain for the Holy Nuns of St. Therese

After my assignment at the Cathedral, I was assigned by the bishop, as chaplain of the Holy Nuns of St. Therese; to offer Masses and hear Confessions at St. Peter's in Lionel City, St. Timothy in Browbeat, and St. Titus in Mustard City parishes; and to help out at the Doorway to Heaven Nursing Center.

While residing at the diocesan priest residence, I offered daily Mass for the Holy Nuns of St. Therese. I came to know their deep love of Our Lady and love of Jesus in the Blessed Sacrament; how they tried to imitate the many saints of their religious order, and their very sacrificial way of life. They were invited by Bishop John Fidelity to start a monastery in the diocese. In many ways it became apparent, chancery personnel, and the people of the diocese unknowingly seriously neglected one of the greatest spiritual resources and treasures. They were a spiritual power house, especially due to their prayers and sacrifices for priests and the bishop.

When some sisters became seriously ill, I discovered they had no insurance, and, therefore, relied heavily on homeopathic remedies, some I believed were "unnatural" and subtly new age. The sisters had no idea they were too overly focused on homeopathic remedies, such that they neglected the ordinary means of proven science and the medical field. Perhaps because they were without insurance, they turned to these remedies for assistance.

For instance, when a sister was diagnosed with gallstones, she was given a homemade mixture of vitamins, supplements, and organic ingredients to remove the stones. The poor sisters didn't realize the local Catholic hospitals would provide free medical care for them. I was able to have a hospital representative explain to the mother superior that they wouldn't be charged for any hospital service, including surgeries and medicine.

The sisters went too far, in their avoidance of city water. They considered city water contaminated by herbicides and pesticides and refused to connect to it. They wanted to avoid drinking chlorine, which they believed would cause cancer, and they asked local people to haul large tanks of water, so they could bathe, drink, and cook with it.

Despite this, I grew close to the sisters and enjoyed offering the Mass partially in Latin. Because some sisters did not understand English, as most spoke only Spanish, and because I didn't know Spanish, I used *Google* to translate homilies into Spanish. I then gave daily written copies for the sisters to read, as I preached the homily in English during Mass.

Many times, when I asked the sisters to pray for a specific intention, their prayers were answered. They were brides of Christ, and He must have been deeply happy with them, because they were faithful to their vows and lived such beautiful lives of holiness, virtue, and self-sacrifice.

I enjoyed driving every weekend to St. Timothy in Browbeat, St. Titus in Mustard City, and St. Peter in Lionel City. Ministering in these parishes gave me the courage to once again become a pastor. The people of all three parishes were very helpful, kind, and loving.

The pastor of the three parishes was a faithful priest, who preached the Gospel, but had great difficulty relating to his parishioners. He apparently suffered from narcissistic behavior disorder. He endured many struggles and difficulties, and most were caused by his foibles. People from all three parishes came to me to complain about him. I did my best to listen, but also tried to support him, and reminded them they needed to visit with him about their conflicts.

Because I listened to his homilies in the sacristy, and would then help distribute Holy Communion, I became aware that in a year's time, he mentioned contraception in every single weekend homily, except one. He even mentioned contraception at the 1st Communion Mass at Lionel.

I ministered every day at Doorway to Heaven Nursing Center and gave out Holy Communion to residents unable to attend Mass. Occasionally, I offered Mass in the nursing home Chapel in addition to the Sisters' Mass. I prayed with the dying and saw firsthand the medical care given to residents of the nursing facility.

Over a period of time, I became more and more aware of a serious problem, the failure of Doorway to Heaven Nursing Center medical personnel to provide nutrition and hydration to residents who could benefit from them. I first became aware of it due to religious sisters, who served there. They made me aware of several residents who were dying without nutrition and hydration, and said, "Even in Panama we do not treat people so cruelly like this."

As the incidents occurred, I began to inform family members of residents not receiving nutrition or hydration as needed, and spoke about the ethical difficulty with a religious sister of Misery, Sister Mary Spinderwebb, who oversaw the spiritual care of the residents. She gave me a handout on Hospital and Nursing Home Ethics by the US Conference of Catholic Bishops, but it failed to mention anything specific about nutrition and hydration. This caused me to realize she did not understand the Church's teachings on this matter.

I documented everything that appeared unethical, called the International Catholic Bioethics Center of America, and spoke with Fr. Tom Broziak and Dr. Mary Hillabeans. I also documented what they said. I looked up information by Pope St. John Paul II including his encyclical, *The Gospel of Life,* and other church sources, such as documents written by a bishop, who wrote a pastoral letter on the subject. I read a document by the Conference of Bishops of Pennsylvania, etc.

With all this information, and after visiting with the director of a Baylor Manner, a Catholic nursing home in Alabama, ran by Sisters of St. Joseph the Caretaker, who followed all Catholic moral principles in their nursing home, it was blatantly clear, I never witnessed any nutrition and hydration that should have been given to patients, who, at times, lived up to 13 or 14 days without any food and water.

I visited with Dr. Bevilaqua, the supervisor of Woebegone Hospice, and told him of my findings. Since he had a Licentiate degree in bioethics in Rome, he was trusted in medical ethics for the dying. However, I soon discovered his view seriously contradicted Church teaching. I asked him to explain when nutrition and hydration should be given. To my surprise, he couldn't. He showed me a chart which showed how when people get older, and how they slowly die, they need less water and food, since, as he said, "their body no longer needs or wants it". I spoke to him about what the International Catholic Bioethics Center of America personnel told me, and how it was clear to them, Dr. Bevilaqua's way of thinking was much different than Catholic teaching.

Not knowing what to do, I spoke to Fr. Quid E Vertitas, the Vicar for Clergy and liaison for Healthcare of the Diocese about the problem, and he suggested I inform the bishop. Therefore, I typed up a comprehensive document explaining the ethical dilemma, and asked the sisters to write letters to the bishop explaining what they had experienced. However, they only agreed to do so without signing the letters, as they feared they may be removed from ministry there. I then mailed everything to the bishop.

Not much later, in an email to me, Fr. Quid E. Veritias said, "You are not the chaplain of the Doorway to Heaven Nursing Center. Bishop said, you are not talk to patients or families or staff about what you perceive to be a nutrition and hydration problem. And if you believe there is an issue, you are to notify me (Fr. Vertias)." I still have his email that states what he said.

I did not realize the depth of the unethical difficulty throughout the diocese of Rolling Hills, until the bishop asked me to be the chaplain at St. John of God Hospital in Tantrum, Idaho. At that truly Catholic hospital, they followed Church teaching concerning Nutrition and Hydration and all Catholic ethics. Never in the two and a half years, I served at St. John of God Hospital, did I ever see a patient die without nutrition and hydration, unless the patient died within a day of being taken off life support.

The State Bishop's Conference provided a document Catholics can sign to indicate their wishes, with regard to death and dying especially concerning artificial nutrition and hydration that clearly explained Church teaching. It states, "Furthermore, if at such time I'm unable to eat or drink on my own (i.e. in a natural manner) food and fluids must be provided to me in an assisted manner (i.e. by tubes or a similar manner) unless: (a) my death is imminent (i.e likely to happen without delay);..."

A bishop from a southwest state, when speaking of dying and the need for nutrition and hydration, stated "imminent" means (3 days or less). Yet, the entire Rolling Hills Diocese community including medical, hospice, and most all clergy, seemed unaware of the injustice occurring at Woebegone Hospice, at Catholic hospitals, and a Catholic Nursing Home in Rolling Hills. Is it because of naivety or some other reason?

Christmas Midnight Mass at St. Titus in Mustard City (2009)

During the time, I was helping to offer Masses and hear Confessions at St. Peter's in Lionel, St. Timothy in Browbeat, and St. Titus in Mustard City on weekends, I offered a Christmas Midnight Mass at St. Titus in Mustard City. To my surprise, as I was offering the Midnight Mass, I noticed my brother and his invalidly married wife, in the congregation. I was grateful they never came forward to receive Holy Communion, especially since she wasn't Catholic, and they weren't married in the Church. They didn't come to my ordination, due to my stance on not attending their invalid marriage, but it was worth it! I was stunned to see them at Mass, as I wasn't expecting them to be there.

As Mass was progressing, I became worried something bad may have happened. When Mass was over, they said they wanted to talk to me, and so we went to the rectory. They said they had a Christmas gift for me. They wanted to obtain annulments from their previous marriages and exchange their marital vows in the Catholic Church. To my astonishment, Lydia, his wife, said she wanted to become Catholic. She said, "I want to have the same faith you do. Since you would not back down on what you believe about marriage, I would like to become Catholic." I was elated. I praised the Infant Jesus for that special Christmas gift.

After a few months, they went through the annulment process, and she took classes to become Catholic from Fr. Kevin O' Murphy and became Catholic. On the day of their wedding, as they exchanged their vows a year later at St. Agatha parish in Fritz, Ohio, I glanced through the glass doors of the church and saw giant snowflakes slowly fall to the ground. It was like a Norman Rockwell wedding, which came about by the grace of God!

#74 ASSIGNED TO IMMACULATE HEART OF MARY WHEATLAND, OHIO

Assigned to Immaculate Heart of Mary Parish in Wheatland

"And you my child, will be called the prophet of the Most High; for you will go before the Lord to prepare His ways, to give knowledge of salvation to His people in the forgiveness of their sins, through the tender mercy of God, when the day shall dawn upon us from on high to light to those who sit in darkness and in the shadow of death, to guide our feet in the way of peace." (Luke 1:76-79)

With the sudden death of Fr. Liberato Modernity at Immaculate Heart, Bishop Traditiones, most likely, had no other choice but to ask me to be their pastor. I hesitatingly, said yes.

Interestingly, I had just spoken with my spiritual director about telling the bishop I believe I am able to do more ministry than my current assignment. By God's providence, it was at this time, the bishop called and asked me to become the pastor of Immaculate Heart of Mary.

Fr. Modernity died from a widow-maker heart attack. I prayed for his soul, and offered many Masses for him. I also encouraged parishioners to daily pray for him. I prayed intensely for wisdom as I began the new assignment, whereby the people were mourning the sudden death of their pastor, who died in the rectory.

His funeral caused their famous German Dinner to be postponed, until the following weekend. Consequently, when I arrived at the parish, it was the same weekend as the German dinner. A few days before the dinner, I visited with the secretary and bookkeeper, both of whom were deeply shocked by his death. Before he died, I had never spoken to Fr. Modernity. Therefore, I had no idea of the ways he pastured the people of the parish. When a new pastor arrives at his new parish, usually the current pastor will share information with the new pastor about the parish. However, due to his death, I had no opportunity to speak to him about the people.

The bookkeeper showed me the exact location she found his body. As odd as this sounds, for months I walked around the spot where he died, and didn't want to step on the place where his soul departed from this life. I felt like it was a sacred spot. I also didn't use his bedroom, but rather, took up the guest bedroom as mine.

There was a strange smell in the living room where he died, and months later I discovered, after his death, he evacuated his stool and no one had cleaned the carpet. I then rented a steam cleaner to clean the carpeted rooms in the house myself.

About a month after I had moved in, the cleaning lady found his pyx in his bedroom drawer with Hosts in it. I immediately took them over to the Tabernacle, and presumed he had been too sick to take them to the church after coming back from ministering at the penitentiary. However, he most likely, had no care or devotion for the Eucharist and treated it as ordinary bread.

An odd event occurred concerning his car that was parked outside in the driveway. As the three of us were talking, as soon as the secretary or the bookkeeper brought up his name, the car started honking on its own. The bookkeeper found his keys, turned off the car alarm, and then we continued to talk. But once again, when his name was brought up in conversation, the car started honking. Later that night, about 3am, a *Twilight Zone* event happened. I was awakened to the car honking again. I grabbed the keys, and tried to shut off the honking, but it wouldn't stop. Out of desperation, I stood by the bedroom window, gave the car a blessing, and, the car immediately stopped honking. I was shocked, to say the least, that the blessing worked. The next day, I told the bookkeeper what had happened, and she thought perhaps Fr. Modernity, from eternal life, was trying to tell us something about the car. We went out to the car and looked through it. We found a glove, hat, and a badge used to gain entry to a nearby correctional facility, where he offered Mass regularly. Had it been left in the car, when it was sold, anyone could have gained entrance into the prison. After the badge was removed, the car never honked again, and was eventually repossessed, since payments hadn't been made after his death.

The parish office was in the rectory, and that made it easy for people to freely walk through the rectory for coffee or do other things, which greatly bothered me. Since it was the place l resided, I felt violated.

While changing a light bulb in the ceiling of my bedroom, the secretary suddenly walked into the room and startled me. Not thinking about what I was saying, and, since I was so shocked she came into my bedroom, I said, "You ought to be glad I had clothes on." What I meant was clerics, rather than pajamas. I was totally embarrassed as to what I said, and so was she. At that moment, I knew the parish office had to be moved out of the rectory. At the next Pastoral Council meeting, we decided to move the office to the parish center.

When everything was moved to the new office, the printer wouldn't work after being reconnected to the computer. We worked on it for hours, but it would not print. Finally, out of desperation, I remembered St. Maximilian Kolbe blessed a broken printing machine, which he said, wasn't working, since "The devil had gotten his tail caught in it." I gave the printer a blessing with the sign of the Cross, just as I blessed Fr. Modernity's car, to stop it's honking. We immediately tried to print and it started working. Thank you, Jesus! Oh, the power of a priestly blessing!

#75 ADORATION CHAPEL AT IMMACULATE HEART OF MARY PARISH FRUITS & BLESSINGS

Adoration Chapel Confusion and Blessing. Parishioner Calls Me Satan.
"He is possessed by Beelzebul," and "by the prince of demons He casts out the demons." And he called them to him and said to them in parables, "How can Satan cast out Satan?" (Mark 3:22-23) "Make every effort to keep the unity of the Spirit through the bond of peace." (Ephesians 4:3)

A few weeks before we were to start the Adoration Chapel, I went on a retreat to the Shrine of the Five Holy Wounds in Bakersfield, Mississippi. Just before I left for the retreat, the secretary asked if the Chapel could be painted while I was away. After giving approval for the paint job, we picked out an off-white color. She wanted the walls to be stuccoed, but I thought the wall surface would collect dust, and suggested it only be painted.

After being on retreat for five days, I decided to return a several days early, and was shocked at what was done to the chapel. The ceiling of the Chapel was open and wires were hanging from it. The carpet was torn up, and walls were being stuccoed by someone I never met. I said, "What are you doing? Stop, right now, what you are doing! Who told you could do this?" To my surprise, she just kept painting walls, and then finally said, "Viola Dubois." I asked Viola to come into the parish hall to visit with me, and when she arrived, I sternly said, "You can't just come in here, and tear apart the ceiling and the carpet. We have to get approval by the Pastoral Council. We are required to use a certified electrician. Who is doing this? Is he an electrician, and who is the woman painting? Why did you tear out the carpet, without talking to me?" I said,

"Viola, I am so disappointed in you. I can't believe you would spend parish money without asking me about it." She said, "Father, you don't understand. We wanted to surprise you. We thought you would be happy to have this done." She departed nearly in tears. I was angry, and didn't know what to think about it all.

A few days later, she and her husband came to meet with me. The first thing I did was apologize for my tone, but I could not understand how they could do what they did without talking to their pastor. Her husband looked at me, and said, "I used to call you father. I used to call you a priest. But, from now on, I will call you Satan!" I was so shocked by what he said, I didn't say anything. Then Viola finally explained. She said their family wanted to remodel the Chapel before it was to open, and they wanted to do it as a surprise for me and the parish. They were paying for everything themselves, at no cost to the parish. They wanted to show me and the people of the parish that they were practicing stewardship. I felt like crawling under the desk, was totally humbled by it, and again apologized. They then said because of my reaction, they were going to go to another parish. Their son was not an electrician, but she said he knew how to wire lights. The woman painter was their daughter-in-law, and did home remodeling for a living. Eventually, we forgave each other, and by God's grace and mercy, it was as though nothing happened between us. They never went to a different parish. Truly, the Spirit of Unity and Reconciliation was at work. I eventually told the parish about the family's stewardship, and publicly thanked them. But, before everyone forgave each other, Viola had written a letter to the bishop, which I didn't know about until years later.

Perpetual Adoration at Immaculate Heart of Mary Parish
Conversions & Answered Prayers

Seven months after I arrived at Immaculate Heart, we started the Adoration Chapel on Oct. 13th, the anniversary of Our Lady of Fatima's last apparition. (See Appendix G - Preparation for Perpetual Adoration for Priests)

A lady from the parish was bound and determined to prevent Eucharistic Adoration. She gave many parishioners her reasons why the Chapel should not be opened. She came to my office, and mentioned seven reasons why we should not start Perpetual Adoration. Since she was trying to convince parishioners, through gossip, to not have Adoration, I wrote an article for the bulletin refuting her seven reasons, though I didn't mention her name. For example, she said, we should not have Adoration, because during the winter, the elderly will fall on the ice. And when there is a snowstorm, there will be car accidents by those on their way to pray at the Chapel. She also said, if someone couldn't make their Holy Hour, some would get upset, since no one showed up. In response, I wrote, "During winter, the Adoration Chapel would be closed at times during inclement weather, and adorers will be called, so they know it will be closed. If someone can't make their Holy Hour, there will be substitutes, or, if necessary, one can call, and ask the person coming after the hour to arrive 30 min. early, and the following hour adorer, to stay 30 min longer. People won't mind when it happens because they love spending time with Jesus."

Don and Mary were a couple from the parish who were divorced years ago, and were no longer living together. Don and Mary, unbeknownst to each other, signed up for a Holy Hour. Over time, both began to practice their faith more. Don began to come to daily Mass, and Mary used to ask me all sorts of questions after her Holy Hour. It was obvious her faith was growing. The two started dating each other, and doing all sorts of things together. Both appeared to have true conversions.

Unfortunately, when they were driving to Idaho to attend a rodeo, a drunk driver crossed the line, and both were killed instantly. We had a double funeral for them at the parish. It seemed, by their time spent with Jesus in adoration, it brought them closer to Our Lord, and brought them back together, to prepare them for their future time in heaven with each other, and with Him.

When the Adoration Chapel started, Ann Chappel signed up for a Holy Hour, persistently prayed for her husband to become Catholic, and prayed her 20-year-old son would start practicing his faith. Without saying anything to either of them, her husband, Garret, on his own, announced he wanted to take classes to become Catholic. Because her son, Roderick, wasn't confirmed, he took RCIA classes with his father, and Ann joined them for moral support. At the Easter Vigil that year, Garrett became Catholic. Roderick was confirmed, and all three began to spend time together with Jesus in the Adoration Chapel. Garrett developed a beautiful devotion to the Blessed Virgin Mary.

Gladys Winterbean called and seemed confused, which was unlike her. Right after our conversation, I went to the Adoration Chapel to pray, and, during my time with Jesus, in the Chapel, I felt the Lord was telling me to call her husband to check on her. The urge became persistent and strong. In response, I called her husband, and spoke to him about my conversation with his wife. He went to check on her, and called me back, saying he thought she needed to go to the hospital, but was refusing. So, I went to their home and spoke to Gladys and her husband. I anointed her, and encouraged her to go to the ER. Later, after she was taken to the hospital the doctor said if she had waited another hour, she would have died. She had a severe infection, which caused her to have back surgery and rehabilitation. Jesus, in the Eucharist, saved her life. Gladys was a faithful adorer of Jesus in the Blessed Sacrament. She had a Holy Hour in the middle of the night from 2am to 3am. Jesus wanted her to be with Him, and so arranged things to save her life and receive the medical help she needed.

A few months after we started our Adoration Chapel, five people quit their Holy Hour. That's a lot of vacancies for a little Chapel that has Adoration from 12pm Sunday to 10pm on Wednesday evening. "Through the Chaplet you will obtain everything, if what you ask for is compatible with My will." (Diary of St. Faustina, #1731)

Not knowing what to do, I went inside the church and prayed to Jesus in the Tabernacle, "Lord, five people quit their Holy Hour, and if I put in the bulletin, there are five openings, the people will lose confidence, and will not keep their Holy Hour. This is your Chapel. If you want to keep it open, you have to help us know what to do. Tomorrow the bulletin needs to be printed, and if I don't find five people tonight to fill those Holy Hours, it will indicate there are five open hours. You said, when we pray the Chaplet of Divine Mercy, whatever we ask, you will grant, if it's your holy will. Right, now, it is the 3 o'clock Hour. I ask that you help me find five people to fill those Holy Hours before we print the bulletin." I then prayed the Chaplet before Jesus in the tabernacle, returned to my office, opened the parish directory, and randomly began calling people asking them to fill particular hours. Each person I called took an hour, and within 15 minutes all hours were filled. I went back to the church, knelt before Jesus, and said, "Forgive me Lord, for I am a sinful man. Thank you, Jesus, for filling the Hours. Truly, this is Your Chapel."

Jesus the King Appears to a Teen in the Adoration Chapel
"Do not come any closer," God said. "Take off your sandals, for the place where you are standing is holy ground." Then he said, "I am the God of your father, the God of Abraham, the God of Isaac and the God of Jacob." At this, Moses hid his face, because he was afraid to look at God. (Exodus 3:5)

Due to foot pain as a result of fallen arches, I was sitting in my office in the evening without shoes, when there was a knock at the door. It was Betty, a grandmother, with her three grandchildren (two girls and a boy). They had a look of shock on their faces. I invited them in, and said, "What happened?" The grandmother pointed to her grandson, and said, "Tell father what happened." The boy said, "All of us were praying in the Adoration Chapel. I was kneeling and looking at the Host, when suddenly Jesus came out of the Host, and stood before me. He was wearing a white tunic, had a gold sash around His waist, and wore a golden crown on His head. Jesus said to me, "Take off your shoes. This is holy ground." The boy said, he took off his shoes, and then, Jesus said to him, "Tell the others to do the same." He then looked at his grandmother, sisters, and told them to take off their shoes. Curiously, they somehow understood something had happened, and did as the boy requested. Jesus then spoke again, and said, "Tell the priest, I want the people to remove their shoes before they enter the Chapel. But, it's up to them, if they want to remove their shoes, or not." The boy then told me, "Jesus, then, went back in the Host."

To determine, if what had happened was of God, I asked the boy how he felt, and he said, "Peaceful. I am humbled, that God had me see Him. I feel unworthy." And then the boy started to cry. I asked why he was crying, and Kaden, said, "I am unworthy."

This event happened within two months after the boy, and his sisters became Catholic. After praying about it, it reminded me of the burning bush, and how God asked Moses to remove his sandals, since he was on holy ground. The boy also had no recollection of the Bible story, nor did he know in some countries, like the Philippines, they traditionally remove their shoes, before entering an Adoration Chapel. The boy said, "I think it's my mission to let other people know the Eucharist is Jesus."

After additional prayer, without telling parishioners, where it happened, during a weekend homily, I explained what was reported, and said it occurred in the Diocese of Rolling Hills. I suggested they remove their shoes before entering the Adoration Chapel, and told them, the event was private revelation, and there is no obligation to believe it. I said it has not yet been investigated by the Church. I said, "I see no harm in removing shoes, as long as no one is offended by odor, and that people may choose to do it, or not." To my surprise, the majority of the people began to remove their shoes before entering the Chapel, out of love and respect for Jesus in the Eucharist.

#76 CONVERSION OF IMMACULATE HEART OF MARY PARISH ADORATION & STEWARDSHIP

"There were no needy ones among them, because those who owned lands or houses would sell their property, bring the proceeds from the sales, and lay them at the Apostles' feet for distribution to anyone as he had need." (Acts 4:34-35)

When I first arrived at the parish, the previous pastor scheduled confessions for 15 minutes before the Saturday evening Mass and was never in the confessional, rather, he would greet people when they came to church. Parishioners had to ask him to hear their confession.

The first months at the parish, I had only one to two confessions each week or 4 to 8 per month. Consequently, I preached about Confession a few times and added confessions 30 minutes before every Mass. By the time, I departed as pastor, four years later, there were 12 to 14 confessions every week or 48 to 56 per month.

When we began continuous Eucharistic Adoration, from Sunday after the 11am Mass until Wednesday, 10pm, except during Mass times, the people began to have conversions and come to confession more frequently. Adoration caused many to learn more about their faith, to pray more, and they received innumerable graces being in the presence of Jesus during Adoration.

The year after we began adoration, I introduced the Stewardship Way of Life, meaning they were encouraged to give their time, talent, and treasure for the glory and honor of God and for the good of their neighbor. People became involved in doing many things for each other. They began to see stewardship was not only about tithing. It was a way of life to give one's love to others, as it was in the early Church.

A parishioner was moved to tears when she learned her volunteer work all those years at the historical society could be attributed to her love of God and neighbor. She had never thought about it in that way.

We had a marble Holy Family statue near the rectory. The Child Jesus in the statue was about eight years old, but one of His hands was broken off. When an atheist woman, who sculptured marble, heard about how many parishioners were excited in doing things for others, she wanted to join in. She spent hours making a marble hand to fit the Child Jesus and reattach it. Her work was so beautifully done, one would never have known it was originally broken off. I used to tell people our stewardship was so successful, an atheist "gave Jesus a hand."

Young people, old people, and everyone in between learned the importance of loving one's neighbor and practicing their faith. Children on their own began to go to confession regularly. 90% of parishioners had a conversion. But, the 10% who didn't, mostly altar society members, would cause heartache and difficulties in the parish.

Once we began ad orientem Masses, I preached that the normal way the Church desires we received Communion is on the tongue. People believed they were required to receive on the hand and were excited to learn they could now receive on the tongue. I told them the Church grants an indult (permission from the Church) to receive Communion on the hand. I said, we may have permission to walk on someone's grass, but the normal way to walk to a front door is on the sidewalk. I explained that if they receive in the hand, they are obliged to look for Sacred Particles on their hand and consume them. I was surprised when over half of the parishioners began to receive on the tongue.

During Holy Communion, at the ad orientem Masses, I placed kneelers near the altar, so anyone who wanted, could receive Holy Communion kneeling. The kneelers were placed there at all weekday Masses and the ad orientem Mass at 11am. Respect for the Eucharist increased, and some ladies began to wear the mantilla on their own. This also caused people to show more reverence by dressing up for Sunday Masses.

But, due to the few complainers, they would paint a picture of the parish that was deceptive and downright false. However, the majority of parishioners were brought closer to Jesus and began to live out their Catholic faith loving and caring for each other.

#77 EASTER SNOW

In 2016, at Immaculate Heart of Mary in Wheatland, one Easter morning, after we celebrated the Easter Vigil the night before, I awoke to see the ground and trees shining and sparkling with two inches of very wet snow. The trees had blossomed recently, and newly sprouted leaves were covered in white. It was like a Norman Rockwell picture. As the morning continued, the snow began to melt. It seemed symbolic of the Lord's Resurrection. When Jesus rose from the tomb, the earth was filled with the sparkling light of His glory. The snow melted fast, but not before I took the wonder of it all in, in late April, an Easter gift to stir hearts for love of Him, who died and rose from the dead for love of us.

#78 GOOD AND BAD EVENTS AT IMMACULATE HEART OF MARY PARISH

"Go to Sally!"

One evening about 9pm, I was returning from Rolling Hills, on my way back to Wheatland, after eating dinner with a couple. Earlier in the day, I stopped by the nursing home, and anointed Sally, a parishioner, who was not doing well. While about two miles from Wheatland, I heard a voice in my head say, "Go to Sally!" I thought, "I can't go to the nursing home this late at night. After all, I anointed Sally earlier in the day". I thought, I must be imagining things, and decided to return to the rectory. As I was driving down a street in Wheatland, Ohio, while passing by the high school, the voice repeated, "Go to Sally!" I said, to myself, "This is stupid. What will they think, if I come this late at night to the nursing home to see Sally? She's probably sleeping, and I don't want to disturb her." I thought, "Well, there is only one way to see if this is of God, I will go, to see Sally."

When I walked through the front door of the nursing home, a nurse looked at me with a shocked look on her face, and said, "Oh Father, you are here to see Sally, right, who called you? We wanted you to come." I sheepishly said, "Jesus." I said, "Jesus told me to come." When I went to Sally's room, her husband just came out, and he said, "Who called you? Sally just died." After telling him about how I came, he said, "I want to come back to church. I haven't attended church for a long time." I then stood by the bed of Sally and prayed prayers for the dead from the *Pastoral Care Book.*

He came back to church and regularly attended Mass. A few weeks after the funeral, he signed up for a Holy Hour, and faithfully kept it every week. He died, as a practicing, Catholic 5 years later after his wife passed into eternity.

Brownies to Kill

There was an elderly lady, Dollie Madison, who, occasionally, made brownies for me. At first, she made some for Christmas. I ate a few, but, gave the rest to the secretary. I needed to stay away from sugar, since at that time, I was becoming diabetic. They were delicious. However, because I told her how good they were, she started to bring them more often, such as my birthday and Easter. I usually ate one or two, and gave the rest away to parishioners.

One day, she made some of her famous brownies and I took a healthy bite of one. But these brownies were different. They were very crunchy. I thought, she added nuts. Since, they were so crunchy, and hard to chew, I spat it out, to see what the nuts were. I was horrified, to see broken chard porcelain glass in the brownies. Because there was so much glass in them, I wondered if she was trying to kill me. After all, I heard she was upset with me about something in the parish. But then, I rationalized, she must have broken a dish and pieces must have fallen in the batter. I wondered if I had swallowed glass fragments, and, if so, would it kill me? I never became ill after eating them.

Since that time, when she gave some to me, I threw them away, since I didn't trust her cooking, didn't want others to get sick, and didn't think it was a good idea to tell her about the porcelain in them.

Ad Orientem Masses

In the diocese of Rolling Hills three parishes went all "ad orientem". The words "ad orientem" means "to the east." It doesn't necessarily mean facing east, but, rather, the priest and the people face God together. The bishop allowed them, by not saying anything to the pastors. Shortly after the three parishes began offering all ad orientem Masses, I decided it would be good for parishioners and I to face God together (east). I gave three homilies on the subject, inserted information in the bulletin, and then sent a letter to every parishioner explaining, that it was the normal way Mass was intended to be offered after Vatican II. A week before we were to begin the "ad orientem" Masses, Cardinal Sarah made it known to all priests, he wanted every parish to do "ad orientem" Masses at the beginning of Advent. I copied his announcement and attached it to the bulletin. Then, the day before we were to begin, the bishop sent out an email to all priests saying he did not want any more parishes to go all ad orientem, but only some Masses could be offered in that manner. Typically, when a priest tries something new, a few parishioners write letters to the bishop to complain. The Bishop called me into his office and told me I could not offer all Masses ad orientem. I said, "Bishop, when I received your email, I decided to offer one weekend Mass, a Wednesday evening Mass and also the Saturday morning Mass. And on feasts and solemnities, we would do it those days too. Is that okay with you? He agreed, despite the fact, he disagreed with Cardinal Sarah, and disagreed with the information I put in the bulletin. I had taken information from the Roman Missal to explain how the Mass was to be offered, but he didn't agree with it. When I was a seminarian, we were told to not follow the rubrics of the Missal. Otherwise, we would be offering Mass "ad orientem."

When I started offering ad orientem Masses, I was surprised at two things. First, it was much less distracting for me to offer Mass and second a lot more people liked it, than I anticipated.

Here is an example of why it's so distracting to offer Mass facing the people. One day, as I was praying the Eucharistic prayer, I noticed an arm go up in the congregation. I glanced to see what happened, and I noticed a man raised his hand to dig in his nose. Then, a few minutes later, I noticed another hand movement and looked again. This time, he removed the finger from his nose and was rolling the booger up into a ball. I tried to avoid looking, but then he moved his arm again, and this time, he was placing the boogers in his mouth. I was grossed out. When he came forward for Holy Communion, the distracting thought occurred to me, "Maybe I should give him a dispensation for breaking the fast." Ha ha. When the people and the priest face the same direction, not only is it less distracting, it is so much more prayerful.

After I was transferred from the parish, the next priest continued offering ad orientem Masses, but not for long, as some people complained to the bishop and did the best they could to get their new pastor transferred, which is what happened to me as well.

Firing of the Parish Secretary

When I arrived at Immaculate Heart of Mary parish, I was astonished to learn the secretary never received a salary from the parish. She worked for free giving her stewardship for the parish. At the end of the year, she made a tax donation certificate for herself, for the amount of money she would have received from the parish had she been paid. She used it for her taxes, as though she took an income.

When the Diocese finance representative completed an audit, as is customary, when a new pastor arrives at the parish, this was discovered, and she was informed by the Diocesan representative, that to create the form, while not getting paid, was improper. She agreed to discontinue. However, the following year, she made out another tax statement declaring she received over $7,000 in salary, but never received money. I reminded her it was illegal, and she agreed. The third year, she did it again, and this time, I realized she was doing it to cheat on her taxes. I asked for advice from the diocesan human resource director, and was told I needed to fire her, since she was asked three times, and was clearly doing something deliberate and illegal.

My heart sank, since I liked her and thought she did a wonderful job as secretary. The day came when I fired her. I told her the diocese told me to do it. Surprisingly, she took it well. I asked a woman from the parish to replace her as secretary, and she agreed. I offered to pay her a regular salary, but she refused. She, too, wanted to give her time and talent to the people of the parish for free. I felt awful over what had happened to the previous secretary. Both times, I was pastor of different parishes, the secretary had to be fired. At least I prepared the next pastors to have good, honest secretaries.

#79 FATHER KAPAUN'S "MIRACLES" AT IMMACULATE HEART PARISH

Fr. Emil Kapaun

While in seminary, I heard about the priest, Fr. Emil Kapaun, a Catholic priest who died as a prisoner of war in Korea. However, I never prayed to him, nor did I have a devotion to him. Then I watched a video about him and became fascinated by his bravery and willingness to die for soldiers in his care, his faith, and his love of country.

After I was ordained a priest, I started to pray to him, asking for his intercession to help parishioners of my parishes. After I became a pastor, it seemed God was favorable to his prayers when they were asked for the good of my people.

Fr. Kapaun Heals a Cat with Cancer

I received a phone call one evening from Margo Armstrong, a parishioner at Immaculate Heart of Mary. She said, "Come to my house. Mark's cat is dying. Come and anoint the cat, so it will be healed." Mark was her 12-year-old son, and his cat was dying. I told her the sacraments were for people, and not for animals. She said, "My husband and children want you to come and bless the cat."

I decided to go to their home, and when I arrived, I noticed the sickly cat, heaving and thin. It had bumps all over its body, including its head. I said, "What's wrong with it?" She said, "It has cancer. It's dying. We took it to the vet, who said it has cancer, and nothing can be done." I told the family I couldn't anoint the cat, since the sacraments are only for people. I said, "However, I can give the cat a blessing." I said, "Why don't we pray to Fr. Kapaun to heal the cat, but we need to accept whatever happens, as God's will."

I extended my hand over the cat, and said, "Lord, if it's your holy will, we pray that through the intercession of Fr. Kapaun this cat will be healed. But, if it's not your will, we pray all may accept what is to come." I made the sign of the Cross, and said the blessing. The cat was so sick, I thought it would die while I was at their home, but it didn't.

Several weeks later, I asked Mark about his cat, and he said the cat was healed, and there were no longer any bumps on it. He said it's fine, except that it's skinny. When I saw Mark's mother, Margo, I told her the cat may have been misdiagnosed, and perhaps, the bumps were pus pockets or something from an infection. She responded saying, "No. I'm a nurse, and the vet said it had cancer, and now, the vet said the cancer is gone." The cat lived for a year. But, they could not find it after that year. They never knew what happened to it, and since they lived in the country, they thought the cat either wandered off or was killed by an animal.

Fr. Kapaun Heals Baby from Immaculate Heart in Wheatland

A Catholic couple, recently married, came to my office with their 6-month-old baby, Alex. The parents were upset because the doctor said their baby had Leukemia. They were on their way to the doctor's office for more lab tests, and stopped by wanting me to anoint their baby. However, I told them only children the age of reason could be anointed. They said Alex was lethargic and had a low white blood cell count. Instead of anointing him, I suggested we pray to Fr. Kapaun. Therefore, we prayed the Fr. Kapaun prayer together, followed by, one Our Father, Hail Mary, and Glory be, for a total healing of Alex. A few days later, the mother called and was ecstatic. She said the lab test results came back and Alex no longer had Leukemia. Without myself making the suggestion, she reported the healing to the diocesan Fr. Kapaun advocate, as a possible miracle.

Fr. Kapaun Heals Baby at St. Patrick's in Pickle Grove

I was visiting Fr. Anthony Birkenstock at his parish when he received an emergency call to come to the local hospital in Pickle Grove. A baby fell out of a high chair landing on his head. I went with Fr. Anthony to the Emergency Room. The baby's vitals were high. His blood pressure was extremely high and had a very fast heart rate. The doctor wanted the baby to be taken to the children's hospital in Ohio City. Fr. Anthony and I decided to ask Fr. Kapaun to intercede before God to heal the baby, and then we prayed one Our Father, Hail Mary and Glory Be, for the baby. As we prayed the three prayers, I watched the monitor and noticed the child's blood pressure and heart rate became normal. The doctor noticed a change, but insisted the child be taken by helicopter to the children's hospital. Later, we found out the child was completely fine. I believed Fr. Kapaun interceded to heal the baby.

#80 NEW LIGHTS AT IMMACULATE HEART OF MARY PARISH STEWARDSHIP & ADORATION

New Lights for the Church, A Symbol of How the Lives of the People Were Changed Through Stewardship & Eucharistic Adoration

"You are the light of the world. A city set on a hill cannot be hidden. Nor do men light a lamp and put it under a bushel, but on a stand, it gives light to all in the house. Let your light so shine before men, that they may see your good works and give glory to your Father, who is in heaven." (Matthew 5:14-16)

At my persuasion, the Pastoral Council voted to purchase and install new traditional looking lights for the church, and we asked parishioners to donate specific lights on behalf of their families. The new fixtures had LED lights and dramatically lit up the church, especially since they replaced ceiling fans with 60 watt bulbs. The people were in awe of the beauty of the church that seemed to have been hidden in darkness.

A week before the lights were installed, a self-proclaimed Satanist entered the unlocked church and sprayed a fire extinguisher throughout it, when the youth event, "Work and Pray" was taking place. Little did the Satanist know, in the basement of the church were high school and college students at the time doing a sleeping over. All were horrified to see the church vandalized, but love came into action, and we prayed for the young man who did it. The youth banded together to clean the church, which took four hours. Carpet and pew cushions were steam cleaned. Statues and the Stations of the Cross, etc. were cleaned. Had the youth not been there to help clean up the mess, the people of the parish, would have been shocked. But, the "Work and Pray" team was a beacon of light out of the darkness of vandalism and evil.

When I arrived at Immaculate Heart of Mary, there wasn't a Finance Council, nor a Stewardship Council, but only a Parish Council. We started all three councils to guide and lead the parish toward a stewardship way of life. The year after the Adoration Chapel began, and with the help of the three councils, there was a tremendous response by the people to begin the Stewardship way of life. Monsignor McDuggle, the former pastor of St. Charles of Sezze parish, started parish stewardship in the diocese. He said, "First, bring the people to Jesus in Eucharistic Adoration. Then they will want to do things for Jesus. That's the way stewardship works." Parishioners were inspired by the youth, who used their talents for the love of God and neighbor. The parish was transformed into a beacon of light by Jesus, the Light of the World truly present in the Eucharist. But the devil continued to cause havoc. He stirred up parishioners against parishioners, and parishioners against their pastor.

#81 "MIRACLES" OF ST. ANTHONY OF PADUA

St. Anthony of Padua Returns – The Finding of Brandon Bratwurst

I was invited for dinner, to the home of a Polish American couple in Glasscow, a small town in the parish boundaries of Immaculate Heart of Mary in Wheatland. When I entered their home, I immediately noticed a large, six-foot statue of St. Anthony holding the divine Child Jesus. I asked how they came by such a large statue in their living room, and inquired where it came from. They said a previous pastor at Immaculate Heart removed the statue from the sanctuary of the church, and was going to dispose of it. To rescue the statue, they asked their pastor if they could keep it. He said they could do whatever they wanted with it. Over time, the statue lost some of its luster and paint was peeling off. They asked me if the statue could be returned to the sanctuary of the church. I told them we will ask the people of the parish to vote to see if they wanted it back in church. The vote indicated the majority wanted the statue returned. The couple volunteered to pay for the refurbishing of the statue.

A parish ten miles from Immaculate Heart parish, recently had some statues repaired by an elderly woman, who specialized in refurbishing them. I contacted her, and she began to repair the St. Anthony Statue in a garage owned by the parish near the Parish Hall. She also repaired the old Nativity scene of the parish, that became damaged over the years.

During this time, a seminarian, Brandon Bratwurst, drowned in Saint Peter and Paul River by saving the life of a young girl in his boat, which tipped over. Brandon's aunt and uncle were members of the parish, as well as some of his cousins. To the heartache of the family, authorities couldn't find his body. As a response to this sad dilemma, at the parish, we prayed a nine-day novena, asking St. Anthony to find the body of Brandon Bratwurst. We prayed the prayer at the end of each Mass for nine days.

The statue was providentially finished on the ninth day of the Novena. I was saddened that on the ninth day, Brandon's body wasn't found, and so, I prayed to St. Anthony, saying, "I'm not going to put you in the sanctuary of the church until the body of Brandon is found. We are placing you in the basement of the church! If you want us to put you in the sanctuary, then help us find his body!"

Immediately after I said the prayer, I felt bad. Who am I to speak to a saint like that? I apologized to St. Anthony, saying, "I'm sorry, for treating you like that. Even if the body of Brandon can't be found, we will put you in the sanctuary,." A few men, including an uncle of Brandon, and I, carried the statue to the church, and placed it on its pedestal. Within an hour, after the statue was set on its pedestal, I received a phone call from Brandon's family, saying his body had been found.

His body was found on the ninth day of the Novena, the same day, St. Anthony returned to his place in the sanctuary of the church. Thank you, Saint Anthony, for returning to the parish and for helping a sorrowing family have peace!

#82 HELPING SICK PARISHIONERS

Jolene Hertzler's Stroke

When I was pastor of Immaculate Heart of Mary parish in Wheatland, the former parish secretary, Jolene Hertzler was living at the local Assisted Living Center, when she had a stroke. Her stroke was severe. She was unable to talk, or swallow, and was paralyzed on one side of her body. Her daughter, Shirley Cartwright, a home health nurse, decided to place her mother on hospice. The family planned to remove her IV. But I convinced Shirley to keep the IV and install a feeding tube on her mother, so she would not die without nutrition and hydration, and I told her I thought she may improve. Within a few weeks, Jolene started to talk. A week later, she began to swallow again. Soon, she was eating and her speech improved. She was transported to a rehab facility in Fig City, and after a few months, was able to walk using a walker. She then returned to the Assistant Living Center. For 3 years, Jolene attended Mass almost every Sunday, and was able to have ordinary conversations with people. At the end of the 3 years, when I began to do hospital ministry in Tantrum, Idaho, she died of a heart attack.

The Happy Death of Annie Oakley at Immaculate Heart of Mary, Oct. 2015
Masses for a Poor Soul and Annie's Last Rites

Annie Oakley's daughter, Ella, asked me to visit her mother, who was living in an apartment for the elderly. Ella said her mother was experiencing strange events at her home. When I went to visit Annie, she described a black figure coming out of her closet, and sitting next to her on the bed when she was lying down trying to sleep. She said the figure attempted to put "his" arm around her, but she pushed it away. She thought it was her deceased husband. I blessed her house, told her to sprinkle Holy Water daily and call if anything more would happen. Each week I went to her home to give her Holy Communion.

A few weeks later, she said the figure again came out of the closet in her bedroom. I said, "Is there anything in your closet that doesn't belong to you?" She went through the closet, found her husband's shirt, and said she was keeping it as memorabilia. I suggested she throw it away to see if the figure would stop coming and also suggested maybe her husband wanted her to have Masses offered for his soul. We scheduled three Masses. The figure did not come back. Over the next few weeks, two Masses were offered. The final day, after the last Mass was offered, I heard an ambulance. I am not an ambulance chaser, but it sounded like the ambulance arrived at either the high school or the elderly apartments, which were several blocks way. I quickly jumped in my car, and found the ambulance near the elderly apartments. There, by Ella's vehicle, Annie, her mother, was lying on the ground. The EMT crew was giving her CPR. I quickly anointed her and gave her the Apostolic Pardon. She died a short time later.

Reflecting on this event, it was by God's inspiration I went to Annie in her need, so she could receive the Last Rites and the grace of a happy death. Before her death, she had three Masses offered for her husband's soul. The last one offered for him was the morning of her death, but not without some previous anxiety for Annie, due to an unwelcome guest.

#83 MORE GOOD AND BAD AT IMMACULATE HEART OF MARY PARISH

Immaculate Heart of Mary Parish Hall Policy For Sacraments and Celebrations
After I was pastor of Immaculate Heart of Mary parish in Wheatland, the first year, on Mother's Day, I promulgated a new policy for the parish hall and for sacraments. The policy was such, there would be no charge for parish hall rental for baptism celebrations or baby showers. I also said there would not be a charge to use the parish hall for weddings, since marriage is a sacrament, and the parish should celebrate with the young couple, and not cause a burden to them. However, a large deposit was required for these functions, so if they did not clean the hall, they would lose their deposit. The parish would also now pay for an annulment for any parishioner. I preferred to not receive funeral, baptism, or wedding fees, but accepted them if it was demanded of me to take them. Today, many parishes and priests charge for such things, which I believe is an abomination, especially for those who are poor and unable to afford it. The parish should celebrate with parishioners and not take advantage of them for financial gain. How much does it really cost to turn up the thermostat for 3 hours and run lights? How crazy! Why not celebrate with the people, rather cause a burden for them as they celebrate their life of faith?

Can You Come to the Church to Help Me Pick Up Something?

While walking downstairs to the basement of the church, I missed a step and fell down the stairs. I was in so much pain, I couldn't get up from the floor to stand. Not knowing what to do, I used my cell phone to call a parishioner, Luke Rodriguez. To not scare him, I said, "I'm in the basement of the church, can you come and help pick up something?" I didn't tell him, it was I, who needed to be picked up. After about 20 minutes from making the call, I was able to stand on my own. Just after I stood up, he arrived, and then I explained what had happened.

After I was x-rayed at the health clinic, the doctor said I had torn ligaments, and needed to use crutches. After 4 weeks, I could walk without them. The following year, I again fell down the stairs going to the church basement, and injured my other ankle and knee, but was able to get up. I was again on crutches for a month. I didn't need surgery from either fall. The pain and suffering was offered up for the people of the parish and the conversion of sinners.

Flowers from Hell

Every year at Immaculate Heart, like most other churches, flowers were purchased for Christmas and Easter to decorate the church. One Advent, many beautiful poinsettias arrived, and with them, came a bill for $1,600! The previous year, the other floral shop in Wheatland charged the church $8 per plant and the bill was $272. However, this year, a parishioner who owned a flower shop, ordered them without talking to anyone in the parish, and sent the bill to the office to be paid. We were charged $47 per plant.

Not knowing the woman ordered them without talking to the Altar Society, I thought the Altar Society ordered them, and would pay for the flowers. Consequently, I called the Altar Society president, who said no one in their organization ordered the flowers, and because the bill was so expensive, they would not pay it. I called the owner of the flower shop, who said someone from the Altar Society said she could order them, and that the Altar Society would pay for them. However, she didn't know the name of the person who gave her permission.

I was in a dilemma. Should I send the flowers back, and if I did, the owner would probably not sell them all by Christmas and lose lots of money? Or should I pay for them to keep peace, yet warn her not to do it again, and this is what I chose to do. Since the bill was so large, and to be a good steward of the parish finances, I sent a letter to the Pastoral Council telling them what happened, and that funds to pay for the flowers came from the parish. To be transparent, I sent a copy of the letter to the owner of the flower shop. She and her husband were furious, and would not talk to me. Just imagine what would have happened if I refused to pay for them. They wrote a nasty letter to me and wrote a letter of complaint to the bishop.

Due to the cost of the flowers, the Altar Society didn't purchase flowers for Easter from that particular flower shop. Instead, the Easter flowers were ordered from the local floral shop and not the expensive shop.

When the husband of the woman who owned the floral shop with the expensive flowers found out, he went to the local floral shop owner and threatened him, that if he would sell the church flowers he would ruin his business by telling all sorts of lies to the people of Wheatland. The Altar Society ended up purchasing Easter lilies from *Walmart*.

#84 HOMILY COMPLAINTS AT IMMACULATE HEART OF MARY PARISH

Homily Complaints –Previewed by the Vicar for Clergy

"Rolling up the scroll, He (Jesus) handed it back to the attendant and sat down, and the eyes of all in the synagogue looked intently at him. He said to them, "Today this scripture passage is fulfilled in your hearing." And all spoke highly of him and were amazed at the gracious words that came from his mouth. They also asked, "Isn't this the son of Joseph?" He said to them, "Surely you will quote me this proverb, 'Physician, cure yourself,' and say, 'Do here in your native place the things that we heard were done in Capernaum.' "And he said, "Amen, I say to you, no prophet is accepted in his own native place. Indeed, I tell you, there were many widows in Israel in the days of Elijah when the sky was closed for three and a half years and a severe famine spread over the entire land. It was to none of these that Elijah was sent, but only to a widow in Zarephath in the land of Sidon. Again, there were many lepers in Israel during the time of Elisha the prophet; yet not one of them was cleansed, but only Naaman the Syrian." When the people in the synagogue heard this, they were all filled with fury. They rose up, drove him out of the town, and led him to the brow of the hill on which their town had been built, to hurl him down headlong. But he passed through the midst of them and went away." (Luke 4:20-30)

Not knowing anything about the previous pastor, I presumed he didn't preach much, or at all about contraception or abortion, since most priests avoid these topics. Consequently, I pastorally decided to wait a year prior to preaching about these topics.

A year later, on the weekend of Roe vs. Wade, I preached about abortion and God's infinite mercy. In Lent, I preached about contraception and God's mercy. During the Fortnight of Freedom (14 days) in June, we were expected to preach about religious freedom and the *Health and Human Service (HHS)* mandate, which forced insurance companies to pay for abortion, sterilization, and contraception. Therefore, I gave one homily on the topic that weekend. Later in July, during Natural Family Planning Week, which our diocese Life Office promotes every year, I preached on *Natural Family Planning (NFP)* and the immorality of contraception. And, in October, during Respect Life weekend, I preached on abortion.

During the Clergy Conference, I was asked to meet with Fr. Veritas. The bishop received letters of complaints, saying I was preaching too much on contraception and abortion, and preaching too much on confession. I said, "Father, I never preached about either topic my first year at Immaculate Heart of Mary. I only preached five times in two years on these subjects." He said, "Well, the bishop said you are preaching about it too often." I didn't say anything, but recalled in "The Catholic Eagle", our local diocesan paper, the bishop said "Abortion is the greatest evil of our time". I thought, doesn't he realize I preached about these topics, only 5 out of 104 homilies in two years? Fr. Veritas continued, saying, "I think it's best I read all your weekend homilies before you give them."

Every weekend from October to April (6 months) I emailed the homilies to Fr. Veritas, before they were delivered. I later found out from multiple parishioners, Fr. Modernity never preached on these subjects. But rather, gave out books promoting President Obama that contained pro-abortion information. Three parishioners also said that Fr. Modernity was never in the confessional. Since he was greeting people, rather than sitting in the confessional, parishioners had to ask him to hear confessions before Mass.

On numerous occasions parishioners said he would preach from the pulpit, "If you miss Mass on Sunday, you don't need to come to confession. Just make an Act of Contrition, since all are welcome to the table of the Lord!"

Just before Easter, Fr. Anthony Birkenstock, whom I asked to read the homilies, called Fr. Veritas, and told him, he felt it unnecessary for me to send Fr. Vertitas the homilies. After all, he said, all of Fr. Leonard's homilies are on-line. Three priests Monsignor James Less, my spiritual director, Fr. Veritas, and Fr. Birkenstock, read the homilies every week for six months! Fr. Veritas never found fault with any homilies except he thought two of them were a bit long. My spiritual director suggested I change a few lines in one homily. But I never told him the those lines were actually word for word, a quote from a saint; but, I had not referenced the saint in the homily. I later discovered the parishioners, who wrote to the bishop and complained about the homilies were pro-abortion and pro-contraception.

#85 GERMAN DINNER AT IMMACULATE HEART OF MARY PARISH

The German Dinner

"Behold, now is a very acceptable time; behold, now is the day of salvation. We cause no one to stumble in anything, in order that no fault may be found with our ministry; on the contrary, in everything we commend ourselves as ministers of God, through much endurance, in afflictions, hardships, constraints, beatings, imprisonments, riots, labors, vigils, fasts; by purity, knowledge, patience, kindness, in a holy spirit, in unfeigned love, in truthful speech, in the power of God; with weapons of righteousness at the right and at the left; through glory and dishonor, insult and praise. We are treated as deceivers and yet are truthful; as unrecognized and yet acknowledged; as dying and behold we live; as chastised and yet not put to death; as sorrowful yet always rejoicing; as poor yet enriching many; as having nothing and yet possessing all things." (2 Corinthians 6:3-10)

The first weekend I arrived at the parish, and because I was new to the parish, I had no idea who were parishioners, and who were guests at the German Dinner. When the dinner began, I volunteered to pray an opening prayer for the meal, and was told by an altar society member, "We don't do that!"

As the dinner went on, patrons became drunk, including servers of wine and beer. I later discovered, they were members of the Knights of Cortez. Not knowing a lady was intoxicated, and after she asked me to sit at her table with her husband and two boys, she suddenly shouted, "I remember you. I had sex with you." She made the loud statement in front of her husband and children. I knew she had the wrong man, because I never had sex with any woman. I was totally embarrassed, and realized she was drunk. I later discovered she was a member of the parish. I asked her name, and told her that I had never met her before. She then quipped, "Do you have a brother by the name of Louis?" I said, "Yes." She then said, "Oh, I had sex with him, and not you. You two look alike." Embarrassed, I quickly left their table.

The CYO was serving food and its director was intoxicated, as well as the Grand Knight of Cortez. A high school youth came up to me, saying, "Father, there is a man in one of the classrooms, and he is drunk. He spilled beer all over the table and the floor." I went to the classroom, and found it just as the boy said. After seeing the mess, I couldn't stand it any longer, and left the dinner. I immediately went to the church to pray, knelt before the statue of Our Lady and wept.

Days after the event, because we had no janitor and each organization was supposed to clean up after their function, the spilled beer and wine evaporated on the floor, and left stains. No one was willing to clean up the mess, even though I repeatedly asked the organizers to do it. I ended up calling a professional cleaning agency to clean it up.

Some parishioners wanted to keep the decorations up all year long, because they were proud of them. I kept asking the Knights and the Altar Society to remove the decorations. They said they would take them down, but didn't. Finally, after the children made their First Communion in May, (four months after the dinner) there was a funeral, and due to all the decorations, the family of the deceased made it known that their father's funeral was no party. She demanded to have the decorations taken down. I ended up taking the decorations down myself. It took about 2 hours.

To discuss the problems of the German dinner, especially the drunkenness of parishioners , who were serving alcohol and intoxicated patrons, I had a meeting with the Grand Knight and the head of the German Dinner. I said there can longer be excessive drinking like that again and said those who serve alcohol should not be drinking while serving. I said, "If this happens again next year, we will limit the drinks to four per person." They agreed, but at the next German Dinner, the following year, some Knights who were serving got drunk, as well as a few patrons.

After the second dinner since my arrival as pastor, at the next Pastoral Council meeting, I asked for their advice about the drinking problem. The council voted to limit drinks to two per person. The Altar Society president, who attended the Pastoral Council, voted in favor of the proposal. After the meeting, I presumed the Altar Society was on board, especially since it was the president of the Altar Society's idea to limit drinks to two. But she failed to notify the leaders of the Altar Society. I wrongly presumed she had, and put a notification in the bulletin. Then came the fireworks. I attended the next Altar Society meeting, and most all ganged up on their president and berated her. She was so upset at the meeting that she quit the Altar Society right then and there, and walked out crying. Then they attacked me. It was truly sorrowful. Their filthy words, their false accusations, their anger. I felt like getting up and walking away, but didn't. I just sat there, and by the grace of God, calmly refuted their false accusations, and distortions of the events that happened. They wouldn't listen to the pastoral council's advice and some raised their voices in anger. They said nobody was drunk at the event, and I made it all up.

The next Pastoral Council meeting was a total disaster. Many of the Altar Society leaders came and some screamed at the Pastoral Council members. There was arguing back and forth. Altar Society wrote letters to Bishop Athanasius Courageous, claiming no one was ever drunk at the German Dinner, and that I made it all up. They told the bishop about the limit of two drinks per person, which they thought was unreasonable. During all this turmoil, I offered Masses for the Altar Society and the Knights of Cortez and tried to bare the suffering for the conversion of those causing the ruckus.

In response, I fasted, prayed Rosaries and Chaplets of Divine Mercy for them, but nothing noticeable seemed come out of it. I felt defeated. I put articles in the bulletin explaining the immorality of excessive drinking and gave a homily on it. But never did I come to know a single heart changed. It was very discouraging.

On several occasions, in order to talk things out, I asked to visit with the new Altar Society president, Ella, but she refused. It was as though all efforts were doomed to fail. God permitted the troublemakers to have the upper hand, and the bishop, without talking to me, gave his approval of the organizers.

If I had to do it all over again, I would do everything the same as before, because I believed what I did was God's will. Even though I felt abandoned even by Him, in my heart, I believed He was supporting me the entire time, because I stood up for the truth. I stood up for Him, who is the truth. My desire was to help people avoid sin, help them to obtain heaven, and for them, to love each other and work with each other, in peace and unity. Sadly, the bishop was duped by the altar society.

#86 IMMODEST CLOTHING & ANGRY PARISHIONER

Immodest Clothing of Extraordinary Ministers of Holy Communion

"Women should adorn themselves modestly and appropriately and sensibly in seemly apparel, not with elaborate hair arrangement or gold or pearls or expensive clothing," (1 Timothy 2:9)

After Mass on Sundays, I overheard men complain about some women Extraordinary Ministers of the Eucharist, who wore revealing and immodest clothing while distributing the Sacred Species at Holy Mass.

As a result of this, I prayed, and decided to send a letter to all who performed liturgical ministry and who had leadership roles in the parish: CCD teachers, secretary, lectors, the choir, organists, greeters, extraordinary ministers of Communion, etc...

In the envelope with the letter, I gave them a copy of the new Dress Code, which I found on the internet from a parish. I quoted diocesan policy in the letter as well and said all are to follow the new dress code. And if not, they would be warned; and, if after they continued to wear immodest clothing, they may be suspended from their ministry.

There were four ladies who wore low-cut tight clothing and all were big busted. None of the ladies changed their attire, so I sent a letter of warning to them. None heeded the warning, so the four received a letter of suspension. But, with the suspension letter was a note asking them to sign it, that indicated from now on, they will follow the Dress Code. And when I received their signed note, they could continue in their ministry. Only one lady signed it and one of the four, wrote a letter to the bishop. Fr. Quid E. Veritas came to the parish to speak to me about the suspensions, and also the German Dinner alcohol policy. I gave him a copy of the Dress Code and the letters I sent. I was very transparent and told him everything, but he failed to support anything I did.

Angry Parishioner

"We are treated as deceivers and yet are truthful." (2 Corinthians 6:8) "Do not let the sun go down while you are still angry." (Ephesians 4:6)

During one of the Pastoral Council meetings, a parishioner asked to address the council. He stood up, and with great anger pointed at me, and yelled, "You are a liar!" "You said we didn't clean after we had our function. That's not true. We did. You also said, Gladys Winterbean was wearing immodest clothing. You are wrong! The letter said she was at the 8:30am Mass, but, she does not attend the 8:30am Mass. She goes to the 11am Mass."

I received a letter in the mail mentioning Gladys was wearing immodest clothing, while distributing Holy Communion, and I sent her a copy. He was referring to the organization, Amagodei (a local group of older men and women, who donate money to charities), and at the end of their dinner, they left their tables and chairs in array. I had thought they also didn't clean up. However, later I recalled, it was the Altar Society's Christmas party, where they left food on tables and didn't clean the floor. I had cleaned up their mess. I later apologized to him, since he was right, as they did clean up. However, they never put away tables and chairs, that needed to be put away before the next day, because the Blood Mobile was going to use the parish hall.

I found out later, he asked the Knights of Cortez to put the tables and chairs back, but they didn't. The Pastoral Council was shocked at his anger and at the way he treated me. It would have been so much better if he and I would have just sat and talked about it in my office. But he decided to unload on me in front of the Pastoral Council, since he wanted to have me removed as pastor.

Shorts at Mass and Adoration Chapel
"O Lord, I love the house where you dwell, the place where your glory abides." (Psalm 26:8)

By way of various letters in the bulletin, I asked parishioners to dress up for Mass, and not wear shorts to Mass or the Adoration Chapel, but to respect Jesus in the Blessed Sacrament and His House. More parishioners wrote letters to the bishop, including the drunk woman, who mistakenly thought I had sex with her, although she didn't mention her behavior during the dinner with the bishop.

I later called the Diocesan human resource coordinator, and asked her, how I could have handled things differently concerning the Extraordinary Ministers of Holy Communion and their immodest dress. She said, I should have asked a woman to speak to each of the women privately. But I told her, "I thought about that, but I had no idea who to ask. Do you think anyone would have actually spoken to them?" The idea sounds good, but practically, seriously, a pastor could not ask a woman to say something to them. They would know the request came from the pastor anyway.

Fr. Vertias, the Vicar for Clergy, came to the parish to visit again. This time, it was about parishioner letters to the bishop. He said, "What is needed is a parish mission". He then asked what he could do to help in these situations. I said, "Father, when you come to know the truth. Stand up for it, and defend me." He said, "How can I know the truth?" I immediately thought of Pilate, who said, "What is truth?"

He said, "Bishop said you should ask for a transfer when the priest assignment papers are sent to all priests." When I filled out the priest assignment paper for that year, I said, "I will do whatever the bishop wants me to do, whether stay or be transferred." But surprisingly, I was not transferred. I never specifically asked for a transfer, but only that I would do whatever the bishop wanted of me. I felt I was being forced to say something I didn't believe. What I really wanted was support from the chancery, in helping to defend the Lord's sheep from sinful behaviors. But that would never happen.

A month later, Fr. Quid E. Veritas came to the parish, spoke at all weekend Masses and gave a talk during a Holy Hour. Although what he said was not harmful to me, or the people of the parish, there was no support for myself or the Pastoral Council. Only eight people came to the "mission". Out of eight only two who came, were involved in the fiasco. The truth of the matter, was there were only about ten people from the whole parish upset by the decision to limit drinks, the immodest clothing, and the other complaints. But there was no support, nor was there an attempt to come to know the truth by the chancery.

#87 MEETING WITH BISHOP ATHANASIUS COURAGEOUS

Meeting with the Bishop

"Because you are God's chosen ones, holy and beloved, clothe yourselves with heartfelt mercy, with kindness, humility, meekness, and patience. Bear with one another; forgive whatever grievances you have against one another. Forgive as the Lord has forgiven you." (Colossians 3:12-13)

The Bishop's secretary called, and I scheduled an appointment with him. The conversation went like this. Bishop: "I was told that you said people could not attend Mass if they wore shorts." I said, "No, that's not true. I said people should not wear shorts to Mass or the Adoration Chapel and I put it in the bulletin, but never preached on it. Perhaps I should have preached on it." Bishop: "People told me there was no one drunk at the German dinner." I said, "That's not true. The Knights of Cortez were serving beer and wine. Some were drunk. One was so drunk, he stood inches from my face when talking to me and I couldn't understand a word he was saying. The Grand Knight was drunk too. The CYO director was drunk, while CYO youth were serving. One CYO youth notified me of a drunk patron, in one of the classrooms, and spilled beer all over a table and the floor. I entered the classroom, I saw a man in his 20s with three young girls. He spilled beer all over the table and floor, and had difficulty walking because he was intoxicated. I mentioned this to the Pastoral Council twice. The first time, I suggested we limit drinks to four per person. The second time, we discussed it a year later, they voted to limit two drinks per person. Then the Altar Society became angry at the Pastoral Council." Bishop: "When I was a pastor, the Knights of Cortez had tents, and it wasn't a problem. They could drink as much as they wanted. It was a good time for everyone. Your alcohol policy is too long; it should just be a paragraph or two." I said, "I will send you a copy of the shorter version you, and you can tell me what you think." He said, "Okay."

Bishop: "In a letter you sent to the homes of every parishioner, you said when the *Roman Missal* came out in English, the wording was not as good as it could have been, and so later, Pope Benedict wanted it be more of an accurate translation. But, that's not true. The English Missal that came out in the 1970s was good for the people of that time. There wasn't anything wrong with that translation."

Bishop: "I received a letter about you suspending Extraordinary Ministers of Holy Communion." I said, "Yes. I heard some men complaining about women wearing very immodest clothing after Mass. I first sent a letter to all who serve at the parish: Lectors, Extraordinary Ministers of Holy Communion, ushers, etc. with a copy of the Dress Code, and told them they needed to follow it, or they may be suspended from serving due to immodesty. But they continued, so I sent the four the same letter again, and indicated this was their warning, or they would be suspended, unless they would follow the Dress Code. But all four continued, so I sent a letter of suspension. However, in the letter, I told them they could be easily reinstated, if they signed the enclosed statement, saying they would follow the Dress Code. One signed it, the other three did not, and remained suspended." Bishop: "The priest should not address something like this himself. It should be a lay person."

It was clear, after our conversation, he didn't believe anything I said. But, I did as he asked. I created a short alcohol policy, and emailed it to the bishop. It was just two paragraphs long.

When I gave it to the Pastoral Council for their approval, they wanted to add many guidelines found in the Diocesan Alcohol Policy and also wanted me to ask Catholic Insurance of America to look it over and obtain their approval. Catholic Insurance of America made suggestions that increased the length of the policy, and before we knew it, it went from several paragraphs to three pages long. After the final version was approved by Catholic Insurance of America with their revisions, I sent it to Fr. Daniel Logger, the Vicar General, who, on behalf of the bishop, rejected it, and made suggestions to eliminate all the Catholic Insurance of America's suggestions, and most of the Diocesan Policy quotes. In the end, the parish policy was devoid of much of Diocesan Policy and devoid of all suggestions by Catholic Insurance of America.

At my request, the Pastoral Council sent the bishop a letter explaining all the controversial events that have occurred in the parish since I became pastor. They supported me. But either the bishop didn't read it, or didn't believe it. A year after I was transferred to Tantrum, I received a copy of the letter the president of the Pastoral Council wrote to the bishop. I was proud of them for telling the truth.

While in Tantrum, Idaho, for those two and a half years of hospital ministry, I tried my best to forgive, and to put behind the angry thoughts towards the people that caused so many difficulties at Immaculate Heart of Mary parish and chancery personnel. Through prayer for the bishop and offering Masses for him, it has helped me understand the Lord forgives the failures of all us, and He expects us to forgive, as He has forgiven us. No one is taught how to be a priest, or a pastor, or a bishop. We learn as we go. And sometimes, we don't realize the consequences of not knowing how to do things, as we ought. God in His mercy sees how we all love and forgive each other, and He works through us, even when we make mistakes or don't do as we ought. He loves us, and forgives us, even when we don't realize what we have done or failed to do, and how actions or lack of actions, may have hurt others. God's mercy triumphs over everything! All of this was one big lesson of Divine Mercy.

"Don't Make Waves" Philosophy & Get Me Out of Here!

Due to the turmoil at Immaculate Heart of Mary in Wheatland, I no longer wanted to be a pastor of a parish in my diocese. In fact, I was searching for a diocese with the hopes of someday being incardinated elsewhere, or at least on loan. The great rule of thumb in our diocese seemed to have been, "under no circumstances should a priest make waves". But, didn't Jesus say, "Do you think that I have come to give peace on earth? No, I tell you, but rather division." (Luke 12:51)

When I was pastor of St. Anthony in Jericho and St. Veronica in Brushwood, I was supported by Bishop Traditiones who would not permit a non-Catholic Freemason's funeral to be held at St. Veronica's parish in Brushwood City. The former pastor, Fr. Jonathon Vanderbilt, wanted to do the funeral of a Freemason at the church, since he was friends with the Altar Society president, whose spouse died, and was a Freemason. And so, I asked the bishop if he would support me, and he did!

Did Jesus make waves when He said things like, "Anyone who divorces his wife and marries another woman commits adultery, and the man who marries a divorced woman commits adultery." (Luke 16:18) Or "If the world hates you, keep in mind that it hated me first." (John 15:18) Or "If any man comes to Me and hates not his father and mother, and wife and children, and brethren and sisters, yea, and his own life, also, he cannot be My disciple." (Luke 14:26)

I emailed Archbishop Andrew Goodshepherd of the Archdiocese of Millsburger, Idaho, and asked if I could serve in his diocese, especially since I knew they had a shortage of priests. I knew Fr. Shannon Blackwater from the Archdiocese of Millsburger, Idaho, because we attended seminary together, at St. Robert Bellarmine Seminary. He died suddenly while on retreat at the Happy Soul Retreat Center in Rolling Hills, Ohio. On my behalf, Archbishop Goodshepherd sent a letter to Bishop Courageous, asking if I could minister in his diocese as a hospital chaplain. However, Bishop Courageous responded, declining his request.

I also called a priest from the Lakota City Diocese, inquiring if I could serve there. But, the Chancellor for the Lakota City diocese later called back, and said, "We don't need you." They had a severe shortage of priests, and less than half were from their diocese. It's a very liberal diocese.

As pastor of Immaculate Heart of Mary, I had the thought, "Just get me out of here! I would rather do hospital ministry, rather than be a pastor." Since the chancery personnel gave me the impression all my decisions were wrong, I believed I was a total failure as a pastor. My spiritual director kept telling me I was a good pastor and successful too! But negative thoughts told me otherwise.

On my last day at Immaculate Heart of Mary parish, when parishioners held a going away reception for me, the scales fell from my eyes. It was only then, God showed me, by His grace, I was a good shepherd who cared for the Lord's sheep.

#88 SACRED HEART OF JESUS BEATING IN EUCHARISTIC HOSTS

Hosts Throb At Nursing Home

When I was about to leave the parish, as pastor of Immaculate Heart of Mary in Wheatland, Fr. Albert Brandmueller, the new pastor, and I were visiting home-bound and nursing home residents, to introduce him to them, and also show him their location. While giving Communion at the Nursing Home in Wheatland, as I picked up a Sacred Host out of the pyx (round metal container with a lid), to give it to a resident, I felt the Host beating. During three instances, with different residents, I felt the Host beat between my fingers. I became unnerved, and asked Jesus to stop allowing me to feel it. But it continued. Finally, I said to Fr. Albert Brandmueller, "Every time I pick up a Host from the pyx, I feel it beating in my fingers, as though it was a Heart. I'm telling you this so it stops." His mouth fell open, and from then on the Hosts finally stopped beating whenever I removed them from the pyx. I think the Lord was trying to tell me He deeply loves each resident. This also happened a few times while doing hospital ministry in Tantrum, Idaho and also at Rolling Hills, Ohio.

#89 DREAMS DURING MY LIFE

Dreams of Color and Dreams of Jesus

"He came to a certain place and stayed there for the night, because the sun had set. Taking one of the stones of the place, he put it under his head and lay down in that place. And he dreamed that there was a ladder set up on the earth, the top of it reaching to heaven; and the angels of God were ascending and descending on it." (Genesis 28:10-12)

Almost every night I dream, and remember them the next morning. If I wake up in the middle of the night, while dreaming, I used to be able to think about what I was dreaming. Then after using the restroom, and falling back to asleep, the dream would continue where it left off.

Over the years, I discovered the reason I remember dreams, is because I am a light sleeper, and those who sleep hard-- don't recall their dreams.

I used to have a reoccurring nightmare, that began when I was a child and continued for years. During the dream, I crawled on top of my grandfather's grandfather clock, and then, the clock started to sway, and just before it crashed to the ground, I awakened.

Another frequent nightmare began in high school. I would see the ground open up, and the devil come out of it. After I went to confession at the age of 27, I never had the nightmare again.

After my conversion, when I started practicing my faith, occasionally I told Jesus I desired to dream about Him. Before I went to bed, at times, I prayed, "Jesus I want to dream about you". The times I did dream about Him, I dreamt about His true presence in the Eucharist. I never saw Jesus as a man in a dream, except one time. As of today, I dreamt about the Eucharist thirteen times. In those dreams, the Eucharist was usually, being mistreated. For example, once I dreamt Hosts fell on the floor, not by me, but by people who were careless, and in the dream, I attempted to pick them up. The last dream about the Eucharist happened last night, when I dreamt a man came to the church during Eucharistic Adoration, removed the Luna from the Monstrance, and fled. In the dream I ran after him to save the Host, but he disappeared before I could reach him in time.

Another dream that I had repeatedly, involved myself searching for my vestment and alb before Mass, and those in the church began to leave before Mass started, because it took a long time to find the vestment and alb. Most of my dreams are in color. It is my understanding that most people dream in black and white.

The one time, I dreamt about Jesus, in His humanity, I saw Him as "Ecce Homo" (Behold the Man) with hands bound by a rope. He had a crown of thorns, and blood was falling down His face. His arms and legs were lacerated due to Him being beaten by the soldiers. He was wearing a red garment, that the soldiers placed on Him. When I woke from the dream, I asked the Lord, who had treated Him so badly. Was it me, by my sins? But there was no reply.

I met a psychologist who had a theory that dreams usually mean one of two things. He said they are either something we are afraid of, or something we desire.

It is my understanding, we are not to place any confidence in dreams or believe in them or think that they foresee future events. Otherwise, we can sin against God's Providence. Dreams are fascinating, and for me, they are like windows into the subconscious, that help the brain to rest or refresh itself, and help us have healthy thinking. In my opinion, we should ignore them, and not place any merit in them. Perhaps I was afraid of Hosts might get mistreated, or afraid I hurt Jesus by my sins. If a spiritual dream makes us happy, we can thank God. God used an angel to speak to St. Joseph in dreams, and He can do that for us. But if that would be the case, I believe we would immediately know it came from God and have no doubts. It's wise to speak to a priest before acting on any dream or ignore the dream.

#90 WHAT IS HEAVEN LIKE?

What is Heaven Like?
"Holy, holy, holy is the Lord of hosts; the whole earth is full of his glory!" (Isaiah 6:3)

Many times, in prayer, I asked the Lord what heaven is like. But I never came to understand what heaven is really like, except for the things we already know. God has never answered that prayer. However, He gave me a small insight.

One day, I repeated to Jesus, "Lord, what is heaven like?" And that day, during Mass, it dawned on me, heaven is like the Mass. At Mass, we worship God with the angels and saints around His throne, the altar. At Mass, we sing with the angels and saints, Holy, Holy, Holy. At Mass, God speaks, and everyone listens to Him in the Scriptures. In heaven, when God speaks, all listen. Likewise, at Mass, we have union with God in Holy Communion, which is a small glimpse of our future union with Him in heaven. At Mass, when the Eucharist is raised above the altar, we see God face to face. In heaven, we will see God face to face in all His glory. At Mass, a priest mediates with God and His people, and offers the prayers and sacrifices of the people to God. In heaven, Jesus, the one mediator, accepts the prayers and sacrifices of the people on earth, and offers them to the Father. At Mass, we give our love to God in Holy Communion, and He gives His love to us, just like in heaven. So, if we want to know what heaven is like, look to the Holy Mass.

#91 DEMONS MAKE THEMSELVES KNOWN

Battle Against Principalities
"Lord even the demons are subject to us in your name!" (Luke 10:17)

During my first trip to Medjugorje, I began to believe I had a vocation to the priesthood. The trip had many special graces with a number of supernatural events. But, also a bad supernatural event.

Terror at 30,000 Feet
A woman from our group and her husband from the Midwest seemed to be good people. But, the longer we stayed, the stranger her behavior became. She would say odd things, but no one thought too much about it. By the time we boarded the plane to leave, her behavior became noticeable by almost everyone in the group.

When we were halfway over the ocean heading towards the US, she suddenly started screaming, saying we were going to crash. She became hysterical, and started cursing. Her husband, who sat next to her, was horrified, and didn't know what to do. I sat directly across the aisle from her. She began making animal sounds and grunting noises. It became apparent something diabolical was happening to her. It appeared as though she may be possessed. In response to her behavior, we started to pray the Rosary for her, which caused her to react even more, with foam coming out of her mouth. The poor stewardess did not know what to do. The leader of our pilgrimage group suggested I pray over her to expel the demon, since, she said, "You have been fasting this whole time." Not knowing what to do, I took my newly purchased crucifix (blessed by a priest) out of my carry-on bag, and told the possessed woman to hold it in her hands. Our group leader sprinkled her with holy water, which enraged the woman. I had no clue what to do, but out of inspiration, I stood up, walked over to the woman, laid my hands on her head and began to pray.

As I started to pray, my voice changed to a deep voice, and I felt the demon come up through my hands, into my neck, and my head. I felt an electrical jolt, and, as I uttered, "In the name of Jesus, I command you to leave her body." It seemed the demon did not want me to say the name of Jesus. It tried to make my voice hideous and distort my words. People who witnessed the event, described my neck and head becoming distorted and stretched. The event terrified the people on the plane, as well as myself. Suddenly, the demon left her, and the woman sat in her chair in a limped manner.

But within a few minutes, it came back. I was so traumatized by it that I went to the restroom to cry. I pulled myself together before I came back out, and sat across from her in my assigned seat. The stewardess used the intercom to ask for a doctor. The doctor witnessed everything and had medicine to help her fall asleep. He injected it into her, but it had no effect. He injected more into her, but there was no effect. The doctor then said, "I gave her enough tranquilizing medicine to put down an elephant." The nearer we came to the US, the worse she acted by screaming and making hideous noises.

Suddenly, the plane blew an engine, and then, about 20 minutes later, the plane blew a second engine. The pilot came on the intercom, said, "Don't worry folks, we are cleared for an emergency landing. We still have two more engines, and this plane can still safely fly with only one." It seemed the flight from hell would never end. Finally, we landed and everyone went their way. Each secretly praying for the woman and her husband, who was beside himself.

Haunted Rectories

When I became pastor of St. Veronica in Brushwood City and St. Anthony in Jericho, the bishop told me to not sleep at the old rectory in Brushwood City, because they were building a new one, which was almost finished. I was supposed to sleep at the old rectory at St. Anthony in Jericho City.

I moved into the old stone rectory, and many parishioners were excited I was their new pastor. I was greeted with food, on the table and in the refrigerator, donated by the wonderful people of St. Anthony.

I stayed in the rectory a week before strange things started to happen. One night, I walked upstairs to go to bed. It was the only bedroom in the old post-rock home. I heard a deep voice laughing. As I kept walking, I heard the voice say, "This is my house. Ha ha ha ha ha!" I said, to myself, "Okay, Fr. Leonard, you must really be tired. You didn't hear that." Then I heard laughing again. I blessed the house, sprinkled Holy Water, and threw Blessed Salt throughout the house.

When I came up to the bedroom to retire, I looked at the beautiful image of Our Lady of Perpetual Help (an old picture, most likely over fifty years old). As I looked at Our Lady, I had blasphemous thoughts about Mary, and heard a deep hideous voice say, "Don't look at her!"

I had no other place to go to bed, and had difficulty sleeping that night. I thought I was either going crazy or something was in that rectory. I decided to call an exorcist, who advised me to offer a Mass at the rectory.

I called the bishop, and told him about the experience, and he believed me. He gave permission to offer the Holy Mass to remove any demonic activity. A few days later, I invited several parishioners and confided to them about the strange occurrences, but I did not tell say exactly what happened. I offered the Holy Sacrifice of the Mass, and never had the difficulty again. I later discovered, the reason the bishop didn't want me to sleep at the old rectory in Brushwood City, was due to Fr. Albert Brandmueller notifying the bishop that he believed the rectory was haunted. Eventually, it was demolished, and no one lived in it again.

In the New Rectory the Rosary Saved Me from a Demon Who Choked Me
When Bishop Traditiones came to bless the new rectory at St. Veronica's, I was excited, to stay in Brushwood City and was the first priest to live in the new rectory. I felt so unworthy. The first months there, I slept in the smaller bedroom, since I felt unworthy to sleep in the larger one. But, there was a smell in that room. I couldn't figure out what it was. I wondered what it could be, after all, it was a new house. Finally, when I washed the bedsheets, I realized, the used mattress in that bedroom smelled like urine. Consequently, I decided to sleep in the larger bedroom with a new bedroom set and new mattresses.

At the beginning of the year in January, we started a Perpetual Adoration Chapel at St. Veronica, and then, in March, we started a Perpetual Adoration Chapel at St. Anthony. In May, I decided to do a Novena of Masses in parishes throughout the diocese to close Schindler's Abortion Clinic. The night the Novena started (May 13th), I had a terrible experience.

As I was preparing for bed, I felt an evil presence in the bedroom, but thought it was my imagination. I turned out the lights, and just as I lay down, darkness came over the room. I felt an evil presence come down on top of me, and began to choke me. As a result, I attempted to cry out the holy name of Jesus, but couldn't. I grabbed a Rosary from the nightstand, and, as I put it around my neck, the evil spirit screamed, and immediately left the bedroom. It went outside the house and screamed by the window. I was so terrified by what happened, I had difficulty sleeping, but eventually fell asleep.

Discernment of Spirits Retreat – Deliverance Events
The Virgin Mary Comes to My Rescue

In October 2019, I was frustrated, due to many personal struggles of overeating and jealousy of the appearance of other men. I also found myself putting a statue of the Divine Child in the closet, since, the Divine Infant didn't answer my prayers, which wasn't good behavior.

Therefore, I decided to consecrate the source of these difficulties to the Immaculate Heart of Mary, trusting the Virgin Mary would help me overcome these temptations. I wanted to do a silent retreat away from the Guardians of the Holy Grail, and other groups present at Our Lady of Good Souls Retreat House in Hodgenville, Georgia. Therefore, I asked the spiritual director if there was some way I could have more of a silent retreat, and he suggested I call Fr. Michael Benedict, who did Ignatian Retreats in Hodgenville at another retreat house. Once I arrived for the retreat, Fr. Benedict made the suggestion, that I do a "Discernment of Spirits Retreat", which I had never heard of before. The retreat went well, but because I just learned how to do it, I don't think I learned to do it well. (See Appendix E – Prayer of Feeling.) Fr. Gadfly's method partially derived from St. Ignatius, *Discernment of Spirits*.

After I finished the retreat in Hodgenville, Georgia, I had another diocesan retreat to attend. The Tantrum diocesan retreat was at a Benedictine retreat house in Montserrat, California. While there, I put into practice the method of prayer I learned from the Discernment of Spirit Retreat.

When I began to practice the meditations, I decided to ask the Lord during one of the meditations, why I was so vulnerable to eat excessively, and, often times jealous, and overly focused on the appearance of other men. As I began the meditation, an incident came to mind I had not thought about for over 45 years.

When I was about ten years old, a girl embarrassed me at the local swimming pool. She pointed at me grabbing the attention of others, saying, "Oh, look at his ribs! You can see his bones. He is so skinny!" I had forgotten about the event, and remembered that I became self-conscious of my appearance due to her embarrassing comments. As a result, even when swimming, I always wore a shirt. I didn't want anyone to see the ribs from my bones. Ever since that embarrassing incident, I believed I was skinny, even when I wasn't skinny later in life.

Whenever I became upset about something, I found myself overeating. During the meditation, I allowed myself to feel (with Jesus) the emotions of embarrassment, fear, anger, and sadness I felt at the time of the incident. I came to understand that I looked at the appearance of other men with jealousy, because I wanted to look like them, rather than accept my appearance. And, as a result, I clung to the false idea, I was skinny.

Just as the meditation began, I heard loud chains going up and down the wall in my room at the retreat center in Montserrat. At first, I thought the noise was coming from the next room. It sounded like someone was taking a hammer, and banging the air conditioner attached to the wall. I could not understand why men were working at 9pm at night. But I later discovered no one was working, and the noise came from my room. There was no rational explanation for the noises. I believe it was an evil spirit.

Just as soon as the noises stopped, I saw in my mind, as though in my room, Jesus hanging from the cross, and blood coming down His hands, feet, and face. I looked up at Him and saw the wound in His side, and His ribs protruding from His side. It was at that moment I remembered what happened when I was a child, when the girl made fun of me. I remembered what my ribs looked like at the age of the embarrassing event. In my heart, I felt as though Jesus was saying to me, "The wound in your side, you received from the girl who made fun of you, is like the wound on my side. The wound you felt, I felt in my side." And it was at that moment, I knew I was healed from that incident. I was delivered from the spirits of immoderation and jealousy.

In fourth grade, I was in the school's *Seven Seas* play. The night before the play, the music teacher asked me to substitute for a man character, who became suddenly ill. But I told her I couldn't memorize all the lines one night before play. She said, "Don't worry, the other main character will whisper the words to you, and you just repeat them aloud." As the play began, the other character didn't whisper the words I was to say. But said them aloud, and then I repeated what he said, causing the audience to laugh every time I spoke. It was humiliating. I thought I ruined the play. When it was over, I wept bitterly behind the stage. For years, I was terrified to stand before crowds, and which was especially true when I offered Mass and gave a homily. I was afraid to stand before a group of people and would literally shake. I realized, during the Discernment of Spirits Retreat the cause of this behavior.

During the retreat, I asked the Lord, why I was so afraid to stand before a crowd, and He brought to mind what happened during the *Seven Seas* play. When I did the meditation, I asked for healing and allowed myself to feel the pain, with Jesus, that I went through when it originally happened.

In the meditation, I pictured myself standing before the audience, and saying, "Shame on you, adults! You should not be laughing at a child. You embarrassed me, and made me cry when it was over. Furthermore, you should know better than to treat children like that!"

226

After I did the meditation, I was healed, and am no longer afraid to stand before a crowd and speak. I was delivered from the spirit of fear.

The third event was much more frightening than the others. After the retreat, when I returned to my apartment in Tantrum, that night, I felt an evil presence immediately after I turned off the lights. I saw a dark figure with red eyes. I fell asleep, but was awakened at 2:30am, and felt the spirit's presence. Then, I asked the Lord what kind of healing He wanted of me.

I started the prayer of feeling, as usual, saying, "Jesus look at me. I am looking at you. Mary look at me. I am looking at you". And then, suddenly, the evil spirit attacked me, and my whole body violently convulsed. I couldn't stop it, and was afraid. I put a Rosary around my neck, but, it continued. Consequently, I began to pray the Rosary, and it continued. I prayed three Rosaries and the Chaplet of Divine Mercy, but it kept shaking and shaking me, and I became intensely frightened. However, I knew Jesus was with me and Mary too. I turned on the lights, and knelt before at statue of Our Lady of Fatima. The more I looked at Mary, the more I was tempted to turn away from Her. I kept praying, "Help me, Mary. Help me Jesus. What is happening to me? What are you wanting to heal?" The violent shaking went on for 45 minutes! The shaking and convulsing were continuous. I felt like the demon was trying to possess me. I was scared, and I attempted to call a priest friend, and ask him to pray for me, but he didn't answer. Finally, I went before the altar within my personal chapel (which did not have the Blessed Sacrament) gazed upon the crucifix, and said, "Jesus, what is happening to me? What healing are you wanting of me?" Since I did not know if it would ever stop, I began to cry. But, I didn't give up. I kept praying. Finally, as I knelt before the large crucifix, and gazed upon it, I remembered the humility of Jesus, and that's when it lost its grip on me. I remembered the Litany of Humility that my spiritual director suggested I pray at the retreat. As I began to pray the Litany, located in the hardback *Roman Missal*, the convulsions slowed, and by the time I finished the prayer, I collapsed on the floor sobbing. It finally left. In my heart, I knew it would not come back. It was at that moment, I realized I was delivered from the spirit of pride.

Benedictine Monastery With A Demon Who Writes With An Ink Pen

I went to the Benedictine Monastery at Archibald, New York, to celebrate Fr. Angelo Strongfaith's, OSB fiftieth anniversary of his priesthood ordination. The night I arrived, I blessed my room and went to bed. When I laid down, I immediately felt an evil presence, and saw a black figure near the bed. I began to pray the Rosary, and then threw Holy Water in the direction of the dark figure. It caused the black figure to back away and go by the door. I kept praying Rosaries and other prayers, but it wouldn't leave. Most of the night, I was awake, but I finally fell asleep.

When I woke up in the morning, there were blue ink lines traced on both forearms. The ink line exactly followed my blood veins. I thought maybe I must have fallen asleep with the ink pen in the bed, but it was on the night stand. I thought that maybe when I carried my suitcase there must have been ink on it, but there wasn't. The ink stopped at the point where both arms bend. I kept trying to rationalize how the ink marked up my arms. I wondered, how the ink followed exactly my blood veins. It absolutely freaked me out. There was no way I would ever mark my own skin. I believe it's sinful to desecrate the body, and at times, I correct others who write notes on their palms and hands, to remind themselves of things.

There was no other explanation. A demon did it. I told Fr. Angelo about it, and, he said, "Yes, there are times when we see that black figure in other parts of the monastery." I was beside myself about the situation, and could not believe a demon could do such a thing. But, evidently, they could, and did.

But the Lord, who is all-powerful, permitted it for a reason. I trust He will take care of me. Jesus is my strength and my courage is from Him. The next morning, I was planning to offer a Mass for my deceased great-grandfather, Leonard Gadflie (Gadfly) and believe the lines of ink on my arms were a plea to offer Masses for the healing of the Gadflie (Gadfly) bloodline. As time went on, Masses were offered to heal our Gadfly family bloodline.

These deliverance examples, the healing of emotions and spiritual maladies are powerful examples of how God gazed upon the misery of my soul, and by His mercy, touched and healed it. Thank you, Lord Jesus, for your incredible and unfathomable mercy!

#92 THE SAD YEAR OF 2017
INVALID MASSES, FAMILY AND FRIEND REVELATIONS

2017 "The Year from Hell & Year of Mercy" (Family, Hometown Parish, & Friend)
"There was a certain creditor who had two debtors. One owed five hundred denarii, and the other fifty. And when they had nothing with which to repay, he freely forgave them both. Tell Me, therefore, which of them will love him more?" Simon answered and said, "I suppose the one whom he forgave more." And He said to him, "You have rightly judged." Then He turned to the woman and said to Simon, "Do you see this woman? I entered your house; you gave Me no water for My feet, but she has washed My feet with her tears and wiped them with the hair of her head. You gave Me no kiss, but this woman has not ceased to kiss My feet since the time I came in. You did not anoint My head with oil, but this woman has anointed My feet with fragrant oil. Therefore, I say to you, her sins, which are many, are forgiven, for she loved much. But to whom little is forgiven, the same loves little." (Luke 7:36-50)

2017 was the 100-yr anniversary of Fatima, and many thought Our Lady would work a miracle during the year. But for me, it was the "Year from Hell", transformed into the "Year of Mercy".

In 2017, I learned my father did something abominable and atrocious when he was drunk, many years ago. O Lord, this information is so despicable, I can't write it down, but I ask in your mercy to help and heal all those involved, including the purification of my father's soul, that departed this life 8 years ago. Jesus, I trust in your mercy!

Also in 2017, I discovered my hometown parish did not have valid Masses for 12 years because the pastors used wine, not made from grapes. Church law requires wine made from grapes. In the years before it was discovered, I unknowingly offered 12 invalid Masses there, including my father's funeral Mass. I give more detail of this event in another location.

In 2017, I tracked down my best friend from college, Kenneth, and discovered he was a bank president. We had a nice conversation over the phone, and he told me about the birth of his granddaughter. However, about a week later, his wife called in tears. She said he came out of the closet and was dating a married man. I could not believe it. He never seemed like he was homosexual. I would never have suspected. He married a good Catholic girl, and they had three children. It was surreal. She eventually left him. This was truly a sad moment for them and me. I felt bad for his children, grandchildren and especially his wife. How horrible! In response to the news, I sent him several letters with information on the necessity of living a chaste life. And sent some CD's on helping homosexuals live their life in accord with Church teaching, but never heard back from him or her. I offered Masses for them, and prayed much for them and their family.

My uncle, who was a priest, now deceased, was a practicing homosexual. In 2017, this was confirmed, when I saw a photograph of him with another priest and was horrified. How disgusting! Who would take pictures of such a thing and then keep them? It was hard for me to understand, especially since he was noted for being orthodox. Lord, have mercy on them.

Also, during the year, I discovered a priest with whom I was doing hospital ministry, and who was at the same hospital for 16 years, made up his own words when anointing the sick, making the sacrament invalid. Even though he did hospital ministry for 16 years, he never even heard of the Apostolic Pardon, therefore never gave it to any patient. Oh, the poor souls, who did not receive the graces and mercy of Jesus, as they ought. O Lord have mercy on the priest and the souls of patients involved.

Sister Mary Snickers "overseeing the priests" lied to the bishop, and allowed that priest to continue his invalid anointings, while at the same time, admitting to me, they were invalid. I spoke to the priest director of Worship for the diocese of Tantrum, and explained the problem of invalid anointings. He agreed it was a serious problem. On my behalf, the priest sent an email to Bishop Thomas Vernacular. But, he didn't want to discuss it with me. I was to do whatever Sister Mary Snickers of the Unholy Sensual Behavior decided.

The anguish I went through, discovering all these things cannot be adequately described. Yet, I believe God in His mercy, somehow, brought good out of it all. For those who did the grievous actions, for me who discovered them, and especially for the people who endured the injustices, God's mercy was available to all. Bringing to light the invalid sacraments helped the people of God to once again have valid sacraments.

All of these events forced me to see God's mercy in a new way. Each person is a sinner, and although their sins seemed grievous, the Lord wanted forgiveness and healing. All of these events caused me to offer many Masses in reparation, and offer prayers of healing. I wondered why God showed me all this, except perhaps, to help those involved and wanted me to console His wounded Heart in Adoration, to offer Masses of reparation, and to pray for mercy and forgiveness. He wanted as many Masses as possible to be offered for those who rightly should have had them. I still shutter to even think of these events, and some of them caused nightmares, even though I had not had a nightmare since I was a child.

O Lord, I am with You. We suffer together. We forgive. We love and bestow Your infinite Mercy on souls suffering miserably. Remember O Lord my sins from the past? How merciful you were, and are, to me? And you bestowed mercy on me despite the sins of my youth. How can I not give your mercy to others? Who am I to judge? For the sake of Your sorrowful passion, have mercy on us, and on the whole world! O Jesus, your mercy is infinite, and my mind is finite. Help me, to see the glory of your mercy, despite, so much human failure!

Carlos Rossi "Blush" Responsible for a 12-Year Eclipse of the "SON" of God
"Think of us in this way, as servants of Christ and stewards of God's mysteries." (1 Corinthians 4:1)

My hometown parish of St. Gabriel in Crossroads, Ohio became the home of a 12-year sacramental disaster, due to the ignorance of its four pastors who served there.

However, on Aug. 11th, the feast of St. Clare, known for her special love of Jesus in the Blessed Sacrament, I offered a funeral Mass for Amelia Schortzenberry, the wife of a cousin, at St. Gabriel's in Crossroads.

During the Mass, when I consumed, what I thought was the Precious Blood, (Catholics believe the Blood of Jesus is transubstantiated from wine at the words of the priest), I noticed the wine was pink, and it tasted sweet. I had not seen or tasted that particular wine used for Mass. Out of curiosity, after Mass, I wanted to see the name of the wine. When I opened the refrigerator in the sacristy, I noticed a bottle of wine labeled *Carlos Rossi Blush*. It was clearly non-sacramental wine. When I returned to my priest residence in Tantrum, I decided to see if the wine was made from grapes, as required by Canon Law.

I was horrified to learn it was made from strawberries and cherries. Only wine made from grapes can be used for Mass; otherwise, the Mass is invalid. I was shocked, as I read, and re-read the ingredients over and over. Since, it was late in the evening, I decided to call the pastor the next day and tell him the wine he was using was made from strawberries and cherries. He responded, "No, it can't be. I will go to look, and then call you back." He never called back. I called a previous pastor of the parish, and asked if *Carlos Rossi Blush* was used when he was pastor, which he affirmed. He gave me the names of the benefactors of the wine, who, from the goodness of their hearts, donated it from their liquor store.

I then telephoned the benefactors of the wine and asked how long they had been donating it. From 2005 to 2017, for 12 years, the church was using it at Mass. Without giving an explanation of why that particular wine should not be used for Mass, I thanked them for their generosity. I could hardly believe it. Twelve years of invalid Masses! This was the parish my father, sister, aunts, nieces, and nephews and hometown friends attended. Since the Masses were invalid, was Jesus not present in the Eucharist either? Did all, who attended Masses at St. Gabriel's, not receive Communion? Did my father not receive Viaticum before he died, as well as countless others? I wondered how many Masses were invalidly offered? The First Communions, the Funerals, the weddings, the Masses for the deceased, even the bishops of the Diocese of Lakota, offered invalid Masses, when they presided over Confirmation for the youth and other celebrations. This was absolutely devastating to me, especially when I realized my father's funeral Mass was invalid, and all the other Masses I offered in that parish as a priest.

I keep track of Masses I offer in a Mass book, and consequently, I unknowingly offered twelve invalid Masses in twelve years, mostly funerals there. My heart sank, and I was overwhelmed with grief. Over a period of a month, I became physically ill and lost ten pounds from the stress of it. I was so distressed. I wondered if my reaction was due to a lack of trust in God's infinite mercy, or were my human emotions getting the best of me. I came to realize God's sheep were spiritually famished by the disaster and I needed to trust Jesus in a way I never imagined.

On August 12th, the day after the horrible discovery, I began to offer Masses of reparation and re-offer Masses offered invalidly at St. Gabriel. Due to the fact, I kept track of every Mass I offered from the time I was ordained, I was able to go through the Mass Record books and re-offer them. I was so glad the Lord inspired me to record every Mass from the time I was ordained. The Sunday Gospel for August 13th of 2017 truly touched my heart, as I read the story of Jesus walking on the water, and calming the storm (Matthew 14:22-33).

Strangely, the next time I discovered more invalid Masses was at a Monastery in 2019, and a similar Gospel for the day was the storm on the lake. (John 6:16-21) Both times, a storm raged in my heart due to these horrible experiences, could only be calmed by Jesus.

It took me two days to compose a letter to the bishop, and that next Monday, August 14th, I emailed it, and also physically mailed a copy of the letter to Bishop Felix Victor of the diocese of Lakota, Ohio.

He responded several days later, indicating he corrected the difficulty of invalid Masses, and said, he would offer a Mass for the souls of my father, a cousin, and an aunt, who I mentioned in the letter.

Amazingly, since the invalid Masses began in 2005, the first valid Mass offered was on August 15th, the Solemnity of the Assumption of Mary in 2017. The invalid Mass issue came to be known on the feast of St. Clare, and resolved on the Assumption of Mary. I believe St. Clare and the Virgin Mary had something to do with helping the parish to have valid Masses again.

A great solar eclipse in the USA occurred the following Monday, August 21st, 2017. To me, it was like the Eucharist was sort of eclipsed for twelve years at the parish. After offering Masses for the parish of St. Gabriel, for the bishop of that diocese, for the pastor, and in reparation for what had happened from August 12th through August 15th, I re-offered my father's Funeral Mass, on August 16th. On Aug. 22nd, the Queenship of Mary, the woman, clothed with sun and moon under Her feet, and on Her head a crown of twelve stars, I offered a Mass for my deceased godmother.

Because I felt they needed to know what they did, I wrote letters to the four past pastors of St. Gabriel's. I told them about the situation and explained that we all make mistakes, and at the time, we may not even realize the depth of our colossal mistake until later. The writing of the letter to the pastors took finesse, and especially with the spirit of mercy. I used words with delicacy, holding back my feelings and emotions, which was absolutely due to the grace of God. None of the former pastors acknowledged the letters.

I obtained Mass intentions for three years of invalid Masses from St. Gabriel's website, and asked several priests to offer the intentions for the Masses. I asked the priests, if they wouldn't mind taking a $5 stipend for each Mass, as it would be expensive for me to pay $10 for each Mass for three years.

Providentially, a few months later, when I was home visiting my mother, the new pastor asked me to offer the Sunday Mass at St. Gabriel's. I was delighted. It was Trinity Sunday. I gave a homily about the mystery of the Trinity, and how we worship the Trinity at Mass. Not thinking about the invalid Masses of the past, I spoke about how Mass is the re-presentation of Calvary. After Mass, it suddenly dawned on me, that when I had said the sacred words at the consecration: "This is my Body" and "This is my Blood", and what I preached about-- became present (the sacrifice on the altar).

Tears welled up in my eyes. The Lord, in His gentle way, wanted me to know He used me to bring back valid Masses. I thanked the Lord for using me, so the little parish could once again have valid Masses.

Now the Holy Sacrifice was present once more, after a twelve-year eclipse of the "SON" of God. I was spiritually overwhelmed and dumbfounded by God's grace, and thanked and praised God for returning the sacrifice of the Mass back to the people of my hometown parish. Oh, God, in your infinite mercy, you bestowed on me the grace to help the people of my parish have Mass again. You looked with pity on the misery of their souls, and granted them the gift of your Holy Sacrifice. Thank you, Jesus!

Interestingly, a few years later, when COVID-19 was at its height, I convinced the nursing home staff to permit me to anoint my aunt who had the virus, and at that time, the man who had donated the wine was dying. I anointed him and gave him the Apostolic Pardon. At that time, the pastor of the parish was not visiting patients for fear of contracting the disease.

#93 TRANSFER TO ST. JOHN OF GOD HOSPITAL IN TANTRUM, IDAHO

St. John of God Hospital in Tantrum (You can't make an Ohioan into an Idahoan)

Due to an agreement between a former Bishop of the Diocese of Tantrum, Idaho and St. John of God Hospital, the Pastoral Department needed to find their own priests to serve as hospital chaplains. This would help alleviate the shortage of priests in their diocese.

The head of the department, Sister Susan, of the Most Unholy Temper, heard about the numerous vocations in the Diocese of Rolling Hills and wrote a letter to my bishop requesting that a priest come to be a chaplain at their hospital.

Bishop Courageous called and asked if I would go to Tantrum, Idaho to serve. I told him I would. Because it came out of the blue, I thought the bishop wanted me out of the diocese. I felt like I was being exiled. Why not minister in the Archdiocese of Millsburger, Idaho, I wondered? He previously asked me to come to his diocese to do hospital ministry, and at that time, Bishop Courageous refused.

Despite the sudden request to minister in a different diocese, I was happy to have a reprieve from being under a bishop whom I didn't understand.

As I began hospital ministry there, I was fearful there would be cases of nutrition and hydration not given to patients who morally should receive them, which is what I witnessed at the Catholic Doorway to Heaven Nursing Home, Mother of Misery Healthcare System, and Woebegone Hospice on Saint Camillus de Lellis campus in Rolling Hills. But thanks be to God, I never witnessed any case of nutrition and hydration not given to patients at St. John of God Hospital in two and a half years. I later discovered a priest and some lay people from the International Catholic Bioethics

Center of America were asked by their bishop to educate physicians and staff at St. John of God Hospital in Tantrum.

How wonderful, patients who died on the cancer floor or the hospice floor at St. John of God died with dignity, unlike "Catholic" institutions in the Diocese of Rolling Hills. Every doubt about how it should be done in Rolling Hills vanished completely after witnessing first-hand Church teaching properly applied at St. John of God Hospital. What a blessing, Bishop Credo understood and implemented Catholic teachings by inviting the International Catholic Bioethics Center of America (ICBCA) to help make their hospital ethically Catholic.

I later asked the bishop of Rolling Hills several times to invite the ICBCA to administer an audit of ethics at the Catholic hospitals in Rolling Hills, but he wasn't interested.

I quickly became awestruck by the many deathbed conversions and ginormous confessions at St. John of God Hospital. Wow! Wow! Wow! St. John Vianney used to say, when he heard someone's confession who hadn't been to confession for many years, he caught a "big fish" now and then. Doing hospital ministry at St. John of God, I not only caught big fish, I caught "Blue Whales"! Unbelievable! Many of them. Oh, the mercy of Jesus! I saw God's providence in sending me there.

In the average parish, the majority of the people who come to Mass go to confession at least once or twice a year or more often. But in the hospital, the priest sees people from all walks of life, some who haven't stepped foot in a church for decades and decades. Who are these people who come to the hospital? Doctors, lawyers, plumbers, farmers, drug users, alcoholics, prostitutes, car salesmen, murderers, saintly men, women, and children. Almost every week, after hearing a confession, deep within my heart, I would cry out, "Yippee! God's mercy is for everyone." I became drunk on God's mercy almost habitually. There was a good number of deathbed baptisms. Just before they died, people who never joined the Church, wanted to become Catholic. Emergency confirmations too. Some received Holy Communion just two or three times after their first Confession, and then departed from this life, to go to their judgment.

By far, the most difficult part of this ministry was seeing children who suffered and died from neglect or abuse. Behind a big fish was usually a big suffering of some sort, and it usually came from the hands of the Sisters of Good Health, or the priests at the hospital.

The things I experienced in the Diocese of Rolling Hills were also similarly experienced by other priests in the Diocese of Tantrum, Idaho, but were handled very differently with Bishop Michael Credo, former bishop of their diocese.

Without mentioning to other priests about the difficulties I experienced, three priests independent of each other, and unbeknownst to each other, mentioned how Bishop Credo, and the Chancellor of the Diocese of Tantrum, always supported the priests when there was parish controversy.

Although I didn't mention anything about my experiences, one priest even had a similar situation as I. The previous pastor at his parish never preached on confession, and when the new pastor began preaching on confession, some wrote letters to their bishop, and he responded in his letters to parishioners saying that the priest was doing well to preach on Confession, and they should do as their pastor suggests. He encouraged them to speak to their pastor when they have a conflict. I never had that experience.

Prayer and more prayer for my bishop and all bishops was needed, to melt my hardened heart, and to give them courage to be sacrificial men for Jesus and His Church. I was needing a conversion of heart, as I had the habit of complaining to priests about these events, which was really a lack of virtue on my part.

"Your Time is Short! Take the Cup of Suffering!"

"I will take the chalice of salvation and call upon the name of the Lord." (Psalm 116:13)

This scripture passage is engraved on the cup of my chalice, donated by the people of the Church of the Ascension. One day, after saying some prayers in the main hospital Chapel, I stood up, genuflected, but then suddenly felt a strong urge to kneel back down and pray. As I knelt, I heard a voice say, "Take and Drink." Then, I suddenly saw a chalice with what appeared to be wine (or the blood of Jesus within it). The voice was strong. I thought it must have been an angel. The voice said, "Drink the cup of suffering." After I consumed the contents, which had no taste, the chalice disappeared, and then, the voice said, "Your time is short." I was bewildered by it all. And did not know what to think. I looked around to see if anyone had seen me drink from the chalice, but no one was in the Chapel, but me. I did not know what it meant, and began to think that I would die soon.

But after reflecting, I think it may have had to do with my time at the hospital and two events that would occur while I was ministering at the hospital. It was not much after that, when I discovered the wine used at my hometown parish was made of strawberries and cherries, which rendered Masses invalid for 12 years. Then, about a year later, I once again discovered the same wine was used at a monastery in Idaho. Both of these events caused me great suffering.

The day after I discovered the wine was made of cherries and strawberries, I called the archbishop of the Millsburger diocese and told him about the wine being used at the monastery, resulting in invalid Masses. And within two hours of the call, I received a call from my bishop to return to the diocese of Rolling Hills.

The two events of discovering invalid Masses remind me of what Jesus experienced as He hung upon the Cross. On the Cross, He was offered sour wine to drink, and tasted it. Every Mass is the re-presentation of Calvary. The invalid Masses I offered, I literally drank wine (not the Blood of Jesus). It was truly my cup of suffering (my

Calvary), where I drank wine at Calvary, not the blood of Jesus, as I should have. I did not know if what I drank, when the Chalice appeared to me, was wine or the Blood of Jesus. When I offered the invalid Masses, I could not have known, until later, if it was the blood of Jesus or wine. One cannot know the deep suffering this caused, especially when I realized my family and the hometown people I grew up with-- did not have a valid Mass and that my father's funeral Mass was invalid. Oh, how great the sorrow! O Mother of Sorrows, the pain you felt in your Heart!

#94 SISTERS OF GOOD HEALTH AT ST. JOHN OF GOD HOSPITAL IN TANTRUM

Sisters of Good Health in Tantrum

The sisters wear their habits and are getting many young vocations. But they weren't getting vocations for their orthodoxy, nor for their mercy. The first year I was at St. John of God Hospital, Sister Susan often told me how she and the sisters loved my homilies. She asked for copies, and then wanted a copy of the Sunday homily every weekend. She would post the homily on the board for the lay "chaplains" to read.

Everything changed, when the hospital president came to Mass on Pentecost. At that Mass, I gave a homily on how the Holy Spirit worked through difficult times through the centuries including recent divisions in the Church, which seemed to have begun under the direction of the Pope. Although, I was respectful of the Pope, I pointed out how some new theology contradicted *The Catechism of the Catholic Church* and the Sacred Tradition of the Church.

The president of the hospital was unhappy with the homily, and told sister I was not permitted to give that kind of homily anymore. There were no problems after that, until I gave a homily during Lent explaining the Ten Commandments. A woman who attended the Mass, wrote a letter to the hospital president complaining. The president told Sister Susan, to tell me, I should not give homilies like that either. I asked my spiritual director and several other priests to read the homilies, and none of them found anything wrong with them. I later discovered the reason the sisters never defended their priests when the hospital president was involved, nor the teachings of the Church, was due to their receiving annually a million dollars from the Sordid Foundation, and they were afraid of losing their money, if they "made waves" by standing against the president of the hospital, rather, than standing up for Church teachings.

When Sister Susan was transferred, a new sister took her place. I had hoped all would get back to normal, but the opposite happened. After multiple Masses, sister Mary Snickers came to my office and said she was unhappy with my homilies. She surely visited with Sister Susan. She said I should preach only about the love and mercy of Jesus and His tender compassion.

One homily she was unhappy with was based on the Gospel for the day, which said the road to heaven is narrow, and the road to hell is wide. I quoted five saints, who said the road to heaven is narrow, and that many do not take it, and ended the homily, inviting the people to strive for virtue trusting in God's mercy. That was the straw that broke the camel's back. She complained about it after Mass, and I said, "Sister, perhaps you should tell Jesus to not say such things, since He is the one who said it." I said, "As of today, I do not want you to give me any more advice on homilies, whether you like them or not, and, if you do, I will notify the bishop." I said this to her, because it was the advice I received from a priest to tell her- if she complained again.

Consequently, I decided to create a tool called a *Memorandum of Understanding*, so the sisters and the priests would agree on the boundaries between us. I felt the sisters many times crossed priest boundaries because they would tell the priests how to do their ministry. I spent hours on it, and believed it very well explained what the Church taught on the relationship between a lay person supervisor of a pastoral care department and priest chaplains.

I asked the priest who was the head of the Office of Worship in Tantrum to read it and make suggestions. He suggested I modify the language a bit, so it would be more amiable to the sisters. I also made an appointment with the Vicar of Clergy of Tantrum, and spoke to him about the sisters, how they ask priests to do things contrary to the rubrics of the Mass during the Triduum and about the homilies. To my surprise, I had his support, something I had never experienced in the diocese of Rolling Hills. He stood up for what was true and right. He looked at me, and said, "Father, remember, read the black, and do the red. As a priest, you are to follow the rubrics of the *Roman Missal*." I felt like standing up and saying "Yes!". Finally, a priest who stands by the Church and the priest. He said this is not the first time, a priest from the hospital came to him about the sisters interfering with the role of the priest at the hospital, and he said he would speak to the bishop about it.

I gave Sister Mary Snickers a copy of the *Memorandum*, asked her to read it, and was looking forward to sitting down and discussing it with her. I thought, at last we would finally put behind our differences and agree. But, that's not what happened at all. After some time, I asked her if I could talk to her about it, and she said, "No, your mind is made up. We will not discuss any of this." I said, "Sister, can't we just sit down and discuss these things together, and come to an agreement?" She angrily said, "No!" I responded, "Sister, I think you should know, the director of Worship for the Diocese approved it and the Vicar of Clergy also read it." She said again, "No". Later, I thought about why she must have been upset. Perhaps, it reminded her the sisters were not so orthodox, and it pointed out how they do liberal things, and she didn't want to be reminded of it.

The Sisters and the Spoiled Wine (Replace Old Wine With New Wine---PLEASE!)

"And no one puts new wine into old wine-skins. For the old skins would burst from the pressure, spilling the wine and ruining the skins. New wine is stored in new wine-skins, so that both are preserved." (Matthew 9:17)

If Jesus were to have seen what the sisters were doing with the old wine, He would have wanted the old wine to be replaced with new wine. The Sisters of Good Health appointed priest chaplains to offer Masses in their convent, and we rotated Masses.

I noticed the wine at the sisters' convent had an odd appearance to it. The wine used at the main Chapel was white wine. But the wine used at the convent was dark red and had a thick syrupy brown swirl floating in it. I pointed this out to Sister Susan, and said, "I think there is something wrong with the wine."

I asked her if I could use a different wine. But she refused. Finally, one day after the consecration, when I looked into the chalice, there was much sediment at the bottom of the chalice and knew something was not right. Because I was so shocked by the contents, during Mass I exclaimed, "There is something wrong with this wine!" It was unlike me to blurt out something like that during Mass, and felt it was the Holy Spirit.

After Mass, I noted the company name who produced the sacramental wine, and called them about it. The company representative told me to discontinue using it, since they said the wine was at least five years old and was in the process of breaking down into a syrupy substance. The date on the box of the wine is the date the wine is created (not the expiration date). Sacramental wine doesn't last longer than five years, he said. I told the sisters what the gentleman said.

However, Sister Mary Pandora said, "Oh, father, you are making that up. You did not call the company." I said, "Yes, I did. I can give you the phone number, and you can call them yourself." She said, "Yeah, right, you did not call them." Because I became angry, I walked away without saying anything. Since then, I secretly brought my own wine with me in a black bag and dumped the syrupy wine down the drain, and then refilled it with fresh wine. I prayed that the Masses offered before I exchanged the wine were valid. Only God knows if they were valid or not. "A jar filled with sour wine was standing nearby, so they soaked a sponge in the wine on a branch of hyssop and held it up to His lips. When Jesus had taken the wine, He said, "It is finished." Then He bowed His head and gave up His spirit." (John 19:29-30)

Triduum Nightmare

Sister Susan, of the Most Unholy Temper, lost her temper before the Mass of the Lord's Supper and literally yelled at me. She wondered why I removed the Hosts from the Tabernacle before Mass because she said the sisters were going to consume all the Hosts after Mass since that's what they do at their mother house.

I told her I was following the rubrics in the *Roman Missal,* and said I didn't believe it was proper to consume many Hosts outside of Mass, as it treats the Sacred Host like bread, and not the Body of Christ.

The Good Friday Service had problems as well. She didn't want to do the procession of the Cross as in the Missal, but instead wanted the priest to do it as they do at the Mother House. The Vigil was even worse. The sisters premarked the Easter candle, so we wouldn't "waste time" doing it at the beginning of the Mass. They also wanted to do multiple things during the Mass at the same time, so that the Mass would be over more quickly. Since I forgot to light the candles during Mass for the Renewal of Baptismal Promises, sister stamped her foot and swung her head. There were only about five people, not counting the sisters, who attended.

A few months after Easter, I told the sisters I would not do any of that again. And so the following year, the sisters didn't ask any of the hospital priests to do the Triduum. But, rather asked a local diocesan priest who was willing to do whatever they wanted, regardless of the rubrics.

#95 INVALID ANOINTING AT ST. JOHN OF GOD HOSPITAL IN TANTRUM

Invalid Anointing of Sick, No Apostolic Pardon
Invalid Confessions at St. John of God Hospital Tantrum, Idaho

"In those times, the sacrament of Extreme Unction will be largely ignored.... Many will die without receiving it, being thereby deprived of innumerable graces, consolation, and strength in the great leap from time to eternity." Our Lady of Good Success in Quito, Ecuador in 1599 "Many shepherds have ravaged my vineyard, have trodden my heritage underfoot..." (Jeremiah 12:10)

In March 2019, it was reported by Catholic News in Brazil, there would be an attempt to use Yucca plant, rather than wheat, when making wafers used at Mass. Obviously, this would be invalid. I wanted to share my dismay with the priests who I minister with at the hospital. Therefore, I mentioned it to Fr. Paul Freeforall and Fr. Bob Virility. However, both said they would support changing the use of wheat to using a Yucca plant substance. They said it would be easier for their culture, since Yucca is more prevalent than wheat, and Jesus used items in His culture during His time. This goes to show their lack of faith in the validity of the sacraments and their disobedience to Church teachings.

When I first arrived at St. John of God Hospital in Tantrum, Idaho, Fr. Paul Freeforall graciously showed me around the hospital as he visited patients. It was then I noticed he was using his own words when anointing the patients. He laid his hands on patients as required. But he didn't use the formula from the *Pastoral Care For Sick* book, which is also found in the *Catechism of the Catholic Church.* He should have prayed, "Through this holy anointing, may the Lord in His love and mercy, help you with the grace of the Holy Spirit. Amen. May the Lord, who frees you from sin, save you and raise you up. Amen."

I spoke to him on three occasions, and all three times he said using the words from the book were not necessary. I reported this to the Vicar for Clergy of the Diocese of Tantrum, who said he would speak to the bishop. But a year later, I found out nothing changed. After the year passed, a patient reported to me that Fr. Paul Freeforall used his own words when anointed.

I spoke to the priest in charge of the Office of Worship for the diocese of Tantrum, who emailed the bishop about it. The bishop told him to tell me to speak to Sr. Mary Snickers, of the Unholy Sensual Behavior, which I did.

Sister Mary Snickers was known for her sensuality. At times, she touched men on their chest or rubbed their backs when talking to them after Mass. After Mass, she kissed (on the neck below the ear) the Vice President of the hospital, who was married. At times, she would give back rubs to male patients and their family members, while visiting them in their rooms.

When I spoke to her, about the invalid anointings, to my surprise, she already knew they were invalid, and knew Fr. Paul didn't give the Apostolic Pardon. She said she wasn't going to speak to him about it, since she said, "the Church supplies" in the cases of invalidity, and it wouldn't do any good, as he was too old and set in his ways.

There are two versions of the Apostolic Pardon in the *Pastoral Care for the Sick* book that may be used during Viaticum (receiving Holy Communion for the last time) and may also be given when a person is unable to receive Holy Communion outside of Viaticum, but many priests are unaware they can give patients the special pardon which remits all temporal punishment due to sin.

The most common form of the Apostolic Pardon prayer states, "By the authority which the Apostolic See has given me, I grant you a full pardon and remission of all your sins, in the name of the Father and of the Son and of the Holy Spirit."

Fr. Bob Virility, only anointed about seven patients out of seventy in a month's time. At times, he wore a pink clerical shirt. He rarely anointed patients, even dying patients, or those who on hospice, or patients in ICU, or having major surgery.

I encouraged him to give the sacrament to patients who needed it, but he indicated he wouldn't change. I sent two letters to the bishop, with no response. He later spoke to both priests, who were furious with me for reporting them to the bishop. Even after they met with him, they continued as before.

Fr. Freeforall's confessions were potentially invalid, since he failed to say all the required words of absolution. Likewise, the confessions of Fr. Doug Garcia, who was pastor of the Holy Ghost parish, not far from the hospital, were definitely invalid. In the letter to the bishop about the invalid anointings, I mentioned this problem to the bishop as well.

At times, Fr. Doug was asked to hear confessions for Spanish patients. However, on one occasion, I went to confession to him, and he used his own words for absolution. He said, "Jesus forgives you. I forgive you. Father, Son, and Spirit. Amen." During my confession to him, I mentioned that he used improper words. I kindly asked him to use the proper formula. However, he became angry and refused. I never came to know if the bishop said anything to him.

Later, Sister Mary Snickers denied saying she knew about father's invalid anointings. She said, "I misheard what you said."

To gain a better understanding of the situation, I visited with one of the Sisters of Good Health, another sister from her own order, who teaches at a seminary in the Archdiocese of Wilmont, Colorado, and also visited with a Canon Lawyer from Cardinal Spellman Seminary, and both teachers said the Church does not supply in cases of invalid sacraments, except for jurisdiction with marriages.

Once Sister Mary Snickers realized what she said was wrong, she told me, "When I told you the Church supplies in cases of invalidity, what I meant was the Church makes them valid. Therefore, Fr. Freeforall's anointings are valid. And so, that's why I told the bishop they are valid anointings."

"Do not let my lying foes rejoice over me. Do not let those who hate me unjustly wink eyes at each other." (Psalm 35)

To convince the bishop, I gave him several lists of patients, but without names to maintain confidentiality. The priest chaplains daily recorded, the sacraments given to patients. Because this information was available on the computer, I was able to give the bishop a list health conditions, as well as the priest who failed to anoint or give patients the Apostolic Pardon.

Even though Fr. Freeforall had been anointing patients for sixteen years, he had never given the Apostolic Pardon. He said he didn't know about it. It makes me wonder what the two priests personal judgments will be like. Were they really ignorant, or not taught properly? Will the Lord show them all the patients who died without being anointed or didn't receive the Apostolic Pardon? I shouldn't even think of such things, for only God can know the true situations and their culpability.

It was with great heartache and tears I left the hospital, since I knew many patients would not receive Anointing of the Sick or the Apostolic Pardon. Yet, I had peace of mind, since I did everything I could for them. It taught me to not judge the priests, for that is only for Jesus to do. I just pray for them and offer Masses for them and pray the patients will receive the graces and mercies they expect from the Church, through priests. I pray especially for the souls of all those who never received the sacrament of the Anointing of the Sick nor the Apostolic Pardon. I plan to offer a Mass for their souls, trusting that God in His mercy, will give them the graces they should have received and expected to receive.

#96 SPANISH CONFESSIONS

Although, I took a summer Spanish class, when I was a religious brother, afterwards I couldn't speak Spanish or read it. However, when I became a pastor for the first time, I typed up an English – Spanish list of sins, used to hear Confessions in Spanish. Originally, I asked the Spanish penitent to point to the sin, and then audibly say the sin on the paper. But later, when I began hospital ministry, I told the penitent to say "Si or No" when I mentioned each sin in Spanish.

I expounded upon the Ten Commandments in Spanish, and then gave a penance in Spanish, telling the person the number of Padre Neustros (Our Fathers) and Ave Marias (Hail Marys) for their penance. I could not give any counsel or advice, since I didn't know Spanish. But, at least their sins could be forgiven. If they couldn't remember the *Act of Contrition* in Spanish I had one for them to read. Using this method to hear confessions in Spanish was very helpful. After all, I could no longer call the Spanish-speaking priest to hear confessions in Spanish, due to his invalid absolution.

#97 CHAPEL AT PRIEST APARTMENT – GREAT GRACE

Apartment (Rectory) Chapel with Jesus in the Eucharist (Beautiful Ave Maria)
The hospital didn't own a rectory for priests, but they rented an apartment in an apartment complex. I considered it a rectory, since I am a priest. There were two women and a young boy who lived in the apartment above me. The women were most likely lesbians. The boy may have been the son of one of the women, or perhaps he was adopted. He was severely mistreated by the younger woman, who would scream all sorts of profanities at him. He was about seven years old. She screamed at him and then talked to him. By hearing footsteps and noises, it seemed apparent, at times, the boy was put in a locked closet and couldn't get out. Since I was worried the child was possibly being harmed, I notified the state of Idaho to have the ladies investigated. One of the women paced every night about 9:00pm for about 20 minutes, and then both women would go to the same bedroom at night. It seemed to be some sort of ritual before they lie in the same bed.

In another apartment, at the end of the building, a woman was shot. Just before that happened, a man attempted to abduct her, so I called police. She ran to me screaming for help and wanted to hide from the man, who she said had a gun. She ran away and ended up in an apartment at the end of my building. The police later said it was a drug deal gone bad.

Due to the bishop of Tantrum, Bishop John Borromeo, known for his liberal ways, I didn't believe he would give permission to have Jesus in the Blessed Sacrament in the apartment. Consequently, the first year I lived at the apartment, I didn't ask. But then later, I found out the previous bishop permitted most rectories to have a Chapel with the Blessed Sacrament. After visiting with my spiritual director, I mustered up the courage to call the bishop and asked if I could have a Chapel with the Eucharistic Jesus. To my surprise, he gave permission. I was absolutely elated.

About a month after Jesus took up His Eucharistic presence in my Chapel, one night I woke up, and heard the most beautiful singing of Ave Maria. It was at an extremely high tone, but incredibly beautiful. I wondered which neighbor was playing the hymn, but realized the singing was coming from the Chapel. I didn't get up to see, but I believe it most likely was my guardian angel singing the Ave Maria. It was truly celestial and heavenly singing.

#98 INVALID MASSES AT ST. MAURUS MONASTERY IN IDAHO

May 2ⁿᵈ, 2019 Carlos Rossi Blush Strikes Again
Invalid Masses at a Benedictine Monastery

While serving at St. John of God Hospital in Tantrum, Ohio, Thursdays were my day away from ministry. One morning, I offered Mass for the conversion of liberals. I decided to have a day of prayer and go to a quite secluded place. As I was driving out of Tantrum, I kept thinking maybe I should not go, since it was a good distance away. After driving for thirty minutes, I almost turned around, but continued the drive to the Monastery.

When I arrived, a sign on the door said, "Gregorian Masses Are Being Offered This Month." A Gregorian Mass intention is a specific Mass intention every day for thirty consecutive days for a particular soul who died. The Gregorian Mass Novena promises the soul to whom the Mass is offered, will go to heaven on the last day the Mass is celebrated.

The monastery was nice and quiet. I prayed before Jesus in the Most Blessed Sacrament in the Tabernacle for several hours and fell asleep. When I awoke, I asked Jesus if He would permit me to eat with the monks, but was fearful of asking them. They would have to ask me. About fifteen minutes later, a monk came up to me, and said, "Would you like to eat with us?" I said, "Sure." I had a nice meal with the monks, and we had good conversations. Due to the closing of St. Maurus University, a monk said, "Oh, the abbot. He makes us pray. We have to pray more now."

After lunch, I walked around the grounds and went back to the Church. I thought I would stay to see how they offered Mass. The way the Mass is offered would tell me many things about their community. About twenty minutes before Mass, a monk asked, "Would you like to concelebrate with us?" I said, "No. I offered Mass this morning." He said, "The Catholic Church permits two Masses in one day. It's okay." I reluctantly said, "Okay." However, I was nervous about how they might offer the Mass. I didn't want to concelebrate a Mass if the rubrics aren't going to be followed properly.

I vested for Mass and concelebrated. I was surprised to see only one lay person attend Mass. The monks did a few odd things during Mass, such as, consume extra Hosts, rather than placing them in the Tabernacle. The wine had an odd color not usually associated with sacramental wine. It reminded me of the wine, *Carlos Rossi Blush,* used in my hometown parish made from strawberries and cherries. I said to myself, "No way, surely it ain't the same wine."

After Mass, when I didn't think the monks were watching, I opened the refrigerator in the sacristy, and to my shock, and horror, *Carols Rossi Blush* strikes again. I immediately realized I offered an invalid Mass with the ten monks who concelebrated with me. Due to the wrong wine not made of grapes, every Monk and I, offered an invalid Mass. Ugh! At first, I was furious. Then I said to Jesus, "You have got to be kidding me. You don't want me to say something to them. No way, I will not do that! You have to find someone else. Please, Lord, not me!" I then thought, "Are you telling me, for those two hours I prayed before the Tabernacle, you were not there! No! No! No! Or Were You there?" Since they used invalid wine for Mass, I had no way of knowing if I had prayed before Jesus or not.

I decided to leave without saying anything. However, a monk came near, and I felt Jesus urging me to say something, and so, I said, "Father, I don't know how to tell you this. But I looked at wine you are using. It's *Carlos Rossi Blush.* Did you know the wine is made from strawberries and cherries?" With a shocked look on his face, he said, "Oh, wow. I guess we just offered an invalid Mass, didn't we?" I said, "Yes". He, then, said, "Do you know where we can get some cheap wine." I said, "Father, I only use sacramental wine." He repeated what he said, and I repeated what I said. Then, he said, "Well, I will tell the abbot when he comes back, and we will just have to make a road trip tomorrow and get some before the next Mass."

I left bewildered, and driving on the way back, started to cry. But then I remembered I had offered my Mass at the rectory for liberals. I understood why the Lord wanted the Mass offered, so they would once again have a valid Mass. I thought to myself, there is no better way to convert liberals than to help them have a valid Mass, and thanked the Lord for using me to help them have valid Masses again. Likewise, I wondered how long they used *Carlos Rossi* wine. Wow! They need to re-offer all Masses in which they used that wine and re-offer all the Gregorian Masses too. Oh, my! No wonder, so few people don't attend Mass. Perhaps, they somehow must have realized they weren't getting much from the Mass. They had no idea the sacrifice of Calvary wasn't present due to the invalid wine. Lord, Have Mercy!

Because of the gravity of this, I believed Jesus wanted me to notify the bishop of that diocese. So, on May 3rd, the Feast of Sts. Philip and James, the day after I discovered the tragedy, I called Archbishop Gooddshepherd of the Archdiocese of Millsburger, Idaho, and told him about it. You have no idea, how scared I was to call the bishop. I felt sick to my stomach. Yet, I knew the Lord wanted me to do it.

I called the chancery of the archdiocese, and asked the secretary to have the bishop call me, and to tell him it was important. The archbishop responded, saying, "This is not going to happen in my diocese. I will call them right now. Thank you for letting me know."

Two hours later, after I spoke with the archbishop, I received a call from my bishop, Bishop Athanasius Courageous of Rolling Hills. I was shocked. I thought, "Oh, no. The other bishop called my bishop. And it's not going to go well". But I soon realized he had no idea what had just transpired, and I wasn't going to tell him either. He called because he wanted me to come back to the Diocese of Rolling Hills, Ohio, to be a hospital chaplain in my diocese.

I wondered how could it be, I discovered invalid Masses with the same non-sacramental wine in less than two years. I told this event to a priest in Tantrum, Monsignor Kevin Glassmasher, who said, "Father, I think after you die, you will be the patron of invalid sacraments." We both chuckled about it. But, I wondered if I would actually become the patron of valid sacraments instead, since I helped to have valid ones. He also knew about the invalid anointings at the hospital, and how I tried to help the priest offer the Sacrament of the Sick validly. But Monsignor didn't know about all the invalid baptisms, I discovered at Mother of Misery Healthcare in Rolling Hills, years previously or the invalid marriages, years before that.

#99 ASSIGNED TO ROLLING HILLS, OHIO "CATHOLIC" HOSPITALS

St. Henry & St. Mother Cope Hospitals (Return of Crucifixes & Triumph of the Cross)
"We preach Christ crucified, a stumbling block to Jews and an absurdity to Gentiles." (1 Corinthians 1:23)

When I was assigned to Mother of Misery Healthcare Center at St. Henry and St. Mother Cope Hospitals in June 2019, I had a meeting with the Pastoral Care Department Manager. He said he heard a rumor about me. The last time I was assigned to the hospitals, he said, "I heard you were unhappy with the crucifixes". I said, "That's true". To show his support, he said, "I don't like the resurrected crosses. I want to replace them." I was surprised he wanted to have ordinary crucifixes at hospitals. He asked if I would help him pick out crucifixes. Over a period of time, I came to understand he really wanted traditional crucifixes. But after some months, it didn't seem like they were going to be replaced.

Since I knew he wanted to replace the crucifixes, I felt comfortable in deciding to remove the strange resurrected crosses, and replace them with real Crucifixes. I purchased, with my own money, one hundred and sixty-five crucifixes to replace the strange looking ones.

Slowly, but secretly, they were exchanged at St. Henry, St. Mother Cope Hospitals and Pool of Siloam Rehab Center. I felt like "007" or "Mission Impossible" slowly exchanging them out and trying not to be seen by staff.

Years ago, when they replaced the real crucifixes with the modern ones, I wondered if they threw them in the trash or gave them away?

One day, I was in an empty patient room, standing on a chair behind the door while replacing a resurrected cross with a real Crucifix, when a cleaning lady suddenly opened the door and hit the chair I was standing on, nearly causing me to fall to the ground. She didn't know what I was doing, and I didn't tell her either.

I even replaced a crucifix in a nursing station where the nurses were almost always updating patient records. But, at that particular time of day, no staff was around, and within a matter of seconds replaced it. I felt like St. Edmund Campion, an English priest martyr, who disguised himself to offer Mass and hear confessions in secret. Replacing the crosses with Crucifixes was like being on a secret mission, and praying not to get caught. Yet, I trusted the Lord was inspiring me to be in certain places, at certain times, to exchange the crucifixes.

Providentially, I was able to replace many on the feast of St. Teresa Benedicta of the Cross. On her feast day, a whole unit closed due to low census, so I went through it and replaced many of them.

Surprisingly, nobody seemed to realize they were being exchanged. At times, even when a patient was in the room, I replaced them. The patients always liked the crucifixes, rather than the strange crosses. In my opinion, they depicted Jesus as a referee at a football game raising His hands for a touchdown.

Despite religious sisters and hospital administrators losing their faith in Jesus Crucified, the faith of the people endures. The Holy Faith cannot be squashed out by liberal attempts to hide the beauty and love Jesus revealed on Calvary. It just so happened, by Divine Providence; the last crucifix installed at St. Mother Cope Hospital was on the Feast of the Triumph of the Cross, September 14th, 2019. "May I never boast except in the cross of our Lord Jesus Christ, through which the world has been crucified to me, and I to the world." (Galatians 6:14)

#100 MEDJUGORJE PILGRIMAGE

Medjugorje Pilgrimages & I Saw an Image of the Virgin Mary

Until now, I went to Medjugorje five times. The first two, I went to Medjugorje before I became a priest. The third time was the first time I went as a priest.

In Medjugorje, I first experienced God's call and now wanted to return to give thanks to Our Lady. It was so moving to return and give thanks to the Blessed Virgin Mary for helping me to become a priest. I was blessed to be the main celebrant at St. James for the 10 am English-speaking Mass. The first reading was about the destruction of Sodom and Gomorrah. During this trip, the US Supreme Court ruled in favor of homosexual marriages. I preached on the topic during Mass.

By God's Providence, I met a young couple who had three children. The wife was dying of cancer and came to Medjugorje seeking a miracle. I gave Polly the Sacrament of the Sick.

As it always seems to happen, after that trip, I had a new mission. The bishop would call and ask if I wanted to help minister in the Diocese of Tantrum as a hospital chaplain. The experience of anointing in Medjugorje seemed to be a nudge to do something new in the future. Polly was from Montana. Polly never received the physical miracle she had hoped for while in Medjugorje and died just a few weeks after the trip. However, she received a special grace at Medjugorje through Our Lady's intercession. When she came to Medjugorje, she said- that when she dies, she can't leave her children behind.

But, by God's grace, on Apparition Hill, as she knelt and prayed before the statue of Mary, she was able to hand her children over to the perfect Mother, the Virgin Mary, Queen of Peace, to care for them, before her death.

The night before we left Medjugorje, I went up apparition hill to ask Mary for some special intentions, and to pray a Rosary. After I finished the rosary, I happened to turn around and caught sight of a woman, who was glowing. She had a long light-colored blue dress and veil. She was hovering over rocks and moving in my direction. She could be easily seen because of the glow. I was so excited. I wanted to cry out, "Look, it's the Virgin Mary!" But I was so aghast by the image I couldn't speak. She kept coming closer and closer to me, until I finally realized it wasn't the Virgin Mary. It was a religious sister with a cell phone that lit up her habit as she climbed over the rocks. This experience reminded me -- women religious are an image of the Virgin Mary. It made me chuckle, as I walked down the hill.

In the evening after the International Mass, the Franciscans led 1 Hail Mary, 1 Our Fathers, and 1 Glory Be, 7 times followed by singing the Salve Regina (Hail Holy Queen).

Then, they began an outdoor Eucharistic Holy Hour with a very large Monstrance placed on the altar and the smoke of incense rose towards the sky to heaven. A small choir led repeated aspirations in different languages as a violin and an electronic organ were played. It was overwhelming to see 10,000 people adoring Jesus outdoors. The silence between hymns was moving even more than the music. (photo on back cover)

On Friday, after the International Mass the Franciscans placed a large crucifix on the altar in what they called "Adoration of the Cross". During that hour, a small choir sung hymns helping the people to reflect on the sufferings of Jesus.

The beauty and power of these devotions made my heart beat ever more fervently in love of Jesus.

#101 RELIGIOUS SISTERS, WHO AREN'T SO RELIGIOUS

Sisters of Misery, Sisters of the Holy Name of Jesus, & Sisters of Good Health
"Then the kingdom of heaven shall be compared to ten virgins who took their lamps and went to meet the bridegroom. Five of them were foolish, and five were wise." (Matthew 25:1-2)

Many religious sisters no longer wear their habits, but instead, wear polyester fashionable clothing, pierced earrings, lipstick, and go to beauty shops. A Conventual Franciscan priest once referred to modern sisters who don't wear habits, as "Sister Poly Esthers of the Most Pierced Ears."

One of my cousins, Sister Jacinta Schwacker, a sister of the Holy Name of Jesus, would have worn her habit if she was able. She said Bishop Basil Braveheart asked the Sisters of Misery and the Sisters of the Holy Name of Jesus to wear their habits. However, she said, both religious communities voted, and told the bishop no.

When Sister Jacinta died, I went to her Funeral Vigil. It was presided over by one of their sisters, while Bishop John Fidelity attended. The bishop wanted to do the vigil, but they told him to be seated, while the sisters did the Funeral Vigil and Rosary. Because of their domineering behavior, the bishop played no role in the Vigil. Due to how they treated the bishop, I decided to not concelebrate her funeral Mass, and offered a private Mass for her soul.

One day, a sister was admitted to St. Henry Hospital. Because she wasn't wearing a habit, I didn't know she was a religious sister, and the patient list didn't indicate she was a sister. When I entered her room, I said, "Are you Julie?" She said, "Yes, I am Julie. I am a sister of the Mother of Misery congregation, but don't call me sister." I introduced myself saying, "I'm Father Leonard Gadfly". One of the sisters who was visiting her said, "Oh, nice to meet you, Len." It seemed the sisters wanted to be known as sisters, so they would be treated as a sister, but not called sister. They also didn't want to call me Father, or use my proper name of Leonard. I came to learn the sisters of this order were behind removing Crucifixes and replacing them with the resurrected Jesus on the cross.

One of the Sisters of the Holy Name of Jesus, Sister Janine Sacerdotis, of the I Wannabe a Priest, is a lay chaplain at St. Marianne Cope Hospital. She prepares items for Mass, and when it begins, she and a lay person stands during the consecration. They also use their personal responses during Mass, rather, than the proper responses as the Church requires.

Sister Janine didn't want laymen to attend Mass, because if they did, she would have to kneel. Mass is offered at St. Marianne Cope's only once a month. This is because she refused to allow me to offer Mass once a week. This is an example of how a sister tells a priest chaplain how to perform his ministry, which is canonically inappropriate, but approved by chancery personnel.

On the memorial of St. Margaret Mary Alacoque, during Holy Mass, when the two sisters were present, I repeated the words of Jesus, who said, "Behold this Heart, which has loved so much, but has received nothing but coldness, indifference, and ingratitude in return. Especially those consecrated to me." I reminded the sisters at Mass, it was religious and priests consecrated to Him, who caused His Eucharistic Heart to be pained so terribly, due to their irreverence, sacrilege, and indifference to His true presence in the Eucharist.

When I arrived at St. John of God Hospital in Tantrum, there wasn't an ablution bowl near the altar, so I purchased one, and then asked Sr. Susan, a sister of Good Health, to dip her fingers in the bowl and wipe them on the towel after she was finished distributing Holy Communion. But she refused to do as I asked. A week later, I explained to her, that each particle, no matter how small, is the whole and entire person of Jesus in the Eucharist. But again, she refused.

A few weeks later, she asked me to type up a brief description for lay chaplains on how to distribute Holy Communion to patients. When I presented the instructions during a meeting, I told them they were to dip their fingers in the ablution bowl and wipe them on a cloth after distributing Holy Communion. Sr. Susan was present during the instructions, and since then, did as I asked.

Unfortunately, when Sr. Mary Snickers first arrived, I had the same problem with her. She also refused to use the ablution bowl after distributing Holy Communion. However, I gave a homily on the Eucharist, and told the people why the Extraordinary Ministers of Communion dipped their fingers in the ablution bowl. It worked, and since then, the sisters began to do it.

The Sisters of Good Health would not help the poor or a priest without health insurance. Here are some examples: I asked the sisters to make a request to administration for a Franciscan priest, who had no money to pay for his surgery or his hospital bill. I asked that they attempt to have the bill forgiven by the hospital, but they refused to do anything. I also asked them if the Franciscan priest could receive free food while he was recovering at Hotel Good Cents. The hotel provided a free place to stay for poor rehab patients, but the sisters refused that as well.

A poor Hispanic family was living in their car in a parking garage, while their father was undergoing serious heart problems. The lay chaplains didn't mention anything to the sisters about their need because everyone knew the sisters would do nothing. The whole pastoral care department rallied around the poor family, donating food, clothing, and money. When the sisters heard about their wonderful charity, they asked why they didn't mention it to them. One of the lay chaplains honestly said, "No one thought you would help."

I noticed Sister Mary Intelligence, breaking hosts into tiny pieces in the sink, and forcing them down the drain. I said, "Sister, what are you doing?" She said, "I was told to break up these old hosts in the Sacrarium and make them go down the drain." She was forcing crumbs from hosts down the drain without using water. I didn't know if the hosts were consecrated, and prayed they weren't. This shows a lack of common sense by her superior, who made the younger sister do something contrary to reason.

On another occasion, I saw Sr. Mary Intelligence pouring Sacred Particles mixed in water from a pyx down the drain of the Sacrarium, and I said, "You should consume those. That is your spouse, you are pouring down the drain. Did you know that Pope St. John Paul II said those who pour Precious Blood down the drain are excommunicated?" She responded by ignoring me.

Besides these examples, there were many young Sisters of Good Health, who showed great devotion and love for patients and the staff. There is great hope for their community in the future, but not until the older liberal sisters go to their eternal rest, or have a conversion, which seems highly unlikely. Unfortunately, the older sisters have a negative influence on the younger ones.

#102 LOTS OF BABIES

July 18th, 2019 – Babies, Babies, Babies

"Then Herod, when he saw that he had been tricked by the wise men, became furious, and he sent and killed all the male children in Bethlehem and in all that region who were two years old or under..." (Matthew 2:16)

July 18th was my day away from ministry. In the morning, I offered Mass to close Schindler's Unborn Baby Disposal Unit in Rolling Hills. During Mass, I prayed for the doctors, nurses, and, all who work at the clinic, would quit. I prayed for those thinking of going to the clinic to have an abortion, would not go. I prayed those who were in the clinic, would change their minds, and leave. I prayed for those who went to the clinic, that they would be open to receive God's mercy and forgiveness.

Just as I finished making my thanksgiving to Jesus in Holy Communion, who came inside my heart, I received a phone call from a lay chaplain at the hospital, who asked me to come to the hospital, since there was a fetal demise (death of newborn) and the family wanted prayers. They forgot that another priest was already at the hospital and on call, and after I mentioned it, he went to help the family. I then went to the abortion clinic, and prayed from 10 am to 11 am.

When I arrived, there was a woman, with her two children, from Freshwater, Ohio, praying. A man from the Cathedral, and another woman from St. Charles of Sezze parish were there. All were Catholic. The man from the Cathedral and I prayed two rosaries, the Chaplet of Divine Mercy, and the Litany of the Saints.

During that hour, separately from each other, two women came out of the clinic, and changed their minds. Both said they were carrying twins. One woman said, "They told me I have twins, and since I can't afford the extra cost of killing two, I thought I would keep them."

Another woman brought her five-year-old daughter, and her forty-year-old mother, with her, to have the abortion. They were in the clinic for about thirty minutes, and then departed in their car. When they pulled up to the gate entrance to leave, the pregnant woman said, "They told me I have twins. I just couldn't abort both of them." Within an hour, four babies were saved from abortion. Praise God and His infinite mercy! The following Saturday, I baptized triplets at Immaculate Heart of Mary in Wheatland.

Three years earlier, I originally prepared the couple, who had triplets for marriage and nine months after their wedding, their first baby died by miscarriage on the exact day the child was to be born. We had the baby's funeral at Immaculate Heart of Mary parish. A year later, the couple was pregnant with twins and I baptized their twins. Two years after the twins were born, they had triplets, and I performed the baptism of their three babies on July 21st, 2019. Since the couple had 5 children under the age of 2, I told them, they have good reason to use natural family planning. God has done great things for us, and we are filled with joy.

#103 ST. JOSEPH

St. Joseph (First Wednesday of the Month)
"Joseph, son of David, do not be afraid to take Mary your wife into your home. For it is through the Holy Spirit that this child has been conceived in her." (Matthew 1:20-21)

In 2019, I heard about ecclesiastically approved apparitions of St. Joseph. On the first Wednesday of the month, St. Joseph promised to grant our petitions. The first time I did the devotion, I asked St. Joseph for the gift of purity, as I continued to have strong lustful thoughts. After I prayed to St. Joseph, on the first Wednesday of the month, I went to confession to Fr. James Samson and confessed lustful thoughts. At times, I wondered, if these thoughts were mortal sins or not. I received absolution, did the penance, went to my car, and drove back to the hospital. On the way back, a demon came inside the car with a horrid voice, said, "I will come back!" After several weeks, I realized, since that confession, I no longer had lustful thoughts like I had previously. Demons are liars. I pray the demon of impurity never comes back, and I thank St. Joseph for delivering me from those temptations. I believe and hope, by the grace of St. Joseph, I was permanently delivered from the demon.

On March, 19th, 2020, I formally consecrated myself to St. Joseph by making the 33-day Preparation for Consecration to St. Joseph by Fr. Donald Calloway, MIC. What a terrific and informational book! (See Appendix B - Consecration Prayers).

#104 HEALTH HEALINGS

My Health and God's Mercy
"O Lord, I cried to you for help and you, my God, have healed me." (Psalm 30:2)

Over the past year, at times I fainted when I moved my head, neck, and back in the wrong direction. A cardiologist had me do a stress test, echocardiogram and wear a heart monitor for a week. A nurse from their office called and said that I needed a pacemaker and she wanted to immediately schedule an appointment. I asked about the results of the heart monitor, but was not given any detailed information. I decided to get a second opinion. I requested the original doctor office to transfer test results to another doctor. After three calls by me and multiple phone calls from the second doctor's office and after three months, they finally sent the results. After reading the results from the tests, the second doctor said, "You do not need a pacemaker." I later discovered the first doctor was known for installing pacemakers in patients unnecessarily. Installing pacemakers is a way to make lots of money.

After an MRI, CT scan, stress test, echocardiogram, carotid ultrasound, the second cardiologist in Tantrum, suggested I may have a blockage in an artery in my brain. He said it may cause sudden death, due to a massive stroke. This was discovered, Thursday, Sept. 26th, the anniversary of my grandmother's birthday. The doctor said he would schedule an arteriogram of the brain with the hope of finding the blockage.

Due to the prognosis, a priest gave me the Sacrament of the Sick and the Apostolic Pardon. After I went to confession, I was anointed, given the Apostolic Pardon, and then offered Mass and received Communion. God in His infinite mercy washed away all my sins and the punishment due to my sins because of this prognosis. The fear of it, was worth having all punishment due to my sins washed away in the ocean of God's mercy.

The arteriogram came out negative. I was then referred to a neurologist who thought I had "Bow Hunter's Syndrome". It can cause an artery in the neck to be kinked and cause a massive stroke, or I could bleed to death if the artery would rupture. Consequently, I made an appointment with a neurosurgeon. All of these doctor visits and all this hype over what "may" be wrong, helped me to have more empathy for patients who deal with doctors and have frightening misdiagnoses.

Since the location of the kinked artery is inoperable, he said nothing can be done about the condition. All these doctors and all these tests ended up in helping me to know I have a condition that medical science can do nothing about.

During my time as a hospital chaplain, I told patients to ask God to heal them. Some said they felt it was prideful to ask God to heal them. I responded, saying, "Have you ever prayed for money?" Most all said, "Yes." Then I would say, "If you pray for money, why don't you pray that God will heal you."

I realized later, I never asked God for the healing of my infirmities and decided to do what I told the patients to do.

Since 1994, I had lactose intolerance, and in 2018, developed diabetes. In 2019, after telling patients to ask God for healing, I decided to ask Jesus to heal me of my own illnesses. I used the "Prayer of Feeling" taught by the Discernment of Spirits Retreat. When I finished, I didn't feel any different. About a week later, I noticed blood sugar levels were normal and decided to stop taking diabetes medicine. I had a strong craving for pizza, but knew I couldn't eat cheese, because it causes gas, pain, and diarrhea. However, I decided to eat pizza, and to my astonishment, it had no effect on me. I am now able to eat cheese, that I was unable to eat for 25 years. Thank you, Jesus!

About a month later, the symptoms that caused fainting disappeared. Healed again! Thank you, Jesus!

Since Jesus healed my body, it gave me confidence that whatever happens in the future, Our Lady will watch over my soul, which is infinitely more important than the body, and will protect it, so that when the hour comes to leave this valley of tears, She will pray for me, now and at the hour of my death, and therefore, I will skip purgatory.

I certainly deserve hell and purgatory, but I trust in God's unfathomable, untold mercy. Many times in my past, I could have died in the state of mortal sin, but God in His mercy saved me.

It's a total gift of God, that His Mercy triumphed in my physical conditions, and I pray it will continue to triumph in me spiritually until I am called to my eternal home. Totally unmerited and undeserved mercy.

#105 REFLECTING ON GOD'S MERCY

God's Promise of Mercy
"He has come to the help of his servant Israel, for He has remembered this promise of mercy, the promise He made to our fathers, to Abraham, and his children forever." (Luke 1:54)

Our Blessed Mother's beautiful words remind me how God's promise of mercy is for all His children, including me. I entrust and consecrate my judgment, purgatory time, and all my time in eternity to You, O Mary. "For we shall all stand before the judgment seat of God, for it is written: As, l live, says the Lord, every knee shall bend before me; and every tongue shall give praise to God. So then each of us shall give an account of himself to God." (Romans 14:11-12) "O Lord, you have shown me my end, how short is the length of days. Now I know how fleeting is my life." (Psalm 39:4) "I have put all my trust in God's never-failing mercy." (Antiphon 3 Wed. Week II) "Lord, I will trust in You" (Psalm 55:23) "Deliver us, Lord, we pray, from every evil, graciously grant peace in our days, that by the help of your mercy, we may be always free from sin, and safe from all distress, as we await the blessed hope and the coming of our Savior, Jesus Christ." (Communion Rite) O Jesus, I await your coming, to take me to Yourself, with the Father and the Holy Spirit, with all the angels and saints in heaven, especially with Mary, my sweet Mother. "Eye has not seen, nor ear heard, nor have entered into the heart of man the things which God has prepared for those who love Him." (I Corinthians 2:9) From the depth of my heart, no matter my future, O Lord, I cry "Jesus I Trust in You." O Lord Jesus, I thank you for the greatest gift—of your mercy—Heaven!

#106 JESUS APPEARS AGAIN

Divine Child's Appearances

During the month of November 2019, the Divine Child began to appear again. This always happens when it's not expected.

As I was walking through a corridor of the hospital, He was wearing His pink gown and lying on my chest and shoulder with His head resting upon me (the same place I was carrying the pyx with the Blessed Sacrament in my pocket). I could see His little Heart beating very fast. It reminded me of the babies in NICU (Neonatal Intensive Care) because their heart rates are much faster than adults.

On a different day, I saw the Divine Child with stitches on His head, in the form of a half-circle on the left side of His head. There were metal like objects (staples) used to help close the wound. I had no idea what that meant. Then a week later, when I was visiting patients at the Pool of Siloam Rehab Center on a Sunday, I saw a patient with the exact wound on her head. I believe Jesus wanted me to understand that He feels and suffers what patients endure. He wanted to remind me to pray for babies in the NICU and pray for rehab patients, perhaps because I neglected to pray for them as well as what I ought.

#107 WEIRD PHARMACY HAPPENING

CBS Pharmacy (Oh What Fun? Not Really!)

I had the bright idea of going to a nearby pharmacy to purchase a neck brace. I hoped it would prevent blood flow problems when sleeping due to artery in my neck getting kinked. While there, I decided to buy a lighter (with a long extension) to light candles at my Chapel, to pick up bottled water on sale, and buy a canister of Christmas popcorn for my step-father.

When I went to the clerk, the young girl couldn't ring up the popcorn, so she called the manager. The manager came and told her to she needed to punch in the product code number, and then it would ring up. She then asked for my driver's license, and said it was company policy, that anyone who purchases a lighter must show their driver's license. I said, "Do you realize I am 56 years old. I lost most of my hair, and it's all gray, and you want to see my driver's license?" She said, "You can't buy it unless you give me your license." I reluctantly gave it to her, and she then scanned the license. She rang up the bottled water, but the price that rang up on the register was a dollar more than the sign posted beneath it. She said, "I need your phone number, so I can sell it to you for sale price." I said, "I am not giving you my phone number." I paid her, and before I left, I said, "I will not come back." The manager heard me say that, and said, "Why?" I said, "You wanted my driver's license to purchase a lighter. The popcorn would not ring up. You wanted my phone number before I could receive the sale price, forget it. I like Belgrens Pharmacy, much better." When I arrived home, I put on the neck brace, and it caused my left arm to go numb, and I had difficulty controlling leg motion. It turned out to be a bad idea, to go to CBS Pharmacy!

#108 DEAD PATIENT'S HEART STARTS TO BEAT AGAIN

Dead Patient's Heart Begins to Beat After Receiving Anointing of the Sick
"Soon afterward, Jesus went to a town called Nain, and his disciples and a large crowd went along with him. As he approached the town gate, a dead person was being carried out—the only son of his mother, and she was a widow. And a large crowd from the town was with her. When the Lord saw her, his heart went out to her, and he said, "Don't cry."Then he went up and touched the bier they were carrying him on, and the bearers stood still. He said, "Young man, I say to you, get up!" The dead man sat up and began to talk, and Jesus gave him back to his mother." (John 7:11-14)

In 2020, during the middle of the COVID-19 epidemic, I was at St. Mother Cope's hospital and received a call from a lay chaplain, saying a patient, not listed as Catholic, but was actually Catholic, was dying at St. Henry's hospital, and the family wanted a priest to anoint him as soon as possible.

I immediately left Mother Cope hospital for the thirty-minute trip back to St. Henry. Upon arrival, I went to Intensive Care Unit. Before entering the room, the nurse said the patient died about fifteen minutes before I arrived.

I decided to anoint the patient, despite the fact he had no heart beat and was not breathing.

There is a thirty-minute window after death in which a person can receive Anointing of the Sick, as mentioned in Jone's *Moral Theology* book. Because it's uncertain when a soul actually leaves the body, the sacrament can be performed conditionally. Only God knows when the soul leaves the body.

When I entered the room, the family was weeping, and the heart monitor indicated a flat line. I immediately laid hands on his head, and just as I made the sign of the cross on his forehead using the sacred Oil of the Sick, his heart began to beat. It kept beating the entire time I was in the room. It was beating erratically, but it was beating.

I began to wonder, "Why don't the nurses attempt life-saving measures since his heart is beating?" I wondered how they could say he was dead for fifteen minutes, when his heart started to beat again? If they took him to the morgue, would he awaken in a body bag during transportation? All these thoughts haunted me.

But later, I had peace, thinking maybe God worked a little miracle to allow the patient to come back to life. This way, his sins could be forgiven through the Sacrament of the Sick and receive the Apostolic Pardon before he went to his judgment. The power of the sacrament was astonishing to me! God's mercy is superabundant, and can even cause a dead man to come back to life, so his judgment would go well.

Divine Mercy Image

I'm scheduled to give a retreat at Happy Soul Retreat House on Divine Mercy Sunday. On the internet, I found a beautiful image of the Divine Mercy, I never saw before, and hope to display it during the retreat. I ordered a four-foot canvas image of the Divine Mercy.

A week later, I was adoring Jesus in the Blessed Sacrament in my Chapel, when I entered into a quiet, peaceful prayer. As I was praying, suddenly in my mind, I saw Jesus as an adult, in the form of His image of Divine Mercy. In my mind, I saw Him walk through the front door of the rectory, and, just as I saw Him in my mind, the doorbell rang, which startled me. I quickly put away the little Chapel Monstrance in the Tabernacle, and went to see who was at the door. When I opened the door, nobody was there, and looked out in the street and saw a Fedup Pony Express driver hop into his truck. It was then, I noticed he left a package on the front steps. I carried the large package into the house, and I discovered it was the Divine Mercy Image I recently ordered. It was the same image of Jesus, I saw in my mind walk through the front door, as I was praying in the Chapel. Thank you, Jesus!

#109 ARTHRITIS HYDROXYCHLOROQUINE & COVID-19

When performing ministry at St. John of God Hospital, I slowly developed psoriasis arthritis without skin irritation. Soon, it became more and more difficult to function due to stiffness and pain. My physician referred me to a good Catholic rheumatologist in Tantrum, who prescribed an anti-inflammatory medicine called Naproxen. However, over time, it became less effective while doing priestly ministry at St. Henry's in Rolling Hills. A year later, it was increasingly more difficult to do ordinary things, such as to put on shoes and socks, or walk up and down the stairs at the hospital. It took fifteen minutes to just put on my socks and shoes.

On Feb. 30th, my birthday, the arthritis doctor prescribed a new medicine called Hydroxychloroquine. It's also the feast of saints Jacinta and Francisco. It was a miracle pill. Within several weeks, I regained motion and pain dramatically reduced. Nearly a month later, on March 17ᵗʰ, St. Patrick's Day, the lock-down occurred, and a week before the lock-down, I contracted COVID-19, but didn't know I had it at the time. Looking back, I could see that when I was placed on the new medicine, the doctor had no idea it could help patients with COVID-19. It was God's way of protecting me by allowing me to suffer arthritis, which resulted in being placed on medicine used to prevent serious COVID-19 complications. It certainly could have saved my life. Thank you, Jesus, for your infinite and providential mercy!

#110 COVID-19 & THE PANDEMIC
PLAGUE OR BIOLOGICAL WEAPON?

Coronavirus

This by far was the most excruciating experience I had as a priest. How horrible! The bishops forbade public Masses. People could not receive Holy Communion. Adoration Chapels were closed due to an infectious virus killing thousands of people worldwide. There were so many sad experiences locally. This was an email from Rod Sterling of Misery Health System, on March 13ᵗʰ, 2020.

I have discussed the issue of patient contact with my esteemed colleagues this morning, and we all agree that regarding chaplains (including priest chaplains), they should not be permitted in a patient room in an active case of COVID-19. The same goes for parish priests. The case for restricting access for non-employed parish priests is even stronger insofar as there is no means by which we can train them in the use of PPE (Personal Protective Equipment). We would not want a priest in the room with, and especially touching, a patient who is a vector and then returning to their parish/community and spreading the virus. The pushback we will likely get is around the importance of touch regarding the sacraments and rites, but it is actually a heresy to assert/believe that the divine work of the Holy Spirit is dependent upon the touch of a human being as its vehicle (or at least my VP, Ethics and Church Relations, told me something to that effect... I'm just a silly philosopher... and will be summarizing it in writing for us later today, citing the appropriate sacramental theology sources).
Thanks,
~RS
Rod Sterling, PhD
Senior Vice President, Healthcare Ethics

Due to this email, I immediately went to the chancery to visit the bishop and asked him if I could give Holy Communion to anyone who asked for it, and he said yes. Due to this permission from the bishop, and since it was given to me personally, my spiritual director said his permission remains enforce until he, himself says otherwise. Then on March 16th, the following email came out. Here is an email that was totally shocking and apparently approved by three bishops of Ohio.

From: Sarah Pickamouse, Todd Stoner

As you know further precautions are being applied as we reconfigure our services to provide safety and care to our patients, families, caregivers and the community. Earlier this week we implemented a Visitor Policy such that patients are allowed one visitor. An exception was made for patients at the end of life when the immediate family is allowed one entry, to then stay in the room through the death. Note that this policy may change based on our experience and learning from other communities.

As you know, Pope Francis issued a decree and a note that provides plenary indulgences in lieu of face-to-face priest ministry for the Sacraments of Reconciliation, Eucharist, Anointing of the Sick and Viaticum. Based on this and the direction of Misery Healthcare Ethics (who have reviewed Canon Law) and the review of Bishop Courageous, Bishop Grunber and Archbishop Lifemann and the direction of Dr. Pandora Socci, Ohio Command Chief representing Infection Control, Risk Management, Medical/Clinical practices the following guidelines have been established for Community Priest and Minister Access and for Priest Ministry within the hospital setting.

Effective at 3:00pm today, the following goes into effect:
Rolling Hills
1. Community priests and chaplains will not be granted access to the facilities. Instead, they will be encouraged to connect virtually with the patient and family if clinically appropriate. In house chaplains are available to arrange for remote access to patients.
2. Fr. Harry Brown and Fr. Leonard Gadfly will continue as in-house priest chaplains. They will, however, for COVID-19 ICU positive tested patients, not enter the room but instead minister the plenary indulgences the Pope has decreed from outside the room. This is a practice that applies to all Misery Healthcare chaplains in Rolling Hills, as well, per Dr. Pandora Socci, Command Chief. Again, this is for the

protection of the patient and the priests who go room to room. It also reserves protection equipment, which to date is a scarce resource.

3. Fr. Harry and Fr. Leonard will continue to broadcast their private Mass at noon to patients in the hospital.

4. Fr. Royal is identifying backup priests for Fr. Harry and Fr. Leonard as the pandemic may intensify, and the duration is unknown. These identified priests may also serve as remote chaplains to patients dealing with COVID-19 in the outpatient or home setting.

5. Fr. Royal is leading communication regarding the Visitor Policy for all priests and encouraging them to be available remotely to administer sacraments to patients outside the hospital that may be under investigation or tested positive, as we know 80% of those tested positive will recover without being in the hospital setting.

Dr. Romana Filburt is recording a video for all priests to learn about COVID-19 and how best to protect themselves and others. This is expected next week and further information will come from the Diocese.

Iceberg / Fort Butter

Mark Menagerie leads our spiritual care at the hospital in Iceberg and the Fort Butter Emergency Room. Mark Menagerie will serve as the in-house chaplain who will arrange for remote sacramental ministry. Father Jack Bequick will take the lead and call on Fr. Cornelius, Fr. Cyprian, Fr. Chrysogonus and Fr. Cosmas who were selected by Fr. Royal and Bishop Courageous as available for remote ministry. These priests will not be allowed access into the hospital for their safety and the safety of those in the hospital, but are available, outside the facility, to minister spiritual care. Please call me or Todd Stoner with any questions in Rolling Hills and in Iceberg call me or Bailey Barnum. Thank you for your flexibility as we all work to make this work and keep safe! We will all be learning, so please bring your learning forward as we work within these new constraints!

Sarah Pickamouse Ext. 0001
Chaplain: Todd Stoner Ext. 0002
Chaplain: Ginger Rogers Ext. 0003
Fr. Matt Royal Ext. 0004

The priests at these hospitals were furious and shocked by this email. Three priests contacted the bishop and Fr. Royal. How on earth do they expect a priest to do sacramental ministry without any contact with patients! I decided I would do what I believed the Lord wanted me to do, and follow my conscience regardless of the consequences. The email showed a lack of understanding of sacraments and the need for the sacraments to gain a plenary indulgence. Fr. Harry and I agreed, we could not obey this email out of conscience and would anoint all seriously ill patients, regardless if they had the COVID-19 virus or not. He emailed the bishop saying, "I will do anything to anoint COVID-19 patients." After about a week of turmoil, the bishop changed his mind, and wanted Fr. Harry Brown to see all COVID-19 patients (Catholic and non-Catholic) and I was to see all Catholic patients in all three hospitals. I was moved by Fr. Brown's willingness to approach the bishop, and to give of himself sacrificially for COVID-19 patients. I later discovered Fr. Harry caved and didn't give any patients Holy Communion, unless they were immediately dying and rarely anointed patients, but only by way of a cotton swab, which the Church permits.

The bishops relied on the medical community to give them advice on the crisis. Not having any scientific or medical background, they were impelled to do as the government requested. Yet, they seriously failed Catholics with regard to their rights to receive the sacraments. At the beginning of the pandemic, the media made it sound like people all over the world were dying by the thousands.

Not knowing what they were dealing with, whether it was a plague, or some freak disease developed in a biological weapon lab, they believed they had to protect the people from physical danger, and thought it imprudent to place the lives of the elderly and weak in serious danger. Government agencies, together with the media, caused deep fear among the people. Looking back after the fact, it is clear to most everyone, the bishops were duped.

While working at Nedley Medical Center, years ago, in the Central Supply department, I learned about biological germs and viruses and was a member of an infection control committee at the hospital. This experience gave me confidence in understanding the difference between what is true or hype during the pandemic. It became apparent something wasn't right, when there was no concern for "universal precautions". The CDC and the NIH never referred to this type of protection for workers or for anyone. To me, this was a red flag. And it made me doubt their information.

In the end, it turned out to be very inaccurate and not logical by the way they treated COVID-19 patients, because it would make perfect sense to treat every patient as if he or she had a disease (universal precautions), rather than to retreat patients differently.

The Iconoclast Sisters

"Do not give dogs what is sacred; do not throw your pearls to pigs. If you do, they may trample them under their feet, and turn and tear you to pieces." (Matthew 7:6)

At the same time of the COVID-19 crisis, the Sisters of Misery revolted against holy objects. Here is an email I sent to a doctor explaining why sacred images in the Chapel were removed.

Dear Dr. Mary Elderberry,

Fr. Harry Brown said Sarah Pickamouse put pressure on bishop to allow contraception to be prescribed by Misery Healthcare doctors. He relented and now allows it, even though, the bishop said he does so reluctantly. An ethics "expert" from Mother of Misery Health System national headquarters, explained to all priests of the diocese their rationale for permitting it at one our spring meetings.

The Sisters of the Mother of Misery, Sister Christy and Sister Moderna, requested the Chapel return to its former appearance, when all items I added, are now to be removed, including the new Stations of the Cross, the new Altar, and the Divine Mercy picture.

Todd Stoner, the Pastoral Care Department head, gave permission to put up the statues, the Stations of the Cross, and to have a new Altar constructed and installed. He said I could do what I wanted in the Chapel, as he said he trusted my judgment. Therefore, I installed the Divine Mercy picture and the other pictures, and then made him aware of the additions by texting photos to him. I told him I would remove them if he didn't like them. After seeing everything, he liked the additions, and said he didn't see anything wrong with them. However, Todd Stoner got in trouble with Vice President, Sarah Pickamouse because he allowed the Altar to be replaced.

On March 19th, Sarah came to St. Henry's to tape Fr. Falloney's Mass on Thursday. Fr. Falloney is a retired priest who helps out when I am away. After she saw the Chapel, she called the Sisters of the Mother of Misery. They were unhappy with the changes and wanted the Chapel to be restored as it was previously.

The sleeping St. Joseph statue was donated by a nurse. Since it was removed at the request of the Sisters of Misery, who have St. Joseph as their patron, I gave it back to the nurse. She said she will check to see if her pastor will put it in her parish. The nurse also helped pay for the refurbishing of the chalice owned by the hospital. She donated about $300 for the Chalice and the statue.

I didn't ask anyone to make an Altar. One day, while standing at the Altar, I leaned against it, and because it's top-heavy, it nearly tipped over. A farmer's wife, who was a former parishioner of Immaculate

Heart of Mary parish, asked how things were going with my new assignment. I happened to mention how the Altar nearly tipped over, and I thought it was ugly. She insisted on asking her husband to make a new Altar. After he completed it, he said, "Father this is your Altar, so if someday it has to come out, it's yours." His words were prophetic.

A daily Mass-goer at the hospital made the wooden prayer box. A lady made altar cloths for the altar and for the shelves near the Tabernacle. The wooden prayer box was removed at the request of the Sisters of Misery. This was all so disheartening. They cared nothing about the time, effort, and money the people put into all of this. For my part, I really should have known this would happen. But I didn't realize the sisters still had influence at the hospital. Why on earth, these brides of Christ, would pick this time during the crisis in the Church, due to COVID-19, to do this, is baffling. It's a work of the devil to desire the removal of the sacred. I pray for them every day. I do not understand their way of thinking. Pray for Todd Stoner, he is a good man. He got in trouble for giving permission to make these changes. I hope he doesn't lose his job. Let's pray for all of them, that they may experience the love and mercy of Jesus.

Here is an email to my spiritual director. In it, it shows how I was struggling to follow my conscience and at the same time trying to be obedient to the bishop.

Dear Fr. Michael Benedict,

Much has happened this past week. The bishop changed his mind and now allows us to anoint patients, but give Communion only to the dying. He is now allowing priests to enter the hospital in Iceberg, Ohio. Previously they were forbidden. I am now seeing all Catholic patients in all three hospitals, except for COVID-19 patients. The other priest in Rolling Hills, who used to be the chaplain of the largest hospital in Rolling Hills, now sees only COVID-19 patients (Catholic and non-Catholic).

A document came out recently that said Communion was not to be given to anyone, unless they were dying. However, if a patient asks for it while in the hospital, it goes against my conscience to not give Jesus to them.

According to canon law, Catholics have a right to the sacraments. Here I am able to lay hands on patients and anoint them, but not give Communion, unless they are dying. Does this practice make sense?

There have been about 4 to 5 people (doctors, nurses, and a lay person), who have been attending daily Mass. I told all of them "with the wink of an eye" the bishop said, they were not to be there.

I can't lock the door and I will not interrupt Mass and ask them to leave. Furthermore, I said if they asked me for Communion after Mass, I would give it to them. And they all want Communion. I feel like I have been inciting them to disobedience and giving a bad example. Yet, at the same time, I feel obligated to give them something they are spiritually wanting. I am their chaplain. They are doctors and nurses, and so, I would think they know better than I, if the virus could be given to them from me during Communion.

They are always, at least six feet from each other, and so, they respect the health guidelines. One doctor flat-out said, it's difficult to get the virus, unless one would sneeze next to another person in close range. She believes people should be able to receive Communion, even on the tongue. She said it was good that I wash my hands before Mass, and so, she is not afraid to receive because of that. I sanitize my hands between each person who receives Holy Communion.

After feeling conflicted, I asked a doctor to not come to Mass as directed by the bishop, and that I would no longer give her Communion. I feel torn by all this. But then later, I told her it went against my conscience to ask her to not come to Mass.

If this wasn't enough heartache, I discovered an abortionist came to the hospital and probably gave an abortion pill to a psych patient. In addition to that, it is believed some doctors also do abortions by induction based upon what is called preeclampsia (excessive high blood pressure) during pregnancy. I think they are illegally reporting on their medical records something untrue (preeclampsia), to do an abortion. The patient actually does not have preeclampsia, but they record it as such. A good Catholic doctor told me doctors were told by the administration to not indicate on medical records that they give contraception to patients, but, rather, mark the medical prognosis as "other". Another doctor said that interns are required to do D & C's before they receive their license. They may do a D & C on a live baby (abortion) or a deceased one (miscarriage), as it was up to each individual doctor. He said the hospital permits both kinds of D & C's.

I am still offering a daily Mass to close the abortion clinic, and, oh my, the demons have come out like flies on honey.

Yesterday, I was called into the office of one of the main administrators over the Pastoral Care Department, and she gave me a list of her complaints, including the new altar, the Divine Mercy image placed in the chapel, etc...

I recently read about St. Ignatius, who spoke about the woman who fights against the man. He said when the man is weak, the woman gets stronger! I experienced that. I decided to do what husbands do to keep peace with their wives, "Sure honey, whatever you want." And boy, as I decided to just let her do as she asked, the more fearlessly she came at me and expressed her opinions (sort of like going for the jugular).

The night before that happened, a demon screamed outside the Chapel of my rectory when I was praying. At first, I thought it was an animal, as it made noises against the side of the house and moved quickly. It kept screaming like a beast saying, "No! No! No!" I couldn't believe it lasted almost five minutes, and moved about in the backyard and then in the neighbor's yard. I kept thinking it must have been a bird squealing, or a possum yelling, or some rabid cat, or some crazy person in the backyard. But, the next day, there were no tracks in the mud near the house.

I think I might discontinue giving people Communion at Mass and again tell them to not come to Mass, since that is what the bishop wants. I pray I am not doing the wrong thing. Thank you for responding to my emails.

Note: In this email I refer to preeclampsia induction, which, according to the International Catholic Bioethics Center of America, is morally permitted. It seems the doctor is reporting preeclampsia, when in fact, there is no high blood pressure, this way he can perform an induction abortion. The patient I became familiar with, was reported to have had preeclampsia, but was dismissed in less than an hour after the induction. According to a good Catholic doctor, this medical practice would lead one to believe the patient never actually had preeclampsia. But rather, the doctor reported it his medical records as preeclampsia to perform an induction abortion. I also personally saw an abortionist at the hospital. A few days later, I recognized her from a photo on the internet as Dr. Rebecca Lovechild, who came to Rolling Hills. The article said, she performed 77 abortions in 2 days, March 19th and March 20th, two days after the lockdowns started, no one could legally attend church, but the governor of our state permits abortions. And the abortionist bragged about it, how many babies she killed.

Fr. Benedict responded to this email, saying:

> Praise God. You are doing a great job in this difficult situation. You are Jesus for them, and even though some want to reject your ways, others want you to continue giving them God's grace. May your angels keep guiding you in the way of the Lord.
>
> God bless you.
>
> Fr. Michael L. Benedict

Fr. Benedict texted me saying:

> You are in my prayers during this Holy Week, that Jesus the High Priest and Victim will help you, as a priest, offer yourself as a victim to the Father to make atonement for sins and bring His mercy to your people. You are a great priest and are important to the Church. Mary is at your side whenever you are on your cross. God Bless You.

Coronavirus Update May 2nd, 2020

"What man among you, if he has a hundred sheep and loses one of them, does not leave the ninety-nine in the pasture and go after the one that is lost, until he finds it? And when he finds it, he joyfully puts in on his shoulders, comes home, and calls together his friends and neighbors to tell them, 'Rejoice with me, for I have found my lost sheep!" (Luke 15:4-6)

In March, the hospital asked me to minister to all Catholic patients in all three Catholic Hospitals in Rolling Hills, except for Coronavirus patients. We were told to give Holy Communion only to dying patients and to anoint only dying patients. But after much prayer, I came to the conclusion this went against my conscience in serving God's people. As a priest, who is ordained to serve and to give the sacraments to the people, and according to Canon Law, the people have a right to the sacraments. I investigated into whether bishops had the right or authority to prevent priests from dispensing sacraments, and preventing people from receiving them. Three canon lawyers, including a cardinal, said bishops do not have the authority to deny the sacraments or tell priests they cannot perform them. Therefore, I believed the Lord wanted me to give out the sacraments and not prevent anyone from receiving them. I decided to anoint all Catholic patients who needed the sacrament and also give Holy Communion to every Catholic patient, who was disposed to receive it and wanted to receive it.

In 6 weeks, I distributed over 1000 Communion Hosts to patients, but I made sure I followed all safety guidelines, especially washing hands, using a sanitizer, wearing of a mask, and wearing a plastic gown. Although it's permissible to anoint using a cotton swab, I chose to use my bare hands to anoint, and then gave patients Holy Communion with bare hands as well.

According to doctors, the virus can be easily eliminated through the washing of hands. And so, immediately after giving a patient Holy Communion, I washed my hands in the sink, sanitized them, and then put on a new pair of gloves. I followed this process between every patient, who I anointed and gave Holy Communion.

In the evening before and the following day, when Fr. Harry took his day off since I covered for him, I visited COVID-19 patients.

Even if the COVID-19 patient was not in ICU, I encouraged every COVID-19 patient to confess their sins. I anointed them, gave the Apostolic Pardon and Holy Communion as Viaticum, because their health could turn worse rapidly, and I may not be able to see the patient before he or she died.

I secretly transported Hosts from St. Henry Hospital to St. Camillius de Lellius Hospital, so Fr. Harry, the chaplain of Saint Camillus de Lellis campus, would not notice any Hosts missing in the Tabernacle at his location. I also didn't record Communions on digital patient records, so Sr. Janine Crowfly, nor any lay chaplains, would know they received it. Otherwise, she, and possibly others, would report this to hospital supervisors.

Once a very furious nurse approached me, and said, "You priests ought to be giving Catholic patients Holy Communion and you are refusing to do so because of the virus." Little did she know, I was giving all Catholic patients Holy Communion and anointing them as needed. But I took the rebuke, so she wouldn't know I was already doing it, lest she would tell others about it.

The first time I anointed a virus patient, I must admit I was frightened, but the Holy Spirit gave me courage, and the tenacity to do it. A Catholic COVID-19 patient became worse, and was transferred to ICU. After putting on all the required protection, I entered his room, not without some dirty looks from some nurses. To my surprise, the man wanted to come back to Church, as he hadn't been to confession for forty years. I heard his confession, gave him the Last Rites including Holy Communion, as Viaticum. What a wonderful blessing! I was so happy when I left his room, I didn't care if I would die of the virus. I felt like a true shepherd willing to search out the lost sheep in difficult places, especially in a desperate situation.

I felt like the sacramental directions we received did not take into consideration the spiritual needs of the desperately ill, who very much needed the sacraments at a time in their lives when they could die and were neglected by almost everyone.

Because I had permission from the Bishop to give Holy Communion to anyone who asked, I took advantage of his permission. Some who were unable to receive Holy Communion in their parishes, were able to obtain the Eucharistic Jesus in their hearts during a terrible and frightful time in their lives.

On Divine Mercy Sunday, I gave 17 non-patients Holy Communion. Between every person and every patient, hands were sanitized, and a mask was worn.

#111 PATIENTS DYING DUE TO LACK OF NUTRITION AND HYDRATION

St. Joseph & the Patients Dying by Lack of Nutrition and Hydration

During a First Wednesday of the month, dedicated to St. Joseph, I asked St. Joseph for a grace. I asked him to end the unethical practice of people dying without nutrition and hydration at Woebegone Hospice and the Doorway to Heaven Nursing Center.

When I was told to minister to all Catholic patients in all three hospitals, I found myself confronted with patients dying at Woebegone Hospice, without nutrition and hydration, who were not imminently dying (within a few days).

A patient, who worked on the cause of a future American saint, was admitted to St. Camillus de Lilles Campus. She was from the diocese of the future saint. She had a stroke. The doctor told her husband she could live for years on a feeding tube and IV. However, the doctor persuaded him to place her on hospice. She lived for nine days without food or water and died a similar death as the future saint, who was also deprived of food and water.

After seeing three patients die like this, I could no longer stand seeing them treated like this any longer, and wrote a letter to the bishop dated, May 1st, the memorial of St. Joseph the Worker. After the letter was delivered to the chancery and given to the bishop, the same day, I received a call from Todd Stoner, my supervisor, who said it was no longer necessary for me to minister at all Catholic hospitals. But, rather, just the two the hospitals I was previously ministering.

It's as though, the Lord said, "Your mission of reporting this to the bishop is complete. This is one of the main reasons why you were assigned to all three hospitals." Todd Stoner had no idea I had just dropped off the letter to the bishop. And there was no way the bishop could have read it, since I had just left the chancery, and the bishop was busy consecrating the diocese to the Immaculate Heart of Mary at the Cathedral.

I saw this event as St. Joseph's intercession in helping this to come about, since it happened on his feast day. As to what will happen of this, I sadly admit I said to Jesus, "I don't trust You." I said these words because I seriously doubted anything would get done. At least it was no longer my responsibility, and now lies in the hands of the bishop. I later told Jesus I was sorry for not trusting Him due to my lack of faith.

#112 SPECIAL GRACES IN 2020

May 31st 2020, Solemnity of Pentecost & Visitation of Mary

May 30th, Feast of St. Joan of Arc. Wow! Unbelievable! Incomprehensible! God's unfathomable, incredible, limitless, unbounded Mercy endures forever! St. Joan of Arc, what an intercessor!!! I can never say what happened on this day. But the Lord knows. Praise God, the Father of mercies!

Solemnity of the Sacred Heart and Memorial of the Immaculate Heart of Mary 2020 (Reconciliation with One of My Sisters)

Due to COVID-19, no one came to Mass, on either of these two days. It was very disheartening. After pondering my family situation, I became upset at one of the 12 promises of the Sacred Heart. One of them says, "I will bring peace to the homes." I had thought it said, "I will bring peace to families." And so, I took out a pen to underline the word "family" and discovered it said "home". I thought, well, I guess I can see why Jesus never said He would bring peace to the family.

There is always unforgiveness, strife, and heartache in families. Some refuse to talk to one another. He is God, but He can't force people to love or to forgive. Then, later that same day, one of my sisters called, and said she was coming to Rolling Hills, and asked me to eat with her and her husband. I really didn't want to go to a restaurant with her. She's the sister who told others I was gay. I suffered calumny from her lies. I decided to tell her I wasn't going to go out to eat with them unless she apologized. When I returned her call, I decided to mention it. She denied ever saying it, and I reminded her of the two times she mentioned it in my presence. She said she had no recollection at all and would never say anything like that, but the truth is, she did. When we went out to eat, she never mentioned it, nor did I, and then, after I came back to the rectory, she texted me saying she was sorry, but she still didn't remember saying it. I told her, "It's all in the past now." I thanked the Lord for the reconciliation that occurred, thanks to the Novena to the Sacred Heart of Jesus. It's a beautiful act of mercy to forgive, even when one fails to admit their fault.

#113 PRIESTLY HEARTACHE AND GRACE AT MASS

Sadness, Yet Rejoice in Suffering

I have been feeling sad lately. Only one or two people come to Mass and rarely does any patient watch the televised Mass. I feel the bishop does not believe I can be a pastor and only wants me to do hospital ministry. I wish I could meet with him to tell him what I believe I am capable of doing. I have asked to meet with him on three occasions, but was denied.

Father Albert Brandmueller, who followed me as pastor Immaculate Heart, was transferred due to parishioners complaining about his homilies. He also preached the fullness of truth.

I pray every day very much for the bishop. I see God's hand in permitting this and rejoice in suffering. I am inspired by St. John of Avila, who said, "I pray God may open your eyes and let you see what hidden treasures He bestows on us in the trials for which the world thinks only to flee. Shame turns into honor, when we seek God's glory. Present affliction becomes the source of heavenly glory. For those who suffer wounds in fighting the battle, God opens His arms in loving, tender friendship, which is more delightful by far than anything our earthly efforts might produce."

New Spiritual Experiences During Mass

At times, during Mass, I see spiritual things. Occasionally, I will see the Holy Spirit in the form of a Dove, come down upon the gifts, as my hands are extended over the bread and wine during the epiclesis. The Dove will cuddle against one of my fingers, to give me consolation. Today, June 21st, 2020, when the Chalice was raised above the Altar, after the Consecration, my hands appeared as though there were nail marks on them. It was a deep dark red color. There was no pain associated with this spiritual experience.

#114 EUTHANASIA – MERCY KILLING

Do I Notify Authorities? Mercy Killing

A patient at the Woebegone Hospice had Alzheimer's disease. He had no other health problems. He was physically healthy. Eating two full meals a day. He could walk around on his own. The family put him on hospice, rather than placing him in a memory care facility. Woebegone Hospice medicated him, to continuously keep him unconscious, until he died due to lack of food and water. I told the bishop how he died. I need to do more to stop these injustices, and so, I'm pondering notifying local law enforcement. It seems to me the crime of mercy killing is occurring especially at Woebegone Hospice on the 8th floor of Mother of Misery Healthcare System, Saint Camillus de Lellis campus. I am hoping to call a lawyer to get advice on how to proceed. Perhaps the lawyer will help me to know what to do.

12 Day Novena to the Hearts of Jesus and Mary to End Euthanasia
Ending June 30, the Last Day of the Month Dedicated to the Sacred Heart

A lay chaplain's mother was admitted to Woebegone Hospice at Mother of Misery Healthcare System, Saint Camillus de Lellis campus on the Solemnity of the Sacred Heart. The family wanted their mother to have an IV and a feeding tube, since she was unable to swallow. The doctor at Woebegone Hospice said they will not do either at the facility. Upset at the hospice, after a few days, the family took their mother home to die.

As a result, the lay chaplain emailed the Bishop on the first Wednesday of the month (the day I have been praying to St. Joseph to stop the terrible problem of euthanasia) telling the bishop she believed it was inhuman to not give patients nutrition and hydration. The woman, who is wealthy, invited the bishop to attend the funeral of her mother, and he obliged. In my opinion, St. Joseph is helping. The bishop listens to lay people. But any help for those who suffer needlessly, seems to be continually delayed. Will anyone ever help these people!

#115 AT ODDS WITH THE BISHOP

Prayer Answered – Misunderstanding by Bishop Courageous

"As King David approached Bahurim, a man from the family of the house of Saul was just coming out. His name was Shimei son of Gera, and as he approached, he kept yelling out curses. He threw stones at David and at all the servants of the king, though the troops and all the mighty men were on David's right and left." (2 Samuel 16:6)

I was having terrible difficulty. I sent a letter to the Bishop in January about the priest assessment for assignments and hoped he would call, so we could discuss the information about misunderstandings when I was pastor of Immaculate Heart of Mary in Wheatland. He never responded.

Finally, I came to the conclusion it is not God's will for the bishop to understand me and the Lord is using the misunderstanding to accomplish His will by my assignment at the hospital, through sacramental ministry, and also the problem with euthanasia.

When Shimei threw rocks at King David, he said God instructed him to do it, so he would basically accept it as coming from God. Though I may never see euthanasia resolved and may never be understood by the bishop, what does it matter? I did what the Lord wanted of me. Prophets of the Old Testament were not listened to, and many of them were persecuted and killed. I proclaimed the truth and that's all that matters. Furthermore, I trust that I will be happy to see the results of it in heaven. Praise God! I have peace, and I am doing God's will to the best of my ability. No more angry thoughts—thank you, Jesus!

#116 FATHER KAPAUN'S WORDS OF WISDOM – ALTAR SOCIETY

Father Kapaun's Words of Wisdom – Chaplain to Stay

I hope to become a pastor again someday, but I believe the bishop's misunderstanding about me will prevent it from happening. I am reminded of the wisdom of Fr. Emil Kapaun. When Fr. Kapaun was a prisoner of war, a man by the name of Bob Wood asked him a question. This is a quote from the book, *The Miracle of Father* Kapaun. "Amid the filth one day, Wood learned, Kapaun could have avoided the perils of the Korean War. Kapaun had served in Burma and India in World War II. After that, Kapaun said he went back to Masses and baptisms in Kansas. "Then how did you end up here?" Wood asked. "I volunteered." "Father Kapaun!" Wood almost shouted. "My God, father! Why did you come back?" "I wanted to come back to men like these", Kapaun said. "Serving in those parishes—it didn't work out." Then Kapaun grinned, and added, "I mean, my God, Bob! Have you ever had to deal with one of those women's committees of a church, the Altar Society?"

As I reflect on the words of Fr. Kapaun, I can honestly say, "What the heck am I thinking? Why would I ever want to be a pastor again and deal with the Altar Society committees? I would rather give the Sacrament of the Sick, hear Confessions, and give Communion to COVID-19 patients risking my death."

#117 FOOT PAIN

Achilles Tendons & Tendons in My Feet

Since 1993, due to fallen arches, there was much pain in my feet, and over the years, I purchased orthotics to put inside my shoes. Recently, perhaps due to all the walking from one nursing unit to another, throughout the hospitals, the pain in my feet has been horrible. I have a hard time keeping my balance and standing at the Altar or at the side of a patient's bed. I try to think about the pain Jesus felt in His feet while He was hanging from the Cross. About a year ago, during the Holy Sacrifice of the Mass, I saw His crucified feet hanging before my eyes during the Consecration.

It reminded me to offer up the pain in my feet and unite my pain, to the pain of His feet on the Cross for the conversion of sinners, in reparation for sins against the Hearts of Jesus and Mary, and for the poor souls in purgatory.

#118 MORE SAINT ANTHONY STORIES

St. Anthony Statues

When I arrived at St. Henry hospital, there was a statue of St. Anthony sitting on a pedestal on the 7th floor near the elevator. I suspect the Sisters of Misery didn't remove it since they never visited patients on the psych floor. The sisters are like iconoclasts wanting to remove pictures and statues of Jesus in the Chapel and in the hospital. I suppose they think they are making the hospital environment, more protestant-friendly. I noticed the statue of St. Anthony had a hole about the size of penny on the top of its head. Consequently, I filled the hole with candle wax and painted over the hole. It looks hugely better.

About 6 months later, I noticed another St. Anthony statue at Mother of Misery Healthcare System, Saint Camillus de Lellis campus, located in the sacristy, along with other statues the sisters removed from the hospital over the years. I asked Todd Stoner, the pastoral care supervisor, if I could make a donation for it. He said I could take the statue without a donation. He said, it most likely would never be used again at the hospital. The statue needed some work and I brought it to a Catholic artist from St. Tarscisius parish in Rolling Hills to have it repaired. Once repaired, I asked a lay person who wanted the statue for a donation of $500, so the money could be used to help a poor family needing dental care.

Saint Anthony Helped Bring Back Cassock and Violet Stole

When my assignment began at St. John of God Hospital in Tantrum, I moved everything into the apartment "rectory". After unpacking everything, I couldn't find a cassock or a violet stole for my violet vestment. I looked through closets four times, including a closet at the hospital sacristy, where I placed some vestments. I decided to drive back to Wheatland and look for them at Immaculate Heart of Mary parish, but couldn't find them. I prayed to St. Anthony and asked him to bring them back, "even if he had to materialize them", I prayed.

A few weeks later, I happened to look in the apartment closet at Tantrum and found both hanging in broad daylight. I immediately presumed the sisters put them there when I was away from the apartment. I previously looked in the closet four times, and so, asked the sisters if they had found the cassock and returned it and the stole in the closet. They were amused I suggested such a thing, and denied it. I truly believe, somehow, St. Anthony put them there.

St. Anthony & the Finding of Bridgette Anderson

I met Carol, the mother of Bridgette Anderson, a young woman who was legally blind, at St. Mother Cope Hospital and administered the sacraments to her. I noticed she was declining, due to some health problem other than COVID-19. There were no visitors permitted due to COVID-19.

The following day, I came to St. Mother Cope's Hospital and stopped by her room to see if she wanted Holy Communion. As I entered her room, I noticed four people who were seated and none of them were talking. I thought Mrs. Anderson was sleeping, but I soon realized, she had just died, perhaps an hour before my arrival.

I prayed with the family, and it was there, I met Bridgette for the first time, and her Catholic friend, Agnes Rangle, who would later marry Aaron Cloogers, my cousin. His grandmother, Violet, was my grandmother's sister. About a month later, Bridgette was admitted to St. Henry Hospital in the psych unit for depression. We had nice conversations. She said her natural father, her step-father, and now her mother died within this last year. She was taking RCIA (Rite of Christian Initiation) classes at Rolling Hills State Catholic Campus Center to become Catholic.

Bridgette had a warm smile and a simple way of trusting everyone. A few months later, I was shocked to see her on a news website, stating she was missing. On the feast of St. Anthony, June 13th, I decided to offer a Mass for her, and prayed through the intercession of St. Anthony, she would be found. A search party found her later that morning, on the feast of St. Anthony, lying dead beside the railroad track. There was no indication of foul play.

Her friends organized a memorial service at Holy Hill Cemetery. The night before the service, late in the evening, Bridgette's friend Agnus called. She wanted me to perform the service. After I prayed the prayers of Commendation, and not knowing I offered a Mass in honor of St. Anthony to find Bridgette, one of her sorority sisters read a beautiful faith filled reflection on how St. Anthony helped locate Bridgette. Because she was young, there were many at the service. I fervently prayed to St. Anthony, asking him to help me give comforting words. Praise God, he did! I had prepared written remarks, but what came out of my mouth was spontaneous and much better than what I prepared. Thank you! St. Anthony!

#119 STANDING BULL – AN AMERICAN INDIAN
Standing Bull, December 15th, 2019 (A Buffalo Bull, Who Stands)

Sometime in the early morning of Dec. 15th, I dreamt people were trying to find the body of Standing Buffalo, and were digging for it. In the dream, I saw the place where he was buried and once his body was to be found, they said he would be a saint. Then in the dream, I heard people exclaim, "We found his body!" I assumed Standing Buffalo was an Indian due to the name.

I woke up from the dream wondering, who is Standing Buffalo? I couldn't recall ever reading anything about the Indian. I decided to do an internet search and discovered he died on December 15th, 1890. Having the dream on the anniversary of his death, seemed to mean something. He was killed by Indian Police. According to various articles, it is uncertain, whether he was baptized into the Catholic faith. However, a priest and a bishop had numerous conversations with him. There are photos of him wearing a Crucifix and a Rosary.

After speaking about the dream to my spiritual director, he suggested I pray for him and ask for his intercession. He also proposed I visit his burial site in Willowdale, Montana. I will pray to St. Anthony of Padua, asking for his intercession. He will help find his true burial site where his body is located. I don't see how he could ever be a canonized saint. Perhaps, when his body is located, he will finally be in heaven, and therefore a saint. Or maybe when I discover his body, it will then be, the moment he is rewarded with the beatific vision forever. I'm not sure what it all means.

Vacation at Willowdale, Montana (Prayer Answered with Imprint of Cross)
I spoke to Fr. Barney Hamster, pastor of St. Joseph in Willowdale, on the phone and told him I was coming to his area on vacation. Because I didn't want to offer Mass in a motel, I asked permission to offer Masses at his parish, which he graciously permitted. I spoke to him about the dream and mentioned my experience in Brushwood City concerning the Indian Burial Ground, and how I offered Mass at the site there for the souls of American Indians buried there. I mentioned that it was suggested by an

exorcist, who is now my spiritual director, that the strange happenings in my parish back then, may have been caused by Indians, who were forced to leave the reservation, and walk to Idaho. It was called the Trail of Tears. He suspected they cursed the ground when the white men took possession of their land. Hearing about this, Fr. Barney thought he would offer a Mass at the Standing Buffalo Monument.

On the way to Willowdale, I stopped in Hodgenville, Georgia, on July 16th, 2020 (Feast of Our Lady of Mount Carmel) to stay at my spiritual director's rectory. I thought I may be able to purchase a plastic folding table at Growdes Lumber Store, in the event I needed to offer Mass at the motel.

As I drove the next day, I had the idea, that maybe the Lord wanted me to offer a Mass at the monument where the Indian is buried. The next day, July 17th, I offered a Mass at the parish at 6:30am, and then drove to the monument to offer prayers for his soul, and if it would be possible, to offer a second Mass at 8 am for the deceased Indian.

While I was preparing for Mass, a great fear came over me. I wondered if local Indians would be displeased if I offered Mass at the burial site. I thought that maybe I should get permission from the local bishop before offering Mass. And, if I did offer Mass, I may get into trouble for not asking the bishop. It was rather windy, and, I noticed a few trucks driving across the roadway about a half a mile away. What should I do? Offer the Mass or not?

As I offered the Mass for the soul of Standing Buffalo, the fear became intense. Consequently, just as Mass was over, I hurried to return Mass items to the car. Then, I returned to the monument, and made my thanksgiving to Jesus in Holy Communion. I prayed to Jesus, "Lord Jesus, is Standing Bull in heaven?" I then prayed the Rosary and the Chaplet of Divine Mercy for his soul. And, since my spiritual director asked, I took photos to text him.

The next day, Saturday, I offered Mass at the Cathedral of the Rockies, dedicated to St. Anthony, in a nearby city. On my way back, I ordered Mexican food, picked it up, and ate it in my "cabin" at the motel. Later that day, I purchased some grapes, a nectarine, and ate them with a taco left over from lunch that I had stored in the refrigerator in the cabin. After eating, I immediately had severe stomach pain. I wasn't nauseated, but the pain was intense. I realized later the grapes were rotten inside, and appeared good on the outside. And maybe the taco for some reason disagreed with me.

Due to the pain, I needed to walk around and decided to go to the local museum. But when I arrived, it was closed. I decided to go to the Indian monument and walk around. As soon as I walked in front of the monument, the pain immediately went away, and I felt completely fine.

Later, I believed the stomach pain was caused by a gallbladder attack that can disappear as quickly as it comes. But it was a one-time event, and never happened again.

I glanced at the monument, gazed over the valley at the lake, and then looked more purposely a second time at the monument. It was then, I noticed a cross was imprinted on the monument.

I didn't remember seeing the cross the day before. I then looked at the photos on my phone that were taken the previous day, and the cross wasn't there. I was awestruck, and thought it was a sign from God. Did someone imprint it, or did God create the cross? Does it matter, if God did it, or a person? No one knew I said that prayer, asking if Standing Buffalo was in heaven, and the cross seemed to indicate, that Standing Buffalo is in heaven. I also thought it meant he was really buried there and could have been baptized before he died. Only God knows these things. I took more photos and texted them to my spiritual director.

He texted back, asking me to obtain a souvenir from the museum and wanted me to touch it to the cross on the monument. I later obtained historic photos of him. I had miraculous medals and touched them to the monument. Furthermore, I picked up small stones on the ground in front of the monument as souvenirs.

After speaking to Fr. Barney about it, he thought it was a miraculous sign and wanted to see it. However, the next day, he thought it was oil someone touched to the monument. To test to see if it was oil, I later touched some Oil of the Sick to a corner of the monument, and it changed the stone's color. But, the imprint of the cross had no oil or substance. The surface didn't appear to be sanded or tampered with. I honestly doubted it came from God. However, the more I tried to disprove it, the more it seemed like God Himself did it.

The day before I was to leave, I met Allisa Johnson, a former Totally Yours youth member. She was just hired by Fr. Barney to help at the parish. She and I happened to meet (providentially). She mentioned she was from Wyoming, and after I told her what happened at the monument, she indicated she goes there often and prays a Rosary for Standing Buffalo. Furthermore, she said a lady from the parish suggested a Mass be offered at the Indian burial site for their souls, due to bad things happening in Willowdale, such as suicides, etc...

Consequently, the next day, I offered Mass at the parish for the souls of all the Indians buried within a 100-mile radius of Willowdale. I suggested Allisa ask Fr. Barney to offer Mass at the Indian Burial site.

Fr. Benedict made the suggestion that I pray to Standing Buffalo for help with various things. I now do pray to him, but, I always preface the prayer with these words, "Standing Buffalo, if you are in heaven or in purgatory, please pray for this....etc..."

Even though the cross image may be a sign he is in heaven, only the Church has the authority to declare it. Could it be, I was healed from the terrible pain in my stomach by the Indian, even though I didn't ask for it? Or did it just happen, the pain went away, as I came to the monument? The postcard I purchased, mentioned he was a "medicine man." Does God want me to ask Standing Buffalo to help heal people to whom I minister? Is Standing Buffalo going to help me minister to patients, or help me do something to close the abortion clinic? Do I need to continue to offer Masses and pray for his soul? I had lots of questions with no answers.

I was certainly terrified to learn the monument was not in the same diocese as Willowdale and I wondered if the Indians or the other Diocese would blame me for defacing the monument.

I now realize, I need to trust that since God imprinted the Cross, either by man or by Himself, it makes no difference what happens, everything will be fine.

There was great joy visiting the Cathedral of the Rockies dedicated to St. Anthony and asked him to help me with my ministry and especially homilies. I offered a Mass of thanksgiving to St. Anthony for the many prayers he answered in the past.

Before I left Rolling Hills and before returning to Willowdale, I decided to bring miraculous medals and hoped to give some away. It just so happened, that while visiting with Fr. Benedict, my spiritual director, on the night of July 16th, he told me about Zane Rex, a Satanist who converted due to the Miraculous Medal. While he was a rehab patient in Rolling Hills, I met Zane about a month before my trip to Montana. Providentially, I had a Zane Rex CD on Abortion, and listened to it when I drove from Hodgenville, Georgia to Willowdale, Montana.

While in Willowdale, I met a man who hadn't been to confession for over thirty years. I gave him a Miraculous Medal. At that time, he wasn't interested in going to confession or coming back to the Church. The next day, he decided to confess and come back to the Catholic Church.

It seemed God wanted me to bring Miraculous Medals for the trip and use them for reasons I never would have anticipated.

#120 THE PROBLEM WITH LAY CHAPLAINS

Catholic Lay Chaplains & A Catholic Lay Chaplain Who Wants to Hear Confessions
Now and then, patients at Siloam Rehab Center told me a black man claimed he was a priest, but was dressed in non-priestly clothing. The man in question wanted to know if the patient wanted to go to Confession to him. At first, I thought the patients were confused, but some were very adamant.

Fr. Dylan Scola, an associate priest, happened to mention that a parishioner of St. Dominic parish told him a black man claiming to be a priest, without clerics, asked the patient, if he wanted to go to Confession. It was then I finally believed the patients, because the chaplain never contacted me to hear any confessions. I notified Todd Stoner, who spoke with him, but he denied it.

Lay Chaplains Woes:
They Bless New Units, Don't End Prayers in the Name of Jesus,
& Give Invalid Sacraments.

A Catholic lay chaplain mentioned she was willing to bless a new hospital unit, if I was unable. I wondered, "How can a lay person, who is Catholic, bless a new unit. And why does she think she has the power and authority to confer the blessing?" Unfortunately, she erroneously thought she could. How sad the hospital hires Catholics like this who don't know the difference between the functions of a lay person and a priest. She also said when praying at the morning nursing staff meeting, I should never pray in the name of Jesus, since non-Catholics could be offended.

Fr. Harry told me Todd Stoner, the pastoral care supervisor, a layman, converted to the Catholic faith about ten years ago. After his conversion, he anointed patients with oil, and, as a Catholic hospital chaplain, he invalidly witnessed the marriage of two Catholics. How sad, "Catholic" hospitals are not really Catholic and cause serious problems for patients.

#121 DISOBEDIENCE TO BISHOP

Disobedience During COVID-19 Pandemic

"What do you think? There was a man who had two sons. He went to the first and said, 'Son, go and work today in the vineyard.' 'I will not,' he answered, but later he changed his mind and went. "Then the father went to the other son and said the same thing. He answered, 'I will, sir,' but he did not go. "Which of the two did what his father wanted?" "The first," they answered. (Matthew 21:28-31)

When COVID-19 caused a lockdown, in April 2020, Bishop Courageous sent an email to priests forbidding outdoor Masses.

I could not understand why outdoor Masses were forbidden and prayed about whether the bishop could forbid this. How could he in good conscience prevent the people from attending Mass when it could be done safely? I decided I was going to offer an outdoor Mass on the farm of a former parishioner, and invite Catholics to attend. Though he didn't tell me not to offer an outdoor Mass, my spiritual director reminded me obedience was a sign of holiness.

I went ahead and planned to offer the Mass, despite the bishop forbidding it, and despite my spiritual director indirectly suggesting otherwise, and kept praying about it.

Finally, believing the Lord did not want me to do so, I changed my mind. Jesus eventually gave me a clear sign. It rained the whole day I was going to offer an outdoor Mass. I felt like the son, who said, "I will not obey", but then later changed his mind. I was disobedient in mind, but obedient in action. I repented of it.

#122 INVALID BAPTISMS, INVALID CONFESSIONS, INVALID MASSES?

Invalid Baptisms, Invalid Confessions, Non-Sacramental Wine (Invalid Masses)?
"Go, therefore, and make disciples of all nations, baptizing them in the name of the Father, and of the Son, and of the Holy Spirit, teaching them to observe all that I have commanded you. And behold, I am with you always, until the end of the age." (Matthew 28:19-20)

Since she was to be married soon, a woman from Texas contacted the Pastoral Care Office wanting a baptism certificate from St. Henry Hospital from her baptism twenty years ago. Preparing to create the baptism certificate, I noticed she was baptized by a lay chaplain, who at that time was baptizing using three different formulas, and two of them were invalid.

Not knowing which baptism formula was used for her emergency baptism, I called her pastor who was going to witness her marriage, and said he needed to do a conditional Baptism and Confirmation before the wedding, and, I couldn't send a baptismal certificate, since it was unknown if her baptism was valid.

I reported the emergency invalid baptisms to Bishop Athanasius Courageous. When Bishop Traditiones was the Bishop of the Diocese of Rolling Hills, eight years previously, he was informed of invalid baptisms and required only priests to perform baptisms.

Baptisms for the next several years were valid, since they were performed by priests. But, eventually the same practice returned and lay chaplains began doing emergency baptisms, rather than requesting a priest to do them. Bishop Traditiones kept secret the invalid baptisms.

Not much after the invalid baptisms were revealed to Bishop Courageous, Bishop Basil Braveheart, the bishop of Rapid Water, Michigan, made it publicly known, a priest from his diocese, invalidly baptized children, and asked all who were baptized by him, to receive the sacrament of Baptism validly.

I sent a letter and emails to all the priests of the Diocese of Rolling Hills warning them of the invalid baptisms and requested they contact specific parishioners who were baptized at the hospital, so they could properly baptize them and depart to them, other sacraments, if needed, such as the sacrament of Confirmation. In the sacramental records book, some indicated which parish the parents belonged when baptized, and so I gave a list of the baptized to each parish.

I later learned, Bishop Courageous was pleased, with the way I notified the priests of the problem. But, I felt he should have it made publicly known like the bishop from Michigan. This way all emergency baptized, during that time period, including those who had no parish, could receive a valid baptism.

Because I wondered whether Standing Buffalo received baptism and since I received a clear indication by the sign on his grave marker he was in heaven, I later wondered if God used this to help me have peace considering all the children not baptized validly over the years. I somehow hoped that God, in His mercy, would bestow on them, what was due to them, if not in this life, in the next.

I also reported to the Bishop, by way of a canon lawyer from our diocese, that St. Valentine parish in Hanover, Ohio, was using non-sacramental wine. There was no response from the bishop. This was all so disheartening and greatly saddened me.

#123 DELIVERED AND FREE OF ENVY

Delivered! Free at Last! Free at Last! Sept. 29th (Feast of the Archangels)
Three times I pleaded with the Lord to take it away from me. But He said to me, "My grace is sufficient for you, for My power is perfected in weakness. Therefore, I will boast all the more gladly in my weaknesses, so that the power of Christ may rest on me. That is why, for the sake of Christ, I delight in weaknesses, in insults, in hardships, in persecutions, in difficulties. For when I am weak, then I am strong...." (2 Corinthians 12:8-10)

For most of my life, I wanted to be free of the sin of envy of other men and I could never seem to get rid of this sin. I didn't ask only three times, as St. Paul asked in his second letter to the Corinthians. Rather, I asked numerous times.

However, I offered a Mass on Sept. 8th, the Feast of Mary's Nativity, for the intention of being delivered from the sin of self-hatred (thinking I was stupid and ugly) and believing no one could love me. For years, I looked at other men with envy. I wanted to be as strong, handsome, smart, and manly as them. I believed most of my life I was ugly, weak, and stupid. I thought no one could love me, and, no girl would be interested in me. These kinds of ideas are contrary to the dignity of the priest. A priest should not want a girl to be interested in him. He should not have self-hatred. Yet, these ideas haunted me from the time I was very young.

Throughout the years, I didn't think I could have friends. Some of this was due to verbal abuse by my father and abuse by the next-door neighbor. I needed to go back and examine these events –with Jesus, and ask Him to heal me of them, and to my amazement--- He did.

Within hours after the Mass, on the Feast of Mary's Nativity, I was assailed with untold temptations and horrible thoughts associated with these sins. These multiplied over the coming weeks, and I felt like I was falling back into these sins from the past. I felt like I had opened a genie bottle and couldn't put the genie back. The horrible anguish, the immense and innumerable temptations, the horrid thoughts. I spoke about this with my spiritual director and even while on the phone with him, the terrible thoughts prevented me from paying attention to him.

Thinking I may have committed mortal sins in my mind, I quickly ran to confession multiple times. I was obedient, to the advice of my spiritual director, and did the St. Ignatius feeling prayers on some intense events from my past, which seemed to ignite an inferno. It was as though evil spirits were sent to crush me, but was permitted by God.

On one occasion, an evil spirit spoke to me and said, "He (Jesus) is not strong enough to deliver us." And I replied, "Yes, He is! He is Lord and God!" There were many times while doing the "feeling prayer" evil spirits would manifest themselves. And many times wanted to give up.

I had many thoughts, most likely from evil spirits, who wanted me to give up on my spiritual director and caused me to be angry with him for doing what he said to do, and I felt like I was sinning by practicing the prayer, which would help deliver me.

Just when I was going to give up on my spiritual director, he would text or email or call. Somehow, he knew I was in the battle of my life and his words were always just what I needed.

Once, during these temptations, I took a relic of St. Padre Pio and placed it on my forehead, asking him to help me and deliver me from these evil spirits. I saw Padre Pio in my mind's eye, praying over me with his wounded hands. And, when he was about to leave, I said, "Padre Pio, please don't leave me. Help me!" He returned, praying over me again.

A few days later, everything suddenly stopped, and I was delivered by Jesus. It was the night of Sept. 27th, 2020, on a Sunday, when I went to bed, and not much after I laid down, I was assaulted by an evil spirit who literally shook my whole body violently for many minutes. My body was bouncing up and down on the bed. Every limb was shaking like a rag doll. All I could do was think of Jesus, who was not far away, since He was in the Tabernacle in my rectory chapel. In my mind, I saw His divine mercy image as the terrible shaking of my body occurred.

In my mind, I kept saying, "Jesus, deliver me." It seemed like it would never end, but when it suddenly stopped, I knew I was free. After that night, on the 28th and on the 29th of Sept. I did the feeling prayer on those wounds from the past, and it was then, I realized I no longer had those kinds of thoughts. On Sept. 29th, the feast of St. Michael and the Archangels, was when I knew for certain, Jesus delivered me. Something I wanted almost my entire life, finally happened. I was free!

"He snatched me from my powerful foe, from my enemies whose strength I could not match. They assailed me in the day of misfortune, but the Lord was my support. He brought me forth into freedom, He saved me because He loved me." (Psalm 18:17-19)

Before all of this occurred, I consecrated these temptations and the source of them, to the Hearts of Jesus and Mary. I fasted for several days to be freed. Oh, the power of the Holy Mass! By God's grace, I am free! I am free! I am free! Now, I am never envious of other men. I am content with the way God created me. I'm not stupid. Furthermore, I'm not ugly. And, so what if I am weak. The battle was worth it. Now I have peace. I cannot thank God enough. I cannot thank Our Lady enough and can't thank my spiritual director enough for not giving up on me. Thank you, Jesus and Mary!

#124 MEETING WITH BISHOP ABOUT ETHICAL ISSUES AT THE HOSPITAL

Meeting with Bishop Oct. 7th, 2020 (Feast of the Holy Rosary) about the Artificial Nutrition and Hydration Problem, More Ethical Issues at Mother of Misery

The bishop's secretary called stating the bishop wanted to meet with me. I was hoping the bishop would talk about the invalid baptisms, and also the problem with the three hospitals, the hospice, and the Catholic nursing home, immorally not providing nutrition and hydration.

I suspected I was in trouble for sending out the email about the baptisms and also suspected he might re-assign me and was hoping he may want to speak about the seven-page letter I sent him in January detailing the truth about Immaculate Heart in Wheatland.

Consequently, I was pleased he wanted to speak about the unethical practice of not providing artificial nutrition and hydration, but was dissatisfied after the thirty-five-minute talk. My impression, though I may have been wrong, was that he didn't understand the seriousness of the problem. He said he planned to meet with hospital staff to discuss it. He wanted to inform me he was working on it.

During the meeting, I again suggested that he call the International Catholic Bioethics Center of America, but he seemed uninterested. Considering invalid baptisms, he said one sentence to me. "Well, you have been working on invalid baptisms with Fr. Gerry Meander. I don't see the need to do anything further." Since he seemed pleased with what I did, it would later move me to let every parish know which parishioners from their parish had potential invalid baptisms. Some baptized babies were recorded in the *Baptismal Register*, but only a few of the true total were recorded.

After the meeting, I decided to call the International Catholic Bioethics Center of America (ICBCA), and wow was I surprised. The president of ICBCA happened to answer the phone and I explained everything to him about patients not receiving artificial nutrition and hydration. I emailed him with a detailed explanation of the situation at all the places in Rolling Hills and, thanks be to God, he reassured me that I should be "sounding the alarm" of these serious situations.

He said, with my permission, he would speak to the head administrators at Mother of Misery Healthcare headquarters. He reassured me those in the top tiers of Mother of

Misery Healthcare System were on board with the International Catholic Bioethics Center of America, and would clean up the unethical situations locally. Likewise, he said they would give Bishop Courageous a call to help him understand the problems. I was so excited. I thought something finally will get done.

He also gave me the phone number of the chief ethicist for Mother of Misery Healthcare System. However, he warned me, that if I went over the heads of the local administrators and spoke directly to the ethicist, the company would fire me, but, that they would resolve all the problems locally. I thought it was worth it.

I was elated! But, after thinking about it, I somehow felt in the end, nothing would get accomplished. I prayed I would be wrong. But, how sad, it all proved true.

At the meeting, the bishop suggested I notify him of new problems as they arise. Later, I sent him a letter about more unethical situations that came to my attention, such as staff referring a patient to have an abortion, contraception pills stored and distributed at Mother of Misery clinics, women getting sterilized by opportunistic salpingectomies, the head of the Pastoral Care Department performing an invalid wedding for a Catholic couple and giving out the Sacrament of the Sick, despite not being a priest, etc. I received no response.

It's no wonder my last name, Fr. Gadfly, fits me. For a priest to grow in holiness, he needs to experience difficulties and at times, the Lord showers sufferings on the priest, so he may be more conformed to Jesus crucified. In many instances, the Lord uses the struggles and heartaches with bishops, to help the priest to grow in love and respect for the man who stands in the place of Christ. By this, a priest will learn to trust in the Lord, to grow in faith, and hope, overcoming discouragement and temptations to give up. But, with God's grace, he may become holy and even a saint. I pray I will become a saint.

#125 A PARISH PRIEST'S TRANSFER & LOOKING FOR MINISTRY

Parish Priest and Retreat at the Shrine of the Holy Innocents

Fr. Albert Brandmueller, the pastor who followed me at Immaculate Heart of Mary parish in Wheatland, was transferred to his new parish in June 2020, due to complaints from parishioners over his orthodox homilies. I can relate to that! It was then I realized we both endured the same people causing problems at Immaculate Heart of Mary in Wheatland. I came to understand the priests on the front-line end up getting wounded by their people.

Poor Fr. Brandmueller was removed from his next parish within six months due to complaints by the people of his parish about his homilies. He preached the truth and ended up being unassigned.

Fr. Brandmueller retained an expensive canon lawyer who requested the Vatican to intervene. Fr. Brandmueller believed the bishop wanted him to resign his new parish and to never allow him to be a pastor again. At first, he was only assigned to teach a 2nd grade First Communion Class in the parish. After being ordained nearly 25 years, he was supposed to only teach 2nd graders. Oh, my.

Now it all made sense, and I came to the realization I was transferred outside the Diocese of Rolling Hills to St. John of God in Tantrum, Idaho, so I would never be a pastor again.

The bishop had no other place for me to minister, except outside of the diocese, because, it seems, he now believed I should never be a pastor again. This caused great turmoil in my soul and anger welled up within me. I wondered if I was really that bad of a priest. Yet, I remembered the huge number of conversions through Eucharistic Adoration and the amazing involvement of parishioners doing stewardship. But, even if that was the case, could it be, I was a bad priest?

In addition to this, the artificial nutrition hydration problem caused me to have great anxiety to see people suffer without food and water, and I felt helpless. What about these poor people who endured their last time on earth, being deprived of ordinary food and water?

I felt like God wanted me to give every effort to bring about proper ethical treatment of the terminally ill and dying at the Catholic hospitals and hospice. Due to these two pressures, and the revelation of bishop's view of me, I didn't believe anything would change concerning the artificial nutrition and hydration dilemma. Therefore, I decided to take a retreat at the Shrine of the Holy Innocents in Bakersville, Mississippi.

I kept thinking that I could no longer endure seeing people die unethically without any way of helping them. I thought maybe God wanted me to serve outside the Diocese of Rolling Hills again, but where? Could it be in the Diocese of Overbrook, Texas? I wondered if their holy bishop would allow me to serve in his diocese.

Consequently, on my way to the Shrine of the Holy Innocents, I stayed in Overbrook, and decided to try to meet with the bishop there. I didn't have an appointment, but I trusted Our Lady would arrange it.

Entrusting it to Our Lady, I soon realized our heavenly Mother made it happen. I was so impressed with Bishop Joseph Trueapostle and immediately felt at home. I explained my current situation and gave my priestly history. To my surprise, without making the suggestion, he asked me if I would be interested in doing hospital ministry in Texas. It was what I had hoped to ask him, but wouldn't. But, he asked me, and I was so excited.

#126 SOUR WINE AT THE SHRINE OF THE HOLY INNOCENTS

Sour Wine and New Wine – Best Wine Last

"Everyone else serves the best wine first, and after the guests have drunk a lot, he serves the ordinary wine. But you have kept the best wine until now!" (John 2:10)

While at the Shrine of the Holy Innocents in Bakersfield, Mississippi, I discovered the wine they were using was comprised due to age. It was made in 1998, far beyond the recommended age to use it. A wine company had told me sacramental wine should not be used five years after date produced. I mustered up the courage and told one of the priests. He immediately addressed the situation by throwing away the old wine and replacing it with new, fresh wine. Why on earth does the Lord keep bringing bad wine verses good wine in my priesthood like this?

To think many Masses over the years could have been invalid was shocking and of all places at the Shrine of the Holy Innocents.

Unlike the wine at the sister's convent in Tantrum, this wine continued to taste like wine, but had a thickened appearance. At any rate, thanks be to God, the Lord wanted the Shrine to use the best altar wine and used me to bring it about. Praise the Lord!

#127 FIRED AT THE HOSPITAL

Stolen Chalice, Roe vs. Wade Jan. 22nd 2021 & "You're Fired!"

"No one pours new wine into old wine skins. Otherwise, the new wine will burst the skins, and it will be spilled, and the skins will be ruined. Rather, new wine must be poured into fresh wine skins." (Luke 5:37)

When I spoke to the president of the International Bioethics of America about the problems at the Catholic Rolling Hills hospitals, he recommended I speak with the head ethicist of Mother of Misery Health System. However, he warned me, that if I called the ethicist and went over the heads of local administration, I would get fired. But, he said they would make the changes. I thought it was worth it to be humiliated to help stop the unethical practices at the hospital. Isn't a priest supposed to be willing to lay down his life for his sheep?

I called Tom Yeradi, a young man, who graduated from Franciscan University of Steubenville with a degree in medical ethics, and explained all the unethical things happening at the hospital: abortion, sterilization, contraception, mercy killing, failing to give artificial nutrition and hydration to patients, who could benefit from them, and encouragement by hospital supervisors to falsify medical records. I explained how the president of the local hospital supported legislation that allocates additional money to Ohio hospitals, but at the expense of paying for abortions.

This occurred during the time of the 2020 US presidential elections. Many believed Democrats stole the presidential election by stuffing ballot boxes with fake ballots. I decided to offer a Novena of Masses for an End to Abortion with the last Mass being offered January 6th, the day the Republicans were going to challenge the election results. On that day, January 6th, the US capital was taken over by an unarmed mob. It was absolutely shocking. It was the final day the Democrats allegedly made stealing the election permanent. And, it was the day a Chalice, and Ciboria were stolen from the hospital Chapel at St. Henry's. This led to a spiral of events.

I believed the Lord wanted me to do everything possible to end the unethical practice of not giving nutrition and hydration to terminally ill and dying patients. I believed He wanted me to directly address the hospice and the nursing supervisor of Mother of Misery Healthcare System, Saint Camillus de Lellis campus, and I did. Therefore, I wrote letters to the director of Woebegone Hospice, and the nursing supervisor for St. Camillus De Lillis hospital. I gave them the CDF (Congregation for the Doctrine of Faith) document, *Good Samaritan,* concerning the treatment of terminally ill and dying patients. During my meeting with the bishop, he suggested I not send out any more letters. But I understood this to mean letters to priests of the diocese.

I kept waiting for a phone call from the nursing supervisor and the hospice director. But no one called. Backlash was expected, and I thought I may get fired because of it, and I did. But what I didn't anticipate was the Mother of Misery Healthcare hierarchy making up false and misleading statements about my ministry at the hospital. I was shocked because they exaggerated and lied to cover up their unethical practice and for them to even possibly prevent an accomplice to the theft (a security guard) from being revealed.

The security supervisor would never reveal the security guard's name who saw me put the keys in a cabinet. Yet, he was able to find out who he was by watching video surveillance. The camera caught an image of the thief, but it became apparent to other hospital staff (radiology), the thief needed help to move about in other places at the hospital. Therefore, the radiology staff believed, a security guard assisted the thief.

The bishop called me to his office for an *urgent* meeting to inform me the hospital wanted my immediate dismissal. During the meeting the bishop with the Vicar for Clergy in attendance, mentioned a list of complaints from the hospital hierarchy against me, though just two weeks ago, the bishop said there were no complaints against myself. One complaint said it was untrue patients were dying without nutrition and hydration. I wondered how they could make that statement? Didn't the bishop meet with them and mention the problem, which he said he would? At the end of the meeting, it became apparent it was a losing battle.

The bishop at first asked if he and I could sit down and visit with them to try to work things out. But I thought it would do not any good to try to explain the artificial nutrition and hydration situation. Consequently, I suggested, to let them have what they wanted. Later, I regretted not meeting with them and the bishop.

It became evident the bishop didn't have another priest to replace me, nor where I would be assigned next. Just before this happened, Catholic Health System from Texas, contacted me for a possible interview at Good Grace Hospital in Longbow, Texas. The bishop preferred I first try to return to St. John of God in Tantrum, since it was known they needed a priest chaplain. I didn't know how this would end, but I had peace because I believed this was all in God's plan. The Lord has a new place for me to go. (New Wine for New Wine Skins).

My spiritual director wisely helped me to see how the letters should have been preceded by meetings with the persons involved to develop a friendship with them before giving them hard-facts about the unethical problems, and I agreed. My imprudence.

At the end of the day, I felt comforted knowing I suffered for human dignity, for the dying, on the anniversary of Roe vs. Wade, a day we are to recall the gift of human life, and its dignity, since it's the day of the horrendous legalization of abortion. There could be no better day to be fired for standing up for the sick, dying and unborn who were dying at the hospital.

The bishop asked the hospital to allow me to continue to minister at the hospitals for the next six months. But no one from the hospital ever spoke to me about the unethical things occurring there. No one ever called. To me, this was a clear sign they didn't want to discuss their unethical practices and wanted to cover them up. They had no problem in ruining the reputation of a priest. An obstetrics doctor later told me the bishop knew about many of the unethical things two years before I brought it to his attention. A group of doctors had spoken with him, asking him to remove the Catholic identity from the hospitals. The bishop may have wanted to preserve having priests hired by the hospital, so that Catholics could receive the sacraments there, though he never mentioned anything like that to me. It was very apparent, Mother of Misery Healthcare System is not a Catholic institution. (See Appendix F – Letter to the Director of Woebegone Hospice).

#128 IMPRUDENT OR PRUDENT

Imprudent of Prudent? Now That's the Question!
"I prayed, and prudence was given to me; I pleaded, and the spirit of Wisdom came to me." (Wisdom 7:7)

During the meeting with the bishop, when I was informed that the hospital wanted my immediate removal, he said I was imprudent to send letters to the Nursing Supervisor and the Hospice Administrator. He said, "You did the same as you did at Immaculate

Heart of Mary with the alcohol policy. Back then, you threw a stick of dynamite to kill a mouse." He said, "You wrote a big, long alcohol policy to address a small problem."

I disagreed with the bishop, but didn't respond to his statement. The parish policy was originally about three-fourths of a page. It was decided by the Pastoral Council to adopt the Diocesan Policy, which was about four pages long. It was adopted word for word. The Pastoral Council also decided to make adaptations of the Diocesan policy to fit the circumstances of the German Dinner parish event at the parish hall. One of the Pastoral Council members asked me to contact the Diocesan Insurance Company to examine our additions to the policy, which I did. The insurance company asked we incorporate two more pages of wording. Therefore, the policy we created was the Diocesan Policy with the Insurance Company's suggestions, and that's why the policy was four pages.

The policy we developed was approved by the Diocesan insurance company. But when the bishop was given a copy of the policy, he asked that we change the policy to be only one paragraph in size, which meant eliminating the Diocesan policy and the insurance company suggestions.

Back then, I told the bishop that the CYO youth director, the Knights of Cortez grand night, other Knights of Cortez members, and several Pastoral Council members were intoxicated at the dinner. His response was, "Well, when we had a parish event with alcohol, boys will be boys. Some drank too much, but no one had a problem with it."

In reference to the artificial nutrition and hydration letters sent to the nursing supervisor and hospice, was I really throwing dynamite to kill a mouse?

I didn't believe it was a little thing parishioners and guests were getting intoxicated at a parish sponsored event, especially since some were leaders of the parish. It's scandalous behavior. It approves of immoderate alcohol consumption. And, it's dangerous for the intoxicated to drive home.

It's not a little thing people never receive artificial nutrition and hydration when hospice patients could benefit from them at any Mother of Misery Healthcare hospital or at Woebegone Hospice located at Mother of Misery Healthcare System, Saint Camillus de Lellis campus. Hospice and hospital patients (such as those who can't swallow due to a stroke), live up to two weeks without artificial nutrition and hydration, and therefore, their death was caused by a lack of food and water, and not the illness or disease. I didn't see it as a little problem that a man was starved to death by purposely medicating him to be in an unconscious state for nine days since the man only had Alzheimer's and was in very good health.

I am not the only source of this information. A staff member's mother and her daughter asked the hospice to give her an IV and a feeding tube, and the hospice doctor said, "We don't do that here!"

Bishop met with various hospital personnel about artificial nutrition and hydration. Todd Stoner, who was present at one of the meetings, said the bishop never mentioned anything about artificial nutrition and hydration. I thought if he had spoken to them about the unethical practice, the letters would be welcomed, and they would have visited with me. But, perhaps, I was wrong.

For me, it would have been imprudent to not address the unethical situations. Wouldn't it be a lack of prudence to not care for the health and souls of real people? Wouldn't it be imprudent for me to not care for the souls of people getting intoxicated at the German Dinner? Likewise, wouldn't it be imprudent for the hospice and hospital staff to not want to know the truth and to help resolve any potential unethical problems in their hospice and hospital? Isn't it imprudent for the hospice or hospital to not desire to know or to ignore Church teachings about artificial nutrition and hydration? Prudence or imprudence, now that's the question.

After reflecting upon all that has happened, I wonder if I am truly very imprudent, but blind to the reality of it. Why is it that I can't see how serious these things are, as I do? Lord, I pray with all my heart, that You will give me the gift of prudence and make up for my failures in my judgments. Not only grant me this gift, but forgive me for my ignorance and inability to judge wisely. O Virgin Most Prudent, pray for me, who have recourse to thee!

#129 FALSE ACCUSATIONS

False Accusations

"Blessed are they, when men shall revile you, and persecute you, and shall say all manner of evil against you falsely, for my sake." (Matthew 10:22)

When I met with Bishop Courageous, he read a list of accusations against me from the hospital as to why they wanted my immediate removal. One allegation said I broke the Health Insurance Portability and Accountability Act (HIPPA) laws. They said I looked at patient records which they said were not permitted by chaplains. When I spoke to Todd Stoner, the pastoral care supervisor about this accusation, he said, "I gave you and every chaplain permission to look at patient records." Every chaplain prints a daily list of the patients, their diagnosis, age, and church affiliation. No one ever told me I couldn't look at patient records. The purpose of looking at patient records is to help staff care for the patient and is not shared with non-staff. How does looking at patient records break any HIPPA law, if the information the hospital provides me, has the same information on it? When I was at St. John of God in Tantrum, the pastoral care staff routinely looked at patient medical records to help assess the patient's condition to help them pastorally.

They said I accused two employees of helping the thief. I did accuse two employees, since only those two, the housekeeper, and security guard, knew where the key was located in the cabinet, and only the security guard had seen where the Tabernacle key was kept. He saw me place the key in its secret place, just two days before the chalice was stolen. I kept suggesting to Justin O' Thief, the director of security, to view video footage to identify the security guard, but he would never do it. How could a thief, who didn't know where any keys were located, find both hidden keys and make off with a chalice and ciboria in eight minutes, as identified in the security video? The thief had to have known where they were located, and only the security guard knew. This was also a theory of radiology. They also had their keys stolen. How would the thief know where the keys were located in both departments?

They said the comment I made in a letter to priests was untrue "Most likely, people are dying throughout the diocese unethically, as they are certainly dying this way in Rolling Hills, at Catholic and non-Catholic hospitals, and nursing homes and in their homes." Despite their opposition to the statement, it's true. I know it's true, because when I was at the Doorway to Heaven Nursing Center (nursing home) for two years, residents did not receive artificial nutrition and hydration, which was reported to Bishop Traditiones, who did nothing about it.

They said I didn't get along with some chaplains in the Pastoral Care Department. There is only one "chaplain" I had difficulty with, Sister Janine. She wanted the statues, the Stations of the Cross, and the new Altar removed. She also defiantly stood during the consecration at Mass. All the other chaplains and I had good rapport. Despite sister's view of things, I thought she and I got along well.

Todd said Woebegone Hospice wanted to sue me for defamation, since I sent the letter to all the priests. I told Todd, "How can they sue me, if everything I said was true?" I told him I met with the Bishop over these problems and sent him letters and emails about it, which the Bishop wanted me to do. Bishop mentioned he met with Todd and other hospital staff about the ethical issues. But Todd said he merely asked questions and never mentioned to them about anything I reported to him that was unethical. The bishop subtly suggested I seek ministry outside the diocese, since he didn't believe me fit to do anything in the Diocese of Rolling Hills. I forgive him, I love him as a bishop and pray for him. To be an instrument of mercy, means to be an instrument of forgiveness and love.

#130 BISHOP THINKS DIFFERENT THAN I

Different Way of Doing Things?
During the meeting January 22nd with the bishop, he said Mother of Misery Healthcare System Hospitals just have a different way of doing things (unlike St. John of God Hospital in Tantrum, Idaho). Does that statement mean morality can be different from Idaho and Ohio?

Does this mean the bishop is saying it is ethically acceptable for Mother of Misery Hospitals and Woebegone Hospice not give patients artificial nutrition and hydration to terminally ill patients who can benefit from them, while at St. John of God in Tantrum it's not acceptable, since they have a different way of doing things? I believe morality is the same everywhere. Surely, I must have misunderstood what the bishop meant.

Blind to Human Suffering and Unethical Practice

Jesus said, 'For judgment I came into this world, that those who do not see may see, and those who see may become blind.' Some of the Pharisees near him heard these things, and said to him, "Are we also blind?" Jesus said to them, "If you were blind you have no guilt; but now that you say, 'We see' your guilt remains." (John 9:39)

How is it, the priest chaplain of St. Camillus de Lillis, who sees Hospice patients at Woebegone Hospice regularly, and a priest chaplain of Doorway to Heaven Nursing Center, who also witnesses patients die regularly, not see the problem? Both were given Catholic Church documents, such as the CDF document *Good Samaritan* about the terminally ill and dying and the necessity to give nutrition and hydration, but they are blind to the problem. To just read the documents and apply them to the situations makes it abundantly clear there are serious unethical circumstances at the hospice, Catholic hospitals, and a Catholic nursing home, and yet they are blind to it. How can one not see the agony of a person who can benefit from nutrition and hydration, and yet not receive any for 9 to 14 days? How can one not see the spiritual and unethical practices, and how it affects not only the bodies of the dying, but also the souls responsible for the unethical practice?

I am a simple man, and a simple priest, and how is it I see these things, as well as the religious sisters from Panama, who take care of the residents at the Doorway to Heaven Nursing Center and the International Catholic Bioethics Center of America president, feel anguish and anxiety over this and yet these two priests do not? What is causing their blindness? Do they have a moral problem? It deeply saddens me they do nothing about it and these poor people suffer so grievously because of their blindness. I pray intensely that, like St. Paul, the scales will fall from their eyes, and they will see. May God's mercy penetrate the depths of their hearts, so they may give His mercy, to those who desperately need it.

#131 DEMONS ATTACK AGAIN

House Cleansing

Almost every night, I had a demon or demons attack me, and wake me up, due to shaking my arm or shaking my leg violently. It was so often, I became almost used to it until I finally prayed about it and realized I never had that happen except in this rectory. I also decided to fight the shaking by resisting it. Wow! That was the wrong thing to do, because the attacks became more violent.

Consequently, I consecrated the rectory to the Hearts of Jesus and Mary, prayed the Litany of Saints, did the Leo XIII exorcism prayer (I have permission from the bishop for other purposes), prayed exorcism prayers permitted by priest to pray, and offered a Mass for the souls of priests for both the living, and deceased, who lived in this hospital rectory.

Just before offering Mass, a demon spoke to me, and said, "Mary was not a Virgin. She committed personal sin, and Catholics make Her out to be someone She's not. Jesus is not God. He never really died on the Cross. His death was just an illusion. Don't offer this Mass for this intention. If you do, we will kill you." Once Mass was offered, the violent shaking of my leg and arm stopped, and it became so much easier to pray in the Chapel, with hardly any distractions.

#132 JESUS APPEARS AS A CHILD

Child Jesus Returns and Shows His Finger

Immediately after I placed the pyx with the consecrated Hosts in my pocket at St. Mother Cope Hospital before going to patient rooms, I saw the Child Jesus. He was larger, "more healthy" than before. He never spoke, but showed His index finger, which was discolored (sort of black). I was very happy to see Him. He always seems to appear when I feel down and out. As I began entering patient rooms, He disappeared. I entered a patient's room, and, sure enough, just as I expected, the patient (an older lady) had an index finger that was gray in appearance due to an infection. I think, the Lord wanted to remind me He suffers in the patients to have more empathy for them, and at the same time, gave me consolation knowing He is partaking in my priestly ministry.

#133 AMAZING GRACE

Baptism Before Surgery, 65 Years of Prayer

I came to a patient room of an 85-year-old man listed as Catholic. After introducing myself, I asked if he was Catholic, and he said, "Yes, but I never became one." He told me he was going to have major surgery the next day due to jaw cancer. His jaw was to removed and replaced with a plate. I asked if he was baptized, and if he had thought about becoming Catholic. He said he was never baptized. He said he would like to receive the sacrament and become Catholic. His wife just left before I arrived, and so I asked if he wanted me to call her back. He said, "No, just do it now." Consequently, I asked Tabitha, a nurse who became Catholic while I was at St. Charles of Sezze parish, to be his godparent. I found out later, just before his wife left, she asked him if he would get baptized. At first, he said no. Then, when I asked, the same question, he said yes. Providentially, I came to his room about thirty minutes after she departed. They just celebrated their 65th wedding anniversary, and she prayed for him all those years to get baptized. After giving him instructions about the sacraments, by the grace of God, he was Baptized, Confirmed, and received Anointing of the Sick. I called his son to tell him his dad received baptism. He said his mother would be elated. Thank you, Jesus!

Six Days of Spiritual Dreams Caused by New Medicine or Grace From Heaven?
I prayed two different Novenas from the conclusion of one, and then began the other, both to the Virgin Mary, asking Her to help me know God's will about my next assignment. The first Rosary Novena was by St. Don Bosco. During the last 6 days of the second Novena to Our Lady of Lourdes, a Rosary Confraternity Novena, I had spiritual dreams every night, that were absolutely joyful.

In one dream, I was at the monastery of the Franciscans of Perpetual Victim Martyrs, and the Child Jesus about the age of ten, was there. He wore a large badge with His Sacred Heart on it, and He sat next to me in the Chapel. Another dream there was a wedding, but the priest was absent, so the adult Jesus officiated the wedding. The parents of the groom didn't come to the wedding, consequently, Mary and Joseph took the place of the groom's parents. In one dream, I saw Mother Annuciata, who had died, and she handed me a long tooth brush. In another dream, I preached to high school students about St. Anthony of Padua, and another dream, I preached on Perpetual Adoration.

I rarely have spiritual dreams, so these dreams were a consolation. I don't speculate as to their meaning. During this time, I started new medicine, which may have caused the dreams. Or, perhaps, the Lord just wanted to give me consolation, with these happy and blessed dreams.

"Lord, What Do You Think?"
"O man of little faith, why did you doubt?" (Matthew 14:31)

After getting fired from the hospital, I wondered what Jesus thought about what I did. So I kept pleading with Him, asking what He thought. His response came from the *Office of Readings*, the Catechesis, by St. Cyril of Jerusalem. "When war comes, fight courageously for Him. Jesus never sinned; yet, He was crucified for you. Will you refuse to be crucified for Him, who for your sake was nailed to the Cross?" A few days after understanding this as a message from Him, I asked Jesus again what He thought about what I did at the hospitals, and again the same quote came to mind.

Then a few days later, I repeated the same question again, and Jesus said, "O man of little faith, why did you doubt?" A few weeks later, I realized there was one thing I did not do. I had offered a novena of Masses, a novena to St. Joseph, and prayed during my daily time with Jesus in the Blessed Sacrament.

Even though, I normally fast on Wednesday and Friday, I realized I failed to fast specifically for Bishop Courageous, Fr. Harry Brown, Fr. Jimmy Tisdale, and hospital administration. As a result, I did a 9-day fast for them. I thought, "This kind (demons associated with blocking them from seeing the truth) can only be driven out by prayer and fasting." (Matthew 17:21)

#134 MY BIRTHDAY AND BISHOPS

A Birthday Gift
Bishop Traditiones Leaves & Bishop Courageous Comes
Bishop Courageous Asks Me To Leave On My Birthday

"Shimei was saying as he cursed: "Get out! Get out! You man of blood, you scoundrel! (2 Samuel 16:7) David and his men continued on the road, while Shimei kept up with them on the hillside, all the while cursing and throwing stones and dirt as he went." (2 Samuel 16:13)

Bishop Traditiones and I certainly had misunderstandings, as well as with other priests. The job of a bishop is enormously difficult. Bishop Traditiones had a temper which he unloaded on me few times.

After visiting with several priests, we decided to pray for a different bishop for our diocese. Without telling anyone, I sent nine Mass stipends to the Cathedral and asked them to offer the nine masses in a row for a special intention. My special intention was that Bishop Traditiones would be transferred, and we would get a new bishop. On the 9th day of the Novena of Masses, it was announced Bishop Traditiones was promoted to become the Archbishop of Battle Creek, Michigan. I was stunned to say the least.

Almost a year later, on my birthday, Feb. 30th, it was announced Bishop Athanasius Courageous would be our new bishop. At first, I thought it was a special birthday gift from Jesus. Then I remembered, Feb. 30th is the feast of saints Jacinta and Francisco. Would this new bishop be a reminder for me to offer sacrifices like the children of Fatima? Would he give out unintentional sufferings to me, so I would have hidden sacrifices to give to Jesus for the conversion of sinners and in reparation for sins committed against the Hearts of Jesus and Mary? I later discovered, it was both a special birthday gift for me, and he would certainly delve out of many opportunities to suffer for Jesus and make sacrifices.

After I was fired by the hospital, Bishop Courageous had nothing for me to do in the Diocese of Rolling Hills. He wanted me to seek ministry on my own outside the diocese. At first, I thought I misunderstood him. However, after I spoke with Fr. Royal, his intention was confirmed, when I received a birthday card in the mail from the bishop, indicating he wanted me to do ministry outside the diocese.

Fr. Royal called to see if I had any success at St. John of God Hospital in Tantrum accepting me, but I informed him they had already found another priest. He then asked about Good Grace Hospital in Longbow, Texas. I told him I was waiting to hear from them. I asked, "What if that does not pan out, what will happen to me? Does the bishop have something else for me to do?" And Fr. Royal said, "No. Bishop has nothing for you to do." To put this into context, I was permitted to continue at the hospitals until the priest change of assignments. My understanding was that the bishop did not want to reassign me in the diocese at the end of the normal cycle, but rather, wanted me out of the diocese. He later accepted a priest from a foreign country to serve in our diocese, as an associate, but didn't want me to serve here.

A few days later, I received a birthday card from Bishop Courageous. Inside the card, he wrote, "I wish you a very happy & blessed Birthday. You remain in my prayers as you figure out what could be next for you! Peace. Bishop Courageous" There it was in handwriting; he was expecting me to figure out for myself what I was to do next. Wow! It was abundantly clear, he had nothing for me to do in the Diocese of Rolling Hills. How disappointing! Not a pastor, not an associate, not to teach. Obviously, not "Catholic" hospital ministry. After a period of anger, prayer, and forgiveness, I came to realize it was a birthday gift from Jesus to experience this heartache. And it was also my fault. Jesus Himself was asking me to leave the diocese, and He wanted me to extend His Mercy to the bishop, which I did, to the best of my ability.

I felt the words of Shimei to King David, were for me. "Get out! Get out! You scoundrel!" Then I recalled the response of King David. "Let him alone and let him curse, for the LORD has told him to..." (2 Samuel 16:11). Do I not deserve to be asked to leave, since I wanted Bishop Traditiones to leave?

I believed the Lord wanted Bishop Courageous to ask me to get out, to leave, and to find my ministry. Everything good or bad, He permits and are therefore from His hands. How can I complain? Suffering and rejection are gifts from God. If the Lord told him to do this to me, it was His way that He wanted me to move on to my next assignment, planned from all eternity by Jesus. I am looking to what the Lord has next. I embrace the suffering, the rejection, and believe I will be rewarded in heaven. The anger abated, and joy filled my heart knowing God loved me enough to pay attention to me, to discipline me, to move me to a new place. Whether it was God's ordaining will, or His permitting will, what does it matter. It's all His will, so who am I to complain. I have peace.

#135 LENTEN RETREAT OF DELIVERANCE
TEMPTATION TO GET DIFFERENT DIRECTOR

Lenten Retreat 2021

"Put on the whole armor of God that you may be able to stand against the schemes of the devil. For our fight is not against flesh and blood, but against principalities, against powers, against the rulers of the darkness of this world, and against spiritual forces of evil in the heavenly places. Therefore, take up the whole armor of God that you may be able to resist in the evil day, and having done all, to stand. Stand therefore, having your waist girded with truth, having put on the breastplate of righteousness, having your feet fitted with the readiness of the gospel of peace, and above all, taking the shield of faith, with which you will be able to extinguish all the fiery arrows of the evil one. Take the helmet of salvation and the sword of the Spirit, which is the word of God. Pray in the Spirit always with all kinds of prayer and supplication. To that end be alert with all perseverance and supplication for all the saints." (Ephesians 6:11-18)

I went to Hodgenville, Georgia for my Lenten Retreat from March 3rd to March 11th. By far, it was the most difficult retreat I ever had. It was difficult for many reasons. I strictly fasted during the 40 days of Lent for two purposes. The first purpose was for the bishop, the priest chaplain at Mother of Misery Healthcare System, St. Camillus de Lellis campus administrators, the priest chaplain, Fr. Lawrence Deathblow of Woebegone Hospice and also Doorway to Heaven Nursing Center, to help them finally see how people are dying unethically and do something about it. The other purpose was to come to know and embrace whatever the Lord was asking of me after my assignment at the hospital. During the retreat, I decided to actively try to find the place the Lord was calling me to minister.

New medicine I began to take and fasting during the forty days caused horrific problems with my stomach, memory problems, and several times my heart went into A-fib. My heart was skipping a beat or two, and I felt weak. I realized I was fasting too much and began to eat more.

During the retreat, I had so many desolations I could not remember to write about all of them at the end of the hour of prayer. During many Holy Hours, I felt my body become contorted. My chest would expand, my arms and legs would stiffen, and many times my whole body would shake intensely. I became so exhausted by these demonic interactions. Yet, when they were over, I believed the demon or demons had left me. On one occasion, a demon said to Jesus, "Son of God! We will never leave him."

The enemy caused me to have doubts about my spiritual director. My spiritual director and I had a disagreement that was exacerbated due to not eating well and taking new medicine.

Many emotional wounds from the past were brought before my mind, including traumatic events, such as car accidents, head injuries, etc. It seemed Jesus wanted to heal emotional and spiritual wounds from the past. I became so fed up with all the demonic actions and due to the misunderstanding I had with my spiritual director, I resolved to leave the retreat early and told my spiritual director about it. Yet, I stayed and was glad I did. For a time, the enemy convinced me to get a different spiritual director. I had hospital ministry taken from me. My diocese was taken from me. And now, my spiritual director too. And through all this, Jesus was silent. Not a peep. I felt abandoned even by God.

I later realized the devil was attempting to cause problems between my spiritual director and myself and to convince me to stop seeing him. But the Lord gave both of us the grace to continue. Thanks be to God! He is the holiest spiritual director I ever had, and I have grown spiritually by leaps and bounds due to his direction. Thank you, Jesus!

During one of the meditations, I realized I had the habit of wanting to know the future of the Church, the pope, and my future priestly ministry. The Lord granted me the grace to see the many times in my life where His Divine Providence took care of all my needs. What struck me the most, was when I was in college, and rarely prayed and seldom attended Mass, God, in His providence, provided everything for me: food, shelter, schooling, a job, a car, friends, a social life, and at that time, I was totally unaware He was doing these things for me. I wept several times due to the realization of His loving care and concern for me. And this caused me to realize the great need, to trust right now, in His Divine Providence, and that my future ministry will be taken care of. I only had to trust Jesus, and truly mean, "You take care of it!"

#136 THE HELL THERE IS!

Meditation on Hell

The man in Luke 16:24 cries: "...I am tormented in this flame." In Matthew 13:42, Jesus said, "And shall cast them into a furnace of fire: there shall be wailing and gnashing of teeth." In Matthew 25:41, Jesus said, "Depart from me, ye cursed, into everlasting fire..."

During the Lenten Retreat, I did a meditation on hell, as prescribed by the Spiritual Exercises of St. Ignatius. During the meditation, I imagined people and fallen angels torturing each other in hell. Whatever caused the soul to go to hell, I saw the soul repeat the sinful action over and over for all eternity. The greedy, who wanted money, jewelry, and riches, never had enough. It would be taken from them, and then they would get it back. They would lose it again, and again. People, who wanted a perfect body, would get the body they wanted. But then, it would turn into decaying flesh, with maggots consuming it, and then they would get the body they wanted, and it would turn into decaying flesh. This cycle was repeated over and over. The stench, the smell, the odor of feces. With sexual sins: they just kept repeating them over and over again. Their greatest pain was their separation from God (from Jesus, the angels, and saints). One damned person said, "We are suffering now for refusing to suffer on earth." Some were mocking the saints and were angry at them for being "righteous". It was amusing that St. Therese appeared above hell and was dropping pedals of roses into it, which infuriated the damned and was a form of torture for them. As the meditation concluded, I opened my eyes, with a feeling warmth on my forehead. The sunlight was shining through the stained-glass window of the Divine Mercy picture. The sun was shining so brightly, through the face of Jesus, I could hardly see His face. It gave me great consolation that if I trust in God's mercy, I will never be damned and gaze upon His face forever.

#137 WHERE DOES JESUS WANT ME, BECAUSE MY BISHOP DOES NOT

Where to Go?

A representative from Good Grace Hospital in Longbow, Texas called and said I needed to be a certified chaplain, which would take years. The sister at St. John of God in Tantrum, never returned my call, signaling I was not needed there. I had reached out to various bishops, asking if they could use a priest in their diocese: Bishop Trueapostle, Bishop Handyman, and Bishop Forthright.

Only the chancellor from Indian Hills was willing to talk to me. It gave me hope I had a place to go. The truth is, Bishop Courageous had a wrong understanding of the ministry I am capable of. He said I am a priest in good standing and would give a wonderful recommendation to whomever will take me. But, he never gave a good recommendation to the Bishop of Indian Hills. He told him my decision-making was often imprudent. It is true, many other priests are better pastors, and at times, I make imprudent decisions. I am truly a wretch of a priest, but I trust in God's mercy and His providential grace.

My heart was in terrible anguish to be treated this way. When I emailed him about Indian Hills, he suddenly wanted me in the diocese of Rolling Hills. Due to my lack of confidence in Bishop Courageous, I prefer to not be a pastor in my diocese of Rolling Hills. I don't believe I could endure getting thrown under the bus another time.

My Easter this year seemed to be a continuation of Lent. I wondered if, and when, I would be vindicated. When will truth prevail? For me, I have nearly lost all hope in having a meaningful relationship with a bishop and ever being able to do the ministry I am capable.

I should not want to be vindicated. I should not care if I am treated justly or unjustly. I desire only what the Lord desires. He may treat me as He wishes, since He knows what is best for my soul.

St. Faustina in her Diary, said, "In prayer I always find light and strength of spirit, although there are moments so trying and hurtful, that it is sometimes difficult to imagine that these things can happen in a convent. Strangely, God sometimes allows them, but always in order to manifest or develop virtue in a soul. That is the reason for trials." (*St. Faustina Diary*, #166)

Is this what God is doing to me? I do believe all is from His hand. With faith, I cry out with all my heart, "Jesus I trust in You, though I do not understand." Do I need to understand? Does it matter if I never do what I am capable? It's all permitted by God, by His hand. So how can I complain? This purification is exceedingly painful. I offer it up for the conversion of sinners, in reparation for sins against the Immaculate Heart of Mary and the Sacred Heart of Jesus, and in reparation for my sins, is my only consolation.

Is all this God's way of answering my prayer? "Lord, I would rather suffer in this life, rather than the next. I don't want to go to purgatory, but certainly deserve it."

Letter Not Sent to Bishop Courageous, An Act of Mercy and Humility
Saturday, April 10th, 2021, the eve of Divine Mercy Sunday, I decided to type a letter explaining to Bishop Courageous my thoughts about his comment. "I throw a stick of dynamite on a situation, like when I created the alcohol policy for Immaculate Heart of Mary parish." I thought it would be an act of mercy to "instruct the ignorant", if I explained the Alcohol Policy was actually mostly the Diocesan Alcohol Policy, as well as recommendations from the Catholic Insurance of America. I wanted him to know his view of me as a priest was in serious error. I believed I had a duty to tell him for the good of the Church, and for my sake and ministry as a priest.

Several years ago, I sent him "Additional Information and Concerns" with the Priest Assessment form in January 2019 that explained the truth of things at Immaculate Heart of Mary parish. But he never replied, and never mentioned it, when I had other meetings with him. Therefore, I created a new letter and again attached the "Additional Information and Concerns" in hopes he would take to heart my words, and maybe spare other priests from what I perceive as an injustice I am going through. I hoped the letter would help him stand up for his priests and stand against immorality and unethical practices. After writing the letter, I went to the Chapel and prayed during a Holy Hour before Jesus in Eucharistic Adoration.

During the hour, it occurred to me, I was trying to justify myself and I should trust the Lord that if Jesus really wanted me to serve in the Diocese of Indian Hills, Montana, He would make it happen without any letter on my part. I had to trust Jesus.

Consequently, I chose not to send the letter. In a book entitled *The Way of Humility* it said, Abba John the Dwarf said, "Who sold Joseph?" A brother replied, "His brothers." The Abba replied, "No, it was his humility which sold him, because he could have said, "I am their brother in objection. But, because he kept silent, he sold himself by his humility. It is his humility, that made him the chief in Egypt." John the Dwarf also said, "We have put aside a light burden which is self-accusation, only to take up the heavy one of self-justification." Due to these words from the book, I decided it was better for my soul and better for Bishop if I never sent the letter. Instead, I chose to make an act of mercy and an act of humility trusting that even if I get an assignment, much less than what I am capable, God will reward me for accepting His humble will. By not sending the letter when I could have, I finally had the Easter joy I was seeking. I had to first die to myself and to my pride, so I could rise with Jesus and share in the joy of His Resurrection!

#138 CARS AND TRUCKS

Cars, Trucks, and Cars (A Modern Horse Trader)

The financial help I gave my family, often times, involved cars and trucks, and of course, money too. My sister Sue's husband, Phillip, was diagnosed with brain and lung cancer. Before his death, wanting to help his wife, and allow himself to enjoy something he had always wanted, he took out a loan on a new car and new pickup. He also took out a loan for a car for his daughter as well. Not expecting himself to die as quickly as he did, the purchases of the vehicles became a burden for his wife after his death. So, when he died, she was responsible for making payments for three vehicles. I paid off the remainder of the pickup and his daughter's car.

About seven years earlier, I donated a car to a nephew, one of their sons. A different sister, Jean, purchased a car, that I later discovered to be a lemon and was saddled with a car that hardly ran. She had a loan of $10,000 on the car. Her ex-husband failed to make alimony and child support payments. She also lost her job resulting in a pile of debt. I paid her bankruptcy fee, and also gave her my Honda Civic, which was a $7,800 gift.

The axle of my brother's car broke, and he had no transportation, so I gave him my Honda Odyssey van that I purchased for $2000.

Then I purchased a Chevrolet Impala, which turned out to be a lemon. I paid $10,000 for the car and paid off the car within eight months. But the car had transmission problems. Consequently, I ended up selling the car for $5,000 and taking out a loan for another car for $8,000. The amount of money spent on vehicles over two years was astonishing.

For years, I sent $200 a month to my brother, Louis, due to his traumatic brain injury, but increased it to $250 a month. Recently, due to gas and food prices, I increased it to $300 a month.

#139 BI-LOCATION

Bi-Location?

There were many times while ministering at Mother of Misery Healthcare System, Saint Camillus de Lellis campus, I seemed to be in the right place at the right time. Cletus, Linus, and Clement, who were lay chaplains, pondered with amazement how I happened to show up at the right place when needed.

For example, one day I went to anoint a Vietnamese patient, whom I visited several weeks before, but was readmitted. Just as I was about to enter his room, Linus and Cletus met me, and said, "How did you know to come?" He said, "The patient just died in the Catheter Lab, and he was just put in his room." As the chaplain was speaking, the patient's family came to be with their father. All of us simultaneously met at the same time. God did not bring me to his room to anoint him, but rather, to be with the family and pray the "After Death Prayers".

On another occasion, I anointed a patient and gave her the Apostolic Pardon. Within just a few minutes after I departed her room, a nurse came to her room and initiated a "Code Blue".

At another time I went to give a patient, who was anointed, but not given the Apostolic Pardon by Fr. Harry. For some reason, I felt like she needed the Apostolic Pardon and gave it to her. A few hours later, she coded, and died.

Due to these events and many others, some began to wonder if I was bi-locating and would ask me if I did. My joking response was, "God only knows if I bilocate or trilocate, but I certainly would never "fornicate", nor "procrastinate." Ha! Ha!

Because every day, I consecrate Anointings, Communions, Confessions, Baptisms, Confirmations, and all ministry of the day to the Hearts of Jesus and Mary, Jesus and Mary providentially brought me to patients at the right time. By the grace of God, I was unknowingly moved by the Holy Spirit to go to the patients God wanted a priest to minister, and when someone wanted a priest to be there.

#140 COME TO MONTANA! BUT, BISHOP FORTHRIGHT CHANGES HIS MIND

Accepted in the Diocese of Indian Hills, but Bishop Changed His Mind

To explore the idea if I could minister in the Diocese of Indian Hills, at the request of the bishop, I had a virtual meeting on the computer with Bishop Forthright and his Chancellor, Michael Alfalfa. I was very tense during the meeting and realized Bishop Courageous had told Bishop Forthright I was not fit to be a pastor and didn't make good decisions. I didn't know how to respond to those kinds of questions, without contradicting Bishop Courageous. Consequently, I agreed my decision-making was faulty, and I should not be a pastor. When the meeting was over, I felt I betrayed myself. It would have been nice if my bishop had told me these things.

However, Bishop Forthright notified Bishop Courageous he had an assignment for me, but wanted to first review my personal file in the chancery. I called Fr. Gerry Meander. He suggested I first look at the file before sending it. When the day came to look through my file, I felt like it was my Day of Judgment. I was terrified to come to know what people wrote about me in their letters of complaint and what the Bishops of Rolling Hills put in my file.

When I looked through the file, I was horrified to see who and how many people said such false things about me. A few people had legitimate and good questions, but I thought if they had come to me first, I could have answered them. The exaggerations and false things said about me were shocking. Several people said I was "creepy". One person said nothing but false things about the German Dinner. In his letters written in response to parishioners, he never suggested that any one speak to me about their complaint before contacting him.

I am very human and this was all very hurtful. I am no saint, who could just brush it off, as if it was nothing. Yet, I trust Jesus. I believe He will give me the grace to love, to forgive, and to put it behind me.

I told Fr. Gerry it was okay to send a copy of the file. I decided to defend myself a little, and sent copies of information that proved there were many unethical things occurring at the three hospitals and the hospice. I also sent an email indicating I was capable of being a pastor, but would accept never being a pastor, if Bishop Forthright preferred it that way. A week after sending the file, I received an email from Bishop Courageous saying Bishop Forthright had changed his mind. Because of this, I was thrown into darkness and sadness and believed I needed to accept the assignment Bishop Courageous would give me, that is, if he would give me one.

A few days later, all during the night, I kept thinking how bad a priest I had been over the years, and thought the letters in my file were proof of it. Did they see in me a bad pastor, which I failed to see because I was blind at seeing myself that way? I began to think, even though what they said was untrue, for them to write such things must have been my fault for failing to be as pastoral as I could have. Therefore, it must have been the case, I am a bad pastor, but ignorant of it.

The next morning as I got out of bed, and entered the Chapel with Jesus in the Tabernacle, the thought occurred to me, none of what I was thinking during the night was true. Rather, I thought I should defend myself and defend the truth, since Jesus desires it of me. He is the truth, and He wants me to defend Him, and His priesthood. I was torn as to remain hidden and rejected, or to tell the truth. Which way was the way of humility? I thought both ways were the way of humility, and that Jesus wanted me to defend the truth.

Consequently, I wrote a four-page letter to Bishop Forthright explaining the truth of things about what really happened in those circumstances. I gave him phone numbers of people to verify everything. I sent the letter via email and was told Bishop Forthright was away the week it was sent, and would get back with me.

I asked the bishop to reconsider, as I explained how the hospital fired me for revealing their unethical practices to a chief ethicist at Mother of Misery Healthcare System headquarters and I revealed some true things about Bishop Courageous, but later I wish I would have kept it to myself. After I sent the letter, I realized Bishop Forthright may send a copy of the letter to Bishop Courageous. I had to trust Bishop Forthright. The information made no difference, and Bishop Forthright didn't want me to come.

Bishop Courageous assigned me to St. Timothy in Browbeat. He said, "I would like you to offer Mass at St. Timothy in Browbeat City. If things go well, after a few years you could become an administrator, and if after a few more years, maybe you could become their pastor. You will need to find a house to live in since there is no rectory, and the pastor of the Church of the Holy Incense would be the pastor of St. Timothy."

I place myself and my future assignment and priesthood in the hands of Jesus and trust in His Divine Providence. "Jesus, I have confidence in your Divine Providence. You take care of it!"

#141 ASSIGNED TO ST. TIMOTHY IN BROWBEAT CITY, OHIO

Assigned to St. Timothy in Browbeat City

I received an email from Bishop Courageous indicating I was assigned to St. Timothy in Browbeat City, Ohio, as a "Sacramental Priest". I was glad to have received the email because I preferred not to have an in-person meeting. The title of "Sacramental Priest" was a clear indication, he had no intention of making me a pastor. I was frankly happy with it, since I prefer to not be one, especially because I am not a very good priest.

During that same week, Todd Stoner, the Pastoral Care Department Supervisor, indicated Fred Wiggle, the head of the ethics committee, told him abortions were occurring at Mother of Misery Healthcare System Hospital.

On Trinity Sunday, the people of St. Timothy were notified I would be their sacramental priest. Also on that day, the anguish I had been experiencing subsided. During this time, from January 22nd until May 30th, 2021 (Trinity Sunday), I felt abandoned by God.

In a letter I wrote to a Norbertine monk, I said, "The Lord revealed to me the beauty of it all. He helped to understand it was a purification process that I had just gone through. In the past, and even not that long ago, I had unknowingly been overly curious about the future, and I was even superstitious about it all. I had always wondered what will happen to me? Where will I minister next? What will happen to the pope and the Church, since we are in such terrible condition at the moment? But, the Lord did not like that. It was a sin against trusting Him and His Divine Providence.

Providentially, I ran across a novena that helped me to trust Jesus more. At the heart of the novena was the desire to truly believe the Lord will take care of everything. I unknowingly was like the people in the desert who wanted to go back to Egypt and didn't trust the Lord to provide food, clothing, to overcome obstacles, and their enemies. I can't say I am now trusting the Lord and His Divine Providence perfectly. But I have abandoned my curious desires, and try to rely on Him for everything now. The Lord used the hospital, the bishop, my spiritual director, and my mistakes to draw me closer to Him. I continue to deeply desire, that the Lord will soon, help all those people who continue to die unethically."

It was five years ago, when Bishop Athanasius Courageous told the priests of the Diocese that he gave Mother of Misery Healthcare System permission to allow doctors to prescribe contraceptives for fear of losing them. Later, he and Fr. Jerry Meander denied giving approval of the hospital's permission to prescribe contraception, even though all the priests present at the meeting understood otherwise, and hospital employees also believed he meant it was okay.

An obstetrics doctor told me that he and some other Catholic doctors spoke to Bishop Courageous about contraceptives, sterilization, and IUDs etc., and were falsely recorded on medical records several years ago. The doctor also had spoken with the same ethicist from Mother of Misery Headquarters in Illinois about the same things I spoke to him, but nothing was ever done. When I learned this, I lost hope in the ethicist and believed what I attempted was a waste of time.

Was the purpose of all this, to be a "Gadfly" "to annoy" the conscience of a few? Is it possible a seed was planted, and in the future, they may actually embrace Church teaching? I did my part and, in the process, my reputation was ruined by people who lied.

I prayed a 9-day Novena of Masses and daily prayed the Holy Rosary and Chaplet of Divine Mercy for the bishop. Imagine the horror of it all: abortions, sterilization, contraceptives, IUDs, not giving feeding tubes and IVs when patients could benefit, mercy killing, giving excessive medication to hasten death, and passive euthanasia in a "Catholic" hospital!

I told the ethicist: "I spoke with a doctor, who told me you knew about everything already. Contraception, IUDs, sterilization, and most likely abortions too. What a waste of time. All that effort and getting "fired" for what purpose. At least I hopefully pricked a few consciences, that is, if anyone has one! I suspect the local non-Catholic hospital, Methodist Regional Medical Center in Rolling Hills, has better morals, at least they don't claim to be something they're not. You lost me."

My last name, Gadfly (one who annoys others and provokes others into action by criticism), and my efforts to warn people of their erroneous ways, reminds me of the prophets of the Old Testament, such as Jeremiah. Almost no one listened to them, and they ended being killed. As Jesus said, "O Jerusalem, Jerusalem, the city that kills the prophets and stones those who are sent to it!" (Luke 34:34) Who knows maybe God sent me as a "prophet" to help them.

I am happy to be considered the least of all priests, as a "sacramental priest". The only one in the diocese. I am the littlest of all priests. I am misunderstood, rejected, and abandoned—Praise the Lord! My last name "Gadfly" even means "Browbeat". St. Therese of Lisieux would love it! I had been praying the Litany of Humility, and by Joe, it certainly helped! To be despised and rejected is much better than being placed on a pedestal and becoming prideful.

It seems to me, Jesus through the bishop, took away one of my three munera (duties), we receive at our ordination, which is to teach, sanctify and govern. God gives and God takes away, blessed be God.

Blessed Father Solanus Casey, never received the gift to preach, or govern, or even hear confessions. His religious order gave him the title, "simplex priest." Yet, he may become a saint, and God used him to work thousands of miracles during his lifetime. A number of years ago, I was blessed to go to Detroit and prayed at his tomb. I'm sure this humble Franciscan is praying for me.

Bishop again gave permission to have a chapel with Jesus in the Most Blessed Sacrament reserved at the priest's house at my new assignment. What a beautiful grace to have Jesus with me! Thank you, Jesus!

#142 CHANCERY FILE

Chancery Personal File – Priest and Victim

Due to Bishop Forthright not wanting me in his diocese after seeing my personal file, my spiritual director suggested I review it and respond in truth to the false information contained within it. After three trips to the chancery and handwriting (the papers could not be copied nor taken home) comments about myself by those who said false things, and after having four priests examine my responses, I responded in truth about comments made by parishioners at Immaculate Heart of Mary parish in Wheatland and about administration at Mother of Misery Hospitals. It certainly was not my idea to even do this, but did it out of obedience to my spiritual director. In fact, I knew the outcome would make things worse.

I sent the information to chancellor, Fr. Gerry Meander, asking him to place the response in my personal chancery file. In the letter of introduction, I noted, "I forgive with all my heart. If God can be merciful to me, I can be merciful to others." I debated whether to send the response, or to delay in sending it, and prayed a Novena to St. Joseph to discern what to do.

Everyone I asked said to send the letter, including a religious priest who was an exorcist, who gave a presentation at the clergy conference in Rolling Hills.

But I believed it would do no good, and would only increase the ire of the bishop. I knew I needed to be prepared to enter more deeply into the victimhood of Christ. I believe the Lord was saying to me, "An ordained man is both priest and victim in imitation of Jesus, who is both priest and victim." Why should I expect anything else, for that is my role? To try to run from being a victim, one runs from the One who the priest is configured. This is who priests are, and we should expect to be both and delight in both.

#143 NEW NON-ECCLESIASTICAL TITLE: "SACRAMENTAL PRIEST"

A Sacramental Priest

In the letter he sent, the bishop gave me the title "Sacramental Priest" with my assignment at St. Timothy in Browbeat. My first thoughts were "What does that mean?" Those I asked including a Canon Lawyer said the same. None of the priests heard of giving a priest such a title. All the priests, with whom I discussed the title, thought the bishop purposely wanted to humiliate me. At first, I was repulsed by it, but then I rejoiced in it. My pride caused me to be offended by it, but now, it's my badge of honor and hopefully my glory in heaven. I don't mind being considered the least of priests, for truly that is what I am. Little did the bishop know, the title "Sacramental Priest" very well fits me. It would have been nice if he would have explained what it meant.

I resolved, the best of my ability, the problem of invalid Baptisms at Mother of Misery St. Henry campus given by lay people and religious sisters who used invalid formulas. The invalid baptisms caused other sacraments to be invalid such as Marriages, Confirmations, and to receive Communions sacrilegiously etc...

I notified Bishop Courageous that there are at least 10 priests in the diocese who potentially give invalid absolution in Confession. They partially use their own words when absolving. They do not say the minimal proper words. "I absolve you from your sins, in the name of the Father, and of the Son, and of the Holy Spirit. Amen."

I stopped a Benedictine monastery in Idaho from offering invalid Masses. I helped my own hometown parish of St. Gabriel's in Crossroads to offer valid Masses. Both places used the same invalid wine, "Carlos Rossi Blush" made of strawberries and cherries.

As a seminarian, I notified Bishop Basil Braveheart of homemade bread with honey and shortening used at Masses for St. Valentine parish in Hanover, Ohio (whether or not it's valid, only God knows).

In two parishes, St. Charles of Sezze in Rolling Hills and Immaculate Heart in Wheatland, I discovered priests performed multiple invalid weddings due to not obtaining annulments and rectified the marriages when possible.

I discovered a lay person was witnessing marriages and anointing the sick, and therefore, all were all invalid.

I called to task a priest at St. John of God Hospital in Tantrum who was making up his own words when giving Anointing of the Sick and reported him to the bishop of Tantrum after trying to convince him to use the proper words from the *Catechism*. After 16 years of hospital ministry (using invalid prayers), he finally anoints validly.

I hope I never discover invalid priestly ordinations, since I had to deal with all the other invalid sacraments. The title "Sacramental Priest" is truly fitting for me.

#144 ST. JOSEPH MOVES

St. Joseph Moves

In the early hours of July 25th, I had a short dream. I dreamt I saw a statue of St. Joseph holding the Child Jesus. The statue started to move. Then it came alive, and I woke up. As I was pondering the dream, I kept thinking I should do a novena to St. Joseph, especially for Dr. Jerome Bevilacqua. He is responsible for the misguided view throughout the diocese of not giving terminally ill and dying patients artificial nutrition and hydration when they could benefit from them.

I resolved to pray a novena to St. Joseph for Dr. Bevilacqua, Mother of Misery Hospitals in Rolling Hills and Woebegone Hospice, with a daily consecration to St. Joseph, as well as the Litany of St. Joseph and the prayer of his holy cloak. I started the novena during my Holy Hour that day, and then later, during the evening of July 25th, I had scheduled (a week earlier) to bless three homes in the city of Montecarlo for parishioners of St. Joseph parish. The three parishioners had serious disagreements with their pastor. And, consequently, asked me to bless their homes. After blessing the last home, the lady of the house gave me a bottle of St. Joseph oil from a convent in Sprocket, Washington, where the oil was placed before a statue of St. Joseph. When I looked on the intranet for the convent from Washington, where the oil came, I was surprised to see the same statue I had in my dream with St. Joseph holding the Child Jesus. When I returned to the rectory in Browbeat, I blessed myself with the oil for each of the nine days.

Nine days later, (Aug. 2nd) on the last day of the Novena, a parishioner of St. Timothy in Browbeat asked me to come to the church to help him *move* the statue of St. Joseph, since he wanted to put petitions under the statue. I gently *moved* the statue just enough, so the parishioner could put the petitions beneath it. Surely, God had all this in mind. I added some of my petitions under the statue. A few weeks later, I decided to place a petition under the statue of St. Joseph, asking him to build a new church at St. Timothy, which is far too small, and frankly, not very aesthetic.

#145 VACCINE MANDATE AND MY CONSCIENCE

Vaccine Mandate and Conscience

The US government, many businesses, and organizations are mandating COVID-19 vaccines. Two vaccine companies, Fitzgard and Mauzedug were supposedly not created by aborted embryonic cells, but were tested on them. Later, it became known they actually were created from aborted embryonic cells. The Johnnybegood vaccine was created and tested on aborted cells. According to the Congregation for the Doctrine of Faith (CDF),

> "The fundamental reason for considering the use of these vaccines morally licit is that the kind of cooperation in evil (passive material cooperation) in the procured abortion from which these cell lines originate is, on the part of those making use of the resulting vaccines, remote. The moral duty to avoid such passive material cooperation is not obligatory if there is a grave danger, such as the otherwise uncontainable spread of a serious pathological agent--in this case, the pandemic spread of the SARS-CoV-2 virus that causes COVID-19. It must therefore be considered that, in such a case, all vaccinations recognized as clinically safe and effective can be used in good conscience with the certain knowledge that the use of such vaccines does not constitute formal cooperation with the abortion from which the cells used in production of the vaccines derive. It should be emphasized, however, that the morally licit use of these types of vaccines, in the particular conditions that make it so, does not in itself constitute a legitimation, even indirect, of the practice of abortion, and necessarily assumes the opposition to this practice by those who make use of these vaccines. At the same time, practical reason makes evident, that vaccination is not, as a rule, a moral obligation and that, therefore, it must be voluntary. In any case, from the ethical point of view, the morality of vaccination depends not only on the duty to protect one's own health, but also on the duty to pursue the common good."

My formed conscience indicated I need to refuse the vaccine, for the following reasons. 1. It would be sinful for me to take a vaccine tested on aborted fetuses, since there is not a grave danger to my health and because the common good is not affected if I were to get COVID-19 without being vaccinated. 2. According to the CDC, the vaccinated and unvaccinated can both cause others to be infected. Therefore, the common good is not affected by whether one is vaccinated or not. 3. Since I had COVID-19 once, and most likely twice, and since both times there were no serious threats to my life, and because I recovered rather quickly, there is not a "grave danger" for myself due to natural

307

immunity. 4. The common good is also not affected, because I would not require hospitalization, which would have affected the ability of others to receive medical care, since hospitals at this time are nearly all full. 5. I prefer not to have anything to do with medicine created or tested unethically on unborn people, who are created in the image and likeness of God.

#146 HAUNTED HOUSE AND ATTACK AT MASS

Unhappy House Happenings

About a month after my arrival at St. Timothy in Browbeat at the house used as a rectory, even after I blessed the house, almost every night between 2am and 3am, I heard what sounded like someone knocking on the back door. I could hear the glass rattle, as the door was knocked. I told one of the parishioners about the knocking, who said it was most likely the water softener machine located in the closet of the chapel. But it turned out to not be the case. I later heard the softener machine, and it didn't sound like that at all. I thought perhaps there were high school youth making the noises almost every night. But then, I decided to throw blessed salt outside the door and I never heard the knocking again.

One day, I was sitting near the computer in the living room and I heard water running in the restroom. I thought maybe it was raining, but discovered the facet was running. I could not imagine leaving the water run after I washed my hands. One day, I went to lock up the church and when I came back to the house, the bedroom light was on. I began to wonder if I was having mental problems. How could I forget I did these things?

Another day, I was terribly physically shaken in the middle of the night. First, my right leg started shaking. Then it went through my whole body. I believed it was an evil spirit since I was preaching so much on Eucharistic Adoration. I began to wonder if these things were auto-suggestive, but later turned out not to be the case, especially after I visited with an exorcist, who assured me, it was not.

Homily on Sign-up Day for Extended Eucharistic Adoration

During Sign-up Day at Mass, after I almost finished the homily, a thought occurred to me. God was going to touch the hearts of all these people through adoration, and He used me to do it. Suddenly, I became emotional and nearly cried. For the life of me, I could not continue on with the homily. While I never had actual tears fall from my eyes, I could not read the homily since I was choked up. I apologized to the people and told them I suspect they never saw a priest cry during a homily, and then I said, "Neither did I". It really shook me up. I finally was able to continue the homily cutting it short and then continued on with Mass, but due to what happened, was very distracted.

Later, as I was thinking about what happened, I thought one of three things could have caused it. 1. The Holy Spirit moved me to become emotional and overwhelmed. 2. I may have had a stroke. 3. An evil spirit attacked me to prevent me from finishing the homily and caused me to be distracted during the rest of the Mass.

Doctor Knows Best

I visited with my spiritual director and told him I was going to see my doctor about the events at the house and also what happened during the homily. The doctor, surprisingly said, "Father, your health is fine. You need to have your house blessed." He said, "You had stroke symptoms, but you should have also experienced paralysis, but didn't." He prescribed baby aspirin. After reflecting upon what happened, I believe it was an evil spirit, since God would not want me to be distracted during Mass. The Lord permitted it, to humble me.

I learned later that Laura Tapper, the owner of the house died in the same room where I normally sleep. I thought, maybe she wanted to have Masses offered for her. Consequently, I scheduled several more Masses and the unhappy house happenings stopped. I also remembered her at the Consecration during Mass.

#147 VACCINE EXEMPTION LETTER

Vaccine Conscience Exemption Letter

A lay Catholic chaplain at Mother of Misery Healthcare System asked me to create a Conscience Exemption Letter for her daughter, who is a nurse at a hospital in Mississippi. I used the Colorado Bishops' Pastoral Letter Template to create the letter and quoted her daughter, who said, taking the vaccine goes against her conscience. The hospital accepted the letter, and she was able to avoid the vaccine. In all sorts of businesses, many were fired for not taking the vaccine.

A few weeks later, Bishop Courageous emailed the priests saying we couldn't give conscience exemption letters. Some bishops permit priests to write letters explaining how a Catholic may choose to object. Other bishops, including our own, did not believe any Catholic could have any conscience objection. How strange is that! Morality can't be different from diocese to diocese.

A couple, who are parishioners at St. Timothy, have two sons in the military. Neither of the men wanted to take the vaccine. The parents asked me to write a letter of exemption for their sons, but I told them I couldn't, since the bishop told the priests they couldn't write them.

I decided to create a letter to put in the bulletin, explaining what the Church teaches on conscience about the COVID-19 vaccine, which would also help form the conscience of parishioners. It was not a conscience exemption letter, but an explanation of what the Church taught on conscience. To create the document, I used the International Catholic Bioethics Center of America Letter for conscience exemption, and also the Colorado

Bishops' template for conscience exemption and added more information. It was placed in the bulletin for all parishioners. The people need to know the Church's teachings on conscience, so they can decide for themselves with a formed conscience. The priest has an obligation to form their conscience. A year later, when the bishop came to our parish for a pastoral visit, a parishioner asked the bishop why priests could not write conscience objection letters. The bishop said, he never told priests they couldn't. The parishioner didn't know if he should believe me or the bishop and consequently, I gave a copy of the email that the bishop sent to us priests, which proved otherwise. Perhaps, the bishop misunderstood his question.

#148 PAGE TORN OUT AND MISSING

#149 6TH TRIP TO MEDJUGORJE 2021

Medjugorje Pilgrimage Sept. 29th through Oct. 6Th 2021

Archie Christopher invited me to go on a pilgrimage to Medjugorje. It was paid by some of his benefactors, who wanted priests to go to Medjugorje. At the time he asked me to go, I was very distraught by the hospital situation, and nothing being done about their unethical actions. I really didn't care whether I would go to Medjugorje. This shows the depth of anguish I experienced, which resulted in me feeling abandoned by God from January 22nd until May 30, Trinity Sunday.

I took the risk of flying even though most countries wanted plane passengers to be vaccinated, and I was not going to do that. By God's grace, all that was needed was to take a COVID-19 test before leaving and before returning.

The required antigen test for COVID-19 was negative. We arrived in Medjugorje, Sept. 29th, the feast of the archangels and had Mass at the Two Hearts Hotel Chapel. The following day, I was the main celebrant for the English-speaking Mass held at the JP II Center in Medjugorje. The JP II Center was large enough to hold at least 800. I hadn't offered a Mass with that many in attendance, since I was at St. Gertrude parish, in the diocese of Rolling Hills.

I created three different homilies, because I wanted to give the best homily possible. The final homily, mostly written in the middle of the night, was said to be fruitful by those who attended. During the Mass, a pilgrim collapsed and doctors were summoned. At the end of Mass, I led the people in praying the Hail Mary for the man, who later expressed his appreciation. I attempted to anoint him immediately after Mass, but he was taken by EMT's before I could get to him.

Just before Mass, Fr. Leland Pentagon and I were talking about the current conditions in the world and the church, and I mentioned I thought a persecution was about to break out. Surprisingly, he mentioned the upcoming possibility of martyrdom for Christians in his short talk before Mass.

The rest of the day was spent in prayer and visiting a few shops to purchase rosaries and holy cards for the people of St. Timothy. I was looking forward to placing the religious items at the base of the apparition, to have them blessed by the Virgin Mary.

Later that evening, I went to Ivan's house. At the beginning of the apparition, he looked up and began to smile. As he spoke to Our Lady, I immediately felt a burden lift from my shoulders and began to pray for as many as I could, especially for the intentions of those I placed in a basket before Ivan. Rosaries and prayer cards were also placed not far from the apparition and afterwards, Ivan said Our Lady blessed all religious objects.

After the apparition, I had a wonderful sense of peace. Ivan said Our Lady appeared with two angels, and left with a white cross in the sky. He said Our Lady gave him a personal message, which caused him great joy. He said Our Lady prayed over the priests and also prayed over the sick who were present.

Other special graces occurred when we went up Apparition Hill as a group. I also went up Apparition Hill, one night and another time during the day. It seemed like every time I went up the hill and started to pray, someone disturbed my prayer. When I was waiting in line to venerate a Crucifix on the hill, a woman bumped up against me with her breasts and then butted in line. My reaction wasn't good. I had a wooden staff with me and placed it in front of her and told her she needed to take her turn. I felt bad about doing such a thing. I could have been more humble and just let her go ahead.

On Oct. 3rd, the eve of the feast of St. Francis, we went to Siroki Brijeg, where over twenty Franciscans were martyred. They were told that if they spit on the crucifix and take off their habit, they would live, but all refused and were killed. Some were burned alive in the underground cave. It was very moving to touch the soil and see the place they were martyred. I prayed, if it would be God's will and by His grace alone, someday, I too would be martyred. In one of the buildings near the site, there was some very strange "religious art". It was sad to see the warped looking images at such a holy place. I was the main celebrant when I offered Mass at the church and preached about the "feeling prayer" although most couldn't hear what I said due to the echo in the church.

At the beginning of the day, Oct. 4Th, we had Mass in the Chapel of the hotel, since we had plans to go up the mountain at the same time the English Mass was offered. On the feast of St. Francis of Assisi, we went up the rocky high mountain called Holy Cross Mountain (Krizevac).

I attempted to walk barefoot, but found myself lagging very far behind, and since I was leading prayers, as we went up, I decided to put my shoes back on. My penance was to accept the fact I couldn't do as much penance as I wanted. The bottom of my feet were very tender due to orthotic shoe inserts I regularly wear. I was unable to tolerate the sharp rocks. Out of humility I had to admit I was unable to do the penance I wanted, and realized the Lord was pleased with me accepting my weakness.

At St. James church, I asked St. Francis to help me come to know if I would ever be a Franciscan religious again. Later that evening, I attended an English speaking Mass on the feast of St. Francis. I was surprised they treated it as a feast rather than a solemnity, since they were Franciscans. The homily given by a Franciscan was similar to the one I gave at the hotel Chapel. At the Mass, I met a priest I went to seminary with at St. Robert Bellarmine Seminary. We both recognized each other, but we could not recall each other's names. I told him I was a Franciscan of Perpetual Victim Martyrs at the time. I thought how fascinating we met on the feast of St. Francis of Assisi.

I met a priest from Ireland, who told me the priests in his diocese have no health insurance, and he hadn't seen a doctor for years because he couldn't afford the appointment. The poor priest had great difficulty walking due to arthritis. I gave him the name of a medicine I use and found very successful. I went to confession to him, and received great advice.

Fr. Petar Ljubicic, who will receive the secrets and reveal them, spoke to our group at the hotel lobby. His words seemed to be directed specifically towards me. He said we can't go on expressing our victimhood, but rather, accept suffering as it comes. He gave the example of a woman who suffered tremendously but never complained. He said that we should want to suffer, and not reject it as it comes.

Three nights I was in Medjugorje, I heard confessions for about 3 to 4 hours. Many confessions were beautiful. I went to confession to Fr. Michael O' Malley and told him about the situation with the hospital and what happened to me due to it, explaining I am now a "sacramental priest". Interestingly, he was sidelined in the early 80s and was never given an assignment. Consequently, he started his apostolate called "Jesus Ministries". He gives talks and is a chaplain for pilgrimages to various places. At the English-speaking Mass, he gave a homily, and when finished, the crowd erupted with applause. He encouraged me stating I wasn't the problem. But rather, he said all who have no faith are the problem. This removed doubts from my mind to help me know what I did at the hospital was pleasing to God.

On October 5Th, the feast of St. Faustina, I was blessed to have been asked to be the main and only celebrant for our group at the Shrine of Divine Mercy, not far from Medjugorje. The Mass was providentially scheduled for 3pm, and so, we prayed the Chaplet of Divine Mercy before Mass. After Mass, we venerated the relics of St. Faustina and Pope St. John Paul II. The image placed above the altar is believed to be miraculous, due to a miracle approved by the Church, which, the director of the shrine said, led to the canonization of Pope St. John Paul II.

Our group was wonderful. There were native Indians from Canada and two were of the Sioux tribe, the same tribe of Standing Buffalo. I showed Rhonda Burner, a native Indian, before and after photos from the monument of Standing Buffalo. The photos showed the before and after imprint of the cross that was added to the monument, after

I had prayed, wondering if Standing Buffalo was in heaven. She exclaimed, "It's a miracle! And will bring about reconciliation."

There are other interesting facts about my trip to Medjugorje. At Medjugorje, I felt inadequate with my devotion to the Blessed Virgin Mary and that the Lord wanted me to invite Mary, into all that I do and grow in my relationship with Her.

There were a few other interesting things about the trip. We visited the site where Fr. Slavko was buried. Our pilgrimage leader mentioned she and Ivan didn't get along since he has an explosive temper. I felt like it wasn't good idea for her to mention that to our group, even if it was true. We are all human.

We visited the Resurrected Christ statue, where supposedly, the legs of Jesus drip water and miracles have allegedly taken place there. However, the parish has officially said nothing supernatural is occurring at the Resurrected Christ statue. Honestly, I think the statue is rather ugly.

There were so many other graces I received at Medjugorje, but these are the ones I chose to write about.

Return From Medjugorje & Weird Things

Since it's located near the airport, before leaving for the trip, I left my car in the parking lot of St. Charles of Sezze parish and when I returned from Medjugorje, someone hit the vehicle. It was scratched on one side, and a rearview mirrored was moved.

The following day after returning from Medjugorje I was attacked by wild dogs. Although I wasn't bitten, the dogs caused quite the ruckus when they tried to bite me. One bit my pants, and as a result, I smacked it in the face with my Breviary that I happen to be carrying with me. The impact from slapping its face caused saliva from the dog to splatter on my hands.

I mentioned the incident to the wrong person, the lady postmaster, who told many what happened. And then, I received calls from people asking if I had been injured.

When I arrived at the church from being out of town for ten days the basement was flooded due to a broken water-line, and it was several inches deep.

Several parishioners complained to Fr. Jeremiah Bullfrog about the vaccination presentation I gave at the parish hall and the document I put in the bulletin explaining the role of conscience for Catholics. The president of the bank and his sister were both Democrats and asked me to encourage the use of masks and vaccines. But I gave a balanced approach at the presentation, and said I only tell people to do whatever the bishop wanted. The president of the bank acted very immature and literally squirmed as I gave the presentation. These poor people don't understand how being a member of the Democratic Party, which promotes communism, socialism, abortion, and homosexual marriage, causes the devil to influence their behavior. The couple decided to discontinue attending Mass at St. Timothy and every weekend, drive 25 miles to another parish.

I haven't heard from Fr. Jeremiah yet, but I am sure when it happens, he will tell the bishop about it.

An Unhappy House, Becomes a Happy House

Before my trip to Medjugorje, I offered a Mass for the soul of Laura Tapper, who died in the house, for all the others who may have died in the house and asked the Lord to remove all demons from it. And since then, I never had any of these kinds of problems again. Praise the Lord!

#150 FOOT OR HAND

Pro-Life Bill- "It's a Foot or a Hand", Summer of Hope and the Incinerator

"Their slain shall be cast out, their corpses shall send up a stench; the mountains shall run with their blood." (Isaiah 34:3)

During the Clergy Conference in 2021, Jesse Waters spoke about the problem of abortion in the state of Ohio. This year, the bishops of Ohio are promoting some limits on abortion. This brought back a flood of memories as to how I progressed in my understanding of the evil of abortion.

Sadly, I helped arrange an abortion for a friend, although the baby died by miscarriage before he or she could be aborted. Back then, when I was 18 or 19, I believed abortion was wrong, but also thought, wrongly, that a person has a right to do what they want. Not thinking that they don't have a right to kill another person or that unborn children have rights.

However, a few years later, I came to understand the fullness of this seriously wrong view and that it is always wrong to harm an innocent person. While I was working at Nedley Regional Medical Center at Fort Hickok, in the surgical and sterilization department one day, when cleaning surgical instruments from a miscarriage, I noticed a tiny hand or foot on a curette.

This event caused me to realize a person is a person, no matter how small. It made me strongly pro-life. I later discovered Bernard Nathanson, an abortionist, who became Catholic, and Abby Johnson, a former director of Planned Parenthood, who also became Catholic, both had conversions after seeing an unborn child die while watching an abortion on an ultrasound image.

Dr. Nathanson described the "Silent Scream" of the unborn baby, as he saw the abortion on the ultrasound. Abby saw the baby move about in the womb until it was killed by the abortionist, with whom she was assisting. All three of us have something in common, we saw something horrifying happen to a baby that caused us to wake up to the truth.

A few years after the event of seeing the tiny foot or hand, I drove to Rolling Hills from Fort Hickcok in what was called the "Summer of Hope". Thousands of people, mostly from Ohio, came to Rolling Hills to protest Schindler's Abortion Clinic. Many were arrested, including priests and religious sisters. Back then, there was a small monetary fine, and once paid, arrested individuals would return the next day to block the entrance of the clinic.

I went to Rolling Hills for the pro-life events and recall going to Schindler's for the first time. As I came to the clinic, there was a horrid smell coming from a machine near the alley. I discovered it was an incinerator used to burn dead babies. When I found out what was causing the odor, I became nauseated and almost vomited.

An anti-abortion rally was held at the stadium. It was packed with thousands of people. Robert Robertson from the Holy Broadcast Network was there and Bishop John Fidelity of the Diocese of Rolling Hills, who also gave a talk. At the event, a man was jumping up and down and acting crazy (certainly mentally ill). Everyone else was orderly and praying in a mostly quiet manner. Yet, on television news that evening, and on the front page of the Rolling Hills Morning Sun, was that crazy man. The media made it appear as though everyone at the event, were radical and crazy like him. That was the first time, I realized the media twists and reports events to make it appear different from what actually occurs due to their liberal way of viewing things.

Fr. Bart Gregarious was giving talks in parishes throughout Ohio, and I secretly hoped I could do the same. But I certainly do not have the gift of preaching as he. At times, I felt I could be doing much more for the pro-life movement, but feel inadequate, perhaps because I really am.

I watched the movie "Unplanned" while in Tantrum, and later discovered it was filmed in nearby Coldwater, Idaho. The movie is about Abby Johnson's story and conversion to the pro-life movement.

Bishop Courageous asked priests of our diocese to preach on abortion, and the pro-life amendment on the weekend of Oct. 24th, 2021.

During the homily at the Saturday evening Mass, since no children were present, I explicitly mentioned how I saw a tiny foot when cleaning surgical instruments many years ago while working in the sterilization department of a hospital. In the bulletin, I also attached a clip art diagram of a partial birth abortion and D and E abortion, so parishioners could see what happens during them.

At Sunday's Mass with children, I didn't mention the foot. But said I saw something that shocked me and then discovered I had cleaned instruments from a miscarriage. I would like to do more for the pro-life movement, but what can I do?

#151 CLERGY CONFERENCE AND DINNER WITH BISHOP

Clergy Conference and Dinner with Bishop

A few weeks ago, during the Clergy Conference, I met Bishop Courageous, who walked up to me, and said, "Oh, Fr. Gadfly. Sometime, I would like to come and visit you at Browbeat. I don't want to talk about anything from the past. I just want to get to know you, so you and I can be friends."

A few days after the Clergy Conference, I received an email from the bishop's secretary, who invited me and some other priests to have dinner at his house. The note said it was a casual event, meaning the bishop expected priests to wear layman's clothes. On November 2nd, All Souls' Day, the bishop invited five priests to have dinner at his house. On that day, I had other places to go in the city, and therefore, wore my clerics to dinner. I was glad I didn't wear my suit jacket to dinner, as that would have been way too formal.

When I arrived at his house, I mistakenly patted the bishop on his shoulder, attempting to express comfort to him, since the day before the dinner, a priest from our diocese, Fr. Tiny Tim, was accused of sexual abuse of a minor. The bishop didn't appear to like the tap on his shoulder.

During the dinner, I made the mistake of interjecting in conversation. The bishop expressed sadness about Gabriel Badsong, who created the hymn, "On Sparrow's Wings". I told the Bishop, that Badsong was known for his pro-homosexual stance, and the bishop stated he doubted that was the case. Based upon his reaction as we discussed the topic further, I had the impression I should have changed the subject.

The conversation finally switched, as several priests spoke about the trials of their leg injuries.

#152 DIVINE CHILD APPEARED IN THE TABERNACLE
MIGRAINES, DREAM, ST. FAUSTINA

Nov. 4th, 2021 St. Charles Borromeo

Yesterday, during the Eucharistic Prayer, I had some terribly wicked, distracting thoughts. But, when I opened the Tabernacle during Mass, I suddenly saw the Child Jesus sitting there and the thoughts vanished. In my mind, I said to Him, "I haven't seen you for a while. I missed you." To keep my mind focused on the Mass, I continued as normal. Perhaps the enemy knew I was going to receive extra grace from Jesus, and so tried to take away my peace. After Mass, I blessed the church and sprinkled it with holy water.

Arthritis and Migraines

I have frequent bad headaches, including migraines. The medicine I'm taking greatly upsets my stomach, but it causes headaches to go away. Since my stomach is so upset, I decided to quit taking the medicine, resulting in more migraines. "O Jesus, I am so weak and turn to medicine so frequently. But the pain is so intense I can't think clearly, and at times, I am confused because my head hurts. I don't suffer well, but I know suffering is so precious in this life, and I wish I could suffer much better than I do. I don't want to take medicine, and to just offer it up. But, do You want me to be confused and disoriented from the pain? O Lord, help me to suffer willingly for love of you, for the conversion of sinners, the poor souls in purgatory, and in reparation for sins committed against your Sacred Heart and the Immaculate Heart of Mary. Jesus, I am afraid the arthritis inflammation will overwhelm me, but I trust in You. Help me, Lord!"

Dream of Red Vestments

A few nights ago, I dreamt about a group of priests who were vesting in red vestments before Mass. I became aware of the reason they were dressing in red, was because they were martyrs of a vaccine mandate. They all had refused to take the vaccine. I was putting on the red vestment as well when I woke up from the dream.

St. Faustina's Diary

While praying during Eucharistic Adoration, I was motivated by the Holy Spirit to look at the *Diary of St. Faustina,* and happened to turn to paragraphs 841 to 848, where St. Faustina saw the Child Jesus at Mass. Jesus said to her, "Oh, what graces I will grant to souls who say this chaplet; the very depths of My tender mercy are stirred for the sake of those who say the chaplet. Write down these words, My daughter. Speak to the world about my mercy; let all mankind recognize My unfathomable mercy. It is a sign of the end times; after it, will come the day of justice. While there is still time, let them have recourse to the fount of my mercy; let them profit from the blood and water which gushed forth for them." (#848)

I believe Jesus wants me to speak of this, but where do I have the opportunity? Our Lord has repeated this to me. That we are in the time of mercy, but His Justice is near, and He wants me to speak of it. As a result, several weeks ago in a homily, I spoke about God's infinite mercy and abortion. Am I to do this in another parish, or at the Happy Soul Retreat House, or here at my parish?

I sent a letter to the priest director of Happy Soul Retreat House and also to a parish priest mentioning I am available to give talks, but neither responded. What do I do? I believe the time is very short, and very near. I must wait on Jesus to show me what to do.

I prayed the Chaplet of Divine Mercy over and over again to resolve the unethical problems while doing ministry at the hospital. But nothing seems to come of it. There was no change in the practice of artificial nutrition and hydration needed by patients, who could benefit from them, and all the other unethical practices at the hospital. Even though I saw nothing good come out of it, Jesus, I trust in You!

#153 CHANCERY FILE REJECTED

Nov. 12Th, Memorial of St. Josaphat, Truth Denied & File Information Rejected

"He who listens to you listens to me; he who rejects you rejects me; but he who rejects me rejects him who sent me." (Luke 10:16)

On Sunday, Nov. 7th, I gave Fr. Gerry Meander a call to see if the information sent to him and the bishop, was placed in my personal file. He said the bishop does not want it my file at the chancery. Fr. Meander said, "I read it and spoke to the bishop about some things that were not true in it." He said, "I know I was there." I said, "What are you talking about, you were not present at Mother of Misery Healthcare System or Immaculate Heart of Mary parish." He said, "You said the bishop gave approval to doctors to prescribe contraception for fear of losing doctors. But that isn't true." Little did he know three priests read the file information before given to the bishop. None disagreed with the statement. All priests, who were at the meeting, knew the bishop gave approval, since he himself said so, during the meeting with the priests. Doctors at Mother of Misery Healthcare also believe the bishop gave approval. Apparently, the bishop never read the file information sent to him.

After visiting with Fr. Meander, I became angry because the truth was denied. Jesus is the truth and Jesus was rejected. Fr. Bob Sorghum read the information before it was sent to the bishop, and consequently, I gave him a call. He is much more sympathetic towards the bishop than other priests. Despite his sympathy, he said, "It was rejected because it pricked their conscience. And they don't want to deal with their conscience." He said, "I admire your courage, and think you are a glutton for punishment."

After this, I tried to deal with anger. I made acts of forgiveness and prayed the Lord would help me to be merciful to the bishop and Fr. Gerry Meander. How difficult it is to be merciful and how beautiful is sacramental grace. Through Confession, we receive grace to open our hearts to be more merciful. If we only take a little step seeking God's mercy and come to Jesus in Confession, He overwhelms us with His mercy, so we can be merciful to others. Our Lady of Good Success, pray for us, who have recourse to thee!

#154 WHO WILL STAND UP FOR JESUS IN THE EUCHARIST?

US Bishops Vote 222 to 8 on Eucharist Document

"Nevertheless, when the Son of Man cometh, shall he find faith on the earth?" (Luke 18:8)

The document on the Eucharist, created by the US Bishops at their summer conference, failed to mention anything about pro-abortion politicians receiving Holy Communion. President Joe Biden said that Pope Francis said told him he could continue to receive Holy Communion. Only God and the two men know if that is true or not.

Vatican News Times interviewed disgraced Cardinal Clampet, who encouraged the bishops not to include anything in the document about the subject.

This event reminded me, when all bishops of England, except St. John Fischer, obeyed King Henry VIII, rather than following the pope, and he became a martyr. How could so many bishops, by their silence, approve of Eucharistic sacrilege? Are they afraid of political consequences for proclaiming the truth?

There was a sign of lack of faith in the Eucharist in our own diocese. Bishop Courageous told a priest from the Diocese of Rolling Hills, "I heard you make a Holy Hour every morning?" The priest responded, "Yes bishop, I do." Bishop said, "What good is that, when you have so many problems in your parish?"

In my opinion, the more difficulties a priest has in the parish, the more often he should be praying before Jesus in the Blessed Sacrament. Priests should turn to Jesus, spending time with Him in Adoration for their every need, and there, they will find consolation in His presence, and grace to persevere through difficulties.

The US bishops declared a Eucharistic revival, but refused to defend Jesus in the Eucharist by permitting radical "Catholic" politicians to promote the killing of unborn babies and receive Jesus in Holy Communion. Some accuse the Vatican of telling bishops to be silent. O Lord, I lift up our bishops to Your throne, and ask You to give them the strength and courage to be witnesses for the faith, even to death, like St. John Fischer.

#155 ALTAR SERVER FROM PREVIOUS PARISH OVERDOSES

Heartbroken Due to Former Altar Server Overdosing Twice in a Week

The parents of Bart Goodboy were deeply hurt and in terrible anguish due to their son's overdose. Only those who endure such a tragedy could understand their pain. The last time he overdosed, his mother, a nurse, saved his life by performing CPR. He stopped breathing and his heart stopped. How could this happen to a former altar server, who is now twenty years old? He comes from one of the most faithful families at Immaculate

Heart of Mary in Wheatland and is now addicted to Fentanyl. It is my understanding some Fentanyl pills are so potent, just one can cause an overdose or even kill the user.

I anointed Bart and gave him the Apostolic Pardon. I also prayed St. John Chrysostom's Exorcism Prayer over him that any priest may pray. I asked his parents to consecrate their son and their family to the Hearts of Jesus and Mary for help and protection.

#156 IRONIES

Ironies and Providential Coincidences

The White Cross. When I was the same age as Bart, who overdosed, a friend offered me "white crosses", a drug. I refused, and told him he would not be my friend anymore if he kept using drugs. If I had taken it, what would have happened? Addicted to drugs? By the grace of God, what happened to the former altar server, could have been me. How ironic, soon after I refused to take the White Cross drug, I joined the Sigh Fi Gamma Fraternity, whose symbol was the "White Cross", as it appeared in the sky for Constantine, "In This Sign You Will Conquer".

$6,900. The amount of $6,900, owed on my college loan, was paid off when I received a $10,000 check from my pension at Nedley Regional Medical Center. The chalice, the people from the Church of the Ascension purchased for my ordination cost $6,900, was the same amount as my college loans paid off by Our Lady.

Transfer Day to a New Assignment. The day I called a bishop in Idaho about invalid Masses in his archdiocese caused by invalid wine made of cherries and strawberries, was the same day Bishop Courageous called, and asked me to be chaplain at St. Henry hospital, where I would later discover invalid baptisms were performed many years by the Sisters of Misery and lay chaplains.

Hospital. Before my conversion, in the 1980s, I was a member of the Infection Control Committee at Nedley Hospital. Interestingly, when the pandemic broke out some 35 years later, I was doing hospital ministry, and needed to wear personal protective equipment to deal with a virus. And therefore, I had basic knowledge about bacteria and viruses that was helpful in dealing with the pandemic.

Dying Grandmother. When I was 26 years old, I was present at my grandmother's death. It helped to bring about my conversion. Later, as a priest, while doing hospital ministry, I witnessed the deaths of many, helped those who were dying to come to conversion before their deaths, and consoled family members at the deaths of their loved ones.

Drugs. When I was the pastor at Immaculate Heart of Mary parish, we set up a video camera and captured high school youth involved in drug deals behind the church. I asked the principal of the school to watch the video to see who the youth were. Five years later, the principal's boy, a former altar server, Bart, overdosed twice in one month.

Crucifixes. Over a period of several months, I replaced all "resurrected" crosses at St. Henry and St. Mother Cope hospitals in patient rooms with a crucifix. The last crucifix replaced was the Feast of the Triumph of the Cross.

Transfer Day to New Assignment. The bishop emailed me my new assignment of St. Timothy in Browbeat on the weekend of the feast of St. Timothy.

Defending Life. The day I was "fired" from the hospital for defending life and speaking up against the hospital's unethical practices, was Jan. 22nd, the Anniversary of Roe vs. Wade. They failed to give artificial nutrition and hydration to dying patients, who could benefit from them, and mercy killing, abortion, sterilization, and contraception.

Cars. Two cars were given to me as a gift when I was a seminarian by my stepfather. I later gave three of my cars away. One to my nephew, one to my brother, and one to my sister, and I paid off the truck of my brother-in-law, who died.

Dilution of Alcohol. I added water to my father's liquor to dilute it, so he wouldn't get drunk so easily. The first Mass I offered as a priest may have been invalid because the pastor mixed large quantities of water with wine (diluting it) due to his diabetic condition.

Holy Sacrifice of the Mass. After twelve years of invalid Masses offered by the pastors of St. Gabriel's parish in Crossroads, and after I unknowingly offered twelve invalid Masses at St. Gabriel's in Crossroads, the first valid Mass I offered in that parish was on Trinity Sunday. The pastor asked me to take the Mass and I preached about the Mass as a sacrifice, but not remembering at the time, they hadn't had the sacrifice of the Mass for twelve years.

Bishops Coming and Going. I had a Novena of Masses offered at the Cathedral for Bishop Traditiones to have him transferred. Amazingly, on the last day of the Novena, he announced he was going to be the archbishop of Battle Creek, Michigan. The announcement of the new bishop, Bishop Courageous, stating he would be our next bishop, was on the same day, as my birthday.

Sacramental Priest. I received the title "Sacramental Priest." When the title was given me, the bishop did not know the Lord used me to help a parish and a monastery have a valid Mass, due to wine being used made from cherries and strawberries. Nor did make the connection of my role in returning valid baptisms at Mother of Misery St. Henry. Or that, I stopped some priests from absolving sins invalidly since they were not using proper words of absolution. Or that I helped a priest to validly anoint the sick, after his 16 years of anointing invalidly. Or helped invalidly married couples, due to liberal priests not obtaining annulments, to exchange vows validly. Or helped a parish, a shrine, and a religious order to discontinue using outdated wine, which may have

321

rendered the Mass invalid. Our Lady of Good Success, pray for us, who have recourse to thee!

Standing Buffalo and Indians. My spiritual director suggested I pray to Standing Buffalo, to know where the Lord wanted me for my next assignment. Ironically, I was assigned to St. Timothy in Browbeat City, whose school mascot is the Indians.

St. Gertrude. When I was a deacon, after praying at the tomb of St. Gertrude asking for a good first assignment as a priest, I was assigned to St. Gertrude parish.

#157 THE PAINS OF A HAPPY DEATH

Pains of a Happy Death (Tragedy, Trauma, and Redemption)

I witnessed a couple's marriage seven years ago. Brayden, the groom, recently called. I had known him since he was a youth, when I was an associate priest at St. Charles of Sezze Parish. When he called, he was in panic mode. In the past month, he said many very difficult things had happened to him and his wife, Millie.

As a police officer, he was required to fatally shoot a man who opened fire on another police officer. The officer's partner was shot in the face and needed reconstructive surgery. The following day Brayden was called to the home of a shooting where an eight-year-old boy accidentally shot his nineteen-year-old brother "blowing his head off". The trauma of these two events was exacerbated due to Millie hearing a voice, calling her name at home. She was a therapist and counseled a teenage girl, a self-professed "white witch". The witch gave Millie a "New Age" rock, which may have been the cause of many difficulties.

Occasionally, Millie saw a figure of a man walk through her bedroom, but no one was there. He came in and out of the closet. I asked Brayden if anything in the closet didn't belong to Millie or him. In the closet was a shirt from Good Hope Free Store, used for a Halloween costume. Due to his wife's strange events, he threw the shirt away. He said a detergent bottle fell off the dryer by itself and the couple heard three knocks in the middle of the night.

Strangely, a few nights before Brayden called, I heard three knocks at the backdoor of my rectory. A few weeks earlier a bottle of detergent fell off the washer and landed on its cap, causing it to burst, throwing liquid detergent all over the cabinets, refrigerator, and floor. How mysterious!

During this time, Millie's father was dying at the hospital. I gave the couple deliverance prayers to pray and encouraged them to confess to a priest. I suggested they ask their pastor to bless their house, and if needed, ask him to offer a Mass at their home. I encouraged Millie to confess that she kept the rock on her desk, and therefore, she gave credence to it. I also suggested, that she throw the rock away and ask a priest to bless her office.

While on the phone, Brayden said when he was a child, he played the Ouija board. I encouraged him to mention it in confession. Their pastor blessed their home, heard their confessions, and offered Mass in their home.

The following day, on Nov. 21st, 2021, her father died. Her father hadn't been to confession for years. But, while in the hospital, he experienced a frightening event saying, "There's a bunch of demons around my bed". As a result to his experience, he went confession, received the Sacrament of the Sick, the Apostolic Pardon, Holy Communion, and prayed the Rosary frequently.

Millie may have been suffering for her father who was dying. The Mass and confessions cleared up their problems in their home. He received the grace of a happy death. Millie and Brayden had their sins forgiven, and were drawn closer to the Lord, who prepared them for the death of her father.

#158 ENEMY ATTACKS

Dec. 20th Night, Early Dec. 21st, 2021 (The Enemy Attacks)

I had difficulty falling asleep, but eventually fell asleep in the wee hours of the night, but then I awoke to an attack of an evil spirit. I had thoughts of lies accusing me of all sorts of vile things which I did not do. I was severely mentally tormented. I began to pray the Litany of Saints with as many saints as I could think of, but the thoughts persisted. I called on St. Michael repeatedly, and my Guardian Angel, and St. Joseph, and the Blessed Mother, all to no avail. The Lord wanted me to suffer for some purpose. Then the evil spirit shook me so hard, I flopped like a fish out of water lying on the bed. It finally stopped, but the mental anguish continued and was unbearable.

Consequently, I got out of bed, and came before Jesus in the Tabernacle and begged Him to help me. I turned on the lights and did the Minor Exorcism Prayer of St. John Chrysostom. As I prayed, the thoughts slowly subsided and disappeared. I thanked the good Lord for helping me in my great time of need.

I wondered if this was due to the Novena of Masses at St. Timothy for our country to overturn Roe vs. Wade, and to end abortion, or was it due to a Guardian of the Holy Grail brother and I, who planted Miraculous Medals around a Masonic Temple in Hodgenville. We placed them at the temple when I was on retreat last week. Could it be the result of praying with a group of people at the abortion clinic there in Hodgenville?

I thought maybe I would have a big fish for confession that morning. I went to church early to get ready for Mass. Then someone came to the church, and I heard their confession. It was a big fish. Now I know why I suffered so dreadfully that night. It was worth it.

Consequently, during Mass, I offered up the terrible experience in union with the sacrifice of Jesus on the Altar, for the conversion of the people of St. Timothy.

I went to confession later that day, and asked a priest friend to pray a minor exorcism (any priest can pray) over me. Afterwards, it was as though these things never happened. Instant peace.

#159 HOLY INNOCENTS & THE SEVEN CANDLES

Dec. 28th, 2021- Holy Innocents & The Seven Candles

"Then Herod, when he saw that he had been tricked by the wise men, became furious, and he sent and killed all the male children in Bethlehem and in all that region who were two years old or under, according to the time that he had ascertained from the wise men." (Matthew 2:16)

Today, I was pondering about my pilgrimage to the Holy Land while I was an associate priest (parochial vicar) at St. Charles of Sezze parish. While in Bethlehem, our group visited the Church of the Nativity, where Jesus was born. Since our group was small, I couldn't offer Mass at one of the main altars, but rather, the altar of St. Jerome's Cave. St. Jerome lived in a cave close to the cave where Jesus was born. There, in his cave, he translated the entire bible from Greek into Latin. The Church of the Nativity was built on top of the cave where Jesus was born and laid in a manger. But it was also built over the cave St. Jerome lived and translated the Bible.

While offering Mass on the altar in the cave of St. Jerome, the Mass intention was for an end to abortion. Interestingly, the night before we came to the Church of the Nativity, I dreamt Dr. Schindler, the abortionist in Rolling Hills, repented of performing abortions. After Mass, the tour guide pointed out, adjacent to St. Jerome's cave, where I offered Mass, the Holy Innocents were originally buried. I was stunned! As I knelt down to pray before the burial site, I thought of all the children who had died at the time of Herod, and all their parents, who wept bitterly over the death of their children. Back then, Herod killed children in Bethlehem, and today abortionists kill unborn children at abortion clinics. Today, political leaders promote the killing of the unborn and push for embryonic stem cell research. At the time of Herod, his soldiers killed the many boys in Bethlehem, causing parents to grieve over their deaths. Today, parents pay "doctors" to kill their child in their mother's womb.

A few years after my trip to the Holy Land, Dr. Schindler suddenly died on May 31, Pentecost Sunday. The 31st is usually the feast of the Visitation of Mary. Did God, in His mercy, give him the grace of repentance before he died, due to that Mass offered for an end to abortion in the Church of the Nativity several years earlier. In the diocese of Rolling Hills, we did a Novena of Masses to close the abortion clinic, and the final Mass offered (though not on the 9th day of the novena), was offered the same day he died suddenly.

On Dec. 28th, 2021, I offered a Memorial Mass for all stillborn, miscarried, and aborted children at St. Timothy parish in Browbeat.

During Mass, it dawned on me, how many relatives had lost infants. Before my brother knew his wife, she had an abortion of a child from her previous marriage. One of her daughters had an abortion. My step-grandfather forced his wife to get an abortion. My great-grandfather on my father's side may have killed his unborn baby and wife by punching her in the stomach. Another sister had an ectopic pregnancy, and therefore, a surgery, to remove a Fallopian tube, which resulted in the death of the baby. Her daughter, my niece, and her boyfriend, came together before marriage which resulted in her getting pregnant, and then she had a miscarriage. Another sister lost her unborn baby due to her husband beating up on her. As I lit the seven candles tonight, I felt like weeping, but wouldn't do it in front of those present. When I was 18, I made an appointment for a friend and his girlfriend to get an abortion, but they miscarried before the abortion.

How incredibly sad are all these events, yet God gave all of us consolation as we came together to mourn the loss of children.

#160 HOPE AT DOORWAY TO HEAVEN NURSING HOME

Doorway to Heaven Nursing Home 2021

In 2009, I was assigned to minister at Doorway to Heaven Nursing Center. While there, I discovered many residents were dying without receiving IVs and feeding tubes when they could benefit from them. Consequently, they were dying due to a lack of nutrition and hydration, rather than from their illness. Back then, I created a report for Bishop Traditiones, who told me to not say anything to anyone about it.

Earlier this year, I discovered a young Catholic man, the new administrator, was on board with doing things ethically right. He and his wife had a premature baby, and while I was ministering at St. Henry's Hospital, I became acquainted with them. I realized he was a good practicing Catholic. Eventually, we discussed the situation, as I knew it back in 2009. He promised to look into the problem, and said he wanted to be trained and certified by the International Catholic Bioethics Center of America. I gave him a copy of the report that I gave to Bishop Traditiones, and asked him to read the document, *Good Samaritan*.

Weeks after our meeting, I learned the diocese took over Catholic Doorway to Heaven Nursing Home, because Mother of Misery Healthcare System was not taking adequate care of patients there, and some were threatening to sue them.

It gave me great consolation the new administrator wanted to be trained by the International Catholic Bioethics Center of America, to be sure the facility would follow Catholic ethics. It can take a long time to see any progress or fruit from a priest's labors. But I have hope, the residents will be treated with the dignity they deserve at the nursing home. It goes to show, a simple layman, is able to understand church teachings and documents and apply them to everyday situations.

#161 A PRIEST'S CHRISTMAS

A Priest's Christmas

"And everyone who has left houses or brothers or sisters or father or mother or wife or children or fields for my sake will receive a hundred times as much and will inherit eternal life." (Matthew 19:29)

After I was ordained, I was astonished at how generous parishioners were to priests. Fr. Bill Cody wanted all three priests at St. Gertrude to sign Christmas cards for every family, which was over 2,000 cards. The people responded with many Christmas cards and usually gave money in them. I received over $1,000 from the good people at Christmastime from their cards. I wondered if it was Fr. Cody's motivation, knowing if we sent a card to every parishioner, we would get a financial boon.

At Christmastime, parishioners donated all sorts of cakes, foods, pies, candies, and meals. I was amazed by it all. We were treated like kings. I felt like we should have donated most of the Christmas food to the poor, but we didn't give any of it away. I rarely ate sweets, and consequently, never partook of it all.

Despite being showered with gifts during the holidays, I missed being with family. But, no one ever called or visited, and I was unable to drive three hours to my home, and return the same day. Yet, I believed this was part of what it meant to be a disciple. To leave our family and receive a larger parish family.

Interestingly, over time, I became closer to parishioners than my own family members. Yet, I had to be careful to not spend too much time with them. Bishop Basil Braveheart told priests we should not go to a parishioner's home more than once a year, and I kept his advice with rare exceptions, that were beneficial for the family pastorally.

The people of St. Veronica in Brushwood City were surprisingly generous as well, despite the fact I didn't believe I was liked there.

At Immaculate Heart of Mary in Wheatland, I sent out 200 Christmas cards to every parish family. I received two cards in return. At first, I was surprised by their lack of interest in sending Christmas cards. Christmas donations didn't cover the cost of the cards. However, over time, more and more parishioners started to send cards in return. It made me realize how selfish and self-centered I was to expect money too to pay for the cards. Over the years, I grew to expect people to give Christmas cards and donations, which was terribly wrong.

Although I used their donations to help the needy, at times I received gifts, but felt uncomfortable taking them. I used to hope to receive many Christmas cards, so I could see the difference in their lives. But, their way of life and following Jesus more closely, is what reveals the fruit of my labors, thanks to the grace of God.

#162 THE GIFT OF THE PRIESTHOOD

High School Blues-- I Have No Gifts
Gifts of Mystery after Ordination & An Epiphany

"And when they had come into the house, they saw the young Child with Mary His mother, and fell down and worshiped Him. And when they had opened their treasures, they presented unto Him gifts: gold and frankincense and myrrh." (Matthew 2:11)

High School days were probably the worst of my life. I felt like no one loved me. Everyone at home wanted to argue. I had no one to talk to. No friends. It was very depressing. I didn't know Jesus and never prayed except for my father to stop drinking. I saw the gifts and talents of other young people my age, and I didn't perceive I had any gifts. I was not good at sports, though I could run fairly fast, and enjoyed long-distance running in the country. Some could sing and others were good at academics. Some had very likable personalities. I perceived other boys my age as being more handsome, more intelligent, and more athletic, and it seemed easy for them to attract girls. I wanted to have a girlfriend so bad. However, I thought, "What girl would want to be around some skinny guy who didn't know how to relate well to others, who struggled in school, and whose shoes smelled like hog manure?" I thought I had no gifts and believed I was a nobody.

The word Epiphany means "manifestation". I had an epiphany moment (revealing of something) on the feast of the Epiphany in 2021. The wise men came to adore the Christ Child and gave Him gifts of gold, frankincense, and myrrh. The drummer-boy played his drum for the Infant Jesus. That was his gift to the Lord. God Himself is a gift, when revealing Himself to us as a baby.

It was not until Epiphany Sunday of 2021, it dawned on me (revealed to me as an epiphany moment) I ended up with greater gifts than all of my classmates. Who, among them, did God give the gift of the ability to change bread and wine into His Body and Blood, or to forgive sins, or to baptize, or anoint, or to preach about Jesus? It is wrong to compare myself with others, and I did that too much when I was young. Now, I am in awe at the supernatural gifts God gave me, unmerited, most likely because He found one of the most miserable of men to manifest His mercy to the world.

Before my ordination, I didn't think I had anything to give. But, after my ordination, He gave me everything when I was ordained a priest. I pray I may use these gifts the way He desires for the good of others, and for the glory and honor of God. At every Mass, each of us can give our gifts, sacrifices, and our total self to God on the altar, with the bread and wine offered to God the Father. How beautiful and powerful, I can give Jesus the gift of my priesthood, all that goes with it, and my very self, at every Mass.

Although I cannot sing well, am not the most handsome man, nor the most intelligent, I have the greatest gift that can be given from God, for God and His people, the gift of the priesthood, and the victimhood that goes with it. As Pope St. John Paul II said, "The priesthood is both gift and mystery."

#163 JESUS SPEAKS

Did Jesus Speak to Me?

Jan. 2nd Feast of the Epiphany this year. During Eucharistic Adoration in my Chapel, I was pondering over everything that failed in my attempt to address unethical situations at the hospital. I told the Lord, "Jesus, perhaps I failed because of my sins. I did the best I could at the time, but I'm sorry if my sins prevented Your will from being accomplished. I am sorry if my sins negatively affected others." Jesus responded, "My will cannot be prevented or impeded. I am almighty and omnipotent. Nothing prevents my will. Trust in my mercy." Oh, what peace came to my soul, when I heard those words!

In speaking about a priest who was suffering much due to an apparent lack of success, Jesus told St. Faustina in her diary (#86), "Write that by day and by night My gaze is fixed upon him, and I permit these adversities in order to increase his merit. I do not reward for good results but for patience and hardship undergone for My sake."

#164 ST. CHARLES OF SEZZE

St. Charles of Sezze- Jan. 6th, 2021

I gave a homily on St. Charles of Sezze on his birthday into heaven, January 6th.

When St. Charles began is autobiography he said, "Because God and my father confessor have commanded me to write the pitiable account of my life, it will be well enough to say, and thereby include everything, that since I have been a great sinner and received a sea of graces from His Divine Majesty, everyone will clearly see the grandeur of His unlimited mercy." His words gave me the "willies". For this is exactly what I thought when I began my autobiography, and why it is entitled "Untold Mercy", for truly when anyone reads it, no doubt they will be shocked at the number, kinds and numerous sins. And yet, God's abundant graces and mercy He bestowed in my lifetime, is unimaginable.

People like St. Charles of Sezze and St. Faustina had such few sins; But my sins are horrific and sadly many, but now I boast of God being much more merciful to me than these saints, since I am absolutely a more miserable human being who needed His infinite mercy to such an immensely greater degree. The greater the misery, the greater the mercy. They received grace to be preserved from depths of misery of sin that I had in my life. How beautiful! I think of St. Mary Magdalene, a prostitute, and yet Jesus forgave her, and even chose to appear to her before the Apostles. As Jesus told St. Faustina, "The greater the sinner, the greater one's right to My mercy". The greater the sinner, the greater the mercy. Jesus, I Trust in Your Mercy!

#165 VACCINE MANDATES

Homily Vaccine Mandates

I gave a homily on the Vaccine mandate on the feast of the Baptism of the Lord. At this time, there is a world-wide tyranny by government leaders to force vaccines when they don't prevent anyone from acquiring COVID-19, nor prevent the spread of the disease. How many people will die from the abortion-tainted vaccines? According to the VAERS (Voluntary Adverse Reporting System), as of today, over 20,000 deaths in the US may have been caused by the vaccine, and nearly 1 million adverse reactions. Several doctors claim COVID-19 vaccines destroy the immune system, causing people to die from faster from ordinary illnesses, whereas they otherwise wouldn't die. Many young people died suddenly, shortly after taking the vaccines. Tyranny throughout the world now seems similar to the early stages of the French Revolution, or similar to what happened at the beginning of the Rwandan genocide. I just wonder how long before an even greater persecution will start.

Some say the virus was a biological weapon purposely released, and the vaccine was developed to help kill, and reduce the world's population. Could this be true? What sad times we are living. If something happens to me, and it appears as though I committed suicide, it wasn't suicide at all. Rather, I could have been killed for being a Christian. I am not depressed, nor am I suicidal. I love life. I love Jesus and I forgive anyone who may kill me.

Vaccine Mandate Misery

Not included in the homily are reports throughout the world that indicate more are contracting COVID-19 after they received the vaccines and then die from the virus, than those who did not get the vaccines.

After I was transferred to St. Timothy's, Mother of Misery Health System mandated every employee to receive the vaccine or get fired. They would not permit conscience objections. Nearly one-tenth of the hospital's staff quit and another 20% were fired. The non-Catholic hospital in Rolling Hills didn't mandate the vaccines and hired many from the Catholic hospitals. It is said only those without a conscience remained at the Catholic hospital. Bishop Athanasius Courageous does not believe in conscience objections for the vaccine. He told priests they could not assist parishioners in obtaining a conscience objection.

Now that I am no longer there, I now see how the Lord protected me from receiving the vaccine and the flurry that would happen if I would reject it. Fr. Harry Brown originally received the vaccine, but later refused the second one, due to becoming ill immediately after taking the first one. Despite his objection to taking the second vaccine, and becoming very ill from it, hospital administration continued to tell him, he must take it. He was transferred the following year to do parish ministry.

A nurse who worked at Montecarlo City Hospital, said the administrator told all nursing staff to record every death at the hospital as a COVID-19 death, because the government will reimburse the hospital for them. Even if the patient died and wasn't tested positive for the virus, nor didn't have the virus, they reported the death, as a COVID-19 death.

Hospitals had a government incentive to report COVID-19 cases. They receive funds from any patient who tests positive. They receive extra funds when a patient is admitted and reimbursed even more when the patient ends up in ICU. And, if a patient dies from it, they receive additional funds. If any hospital fails to comply with requiring all employees to receive the vaccine, the hospital loses financial aid from the government. Some doctors and nurses are now saying hospitals have become death camps and should be avoided.

#166 BISHOP NOW ALLOWS CONSCIENCE EXEMPTION FOR VACCINES

The priests received an email from the Vicar General stating the bishop now permits vaccine exemptions. A template was provided for the priests to use. Praise the Lord! However, how sad for all who lost their jobs because it was not permitted. How difficult it must be to be a bishop and navigate through our difficult times.

When the bishop came to St. Timothy for a pastoral visit, a parishioner asked the bishop why conscience objections were never given. The bishop replied, "They were never forbidden. I always gave them out." The parishioner then questioned me and asked why I said conscience exceptions were forbidden. I replied, "They were." I then showed him a copy of the letter with the bishop's signature, stating he forbade priests to give them out. Who knows, maybe the bishop was confused when he responded to the parishioner's question.

#167 MIRACULOUS MEDAL AND ST. CHARLES OF SEZZE

Jan. 18th Feast of St. Charles Sezze? A Miraculous Medal

One source, *The Franciscan Book of Saints* states the feast of St. Charles Sezze is January 18th.

It was cold the morning of January 18th 2022 when I went to unlock the church. I decided to water a few poinsettia plants remaining from the Christmas season. As I was carrying a water jug in one hand, and with the other hand, I attempted to pick up dead plant leaves on the floor. As I bent down, the hood from my coat accidentally flipped and covered my head. About a second later, a Miraculous Medal landed on my shoulder and fell to the floor. I was stunned. There wasn't any way, a medal could have fallen out of my hood, because I had just worn the hood from the house to church. I looked around to see if anyone was in the church, but no one was there, especially since I just unlocked it.

The previous night, January 17th, I was pondering, on dropping medals on the grounds of the masonic building in downtown Browbeat. If the medal hadn't fallen out of nowhere, hit me on the shoulder, and landed on the floor in front of me, I probably would have tossed some there.

There is no better way to describe this event, except to say, it startled me to the core. There seemed no reasonable way, the medal could have landed on my shoulder and fallen on the floor in front of me.

I was so astonished by the event, after Mass I called a priest friend exorcist, and he told me I should not drop the medals near the masonic temple, since he said the ground in itself is not good to walk on. He said part of a deliverance prayer mentions praying for deliverance for those who walk on the grounds of a masonic temple. I told him I did something similar a few months ago, in Hodgenville, Georgia, where I walked on the grounds of the masonic temple near a friary and dropped Miraculous Medals there. By the time we ended our conversation, I realized I needed to do deliverance prayers for walking on Masonic grounds in Hodgenville. I believe Our Lady, through the intercession of Her Miraculous Medal, prevented me from doing the same thing again.

Later that day, a priest passing by on his way to Rolling Hills, stopped to visit and happened to (providentially) give me a holy card of St. Maximilian Kolbe, who promoted the Miraculous Medal, and was very opposed to the Freemasons of his time.

On the feast of St. Maximilian years ago, I made my perpetual profession with the name Br. Antonio Maria. It became apparent, through Our Lady's intercession, and the prayers of St. Maximilian Kolbe, and St. Anthony of Padua, I was being protected.

St. Maximilian must be pleased that we pray his exhortation, and other prayers before every Rosary at St. Timothy, "O Mary Conceived without sin, pray for us, who have recourse to thee, especially, the Freemasons, Communists, Heretics, Schismatics, and Marxists." We started doing this, because some believe the Freemasons and Communists allegedly infiltrated the Church and society today. I also believe Our Lady wants me to distribute more medals.

#168 MIRACULOUS MEDAL BRINGS BACK FALLEN AWAY CATHOLIC

I gave a blessed Miraculous Medal to a practicing Catholic woman, asking her to give the medal to her daughter, who hasn't been to Mass or Confession in over twenty years.

The woman said her daughter was arrested for selling narcotics and isn't interested in the Catholic faith. I told the woman to pray for her daughter, to offer her attendance at Mass, and offer her Holy Communion for her. After she did this, she gave her the medal. I offered a Mass and fasted for her. I then asked the mother to invite her daughter to attend Mass with her. She invited her daughter and she came. After attending Mass for several weeks, the young woman went to Confession and is now a practicing Catholic. Thanks to Our Lady and Her Miraculous Medal, the young lady returned to church.

#169 GOD'S PROVIDENCE ANOINTING 2 PEOPLE, SAME SURGERY, SAME DAY

Anointed Two Having Surgery on Their Shoulder, the Same Day at the Same Place
I anointed a parishioner, who will have shoulder surgery on Tuesday, January 25th. The following day, I anointed a priest who will have shoulder surgery on the same day, January 25th, at the same facility. What is God trying to tell me? At least to pray for them.

#170 POOR MAN GETS A RECLINER

Recliner for a Poor Man
"Therefore I tell you, do not worry about your life, what you will eat or drink; or about your body, what you will wear. Is not life more than food, and the body more than clothes?" (Matthew 6:25)

A poor non-Catholic man living in Browbeat said he has to sleep on the floor with his head propped against his recliner. Since his recliner is broke and due to severe back problems, his head needs to be propped up when sleeping. He said many times his mother told him, she wished she would have aborted him. He said she physically abused him often as a child. How sad!

To help him out, I decided to purchase, with my own money, a recliner with an electric power lift. A new recliner cost $75, as advertised on the internet. Although I had not purchased it, I later discovered it was a scam. The cost of a new power lift recliner from Walmart is $400. A couple happened to give me $200 in thanksgiving for renewing their vows during Mass. I was going to pay the remaining $200 myself for the recliner. But, I received $175 for offering two Masses at Church of the Holy Incense parish in Waterbury. I later told the pastor of that parish that in the future, I prefer not to be paid when offering Masses or hearing Confessions in a parish. I told him I already receive a salary from the parish. A lady gave me $20 for traveling to Rolling Hills to attend a prayer group. I tried to refuse the money from her, but since she insisted, I took it. I thought it would be charitable to humbly receive it, and then use it, for a holy purpose.

Consequently, my total payout for the recliner out of pocket was $5. God's providence is magnificent! He wanted me to know, I shouldn't worry about money. But, trust Him, since He will take care of what is needed to help the poor. The Lord saw the misery of the poor man and through the mercy of others relieved it.

#171 WHAT INFLUENCED ME TO BECOME PRO-LIFE?

Family Difficulties with Babies Influence Respecting the Unborn
"For I know well the plans I have in mind for you—plans for your welfare and not for woe, so as to give you a future of hope." (Jeremiah 29:11)

When I was 18, my oldest sister, Anne, gave birth to a three-month premature baby, Marlene. On hearing about the untimely birth, I rushed to Hasten County Hospital to be with family and see tiny little Marlene. She was so small and her skin was dark. She hardly moved on her own. A special ambulance from Fort Hickok with a Neonatal Incubator took her to the larger hospital there. The ambulance seemed to take a long time, and when it finally arrived, my father raised his voice at the crew. "What took you so long? If anything happens to this baby, you're going to hear about it." I tried to follow the ambulance to Hickok, but couldn't keep up since they were driving over ninety miles an hour. Marlene was then flown to Methodist Regional Medical Center in Rolling Hills. She was in the Neonatal ICU for a month and happily came home with no adverse problems.

A few years later, my sister, Sue, had an ectopic pregnancy. During a bad winter storm, she was living on a farm, near Gulleywasher City, Ohio. An ambulance was called. However, due to deep snow, a snow plow prepared the way for the ambulance to arrive at their farm, to travel to the hospital. She needed emergency surgery because the unborn child had attached to her Fallopian tube and was growing. If the tube would break, my sister, and the baby, would die. To save Sue's life, the Fallopian tube was removed, which had the side effect of causing the death of the baby. Either way, the baby would never live.

These two events involving very young babies were scary. We prayed for Marlene, so she would survive. The death of my little unborn niece or nephew was sorrowful. These events helped to mold my way of thinking about unborn babies and the need to protect them.

After a man becomes a priest and sacrifices not being married or having children, the protective mode of a man kicks in, when children are in danger or threatened.

These events, as well as my regret of scheduling an abortion for a friend (though it never took place) and the event of seeing a child's foot or hand in a surgical instrument tray while cleaning instruments, helped me see the beauty of life, and the need to do everything I can, to help save babies.

Homily Miscarriage and Contraception
"Before I formed you in the womb, I knew you." (Jeremiah 1:5)

From the time I was at St. Tarcisius parish in Rolling Hills, pastor of St. Veronica in Brushwood City, St. Anthony in Jericho City, pastor of Immaculate Heart in Wheatland, and now here at St. Timothy in Browbeat, I have given a homily on how some contraceptives: the pill, IUD, the shot, and the patch, cause the death of an unborn child within five days of conception. When these homilies are given, I always speak much about the Mercy of Jesus. Remarkably, every time I preach on this topic and make confessions available afterwards, they last for hours. Much fruit! Praise the Lord! But the enemy doesn't like this homily. I am going to mention this, during the homily this weekend at St. Timothy, and also at Church of the Holy Incense.

The night before I gave the homily, I was attacked again, mostly with violent shaking. But then, the demon angrily spoke to me, and said, "If you give that homily this weekend, I will kill you." I believe this is a lie, since two exorcists in the past told me God does not permit demons to kill us.

#172 THE AMAZING AUTOBIOGRAPHY OF ST. CHARLES OF SEZZE

St. Charles of Sezze Autobiography
I am re-reading the *Autobiography of St. Charles of Sezze*. I read it about 25 years ago, when I was a novice, with the Franciscan Perpetual Victim Martyrs. I am amazed at the similarities, and also the many differences between his life and mine. His writings help me to know how far I am from his humility and virtues.

At the beginning of his autobiography, St. Charles spoke about God's mercy. I did the same. His humility is revealed in his words. But, the manner I write, compared to him, reveals my pride. When he was very sick, his father made a wooden cross for him. When I was a child, I carved a wooden cross out of a piece of wood and still have it. He didn't feel worthy to become a priest, and he told the story of how St. Francis of Assisi didn't feel worthy either. And, that is why he never studied to become a priest. I felt unworthy to become a priest and backed out of my deacon ordination. But later, recognized it was God's will.

God works through each of us, and he can make a saint out of anyone. Some greater saints are raised to the altar, to be an example for others. And some smaller saints, although great sinners, by God's grace and infinite mercy, made it to heaven to receive their glory.

To be honest, I would love it, that after I am in heaven, people would ask for my intercession. I want to help, as many as possible to endure their struggles similar to what I went through. Since I have not been very successful in this life bringing very many souls to Jesus, in the next life, I pray, the Lord will grant this gift.

There were times I felt saints didn't help much, when I asked them for help, except for St. Anthony of Padua, but I'm sure they did. I want to be someone people can trust, who will help them when they ask for it, although I know it is all contingent on God's holy will and Mary's intercession.

Why not trust that God can make me a saint? I seem very far from it and most likely would not even be aware of it until my judgment. This way, God helps me to be humble and avoid pride. I want to "go for the Gold" of God's glory! And become a real saint!

#173 PEACE OF HEART
THANKSGIVING FOR GOD IN HELPING OVERCOME SINS

Thanksgiving Overcoming Sins and Peace of Heart

During Eucharistic Adoration today, my heart leaped with joy at the thought of so many mercies bestowed upon me by Our Lord. My spiritual director, Fr. Michael Benedict, has helped me in so many ways to overcome my sins, and the tendency to commit these sins. The method of prayer he taught to battle against temptations has been unbelievably successful. Truly, I am a different man. I believe I can say, "It is no longer I who lives, but Christ who lives in me." (Galatians 2:20) I am no longer jealous or envious of the appearance and gifts of other men, which caused self-deprecating and worthless thoughts about myself. I used to think most men were smarter than I, better looking, stronger, and even if that were the case, today, it would not matter. I no longer purposely over-eat when upset, nor do I desire love or affection as I had in the past. I no longer have many fears, such as the fear to speak in public, or the fear of doing something new. I gave a talk yesterday for the Forty Days for Life group and was not nervous or fearful. How different from the past, when I needed to read notes, to just say the smallest thing in front of a group. I no longer have such terrible lustful and impure desires. Oh, the mercy of God! His infinite power worked many miracles in my soul.

When I had my conversion at twenty-seven, I came back to Confession and started to receive Holy Communion. Back then I had profound insights and spiritual feelings when Jesus came inside my heart during Communion. There were times I felt like I was in Heaven. The joy of receiving Jesus moved me to receive Him more often. At times, I attended two Masses a day, so I could receive Holy Communion twice in a day. Oh, the delights I had back then! Though I feel utterly dry now when receiving Holy Communion, I have the joy of overcoming so many sins. Today, Jesus wants me to desire to receive Him by faith and not by feelings. Yet, I know I still have many more sins to work on.

For so many years, I had disdain for the current bishop and former bishop. This grieved my heart and caused a deep wound that took years to be healed, and in fact, my heart only bled over the years. I offer up this anguish for the salvation of souls. I care about them!

At times, the bishops made public statements in the local diocesan paper that seemed to support priests or stand against unethical things. I still wonder about all the unethical things occurring at Catholic hospitals and know people are suffering and dying, since nothing was ever accomplished.

But I trust in God's mercy. These words are short, but have deep meaning. I trust in God's mercy, that He is taking care of those dying unethically. And those responsible, I trust, He can bring to salvation. I trust in God's mercy, despite apparent colossal failures of all involved, they can hopefully enjoy heaven. For truly, they do not know what they are doing or fail to do.

Whether its ignorance, or a lack of courage, or whatever causes hospital staff to not seem to care for the salvation of souls, is not up to me to figure out, or to know, for truly God can still make all things good for them, and the people to whom they are obligated to serve. If only, they can see what they are doing.

I keep hoping the day will come ,when by God's grace and mercy, I can be martyred. Will it be at an abortion clinic, or in the parish, or some other place? Or will it never happen at all? I have had many white martyrdoms, especially due to those who have authority over them. I realize much penance is needed to skip purgatory. Many opportunities were offered to me. But, whether I corresponded to those graces in the manner God desired, I know not. However, I trust in God's mercy.

O most merciful Jesus, You said, the greater the sinner, the greater the right one has to your mercy. You are most pleased when we plead mercy for sinners. You even bestow more mercy than we ever ask for. So, from the depths of my heart, I cry to Thee, O Jesus, I trust in your mercy, and believe I will not be disappointed. By your mercies, you have already purified my soul, in so many ways, from sins, and their inclinations, and truly, all through the hands, prayers, and graces of the Mother of Mercy, my Queen! O blessed Lady, why have you been so good to me? I know not. But, I thank you, and your dear Son, with all my heart! I thank you, O Jesus, for the gift of having suffered for You. And, although, I could have suffered more, and better, You make all things good, my loving God. I trust, in St. Louis de Montfort's promise, that when we consecrate our self to our Lady, She keeps, and protects all graces, we received. And, therefore, O Mary, I trust you! That you will not allow any grace to be lost. Amen.

#174 EXPENSIVE NATIVITY SET AND BIRTHDAY PARTY

Nativity Set for $8000

A woman from St. Timothy parish wanted to repair the parish life-size nativity set, since there are many chips and marks on the statues. She and her husband took the statues to Rolling Hills to have an artist give an estimate for their repair. The repair estimate was $6,900. Instead of repairing them, the woman asked Fr. Jeremiah Bullfrog, the pastor of St. Timothy, to purchase new ones. She found a life-size nativity set on the internet for $8,000. Without approval or knowledge of the Pastoral Council, the statues were ordered by the pastor and arrived. The Pastoral Council president was shocked at the cost for a parish of fifty families. Nevertheless, he signed the check. Some parishioners were upset with the woman's aggressive in way she obtained the statues, without anyone's knowledge. Parishioners were also upset with the pastor for not talking to anyone about it before he spent parish money. Although the pastor has the authority to purchase items, it seemed imprudent to spend such a large sum of money.

Herod's Birthday Party and a Pastor's Birthday Party

"On his birthday Herod gave a banquet for his high officials and military commanders and the leading men of Galilee. When the daughter of Herodias came in and danced, she pleased Herod and his dinner guests. The king said to the girl, "Ask me for anything you want, and I'll give it to you." And he promised her with an oath, "Whatever you ask I will give you, up to half my kingdom." She went out and said to her mother, "What shall I ask for?" "The head of John the Baptist," she answered. At once the girl hurried in to the king with the request: "I want you to give me right now the head of John the Baptist on a platter." The king was greatly distressed, but because of his oaths and his dinner guests, he did not want to refuse her. So he immediately sent an executioner with orders to bring John's head. The man went, beheaded John in the prison, and brought back his head on a platter. He presented it to the girl, and she gave it to her mother. On hearing of this, John's disciples came and took his body and laid it in a tomb." (Mark 6:21-29)

To celebrate the birth of Jesus, the pastor of Church of the Holy Incense parish, in Waterbury, Ohio, asked his employees to send out a Christmas card to all parishioners of his three parishes. A group of ladies from Church of the Holy Incense decided to throw a surprise 40th birthday party for Fr. Jeremiah Bullfrog. They included an invitation to a luncheon with cake in February.

Several weeks before the party, the secretary of their parish sent out an email to three of us from St. Timothy. It suggested each organization donate $1,500 to $2,000 to help pay for the cost of the catered meal, which cost $6,000. However, there is only one organization at St. Timothy, the Altar Society. They have one fund-raiser a year and take in about $1,000. The suggested donation from the secretary of the Church of the Holy Incense is very unjust for the parish of St. Timothy, with only fifty families. St. Margaret of Cortona and Church of the Holy Incense parishes in Waterbury, Ohio, have at least 1,300 combined families, and therefore, the donation requested for the size of the parish is greatly disproportionate. The donation should not be more than 3.7%, not even 4% of the total. And yet, they were asking St. Timothy to pay 33% of the cost.

Jokingly, I made a comment to a priest friend saying, "Herod's birthday party didn't cost that much!" The funny thing was, the next day, the Gospel was about Herod's birthday party. I usually read the Gospel in advance, but didn't. It was the feast of St. Agatha, and I wanted to preach about her, rather than the Gospel for the day.

It was truly a surprise birthday party for Fr. Jeremiah Bullfrog, who was unaware of the expensive and scandalous cost of his own birthday party. The poor women, with good intentions, believed they were doing something nice for their pastor. I wanted to call Fr. Jeremiah, in case he may want to cancel the catered meal, and not waste so much money, especially since the Catholic High School in Waterbury and Church of the Holy Incense parish, were both having serious financial difficulties.

I spoke with two priests about the party, and both recommended not saying anything to Fr. Bullfrog. If I were in his shoes, I would want another priest to tell me about the extravagant expense, cancel the catered meal, and have only cake and drinks. But I decided to do what the other two priests suggested.

It was hilarious to discover the party is a week after my birthday, so I'm looking forward to getting a tasty meal under the disguise, of a super-secret birthday party. How selfish is that! How many poor people and families could have enjoyed a nice warm meal costing $15 per person? I called Fr. Sam Bullfrog, an uncle of Fr. Jeremiah, and asked his opinion. He thought I should let things play out and not tell Fr. Jeremiah, less his surprise be ruined and upset the ladies who organized it. He said, after all, it was "only" $6,000. I think Fr. Sam and the other priests think it is better to spend $6,000 than to cause people to get upset. Why not just cancel the expensive dinner and have cake and ice cream, I wondered? Oh my, how different I think than other priests. Truly, I am praying this all comes to a good conclusion.

#175 THE SQUIRREL AND THE SEWER

Sewer Surprise
"Do you not realize that everything that goes into a person from outside, cannot defile, since it enters not the heart, but the stomach and passes out into the latrine?.. But what comes out of the man, that is what defiles him. From within the man, from his heart, come evil thoughts, unchastity, theft, murder, adultery, greed, malice, deceit, licentiousness, envy, blasphemy, arrogance, folly. All these evils come from within and defile." (Mark 7:17-19)

On a very cold winter day, in 2022, I heard what sounded like a squirrel crawling down a metal sewer pipe from the roof. With a hammer, I banged on the pipe, but whatever it was, didn't leave. Finally, after a while, there was silence.

The next day, when the toilet was flushed, it overflowed. After plunging multiple times, the toilet water finally started to go down. Then, whenever I flushed the toilet, waste water came up through the sink and bathtub. A handyman came and ran a metal sewer snake through the pipe from outside and out came part of a dead squirrel. After it was removed, the toilet flushed properly. A squirrel had crawled down the pipe protruding from the roof and ended up in the sewer plugging the toilet. And remarkably, the Gospel reading for the day, stated that what passes into the latrine, does not defile, but rather, what comes out of the man's heart, defiles him.

#176 MORE THOUGHTS ON ST. CHARLES OF SEZZE'S AUTOBIOGRAPHY

St. Charles of Sezze's Autobiography Thoughts

"Be angry, but do not sin; do not let the sun go down on your anger." (Ephesians 4:26)

St. Charles discussed how he, and two religious brothers from his community, were seeking to enter religious life with the Franciscans, but were told to leave the community. You would think he would have been angry. But he wasn't. Do saints not have feelings and emotions? Or, did he fail to mention them? Or, did he completely trust in the Lord, and accept whatever would happen? For one to not have some sort of anger, for being rejected, it makes me wonder why not? Was it all grace? Yet, is it not also meritorious, to battle against angry thoughts, to pray for those who hurt us, and to overcome them by God's grace as well? There are many ordinary people, who valiantly and heroically, overcame the weakness of their wounded emotions, and gave God the credit for making it happen.

Later, in another part of his autobiography, he revealed his anger towards someone. But, as an act of penance for his anger, he carried his habit around his neck. Oh, what humility! On another occasion, he said, he was tempted to choke, one of his superiors, but overcame the temptation. I find this so inspiring. Once I confessed that I had the thought of spanking the bishop with a paddle for not doing something about the injustices at the hospice and hospital. What a terrible thought and lack of reverence for the sacred office of the bishop. To physically harm a bishop, one could be excommunicated. I certainly would never do such a thing, since I truly do love and respect the bishop. Oh, how human we are with our crazy thoughts. Saints and sinners are very human.

#177 THE DEADLY VACCINE AND A HOMILY

Vaccine Homily & Niece Loses Baby Due to Vaccine

My niece, Susie Chapstick, became pregnant out of wedlock. Due to her pregnancy, she was rushing to get married. She, her boyfriend, and I met. We discussed their wedding plans and their unexpected baby. Later, after they left, I texted my niece warning her to not take the COVID-19 vaccine, since it's known for causing miscarriages. She either received the text too late, or disregarded it, and took the vaccine. When she received the vaccine, she fainted thirty minutes after getting the jab and was taken to the hospital. After running tests on her and her unborn baby, the doctor said both were fine.

However, a month later, the baby died, presumably from the vaccine. Perhaps I should have warned her sooner. Or, maybe she received the text, but disregarded it. It's possible, the baby's death was caused by something else. I didn't believe it was best to ask her. How sad for her and her fiancé, and especially the baby. Due to this event, they postponed their marriage for six months and will be getting married without any pressure.

According to the VAERS website (Voluntary Adverse Reaction Reporting System) at least 3,900 miscarriages have occurred due to the vaccine. Tragically, the US government continues to indicate the vaccine is safe! Due to this event, that same weekend, I preached on the dangers of the COVID-19 vaccine. I was terrified to give the homily, due to a possible negative reaction from parishioners who might go to the bishop to complain. I gave the homily anyway out of love for the people, and took the risk of upsetting some parishioners, and the bishop. The three parishioners, who most likely would complain, the Lord prevented them from attending Mass at St. Timothy. They attended Mass at a different parish this weekend.

Homily Response by Parishioner- Storm on the Lake

"And when he got into the boat, His disciples followed him. And behold, there arose a great storm on the sea, so that the boat was swamped by the waves; but He was asleep. And they went and woke Him, saying, "Save us, Lord; we are perishing." And He said to them, "Why are you afraid, O you of little faith?" Then He rose and rebuked the winds and the sea; and there was great calm. And the men marveled, saying, "What sort of man is this, that even winds and sea obey Him?" (Matthew 8:23-27)

On my day away from ministry, I decided to drive to Ohio City State Lake, and attempted to take a direct route via dirt roads. But it turned out, not so direct. According to the internet map, there should have been a continuous road taking traffic to a highway. But, I ended up having to take all sorts of turns and wondered for a while if I was lost. Nevertheless, I came out on the exact road to take me to the lake.

When I arrived at the lake, the wind had drastically picked up and the waves were crashing on the shore. It reminded me of the storm on the lake with the apostles. I thought Jesus was saying to me, "A storm is brewing in the parish." But I reminded myself, just as Jesus calmed the storm with the apostles, He would do the same at the parish.

On the way back, I thought of a parishioner whose family often misses Catechism classes due to sports. On many Sundays, they don't attend Mass, at least not here. The same mother of the family was upset about an animated, non-bloody abortion video I showed to the high school class.

As I was returning to Browbeat, the thought occurred to me an evil spirit was active in the life of this woman, causing her to place sports as an idol, over the worship of God, and the religious education of her children. Consequently, I decided to pray a Rosary for her and her family, as well as pray the Chaplet of Divine Mercy on the way back from the lake. Shockingly, when I arrived back at the house and checked my email, she had emailed me and the pastor, complaining about the homily and the abortion video.

I prayed deliverance prayers for her and her family. The pastor emailed me, saying, although the homily was accurate and true, I lacked pastoral sensitivity. I responded back to the lady's email explaining the reasons for the homily and told her I was sorry for not knowing she and her children had received the vaccine. She said the homily caused her children to doubt the authority of their parents and made them fearful they might die from the vaccine. In response, I told her I would have worded the homily differently, had I known any children who attended Mass already received the vaccine. Instead of sending an email, I would have rather talked on the phone, or in person. But since she emailed the pastor and I with her complaint, I responded back with an email and told her I would be happy to talk to her on the phone or in person. Before giving the homily, I emailed a copy to three doctors and three nurses, asking for their opinion. None suggested making any changes.

#178 GOD'S LOVE & CARE FOR AN ELDERLY LADY & SEXUAL PREDATOR

An Elderly Parishioner Saved from a Sexual Predator by God's Inspiration
While visiting her family in Florida, an elderly woman from St. Timothy ended up in the hospital. Although it was a Catholic hospital, and despite requests from family, a priest never came to anoint her. After being dismissed, she returned home, located several miles out of town in the country. By God's inspiration, I asked her son if she would like to receive Anointing of the Sick and Holy Communion, because she was unable to come to church due to her health. By God's inspiration, we set a time for her son to meet at his mother's home.

It just so happened, a registered sexual predator came to her house just before we arrived, while another woman was also visiting the elderly parishioner. The parishioner's son and his wife arrived not long before I came. Thinking the man was a friend of the family, I didn't suspect anything at all. Consequently, I anointed her, gave her Holy Communion, and then departed.

The next day, her son told me the man had no relationship with his mother and was a sexual predator who previously lived at Browbeat. He said when he came inside the house, the man was kneeling before his mother, with his hands in her hands. The son warned the man to never return to his mother's home again, and called the police to report what had happened.

Through all this, God was working to protect the lady, to warn the man to not prey on anyone, to help the son and his wife know his mother needs them, and to remind me, He is still using me to help others, at times, in ways I don't know.

#179 INNER TURMOIL & DEMONS THROW ME TO THE GROUND

Inner Turmoil

My soul at times is thrown into terrible turmoil when I do something like give a homily I believe is inspired by God, such as the dangers of the vaccine homily, and am convinced it is what the Lord wants. Then after the homily, if someone complains or is upset by it, I start to doubt whether it was originally what God wanted of me. I don't want to offend or upset anyone, desire to be pastoral to the best of my ability, and to always give homilies with love, mercy, and the fullness of truth. But the turmoil that takes place after someone complains is very difficult to endure. I believe the enemy is behind some of this turmoil. First, the enemy tries to convince me to not give the homily. Then after it is given, when someone complains or is upset, he makes me feel like I was a total failure. At times people can bring attention to something that came across, in a way I didn't see. Their words can be helpful when giving correction, even when it's not objectively true what they are saying. At least it helps the priest to avoid pride and grow in humility.

When reading the book, *The Priest the Man of God His Dignity and Duties*, by St. Joseph Cafasso, these words by the saint greatly consoled me: "cast away all fear and alarm; if you cannot apply yourself, or succeed in anything at all, that does not matter. It is a sign God does not demand success from you. He will see your good will. He will see you are trying, that you are making an effort, and that nothing comes from your effort. By these efforts, you have already conquered, the glory of God has been safeguarded and in addition, you have the merit that comes from the pain and sorrow you experience from seeing yourself incapable and powerless to labor for God, from being aware that your efforts are useless and vain, since the Lord knows how much a zealous priest suffers and grieves in these circumstances." (pg. 258 to 259)

As insignificant it may sound, it's a slow martyrdom. It's something I can place on the altar to give to the Lord as a sacrifice of love. There are some fears that cause anxiety: the fear of what the bishop thinks of me; the fear offending others; and the fear of having my priestly ministry reduced to a lower state. All these fears are so very painful. Behind this fear within me is pride. But the Lord desires to crush my pride, to make me a pleasing and acceptable sacrifice of humility, which seems almost impossible. But I trust in His mercy. I wish I could give every priest a copy of St. Cafasso's book. It has been so very beneficial to my soul.

A Demon Throws Me Backwards While Kneeling Before Our Lady

When kneeling before a large statue of the Blessed Virgin Mary in my Chapel, asking Her for the grace to overcome jealousy of a boy who stole my girlfriend in 8th grade, my body began to shake violently, causing me to pray more intensely to Our Lady. Suddenly, I was thrown backwards in the air and landed on my back. It was at that moment the demon left. I felt his fury and anger. But I got back up, and knelt once again before the statue of Our Lady. Since then, I have not had any more spiritual attacks at night. That demon was fierce and strong. And, it made me know, it was exceedingly unhappy when I was kneeling before a statue of Our Blessed Mother. The Queen of Heaven and Earth delivered me from that demon, I hope and believe permanently. Thank you! O Mary!

#180 THE BEAUTY OF ST. FAUSTINA'S DIARY

Diary of St. Faustina Gives Me Peace

I have been reading the *Diary of St. Faustina.* There have been many times it has greatly helped me to have peace. I have often wondered if I should avoid taking medicine to alleviate pain and consequently, suffer as much as possible for Jesus by uniting my sufferings to His on the Cross for the conversion of sinners. Yet, my headaches become so intense, I can't think straight and become exceedingly confused.

In #1276, St. Faustina describes how she takes medicine, but it does no good. By reading this, I came to understand the Lord desires me to take medicine. But, if it were to not work, then it would be His will for me to suffer that intensity, which I am willing to do, if that is what He wants. I prolong not taking medicine as long as possible, until it becomes clear, I become confused, and have great difficulty enduring it. Nevertheless, I need to fulfill my duties as a priest, so the people I serve aren't negatively affected by me not taking care of myself.

In #1317, of her Diary, Jesus told St. Faustina, "I know, My daughter; that you understand it and that you do everything within your power. But write this for the many souls who are often worried because they do not have the material means with which to carry out an act of mercy. Yet spiritual mercy, which requires neither permissions nor storehouses, is much more meritorious and is within the grasp of every soul. If a soul does not exercise mercy somehow or another, it will not obtain My mercy on the day of judgment. Oh, if only souls knew how to gather eternal treasure for themselves, they would not be judged, for they would forestall My judgment with their mercy."

So many times, I feel inadequate, like I should be doing something for others, by doing some sort of work. But, these words help me to realize, that spiritual works of mercy are more meritorious. I will try harder to do more spiritual works of mercy.

#181 SYNOD OF SYNODALITY AVOIDED BY RETREAT

Convocation Avoided by Short Retreat

I didn't want to attend the spring convocation. We were supposed to participate in the Synod of Synodality, by discussing their topics. Nor did I believe the Lord wanted me to go either. Consequently, I scheduled a five-day retreat at Our Lady of All Saints Monastery in Gasper, Nebraska and received permission from the Vicar General to miss the convocation.

During the first Mass celebrated by Fr. Barry Canopener, after I received Holy Communion, I had an interior vision of the Child Jesus sitting on a cloud. He was chubby and behind His head was a triangle that was light blue. He had a darker blue cape that flowed with the wind. In His right hand was something like a torch, with fire coming out of the end. It was truly a beautiful sight.

When I arrived at the monastery, I began to have a great deal of anxiety due to the bishop saying I was imprudent. All of us are imprudent at times.

However, I didn't perceive myself as imprudent, as he suggested. I began to think everything I had done, even small decisions, were imprudent, but blind to it, and that maybe I should retire.

I went to confession to Fr. Canopener. He recommended I read the writings of St. Thomas Aquinas, on the subject of prudence, in his, *Summa Theologica.*

Immediately after receiving absolution, the thoughts vanished, as though I never had the problem or anxiety.

It was clear to me the devil was the source of these tormenting thoughts. Since then, I have begun to pray much to Our Lady and the saints for prudence.

During the retreat, I was inspired to read about the life of St. Charles of Sezze. His life is a great inspiration to me. Oh, how many times, I wish I could live the life I abandoned, as a Franciscan Perpetual Victim Martyr. I think about it almost every day.

On the way back from the retreat, I visited with my mother, who was not doing well. Due to viral pneumonia, she had to go to the hospital, but was dismissed the same day. After two weeks, there was little improvement.

When I returned to the rectory, I decided to watch the Extraordinary Form of the Mass to try to learn how to do it. I wanted to offer Masses for my mother, for the grace of a happy death, but also prayed, it would be God's will, she may be healed.

#182 SIMILARITIES OF LIFE OF ST. CHARLES SEZZE

Similarities of Life of St. Charles of Sezze

I continue to obtain tremendous inspiration from the life of this holy saint. There have been so many similarities in my life and his, that it truly dumbfounds me.
His priest uncle was murdered. A new seminary friend of mine was murdered.

His heart was touched by love before the Eucharist, and so was mine in Adoration.

He ministered in a plague. I ministered during COVID-19.

He had a vision of the Virgin Mary holding the Child Jesus, and so did I.

He asked Blessed Salvator Horta to work miracles, I did through Fr. Kapaun.

An illness of his was miraculously cured, and so did I.

He had demons attack him, so did I.

He charitably confronted women, who wore immodest clothing, so did I.

His autobiography opening comments were about God's mercy, so are mine.

His superiors persecuted him, I felt my superiors did this to me, but I may be wrong.

But his heroic virtue sets us apart. I certainly try very hard to practice virtue, but don't see how it's heroic. Many times I confided to priests, and a few lay people about difficulties; it took a long time for me to finally be able to have peace. Years ago, I prayed I would become a saint, and when I prayed the prayer, I asked Jesus that if I would become a saint someday, I wouldn't know it in this life. He sure answered that prayer. But, I hope to become a saint, even though it seems like I can never be one!

#183 SPIRITUAL DREAMS AND SUBMITTING TO GOD'S WILL & SUFFERING

Spiritual Dreams, Night of March 9th, early March 10th, 2022

The night I returned from a short retreat, I had two dreams. In one dream, I died and was being placed under a marble floor. There was a young man and an older lady who also died. The three of us could talk to each other, though we were dead. None of us wanted to be buried beneath the marble floor. I thought the floor was either at a chancery or in a church.

During this dream, I was partially awake, and realized a demon was shaking my arm. It then moved to my leg and then began to shake my leg. I was sleeping and dreaming, yet awake, and aware of being attacked by a demon while dreaming.

The other dream involved offering Mass, and during the Consecration, the Host miraculously came out of my hands, and went high in the air in the church. Someone then received Communion from me. When they received Communion, Particles from the Host, put in their mouth, fell on my arm, because they consumed the Host irreverently, crunching it in their front teeth, rather than trying to dissolve it when placed in their mouth.

Wisdom from St. Faustina – Submit to God's Will & Have Peace in Suffering

#1394 "Whatever God sends me, I accept with complete submission to His holy will. Wherever He puts me, I will faithfully try to do His holy will, as well as His wishes, to the extent of my power to do so, even if the will of God were to be as hard and difficult for me as was the will of the Heavenly Father for His Son, as He prayed in the Garden of Olives. I have come to see that if the will of the Heavenly Father was fulfilled in this way in His well-beloved Son, it will be fulfilled in us in exactly the same way: by suffering, persecution, abuse, disgrace. It is through all this, that my soul becomes like unto Jesus. And the greater the sufferings, the more I see I am becoming like Jesus. This is the surest way. If some other way were better, Jesus would have shown it to me. Sufferings in no way take away my peace. On the other hand, although I enjoy profound peace, that peace does not lessen my experience of suffering. Although my face is often bowed to the ground, and my tears flow profusely, at the same time, my soul is filled with profound peace and happiness…"

I can very much relate to this. Many times, I struggle to have complete submission to His holy will. How many times my face is bowed to the ground, or at times weep tears on my pillow, or before Jesus in the Blessed Sacrament during Adoration, due to persecution, abuse, suffering or disgrace, not being treated as I desire to be treated, which is worldly. And in the midst of it, peace is there. But at times, it is hard to see peace. It is true mental torture. To be at peace and be happy in the midst of suffering, knowing I am slowly being conformed to Jesus Crucified, gives joy to my soul, and yet outwardly, I am in torment. To feel despised, misunderstood, not accepted or believed, and this causes me to feel a lack of confidence in myself. Hopefully, this purifies my trust in Jesus and in His Mercy, for, I only want to please God and not man. I desire to have complete confidence in Him.

#184 WINDOW INTO MY SOUL

Depressed or Not? Opens a Window into my Soul

Lately, I have been feeling down or sad, but was unable to figure out why. I confessed my despondency to a priest. But later discovered the source was caused by a pre-diabetic condition, such that when my blood sugar was elevated, I felt sluggish and tired, and at times very drowsy. But, I also felt down. For the most part, I avoid sweets. However, I had been eating some high carbohydrate meals. Although I felt sad and tired, I had a sense of peace about myself. And this was when I was able to look, as through a window, into my soul.

The activity of the soul is different from the activity of the body, and the feelings we have. I had always wondered how St. Faustina often times mentioned this or that about her soul.

Now I understand. To come in contact with the soul, one needs to understand the inner workings of one's own conscience, and peace of mind a person has at the time.

This special grace helped me to soar above feelings, emotions, and outward disturbances that occur in one's life, and by this knowledge, one has a greater depth of peace. To know what pleases the soul and what makes the soul out of sorts is so very helpful to one's state of mind.

Sin and worldly comfort cause the soul to be disturbed, while suffering and its acceptance as well as prayer, works of mercy, and love, cause the soul to be delighted, despite one's health or one's feelings or emotions at the time.

O blessed soul, how I have finally discovered, who you are, and what you want. Your greatest joy is God Himself, and possessing Him, and even the consolations He gives, are only a mere shadow of Himself. A mirror reflects an image, but if the image itself, is "I AM, WHO AM", then it fulfills the deepest longing of the soul, to be one with God forever. O soul, how you long to be with your Creator.

#185 NEW KIND OF PRAYER

Prayer Change

I have felt so sluggish in prayer, but this was mostly caused by praying after I ate. After eating, I felt sad, and tired, and often times fell asleep while praying. I realized my prayer was not very fervent and lacked reverence. Therefore, I asked Jesus to help me have a more fervent prayer, and He gave it to me. But the enemy never sleeps; and when he sees a person given extra graces, he tries to thwart them. On several occasions, my prayer has moved to a greater intensity and I felt inspired to say things to Jesus, I hadn't said since my early conversion. I have been asking that our wills become one. I ask that I may have His Heart and He may take mine, and that our hearts will become one.

Thanks to the *Autobiography of St. Charles of Sezze*, I was able to see how I rebel against the smallest things God wills. But I desire to accept these things and embrace the crosses that go with them.

I have renewed my prayer of asking to be martyred; but of course; it would be a total grace, unmerited and undeserved. When St. Charles health started to decline, he came to the point of total surrender, and told the Lord, if he would lose his eyesight, or a leg, he would accept it for the love of Jesus. By the grace of God, I told the Lord the same thing, but that only with His grace of acceptance would I be able to endure such things.

The enemy, somehow, picks up on this type of prayer and attacks terribly, torturing the mind to make oneself feel unable to perform one's current duties. Thoughts such as, being so weak, one should just give up, and retire, or to accuse me of thinking everything I do is imprudent-- can come from the enemy.

But, God's grace abounds. The Lord gave much consolation. While praying in this manner, I had a very quiet soul. When I came before a statue of Mary, She unexpectedly gave me such a wonderful feeling of consolation, as though She put Her arms and mantle around me, as a mother comforts a hurting child.

#186 ONCE WAS LOST, NOW IS FOUND-- A CRUCIFIX

After 40 Years a Lost Crucifix is Found?

After my great-grandfather, Paul Schwinderspoon's death, a relative gave me a wooden crucifix formerly owned by him. The wooden crucifix had a plastic corpus that glowed in the dark. I greatly cherished it, and hung it on the wall in my bedroom. But I couldn't find it, that is, until last Monday, March 14th, 2022. I stopped by St. Gabriel's church in Crossroads, and as I looked through the freebie section, there it was. I noticed the nick on the top back of the crucifix. I couldn't believe what I was seeing, as that's how I remember it looking. How in the world it ended up at the church, and how I happened to stop by to find it, in the freebie section, was unbelievable. I could hardly believe it. I kept thinking, it can't be. Maybe, it just looks like it, or it really was my old crucifix. I immediately thanked Jesus and kissed His wounds. God is so good. If it isn't the same one, at least God wanted me to remember it, who it came from (grandpa), and He wanted me to have it again.

This inspired me to purchase a crucifix for each child at St. Timothy, as an Easter gift. Frequently, I use my own money to donate items like these to the people of the parish. Since my arrival here last year, I have donated scapulars, miraculous medals, a New Testament bible, the book, *Jesus Our Eucharistic Love,* and Crucifixes. The cost for the crucifixes was $1,000.

#187 HOW A SAINT DEALS WITH IMMODESTY

St. Charles & Immodest Women

"Likewise, I want women to adorn themselves with proper clothing, modestly and discreetly, not with braided hair and gold or pearls or costly garments, but rather by means of good works, as is proper for women making a claim to godliness." (1 Timothy 2:9-10)

When I read the following paragraph, from the *Autobiography of St. Charles of Sezze,* I laughed, and laughed, and laughed. I hope it wasn't disrespectful to Jesus in the Blessed Sacrament, since I was reading the book in the chapel, and consequently, laughing aloud at the time.

What I am going to relate here is a completely different experience he had, than mine, in addressing a modesty problem, which shows how a saint is beloved by God in a special way, and how a non-saint's experience (me), is so much different.

Pages 274-275 of his autobiography, read, "One woman who had been educated in a convent was given to this vanity, and, besides dressing immodestly, bathed everyday in perfumed water. God punished her for this, and for the bad example she was giving, by taking her husband away in death and sending on her, a horrible sickness that covered with suppurating sores, those members of her body through which she had been immodest. This even disfigured one of her eyes. Whereas she had formerly dressed vainly and immodesty, she now had to clothe herself fully out of necessity. The other case of a woman, whom I corrected charitably, asking her to dress properly, pointing out by some examples how much this displeased God, as well as that she was giving scandal. I promised I would pray for her if she did this. Seeing how obstinate her blindness made her, I said, with a particular feeling that came from our Lord: "The time will come when you will have to dress properly!" Because of a lawsuit not long after that, she lost all she possessed, and became terribly sick. Since the courts had taken everything, even mattresses and clothing, she was reduced to using an abandoned straw bed, and for clothes, she had to do with some dirty rags, that had once been a sheet. When finally she sent for me, I found her in the greatest misery. She was sorry for her sins and begged God to pardon her. Then she asked me, out of charity, to find her a blouse and a clean sheet. For the following day, she was to receive Holy Communion. I asked my companion what he thought about this. Because it was getting late, and we were on the slope of Monte Cavallo, a great distance from our monastery of Monte Cavallo, a great distance from our monastery of St. Peter in Montorio, he judged it would be better to go back home, and not give the Superior reason to punish us for returning at night. I told him to have no fears about that. Every time we are ready to show charity, our Lord will even permit the sun to stand still and not advance. O how wonderful is God! How much charity pleases Him! We went to find a blouse, brought it to the woman, and then returned to the monastery; and our Lord caused it to happen that we saw the sun in the very same position it had been, when we left the sick person for the first time. The next day, I found sheets for her and another blouse, a modest one, with some other alms. This is how God corrects and punishes sins of vanity in this life. It makes us think, too, of the next!"

My experience was much different from St. Charles of Sezze, due to my charitably correcting of a woman at St. Veronica in Brushwood City. I previously mentioned this in my diary, "the sun kept moving", and my superior (the bishop) corrected me, explaining that I should have never visited with the woman about it. I always thought saints suffered more than non-saints. Well, I guess that's not always true! At times God wants us to suffer for the love of souls, even if the person to whom we are suffering doesn't seem to be positively affected by it in this life. I was told a priest should never speak directly to a woman about her immodest clothing, but didn't listen to the advice. I felt my conscience was telling me otherwise. These words from St. Charles help me to know what I did was right, despite suffering for it. I think one of the reasons why I wasn't successful, is that I failed to do as St. Charles, which was an act of charity as well (buying a modest blouse) for the women who needed it! Just kidding. For a priest to purchase a piece of clothing for an immodest woman wouldn't be taken well at all, unless you're a saint. Ha Ha Ha!

#188 BLIND GUIDE

Blind in One Eye and Can't See Out of the Other

"Jesus said, "For judgment I came into the world, that those who see may become blind." Some Pharisees near Him heard this, and they said to Him, "Are we also blind?" Jesus said to them, "If you were blind, you would have no guilt, but now you say, 'We see', your guilt remains." (John 9:30-31)

In the past, those in authority over me, made it clear a priest should not directly address immodesty. But rather, pay no attention to the problem. But, I believe, if that were the case, the priest is not caring for the salvation of the soul of the immodest dresser, nor the men tempted because of it.

I prayed for one of the priests who said priests should do nothing about immodestly dressed women, and prayed he would see his all the spiritual consequences of failing to help a misguided soul, and also the truth of those dying unethically, without artificial nutrition and hydration, who could benefit from them, which he did not think was a problem.

Sadly, he developed an eye infection, didn't take care of his eye, and then, lost his eyesight in it. How sad to lose an eye. Unfortunately, it reminds me of the saying, "Blind in one eye and can't see out of the other." For truly he, and the others, are "blind guides."

I pray that his suffering in this life will prevent his need to suffer in the next life due to being spiritually blind by failing to be concerned about the salvation of souls, and for his obligation to help the dying obtain food and water, when they would benefit from them. He has a degree in moral theology, with an emphasis on medical ethics.

#189 FALLEN AWAY CATHOLIC HELPS DYING MAN

Fallen Away Catholic – Helps Dying Man

"A man was going down from Jerusalem to Jericho, when he was attacked by robbers. They stripped him of his clothes, beat him, and went away, leaving him half dead. A priest happened to be going down the same road; and when he saw the man, he passed by on the other side. So too, a Levite, when he came to the place and saw him, passed by on the other side. But a Samaritan, as he traveled, came to where the man was; and when he saw him, he took pity on him. He went to him and bandaged his wounds, pouring on oil and wine. Then he put the man on his own donkey, brought him to an inn and, took care of him. The next day he took out two denarii and gave them to the innkeeper. 'Look after him,' he said, 'and when I return, I will reimburse you for any extra expenses you may have.'" (Luke 10:30-35)

The local postmaster is a woman. I was offering Masses and praying for her and other fallen away Catholics in our parish to come back to church. She is living with a man outside of marriage, and after we had a few conversations, she finally decided to move out, and buy a house, so she could live a good moral life. On the way to signing the deed to her new home, she saw a man lying on the road, due to a motorcycle accident. She stopped to help him and called an ambulance.

She then called her realtor, and said she would be late due to helping a victim from a motorcycle accident. She knelt before him, prayed for him, and then removed her jacket to support his bloody head. The ambulance arrived and took him to the hospital, where he died. She then called her realtor, and told her she had a terrible day, and the realtor said, "Me too. I just found out a friend of mine died." It was the same man the postmaster helped on the road. If she hadn't decided to live a good moral life, and hadn't moved out after buying a home, would anyone have been there at the man's last hour? The postmaster surmised his sudden death was caused by the Covid-19 vaccine.

#190 CONSECRATION OF RUSSIA AND
ST. FAUSTINA'S SPIRITUAL CHILDHOOD & TRUST IN GOD'S MERCY

Consecration of Russia, Ukraine, All Humanity & the Church
to the Immaculate Heart of Mary

Due to the invasion of Russia into Ukraine, and the killing of so many innocent people, the Ukraine Conference of Bishops asked Pope Francis to consecrate Russia and Ukraine to the Immaculate Heart of Mary. Pope Francis, in union with all the bishops of the world, including priests and lay faithful, did the consecration on March 25th 2022, the Solemnity of the Annunciation.

At St. Timothy, we had a Eucharistic Holy Hour from 10:30am to 11:45am. Then we consecrated the parish, our families, and ourselves to the Hearts of Jesus and Mary, and to St. Joseph, and then prayed the Litany of the Blessed Virgin Mary. At noon, we had Mass and after Mass, we did the prescribed Consecration prayer at 12:30pm, the same time Pope Francis and the bishops at 6:30pm in Rome. What a beautiful grace! The world is watching and hoping now, that the consecration occurred as Our Lady requested. Surely, this will inaugurate the Triumph of the Immaculate Heart. We hope and pray.

St. Faustina's Diary Helps Again
Spiritual Childhood & Trusting in God's Mercy Despite My Sins

I was contemplating why Jesus appears to me as a child, and not as a man, and I finally received the answer to my question. In #1481, of St. Faustina's diary, she said, "Although You are so little, I know that You are God. Why do You take the appearance of such a little baby to commune with me?" Jesus responded, "Because I want to teach you spiritual childhood. I want you to be very little, because when you are little, I carry you close to My Heart, just as you are holding Me close to your heart right now."

Jesus desires to teach me spiritual childhood. Thank you, Jesus! These words from her diary #1485 also spoke to my heart: "Soul: Lord, I doubt that You will pardon my numerous sins; my misery fills me with fright. Jesus: My mercy is greater than your sins and those of the entire world. Who can measure the extent of my goodness? For you, I descended from heaven to earth; for you, I allowed myself to be nailed to the cross; for you, I let my Sacred Heart be pierced with a lance, thus opening wide the source of mercy for you. Come, then, with trust to draw graces from this fountain. I never reject a contrite heart. Your misery has disappeared in the depths of My mercy. Do not argue with Me about your wretchedness. You will give me pleasure if you hand over to me all your troubles and griefs. I shall heap upon you the treasures of My grace."

O, Jesus, I do trust, that no matter how miserable my soul is in your sight; that when I depart from this life, not only will my sins be forgiven, but the punishment due to them as well. Oh, Jesus, how I want to go directly to heaven. I would rather suffer in this life, and not in the next. Yet, your mercy is so infinite. To suffer in this life, to atone for sins, You can even do away with these as well.

In #1488, Jesus also told St. Faustina, "My child, know that the greatest obstacles to holiness are discouragement and exaggerated anxiety. All temptations united together ought not disturb your interior peace, not even momentarily. Sensitiveness and discouragement are the fruits of self-love. You should not become discouraged but strive to make my love reign in place of your self-love. Have confidence, my child. Do not lose heart in coming for pardon, for I am always ready to forgive you. As often as you beg of it, you glorify my mercy."

When I read these words, it was as though a veil was lifted from my spiritual life. I have much more peace, when recognizing, why I do, what I do; and because I am trying to overcome these faults and sins. Thank you, Jesus!

#191 PENNY FOR YOUR THOUGHTS
& QUARTERS FOR GOD'S MERCY
THE HABIT (ROBE)

When I was a child, my father used to say at times, "A penny for your thoughts." He would say this because he wondered what I was thinking. I decided to go to Confession today in Waterbury, and then drive to Rolling Hills to pick up my habit. I ordered a Franciscan habit, and needed to have it hemmed. It was ready to be picked up at the dry cleaners. The habit (robe) will only be used when I get out of bed, so I can visit Jesus in the Blessed Sacrament and consequently, wear decent clothing when entering the chapel. It's easy to put on, without the need to put on pants and a clerical shirt when I make visits in the middle of the night.

While the desire of my heart is to once again become a Franciscan, at my age it's impossible. After I picked it up, I decided to purchase a hamburger at Panjellies Restaurant and went inside to use the restroom. The poor clerk said that the restaurant ran out of quarters. I told her I had a jar full of quarters in the car. I returned with them and the workers happily received them in exchange for dollars. The Lord helped me to know that He cared about their lack of quarters, and guided me to that restaurant, so I could help them and at the same time, unload my coins. The Lord saw their misery and allowed me to give them mercy, helping them in their need; and, He saw my misery, of having too many coins, and allowed me to receive mercy from them, by exchanging the quarters for bills.

Jesus wanted to teach me the definition of mercy is to become aware of the misery of another and to relieve their misery with an act of mercy, and at times, there is an exchange of mercy, from one person to another. His Heart was opened to see the misery of our sins on His Cross and He relieved our misery, by His mercy.

#192 THE OWL

There is an owl that can be heard almost every night about 10 pm while it hoots outside my bedroom window. I believe the Lord wants the owl to visit me. It is so soothing to hear his hooting. At times, he stays for a while, and other times he comes just for a few minutes. God's creatures fulfill His will and help us in our lives, to become aware, God watches over us and cares about us. And at times, though rarely, the owl returns at about 2 am. God's creatures are a joy. They raise my spirit at the sound of their voices as they praise the Lord.

#193 REVEALING THE TRUTH OF COVID-19

A video by Dr. Billy Reed claims he discovered the truth about COVID-19. He states it's a derivative of snake venom created in a biological weapon laboratory. He claims the vaccine contains snake venom derivatives. And this derivative is also found in an FDA-approved drug, Remdesivir, that allegedly causes deaths of COVID-19 patients in ICU. The horror of it all. He states doctors should treat COVID-19 patients as though they were bitten by a snake. According to him, snake bite victims lose their sense of taste and smell. They have difficulty breathing. COVID-19 patients develop strokes, paralysis, and myocarditis (inflammation of the heart), which is what snake bite victims contract.

He recommends medicines such as Hydroxychloroquine, Azithromycin and Zinc in early treatment. He also claims nicotine is like an antidote. He believes there is a world-wide plan to decrease the population. I forwarded the information to doctors and nurses, and spoke about it to some lay friends and several priests. Can this be true? What a terrible time we are living in. If this is true, then perhaps it's a punishment for the killing of the unborn that so few seem to care about. Or is this fake? And, if so, it could deeply harm believers of it.

#194 THE O-RING

A wealthy goodhearted Catholic purchased a Processional Cross for St. Timothy in Browbeat. The current Processional Cross is old and broken. The corpus moved about and the metal is tarnished. I tried to polish it, to no avail. When the new cross arrived with the base for the Processional Cross, it was beautiful to behold. But, when the cross was placed in the base, it made a loud bang. I said this prayer, "O Jesus, what can I do to stop the loud bang when the cross is placed in its holder?" The thought occurred to me, a rubber O-ring used for connecting pipes would work.

I went to the hardware store in Montecarlo City, and found O-rings, and when I placed them on the base, they fit perfectly. After installing them when I left the church, I walked past the metal statue of Jesus with children and happened to look down on the ground. You guessed it. It was an O-ring the exact size I just purchased and installed. I was astonished, and wondered what the Lord was trying to tell me. Surely, I think He was pleased I came to Him in a childlike way asking Him how to solve the Processional Cross banging problem. He wants us to ask Him for everything, as a little child, even a little O-ring, and let me know He will provide for it.

I believe He also wanted me to know it was His idea and not mine. Jesus inspired me to pray for help when I had the difficulty. He inspired the idea to purchase the O-ring and He cares about the smallest details of our lives.

But, I believe there was an additional meaning for me. A few days later, I recalled, that back in 1986, a Catholic teacher was a passenger on the Challenger rocket. However, an O-ring used for the rocket was bad, and she, as well as the whole Challenger crew died in a midair explosion. The nation's children watched on television in horror when it happened. Back then, being young, and not so smart, there was a joke about her. People and I used to say, "Do you know the color of Sharon's eyes?" The other person would say, "No", then the joke-teller would say, "They were blue. One blew this way and the other blew that way." The Lord helped me to understand who terrible it was to joke about it, and He wanted me to repent of it.

She said this in an interview. "I'm Catholic. I teach catechism to eighth graders. I don't know whether 200-miles above Earth, I'm going to feel that I'm closer to God. I've never taught my kids or tried to make people believe that God's up there somewhere. I believe that He, or should I say She? -- has always been part of our lives. And it's the way, that you treat one another that manifests good will."

I think the Lord wants me to pray for her soul, though it has been many years since she died. To call God, "She" publicly was not good. She went to her judgment shortly after she made that public statement. The Lord uses even a tiny O-ring, to bring about good for others, repentance from a sin committed years ago, and can help a deceased soul needing prayers. Oh, the infinite mercy of God, who desires to help souls in their misery.

#195 CHRISM MASS

Every year, all diocesan priests are obligated to attend the Chrism Mass, where the bishop blesses the Holy Oils used for parishes. They are the oil of the sick, chrism, and the oil of catechumen. At the Mass, priests renew our promises made at the time of our ordination. During Lent, I didn't want to go to the Chrism Mass because, I didn't want to be around the bishop. But by the grace of God, I was finally able to see the event as an opportunity to put behind the wounds and pains of the past, and see it as an act of obedience to Jesus. And, do it for the love of Jesus, who would make it sweet.

When the priests were processing in the Cathedral for Mass, the bishop stood near the front of the loggia, watching as the priests processed by. He turned his gaze towards me and stared. I did something totally unexpected. Rather than turning my head and acting as though I didn't see him, I looked directly back at him, smiled and waved. I kept waving with a big authentic smile on my face. I was so happy to be able to see, in the present moment, the opportunity of showing my love and respect toward him and seeing Jesus in him. His eyes followed me, as I walked past. He had a rather blank look on his face, with an expression I will never forget. But I overlooked his unusual facial expression and kept smiling with love. What a grace from God! Thank you, Jesus! This Lent, turned out much better than I anticipated, and it prepared me to celebrate the glorious Resurrection of Jesus on Easter. It was pure grace, that I did this act of mercy.

#196 HOLY WEEK & GOOD FRIDAY – TO REMEMBER

On Passion Sunday (Palm Sunday), as I was leaving the Chapel at the rectory, I heard in my mind, "You're going to get the stigmata." Because the thought caught me off guard, I replied, "Only if it's God's will." Then I said, "I have already received the stigmata (was wounded) on Jan. 22nd (2021) when I was told I was fired from the hospital." I then forgot about hearing those words.

However, on Holy Wednesday night, early in the morning on Holy Thursday, I woke up with excruciating pain in my left arm and hand. My fingers were closed, and I could not move them at all because they were so stiff. The pain in my hand and arm was unbearable. I don't think I had such physical pain before. My arm was numb and stiff. I slowly used the other hand to move my arm and hands. The pain finally went away. I don't understand what happened. I first thought maybe I had a blood clot in my hand or arm. Then I wondered if maybe the arm fell asleep, due to the way I was laying. But never had I had such terrible pain like that before.

Then, early in the morning on Good Friday, April 15th, 2022, I woke up, and began to feel pain in the middle of my right hand steadily increasing. It became intense, that lasted five to ten minutes, then slowly went away. I don't understand what happened with either of these events.

Later, on Good Friday, as I was doing my meditation on the sufferings of Jesus, Our Lord allowed me to feel, in a small way, what He went through, while hanging from the Cross. I don't know the cause of these pains.

It was not until Holy Saturday that I remembered the words from Passion Sunday. I don't know what to think about all this. Could it be the enemy is trying to make me prideful? The enemy knew what would happen later in the week, and so maybe wanted to take something natural, that occurred for some health reason, to make me think I would receive the stigmata.

Or, was all this from God, who for some reason chose these events, so that I may offer up these sufferings for the conversion of sinners, the poor souls in purgatory, and in reparation for sins against the Hearts of Jesus and Mary?

While we were at church at 3 pm on Good Friday, we prayed the Chaplet of Divine Mercy, a Novena prayer, and then the Rosary. I returned to the priest's residence about 3:40 pm and a delivery truck arrived. It was the crucifixes I ordered. How wonderful they came during the hour we celebrated Jesus dying on the Cross on Good Friday. I had hoped to give them to the children, and people of the parish on Passion Sunday (Palm Sunday), the previous Sunday. But the Lord wanted them to arrive the hour and day we celebrate the day He suffered and died. What an amazing gift!

Later that evening, I celebrated the Passion of Jesus. When I elevated the pre-consecrated people's Host, from a previous Mass, that was taken from a ciborium reserved in a tabernacle located in the sacristy from Holy Thursday night, and as I said, "Behold the Lamb of God, behold Him who takes away the sins of the world", I felt the Host beat between my fingers, as though I was holding the Heart of Jesus. It was completely unexpected, and I was astonished by what had happened. Just like in the past, the Lord Jesus wanted to remind me, He is truly there! Thank you, Jesus.

I will be sure to tell my spiritual director about these events. He is my protection.

#197 WHOLE LOT OF BULL

Today, I remembered several bull stories. The first story happened during the summer I graduated from high school. The local tavern "beer joint", called "Red's", was named after Michael O'Malley. Everyone called Michael "Red" due to his red hair. He rented a mechanical bull for men and women who would pay to ride it. The mechanical bull became popular in bars and traveled from tavern to tavern, as a result of the movie, *Urban Cowboy*, starring John Travolta. I paid the nominal fee to ride the mechanical bull. They turned up the speed as high as it would go, but I didn't get bucked off. The rider could hold on to a saddle strap with only one hand, while the other hand couldn't grasp anything and was raised in the air when the bull was bucking. There was a lot of hollering by the onlookers cheering me on. While ridding the bull, I wore my cowboy hat given by my mother for my high school graduation.

A few years later, when I was working at Bob Gart's Grocery Store in Fort Hickok, a tornado was spotted not far from the city. No one was injured. A few days after the tornado went through, an old farmer, Anthony Legee, came to the store. He told the cashier what happened at his farm. As he was talking to her, I was bagging groceries for another patron. He related this story. He said, "Did you know a tornado went through my pasture?" The clerk responded, "I heard about it." In a slow German accented voice, he said, "Well, after it went through my pasture, I went to check the cattle, and I couldn't find a bull. I looked down by the creek, and he wasn't there. I looked by the barn, and he wasn't there. I looked by the pond, and he wasn't there. I looked everywhere, and couldn't find my bull anywhere. When I "headed" back to the house, I walked under a tree and looked up. And there it was, a two-thousand-pound bull hanging in the tree."

#198 SPIRITUAL DIRECTOR & THE STIGMATA

My spiritual director called today at the regularly scheduled day and time. During our conversation, I mentioned what happened during Holy Week and asked what the thought about the stigmata incident and also about the time I felt pain in my arm and hands. He wisely suspected the evil one was at work. The enemy was trying to make me proud. What a gift it is to have a spiritual director, who stands in the place of Jesus and is able to protect the soul from the enemy.

#199 DIVINE MERCY IMAGE DISTRIBUTION

Every year, I look forward to the many special graces received on Divine Mercy Sunday, and as a priest, I have always preached about it, and when able, held a Holy Hour at 3 pm. One year, I was invited to do the Divine Mercy Holy Hour and Mass at the Cathedral.

The year Pope John Paul II was canonized, I was invited to offer Mass and lead a Holy Hour at St. Charles of Sezze parish in Rolling Hills.

At every parish I was pastor, I placed a large Divine Mercy Image in the parish. It was placed in St. Veronica Giuliani in Brushwood City (in the church); St. Anthony in Jericho City (in the church); Immaculate Heart of Mary in Wheatland (in the gym) because there was already one in the church. At St. Timothy in Browbeat, a parishioner and I each paid half the cost of the image that was placed in the church near the statue of Mary.

I asked permission to place a Divine Mercy image in their chapel called "Divine Mercy Chapel" at the Doorway to Heaven Nursing Center. But Sister Agnes Rangle didn't want such an image in their "Divine Mercy Chapel". She thought it was unnecessary to have a picture of Jesus in the chapel.

At Mother of Misery Healthcare System at St. Henry Hospital, I asked permission to place a large image of the Divine Mercy in the Chapel, and received permission from the Pastoral Care Department supervisor. But a sister of Misery, who complained about it, had it removed several months later.

I donated a large Divine Mercy image for the grade school of Holy Angels parish. In every parish I was pastor, I placed 8 by 10 photos of the Divine Mercy image in frames and gave them to parishioners, either on Easter or Divine Mercy weekend. Everyone was able to receive an image. This also included the Divine Mercy services at St. Charles of Sezze parish and every parish I was assigned. I gave away thousands of the images.

At Immaculate Heart of Mary parish in Wheatland, we had a float for the Old Prairie Parade. Our church youth walked beside the float giving away free Divine Mercy pictures to people in the crowds along the streets. Most non-Catholics took them.

#200 GOD'S MERCY THROUGH FORGIVENESS

"Put on then, as God's chosen ones, holy and beloved, heartfelt compassion, kindness, humility, gentleness, and patience, bearing with one another and forgiving one another, if one has a grievance against another; as the Lord has forgiven you, so must you also do." (Colossians 3:12-13)

Everyone sometime in their life has to forgive others. By God's grace, and through much prayer, confession, and especially His divine mercy, I forgave all who have ever hurt me. I pray, by God's grace, I will forgive everyone in the future, who may harm me, because I love everyone, and want all to obtain heaven. O Jesus, with all my heart, I forgive. I thank You, Lord, for the mercies You bestow on them, through me, that flows from the very depths of Your Sacred Heart. Thank you, O Lord, for creating an icon of mercy within my heart. You know very well I could not have forgiven everyone had it not been for your grace and inspiration. You know all the untold mercies, never mentioned. But, You, and I, hold within our hearts, the love for each other, which is so tender. Your mercy endures forever.

#201 THE BIGGEST FISH I NEVER CAUGHT

"When they arrived at shore, Peter went back into the boat to help them collect the fish, and they counted 153 fish—and large fish, at that. While there were so many fish, the net did not break." (John 21:11)

This weekend, the 3rd Sunday of Easter, the Gospel is about Jesus appearing on the side of the shore and the apostles who caught 153 large fish. This reminded me of our high school class of 1981, Senior Skip Day. Senior Skip Day was approved by parents and the school. For Skip Day, my class decided to go camping and fishing at Cherry Wood Bluff reservoir, in western Ohio.

During Skip Day, I caught the largest fish I ever caught, without a fishing pole or a fishing net.

The way most people in Ohio go fishing, is with a fishing pole. In the time of Jesus, fishing businesses used large nets to throw off the side of the boat. I never brought my fishing pole or a net to Cherry Wood Bluff Reservoir.

I decided to sleep in my sleeping bag on the ground outdoors. In the morning, a friend and I walked along the shore of the lake, and right in front of us was a large dead fish in the water. I took it out of the water. We surmised the fish died due to getting hit by a boat. We brought the large fish to the Dam Store and I told a fish tale. I told the owner I caught the fish. He weighed and measured the fish, and it was the largest fish "caught" so far that year at Cherry Wood Bluff Reservoir. Therefore, it's true, I caught a fish without a fishing pole or a net. But it was an easy "catch", since it was already dead.

#202 BASKETBALL CHAMPIONSHIP WON. FAMILY CONSECRATED TO THE HEARTS OF JESUS & MARY RESOLVES DRUG ADDICTION

When I was pastor of Immaculate Heart in Wheatland, the wife of the Catholic principal was upset because Wheatland High basketball team was experiencing turmoil. A new Catholic coach, formerly from a Catholic High School in Rolling Hills, became the new boys' basketball coach for the public high school. His new ways caused many of the players to drop out. Consequently, only six players remained. The players who left, said the team would lose all its games because of the new coach.

Only one player, Bart Goodboy, and the coach were Catholic. Cammi, Bart's mother, came up with the idea to consecrate the team to the Hearts of Jesus and Mary. And so, one afternoon the coach brought the team to church. The coach, Bart, and the non-Catholic players, as well as Cammi, and I, recited the prayers of consecration, asking for God's help and blessing for the team.

On January 1st of that year, I was transferred to St. John of God Hospital in Tantrum and the team finished the season rather well. The following year, the basketball team did extraordinarily well, losing only two games the entire season, and they went to state.

At the state basketball championship, when the score was tied, Bart made a basket, with a layup, just as the buzzer sounded, causing Wheatland High to win the 3A state championship by two points.

After the game, no one could find Bart. Finally, about an hour later, he came home. When his parents asked where he had been, he said, "I went to church to thank Jesus in the Tabernacle for allowing us to win. And I thanked him for allowing me to make the final points that made it happen." When I heard what he said, it moved me to tears, because as the former pastor of the parish, I helped many parishioners to come to know and love Jesus in the Eucharist. Bart and his family had a weekly Holy Hour.

Several years later, after Bart had graduated from high school, he became addicted to drugs and almost died twice. Due to his addiction, I told the family to consecrate themselves to the Hearts of Jesus and Mary, and told John, Bart's father, to be sure Bart would do the consecration too. And he did. Today, he is now living in Arizona, and doing well, drug-free.

#203 FUNERAL & SOLEMNITY WITH NO INCENSE

The family, of a former parishioner in Wheatland, asked me to give the funeral homily of her mother. I had kept in contact with the family over the years. The daughter of the woman who died was allergic to incense.

Years previously, while I pastor of Immaculate Heart of Mary, at the evening Saturday Mass, I didn't use incense, except for two Sunday Masses and on special occasions, so those who had a problem with incense would be able to attend Mass. Now, at the death of her mother, Betty, her daughter requested I not use incense at Mass. Otherwise, she may get a migraine.

This event reminded me of my first Solemnity Mass as a priest. On Aug. 15th, the Solemnity of the Assumption of Mary, at St. Gertrude Parish in Rolling Hills, I planned to use incense. Before Mass, I explained to the servers how to use incense. When we were ready to begin Mass, I waved to the organist to start the music for Mass to begin. As the congregation was singing, I opened the thurible, and the charcoal wasn't lit. Not knowing what I do, I wrongly told the altar server to walk down the aisle, without it being lit. As we processed down the aisle, with the unlit charcoal, a woman at the back of the church, saw the thurible, and as we walked by, she started coughing.

Stupidly, and since I was nervous, I walked around the altar swinging the unlit charcoal in the thurible and then told the altar server, we would not use it for the remaining part of the Mass.

When Mass was finished, and after we had processed out, the woman who was coughing, approached me, and said, "Father, will you please not use incense in the future, it causes me to cough." I responded, "But Ma'am, it wasn't lit." To see the astonished look on her face was absolutely hysterical. I never laughed in front of her, but when I was in the sacristy, I couldn't help but let it out.

This crazy event caused me to realize, that for some, it's more psychological than natural to cough when incense is used. It also made me realize, I can do really dumb things when nervous. But in the end, God brings good out of everything, such as, to teach me humility and also help a parishioner understand why she thinks she needs to cough.

#204 ADDITIONAL PENANCE – FALLEN AWAY COME BACK DURING LENT

I received permission from my spiritual director to wear a Franciscan cord with three knots, to be worn, under the pants for penance. The children of Fatima wore a cord during the day as a penance, but the Virgin Mary told them to remove it, while sleeping. I find it annoying, but not painful. I also asked permission to do an additional fast day, every week on Saturdays, which is in addition to fasting on Wednesday and Fridays. St. Charles of Sezze and many other saints and non-canonized Catholics fasted on Saturday in honor of the Blessed Virgin Mary. My spiritual director told me to not fast on Saturday during the Easter season.

Over years, I regret my sins the most, but second to them, I regret not suffering as much as I could for the conversion of sinners, in reparation for sins committed against the Immaculate Heart of Mary and the Sacred Heart of Jesus, and for the poor souls in purgatory. To accept daily suffering as it comes is more difficult than voluntary penance. It's not as easy at times to not adjust the thermostat or to accept people or situations that cause suffering.

During Lent, I fasted three days each week, (Wednesday, Friday, and Saturday) and offered Masses and Rosaries and Holy Hours to bring back the fallen away. There were five fallen away parishioners at St. Timothy who came back to the Church during Lent. The Holy Hours of Adoration by the people could have been the greatest contributing factor. Praise the Lord!

#205 PAGE TORN OUT AND MISSING

#206 ANNULMENT NIGHTMARE FOR COUPLE

At St. Timothy, a couple who conceived a child out of wedlock, decided they wanted to get married in the Catholic Church. Due to no resident pastor at St. Timothy, at the time, the couple went to St. Peter's Church in Lionel to fill out the paperwork for their annulment. The young man isn't Catholic, but she is. I helped him finish the process, except he needed to fill out the Marital History Form and to obtain the marriage license from the priest from Lionel, since he had given it to him. However, the priest was reassigned to St. Cecilia in Bluesville, Ohio, and took it with him.

The couple moved between Port Apotty City, Ohio, located on the shore of Lake Erie, and Wiennerfield, Ohio, about 20-miles south of Port Apotty. They wanted to do the annulment process with their priest at their new parish. I called the priest, from St. John Vianney parish in Wiennerfield, who said he would take over the case. But he later changed his mind, and transferred the information to the priest at Seven Sorrows Parish in Port Apotty.

The priest from Wiennerfield delayed in doing anything for almost a year, even though the couple and I kept encouraging him to work on the annulment. Out of desperation, they asked if I would be their advocate again with the annulment. During this year, the couple had another child.

The young man was interested in becoming Catholic, and I told both priests his desire. But neither spoke to him about the possibility of him becoming Catholic after he would receive the annulment. The priest at Wiennerfield said he wants to now help with the annulment.

Unfortunately, neither priest seemed interested in helping him become Catholic, nor helping him to obtain an annulment. They're too busy to help their sheep. How sad is all this! A pastor of souls, what does that mean? Perhaps it means, a pastor of a little white ball used on a golf course! The priest finally sat down with him and completed the forms. Amen! But then, he never mailed it for six months! Lord, have mercy, on his failure to do an act of charity.

#207 HIDDEN SUFFERINGS

Everyone has hidden sufferings. My mother hides her sufferings exceptionally well by not telling anyone about her physical illnesses. Because of the way I walk at times, and due to their questions about it, I need to disclose to others I have arthritis. It is often very painful in my back, hips, neck, ribs, etc. and is responsible for migraines. When I wake up at night to use the restroom, I need to use a cane, or I could easily fall. As I walk, I grab on the walls, the dresser, and the sink to keep standing. With bad fallen arches, severe stiffness in my body, the pain makes it very difficult to walk in the middle of the night and early in the morning. This can also happen during the day, when a cold front is approaching or has arrived.

Due to a laxative needed for constipation, at times, I have sudden bowel movements after I eat food, including immediately after consuming the Host and drinking the Precious Blood at Mass. At times, I end up making my thanksgiving after receiving Holy Communion sitting on a toilet. A pretty humiliating experience, especially since the King of Kings just came into the throne of my heart, and I have to sit on a porcelain throne (toilet) thanking Him and enjoying His divine presence and love.

While doing hospital ministry at St. John of God Hospital in Tantrum, my doctor suggested, I take a sleep lab test. During the sleep tests my heart rate drops to the upper 40s. I also have difficulty breathing at night and the inability to sleep well. Several times the technician tried to adjust the breathing machine. But for some odd reason, my body rejected it. I'm one of the few who can't use the machines.

Due to sleep apnea causing low oxygen, a low heart rate, and not getting much sleep, in the mornings I can wake up confused and unable to think clearly. All this is exacerbated when I also wake up with a migraine caused by arthritis. The combination of these makes my early mornings make it difficult to function well. During Mass, I rely on reading my homily and carefully praying the prayers of the *Roman Missal*. I unite all this to the Cross of Jesus at every Mass for the conversion of sinners.

There are occasional conflicts with priests, whereby most all priests think one way, and I think differently. This kind of suffering entails wondering if my view is in error, but normally, it's not. For example, almost every priest had no problems watching the R-rated movie of Fr. Stu Long with its terrible cussing and a sex scene. I wish I hadn't watched the movie, and suggested the Catholic youth of the parish don't go to it. I don't think the CYO leaders should organize the youth to attend. However, despite my attempts to persuade parents to avoid taking their children, almost every parent and almost every priest thought it was not an issue for 8th grade through high school to watch it.

I know of only two other priests who agreed with me. Some parents of this age group had an issue with their child watching an animated abortion, without blood, but didn't think it was a problem, if their child watched a sex scene and horrific cussing.

I suffer when people don't understand the consequences of exposing children and even adults to see a movie that isn't good for the soul. I suffer when I know other priests don't see the problems of it. At times, I feel rejected and not liked. But these feelings are very worldly. However, it's painful, since if people don't like the priest, they won't listen when he speaks about morality or virtue.

The agony of doubting oneself is very keen and cuts to the heart. But, when I turn to Jesus and cry out, "Jesus I trust in You", He restores peace to my troubled heart. Perhaps the reason my conscience is so sensitive, is due to living in the dark side of the world without confession for twenty years. However, after returning to Confession in 1991, I confess weekly, while most priests and laypeople go to Confession once a month or less. My point, is not that I am any better than they, but that frequent confession sharpens the conscience.

I thank the Lord for His goodness and mercy and continue to daily ask Him to help me carry my crosses, embrace them for the love of Him, and for the conversion of sinners. I am no better than others. But I have received special grace, to more easily distinguish evil versus good.

#208 ST. PADRE PIO DREAM

On the night of May 7th, 2022, the last day of a novena for Bishop Courageous in which two priests and I prayed for him, I dreamt St. Padre Pio was smiling. I asked if I could kiss his wounds in his hands, and he held one out, but the wound was no longer there. In its place was scar tissue, and he smiled at me. The dream was vivid and in color. In the past, it seems, whenever there was any interaction with St. Padre Pio, it had to do with my obedience to the bishop. Obedience is the virtue I most admire in him. He suffered in obedience without complaining. I think he was pleased I was the instrument to help other priests to pray for the bishop. He was unable to offer public Mass or hear Confessions for ten years and never complained. He and other saints are good examples of how "Canceled Priests" should act when their bishop treats them unjustly. My vote is to make St. Padre Pio the patron of Canceled Priests.

#209 NIGHT TIME VISITS TO JESUS

Every night I wake up to go to the restroom. After using the restroom, I put on the Franciscan cloak (habit) and go to Jesus in the Tabernacle. I tell Him I love Him and am so happy He is here in this house with me. Then I pray either the Chaplet of Divine Mercy or the Chaplet of Tears for various intentions, usually for the bishop. But, at times, I pray for the seriously ill and dying or for people who are tempted to commit suicide.

#210 EXTOL MY MERCY

As I was praying before Jesus in Eucharistic Adoration at the rectory, I distinctly heard the voice of Jesus in my mind, say, "I desire that you extol my mercy." I responded, saying, "I'm sorry, Lord, I don't know what extol means." He didn't say anything in return. I looked up on the computer the word "extol" and it states, "to give glory and praise".

I am uncertain as to the ways the Lord wants me to give glory and praise for His mercy and believe He will let me know, since I trust that if the words were from Him, He will help me to do what He is asking of me. Perhaps, one way is to publish this autobiography. But, if so, it must be done in a way, no one will know it is me.

#211 HOSPITAL MINISTRY REFLECTION

I was reflecting on the many ways God used me to bestow His mercy. Most especially, this occurred during hospital ministry over five years as a chaplain. I am certain the Lord Jesus saved hundreds and hundreds of souls who were away from the sacraments for many years. Just before death, many went to Confession and came back to the Church. They received Holy Communion and the Apostolic Pardon. I am always very private about these things, but God wants His mercy to be known. At times, at the end of the day, I was so happy and joyful to be in the right place, at the right time, just before a patient died. A good number of them received God's infinite mercy after being away from the Church for decades and decades.

#212 FR. STU LONG'S STORY AND MY STORY

After reading more about the life of Father Stu, it amazed me how his story and mine are similar. He liked "Bigfoot". I was a fan of the movie *Big Foot*, the first movie I ever watched at the theater in my hometown. It's sad to say, but I committed worse and more grievous sins than he. He boxed, and I did karate kick boxing, but only for a few months. I also wrestled in grade school in PE class and was undefeated until the last match against a heavy boy. I threw the match as mentioned earlier. Fr. Stu had a motorcycle accident and I had a car accident due to excessive drinking of alcohol. He cussed like a sailor, and so did I. He had a terrible struggle with an illness, but I have never had such a thing. His illness brought him, and others, closer to Christ. I am sure my trials and difficulties endured in life have brought me closer to Jesus, and for them, I thank the Lord. Fr. Stu's bravery is inspiring. He went through much to become a priest.

The point of all this, is that God's mercy was abundant in His life, and out of humility, it seems His mercy towards me, was more abundant, since the misery of my life was much worse than his. I wonder if the revealing of my life would be a good way to Extol God's mercy, but I would need to do it in such a way as to not hurt or offend others. Perhaps I could change the names and places within it. O Lord, Thy will be done. Give me the grace to do as you desire. Fr. Stu's story gives me inspiration to share my story, and "Extol Your Mercy."

#213 SPIRITUAL HEALING OF MENTALLY ILL THANKS TO CHILD JESUS

A friend, I have known since 1991 is mentally ill. Many years ago, she was diagnosed with multiple personality disorder. She said she was a victim of Satanic ritual abuse. She claims there are children "inside her", and has never been able to pray to Jesus. In the past, she has even said she hates Him. However, she loves the heavenly Father. She said someone who dressed as a priest abused her when she was a child. She said, since the priest represents Jesus, she wants nothing to do with Him. It is my opinion, her abuser, may have been a Satanic priest.

I suggested she pray to the infant Jesus. She was able to pray to Him as a child. And since then, she now loves Jesus, and has found healing. Praise the Lord! I gave her a small statue of the Divino el Nino, holding out His Heart.

She said she called Bishop Courageous just before the last presidential election and asked him to make a statement telling the people of the Diocese, they shouldn't vote for a pro-abortion candidate, when at the same time, the other candidate is pro-life. She asked him to tell the people it would be a sin to do so. Furthermore, she told him abortion is a very grave evil that outweighs the other issues and because of its gravity, one could never vote for a pro-abortion candidate if the other candidate is pro-life. I believe what she said is right. A priest from our diocese said he published a homily on his parish website that said one cannot vote in favor of a Democrat, who is a pro-abortion candidate, while the other candidate is Republican, and is pro-life. He said the bishop told him to remove the homily from the parish website.

#214 TO BEE OR NOT TO BEE. TO RAMBLE OR TO RUMBLE.

A woman from Waterbury, Ohio, called the rectory and said she was coming to Browbeat, to see if she could find a grave at Poor Souls' Cemetery, near St. Timothy. She said she was looking for an autobiography of a relative and believed it was located at the Methodist church here. I visited the Methodist pastor to see if he knew anything about it. He said, "No. I'm perplexed and think this woman just has a bee in her bonnet." I thought his bee expression was funny, but didn't say anything to him. He said he would ask their church historian to see if she knew anything about it, and then get back with me.

The woman wanted to visit with me. When she came to the parish it was clear she was mentally ill, but a very nice lady. She changed the subject so many times I couldn't keep up with her conversation. I wondered, "The way this woman is rambling, if there's a bee in her car, it surely would be dying from heat, since it's so hot outside." When we were finished talking, I went outside and noticed she had a bright yellow pickup. She said, "How do you like my Dodge Bee Rambler?" I said, "What?" She said, "That's the name of this truck. They only made about 10,000 of them". I then noticed painted on the back of the truck was a large bee. I did everything I could to not laugh aloud and figured, "I got stung by that one! It ain't in her bonnet, but it's on the side of her truck! And she was rambling just like the name of her truck." All in the life of a priest. Despite the situation and her odd behavior, I treated her with respect and dignity, and believe the event was an act of mercy God wanted on my part. I later discovered it's actually called a "Dodge Bee Rumble".

#215 NIGHT VISITS MUST BE SHORT

Since I was unable to go to sleep and could sleep for only several hours, which would affect my ministry as a priest, I abandoned the practice of making night visits to Jesus in the tabernacle. When I go to the restroom, I first briefly stop at the chapel, say a prayer, and then use the restroom. At times, we have to accept our limitations, which is more pleasing to God, then if we were to do something that causes difficulties in the priestly life caring for the people.

#216 PRIEST UNCLE KNOCKING IN A CLOSET FOR MASSES

"I saw my Guardian Angel, who ordered me to follow him. In a moment I was in a misty place full of fire in which there was a great crowd of suffering souls. They were praying fervently, but to no avail, for themselves; only we can come to their aid. The flames which were burning them did not touch me at all." (Diary of St. Faustina, #20)

The night of May 19th, as I was praying during my daily Eucharistic Holy Hour. I heard a loud knocking behind me in a closet with two sliding doors. I thought maybe a sliding door was rattling, due to moving my chair. I suspect the vibration on the floor from the chair caused the knocking in the closet. But even when I didn't move, the knocking continued. I put the Chapel Monstrance in the Tabernacle and went to see where the noise was coming. As I was looking at the closet door on the right, I heard the knock from behind the door on the left. When I opened the left sliding door, I realized the knocking was coming from behind the chalice box containing the chalice that I received after the death of my uncle, Fr. Ferdinand Tomserck. I went outside to see if anyone was knocking on the wall outside by the carport, located behind the closet on the other side of the wall. But, no one was there. When I opened the door and looked at the chalice box, the knocking stopped. The next morning, I decided to look on the computer to see if it was my uncle's birthday or the day of his death, but discovered neither was the case. Amazingly, it was the day of his ordination, May 20th. Consequently, I thought he might be knocking to have a Mass offered on the anniversary of his ordination and to offer more masses for him.

Over the next few weeks, I offered three Masses for his soul and began to use his chalice at church, rather than use the chalice donated by the people of the Church of the Ascension and to daily remember him during the Consecration (*Momento*).

#217 PRIEST BLESSINGS & THE HOUSE OF HORRORS

"He went to heaven and is at God's right hand, with angelic rulers and powers subjected to Him." (1 Peter 3:22)

Sunday, May 29th, 2022, the 18th anniversary of my priestly ordination, the Solemnity of the Ascension of Jesus into heaven, I preached on Christ's Blessing just before He ascended. I told parishioners, Jesus blesses us today through the priest including personal blessings, house blessings and all sorts of blessings from the *Book of Blessings*. I said, although He ascended to heaven, He is still with us in the priest and Jesus performs the Sacraments through priests today, such as Confession, Mass, Baptism, Anointing of the Sick, etc...

Later in the day, I drove to Tucom, Ohio to baptize my niece's baby boy. And, since it was Memorial Day weekend, I decided to visit the graves of deceased relatives at Holy Moses Cemetery at Tucom. Then I went to St. Gabriel's Cemetery in Crossroads to visit my father's grave and the graves of other relatives.

On the way to the cemetery, I drove past the house, where I was raised as a boy. I noticed a Rental Haul Trailer. Since I became a priest, I always wanted to bless our old family home, but never had the opportunity, since I didn't know who owned it or lived in it. Without thinking at all about the homily given at Mass this morning, I decided to stop and visit the people at the house to see if they would allow me to look inside. We had a nice visit, and they permitted me to enter the house. With the exception of a bathroom modification, the house looked just as it was over 20 years ago and the memories began to flow.

They mentioned "weird things" happening in the house, including a doll that moved by itself on the floor. They said a porcelain angel fell and broke on its own. A ball of light moved around the house. A ceiling fan in the bedroom suddenly kept running faster and faster until it flew off. Young children saw visitors in the house, who would suddenly appear and then disappear. A child said one visitor was a man with horns. The adults also saw odd things in the house.

When we were children, we played the Ouija board in the house. Back then, we too experienced strange events. Growing up in the house, I had repeated nightmares of the devil and in the nightmares, and I saw hell beneath our home. I saw faces of people in the closet. Years ago, my brother saw a glowing ball outside. There were also many terrible events that happened in the house. Dad's alcoholism and verbal abuse. Dad doing atrocious other things that cannot be mentioned. Parents fighting and their divorce. Siblings arguing with each other. Mom attempting suicide. To think all those years after we had moved out of the house and all the people who lived in the house may have also had bad experiences was very disturbing to me. I had heard that some didn't want to live there due to the house being haunted. My mother said the house was on the market for only $37,000, and it was worth at least twice that amount.

I asked the renters, who were non-Catholic if I could bless the house. With their approval and the approval of the owner who lived next door, I blessed the house and everyone was grateful and overjoyed.

For all those years, I wanted to bless the house. Finally, on the 18th anniversary of my ordination, by God's grace and His power, the Lord kicked the demons out. Without thinking, it would happen, I fulfilled what I said at Mass, "Jesus, through the priest blesses people and houses. "

It is as though the Lord gave me the opportunity to undo what I mistakenly and unknowingly did as a child, playing a demonic game. How sad to think what all people and families who lived in the house went through during the 40 years after my family moved out. They had to deal with demons, perhaps caused by the Ouija board or maybe other sinful actions of other residents through the years. Jesus, have mercy on us! Thank you, Jesus, for these wonderful years of priesthood and for using me to bestow Your mercy and graces on people and things, including my childhood home.

#218 ADVICE TO NEW PASTORS

"He shall feed his flock like a shepherd: he shall gather the lambs with his arm, and carry them in his bosom, and shall gently lead those that are with young." (Isaiah 40:11)

At times, I gave unsolicited advice to new pastors. I would say, "When you become a pastor, it's like a new and different way to pastor sheep. It's like when you are first ordained, you learn how to play basketball and then when you feel comfortable in handling the ball, you score points. But, at times, you foul or others foul you. Then, when you become a pastor, it's like a whole new game you never played before, and you're not told the rules. It's like the difference between basketball and rugby. Therefore, you better be prepared for playing hard and getting beat up.

When you become a pastor, it's like, a shepherd who loves his sheep and will do everything to help them. He will seek the lost, but some want to remain lost. He reaches out his hand to help take them off of the cliff, but, in turn, they bite your fingers. But finally after some patience and love, you convince some to come into your arms, where you press them to yourself and give them the love and mercy of Jesus.

It's also like a shepherd in a sheep pen. When he stands gazing at the sheep, he suddenly feels a warm liquid run down his leg, as one of the sheep just urinated on him. At times, the back of his shoes are nibbled by the sheep. And other times, smelly manure will have landed on your shoes. Once in a while, a sheep or two will bite the back of his pants and tear holes in them. Some sheep refuse to follow you. It's also like

369

when a sheep runs up to the shepherd and rams him from behind causing him to tumble into a pile of manure. But he loves them all despite how he is treated.

And, it can be that a high standing old ewe (female sheep), will complain about you to the chief shepherd, who won't believe, nor even want to hear, what you have to say. The chief shepherd will not pay any attention to your success. But, only focus on the two disgruntled sheep, who the chief shepherd does not know had bitten their shepherd, urinated on him, caused division among the sheep, and ran off to a different pen.

And all your successful accomplishments and all the sheep who consistently followed you, and who grew deeply in their faith, including some you helped to come to the eternal pasture with springs of living water, none of these will be acknowledged by the chief shepherd. Therefore, be prepared to be removed from the pen, cast outside, and go to a place, you would rather not go. But through all this, the shepherd who pastured the sheep will be conformed to the Good Shepherd, Jesus Christ crucified, as a victim, and transformed into a living image of Jesus in the Sacred Host."

#219 ORGANISTS WHO PLAY A DIFFERENT TUNE

Over the years as a priest, I have come to know some well talented organists. Most of them were very accomplished. But, the majority were stubborn and desire constant recognition and applause for playing hymns at Mass. Two organists (pianists) at St. Timothy parish will play only modern songs and rarely Catholic hymns, even after I asked otherwise. One of them purposely tries to annoy me during Mass. For example, because she desires everyone to shake hands at the sign of peace, there will be a long delay before she begins to play the "Agnus Dei" Lamb of God.

Even though I left her a note on the piano before Mass, indicating there is a Sequence on Pentecost and will be read by the Lector, the pianist acted bewildered when the Lector read it. She acted as if she never knew anything about it. Every time she plays the piano she wants to grab attention or to disrupt the Mass. For example, she will bellow out an announcement before the final hymn without telling me about it, whereas I could have mentioned it with the regular announcements, had she mentioned it to me.

I honestly believe the devil is constantly at work in that poor woman. I can't stand when the organists play the piano. An organ raises the heart and mind to God, but the piano makes you fell like you're in a protestant church or a supper club.

When I was an associate at the Cathedral, an organist delayed Mass even though the priest gave the signal to start Mass. While at the Cathedral, when the choir and organist were not playing because they delayed Mass for an unusual amount of time, I told the servers to begin processing. Other priests at the Cathedral have the same problem, even today, ten years later. Their willfulness and desire for attention is nauseating.

How rare are organists who want to play Catholic hymns and listen to the priest's advice. The devil uses pride to attack the Mass and the priest. Almost none of them know how, nor do they want to know how to play Gregorian chant, which is most proper and exceedingly beautiful when played and sung at Mass.

#220 NOVENA TO MAKE OUR STATE ABORTION FREE

I sent out an email to the parish secretaries throughout the Diocese asking them to schedule a Mass in their parish. The email mentioned, I would pay the Mass Stipend with the intention to "Make Our State Abortion Free". One of the secretaries must have notified a priest, who was at angst with the Novena. I received a call from the Ohio Conference of Catholic Ecclesiastics coordinator, who said, "Father, I read your Novena. You can't call that Novena "Make Our State Abortion Free". We (Ohio Bishops' Ecclesiastics) support current legislation allowing for some abortions. If people think we want no abortion in the state, then they won't vote for this bill. We want to allow for some abortions.' I said, "That is ridiculous!" He responded, "Listen, Buddy, I will call the bishop and the head of the Pro-Life office for the diocese, and they will call you, and change your mind!" Consequently, I changed the name of the Novena but still had the personal intention of making our state abortion free.

#221 ROE VS. WADE OVERTURNED

Wow! Unbelievable! Finally, after almost 50 years the Supreme Court overturned Roe vs. Wade today. It's time to celebrate, especially since it occurred on the Solemnity of the Sacred Heart, June 24th this year. Today would have been the Nativity of John the Baptist. This year, the Solemnity of John's birth was transferred to June 23rd. But, every year, after this year, the overturning of Roe vs. Wade will be celebrated on St. John's Feast Day. It is as though the Lord wanted the birth of John the Baptist (June 23rd) to remind us to repent for the sin of abortion (June 24th) on the Solemnity of the Sacred Heart of Jesus. At the same time, the Lord wants to give us His love and mercy flowing from His wounded Heart to those who have been wounded by abortion. At the visitation, John the Baptist pointed out the unborn Jesus, when he was in the womb of his mother, St. Elizabeth. He leapt for joy at the presence of the unborn Jesus, who was in the womb of the Virgin Mary.

#222 EUCHARISTIC HEARTACHES

"Therefore whoever eats the bread or drinks the cup of the Lord unworthily will have to answer for the body and blood of the Lord. A person should examine himself, and so eat the bread and drink the cup. For anyone who eats and drinks without discerning the body, eats and drinks judgment on himself." (I Corinthians 11:27-29)

There are many Eucharistic heartaches caused by priests. Here is a list of some of them.

The priest is saddened and disappointed because he is required to face the people, and therefore, has continuous distractions during Mass. Once, during Mass, as I was praying the prayers at the altar, facing the people and trying to read from the *Roman Missal,* I saw a movement in a pew, near the front of the church that caught my attention. It was as though someone waved at me. When I glanced to see what was going on, I noticed a man raising his hand to dig in his nose. As Mass progressed, he rolled up his boogers and ate them. What a gross distraction! Shouldn't we all face the Lord during Holy Mass? Many bishops do not allow priests to offer the Holy Mass Ad Orientem (facing east, away from the people). It is my understanding they do not have the authority to prevent priests from offering the Mass Ad Orientem because its universal liturgical law. However, respecting the bishop's authority and his office, we obey. Some view the Mass as a show to watch, rather than being present at the Sacrifice of Calvary. They talk before, during, and at the end of Mass in the sanctuary. People want the priest to tell jokes. They want him to move about around the church abandoning the Ambo, so, he can "be with the people" and become the center of attention. The presider's chair at times, is in front of, or near the Tabernacle. The people and some priests want the Mass completed in the shortest time possible, so they do other things. In many parishes some come late and leave early. Some leave after receiving Holy Communion without returning to the pew to make their thanksgiving.

Most likely, many receive the Eucharist sacrilegiously, due to being in a state of mortal sin. Perhaps this is caused by missing Mass on Sunday, impurity, or using birth control, and they think nothing of offending the Lord, and at the same time, bring condemnation to themselves when they receive the Eucharist sacrilegiously.

Most bishops refuse to allow priests the use of Altar Rails and prevent them from being installed.

If anyone complains to the bishop that the priest is the only distributor of Holy Communion, the bishop requires the priest to have Extraordinary Ministers of Holy Communion, even if he can offer the Mass and distribute Holy Communion in less than an hour. Many parishes use "wheat" hosts, unlike "white" hosts. Both are made only of wheat. But the "white" hosts prevent Sacred Particles from falling to the ground, whereas wheat hosts cause a great quantity of particles to shed from the Host, that oftentimes fall to the ground.

In most parishes, 90% or more of Catholics receive Communion in the hand and tiny particles of the Host, that remain on the hand, fall to the ground, most especially when the "wheat" hosts are used. Some parishes don't use Ablution Bowls used after the Extraordinary Ministers of the Eucharist give out Communion to wash Particles from their fingers.

May I ask this question? Why do they want to receive on the hand? What is the purpose? Does it show more reverence, no. Is there a less probability of dropping the Host, no. Are they afraid the priest will touch them and give them germs? When distributing Communion in the hand, the priest or extraordinary ministers hand almost always touches the hand of the communicants. Can the tongue be accidentally touched? Yes, but is extremely rare. So, why do people want to receive in the hand? Could it be pride and or a lack of faith or to have power to touch Jesus? O humble humility, where art thou? There is homily given by a priest in Medjugorje that explains why Communion on the tongue is better than on the hand. (See Appendix H)

Some bishops won't allow priests to even "recommend" to their parishioners receive on the tongue. According to the Council of Trent, every Particle, no matter how small, is the whole and entire person of Jesus. The ordinary manner in which the Church desires we receive Communion is on the tongue. It's an indult, a permission, to receive on the hand.

Another heartache of irreverence during Mass, is caused by organists, who either only know modern songs and/or refuse to play traditional Catholic hymns. In many Catholic parishes, Protestant songs are played more often than Catholic hymns. Some Protestant songs have heretical lyrics. Most organists won't play hymns requested by the priest. They refuse to learn Latin or play Gregorian chant.

Today, in some parishes, the Holy Sacrifice of the Mass has taken on Protestant adaptations. Some bishops restrict priests in offering the Extraordinary form of the Mass in Latin. Sadly, kneeling to receive Holy Communion, is not permitted by many bishops or pastors. Many parishioners don't make a sign of reverence, such as the bow of the head, the Sign of the Cross, or kneel before receiving Holy Communion, as required by the Church.

Some receive the Eucharist as though it were ordinary bread.

An organist, here at St. Timothy, receives Communion and immediately bites the Host as a child eats crackers.

Oh, how the Heart of Jesus must be so deeply saddened, to see the Holy Sacrifice and His Precious Body and Blood treated with irreverence, disrespect, and sacrilege.

When I was a seminarian serving at Church of the Ascension in Rolling Hills, after the Extraordinary Ministers of Holy Communion finished distributing the Precious Blood in communion cups, they carried the cups to the Sacristy and the remaining Precious Blood was poured down the drain. A few years later, Pope St. John Paul II declared those who pour the Precious Blood down the drain can be excommunicated from the Church.

When I was a religious brother, I saw the deep love and respect of the nuns for the Holy Eucharist. If a Host accidentally fell to the ground, the priest placed a white Purificator over the spot. Then, after Mass a wet Purificator is used to dampen the spot Sacred Particles may have fallen. I try to do that as well.

Chalices, Ciborium, and Pyxes are often times not purified and placed in the cabinet with Particles or dried Precious Blood within them. In some parishes, the same Ciboria is continuously used without ever being purified, leaving the bottom covered with tiny Sacred Particles from the Hosts and then placed in the cabinet.

During the Fraction at Mass (the breaking of the celebrant's large Host), the priest will not consume the entire Celebrant Host, as he ought. But rather, some priests place portions of the Host in the Ciboria to give to the people. It's my understanding the priest is required to consume the entire Celebrant Host to complete the Sacrifice he has offered.

How many priests use only Eucharistic Prayer II for all Masses at all times to complete the Mass as quickly as possible. It is said, that two priests developed Eucharistic Prayer while they were in a bar and then the Congregation for the Liturgy added it to the *Roman Missal*. According to *The General Instruction of the Roman Missal*, only for pastoral reasons should Eucharistic Prayer II be used on a Sunday. The beauty of Eucharistic Prayer I is completely overlooked, such as to pause and pray specifically for the living and the dead. And the Roman Canon (Eucharistic Prayer 1) invites saints and martyrs to pray for us and is powerful. I only use Eucharistic Prayer I.

When I was a parochial vicar at St. Charles of Sezze parish in Rolling Hills, even though the Sunday Mass was less than an hour, the pastor demanded that I never use Eucharistic Prayer I. When I refused and cited the documents of the Church, he gave me the silent treatment and never spoke to me for weeks, until I finally relented. While offering Masses at a convent, I always used Eucharistic Prayer I. Consequently, the mother superior demanded I stop using it, because it added an extra five minutes to the Mass. She said the sisters needed to immediately leave for their apostolates. So what about thanksgiving after Mass? Why not start the Mass earlier?

Many parishes do not use server patens, which prevent Hosts and Sacred Particles from falling to the ground during distribution of Communion. (See Homily on Receiving Communion on the Tongue Appendix H)

I pray, in the future, the Church will elect a pope, who will appoint bishops, who will allow priests to offer the Mass Ad Orientem and the Extra Ordinary Form of the Mass. And allow priests to use and install altar rails, to use Latin Mass parts and Latin hymns. I pray, Gregorian chant will return to Mass, and pray guitars and pianos will be discontinued at Mass and pray for the return of the use of organs.

I am hoping to learn the Extraordinary Form of the Mass and believe someday soon, the Church will have a liturgical revival, but only after it goes through its persecution of the faithful and purification of priests, bishops, and cardinals.

O dear and loving God, help bishops and priests to offer the Mass worthily, with reverence and never hurriedly, to help the people to love and respect the Mass and Holy Eucharist. May they respond in love.

#223 GODPARENTS

"Train up a child in the way he should go; even when he is old, he will not depart from it." (Proverbs 22:6)

I have five godchildren. Two are nieces. Three are cousins. Recently, I reflected upon my bad example over the years, such as my failure to attend Mass or go to Confession when I was younger. I lived a terribly sinful life before my conversion.

A woman from the parish recently asked if she could change a godparent for her ten-year-old daughter since the godparent is not living in accord with the Church. I told her she couldn't. But, I said, God's mercy is infinite, and if you keep the godparent in your prayers, he may return to the Church. God can change the hearts of sinners as he changed mine, and he can even become a saint.

I pray for my godchildren every day and have Masses offered for them. I should have been more active in their lives. Even as a priest, I failed to help them grow in their faith. Although separated by distance, I could have called and sent more letters, cards, and gifts to them, and encouraged them in the Catholic faith. I gave each a Bible, rosary, statue of Mary, a catechism, and other religious articles over the years.

As a priest, when a person wanted to be a godparent, and asked me to sign their paper saying they were practicing, but in fact were a non-practicing Catholic, I first made sure they were able to go to Confession, and receive Holy Communion. If they said they were not practicing, not attending Mass very often, I would say, "Well, you can't become a godparent unless you are a practicing Catholic. But, if you desire to be a good godparent, and to practice your faith starting today, let's do your confession now, so I can sign your paper saying you are a Catholic in good standing who practices his faith." This was hugely successful. Many times, I heard their confession, right then and there, and what a joy it was, they returned to practice their faith.

#224 "L" OF A BUNCH

The phrase "L of a Bunch" is a take-off from the phrase, "Hell of a Bunch". I concelebrated a funeral today in Apache, Ohio. It was for Lonnie Ball. He and his friend, Lambert came to my deacon ordination at Mary's Meadow Seminary by way of Amtrak. I came to know Lonnie, when it was discovered, as an Extraordinary Eucharistic Minister of the home bound, he gave Holy Communion to my former babysitter, Leonella. She was an interesting woman. Although married, she invited her boyfriend, Walter, who was married, to live with her and her husband, John. She had a large purse and always carried a bottle of whiskey and a plastic cup in her purse. She said she never knew when she might need a drink. Soda and water was all she needed to mix herself a drink. Although I never saw her intoxicated, there were times her eyes were watery from too much alcohol. The name of Lonnie's son is Lambert. Lonnie gave Holy Communion to Leonella. Therefore, Lonnie, Lambert, Lance and Leonella, made up the "L" of a bunch, he said.

Later in her life, as a resident of the nursing home, Leonalla would visit other residents of the home, whose families would never come to see them. She took the time to visit with those who never received visitors.

Lonnie used to write letters and occasionally send a check for financial assistance. The families of most seminarians would give money to their son or relative who was in seminary, but my family was poor, and I could never ask them for help. Lonnie also prayed for me and the many other seminarians who he helped support through seminary. Leonella and Lonnie are unsung heroes and hidden saints, I like to recall on All Saints Day.

Priests have a saying about the "Ls". The four "Ls" are constant worries for priests. They are leaks, locks, loons, and lights. Roofs and pipes leak and are in constant need of attention.

The priest often worries about who will lock up the church and when it will be locked and unlocked, especially if he is away. The locks for the church, parish hall, and school, can result in a pocket full of keys for each place. Lights are constantly burning out, and need to be replaced. Or they are left on all night. Electric wiring can be a headache.

Priests come in contact with everyone from panhandlers, drug addicts, excessively rigid, or liberals, and every kind of person from every walk of life.

There is the rigid woman who just can't stand when a priest holds his hands out past his shoulders, or the liberal who desires the priest to come down from the sanctuary and shake hands during the sign of peace.

Loons refer to parishioners, or anyone who may be unstable or excessively demanding, and therefore a pain in the neck. Some are "high maintenance" (more needy than most). No matter what you do, the more you help, the more is needed to help them. Some priests refer to the mentally ill as loons, which I very much dislike. They can be very taxing and demand much attention from the priest. Some believe Jesus was reincarnated, or they think Jesus told them to start a community service project that will save the world from aliens. Loons are really Jesus in disguise, and should never be called as such. One's mental abilities, or lack of them, does not define who they are. Every person has human dignity, but suffers from their human frailties. A man born with a withered hand or a bipolar woman, each suffer from a human condition, they cannot help and both are crosses for them.

All the "Ls" for priests are really modes of sanctification for him, and are ways to help the priest to grow in love and charity towards others. Rather than viewing them as a pain in the neck, he should see them as Jesus sees them with loving attention.

There is another kind of "Ls". Some priests desire to be liked, loved and listened to. When many are young, perhaps in their teens, they may experience not being liked, loved, or listened to. If these wounds aren't healed, and if the man becomes a priest, the priest can end up searching for these in all the wrong places. We are not here in this world to be liked, loved and listened to our every word. We are not the center of the universe. Jesus is the center of the universe.

Because of these "Ls", a priest may want to make his mark by accomplishing something great, so that all will praise him, or draw attention to himself. Their inordinate desires can also be a danger to celibacy.

However, if a priest applies the "feeling prayer" to his wounds from the past, and sees Jesus, as the one to please, to love and to listen, he will have peace, and not search for something only God can fulfill because God alone fulfills all our desires.

Christians should want to be rejected, despised, scoffed at, rather than to be praised, esteemed or exalted, to be more conformed to Jesus crucified. Praying the Litany of Humility regularly can help remedy these inordinate "Ls".

#225 INVALID MASSES AGAIN AND BAD WINE

At the funeral of Lonnie, as I was concelebrating, I noticed some concelebrating priests were not saying the words of consecration in a manner that was audible. To be sure, I wasn't mistaken, I turned my head and looked directly at them and noticed the other three concelebrants weren't moving their lips when the prayers were being prayed. According to the *Roman Missal*, #218, it states, "The parts spoken by all the concelebrants together, and especially the words of consecration, which all are bound to say, are to be said in such a way, that the concelebrants speak them in a very low voice, and that the principal celebrant's voice be clearly heard. In this way, the words can be better understood by the people." Fr. Edward McNamara, a liturgical expert, said, "For a concelebrant's Mass to be valid, the words of consecration, recited in a low, but audible voice, is strictly necessary."

More invalid Masses. This angered me. Poor Lonnie had just two Masses offered for him at his funeral, the celebrant, and mine. The other three were invalid. How sad! Lord have mercy! Amazingly, two of the three priests, who didn't audibly pray at Mass, are the same former pastors, who used invalid wine (made of cherries and strawberries) at my hometown parish. The devil is having his way in that diocese, due to ignorant and careless priests.

A parish priest, from the church where the funeral was held, asked me to distribute the Precious Blood. Some are still becoming ill from COVID-19 and yet, these pastors in the Lakota Diocese are allowing people to receive from the same cup. However, in the Diocese of Rolling Hills concelebrating priests continue to dip the Host into the Precious Blood rather than consume from the same chalice. I guess liberality includes being liberal in other ways.

At the funeral Mass, as I was distributing the Precious Blood, I noticed what appeared to be coffee grounds swirling in the bottom of the chalice. There was a large amount of sediment, due to the old wine they were using, and its deterioration. After the distribution of Holy Communion, I consumed two cups of the remaining Precious Blood and wondered what type of wine they used. It didn't taste like any wine I used for Mass before. But when I checked the bottle, it was *Rosato*, the same wine we use at St. Timothy. However, it tasted far different, since it was old. Was it a valid Mass? Only God knows. I mentioned the wine problem to the "pastoral associate", a lay person (who I later found out is a practicing homosexual) and told him he needed to order new wine and throw out the old. I told him he should speak to his pastor about the sour wine.

What do I do to address the invalid Masses by the concelebrants who don't audibly pray as they ought? Can you imagine their reaction, when I sent letters to them several years ago, informing them of the twelve years of invalid Masses at the parish where they were pastors. And now telling them, every time they concelebrated without saying their part at Mass, those Masses too are invalid! I pray the Lord will help me to know what to do.

#226 NO ONE BETTER

Today, I prayed in my rectory chapel before Jesus in Eucharistic Adoration about all the unethical situations that continue at the supposed "Catholic" hospitals and the hospice and how the injustices continue. Patients keep dying day by day without artificial nutrition and hydration, when they could benefit from them. They are dying of starvation and lack of hydration, rather than their illness. Likewise, many are affected by the hospital giving out contraceptives, implanting IUDs, doing sterilizations and abortions. Yet, I failed to make any changes there. The current priest chaplain at those facilities allows all the unethical things to continue and doesn't even see a problem with them. The former head of the hospice, responsible for this erroneous way of treating the dying, hasn't had a change of heart, and continues his instructions to staff and families, that are not in accord with the Church. The bishop knows everything. Yet, nothing is getting done.

I became exceedingly frustrated and wept very hard with loud lamentations. Out of exasperation and anger, I said to Jesus, "Why did you set me up to fail? You duped me! You knew nothing would be accomplished. Why didn't you send a better priest, who has better personal skills, who knows ethics and could make changes?" Our Lord responded, saying, "I did. I sent the best." I responded, saying, "If I'm the best, it's no wonder the Church is in such terrible condition as it is today."

I later apologized to the Lord for the inappropriate and irreverent manner I treated Him.

#227 HAPPY SOUL RETREAT CENTER

"And Jesus went into the temple of God, and cast out all them, that sold and bought in the temple, and overthrew the tables of the money changers, and the seats of them that sold doves. And said to them, it is written, My house shall be called the house of prayer, but you have made it a den of thieves." (Matthew 21-12-14)

Because I was in the area, I stopped by Happy Soul Retreat Center to pray a Holy Hour before Jesus in the Tabernacle. When I entered the chapel, I genuflected, and after thirty minutes of prayer, noticed the red sanctuary candle in the chapel was missing. There were also Protestant hymnals in a box in the front of the church. It seems the chapel was used by non-Catholics for their "worship" service. The priest must have removed Jesus in the Eucharist from Our Lord's own house to make room for heretical hymns to be sung in His house. How ecumenical! Doesn't that make us all feel united? At least the priest didn't permit them to do it in His divine Eucharistic presence. While I know the Church permits such things, is it really a good thing to do regularly? Why allow it, except, of course, for money, and false unity? Other diocesan retreat houses permit only Catholic organizations to use their sanctuary and facilities.

There was a Rabbi, a Catholic priest, and a Protestant minister eaten by a lion. Do you know how it all came out? The lion had an ecumenical movement. Ha! Ha!

The retreat house has another chapel with a hideous looking tabernacle. Frankly it looks like a darkened metal trash can. It reminds me of a body darkened by a soul in mortal sin, and then forcing Jesus to come inside by receiving Communion when the person should either abstain from the Sacred Host or go to Confession. Oh, how I wish we could replace that ugly tabernacle with a tabernacle made of precious materials worthy of the true body of Christ, the resurrected Jesus!

#228 THE CANDID RCIA CANDIDATE

"Beware of false prophets, who come to you in sheep's clothing, but inwardly are ravenous wolves." (Matthew 7:15)

I just finished the last class for several of the Rite of Christian Initiation (RCIA) candidates, a lady, and her husband. When they started taking classes, they said they weren't interested in becoming Catholic, but wanted to learn more about the Catholic faith. I hoped they would overcome their obstacles during the year, and they overcame many. She believes in the true presence of Jesus in the Eucharist and comes to church, once a week, to pray a Holy Hour.

At the last class, I presented the Church's teachings on homosexuality. At the previous class, she informed me that she does not believe in the Church's teachings on homosexuality. She also does not believe that Sacred Tradition is equal to Sacred Scripture and said she cannot, at this time, venerate the Virgin Mary as Catholics. Needless to say, she and her husband won't be coming Catholic until they overcome these obstacles. I explained from scripture and the *Catechism of the Catholic Church*, how homosexual actions are immoral. She responded, saying, "That was those days, many years ago. Scripture has a different meaning today." This way of thinking is another reason why she can't become Catholic now. She unknowingly fell into the modernism heresy.

I pressed her, to see where she stood on homosexuality. I said, "Some people don't understand what goes on behind closed doors of homosexual partners and how homosexual men do impure things to each other." "If they were to adopt a child, it could greatly harm the child's understanding of true marriage and their identity." The woman responded, "I don't see anything wrong with homosexual actions, and as a mental health professional, who counsels people every day, I disagree. I don't believe children would be harmed by a homosexual couple." She said, "We go to a Congregational church at Montecarlo that openly accepts all homosexual couples. As long as they aren't promiscuous (unfaithful to their homosexual partner), I don't see a problem with homosexual marriage."

The RCIA's sponsor jaw dropped, and I struggled to keep my face from showing shock. I wondered how could a Christian minister lead a whole congregation to such immorality. Leading people astray by justifying sin, is a serious consequence of being a wolf in sheep's clothing. May her "pastor" and his congregation come to see the truth of homosexual immorality and begin to walk in the light of Christ.

#229 DIOCESAN RETREAT

At the end of June, we had a voluntary diocesan retreat at Happy Soul Retreat House. Bishop John Handyman was the retreat master. He was one of the bishops I requested if I could do ministry in his Diocese of Land-O-Lakes, Arkansas. His presentations were very practical and very helpful. It was one of the best diocesan retreats I ever participated.

I decided to make it an all-silent retreat and consequently, sat away from the other priests during meals. During these diocesan retreats almost every priest mingled with other priests, and therefore didn't maintain silence. They enjoy their time away from the parish and look at this as an opportunity for fraternity. While I enjoy fraternity on a retreat, I like to maintain silence to allow Jesus to speak to my heart.

An evening meal, during the week, is considered a banquet style dinner with steak or some sort of fancy food, which volunteers serve for the priests on retreat. After every dinner there is always a social with about twenty kinds of alcohol beverages available for priests. There are also snacks that go with the beverages. I find this atmosphere for a retreat distasteful. It seems some priests are trying to find comfort in friendship, food, and drinks.

Some have an attitude of superiority, worldliness, and arrogance at the expense of others, whom they deem less important. This kind of thinking finds its home in hearts not seeking the Lord, who is the only true consolation in this life. The spirit of entitlement sneaks into the lives of some priests, and are oblivious of it.

Some misdirected seminarians would say, "We are meant for chalices, not callouses." By this, they mean, they are excused from manual labor due to their dignity as a priest, which is really a warped view of the priesthood of Jesus, who said, "I came to serve, not to be served."

However, many priests genuinely try to live a holy life and see their time together with other brother priests as a time for fraternity, friendship and to relax.

#230 GOD'S MERCY IS FOR EVERY WRETCH, LIKE ME

I don't watch television, but obtain news from the internet. Over the past several weeks, some events caught my attention and remind me of how merciful the Lord has been in my life.

A young man in his twenties, high on drugs, drove his car onto a sidewalk, hitting a family, killing the father, causing a traumatic brain injury to the mother; his daughter received a broken back, and two other children escaped unharmed. If it wasn't for the grace of God, there go I. When I was in high school to gain attention and to scare people for fun, I drove my car on a sidewalk in front of a grocery store. I thought it would be funny if people jumped out of the way. Thanks be to God, no one came out of the store.

There was a man driving down a main roadway in Rolling Hills. The speed limit was thirty miles an hour. But he chose to speed with his seven-year-old son riding with him. According to reports, he was traveling over seventy miles an hour when he hit a dip in the road causing the car to go airborne and crash. His son died, but he escaped with minor injuries.

If it wasn't for the grace of God, there, go I. How frightening, when I was intoxicated on prom night and drove over seventy miles an hour in a twenty mile an hour zone causing my car to go airborne. Three friends were in the car with me. We could have all died due to my stupidity. By reading this diary, can't you see the wretch of a man I am? But, can you also see, God chose me, the most unlikely miserable of all, to extol His mercy?

St. Faustina spoke of herself as a wretch. She said, "I spent the whole day in thanksgiving, and gratitude kept flooding my soul. O my God, how good You are, how great is Your mercy! You visit me with so many graces, me who am a most wretched speck of dust. Prostrating myself at Your feet, O Lord, I confess with a sincere heart that I have done nothing to deserve even the least of Your graces. It is in Your infinite goodness that You give Yourself to me so generously. Therefore, the greater the graces which my heart receives, the deeper it plunges itself in humility." (#1661) She said, "Oh most sweet Jesus, who, in Your incomprehensible kindness, have deigned to unite my wretched heart to Your most merciful Heart. It is with Your Heart that I glorify God, our Father, as no soul has ever glorified Him before." (#836) "O my Lord, my soul is the most wretched of all, and yet You stoop to it with such kindness! I see clearly Your greatness and my littleness, and therefore I rejoice that You are so powerful and without limit, and so I rejoice greatly at being so little." (#1417) "I acknowledged that she was right, because I am indeed a wretched person, but still, I trust in God's mercy. When I met the Lord, I humbled myself, and said, "Jesus, it seems, that You do not associate intimately with such wretched people as I." "Be at peace, My daughter, it is precisely through such misery that I want to show the power of My mercy." (#133) "Holy Hour. During this hour of adoration, I saw the abyss of my misery; whatever there is of good in me is Yours, O Lord. But because I am so small and wretched, I have a right to count on Your boundless mercy." (#237)

How much more merciful God has been to my soul that was in more immeasurable misery than St. Faustina, and who most likely never committed a mortal sin in her life? O, God, you are so good and merciful!

#231 MORE ALTAR SOCIETY WOES

I received a phone call today from the president of the altar society. She and two other members wanted to meet with me about ordering candles. Over the past year, I drove to Rolling Hills and picked up candles for the parish as needed. I had noticed the altar society was collecting the money from the votive candles, but were not paying for them. Therefore, I suggested they pay for some candles, especially for ones, they were collecting money in the metal box located under the statues.

At the meeting, they informed me the church should not be purchasing beeswax candles for the sanctuary candle. They don't want four candles lit during Eucharistic Adoration. They want the Pastoral Council to approve all purchases, including candles, cruets, and a chalice paten that was purchased recently. A family had donated four candle sticks for the altar at a cost of $4,000, which was approved by the pastor. The altar society thinks the pastor should have gotten the approval of the pastoral council before the candle sticks were donated. In response to their requests, I volunteered to pay for the paten and the cruets, which seemed to surprise them.

A parishioner is making a Corpus Christi canopy and I suggested the altar society help pay for the canopy. To purchase a new one would cost $3,500, but to make a homemade one would cost $500. The altar society has $5,000 in their account. They decided not to help pay for it. All this speaks for itself. Fr. Kapaun, you were so right about the altar society!

#232 NOT IN A CORD

I received permission from my spiritual director to wear a Franciscan cord out of penance. But after wearing it a few times, I can no longer do so. The cord keeps falling down and sticks out of the bottom of a pant leg. I can't let others see this happen. Therefore, I am no longer able to wear it. Perhaps, I can obtain a rougher and more durable cord that won't move about so easily. Or may be, it is not God's will for me to do this kind of penance.

#233 JESUS COMES TO THE ABORTION CLINIC

I was asked the lead the Rosary at an abortion clinic in Rolling Hills. We pray all four mysteries of the Rosary and the Litany of the Blessed Virgin Mary. I need to offer the First Saturday Mass an hour earlier at 7am to make it to the Rosary which starts at 9am.

After Mass, just before leaving the parish, I made sure there were three Hosts in the pyx to be used for my weekly Sunday visit to the nursing home to give Holy Communion to the residents there. I placed the pyx in the tabernacle, genuflected, and then left to drive to Rolling Hills.

After arriving at the clinic, and after completing four Rosaries with the people, I went to my car and felt something in my pocket. It was the pyx. I could not understand how I placed the pyx in my pocket. Little did I know, I drove with the Eucharistic Jesus in my pocket from Browbeat to Rolling Hills and then prayed four rosaries with Jesus in my pocket at the abortion clinic. I'm fearful of calling this a miracle, but I don't understand how the Eucharistic Jesus showed up in my pocket. Perhaps, I was forgetful and just didn't realize I put Him in my pocket, rather than the tabernacle, but don't see how I could have done this.

At any rate, we were blessed to have His physical presence with us at the abortion clinic, and I was blessed to make a Holy Hour with Him in the car on the way back to the parish. Interestingly, I had been wanting to bring the Host to the abortion clinic, but felt I needed to ask the bishop permission. Well, I guess Jesus, decided He wanted to come. Thank you, Jesus, for coming to be with Your people at the abortion clinic and gracing us with Your true presence in the Most Blessed Sacrament, and please forgive me if I was forgetful and negligent.

#234 ST. MONICA, AUGUST 27th WAILING WAYLON

Erroneously thinking August 26th was the memorial of St. Monica, during Mass, I gave a homily on St. Monica and prayed the collects, on what was supposed to be a ferial Mass for the day, which had no saints associated with it. Basically, I unknowingly offered a votive Mass for St. Monica, on the day that preceded her actual feast day.

On August 26th, a Friday, after eating breakfast, I traveled to the nearby city of Montecarlo to go to confession to the pastor of St. Joseph parish. After introducing myself to the secretary, she suggested I be seated, as she called the pastor to see if he was available.

After I sat down, a little boy and his teacher came into the office. The boy's eyes were red, and it was clear he had been crying. Thinking maybe the boy had gotten into trouble and trying to cheer him up, I spoke to him and discovered he was five years old, and just started kindergarten at the Catholic school. He was crying because he missed his parents. His name was Waylon.

The following day, on the actual memorial of St. Monica, I preached on the Gospel of the day for Saturday, since I erroneously preached about her the day before. The last sentence for the Gospel of the day said, "And throw this useless servant into the darkness outside, where there will be wailing and grinding of teeth." St. Monica was known for her many tears, and she surely wailed much before the Lord on behalf of her son, St. Augustine. So, here we had a boy, who came to the office wailing, and whose name was Waylon, and on a day, I offered a votive Mass for St. Monica. But it preceded, the actual day of her memorial, and the Gospel spoke about "wailing".

#235 THE HOLY EUCHARIST

When I placed unconsecrated hosts in a ciborium, as I opened the package, some hosts flew in the air and landed on the counter and the floor. I picked up the unconsecrated hosts, broke them into pieces, and threw them in the trash.

Later, that day, I placed a pyx with consecrated Hosts in my pocket and then gave Communion to a woman at her home. I returned the pyx with the consecrated Hosts in the tabernacle. Later that evening, as I offered Mass, I felt a spiritual attack during Mass and became easily upset over trivial things during Mass. I felt there was some demonic influence causing me to be agitated.

Later that evening, I made a Holy Hour before Jesus in Eucharistic Adoration in the chapel in the rectory. When I was going to bed, I noticed something in my pocket. It was a host. I wondered if the host fell out of the pyx or was it a host that flew in the air after I opened the package earlier in the morning. Since no Host ever fell out of a pyx before, I had certainty it must have flown out of the package of unconsecrated hosts and landed in my pocket.

After I went to bed, I dreamt I gave Hosts to people and then a priest gave me Holy Communion. In my dream, I thought, "I can't give myself Communion". What an odd dream.

The next morning before Mass, due to the disturbance at Mass the previous day, I blessed the church and sprinkled it with holy water before the 8 am Mass. During Mass, I had difficulty removing to the lid of the ciborium with the Hosts, that I had taken out of the tabernacle. Because it was so tight, I had to pull hard to remove the lid, causing the ciborium to be knocked over and consecrated Hosts fell on the altar and the floor. It was a terrible and sad situation. I felt horrible. Yet, I knew it was not done on purpose. I picked up the Hosts off the altar and those that fell to the floor. I immediately consumed the Hosts that fell on the floor.

I then took a Purificator dampened with water, and wiped the floor where the Hosts fell. After Mass, the altar cloth was replaced with a clean one. The altar cloth and corporals affected by the Hosts that fell on them, were placed in a bucket of water to be soaked in order to dissolve Sacred Particles that may be on them.

I can't understand why these things happened in rapid succession. Truly, the Lord wanted me to grab my attention about the Eucharist. O Jesus, truly present in the Blessed Sacrament. I love You and never want to offend You. Please forgive me for my negligence and carelessness.

#236 END OF LIFE NEAR?

About a week before leaving for a Medjugorje trip, I began to think about my life in general and the idea came to mind, that I most likely will die soon. That very day and time I was thinking about dying, I received a text from a priest friend who informed me that a seminary priest professor died suddenly. I told him perhaps maybe the Lord was trying to tell me something about my own future death.

#237 MEDJUGORJE 7th TRIP – BRUSH WITH DEATH

I was invited to be a chaplain of a pilgrimage group to Medjugorje. I was so excited and looking forward to doing all sorts of things there, especially hearing Confessions, concelebrating Masses, and perhaps the main celebrant of a Mass and give a homily. Furthermore, I had hoped to attend an apparition since we were to stay at visionary Maria's house. I had trepidation, since usually when I go to Medjugorje, I come back with something new that the Lord wants me to do. At times, there is some mission the Lord has for me after returning from Medjugorje, though it is not revealed until a later date. Several months before the pilgrimage, I began to have difficulties urinating and went to a doctor, who prescribed a medicine he believed would reduce the size of my prostate due problems urinating. A month later, I continued to have problems and scheduled an appointment with my new doctor to include an annual checkup. I told my doctor I was going to Medjugorje and the previous doctor suggested I take a self-catheter for the trip, that I could insert myself if needed on the trip. She didn't like the self-catheter idea and didn't recommend it. I was hoping either doctor would refer me to a urologist, before going to Medjugorje, but neither did.

The day that I left for Medjugorje, while at the airport in the US, I had difficulty urinating. From the time, the plane left until I landed in Split, Bosnia-Herzegovina, I was unable to urinate for sixteen hours. I was very uncomfortable and had terrible pain. When arriving at the airport, I disclosed my condition to the pilgrimage director, who recommended I go to the hospital. The airport had a doctor, told me to take an ambulance to the hospital, but I took a taxi.

After I arrived at the hospital, two doctors attempted to insert a catheter, but could not. As a result, a doctor performed a supra-pubic procedure because of a stricture. I was injected with a local anesthesia, but it didn't work at all. There was absolutely no numbing effect, and I felt everything. Before he started, he quipped, "If you feel like screaming, go ahead." I thought, why would he say that, if he was going to use a local anesthetic? He must have known there was no numbing effect.

After slitting my abdomen with a blade, I painfully felt, he forcefully took a spike like device, a trocar, and thrust it through my abdomen into my bladder, causing urine to gush out all over the bed, floor and on me. I thought I was going to die. When he sutured the area, I felt every time he stuck me with the needle. Ouch!

A priest, wearing secular clothes, visited me just after the procedure, but refused to give me anointing of the sick. I was dismissed and spent the night in a hotel, because the doctor wanted to check the next day, to see if the catheter was working and if the bleeding stopped.

Oct. 4th, the feast of St. Francis of Assisi, was the second time in eighteen years, I was unable to offer Mass. The staff demanded immediate payment for the procedure and would not take a credit card, nor euros, nor American dollars. A woman patient who spoke English, volunteered to charge it to her credit card, and I reimbursed her in euros. Thanks be to God for this charitable woman. The hotel also would not take euros, and then went to the bank to convert euros to their currency called Kuna. They allowed me to stay at the hotel without paying them until the following day. Truly, the Lord in His Mercy and Our Lady took care of me.

The taxi trip from Split to Medjugorje cost $200 US dollars. The surgery and visit the following day cost, $175 US dollars. In the US, I was later told the cost would have been $2,000 to $10,000 for the surgical procedure.

Within a day after I came to Medjugorje, I developed a severe infection. My private parts turned black, which was extremely painful. Every time I even moved just a bit, it felt like hundreds of pins and needles were sticking me. I was glad I brought the remaining antibiotic pills, that I didn't finish from a prescription due to a finger infection months previously. We're not supposed to stop taking antibiotics, but I saved some for the trip.

The local pharmacy in Medjugorje had a strong three-day over the counter antibiotic. The antibiotics didn't help the infection to go away. However, they kept it from worsening.

Thanks be to God, I arrived in Medjugorje several days before the pilgrimage group, so I had time for some recuperation. When I arrived, I was able to concelebrate the International Mass on the feast of St. Faustina. I attempted to do everything with our pilgrimage group and didn't tell anyone what had happened except the pilgrimage leader, and then later sought advice from a nurse and a physician assistant who were pilgrims in our group.

The following day, I was blessed to be present at Ivan's apparition of the Blessed Virgin Mary. What a gift to be with a chapel full of priests and religious sisters during the apparition. The following day, the group went up apparition hill, but I was too weary, and thought the hike might tear stitches, or I may fall down while trekking up and down the rugged hill.

After a few days, and when feeling better, I went on my own up apparition hill and had no problems. It was such a peaceful time with Our Lady despite many pilgrims going and coming at the time. I prayed the Rosary for the many people who asked me to pray for them.

At a nearby shrine, dedicated to St. Anthony, one of my favorite saints, I offered Mass and gave a homily on Saturday. What a blessing! Our Lady knows how to tickle me spiritually.

A few weeks before traveling to Medjugorje, after completing my diary and sending it to a publisher, I began to think maybe the Lord wanted me to join the Order of Mary's Men, a religious order, known for their devotion to the Blessed Virgin Mary. I surmised the Lord wanted me to attend a vocational retreat scheduled by their community. Before I sent the email, I told the Lord, "I'm too old. They will never take me." But I believed Jesus encouraged me to send it anyway. A few days later, I received a reply, saying, "Sorry, brother, you're too old." When I read it, I said to Jesus, "I told you. I'm too old." A few weeks later, I said to Jesus, "I'll bet I know what's going to happen in Medjugorje, I will meet a priest from the OMM (Order of Mary's Men)."

Sure enough, a priest in our group was from the US, and a member of the OMM congregation. We confided to each the struggles within our priesthood. Our conversation encouraged both of us. I later discovered the priest and his mother contracted food poisoning, most likely from a restaurant in Medjugorje.

Two days before leaving, I was able to attend Maria's apparition (the visionary) at her home, called "Magnificat", and there I met another priest, whom we attended seminary together.

While in Medjugorje, the OMM priest spoke with his vocation director, and then gave me the vocation director's information. I told him I would first visit with my spiritual director before giving him a call. Is God calling me to join a religious order? Surely not during this time of my life.

Thank you, O Blessed Lady, who cared so much that you helped me receive the medical care I needed in a foreign country, I was unable to obtain it in the US. Oh, how you care for each of us and our needs. You will even bring us halfway around the world to help us. Please, O Holy Mother, help me to do God's will and lead me toward the path of heaven. Help me so I don't disappoint you. When I die, take me straight to heaven. I look at this experience as eliminating some of my purgatory time, especially due to impurity when I was young, and most especially, I offered it up for the conversion of sinners. And through Your hand, I pray many will be converted.

#238 SURGERY AND INVALID ANOINTING OF THE SICK

Three days after returning to the US, I witnessed my niece's marriage, never telling any family member about my health issue. No one suspected, I had a catheter hanging out of my abdomen as they exchanged their vows. The day after I returned from Medjugorje, I was able to make an appointment with a urologist to have the stricture dilated during a surgery. The doctor said the stricture was most likely caused by scar tissue due to an injury many years ago.

I presume the stricture could have been caused by a bicycle accident when I was about ten years old. I used to drive very fast around the neighborhood block. One day, I happened to see a rabbit in someone's yard and failed to look directly ahead as I went around the corner. I was going about thirty-five miles an hour, when my bicycle collided with a parked truck. Besides other bruises, I was injured in the area of my urethra. As a child, I never told anyone about the accident, nor saw a doctor. The front wheel of my bicycle, and parts of it, were so damaged they were irreparable. I had to get a different bicycle.

Due to the urethra stricture, my bladder couldn't empty fully. The hole was tiny and therefore caused a bladder stone to develop, which prevented urination. While in Medjugorje, I painfully passed the stone. When it was dispelled, I was then able to urinate even with the catheter in my abdomen. When the doctor in the US attempted to perform a cystoscope, he found the stricture and was unsuccessful to look into the bladder because the urethra hole was too small. The surgery is to dilate it, so I could urinate properly. If it fails, I may need to be on a suprapubic catheter for the rest of my life.

Since I was to be under anesthesia, I asked a priest to anoint me. But, he may have anointed invalidly. Ugh! For a valid anointing the priest must do three things: lay hands on the person, recite the proper prayers, and anoint the priest's head and hands. He failed to lay hands on me. A priest should not cause doubt to the one receiving a sacrament. I called a priest friend, who anointed me two days before the surgery. He did not rush. He was reverent and performed the sacrament in the manner required by the Church.

#239 LIFE SPARED FOR NOW

"Hear my voice in your mercy, O Lord; by your judgment, give me life." (Psalm 119)

Had I decided not to go to the hospital and went straight to Medjugorje, and then later travel to the hospital, I most likely would have died because my bladder would have burst. The urgency in which the doctor at the hospital preformed the supra-pubic catheter and the urgency in which the doctor in the US performed the surgery helped me to understand that without those procedures, I would have died.

When it was happening, during anxiety and terrible pain, I repeatedly prayed, "No matter whether I live or die, Jesus, I have confidence in You." I thought I was going to die in Croatia, and was going to tell a priest friend to have my body buried there and have a memorial Mass for my soul back in the US.

If the surgery doesn't work, I may end up with a permanent abdominal catheter, or perhaps may die. Whether I live or die, I belong to the Lord and trust Him and can't wait to see His face.

Thank you, Jesus and Mary, for allowing me to live longer. In Your mercy You sustained my life, by preventing death. In Your mercy You helped me trust and have confidence in You, when death was a possibility. In Your mercy, You helped me to accept sufferings. Due to the pain in that bodily area, in your mercy, you allowed me to make reparation for sins of impurity from the past. In Your mercy, You provided people and technology to save my life. In your mercy, you gave me consolation knowing Mary was with me and helping me.

#240 CONFESSION – EMPTY YOURSELF

"Though He was in the form of God, did not consider equality with God something to be grasped, but rather emptied Himself, taking the form of a servant,being made in human likeness." (Philippians 2:7)

During the several weeks with the abdomen catheter, many times I needed to empty my bladder manually through the catheter, because I couldn't urinate properly. At times, I felt that I needed to empty my bladder, but due to the sensation of the spasms, I couldn't tell the difference. Consequently, I tried to empty my bladder, but nothing happened. I was constantly trying to empty myself.

After the catheter removed and was in the process of healing from the abdomen surgery, I went to confession to a young priest. Before my confession, I prayed, "Dear Jesus, please speak to me through this priest." After I had made my confession, when the priest gave counsel, he said, "I feel like the Lord wants me to tell you something. He wants me to say to you, "Empty yourself. You need to decrease and allow Jesus to increase, like John the Baptist." I think the spiritual message from the health issue was simple and clear, "empty myself" and allow Jesus to be seen through me.

#241 DEMONS ON THE ATTACK – BIG GRACES COMING

A few days before leaving for Medjugorje, I was awakened in the middle of the night by the banging and rattling of my bedroom window. The night I returned from my trip to Medjugorje, it occurred again.

A few minutes later, an unknown force raised both legs off the bed, and were suddenly dropped. This picking up of my legs and dropping has happened twice before. These events always precede good spiritual occurrences. For example, one time, the day after it happened, I gave a televised Mass with a homily that literally went around the world. During the homily, I spoke on the Eucharistic Heart of Jesus. Despite the homily televised ten years ago, it can still be found on the internet.

Due to immense suffering from health problems, and demons attacking me, most likely some big grace will be granted soon. I suspect it has to do with the publication of this diary, which I pray will touch the hearts and minds of many Catholics and draw them closer to Jesus and Mary. And, I pray, they will come to know a farthing of God's infinite mercy. May He increase and I decrease.

#242 THE GIRL WHO BELIEVES IN MIRACLES

During my daily Holy Hour, I decided to meditate on Jesus raising Lazarus from the dead. I read John 11:1-46. I especially contemplated the words of Jesus, who told Martha, "I am the resurrection and the life. The one who believes in me will live, even though may die; and whoever lives by believing in me will never die. Do you believe this?" "Yes, Lord. I believe that you are the Messiah, the Son of God, who is to come into the world."

After the meditation, I decided to watch a YouTube video entitled *The Girl Who Believes in Miracles*. As I left the chapel to watch the movie, I said to Jesus, "Lord, come with me to watch the video."

As the movie began, there were scenes in it of a young girl who prayed that a dead bird would come back to life, and then later in the video, the same words I was contemplating were quoted by the priest in the movie, "I am the resurrection and the life. The one who believes in me will live, even though they die; and whoever lives by believing in me will never die." I was very much startled by all this and stopped the video and returned to the chapel saying, "Lord, you are scaring me. What are you trying to tell me?"

I perceived He wanted these words included in the diary, but more importantly to encourage me on the road to salvation and to help others as well. He wanted to increase my faith, give me hope and help others increase their faith in His resurrection. He truly listens to our prayers and is always with us. Thank you, Jesus!

#243 JESUS IN THE DISGUISE OF A POOR MAN

When entering a convenience store, at Rolling Hills, I noticed an older poor man sitting on the pavement leaning against a wall of the building. He was obviously hoping someone would give him money.

I stopped to visit with him, and he asked for money saying he was hungry. Instead of giving him money, I said I would purchase food for him. I asked what he wanted to eat and drink, and he replied saying he would like Mexican food. I purchased several burritos and warmed them in the microwave at the store. I also purchased a bottle of soda for him. He was elated and immediately began to eat the food and drink his soda.

About a week later, I stopped at a gas station at Montecarlo city and noticed freshly made burritos. I asked the clerk for one. She handed it to me, and said, "No charge, father". I said, "What?" She said, "It's yours. You don't need to pay." I was humbled and thanked her. Then I recalled the poor man, whom the Lord inspired me to give burritos. And, I was acutely aware, the woman did her act of charity for Jesus, whom she loves and not for me, whom she does not know.

#244 COLLECTION WOES

Due to COVID-19, the pastor of my parish decided to avoid numerous people touching the collection basket passed around during the offertory time, so he wanted it to be placed at the entrance of the church instead. This way, when people arrive, they place their donations in the gathering space. But there was no watchful oversight of the basket. During Mass, as we were singing the Gloria, and on another occasion, when giving a homily, I saw a woman with a major role in the Altar Society repeatedly steal cash from the collection.

Once, she took a sealed bag from the safe downstairs and opened it during Mass. She and her husband normally arrive late to Mass. Because they come late, it's a window of opportunity to steal. On another occasion, I saw her put her hand in the collection basket and put something in her pocket, most likely cash.

I repeatedly asked the bookkeeper and the bulletin coordinator to schedule two persons to count the collection. She counts the collection often by herself. But the bookkeeper and bulletin coordinator wouldn't do as I told them. I finally informed the pastor of the woman's thievery and suggested we remove opportunities for theft. He agreed. We didn't think it prudent to visit with the woman unless there's video proof, which we do not have. Otherwise, it would be her word against mine.

I suspect the woman's husband is aware that she has a problem with spending, and so limits the money she is allotted, and therefore, she tries to find other ways to obtain money for herself. Once, she left a note saying she took a package of batteries, but never replaced them. She could have easily purchased some at the local grocery store, just two blocks away. Now three months later, no batteries. Kleenex and other items seem to disappear. While it's shocking, someone would steal from the church, it's an act of mercy to remove occasions of sin, from those who have the habit of stealing, and pray for them to be freed from their addiction.

#245 PASTORAL ACTIVITIES INCREASE – THE JOY OF BEING USED BY GOD

In a parish of only 50 families, often there is little activity. Since school started, however, I now have: a weekly adult initiation class; a children's rite of initiation class; an adult faith formation class; I visit CCD classes every week and give Communion to Catholic nursing home residents on Sundays. Mass is offered daily, including on my day away from ministry, so people can still have Mass and receive Jesus in Holy Communion. Why offer a private Mass on my day away, when they can come to the Holy Sacrifice and receive Our Divine Lord in Holy Communion? Today, Sunday, I had a baptism for a two-week-old baby boy, whose parents are not married, but who will raise the child Catholic once they obtain an annulment and get married in the Church. Before every Mass, we have Confessions. Also, today before Mass I had a big fish! Praise the Lord!

I go to the local nursing home and visit four Catholic residents and periodically pray the Rosary with them. Before we pray the Rosary, each can state their intentions. Some residents feel they are no longer needed or wanted or loved. I pray more people will visit them as an act of mercy.

For specific fallen away Catholics, I first fast as much as I am able (three small meals) for as many days as the Holy Spirit leads me, then I offer a Mass for them, remember them during the Consecration at Masses, and consecrate them to the Immaculate Heart of Mary and the Sacred Heart of Jesus. For some, the Lord wants me to give them a miraculous medal to wear. Then I visit with them and subtlety attempt to get them to go to confession and return to regular church attendance.

During Eucharistic Adoration when parishioners pray their Holy Hour, they gaze upon the face of Jesus for an hour each week. Jesus is slowing touching the hearts of people and bringing back the fallen away. By the grace of God we have been hugely successful. We have continuous adoration after the 8am Sunday Mass until Tuesday morning before the 7am Mass. Forty-three out of fifty families signed up to be with Jesus an hour a week. Praise the Lord! Each adorer becomes a fountain gushing forth mercy, in their soul, their family, the parish and the whole world.

Being active in my priesthood gives me great joy, but I realize, I am like a broom, whom the Lord can take out of the closet and use, or put back in the closet, and wait to be used, when He so chooses, as St. Bernadette used to say. I should be content with either. But, I admit, it is a great joy to be used by God for the salvation of souls, and to see how the Lord uses me.

While I spend two or three hours of daily prayer before His Eucharistic Heart, He does not permit me to see how I am a channel of grace.

#246 PUBLICATION OF THE DIARY

I believe the Lord wants this diary to be published, so His mercy can be extolled. I am praying to St. Faustina daily, and pray an additional daily Holy Hour during the Hour of Mercy at 3 pm.

During that hour, I think about the Lord's Passion, pray the Stations of the Cross, pray three chaplets of Divine Mercy with the novena prayers, and also pray the Sorrowful mystery of the Rosary, and I trust many souls will come back to the Lord and His mercy will be extolled as He asked of me.

#247 TIME IS SHORT?

I continue to have more health problems. My urination is erratic. My esophagus keeps closing off, and I choke on food. I chocked again several days ago and thought I was going to die. Just as I asked my guardian angel for help, I was able to swallow that small piece of bread. I even at times choke on a pill, which gets lodged in my esophagus. I don't think I have much time left. Perhaps I won't see the book's publication in my life. But, that's okay, it's in the Lord's time. Whether I see it or not published, is up to Him. It's all for His glory and honor. I must decrease, while He increases. Lord, please help me to become a saint. Please, Jesus, do what is needed to remove my temporal punishment from sin. Through the intercession of Mary, I want to go straight to heaven. I think this is why I often want to be a religious, because I think that would help me to become a saint easier, but apparently, it is not His will. But I trust, He can still make me a saint.

#248 CONTACTED VOCATION DIRECTOR AGAIN

I emailed the vocation director who the OMM priest said he had visited and who he suggested I contact again. The vocation director replied to my email, "Fr. Gadfly, Thanks for the email. Sounds like the pilgrimage was a great blessing! Regarding discerning with the Order of Mary's Men, Fr. Gabriel Pâtisserie means well (he's a great guy and a dear friend) but we have a policy that I can't break. The age limit for priests who are interested in joining us is 50. There's nothing I can do about that since it is our policy and was put into force quite a few years ago by the leadership team. Again, I apologize for the bad news. May Our Lady and St. Joseph place their mantle and cloak over you and guide your discernment. Fraternally, Fr. Ben Stowaway, OMM." I wanted to tell Jesus, "I told you, I was too old" again, but I am sure He knew all along the answer would be no, but He only wanted me to be told so. I am content with whatever God wants.

#249 MORE HEALTH PROBLEMS

The NSAID anti-inflammatory I take is causing terrible stomach pain, especially when I eat citric foods, such as grapefruit. I belch throughout the day. At times, it is a source of humiliation. I discovered the drug also causes esophageal problems such as an inability to swallow and urine retention because it causes the bladder to not empty properly. If I don't use the anti-inflammatory, I develop migraines caused by arthritis in my neck and also have great difficulty walking and limb flexibility. Oftentimes, when walking to church in the morning, I use a walking stick to keep from falling down. I hope to try omega pills and eat fish frequently because they have anti-inflammatory properties. If I were to not have medicine, there is no doubt, I would become debilitated soon.

O Jesus, I accept my health issues for love of you, for the conversion of sinners, in reparation for sins committed against Your Sacred Heart and the Immaculate Heart of Mary and for an end to abortion in my state and my country. Amen.

#250 HEALTH & CONFUSION

Three weeks ago, my doctor said I have three or four hernias and need to see a surgeon in a few weeks. At that same time, I began to develop severe pain in my back and right arm (pain level between 7 and 8). I suspected the cause of three-weeks of high pain was a very bad arthritis flare-up. Since some physical therapy exercises curtail the pain, and they were not helping, my mind began to wonder if it was something worse. I wondered if I have a sepsis infection or possibly cancer.

At another doctor appointment two weeks later, my doctor explained the pain is caused by arthritis and prescribed a steroid, an antacid for stomach pain, and physical therapy. Due to difficulty in swallowing and stomach pain, most likely caused by the NSAIDs, I will also see a gastroenterologist. An elderly man once said, "Getting old isn't for sissies." The enemy takes advantage of our weaknesses and tries to frighten us and lose our peace. The older we become, the more we need to learn to embrace the cross of suffering and turn to Jesus to protect us from irrational fears.

#251 ADVENT BLESSINGS

"Let the little children come to me and do not hinder them, for the kingdom of heaven belongs to such as these." (Matthew 19:14)

During Advent, after I gave lessons to several children, an eight, and ten-year-old were Baptized, Confirmed, and received their First Holy Communion just before Christmas. I requested at least one parent attend class with their child and gave the children a shortened number of lessons. They were taught everything they needed to know for their age before receiving the sacraments.

The parents of the girl rarely attended Mass. Her father married previously, and he is now in an invalid marriage. But, since he is attempting to obtain an annulment, there is reasonable hope the daughter will be raised Catholic. Last year, she took special lessons to receive the sacraments. But she stubbornly resisted learning about the Catholic faith. She threw a rosary on the floor, refused to genuflect before Jesus in the tabernacle, would not dip her hand in holy water, and wouldn't participate with other children. She said, "Why should I do these things if my parents don't attend church?" I thought she had a good point. I told her father what she said, hoping it would encourage him to start attending Mass, but he still doesn't come. At times, her grandmother takes her to church. The girl's mother is non-Catholic, and, I am told, she's anti-Catholic. What an environment for the poor child!

This year, her parents placed her in the CCD class with other children her age. One day, during class, the non-baptized girl asked the other children, "Is it true, people who aren't baptized, can't go to heaven?" A boy responded, "That's true. They can't go to heaven." Since then, she began to ask her catechism teacher, if she could receive Baptism. Because of her desire, I gave her lessons with the eight-year-old boy. I spoke with the girl's twenty-five-year-old brother. He is very good practicing Catholic. I asked him to try to positively influence her toward the Catholic faith and help her to do the things she was refusing. Not much later, the parents of the girl began to attend Mass regularly. Apparently, the young man asked his father and step-mother to attend Mass with their daughter. She finally received the sacraments on Dec. 23rd and took Kateri Tekakwitha, as her Confirmation saint name.

When I began to give the two children lessons, the boy did not want baptism. During class, he made snide remarks. His mother recently returned to the practice of her faith, and she wanted her son to receive the sacraments. Thank God she came to the lessons with him. But his father, a non-Catholic, who has shared custody, was not supportive of anything spiritual. After showing the two children a children's video on First Communion, he suddenly changed his mind and wanted to receive the sacraments. I also believe it was helpful, that I prayed the prayer of exorcism for unbaptized children over them. Whenever I prayed the prayer, the children stopped fussing and immediately seemed at peace during class. Oh, the grace of God!

When children and adults receive Baptism, Confirmed, and make their First Holy Communion, I always schedule a day and time, about a month after their baptism, so they can make their First Confession. If not scheduled, they may not do Confession for a long time. I always have a practice in advance.

During separate Masses, due to parents of each having schedule conflicts, the two children received the sacraments, and after Mass, were enrolled in the Scapular of Our Lady of Mount Carmel.

At the weekend Masses, I announced the day and time of our Parish Penance Service and told them of a nearby parish having their service a few days earlier than ours. So that I too could go to Confession, I went to the neighboring parish Penance Service and noticed five of our parishioners there. I was elated and happy to see they went before Christmas even if they went to a different parish.

#252 CHRISTMAS BLESSINGS

"And this will be a sign to you, you will find an Infant wrapped in swaddling clothes and lying in a manger." (Luke 2:12)

The Babe's Beating Heart

What a joy to see the two children, who were just baptized and confirmed, now attend the Christmas Vigil Mass and receive Holy Communion. Jesus must have been thrilled to be able to come inside their pure hearts.

During the Christmas Vigil Mass and also the Christmas Midnight Mass, immediately after praying the words of consecration of the Host, and when the Host was elevated above the altar, I felt the Host beat between my fingers, as though I was holding a Heart in my hands. I was so astonished, it took much effort to not weep in the presence of the people.

Then again, at the Midnight Mass, after I preached about Christmas miracles and after the consecration of the Host, I once again felt the Host beat between my fingers. The throbbing feeling didn't happen at the Christmas morning Mass. After the midnight Mass, I lifted my hands and pressed my fingers together, but could not re-enact the feeling of beating between my fingers. I thought maybe there was some physical reason why it was happening. But I could not find one.

The Babe with Red & White Rays of Mercy

During the Christmas Midnight Mass, as I held the Sacred Host above the altar at the consecration, in place of the Host, I saw in my hands the baby Jesus wrapped in a blue blanket. From His chest, I saw white and red rays coming forth out into the whole world. To the right of the Child Jesus, I saw the face of Saint Faustina.

Oh, baby Jesus, why do you do such beautiful things for me? I love and adore your Eucharistic Heart beating and throbbing for me, for parishioners, and the whole world! O Lord, what a tremendous act of mercy that God the Father sent you into the world as a little baby and from Your birth we receive untold mercies. O Lord, you saw the misery of our human condition and came as a baby to show us You love us, to not fear You, to forgive our sins, to restore our friendship with You, and to give us a share in Your divine life, that we experience here on earth and will eventually experience perfectly in heaven.

St. Bernard said, "Before the Son of God became man His goodness was hidden, for God's mercy is eternal, but how could such goodness be recognized?" "How could He have shown His mercy more clearly than by taking on Himself our condition."

The feast of the Holy Family antiphon for Evening Prayer, states, "He had to become like His brothers in every way to show the fullness of His mercy."

The Baby Jesus Placed in the Manger

For both the Christmas Vigil and Midnight Masses, I chose a little child from the congregation to carry the infant Jesus in procession at the beginning of Mass. Once at the altar, the child placed the baby Jesus in the manger. After the Christmas Vigil, I remembered the divine Child statue from the large outdoor nativity set had not yet been placed in the manger. I felt bad that I forgot to ask someone to do it. It's a special privilege to be chosen for such a task. Apparently, no one noticed the baby wasn't laid in the manger. After Mass, I took the handcrafted statue of the baby Jesus and laid it in the outdoor manger myself. I believe Jesus chose me to do it. I felt honored and humbled He wanted me to do it out of love for Him. I guess He is telling me to be like a little child.

Christmas Dinner with Mom & Stepfather

Since my mother is having surgery next week, I was so happy to be able to go home on Christmas Day and have a Christmas dinner with her and her husband. At the age of 81, it may be my mother's last Christmas. Before next Christmas, either I may be called home to heaven or perhaps she could too. Her oven-baked turkey, homemade stuffing, mashed potatoes and gravy, sweet potatoes, cranberry sauce, and strawberry rhubarb pie were all very special. When I was a child, after every Christmas Mass, my mother would bring us children to the nativity set at the front of the church, and she would want us to gaze upon the poor scene in silence. What a profound memory and how much meaning it was for me, many years later.

A Reminder to Pray to My Guardian Angel & St. Michael

On the way to visit my mother and stepfather on Christmas Day, I partially drove off the road while looking at a map. I could have been a "goner". On the way back, several times, I nearly hit deer, as they jumped in front of the car. Then, once I returned to the parish, a few hours later, the roads iced over, and I fell before entering the church. Due to the ice, we discontinued Eucharistic Adoration on Christmas day in the evening. When ice melted enough for safe arrival at the church, we started Adoration at the 3 pm the day after Christmas.

I later recalled that I recently changed my prayer routine. In the morning I used to pray to my guardian angel and St. Michael. I will return praying these very important prayers asking for their heavenly intercession for protection and to help me to grow in holiness.

Joy of Being with Jesus on the Feast of John the Apostle

What a joy it is to have the Eucharistic Jesus in a tabernacle on an altar in nearby room (a chapel) at the rectory. Yesterday, I spent 4 hours before Him in the Most Blessed Sacrament. Oh, thank you, Jesus, for the graces, parishioners, my family, myself, and the whole world receives when anyone is basking in the light of the Eucharist.

Christmas Money from Generous Hearts

This year, I received $675 dollars inside Christmas cards and will give the money to the poor. I also received gift $160 of certificates for local businesses, such as the grocery store and a restaurant. I will see if they can also be given to the poor. Most are written in my name. Can I still give them to someone else? Thank God for the generosity of parishioners. May the Lord bless them for their generous hearts. One act of mercy opens the door to more acts of mercy.

#253 DISAPPEARING DOUBTS & GRACES FROM THE RETREAT

"Another goes his way a weakling and a failure, with little strength and great misery. Yet, the eyes of the Lord look favorably upon him. He raises him free of the vile dust, lifts up his head, and exalts him to the amazement of the many." (Sirach 11:12-13)

I was doubting if this diary should be published. Yet, I believed the Lord desires to use me as a witness to His divine mercy. At the beginning of the retreat the doubts vanished, and I had peace when I read Sirach 11:12-13. Just as the retreat was about to start, I finished reading the book, *A Mother's Plea*. Today a sentence struck me to the heart, on page 333. Fr. Anthony Bus, CR, quoted Pope St. John Paul II, who said, "May you be a witness of mercy." I felt like these words were for me. Through much of my life, I viewed myself as a weakling and a failure, with little strength and great misery, and especially now I feel that way. But many times, the Lord came to my misery and relieved it with His mercy, which flows from His Sacred Heart through the Immaculate Heart of the Mother of Mercy.

At the retreat house, I had spiritual direction daily with my spiritual director for an eight-day Ignatian Retreat. He asked me to use the book, *The Virgin Mary in the Kingdom of the Divine Will*, by the Servant of God, Luisa Piccareta. Some imagery in the book moved my heart to a great love of Our Lady. But, due to some odd words and phrases, with my spiritual director's permission, I switched to the book, *The Glories of Mary*, by St. Alphonsus Ligouri.

I didn't realize another retreat group would start a few days after I began my retreat. The group's silent retreat was called "Apostles of Mercy". With God there are no coincidences. It was all in God's plan, and with the permission of my spiritual director, while doing the Ignatian Retreat, I listened to the conferences about divine mercy.

St. Alphonsus speaks of Mary in many chapters, as Our Lady of Mercy. I felt like the Lord wanted me to drink from the well of mercy, through the eyes and Heart of Mary during the retreat.

As the retreat began, I was sad because I felt my devotion to Mary was so pitiful. She has brought me to many of Her apparition sites, such as Lourdes, Fatima, Guadalupe, the Miraculous Medal, and Medjugorje seven times, and She allowed me to witness apparitions by seers in Medjugorje.

Although I pray three or four Rosaries a day, wear Mary's scapular and Miraculous Medal, am consecrated to Her, and kneel before Her image daily, I feel I lack a personal friendship with Mary as I ought.

But, the book, *The Glories of Mary,* moved my heart, so many times I finally felt, Mary and I are like a real mother and son and even more than a natural mother and son could be.

O blessed Lady, help me to love You, honor You, and reverence You. With all my heart, I want to have an unlimited devotion to You! I would be so humbled if, as a witness to God's mercy, He would use me to help others to come to know His unfathomable mercy. I am such a poor miserable priest, which makes it easier for all to see God and not me.

The stories of St. Alphonsus were very helpful in creating a special friendship with Mary. I believe I should use more stories in my homilies, to help listeners better understand the message given.

I realize now, by God's grace, how I have failed miserably to see and "feel" the misery of those I have served. This retreat has moved me to have more compassion by doing what I can to relieve their misery, allowing my heart and actions to overcome judgmental and critical thoughts of others by way of merciful thoughts, prayers, and deeds.

While looking at the tabernacle in the chapel of the retreat house, I kept seeing the word, "Amodeus". Not knowing what the word meant, I told my spiritual director that I kept seeing the word, "Amodeus" when looking at the tabernacle. He said the word means, "I love God." I should have known that, as I do know some Latin.

Then, later that night, when I was reading from *The Glories of Mary*, St. Alphonsus quoted "Blessed Amandeus", who said, "That our Queen is always before the Divine Majesty, interceding for us with Her prayers. And since in heaven, She knows perfectly our miseries and necessities, She cannot but have pity on us; so with the affection of a mother, moved by compassion for us, She kindly and mercifully endeavors to relieve and save us. So great is the pity which Mary has for our miseries, and so great is the love She bears us, and defending us from evil with Her prayers, and obtaining for us favors—She is never satisfied with defending us."

One night during the retreat, when I went to bed, and after I had prayed the feeling prayer while lying in bed, I asked Our Lord to shine His light on the wounds of my soul. About ten minutes after praying that prayer, and I was just preparing to fall asleep, my room was filled with light. I presumed a light came from outside my window shining through the closed curtain to light up the room. I wondered if a car was shining it headlights in my room or if a nearby outdoor light had come on. It lasted about three minutes and then stopped. But the next day, I realized a car couldn't shine its light in the direction of my room, nor was an outdoor light near my window.

A few days later, after I went to bed, and as I was preparing to fall asleep, an unknown light lit up my room again, but it went out, and after a few seconds, it lit the room back up again. The light kept lighting up the room and going out. It lasted for about three minutes. I didn't get out of bed to see where it was coming from. I just allowed myself to experience it and felt peace about it.

The next morning, I happened to notice a pamphlet called, "The Litany of Light" in the chapel and picked it up and prayed it. That day, as I met with my spiritual director, he opened the Bible and read, "The Lord is my light and my salvation." I then told him about the events. At the conclusion of the retreat, I returned *The Glories of Mary* to the library. I placed in back in the exact location I originally removed it, and next to it was a book called, *Our Lady of Light*.

#254 SURGERY & UNVACCINATED BLOOD

I'm scheduled to have surgery on Jan. 24th for hernia repair and an exploratory laparoscopy. My general doctor believes I have at least three hernias.

The surgeon can't tell whether it's one hernia or multiple hernias and wants to explore my abdomen. He believes there may be lipomas in the pain areas and wants to remove them. Though he didn't say so, he suspects I may have cancer because there are so many locations of pain in my abdomen.

I informed his nurse, that I would not consent to take blood from those who had the COVID-19 vaccine. I do not want baby body parts in my blood, that are in some vaccines. Some doctors are saying the COVID-19 shot is causing blood clots, myocarditis, sudden death, and causes the immune system to be comprised, which does not allow the body to fight off viruses.

In my parish, when the vaccinated contract the flu, they have the flu for up to three weeks, while the unvaccinated have the flu for three or four days. In the previous six months, I know of three people who were COVID-19 vaccinated, and each then contracted pneumonia and died within three days because antibiotics and their natural immune system were not effective.

My sister, Sue, had a ruptured appendix this week, and previously had the COVID-19 vaccine. She had the flu for three weeks. After originally receiving the vaccine, a few weeks later she had convulsions. The same day, she had a drainage device installed due to the ruptured appendix, and several hours after the surgery, she went into convulsions again. Some family members believe she may not live long because her compromised immune system can't fight off the infection. Lord have mercy. Over a year ago, I warned my family members and some parishioners to avoid COVID-19 shots and was recently heartbroken to learn my mother didn't listen to me and had the vaccine and booster.

It's now proven that several of the COVID-19 vaccine manufacturers have tiny unborn baby particles in every shot. All other manufacturers of the COVID-19 vaccine, while they do not have unborn baby parts in the shot, were developed and manufactured using unborn babies, who were aborted alive, and their organs removed while alive in order to perform tests on them.

The horror of it all. How sick that we treat baby humans with no dignity, and even treat them less than animals.

I refuse to have anything to do with receiving blood from vaccinated persons, and will not take the vaccine, even if it means I cannot have life-saving blood. I would rather die during surgery than receive blood containing aborted tissue or blood from the COVID-19 shot that can cause complications to those who would receive it.

Instead of killing babies to save our lives, I would rather give my life to help save unborn babies.

#255 HEALTH UPDATE & MORE HOSPICE WOES

About six weeks after surgery, I'm writing about the last doctor visit. The first remark from the surgeon during the follow-up visit after the surgery was, "You don't have cancer." While I was happy, it also showed, he suspected I had cancer. Unfortunately, I now have a large elongated lump in the area of the surgery. He said it was swelling that would go away, but now it is apparent, it's either another hernia or some sort of problem associated with the surgery. Now what do I do? Should I go back or just leave it as it is? In your hands O Mary, I entrust this to you.

This evening I went to a talk on ethics and end of life issues. The former doctor of Woebegone Hospice, Dr. Bevilacqua's son, a priest, gave a talk at a nearby parish. About two years ago, I sent the priest, and all the priests of the diocese, information on Church teaching and end of life issues.

I was wondering if he would proclaim the Church's teachings on the subject in accord with documents of the Church by the CDF, several US state bishop's conferences, several bishop's pastoral letters and the International Catholic Bioethics

Center of America, specifically with regard to artificial nutrition and hydration, or if he would give his father's view, which departs from Catholic teaching on the subject.

I was deeply saddened and angered he chose his father's view, which has utterly devastated our diocese with regard to the subject. How many in our diocese have died as a result of not having nutrition and hydration when they could have benefited from them?

During his talk, Father Paul Bevilacqua gave a list of Catholic principles, but with a distorted view on the subject heavily favoring avoiding all extraordinary means and was very negative when speaking of giving patients IVs or feeding tubes at the end of their life. By the way, "Bevilacqua" ironically means "drink the water."

Sometimes extraordinary means, such as a ventilator, can temporarily be used to allow a person to overcome an illness and be restored to health.

At the talk, a goodhearted parishioner from their parish recently lost his father and asked a very good question. He said, "Toward the end of my father's life, the hospice didn't want to give him an IV or a feeding tube. But, it is my understanding, the Church teaches a patient should die of the disease or illness and not due to a lack of food or water." The priest responded saying, "Well, if he had received an IV, he would have eventually died of too much water in his system." But, the problem with his reply, is it's not always the case that a person will die from too much water, and he knew nothing about patient's medical condition. He made a statement presuming the IV would cause his death. However, many benefit from an IV and a feeding tube at the end of their life. The priest's reply indicated he had a presupposition that all patients who are dying will not benefit from an IV. He also said, "My dad has a principle that he always tells the people who are going through similar situations. He will say, 'If the action you are performing won't bring him to eat at the supper table again, then why do the action'?"

He clearly has a negative attitude towards anyone who needs to be on an IV or a feeding tube for a long period of time or even a short period of time when he or she could benefit from it. He also made sound like, if a person does not have quality of life, then why bother with feeding tubes or IVs. However, the Congregation for the Doctrine of Faith document, *Good Samaritan*, #3 states:

> "When the provision of nutrition and hydration no longer benefits the patient, because the patient's organism either cannot absorb them or cannot metabolize them, their administration should be suspended. In this way, one does not unlawfully hasten death through the deprivation of the hydration and nutrition vital for bodily function, but nonetheless respects the natural course of the critical or terminal illness. The withdrawal of this sustenance is an unjust action that can cause great suffering to the one who has to endure it. Nutrition and hydration do not constitute medical therapy in a proper sense, which is intended

to counteract the pathology that afflicts the patient. They are instead forms of obligatory care of the patient, representing both a primary clinical and an unavoidable human response to the sick person. Obligatory nutrition and hydration can at times be administered artificially, provided that it does not cause harm or intolerable suffering to the patient." #4 states, "In addition, palliative interventions to reduce the suffering of gravely or terminally ill patients in these regulatory contexts can involve the administration of medications that intend to hasten death, as well as the suspension or interruption of hydration and nutrition even when death is not imminent. In fact, such practices are equivalent to a *direct action or omission to bring about death and are therefore unlawful*. The growing diffusion of such legislation and of scientific guidelines of national and international professional societies, constitutes a socially irresponsible threat to many people, including a growing number of vulnerable persons who needed only to be better cared for and comforted but are instead being led to choose euthanasia and suicide."

To presume all dying patients or in a vegetative state would not benefit from an IV is contrary to Church teaching. When speaking of patients in a vegetative state, #8 states, which states:

"One must never forget in such painful situations that the patient in these states has the right to nutrition and hydration, even administered by artificial methods that accord with the principle of ordinary means. In some cases, such measures can become disproportionate, because their administration is ineffective, or involves procedures that create an excessive burden with negative results that exceed any benefits to the patient."

Pontifical Council for Pastoral Assistance to Health Care Workers, *New Charter for Health Care Workers*, n. 152:

"Nutrition and hydration, even if administered artificially, are classified as basic care owed to the dying person when they do not prove to be too burdensome or without any benefit. The unjustified discontinuation thereof can be tantamount to a real act of euthanasia: 'The administration of food and water even by artificial means is, in principle, an ordinary and proportionate means of preserving life. It is therefore obligatory to the extent which, and for as long as, it is shown to accomplish its proper finality, which is hydration and nourishment of the patient. In this way, suffering and death by starvation and dehydration are prevented.'"

1986 document of the US Catholic Conference bishops sums up the current Church understanding of the administration of nutrition and hydration for all patients:

> Because human life has inherent value and dignity regardless of its condition, every patient should be provided with measures which can effectively preserve life without involving too grave a burden. Since food and water are necessities of life for all human beings and can generally be provided without the risks and burden s of more aggressive mean s for sustaining life, the law should establish a strong presumption in favor of their use. Committee for Pro-Life Activities, NCCB, "The Rights of the Terminally III," Origin, vol. 16 no. 12 (June 1986): 222.

"Care for Patients in a 'Permanent' Vegetative State," May 2004, Saint John Paul II in #4, said,

> "The sick person in a vegetative state, awaiting recovery or a natural end, still has the right to basic health care (nutrition, hydration, cleanliness, warmth, etc.), and to the prevention of complications related to his confinement to bed. He also has the right to appropriate rehabilitative care and to be monitored for clinical signs of eventual recovery. In this regard, I recall what I wrote in the Encyclical *Evangelium Vitae*, making it clear that "by *euthanasia in the true and proper sense* must be understood an action or omission which by its very nature and intention brings about death, with the purpose of eliminating all pain"; such an act is always "a *serious violation of the law of God*, since it is the deliberate and morally unacceptable killing of a human person" (n. 65).

In response to the priest who gave the misinformation when he said, "If grandpa is unable to sit down and have a meal, what good would it be if he is unable to participate? Why bother with an IV and Feeding Tube or other medical interventions?" #5, *Good Samaritan* said,

> "Considerations about the "quality of life", often actually dictated by psychological, social and economic pressures, cannot take precedence over general principles. First of all, no evaluation of costs can outweigh the value of the fundamental good which we are trying to protect, that

405

of human life. Moreover, to admit that decisions regarding man's life can be based on the external acknowledgment of its quality, is the same as acknowledging that increasing and decreasing levels of quality of life, and therefore of human dignity, can be attributed from an external perspective to any subject, thus introducing into social relations a discriminatory and eugenic principle. Moreover, it is not possible to rule out *a priori* that the withdrawal of nutrition and hydration, as reported by authoritative studies, is the source of considerable suffering for the sick person, even if we can see only the reactions at the level of the autonomic nervous system or of gestures. Modern clinical neurophysiology and neuro-imaging techniques, in fact, seem to point to the lasting quality in these patients of elementary forms of communication and analysis of stimuli."

Note: A person's right to the normal human need of food and water, should never be rejected based upon "Quality of Life".

Are Feeding Tubes Required?, National Catholic Bioethics Center, Rev. Tad Pacholczyk, PhD, said,

"As a general rule, we ought to die from a disease or an ailment that claims our life, not from an action (or inaction) by someone that intentionally causes our death. Our death, in other words, should result from the progress of a pathological condition, not from a lack of food or water if it could have been readily and effectively offered to provide comfort and support to a patient."

The Pennsylvania Catholic Conference, *Nutrition and Hydration Moral Considerations*, Dec. 12th, 1991, Revised 1999, said,

Is the procedure (supplying of nutrition and hydration) beneficial to the patient in terms of preservation of life or restoration of health? Supplying nourishment sustains life; it does not of itself restore health to a former state. However, it is clearly beneficial in terms of preservation of life, since death would be inevitable without it and life will continue with it. Is it serving a life-saving purpose? There is no doubt about the fact that it is, since the patient could not survive without it and is unable to supply it for himself. *Is it adding a serious burden?* In almost every case the answer is negative. The means of supplying food in themselves are all relatively simple and — barring complications — generally without pain. While there should be a

406

presumption in favor of medically assisted nutrition and hydration, the judgment can legitimately be made that, in a particular case, they can be extraordinary. (This last sentence clearly indicates it would be an exception to not give medically assisted nutrition and hydration based upon being an excessive burden. However, today, many hospitals and hospices see this exception, as a rule, and therefore, every patient who could benefit from medically assisted nutrition is denied ordinary nourishment to sustain their life. And so thus becomes a subtle form of euthanasia.)

Address of Pope Saint John Paul II to the Participants of the International Conference on "Life Sustaining Treatments and Vegetative State: Scientific Advance and Ethical Dilemmas", #4, March 20, 2004,

> "I should like particularly to underline how the administration of water and food, even when provided by artificial means, always represents a natural means of preserving life, not a medical act. Its use, furthermore, should be considered, in principle, ordinary and proportionate, and as such morally obligatory, to the extent to which, and for as long as, it is shown to accomplish its proper finality, which in the present case consists in providing nourishment to the patient and alleviation of his suffering.".

A reason, I believe the Lord wants this diary published, is to bestow His mercy on the dying. He wants to alleviate their hunger and thirst, as Jesus said, "When I was hungry, you gave me food, when I was thirsty, you gave me drink." (Matthew 25:35)

I wonder, and fervently pray, "Why, O Lord do you delay? I trust you, but I am in deep anguish when I know this terrible anti-life view is promoted, and I am unable to do anything. There are priests who promote it. A Catholic hospital who does not follow Church teaching. A hospice in a Catholic hospital, where people keep dying due to a lack of food and water, when it would benefit them."

Open wide the door of Your mercy, O Lord, show me or someone, anyone the way. Please, O Lord, my heart is torn, and yet, I will praise you in the storm. I remember when you heard my cry before, when my strength was almost gone. Awake, O Lord, from the storm. Stand up and raise your hand and say, your holy words, "Quiet, be still." And move hearts to bring about your tender mercy for the sick and dying. For I know, You love and care for them, even more than I could ever imagine. Here I am Lord, I come to do your will, show me or someone, or anyone the way.

#256 THOSE I CAUSED PAIN & SUFFERING

While in Eucharistic Adoration, the Lord showed me many who I hurt in the past and my failure to pray for them and make up for what I did to them.

I prayed for the young man who was with me when I wrecked two vehicles due to drunkenness, and my classmate and his girlfriend who were in the other vehicle. My passenger surely had a concussion since his head cracked the windshield and glasses were broken. Today, I mailed a $200 check to pay for his glasses, broken over 40 years ago.

I offered three Masses, for the boy, who I threw a brick at him and hit his head. Did he have permanent brain damage or seizures? Lord, have mercy, I was young and stupid. Did I ruin his life?

For the classmate in 7th grade, as I caused his appendix to rupture during football practice, I prayed and will offer a Mass for him.

In the past, I prayed for the two 16-year-old friends who I scheduled an abortion for their baby, and especially for the baby and offered Masses for them. I still felt the Lord wanted more prayer and Masses for them.

I offered a Mass for each of the two guys I got into fights with. I prayed for and offered Masses for the two boys I punched in the gut in grade school. For my brother, who I body slammed and made him feel helpless by overpowering him when wrestling. For the boys in high school I hit as hard as possible during Karate boxing. And many more.

I started to offer an extra Mass every day for specific people from my past, who I have hurt, asking the Lord to heal them, in any way I caused them pain or scandal and that Jesus would give them His love and mercy. Oh, how I should have apologized to them and prayed for them in the past.

O Lord, in your mercy make them whole and help them to get to heaven. Heal them of any physical and or emotional trauma I caused. Let your light penetrate the depths of their souls. I trust in your unfathomable mercy.

#257 WOMAN CASTS OUT DEMON FROM SON, INVALID ANOINTINGS, SMOKE DETECTOR GOES OFF

A woman from the parish told me about her two sons, Bob and Bill, who live together. One of the two sons, Bob, has custody of his daughter, Maggie, and son, Van, who live with their father and uncle. The adult brothers are alcoholics. Bob's brother, Bill is mentally slow and has health problems which prevent him from working. Bob purchases all the liquor that Bill wants, rather than trying to help him not get drunk. Since each drink, at least, a six-pack of beer a day and smoke at least one pack of cigarettes a day, they spend $20 a day on alcohol and beer and don't have enough money to pay the rent. They spend $7,300 a year on beer and cigarettes, the exact amount of money needed to pay their $600 a month rent for an entire year. Although he is thirty years old, Bill hasn't worked for several years and has never attempted to get disability.

Bob's boy is sixteen and his daughter is twelve. The girl started thinking she was homosexual and decided to be transgender. What is she to think, when living with two alcoholic men and a brother? Sadly, she attempted suicide and was admitted to a mental hospital. In the winter, a few days after her admittance, the boy ran away from home, but has been found and returned a few days later. Their mother used to severely beat the boy, and so he hid in wall compartments in their former house to prevent her from hurting him. The children were named after characters in a video game from the 1990's. Their parents divorced five years ago, and their alcoholic father was awarded custody. While at school, the girl had a mental breakdown running through the halls screaming and cursing, causing the school to be put on "soft" lock-down. She was taken to a mental hospital again and then handed over to foster parents. Due to this traumatic activity, Bob had a mental breakdown. When his mother went to his home, she said his body became stiff, his eyes rolled to the back of his head, his teeth clenched, he started grunting, and foam came out of his mouth. She said, "I got on top of him and placed my hands on his face. Then I said, 'In the name of Jesus, and through the intercession of the Virgin Mary, I command you, Satan, leave.' and my son immediately became better." I never mentioned to her, I was praying deliverance prayers for him to be freed from his addiction and that he would come back to the sacraments. Unbeknownst to either of us at the time, it seems like the Lord used both of us to cast out the enemy. I recently blessed the house just before he was delivered.

A priest and I spoke on the phone today. He discovered that when the priest chaplain of the very liberal religious order of sisters, Sisters of the Holy Name of Jesus, is away, a sister will give their monthly anointings of the sick to her religious sisters. Or if a sister has a turn to the worse, rather than call another priest, she will anoint the sick sister. Lord have mercy, invalid anointings.

A few nights ago, about ten minutes after I laid down to sleep, the fire detector went off. However, I didn't smell smoke. I walked through the house and there was no smoke anywhere in the house. When I opened the door to the chapel the alarm immediately ceased. Then, when I laid back down in bed again, I remembered I had not set the alarm clock. So, I got out of bed again and set the alarm. The smoke detector had never gone off before and has never gone off since. I believe the Lord made it go off to remind me to set the alarm clock, so I would not sleep past the time to offer the Holy Mass and hear confessions in the morning at the parish. Thank you, Jesus!

#258 WAS MY FATHER POSSESSED? FREEMASONRY CURSE?

The priests of the diocese listened to a talk by an exorcist. When the priest exorcist spoke about the effects of freemasonry on family trees, it was like a light came on. I was able to clearly see most likely a family member in the past must have been a Freemason. Some signs the priest mentioned included: molestation, incest and ailments that doctors can never seem to identify.

I was molested two times, once by my father and another by a neighbor. There are other events involving family, that can never be written here, that would lead one to believe someone in the family was a Freemason.

My brother had blood in his stool for at least five years and no doctor has ever diagnosed the cause of it.

According to a priest exorcist, when a member of the family becomes a Freemason, the entire family is cursed for five generations. If it was the case, one should pray the "Prayers to Break the Freemasonry Curse", which will remove the curse from the family. It's to be prayed three times and ratified each time in the presence of a priest. I asked a priest, if he would witness the prayer and ratify it. A few weeks later, we met, I prayed the prayer, and he ratified it.

Within a few days, my brother was diagnosed with internal hemorrhoids causing severe bleeding and blood-clotting.

A few months later, I watched the movie, *Nefarious*, that accurately explains what happens when a man is possessed. The movie caused me to believe, most likely, my father, at times, became possessed when he became drunk. I don't believe this is something that normally happens to alcoholics. I have seen a lot of drunk people, but have never seen anyone act like my father when he was drunk. My father said he had periods, during drunkenness, when he couldn't remember what he did. He called the episodes blackouts. While this happens to other alcoholics, his personality seriously changed when he was drunk. He was mean, vicious, condescending, and it was at these times he did atrocious things. He would sleep-walk without any clothes on.

The movie gave me hope, that my father may not have been responsible for his behavior because it could have been a demon acting through him. Strange phenomena occurred in the house we were raised. Marie, my sister, recently shocked me. She said when she was ill as a child, she saw faces in the closet laughing and mocking her. When I was a child, and was ill, I saw faces in the closet, laughing and mocking me too. What are the chances both her and I, who had never discussed the topic, would both see the same thing in the closet when we were children?

I have concluded that our childhood home was haunted, even before we moved in and not when we began to play the Ouija board. However, playing the Ouija board made things worse. I suspect Dad became possessed there, which would reduce the culpability of his actions. It's possible it was not my father performing all those wicked things, but a demon, who had possessed him. And therefore he did not himself choose those actions. This gives me hope, that God in His mercy, may have granted my father salvation. How could God condemn someone whose actions may have been performed by a demon and not the person possessed? I trust in the mercy of Jesus.

#259 STOP WRITING?

The next time I visit with my spiritual director, I'm going to ask him if I can discontinue writing in my diary. It seems there were multiple purposes for writing it. It helped me to know myself better and understand how God was so merciful and good to me on my life. It helped me to look back in my life and make amends to others. I can now see the many times the Lord bailed me out of situations and how many times He used me as an instrument of mercy. Perhaps, one purpose of this diary will be to help priests, seminarians, religious, and lay people. All of these ways and many more humbles me.

It was Jesus who helped me to forgive the many people in my life. I never could have forgiven my father, who did atrocious things to others as an abusive alcoholic. Or forgive a molester, murderers, bishops, priests, former friends, parishioners, religious sisters, hospital administrators, doctors, and, forgive myself, if it wasn't for God's untold mercy.

How many Catholics run away from Jesus, and don't realize they are? If only they would regularly come to Confession, attend Mass as often as possible, receive Holy Communion, and spend time with Jesus in Eucharistic Adoration. If only they would daily pray to Jesus and come to truly know Him and not just about Him. If only they could understand the love of the Virgin Mary, the power God has given Her to help us in our daily lives, especially through Her Rosary and Consecration to Her Immaculate Heart.

Jesus wants to heal souls, their wounded hearts, emotions, traumatic experiences, and even physically heal through the sacraments and prayer. Jesus wants to deliver us from evil spirits and help us to live in freedom and peace.

There are untold mercies that are not bestowed, who otherwise could be helped and healed, simply because they do not come to the primary means God intends, through the Church, the sacraments, and the saints. God can help us and heal us outside of the sacraments, but His primary way, and the easiest and most sure way for us, is through the sacraments and the Church.

This life is a battle. That's why we are the Church militant, but we have nothing to fear, because the Lord Jesus and His Mother are leading the battle. May Jesus and His holy Mother bestow His untold mercy upon us, until we see Him face to face.

(Note: Father Gadfly has multiple health issues. Most likely his life on earth is nearly complete. When you read this, pray for his soul, whether living or deceased, that God may grant his desire of skipping purgatory and being with Jesus, Mary and all the angels and saints in the Father's house.)

#260 THE TRADITIONAL LATIN MASS

My spiritual director agreed this is my last entry, but my private diary will continue.

I am convinced the ancient Latin Roman Mass can never be abolished. An author of a book, that I just read, states no pope, nor any bishop has the authority to abolish the Traditional Latin Mass. The Novus Ordo Mass opens the door to many abuses. I gave my Eucharistic rant previously. Despite many problems with the Novus Ordo Mass, it can be done in a worthy and reverent manner, with Gregorian Chant, and all in Latin, but it lacks the fullness of beauty in the way the Mass can be offered. My bishop does not permit every Novus Ordo Mass to be offered in Latin, with Gregorian Chant and ad orientem. Although my bishop permits the Mass to be offered ad orientem, when he becomes aware of it, he will transfer the pastor and ask the new pastor to not offer the Mass that way. Does he have the authority to prevent a priest from offering the Mass in the manner the Church intends?

Due to the possible future meddling with the Novus Ordo Mass, or an outright eliminating of it, and making another "new" Mass, some suspect the Church may go underground because those in authority may actually invalidate the consecration. If that happens, will the Traditional Latin Mass be the only valid Mass faithful Catholics will be able to attend? I tried learning the Mass about 10 yrs ago, but Latin was extremely difficult.

O, Jesus, eternal high priest, if you want me to offer the Traditional Latin Mass, help me.

CONCLUSION: QUEEN OF PEACE & MOTHER OF MERCY

Mary is the Queen of Peace, as St. Albert the Great makes Her say, "I am the dove of Noah, which brought the olive-branch of universal peace to the Church." And St. Bernadine of Sienna says, "Mary is the bow (rainbow) of eternal peace; for, as God on seeing it remembers peace promised to earth, so does He, at the prayers of Mary, forgive the crimes of sinners, and confirm His peace with them."

Mary is the Mother of Mercy, as St. Bernard said, "Ah, truly, O great Lady, does the immensity of thy mercy fill the whole earth." St. Bonaventure said, "Mary is the throne, at which all—just and sinners—find the consolations of mercy." St. Bridget heard Jesus addressing His Mother in heaven, and said, "My Mother, ask of me what thou wilt." And Mary said, "I ask mercy for sinners. My Son, thou hast made Me, the Mother of

Mercy, the refuge of sinners, the advocate of the miserable; and now thou tellest me to ask what I desire; what can I ask, except for mercy for them? I ask mercy for the miserable."

FINAL PRAYER

O greatly Merciful God, Infinite Goodness, today all mankind calls out from the abyss of its misery to Your mercy---to Your compassion, O God; and, it is with its mighty voice of misery that it cries out. Gracious God, do not reject the prayer of this earth's exiles! O Lord, Goodness beyond our understanding, Who are acquainted with our misery through and through, and know that by our own power we cannot ascend to You, we implore You: anticipate us with Your Grace and keep on increasing Your mercy in us, that we may faithfully do Your holy will all through our life, and at death's hour. Let the omnipotence of Your mercy shield us from the darts of our salvation's enemies, that we may, with confidence, as Your children await Your final coming -- that day known to You alone. And we expect to obtain everything promised us by Jesus in spite of all our wretchedness. For Jesus is our Hope: Through His merciful Heart, as through an open gate we pass through to heaven. Amen. #1570

O incomprehensible and limitless Mercy Divine, to extol and adore You worthily, who can? Supreme attribute of Almighty God, You are the sweet hope for sinful man. Into one hymn yourselves unite, stars, earth and sea, and in one accord, thankfully and fervently sing of the incomprehensible Divine Mercy. #951

APPENDIX A

ST. AUGUSTINE
PREPARING FOR JUDGMENT & THE SECOND COMING BY WORKS OF MERCY*

He has come the first time, and he will come again. At his first coming, his own voice declared in the gospel: *Hereafter you shall see the Son of Man coming upon the clouds.* What does he mean by hereafter? Does he not mean that the Lord will come at a future time when all the nations of the earth will be striking their breasts in grief? Previously he came through his preachers, and he filled the whole world. Let us not resist his first coming, so that we may not dread the second.

What then should the Christian do? He ought to use the world, not become its slave. And what does this mean? It means having, as though not having. So says the Apostle: *My brethren, the appointed time is short: from now on let those who have wives live as though they had none; and those who mourn as though they were not mourning; and those who rejoice as though they were not rejoicing; and those who buy as though they had no goods; and those who deal with this world as though they had no dealings with it. For the form of this world is passing away. But I wish you to be without anxiety.*

He who is without anxiety waits without fear until his Lord comes. For what sort of love of Christ is it to fear his coming? Brothers, do we not have to blush for shame? We love him, yet we fear his coming. Are we really certain that we love him? Or do we love our sins more? Therefore, let us hate our sins and love him who will exact punishment for them. He will come whether we wish it or not. Do not think that because he is not coming just now, he will not come at all. He will come, you know not when; and provided he finds you prepared, your ignorance of the time of his coming will not be held against you.

All the trees of the forest will exult. He has come the first time, and he will come again to judge the earth. He will find those rejoicing who believed in his first coming, for he has come.

He will judge the world with equity and the peoples in his truth. What are equity and truth? He will gather together with him for the judgment his chosen ones, but the others he will set apart; for he will place some on his right, others on his left. What is more equitable, what truer than that they should not themselves expect mercy from the judge, who themselves were unwilling to show mercy before the judge's coming.

Those, however, who were willing to show mercy will be judged with mercy. For it will be said to those placed on his right: *Come, blessed of my Father, take possession of the kingdom which has been prepared for you from the beginning of the world.* And he reckons to their account their works of mercy: *For I was hungry, and you gave me food to eat; I was thirsty, and you gave me drink.*

What is imputed to those placed on his left side? That they refused to show mercy. And where will they go? *Depart into the everlasting fire.* The hearing of this condemnation will cause much wailing. But what has another psalm said? The just man will be held in everlasting remembrance; he will not fear the evil report.

What is the evil report? *Depart into the everlasting fire, which was prepared for the devil and his angels.* Whoever rejoices to hear the good report will not fear the bad. This is equity, this is truth.

Or do you, because you are unjust, expect the judge not to be just? Or because you are a liar, will the truthful one not be true? Rather, if you wish to receive mercy, be merciful before he comes; forgive whatever has been done against you; give of your abundance. Of whose possessions do you give, if not from his? If you were to give of your own, it would be largess; but since you give of his, it is restitution. For what do you have, that you have not received?

These are the sacrifices most pleasing to God: mercy, humility, praise, peace, charity. Such as these, then, let us bring and, free from fear, we shall await the coming of the judge who will judge the world in equity, and the peoples in his truth.

*An excerpt from St. Augustine's Discourse on Psalm 95 (14 & 15: CCL 39, 1351-1353)

APPENDIX B

CONSECRATION PRAYERS

Act of Consecration to Mary by St. Louis De Montfort

I,_____a faithless sinner, renew and ratify today in thy hands the vows of my Baptism; I renounce forever Satan, his pomps and works; and I give myself entirely to Jesus Christ, the Incarnate Wisdom, to carry my cross after Him all the days of my life, and to be more faithful to Him than I have ever been before. In the presence of all the heavenly court I choose thee this day for my Mother and Mistress. I deliver and consecrate to thee, as thy slave, my body and soul, my goods, both interior and exterior, and even the value of all my good actions, past, present, and future; leaving to thee the entire and full right of disposing of me, and all that belongs to me, without exception, according to thy good pleasure, for the greater glory of God in time and in eternity.

Act of Consecration to the Immaculate Heart of Mary

Queen of the Most Holy Rosary, and tender Mother, I forever entrust and consecrate myself, my family, my parish, my personal intention_____, my country and the whole human race to your Immaculate Heart. Please accept my consecration, dearest Mother, and use me as you wish, to accomplish your designs upon the world. O Immaculate Heart of Mary, Queen of Heaven and Earth, rule over me, and teach me how to allow the Heart of Jesus to rule and triumph in me and around me, as it has ruled and triumphed in you. Amen.

Act of Consecration to the Sacred Heart of Jesus

Most Sacred Heart of Jesus, I forever consecrate myself, my family, my personal intention_____, my country, and the whole human race to Your Most Sacred Heart. Take possession of my whole being; transform me into Yourself. Make my hands Your hands, my feet Your feet, my heart Your heart. Let me see with Your eyes, listen with Your ears, speak with Your lips, love with Your heart, understand with Your mind, serve with Your will, and be dedicated with my whole being. Make me Your other self. Most Sacred Heart of Jesus, send me Your Holy Spirit to teach me to love You and to live through You, with You, in You and for You. Come, Holy Spirit, make my body Your temple. Come, and abide with me forever. Give me the deepest love for the Sacred Heart of Jesus in order to serve Him with my whole heart, soul, mind, and strength. Take possession of all my faculties of body and soul. Regulate all my passions, feelings, and emotions. Take possession of my intellect, understanding and will; my memory and imagination. O Holy Spirit of Love, give me an abundance of Your efficacious graces. Give me the fullness of all the virtues; enrich my faith, strengthen my hope, increase my trust, and inflame my love. Give me the fullness of Your seven-fold gifts, fruits, and beatitudes. Most Holy Trinity, make my soul Your sanctuary. Amen.

Act of Consecration to St. Joseph by Fr. Donald Calloway, MIC

On this day, before the great multitude of heavenly witnesses, I, _____, a repentant sinner, consecrate myself, body and soul, my family, to you, St. Joseph. I turn to you as my spiritual father and place my life and my salvation into your hands. Confident in your goodness, I place myself under your paternal cloak and ask you to protect me from the world, the flesh, and the devil. St. Joseph, you are the virginal husband of the Mother of God! Help me to love her with tender affection and filial devotion. Mary is my spiritual mother and the surest, fastest, and easiest way to Jesus. Keep me close to her and, together with her, bring me closer to Jesus. Never depart from me, St. Joseph. Nourish me with the Bread of Life, instruct me in the wisdom of the saints, help me carry my cross, and keep me always in the Catholic Church. When I die, take me into the Kingdom of Heaven to see Jesus and Mary. From this day onward, I will never forget you. I will speak of you often, spend time with you in prayer and, with your help, earnestly strive to sin no more. Should I fall, help me to repent and go to Confession. Should I go astray, guide me back to the truth. Before heaven and earth, my soul cries out: Praise to the Holy Trinity who has made you prince over all their possessions! Praise to the Virgin Mary who loves you and longs to see you loved! Praise to you, my spiritual father, the great St. Joseph! I give everything to you, St. Joseph. Take me as your own. I am yours. Amen!

APPENDIX C

FIRST HOMILY GIVEN AS A PRIEST ON CONTRACEPTION, AUGUST 1st, 2004

Sunday 18th Week Ordinary Time, Year C
"If today you hear His voice, harden not your heart!"

Have you ever danced with the devil? When the rich man asked Jesus to help him to gain his inheritance, Jesus said, "Take care to guard against all greed... one's life does not consist in possessions." Our Lord then told the parable of a rich man, who built a larger barn to store his grain, rather than sharing his excess with others. The man said to himself "rest, eat, drink and be merry", but God said to the man, "You fool, this night your life will be demanded of you, and the things you have prepared, who will they belong? Thus, it will be for all who store up treasures for themselves but are not rich in what matters of God." It is true, we do not know when our life will come to an end. Many today have been duped by society, believing they must live a certain lifestyle, and so worship the gods of greed and materialism.

Some married couples will say, "Now is not the right time for me. If it should have a child, I may not be able to advance in my career. Let us plan to have children after we are married five years. And then, we will have one or two at the most. In these five years, we will be free to go places we want, build a larger dream house, and see the world". Turning to the pill, which they believe will give them their dreams, they dance with the devil, and so succumb to the temptation of contraception, and immorally plan their family.

Perhaps some have not heard Natural Family Planning (NFP) is 99% effective, which is more effective than contraception and is morally acceptable. Some think NFP, is the calendar method, not knowing the Billings or the Sympto-Thermo methods of NFP, which is new and much more accurate. The *Catechism of the Catholic Church*, states, "Birth regulation based upon self-observation ... respects the bodies of spouses, encourages tenderness between them and favors the education of authentic freedom. On the other hand, every action... which renders procreation impossible is intrinsically evil... (#2370)."

"One cannot give oneself totally in love, by contraception, and it is a positive refusal to be open to life." Perhaps not knowing the truth, many convince themselves contraception is not morally wrong. The Church, in Her wisdom, has said, the use of all contraceptives is a serious sin. Pope John Paul II, said, in his document, *Evangelium Vitae*, #13, "contraception and abortion are the fruit from the same tree". Because the use of contraceptives, including prophylactics, is a serious sin, one is not permitted to receive Holy Communion, unless one confesses to a priest. Taking the pill, which poisons the soul, is a dance with the devil for worldly dreams and desires. But "Vanity, is vanity, all is vanity!"

Others will think, "the Church should stay out of my bedroom", perhaps not recalling the Holy Spirit, who is God, entering the bedroom of Our Lady, resulting in Our Savior entering Her womb. Still others believe it is wrong, but, use it anyway.

They may subconsciously think, "I will just dance with the devil and go to confession later, after all, it's my conscience", or they may think, "I don't need to confess my sins to a priest, I can confess my sins straight to God."

And so, some will forsake their Holy Catholic faith, for the pill, which poisons the soul, but promises material objects and dreams. And, to pacify their conscience, will do away with the sacrament of confession instituted by Jesus Christ.

"Today, if you hear His voice, harden not your heart!" Listen carefully, many will not be aware of what I am about to say, but it is the truth, which must be proclaimed for the salvation of many and to save innocent lives. Listen carefully, according to One More Soul.org, in the pamphlet, *The Harms of Contraception*, "All oral contraceptives, Norplant, Depro-Provera and IUDs cause abortions before a woman even knows she's pregnant."

These pills do not allow a fertilized egg, which is a tiny child, to be implanted in the womb. Each of these drugs have what is called contraindications, which is a label with warnings indicating side effects. On the label it may say, "the fertilized egg" or it may say "zygote", (which we know to be a tiny child) is prevented from being implanted. And therefore, it kills an unborn child. Many, who have taken these contraceptives, have unknowingly killed their unborn children. Some most certainly may have not heard this before, and it may come as a shock. We must forgive those who have encouraged us to take them.

Whether it be our self, our spouse, our doctor, parents, teachers or friends, since all of us have been duped by society. When I say duped, I mean that we unknowingly have followed the path of society doing something, we did not know was seriously wrong. Our God is a God of mercy, who loves us, forgives us, understands us, and desires to save us. He knows we were duped, and He feels for us and cares for us and desires to lead us to Him and to His truth and love. My dear people, who were duped by the world, and the devil, God forgives, and so we must forgive ourselves, for what we have done.

And now that we know, we must immediately discontinue using contraceptives and come to Jesus in confession, who waits for us to give His mercy and His love. There are also those who are single and contracepting. Having a false sense of security, they use it to enjoy a passing moment of what they think is love. Vanity, is vanity, all is vanity! But there is no love, based upon sin and evil, and so they too dance with the devil. They flee from the commitment of marriage, not knowing true love is based on sacrifice. Unknowingly, they may assist the other in mortally wounding their soul. Thereby destroying love, which comes from God, who is love, and so they commit serious sins of fornication and contraception. They, too, have been duped by society, by way of television and movies.

My dear people, as teenagers, most of us longed to have that dance with the person of our dreams. We wished the dance would never end. At that moment, we thought we could have all we wanted by that one dance.

We wanted the moment to last forever, but when the song was over, we realized it was only a dream and just a fleeting moment of time. O vanity of Vanity, all is vanity! All material things on earth are like that wisp of smoke; they disappear.

And so, it is with contraception, we dream that if we dance with it, it will make all our dreams come true. But, know for sure, when one takes contraceptives, one is dancing with the devil, who may give us our worldly dreams, through greed and sin. However, all is vanity or a passing vapor, if there is no eternal life. And if we have the last dance with the devil, he will destroy our deepest dream of living with God in heaven forever. True wisdom is to put everything, including our earthly materials and desires, in the context of eternal life. If we fail to do this, we will dance with the pill of poison, which will be a "dirty-dance" with the devil. We may "grasp the hands" of the devil, and "side-step" away from God. As St. Peter Chrysologus said, "Anyone, who dances with the devil, cannot rejoice with Christ."

Because we know not, when our life will be demanded, and, if therefore, it should happen to be our last dance, the devil may give us a final "dip during the dance" and unexpectedly drop us into a place (hell) we would rather not go.

As St. Paul tell us, "...Seek what is above, not what is on earth." "Put to death, then, the parts of you that are earthly: immorality, impurity, passion, evil desire and the greed that is idolatry. Put on the new self." My friends, many of us have been duped by society, but we can put on the new self. We were lied to, and we have not been told the truth, and so, we need to remember that we are poor wounded men and women, whom God loves dearly.

When we made our vows at baptism, we renounced Satan, all his pomps, all works and all his empty promises. We professed, we believe in Jesus Christ and His Holy Catholic Church, as well as the forgiveness of sins, and so, we are called to live out our vows, by coming to Jesus in confession and following the light of truth given to us by the Pope and the Church.

May those who have danced with the devil, "turn" to Jesus, who truly loves us. He will "embrace" us by His love, "flatter" us with His grace, and "gaze into the eyes of our soul", and we will be "touched" by His "mercy and forgiveness" in the Sacrament of Confession.

Come to Jesus, whose tender, loving Heart waits for you in the sacrament of Confession! When you dance with the Lord, it will be a dance, that will last truly last forever, since He will "sweep you off your feet" and bring you safely into heaven, where all your dreams will come true. "If today you hear His voice, harden not your heart!"

APPENDIX D

ST. JEROME
A COMMENTARY ON JOEL

Return to me with all your heart (Joel 2:12) and show a spirit of repentance *with fasting, weeping and mourning* (Joel 2:12); so that while you fast now, later you may be satisfied, while you weep now, later you may laugh, while you mourn now, you may some day enjoy consolation (Luke 6:21; Matthew 5:4). It is customary for those in sorrow or adversity to tear their garments. The Gospel records that the high priest did this to exaggerate the charge against our Lord and Savior; and we read that Paul and Barnabas did so when they heard words of blasphemy. I bid you not to tear your garments but rather to *rend your hearts* (Joel 2:13) which are laden with sin. Like wine skins, unless they have been cut open, they will burst of their own accord. After you have done this, return to the Lord your God, from whom you had been alienated by your sins. Do not despair of his mercy, no matter how great your sins, for great mercy will take away great sins (Luke 7:41-47).

For the Lord is *gracious and merciful* (Joel 2:13) and prefers the conversion of a sinner rather than his death. Patient and generous in his mercy, he does not give in to human impatience but is willing to wait a long time for our repentance. So extraordinary is the Lord's mercy in the face of evil, that if we do penance for our sins, he regrets his own threat and does not carry out against us the sanctions he had threatened. So by the changing of our attitude, he himself is changed. But in this passage we should interpret "evil" to mean, not the opposite of virtue, but affliction, as we read in another place: *Sufficient for the day are its own evils* (Matthew 6:34). And, again: *If there is evil in the city, God did not create it.*

In like manner, given all that we have said above – that God is kind and merciful, patient, generous with his forgiveness, and extraordinary in his mercy toward evil – lest the magnitude of his clemency make us lax and negligent, he adds this word through his prophet: *Who knows whether he will not turn and repent and leave behind him a blessing?* (Joel 2:14). In other words, he says: "I exhort you to repentance, because it is my duty, and I know that God is inexhaustibly merciful, as David says: *Have mercy on me, God, according to your great mercy, and in the depths of your compassion, blot out all my iniquities* (Psalm 51:1). But since we cannot know the depth of the riches and of the wisdom and knowledge of God, I will temper my statement, expressing a wish rather than taking anything for granted, and I will say: *Who knows whether he will not turn and repent?* (cf Joel 2:14). Since he says, *Who*, it must be understood that it is impossible or difficult to know for sure.

To these words the prophet adds: *Offerings and libations for the Lord our God* (Joel 2:14). What he is saying to us in other words is that, God having blessed us and forgiven us our sins, we will then be able to offer sacrifice to God.

*From a Commentary on the Book of Joel by Saint Jerome, priest (PL 25, 967-968)

APPENDIX E

PRAYER OF FEELING

My spiritual director, an exorcist, said demons attack us most frequently through wounded emotions and traumatic experiences. We can unknowingly enter into relationships with them through these ways. For example, if someone were to call us stupid, and if it were to deeply hurt us, we can begin to think we are stupid. The demons can come at us through emotions such as sadness or loneliness or jealousy of others who are more intelligent. We can then allow demons to tempt us to think we are stupid, to feel sad, or lonely, or be jealous of others. By bringing wounded emotions and traumatic experiences into the light of Christ, and by asking Jesus to heal them by re-experiencing them, as we originally felt them, through the "Prayer of Feeling", then Our Lord can permanently heal those wounds and prevent demons from acting through those wounds in the future. The relationship we developed with a particular demon is then severed. Most importantly, we should confess these temptations and sins in the sacrament of Confession.

Fr. Gadfly's method partially derived from St. Ignatius, *Discernment of Spirits.*

1. Preparatory Prayer: "I beg you God, my Lord, for the grace that all my intentions, actions, and operations may be directed purely to the praise and service of Your Divine Majesty."

2. Close your eyes and picture Jesus and Mary standing before you.

3. Pray "Jesus, you are looking at me, and I am looking at you. Mary, you are looking at me, and I am looking at you." (Repeat this prayer slowly three times)

4. Read a scripture passage about the life of Jesus or if you don't have a bible with you, recall the scripture you want to think about. Picture yourself in the bible story, such as being in a boat with the apostles, tossed about in the wind and Jesus sleeping in the boat. One of the apostles wakes us Jesus, and says, "Lord, save us". Imagine the waves crashing over the side of the boat, and you see the fear of the apostles. You speak to Jesus and say, "Lord, I am afraid. Help me." You then see Jesus stand, raise His hand, and immediately the storm ceases and the waves come to a hush. Jesus then says, "You of little faith, why were you so afraid?"

5. Then ask Jesus what you desire to be healed.
"Jesus, I desire to be healed of this……….. traumatic event."
Or anger, Or depression, etc… Or "Jesus, I desire to be healed of my mental Illness."

Or if you desire to pray for a physical healing pray, "Jesus I desire to be healed of my high blood pressure." Or "I desire to be healed of cancer."

Repeat the prayer, "Jesus, you are looking at me, and I am looking at you. Mary, you are looking at me, and I am looking at you."

Then allow yourself to feel the emotion in the presence of Jesus and continue with the emotion until it dies away. Stick with the emotion. It will be a temptation to shy away from it, because of its painful experience: anger, sadness, fear, etc. If you relive the bad event (with Jesus) and allow your emotion to be expressed with Jesus until it dies away, then Jesus will heal you. Some events and emotions need to be repeated for a more complete healing.

6. Say this prayer slowly, "Jesus, let your light shine on my blood pressure." or "this traumatic event." Or "Jesus, let your light shine on my cancer." Or "Jesus, let your light shine on my suicidal thought." Or "Jesus, let your light shine on my brain, so I may think properly."
And repeat the prayer "Jesus, let your light shine on the source of this emotion." for about ten to fifteen minutes.

7. Picture yourself, at the foot of the Cross and look at Jesus hanging on the Cross and say, "Thank you, Jesus, for healing me." "Jesus, what can I do for you, for you have been so good to me." And, if you didn't receive a physical healing, pray, "O Jesus, help me to carry this cross of my illness and all the suffering that goes with it."

LETTER TO THE DIRECTOR OF WOEBEGONE HOSPICE

01-18-21

Woebegone Hospice

My name is Fr. Leonard Gadfly. I am a chaplain for Mother of Misery Healthcare System, and I see patients at Woebegone Hospice at St. Camillus de Lellis Hospital. Since your Hospice is non-Catholic, and because I visit Catholic patients, I would like to help your hospice understand Catholic ethics concerning the terminally ill and dying. There is a new document that came out by Congregation for the Doctrine of Faith in Sept. of 2020, entitled, *Good Samaritan.* It is enclosed.

This document is a wonderful blessing to help hospitals and hospices understand more clearly Catholic ethics for the terminally ill and dying. I have enclosed the entire document and also presented several excerpts in this letter.

In the past two years, I have noticed there are never any patients with an IV or a feeding tube at the hospice. This was not the case when I did hospital ministry at St. John of God in Tantrum, Idaho. They also had a hospice floor, which I regularly visited.

When a patient can benefit from artificial nutrition and hydration, the hospital and the hospice are morally obligated to provide them for the patients. Otherwise, the death of some patients could be the result of a lack of food or water, and not the illness or disease. Food and water are considered ordinary care, and that is obligatory. That is, unless they are futile or excessively burdensome. In #3, of *Good Samaritan,* it states:

> "A fundamental and inescapable principle of the assistance of the critically or terminally ill person is the continuity of care for the essential physiological functions. In particular, required basic care for each person includes the administration of the nourishment and fluids needed to maintain bodily homeostasis, insofar as and until this demonstrably attains the purpose of providing hydration and nutrition for the patient. When the provision of nutrition and hydration no longer benefits the patient, because the patient's organism either cannot absorb them or cannot metabolize them, their administration should be suspended. In this way, one does not unlawfully hasten death through the deprivation of the hydration and nutrition vital for bodily function, but nonetheless respects the natural course of the critical or terminal illness. The withdrawal of this sustenance is an unjust action that can cause great suffering to the one who has to endure it. Nutrition and

hydration do not constitute medical therapy in a proper sense, which is intended to counteract the pathology that afflicts the patient. They are instead forms of obligatory care of the patient, representing both a primary clinical and an unavoidable human response to the sick person. Obligatory nutrition and hydration can at times be administered artificially, provided that it does not cause harm or intolerable suffering to the patient."

The relationship with the Catholic hospital and the hospice should be such that both clearly understand how patients are ethically cared for. By this, I mean, the hospital should know, that when a patient is going on "Comfort Care", it would not mean the IV's and feeding tubes would be discontinued, if the patient can benefit from them. So, practically speaking, that would mean, when a hospital patient is transferred to the hospice, both the hospital staff and the hospice would know that artificial nutrition and hydration would need to continue, and so these would not be removed when the patient is benefiting from them. The hospital staff would likewise help the hospice staff know if it is futile to give the patient artificial nutrition and hydration.

Because some patients may not be receiving artificial nutrition and hydration while on hospice, when they can benefit from them, and therefore, it can cause additional suffering from dehydration and malnutrition. From what I have seen, this added suffering seems to be "subdued" by giving more medicine to alleviate this extra suffering caused by malnutrition and dehydration. But excessive medicine can hasten death, though it may not be intended. It would also be unethical, if excessive medicine intends to hasten death.

Last year, at Woebegone Hospice at St. Camillus de Lellis, there was an Alzheimer's patient, John Doe, whose health, according to his wife, was fine. I met John, when he arrived at the hospice, and was surprised at his robust physical health. He needed a sitter, so he would not leave his room. However, the man suffered greatly from dementia. According to his son, medicine was given to his father to keep him sedated. Apparently, he was so heavily sedated for nine days, he was kept unconscious. Whereas before, his wife said he was eating two full meals a day. His wife said she was actively trying to find a memory care unit, since she realized hospice was not the place for her husband. She said a representative from Woebegone Hospice, convinced her to put her husband on hospice, despite the fact, his physical health was fine, and that he was eating normally. Therefore, the man's death was caused by heavy sedation, which prevented oral food and water.

The document #4 of *Good Samaritan* states,

> "In addition, palliative interventions to reduce the suffering of gravely or terminally ill patients in these regulatory contexts can involve the administration of medications that intend to hasten death, as well as the suspension or interruption of hydration and nutrition even when death is not imminent. In fact, such practices are equivalent to a direct action or omission to bring about death and are therefore unlawful. The growing diffusion of such legislation and of scientific guidelines of national and international professional societies, constitutes a socially irresponsible threat to many people, including a growing number of vulnerable persons who needed only to be better cared for and comforted but are instead being led to choose euthanasia and suicide."

It is my hope, and desire, that I can help you and Mother of Misery Healthcare System, St. Camillus de Lellis hospital, to work together to protect the innate human dignity of each person.

Life is precious and valuable and your staff, in my opinion, do a very fine job of taking care of not only the patient, but also the family in their time of distress and helping to prepare the patient for the next life. I have always had good and positive interactions with the staff at the hospice. Truly special people, who are very caring.

I would be happy to discuss this with you. Please give me a call at your convenience and also, please read the enclosed document and distribute the document to hospice staff.

With prayers,

Fr. Leonard Gadfly

APPENDIX G

PREPARATION TO START PERPETUAL ADORATION FOR PRIESTS

1. Permissions.

Everything must be done under obedience, then the graces will flow.

Speak to your spiritual director and obtain his permission.

Speak to the bishop or write him a letter and ask his permission.

As pastor, formally Consecrate Perpetual Adoration to the Immaculate Heart of Mary, the Sacred Heart of Jesus, and Most Chaste Heart of St. Joseph.

2. Purchase, *Jesus Our Eucharistic Love,* by Fr. Stefano Manelli.

Books to be given to each parishioner 6th grade and older. Book price $2 per book when ordering one box of 30, you save 60%.

Academy of the Immaculate

https://academyoftheimmaculate.com/products/jesus-our-eucharistic-love

3. Kick Off Weekend.

A. In all the pews place prayers of Consecration of the Parish, its ministries, parishioners, etc... and give a short homily for the day, but at the end of all weekend Masses pray all three Consecration Prayers together as a parish: Sacred Heart, Immaculate Heart, St. Joseph.

B. Give an explanation to the Parish of your vision of starting Perpetual Adoration and how it will positively affect the parish.

C. On this weekend have pre-prepared in each pew a prayer to be prayed at the end of every Mass, including weekend Masses. They can be taped to a missalete back cover.

D. Pass out books at the end of all Masses. *They should be <u>handed out</u> to every person above 6th grade. Some people won't take them unless they are specifically handed out to them.* Altar Servers, Ushers, and/or Greeters can hand them out.

These are good to mail to fallen away Catholics, as well as, a Rosary, How to Go To Confession with Examination of Conscience, bulletin with Mass and Confession times.

E. Prayer to be Prayed at the End of Every Mass.

Prayer For Perpetual Adoration

O Lord Jesus Christ,/ you who are really and truly present/ in the Most Blessed Sacrament./ We humbly come before your divine majesty,/ imploring and beseeching you with all our heart,/ for the grace to bring many parish family members/ to Your real and true presence in Eucharistic Adoration./ Touch the hearts and minds of many souls/ and instill in them a great love and devotion/ to your true presence in the Eucharist./ Grant them the grace to make the commitment/ to sign up/ and faithfully spend one hour a week with You in adoration./ We ask this through the intercession of Mary and in your name, Jesus Christ, Our Lord. Amen.

4. Perpetual Adoration Talk or Homily by Guest Priest or Pastor.

Explain How Perpetual Adoration Works, How Leaders Are Needed, etc...

In a homily, or after Mass, ask for people who may be interested in helping start Perpetual Adoration. A guest priest or the pastor can give a homily at all Masses.

Ask people who would like to help start Perpetual Adoration to sign up. The sign-up sheet to help start Perpetual Adoration should be in a location easily visible.

Give those who sign up to help start Perpetual Adoration, Prayers of Protection to pray daily. Don't frighten them, but just let them know the devil doesn't want Perpetual Adoration, and the prayers can protect them.

Then set a day and time you will meet. Usually, the same Sunday so the guest priest can give instructions on: fasting, prayer, explain what leaders do, future meetings with the pastor, etc...

Whenever you meet, pray a Holy Hour before the meeting, then after the Holy Hour meet with the potential leaders. Do a Holy Hour every week at a specific day and time. You don't need to meet after every Holy Hour. Plan your meetings.

Invite all parishioners to come to the weekly Holy Hour. Don't be discouraged if just a few people come to the Holy Hour. The purpose of that Holy Hour is to pray and ask the Lord for guidance on how and when to start Perpetual Adoration. Pray the Prayer that will be prayed at the end of every Mass during the Holy Hour. Also, pray a Rosary and Chaplet of Divine Mercy during the Holy Hour. There should be silence during the Holy Hour too.

At the first meeting, ask the group to fast for 40 days before Adoration begins. Fast means one meal a day and if necessary two smaller meals that don't equal a meal. Some may be able to fast more strictly such as bread and water (the best kind of fast). They should also Fast from TV, wasting time on computer, sweets, etc... Ask the group to go to Confession and come to daily Mass and offer their Masses and Communions for the intention of Perpetual Adoration.

DO NOT TRY TO START PERPETUAL ADORATION WITHOUT 40 DAYS OF FASTING AND PRAYER. This is essential! Even if you just have 3 or 4 people praying or fasting, the Lord will use their sacrifices and prayer to touch hearts to sign up.

At that first meeting, on the same weekend, the guest priest or the pastor can explain to the group what they will need to do. How specific sections of hours will need a leader: 12 am to 6am, 6am to 12 noon, 12 noon to 6pm, 6pm to 12 midnight.

Be very careful in choosing the leaders of the hours. Leaders should also be willing to substitute during their 6 hours if a regular substitute can't be found. Those who won't or shouldn't be leaders, tell them they are the prayer warriors for Adoration. Their apostolate is to help bring souls to Jesus in the Eucharist.

5. Think and Pray about whom you might want to be Coordinator.

This is one of the most important things you do. If you choose the wrong leader, lots of problems will occur. It could be disastrous. The person needs to be very kind and compassionate, and allow people to make mistakes in missing their hour. Yet, the person needs to not be afraid of asking others to take an open hour or to substitute.

6. Spiritual Power Houses.

Offer Masses specifically for the intention of drawing as many as possible to Jesus in the Eucharist.

Send letters to monasteries of nuns, sisters, and religious brothers and ask them to pray for this intention. Give them the specific sign-up day, so they know what day people will be inspired to sign-up.

7. Send Letter to All Parish Individuals and Families.

Choose a weekend for Sign-Up Day. Send a letter to every parishioner of the parish, so they know in advance when Sign-Up weekend will be. Also in the letter give them a brochure explaining what Perpetual Adoration is and its fruits and benefits. In the letter, indicate if they will be away on Sign-Up Weekend, to let a specific person know in advance. Or if it happens they can't come due to an unforeseen circumstance, they will still be able to sign up later. It's okay if anyone wants to sign up in advance. *Assign every person who signs up a specific hour.* This is important because there will be some who want to sign up, but won't be there at the Mass.

Through the letter or by an inspiration of the Holy Spirit, the Lord will bring fallen away Catholics to that Mass, and they will sign up, even though they may not have been to Mass in months or years. Then, once Adoration begins, you will see what happens, how the Lord will change their hearts to want to attend Mass, to go to Confession and may even become evangelizers etc...

8. Choose a Typist from the Volunteer Group.

Ask someone from the leader group who likes to type to make the sign-up sheets and also who will make the sign-in notebook. This person should be able to make future changes to update the sign-up notebook and who will also give new people a packet of information.

9. Before Sign-Up Day.

Put in bulletin what will happen if: Snow, Tornado Warning, What to do if someone doesn't show up, Method of Asking for Someone to Substitute for Their Hour.

First ask family member or friend to take the hour. It that's not possible, switch with another adorer, or call a substitute. If no substitute ask each person before and after your hour to take an extra 30 min. Asking non-practicing Catholic family member to substitute for the person's hour, is a great way to allow Jesus to touch their hearts and bring them back to the Church.

10. Sign-Up Day.
Place Sign Up Sheets in Pews abundantly in areas that are easy to access. Be sure there are many extra papers and pencils that will be available. They should list first, second, and third choice of group of hours. Don't just place the sheets at the end of the pews. Place also in the middle of the pews. After the homily, do the sign-up. Don't do it at the end of Mass, because people will leave after Mass and won't sign up. The Mass will be longer than usual, but they will understand since it's a special Mass. Don't rush them when signing up. Give them time to sign up and pray Hail Marys when they are signing up. When it appears all are finished filling out the papers, have them pass them to the end of the pews and ask ushers or altar servers or greeters to pick them up.

11. Prepare A Packet of Information for Every Adorer.
Include: Total list of adorers, their hours, and phone numbers. List of Substitutes. List of leaders and their phone numbers. Name and Phone Number of Coordinator or Perpetual Adoration. Explanation Letter with this information:
1. Never abandon the Sacred Host
2. Phone will be available at Adoration Chapel and phone number.
3. Rules of Conduct (dress code, no talking on phone or texting, unless it's an emergency, don't play music, never touch the monstrance, what to do in case of Tornado Warning, Blizzard and cancellation of Perpetual Adoration, and how they will be notified, etc..)
When Adoration starts, have these packets available with their names, on each packet outside the Adoration Chapel.
This packet should be always be given to new adorers, as soon as they begin adoring.

12. What to Do If Someone Does Not Come to their Hour Regularly.
Never cut them off or remove their name unless they ask for it. Find another adorer to do the hour with them, so there will be two for that hour.

13. Suggested Homilies.
What is the Eucharist?; Who is the Eucharist?; Personal Relationship with Jesus; Real Presence; Transubstantiation; Sacrifice of the Mass; re-presentation of Calvary, importance of offering Masses for living and the dead; Benefits of Receiving Holy Communions; 15 min of union with Jesus (heaven on earth); Benefits a Weekly Hour, for adorer, family, parish, community, (deters evil in the area), and the world; What is Perpetual Adoration?" Explain How It Works; What to do if someone forgets their

Hour- "Be Merciful", we are all human and most of us will forget once in a while, especially before the habit is made; Eucharistic Miracles Approved by the Church; What To Do During the Hour 1. Pray with the Heart 2. Read and Meditate on Scripture 3. Pray the Rosary and Chaplet 4. Sit in Silence (Not a good idea to read the entire time of the hour), Jesus wants us to pray to Him. 5. Method of Prayer ACTS Adore, Confess, Thanks, Supplication (pray for own needs and needs of others); *Make Available papers of the ACTS method in the chapel*; Explain Dryness of Prayer, don't stop praying, don't stop adoring, rather find additional devotionals to help inspire, etc... Dryness leads to faith, to pray without feeling consolation; Homily on Saints and Adoration and their devotion to the Eucharist; Scriptural Foreshadowing: Manna and Quail in Desert, the Passover, Melchizedek, Multiplication of Loaves and Fish, Road to Emmaus, Last Supper, John 6 Eucharistic Discourse, etc..., Acts of Apostles Breaking Bread; Receiving the Eucharist Worthily, fasting an hour, St. Paul 1 Corin. 11, etc.... Receiving on the tongue vs on the hand.

14. Preach about the beauty and graces of those who take night hours.
Ask men especially to take the hours because women can be fearful to take them.

15. Prayer Books, Reading Material, Spiritual Books, Bibles, etc.
Careful to not allow secular books or magazines, etc... in the library located either outside the chapel or directly in the chapel. Also be careful to not allow parishioners to add books unless the pastor approves, as some may have theological problems, or be books written by dubious authors.

16. Door Code, Telephone, Restrooms, Sign In Sheet, Prayer Request Notebook (this allows adorers to pray for each other's intentions). These need to be planned out.

17. Adorers Who Give Up Their Hour.
Usually within the first few months, there will be a handful of adorers who give up their hour, or who will want a different hour. Don't fret. This is normal. Trust Jesus! The Lord will provide for the hours that open up. It's important at the beginning to not put a bunch of open hours in the bulletin. Rather, the pastor or a priest most especially should ask specific parishioners. (He should be an evangelizer to bring people to Jesus) to take specific hours. This is by far the best way to fill hours. To just put them in the bulletin without asking specific people is not a very good way to keep the chapel open. Ask the one who gave up their hour, if they would like a more convenient time or ask them if they can be a substitute, and if so, what group or groups of hours. Then be sure to add them to the list of substitutes. Some adorers lives will change, such that they have different work hours, or they have to move, some will die, or their children have activities, etc.. We need to be flexible with them.

18. Leaders - What To Do When an Hour Opens Up.

Pray and ask Jesus, whom He wants to take the hour. When someone comes to mind, FIRST, before asking the person, pray for them to be open taking the hour. When you believe you have prayed sufficiently for them, then ask the person and be ready to give them a packet explaining everything when they say yes. The Perpetual Adoration Chapel is the work of Jesus Himself. It's His chapel, He will make sure it continues. We just need to be open to understand what He wants. Sometimes, Jesus does not want to fill an hour immediately because He wants substitutes to spend more time with Him. Sometimes, the person He wants to do the Hour is not yet ready. We have to be patient and trust.

19. Tactics of the devil.

(Discouragement, Fear, More Important Things, Pride Among Leaders who try to tell others what to do, etc…) Humility, Humility, Humility keeps the devil at bay!
The devil will try to discourage people from coming and try to convince them that they could be doing more important things. They will begin to think, it's a waste of time sitting there. He tries to cause fear (the chapel will not continue, somebody might get hurt due to weather or intruder etc... or someone might miss their hour and cause me to lose my job, etc…) Fear and discouragement are the biggest things the devil uses to try to convince people to quit. Address fears and discouragement in a pastoral letter in the bulletin, or preach about it at Mass, etc... Use the bulletin heavily to explain what is expected and what will happen.

20. Remove snow and ice etc…

 Volunteers can remove ice and snow. Or the parish may pay someone to do it regularly. Fear of elderly falling. Don't be quick to cancel Perpetual Adoration, due to weather, ask substitutes when elderly are afraid to come due to weather. Some people like to take multiple hours. However, be prudent. Ice is the most dangerous when driving or walking to the chapel. People are adults, we should treat them as such, and believe they will use their own common sense to come or not if the weather is frail. Canceling Adoration. Some parishes don't have adoration on Christmas or Easter, etc... However, in some parishes the people like to have their hours on those days. First try to have it on those days and see what happens. It may be that some will take two hours, but they like to do that.

21. Sign-Up Day.

All hands on deck. Tell parishioners It's important to answer their phones and be ready for them and give them a rough time of hours and someone will call them such as between 12 noon and 6pm on that day. Tell them to be sure to let you all know if they signed up and don't get a call. Papers can accidentally be lost. Unanswered phones can cause some people to not get the hours they would like. Meet with leaders to assign hours. Be ready for them to call individuals and ask them to take specific hours. You should have a large board with all the hours with specific names listed once they agree to an hour after they are called.

If someone wants multiple hours, be careful! If you assign them 3 hours because that's what they want, then if the person dies or becomes sick, or moves, you will have 3 hours open. It's a good rule to not allow one person to sign up for more than 2 hours. They can always adore with others at a time convenient for them.

If you require two people per hour for every hour of adoration, it can be problematic. This usually cannot be done, even in very large parishes. If two people are assigned the same hour, they must get in the habit of notifying the other adorer, when they won't be able to do their hour. Otherwise, both will think the other be there and neither will show up.

VERY IMPORTANT: Every person who signs up should be called personally and should be given an hour. If someone who signed up and is never called, it will have a ripple effect and cause problems. But most importantly, failing to call someone may result in the person never being with Jesus in the Eucharist, who otherwise could have been adoring Jesus every week for years.

Do not prevent non-Catholics from being assigned a Holy Hour, but there should be (but not required, if you know them) a Catholic also assigned with their hour. Allowing non-Catholics (spouses of Catholics, etc...) to sign up, almost always leads to their conversion to the Catholic faith. Non-Catholics spouses can be asked by their spouse to take their hour when they will be away.

22. Substitutes, All Adorer Information.
Put the list of all adorers, substitutes, and phone numbers on the parish website, so its easily accessible, but be careful so the information will still be private. This way, if they lose their own lists, they have a way to look them up.

23. Expect panhandlers and people asking for money or help, who may come to the chapel.
Tell parishioners how to charitably handle a panhandler. Tell them what to do in advance. If anyone gives them money, they will be back. Some may be legitimate, most are not. Pastorally handle these situations, in a preventive way, will be very helpful to allowing people to have peace and to know what to do if it happens.

24. Be Attentive to Small Miracles.
People will be coming back to Church, going to Confession, Praying More, Answered prayers, learning their faith better, etc... The Lord will often times get people to become

more involved in the Church. New avenues of stewardship will come about. Be ready to find more stewardship possibilities. Put Adoration on the Stewardship forms. See the silent graces flow!

25. Offer Mass of Thanksgiving for Those Who Signed Up.

26. Prayers of Protection.
St. Michael Prayer
St. Michael the Archangel defend us in battle. Be our defense against the wickedness and snares of the Devil. May God rebuke him, we humbly pray, and do thou, O Prince of the heavenly hosts, by the power of God, thrust into hell Satan, and all the evil spirits, who prowl about the world seeking the ruin of souls. Amen.

O glorious prince St. Michael, chief and commander of the heavenly hosts,
guardian of souls, vanquisher of rebel spirits, servant in the house of the Divine King
and our admirable conductor, you who shine with excellence
and superhuman virtue deliver us from all evil, who turn to you with confidence
and enable us by your gracious protection to serve God more and more faithfully every day.
(from The Chaplet of St. Michael)

Prayer against Retaliation
Lord Jesus Christ, in your love and mercy, pour Your Precious Blood over (me, parish members, my family, co-workers, etc...) so that no demon or disembodied spirit may retaliate against us. Mary, surround us with the mantle, blocking any retaliating spirits from having any authority over us. St. Michael, surround us with your shield, so that no evil spirit may take revenge on us. Queen of Heaven and St. Michael, send down the legions of angels under your command to fight off any spirits that would seek to harm us. All you Saints of Heaven, impede any retaliating spirit from influencing us. Lord, You are the Just Judge, the avenger of the wicked, the Advocate of the Just, we beg in Your mercy, that all we ask of Mary, the Angels and the Saints of Heaven be also granted to all our loved ones, those who pray for us and their loved ones, that for Your Glory's sake, we may enjoy Your perfect protection. Amen (Ripperger, *Deliverance Prayers, For Use of Laity*, pg. 37)

O Mary, Conceived without sin, pray for us, who have recourse to thee.
(Pray 3 times and any other time when tempted)

APPENDIX H

HOMILY ON RECEIVING COMMUNION ON THE TONGUE

Praised be Jesus and Mary!

In the Gospel today, Jesus knew Pharisees were soon going to kill him. He said, "I will send them as prophets and Apostles; some of them they will kill and persecute in order that this generation might be charged with the blood of all the prophets..."

Jesus is the prophet of prophets, and, He, like those before Him will be persecuted and killed.

Scripturally, a prophet not only predicted future events, but spoke to God's people on behalf of God. In the Old Testament, after the people went astray, God sent a prophet to call them to repentance and back to God. But, usually, prophets were persecuted and killed, including Jeremiah, Zechariah, and John the Baptist.

Today in the United States is the feast of Saints John de Brebeuf, Isaac Jogues and companion martyrs in the 1600's. These Jesuits evangelized Indians, provided settlers with the sacraments and were faithful to the deposit of faith passed down to us from Jesus and the Apostles. By their teaching and preaching the faith, as prophets they spoke on behalf of God, and died for the faith.

There are subtle prophecies from Fatima, with regard to the Mass and the Eucharist. In 1916, a year before Mary appeared, an angel appeared to three children holding a Chalice in his hands. A Host was suspended over the Chalice, and drops of blood fell from it into the Chalice. While the Chalice and Host were suspended in the air, he prostrated on the ground and repeated three times: "Blessed Trinity, Father, Son and Holy Spirit, I adore you profoundly, and I offer the Precious Body, Blood, Soul and Divinity of Our Lord Jesus Christ, present in all the Tabernacles of the world, in reparation for the offenses, sacrileges, and indifferences by which He is so offended. And by the infinite merits of your Sacred Heart and the Immaculate Heart of Mary, I ask for the conversion of poor sinners." Then the angel, took the Host, gave it to Lucia, and the contents of the Chalice to Jacinta and Francisco, saying: "Eat the Body and drink the Blood of Jesus Christ, horribly offended by ungrateful men. Make reparation for their crimes and console your God."

Years later, Sister Lucia had a vision in the convent chapel at Tuy, Spain. She saw the Virgin Mary holding a Rosary, pointing to Her Heart surrounded with thorns. She stood next to the Blessed Trinity, who were above the altar. She saw God the Father looking down upon Jesus hanging on the Cross and the Holy Spirit between the two. From the crown of Jesus and His wounded Heart dripped blood onto a suspended Host, which then dripped into a chalice.

The apparitions of the angel and the vision at Tuy, are subtle reminders, of our times that there is loss of faith in the Eucharist causing indifference, sacrileges, and offenses.

The Tuy vision showed us truths about the Mass. That Mass is a Holy Sacrifice. It's the re-presentation of Calvary on the altar. The Holy Mass is the worship of the Blessed Trinity. The bread and wine are totally changed into the body and blood of Christ at Mass. During the time of the apparitions, no one, except the priest received Communion in the hand. That's why the children received Communion on the tongue, as an example for us today.

Today, there is a lack of reverence by treating Our Lord causally, by handling the body of Christ as mere bread.

However, when the Eucharist is received on the tongue, there is humility & reverence. It's a fact, the Church teaches, the ordinary manner to receive Communion is on the tongue. I repeat, it's a fact, the Church teaches, the ordinary manner to receive Communion is on the tongue.

Most bishops give an indult (a permission), to receive on the hand. In some dioceses bishops don't allow Communion in the hand.

Another problem with receiving Communion on the hand, is that it makes it easy for people to steal Hosts, which happened in one of my former parishes.

Another problem with receiving Communion on the hand is that tiny particles fall from hands and are dropped on the floor. In my diocese, most every parish uses server patens, which altar servers hold beneath the chin to catch a dropped Host or small particles that fall when Communion is distributed. At most Masses particles fall on the paten during Communion. Just ask the deacons here at Mass when Communion is over, how many particles are in the gold bowl, called a Ciborium.

The Church teaches every particle no matter how small is the entire person of Jesus.

During Covid-19 a doctor scientifically tested to see if it was safer to receive Communion in the hand or on the tongue. He concluded it was more hygienic to receive on the tongue, because the person who distributes Communion often times touches the hands of the communicant.

Treating the Body of Christ like bread, is a sign of a lack faith in the true presence of Jesus, and is a subtle reminder Fatima prophecies are fulfilled.

Catholics believe the bread is totally transformed into Jesus Himself. The Eucharist is the real presence of Jesus in His physical resurrected body.

Peter Julian Eymard said in the Sacred Host is the beating Heart of Jesus Christ. Many Eucharistic miracles approved the Church attest to blood coming from living Heart tissue. It's Our Lord's true flesh, as He said, "Whoever eats My flesh and drinks My blood has eternal life... For My flesh is true food, and My blood is true drink."

St. Thomas Aquinas said that Holy Communion lasts until the Host is assimilated. Saint Louis De Montfort says that Communion lasts at least 10 to 15 minutes. There is no greater moment on earth than when we receive Jesus in Holy Communion because our Heart is united to the Heart of Jesus.

I know of a priest, who felt the beating Heart of Jesus in His hands when holding the Sacred Host.

Before receiving Communion, we should first confess our mortal sins, such as sex before marriage, adultery, missing Mass on Sunday, homosexual actions, impure actions, pornography, birth control, etc... Every mortal sin must be confessed before receiving Holy Communion. Otherwise, if we receive the Eucharist in the state of mortal sin, we commit a sacrilegious communion, another mortal sin. We should have the intention not doing the sins in the future. We receive absolutely no graces from Communion when we receive the Eucharist in mortal sin.

Ladies, I'm going to tell you something that is painful for me to say and painful for you to hear. Did you know the IUD, the Pill, the Patch, and the injection can cause the death of newly conceived baby? What happens is all of these irritate the womb and the baby is unable to attach to the womb within 5 days of conception. The baby dies, and the mother didn't even know she was pregnant. It's sad for you to learn that you may have lost multiple children while taking birth control.

But, Jesus is infinitely merciful. Jesus forgave Bernard Nathanson, an abortionist who did over 70,000 abortions. His sins were all washed away and the punishment due to his sins were all washed away, when he was baptized by Cardinal O'Conner at St. Patrick's Cathedral in New York, City. If Jesus forgave him, he will forgive you for using birth control and committing sacrilegious communions when you received Communion while on birth Control. Jesus washes all sins away and the punishment due to sins, on the Sunday after Easter called Divine Mercy Sunday. All one has to do is confess their sins sometime during Lent and/or up to and including Divine Mercy Sunday and receive Holy Communion on feast of Divine Mercy. All will be washed away in the ocean of God's mercy.

Because of a lack of faith in the Eucharist many also do not obey Church teachings. This is why the angel asked the children to make reparation for sacrileges and offenses against the Eucharist.

In our day, Fr. John Hardon, a Jesuit, from the United States, is on the road to sainthood. He was a pillar of faith for Catholics, when the faith was being undermined by other Jesuit priests. He said the greatest reason for the loss of faith in the Eucharist, was caused by another Jesuit, Fr. Karl Rahner, who falsely taught transignification, meaning the Eucharist is merely a symbol. However, Catholics always believed in transubstantiation, the entire substance of bread and wine are changed into the body and blood of Christ and NOT a mere symbol. What was true 2000 years ago, is true today.

Fr. Hardon was persecuted and rejected by his own Jesuit confrères, causing his white martyrdom. Like his fellow North American martyr Jesuits, Fr. Hardon firmly taught the faith passed down to us from Jesus and the Apostles. He is on the road to sainthood. But Karl Rhaner caused a loss of faith in the Eucharist and will never be a saint. There are good Jesuits, loyal to the Catholic faith, and who preach and teach the truth. There are bad Jesuits, who try to change the faith. Karl Rahner's non-Catholic views will never succeed. The truth always wins.

Karl Rahner is wrong, he is a false prophet, and did not speak on behalf of God on the Eucharist, because the Eucharist is not mere a symbol, as Protestants believe.

Because of their lack of faith in the Eucharist, many do not obey Church teachings. This is why the angel asked the children, to make reparation for sacrileges and offenses against the Eucharist.

The prophecies of Fatima warn us of a loss of faith in the Mass and the Eucharist. As a priest, I am speaking as a prophet on behalf of God. And so, I say to you, console the Hearts of Jesus and Mary, by attending Mass as often as possible. Ask Jesus if He wants you to receive on the hand or on the tongue. If you receive on the hand, look for particles, pick them up and place them in your mouth, so they don't fall to the ground.

Only receive the Eucharist in the state of grace. Offer your Holy Communion in reparation for sins committed against the Hearts of Jesus and Mary. Adore Jesus in Eucharistic Adoration not just one Holy Hour a week, but as often as possible. If you don't have adoration, spend time with Jesus before the tabernacle. If you have never confessed using birth control and receiving Communion sacrilegiously while on birth control give these sins to Jesus in Confession, so He can give you His infinite mercy.

Give Jesus in the Eucharist the greatest reverence possible, to make up for the sacrilegious, indifference and offenses He Himself is offended in His Eucharistic Heart.

The Church asks us to make a sign of reverence before receiving Holy Communion, such as to bow our head, or make a sign of the Cross. Some churches use kneelers and altar rails for Communion. According to the Vatican Office of Divine Worship for the Sacraments, a priest may not deny Communion to those who kneel.

When you return home to your countries, be a witness to the true presence of Jesus in the Eucharist. Don't be afraid to suffer persecution for your faith in the Eucharist.

The word "witness" means martyr. Be a prophet, a witness, and a martyr for your faith in the Eucharist. You can either be white martyr like Fr. John Hardon or you can be a red martyr for the faith like St. Isaac Jogues, St. John de Brebuff and companions.

Our Catholic faith is our greatest treasure. Are you willing to suffer and die for our unchanging faith, like the prophets before Jesus and like the saints after Jesus? Are you willing to be a witness to Mary's love of Her Son in the Eucharist? Do not listen to false prophets who try to change our faith passed down to us from Jesus and the Apostles.

Did you know Mary was sad every time She appeared to the children of Fatima? Let's console our Mother's Heart and give Her Son, in the Eucharist, the greatest possible reverence and help others to grow in their faith and do the same.

Surely, the Virgin Mary received Communion kneeling and on the tongue from St. John the Apostle, whom She lived. What joy for Her to be united to Her Son, Jesus. What joy for us to be united to Our Lord in the Most Blessed Sacrament.

THE END

"Be exalted above the heavens, O God; above all the earth be your glory!" (Psalm 57:12)

Made in the USA
Columbia, SC
20 January 2024

29880210R00241